THE
UNITED
MINE WORKERS
OF
AMERICA

With the publication of this book, The Pennsylvania State University wishes to draw attention to the United Mine Workers of America Archive, the newest addition to Penn State's Historical Collections and Labor Archives. This archive, which was donated by the UMWA to Penn State in 1994, consists of nearly two thousand cubic feet of historical documents. Materials will continue to be transferred from the UMWA headquarters in Washington, D.C., to the University Libraries. Penn State is honored to have been chosen by the UMWA for the responsibility of organizing and preserving this significant documentary heritage. By placing these research materials in an academic library, Penn State hopes to open many new opportunities for research in American labor studies. Furthermore, scholars will find Laslett's *The United Mine Workers of America: A Model of Industrial Solidarity?* an indispensable research tool for working in this collection.

THE
UNITED
MINE WORKERS
OF
AMERICA

A MODEL OF INDUSTRIAL SOLIDARITY?

EDITED BY
JOHN H. M. LASLETT

Published by
The Pennsylvania State University Press
in association with
The Pennsylvania State University Libraries
University Park, Pennsylvania

Library of Congress Cataloging-in-Publication Data

The United Mine Workers of America : a model of industrial solidarity? /
  edited by John H. M. Laslett.
      p.   cm.
    Eight of the twenty-two chapters consist of revised papers that were delivered originally
  at the Centennial Conference of the United Mine Workers of America, held at the
  Pennsylvania State University in October 1990.
    Includes bibliographical references and index.
    ISBN 0-271-01537-3 (alk. paper)
    1. United Mine Workers of America—History.   2. Strikes and
  lockouts—Coal mining—United States—History.   3. Coal miners
  —United States—History.   4. Labor movement—United States—History.
  5. Industrial relations—United States—History.   6. Coal mines and
  mining—Law and legislation—United States—History.   7. Labor laws
  and legislation—United States—History.   I. Laslett, John H. M.
  II. United Mine Workers of America.   Centennial Conference (1990 :
  Pennsylvania State University)
  HD6515.M616U5584   1996
  331.88'122334'0973—dc20   95-39732
                                                                        CIP

Copyright © 1996 The Pennsylvania State University
All rights reserved
Printed in the United States of America
Published by The Pennsylvania State University Press,
University Park, PA 16802-1003

It is the policy of The Pennsylvania State University Press to use acid-free paper for the first
printing of all clothbound books. Publications on uncoated stock satisfy the minimum
requirements of American National Standard for Information Sciences—Permanence of
Paper for Printed Library Materials, ANSI Z39.48-1992.

CONTENTS

PART I
Founders and Leaders of the
United Mine Workers in Its Heyday, 1890–1960

PART II
Work Habits, Miners' Health,
and Coal Company Paternalism

PART III
Strikes, Minorities, and the Role of Female Activists

PART IV
International Comparisons

PART V
Developments Since 1960, and the Struggle for Renewal

LIST OF TABLES

FOREWORD

The story of the United Mine Workers of America is, in many ways, the story of America. And it's a story, still unfolding, of struggling to fulfill the American dream. It's a story of immigrants to the United States and Canada, a story of those who dug the "black gold" that fueled the industrial revolution, a story of harsh exploitation that consumed the lives of men and boys, a story of grieving widows and orphans, a story of company gun thugs and union martyrs, a story of heroism and solidarity and epic industrial conflicts that changed America.

Much has been written about the history of the UMWA over the past century, and much remains to be written. As John L. Lewis said, "Who can measure the sum total of human effort and human hopes and human tragedy that have been wrapped up in the history of this organization?" Still, it's a history that too often is given short shrift in our schools, colleges, and libraries.

The story begins on a cold winter day, on January 25, 1890, in a dusty meeting hall in Columbus, Ohio, where some two hundred miners from two rival unions put aside their differences to unite in a single organization, the UMWA.

The new union was the first to understand the destructive impact of racism, and its constitution banned racial, ethnic, and religious discrimination. Recognizing the importance of organizing beyond the confines of a single craft, the union opened membership to anyone who worked in or around the mines. Also, the constitution gave the rank and file the right to elect those who would lead the union.

Early on, the UMWA gave wings to the concept of solidarity as a close-knit union family was formed from the unlikely ranks of poor immigrants speaking several languages and the sons of former slaves transported to America's coalfields by ruthless coal barons seeking to exploit cheap labor and ethnic divisions. The unique combination of vision, practicality, and militance that characterized the UMWA would come to redefine the labor movement. The union dared to dream impossible dreams and persevered to make them come true. Examples include the strikes that overcame blacklisting, eviction, and hunger to win the first coal industry contract in 1897 and, a year later, the eight-hour workday during a period when labor unions were an illegal "restraint of trade."

Other examples of how hope, sacrifice, and solidarity triumphed over the odds:

- After a decade of losses and defeats during the anti-union 1920s, labor won the legal right of collective bargaining in 1933. The same year, the UMWA organized three hundred thousand new members and won its first national agreement that, among other gains, banned child labor.
- In the face of the conventional wisdom and the belief of AFL craft union lead-

ers that low-wage manufacturing workers could not be organized, John L. Lewis committed the union's energy and resources to organizing millions of auto, steel, rubber, electrical, and other workers into a new labor federation, the CIO. Thus was created the modern trade union movement and the great American middle class.

- The coal mine walkouts directed by Lewis in 1946 and 1947 won the first union health and pension plan in defiance of presidential edicts, court injunctions, and massive fines.
- The Farmington, West Virginia, mine disaster of 1968, which killed seventy-eight miners, galvanized coalfield communities to demand that Congress pass and President Nixon sign the landmark federal Coal Mine Health and Safety Act of 1969.
- Early in 1990, the UMWA emerged victorious from a bitter nine-month strike against Pittston Coal. Mobilization by the whole labor movement and allies in the community against a symbol of corporate greed and a sophisticated ''corporate campaign'' that challenged the company on its own turf were able to triumph over Pittston and a hostile judge, governor, and state police.
- Despite warnings that the political winds were unfavorable, the UMWA mobilized its retired and active members to achieve the enactment of the 1992 Coal Industry Retiree Health Benefit Act, protecting the health benefits of pensioners and widows from companies that tried to shirk their obligations to their former workers.

Despite our past victories, today we face challenges that are as great as any faced by our forebears. Like the coal miners who formed a new union in 1890, we are confronted today by corporate power run amok and by politicians in the pocket of a privileged few. We are confronted by a Congress that is working to bring back company unions and to roll back decades of hard-won gains in workplace, health and safety, education and job training, and other vital areas.

In defending past gains and in fighting for goals such as universal health care and the right to join a union freely and go on strike without getting fired, we must mobilize labor's ranks to wage once again the kind of struggles that produced yesterday's victories.

Unlike the coal industry of yesteryear, mining in the 1990s represents only a small part of the operations of mammoth multinational corporations with large holdings in oil, gas, chemical, and other interests. Responding to the new challenges of these corporate operators has required the union to develop innovative strategies unknown in the days of Mother Jones, John Mitchell, or even John L. Lewis. The UMWA and other unions now use corporate campaigns in collective bargaining and organizing in order to generate public support and put pressure on the noncoal interests of recalcitrant multinationals.

The UMWA-led Shell Oil boycott in the successful campaign against South African apartheid is an example of an international corporate campaign. Working through the International Confederation of Free Trade Unions and the Miners' International Federation, the UMWA is addressing the challenge of global corporations by establishing important new alliances with unions overseas similar to those already formed with miners in Australia, South Africa, Poland, Russia, and Colombia.

Fight when we must, we seek to cooperate whenever we can, especially when our jobs are at stake. In the 1993 contract with the Bituminous Coal Operators Association, the UMWA won the establishment of a Labor-Management Positive Change Process. This has empowered our members with a say in mine operations—improving the productivity and economic competitiveness of unionized mines and creating jobs.

To maintain and expand our union's strength, the UMWA in recent years has reached out to organize the unorganized throughout the coalfields and beyond, regardless of their workplace. On the crucial political front, we are reviving the UMWA's tradition of aggressive action to elect pro-worker candidates to public office throughout the United States and Canada.

For the UMWA, the mission of our second century is to build upon one hundred years of pride, commitment, and solidarity to meet the challenges of change. It's a mission that will draw on the experience, vision, and hopes of each of its members, and a mission that will require the commitment of all of its families.

Washington, D.C.   Richard L. Trumka
August 1995   Former President, United Mine Workers of America

PREFACE

The idea for this collection originated at the Centennial Conference of the United Mine Workers of America, which was held at the Pennsylvania State University in October 1990 to mark the hundredth anniversary of the union. This three-day meeting, sponsored partly by the UMWA and partly by Penn State, was somewhat unusual: besides professional historians, it brought together more than one hundred students, social activists, and UMWA members to hear and comment upon a wide range of papers dealing with the history and policies of the union during its first hundred years. Former UMWA President Richard Trumka delivered a stirring Philip Murray Memorial Lecture on the general prospects for American trade unionism. He, along with other UMWA members and labor activists, also shared their practical experience of mining trade unionism by contributing from the floor. Their ideas added much of value to the papers published here.

Although it was partly sponsored by the UMWA, this collection does not reflect the official views of the organization. Although respectful of the union and its achievements, some of the essays are quite critical of it. The book attempts instead to present a balanced portrait of the coal miners' union and its history, and to provide insight into the lives of rank-and-file miners and the nature of the industry in which they worked. Eight of the twenty-two chapters consist of papers that were delivered at the conference. Four are taken from previously published works on the UMWA and the mining industry. Each of these has been revised by its author. The remaining ten essays were specially commissioned by the editor for this volume. The concluding chapter, by Maier Fox, brings the story up to date by filling in the union's history between 1990 and 1995.

Three out of the ten commissioned essays are by authors who either worked for the UMWA or were close to it. Besides Maier Fox these are George Goldstein, who wrote on the UMWA's Health and Retirement Fund (Chapter 10), and Marat Moore, whose Chapter 20 deals with the experiences of women miners underground. See Notes on Contributors for details.

"A Model of Industrial Solidarity?" the opening chapter from which the book takes its name, has three purposes. It introduces the essays that follow; it provides the general reader with a chronological overview of the UMWA's past; and it offers an analytic—and, I hope, provocative—framework within which to interpret the union's first hundred years. Besides dealing in depth with the lives of three of the union's best-known leaders, the remainder of the collection takes up such issues as coal-company paternalism, the mechanization of the mines, the UMWA's health and retirement system, and its racial and ethnic composition. Another original feature is the section that examines the history of the UMWA in a comparative and international context. A third is the attention given to the role of women in the mining industry.

Despite its length, this work is not fully comprehensive. Perhaps no collection on the history of the United Mine Workers could be, given the critical role it has played in the history of the American labor movement. No single chapter, for example, focuses exclusively on the miners' community life, although many of them touch on it. Nevertheless this work is, I believe, the most extensive collection of original essays ever to be published on the history and fortunes of a single American union.

Besides the United Mine Workers itself, thanks are due to Marat Moore, James R. Green, Stephen Brier, Maier B. Fox, and Peter J. Potter of the Penn State Press, for their help in the preparation of the book. Chapters 7, 11, and 12 reprint material taken from the following books, and is reproduced with permission from the publishers: Keith Dix, *What's A Coal Miner To Do? The Mechanization of Coal Mining* (Pittsburgh: University of Pittsburgh Press, 1988); Joseph W. Trotter, *Coal, Class and Color: Blacks in Southern West Virginia, 1905–32* (Urbana: University of Illinois Press, 1988); and Ronald Lewis, *Black Coal Miners in America: Race, Class and Community Conflict* (Lexington: University Press of Kentucky, 1987).

John H. M. Laslett
University of California at Los Angeles
January 1996

ABBREVIATIONS

AALL	American Association of Labor Legislation
ACW	Amalgamated Clothing Workers Union
ADAH	Alabama Department of Archives and History
AFL	American Federation of Labor
AMO	Area Medical Office
ARHI	Appalachian Regional Hospitals, Inc.
BCOA	Bituminous Coal Operators Association
BNWS	Bureau of Negro Welfare and Statistics
CBLS	Colorado Bureau of Labor Statistics
CCF	Central Competitive Field
CCMC	Committee on the Costs of Medical Care
CEO	chief executive officer
CEP	Coal Employment Project
CF & I	Colorado Fuel and Iron Company
CIO	Congress of Industrial Organizations
CIR	Commission on Industrial Relations
CNG	Colorado National Guard
CSHS	Colorado State Historical Society
CW & V	Chicago, Wilmington and Vermilion Society
CWP	coal workers' pneumoconiosis
CWST News!	Coalmining Women's Support Team News!
D & H	Delaware and Hudson Railroad
DL & W	Delaware, Lackawanna, and Western Railroad
EESP	Employment and Economic Security Pact
ERISA	Employees Retirement Income Security Act
GM	General Motors
HCFA	Health Care Financing Administration
HMO	health maintenance organization
HRFA	Health and Retirement Fund Archives
IEB	International Executive Board
ILGWU	International Ladies' Garment Workers' Union
ISFL	Illinois State Federation of Labor
JMP	John Mitchell Papers
K of L	Knights of Labor
NPL	Labor's Non-Partisan League
LCMU	Lanarkshire County Miners Union
MA	Master Alphabetical
MCCRO	McDowell County Colored Republican Organization

MFD	Miners for Democracy
MFGB	Miners Federation of Great Britain
MP	Member of Parliament
NA	National Archives
NAM	National Association of Manufacturers
NBCWA	National Bituminous Coal Wage Agreement
NBW	National Bank of Washington
NCF	National Civic Foundation
NIOSH	National Institute for Occupational Safety and Health
NIRA	National Industrial Recovery Act
NLRB	National Labor Relations Board
NMU	National Miners' Union
NRA	National Recovery Administration
NWLB	National War Labor Board
OAW	Office of Allied Workers
OCAW	Oil, Chemical, and Atomic Workers
OFCCP	Office of Contract Compliance Programs
PHS	U.S. Public Health Service
PM	*Progressive Miner*
PMA	Progressive Miners Association
PP	Parliamentary Papers
PWA	Provincial Workmen's Association
RMN	*Rocky Mountain News*
SLU	Southern Labor Union
SNF	Straight Numerical Files
SP of A	Socialist Party of America
SWMF	South Wales Miners Federation
SWOC	Steel Workers Organizing Campaign
SWP	Socialist Workers Party
TCI	Tennessee Coal, Iron and Railroad Company
TVA	Tennessee Valley Authority
UAW	United Auto Workers
UE	United Electrical, Radio, and Machine Workers of America
UMWA	United Mine Workers of America
UMWJ	*United Mine Workers Journal*
URWA	United Rubber Workers of America
USWA	United Steel Workers of America
WBA	Workingmen's Benevolent Association
WHD/DPL	Western History Department, Denver Public Library
WVBNWS	West Virginia Bureau of Negro Welfare and Statistics

CHAPTER ONE

INTRODUCTION
"A Model of Industrial Solidarity?"
Interpreting the UMWA's
First Hundred Years,
1890–1990

JOHN H.M. LASLETT

I

The United Mine Workers of America was for more than forty years the largest, the most powerful, and in many ways the most progressive trade union in America. Its initial membership, which came to only 17,000 when the National Progressive Miners Union first joined with Knights of Labor Assembly 135 to establish the UMWA in January 1890, consisted almost entirely of native-born or British immigrant pick miners who dug soft coal in an arc of states running east from Illinois to West Virginia, and then south into Alabama.[1]

---

1. As indicated in the recommended list of further readings, the best overall narrative history of the United Mine Workers of America is Maier B. Fox, *United We Stand: The United Mine Workers of America, 1890–1990* (Washington, D.C.: United Mine Workers of America, 1991). Two other useful works are McAlister Coleman, *Men and Coal* (New York: Arno and The New York Times, 1969), and Priscilla Long, *Where the Sun Never Shines: A History of America's Bloody Coal Industry* (New York: Paragon House, 1989). The latter work goes up to the First World War. For a critical history of the union in recent years, see Joseph E. Finley, *The Corrupt Kingdom: The Rise and Fall of the United Mine Workers* (New York: Simon and Schuster, 1972).

The UMWA's first great success came in 1898, when President John Mitchell negotiated the so-called Central Competitive Agreement. This brought wage increases and union recognition, as well as competitive equality for coal operators in the five main midwestern states. He followed this up by leading a successful strike of the anthracite miners of eastern Pennsylvania in 1902, most of whom were recently arrived Italians and Slavs. As a result, the UMWA's membership jumped to 263,000 in 1908. By 1914 the union had enrolled 377,688 miners who dug coal in more than twenty states stretching all across the continent. In 1919 this figure again almost doubled, making the UMWA by far the largest and most powerful industrial union in the AFL. The only other occasion on which membership passed the half-million mark came during the period of full-time employment surrounding the Second World War.[2]

By this time the Anglo-Saxon pick miner's skills, except for detailed work, had become largely obsolete. They were undermined by coal-cutting machines, which were introduced at the turn of the century, and then by machine-loaders, which came in about thirty years later. These machines dramatically increased productivity in the coal industry, while at the same time reducing the need for labor. In turn these developments, coupled with a rapid growth in the output of nonunion strip mine coal in Wyoming and elsewhere, has caused the UMWA to shrink. Today it has fewer than one hundred thousand members working mainly in Appalachia, Illinois, and in a few western states. But the small size of the present-day UMWA cannot obscure the achievements of its past. Even in recent times, it has continued to innovate. In the Pittston strike of 1989, for example, the UMWA helped revive the spirits of the much weakened AFL-CIO by developing a new, community-based form of trade unionism, based in part on the social movements of the 1960s.[3]

Building on the militant and inclusive traditions of the Knights of Labor, the UMWA also pioneered industrial unionism in the AFL. It enrolled large numbers of southern and eastern European peasant immigrants into the American labor movement, most of them for the first time. With its considerable political clout, it successfully lobbied Congress, as well as numerous coal-state legislatures, for mine safety and other progressive legislation. Most impressive of all, it provided much of the money and organizing talent that developed the Congress of Industrial Organizations in 1935–36.[4]

During the course of its history the UMWA also produced several of America's most interesting and influential labor leaders. Among these the beetle-browed and charismatic figure of John L. Lewis, who dominated the UMWA from his assumption of the presidency in 1919 until his retirement in 1960, was by far the most important. In the 1930s and 1940s, as a result of his complex and stormy relation-

---

2. Coleman, *Men and Coal*, 58, 80, 88, 139.

3. For details of the Pittston strike, see James R. Green's analysis in Chapter 21.

4. David McDonald and Edward Lynch, *Coal and Unionism: A History of the American Coal Miners Unions* (Indianapolis, Ind.: Lynald Books, 1939), passim.

ship with Presidents Roosevelt and Truman, as head of the CIO, President Lewis was for a time one of the most powerful men in America.[5] Hence he receives two essays in this book. Besides Lewis there was also John Mitchell, president of the UMWA between 1898 and 1908, who also played a pioneering role in the development of America's system of industrial relations.[6] Also important were Scots-born Philip Murray, who succeeded Lewis as president of the CIO in 1940, as well as John Brophy. After playing a significant role as radical counter to Lewis's conservatism in the UMWA of the 1920s, Brophy too exerted a significant influence over the growth and early development of the CIO.[7]

Reviewing the careers of these important labor figures, and the union they led in the first half of the twentieth century, constitutes the rationale for Part I of this book. Parts II–IV are distinguished by theme rather than chronology. Part II deals with the work habits of the individual miner, the company town, changes in mining technology, and the question of safety and health. Part III concerns strike action and the issue of violence in mining strikes, as well as relations between Anglo-American miners and minorities, both Southern and Eastern European, and black. The role of women as auxiliaries to the Illinois Progressive Miners Association of the 1940s is also dealt with here, in the only chapter in the book that goes outside the UMWA as such. Part IV explores the international context in which the UMWA operated. Its three essays shed new light on the UMWA's organizing philosophy by comparing it with that of coal unions in the two coal-producing countries whose outlook most closely approximated its own: Great Britain and Canada.

Part V returns to a chronological approach. It deals with several of the most important strands in the UMWA's life since 1960. This was the year that marked both President John L. Lewis's retirement, and the beginning of major changes both in technology and in the marketing of coal that signaled the union's numerical decline. Topics analyzed here include the struggle for democratic reform in the wake of Lewis's departure, the new role of women as underground miners, and the galvanizing effects of President Trumka's leadership in the critical Pittston strike of 1989.

II

The remaining sections of this chapter, however, have a different purpose. Their intention, following the subtitle of the book, is to determine whether the UMWA has been the creator and preserver of a special form of labor solidarity. Throughout

---

5. The standard biography of Lewis is Melvyn Dubofsky and Warren Van Tine, *John L. Lewis, A Biography* (New York: Quadrangle/New York Times, 1977).

6. For John Mitchell, see Craig Phelan, *Divided Loyalties: The Public and Private Life of John Mitchell* (Albany: State University of New York Press, 1994).

7. John Brophy, *A Miner's Life* (Madison: University of Wisconsin Press, 1964).

industrial history many people have argued that mining communities, and the unions
they have created, have constituted what Marxist commentators used to call the
vanguard of the working class. Such people, who include both labor activists and
academic commentators, have suggested that the underground nature of mining as
an occupation—coupled with the rural isolation of the mining community—has
mandated a special form of labor solidarity that puts colliers in a different category
from other elements of the working class.[8]

How true is this? Is there, in fact, a special form of miners' solidarity? Or does it
differ only in degree from the sense of comradeship and class consciousness that
has spawned America's other trade unions? In other words, is the UMWA now, or
has it ever been as some of its supporters claim, a model of industrial solidarity?

At first glance both the influential role the UMWA has played in America's labor
history and the special circumstances of the miner's life seem to compel affirmative
answers to these questions. The rural concentration of coal-mining communities into
limited geographical areas, coupled with the underground isolation of the collier
and the peculiar dangers of his task, has seemingly created a special bond among
miners greater than that binding other workers. Despite ongoing improvement in
safety, all miners, whether they be shot-firers, hand-loaders, man-trip drivers or
hoisting engineers, are subject today—as they have always been—to the deadly
discipline of the mine. They ignore it at their peril. To neglect pit rules, or risk a
fellow miner's safety by working in a gas-filled room, is to court not simply a hand
injury as it might on the auto assembly line, but the instant death of hundreds of
men.[9]

From these dangers peculiar to the miner's life, the argument runs, stem both the
special bonds that tie mining communities together, and the militant traditions of
the UMWA itself. Despite some initial prejudice the union has usually—unlike most
AFL craft unions—accepted into its ranks any and all colliers who sought to join it,
of whatever race or creed. It has been willing to defend their interests in a manner
few urban unions, whose members are divided up by neighborhood and by the
intervening members of other social classes, have managed to emulate.

In support of this argument one can cite the extraordinary sacrifices that UMWA
members in different parts of the country have historically been willing to make for
fellow miners in distress. These include sympathy strikes by one district of the
UMWA in support of another district; defiance of court injunctions bearing extensive fines by one mining community in order to win a strike in another; eviction
from company housing by miners in one part of a coalfield so as to ensure the
success of a stoppage elsewhere; or the sacrifice involved when an individual min-

8. For a discussion of this point, see the introduction by Royden Harrison to his edited book, *Independent Collier: The Coal Miner as Archetypal Proletarian Reconsidered* (New York: St. Martin's,
1978).

9. A good analysis of the dangers of coal mining and the legislation that was enacted to deal with
them can be found in William Graebner, *Coal-Mining in The Progressive Period: The Political Economy
of Reform* (Lexington: University Press of Kentucky, 1976).

er's family donates hard-won furniture or food to a fellow miner's widow. The UMWA's members include not only all underground workers from a wide variety of nationalities, but most surface workers as well. To Samuel Gompers's distaste, the UMWA's unique claim to be seen as a model of industrial solidarity was ratified in the Scranton Declaration of 1902, which gave it official permission (granted to no other union) to organize all workers "in and around the mines."[10]

This solidaristic image of the mining community, and of the colliers' unions it has spawned, was for many years upheld not simply by radical activists, but by a wide variety of scholars and historians. Among academics two ideas, in particular, have helped to give it shape. One was Charles Kerr and Abram Siegel's notion, first promulgated in 1954, that miners as a body constituted an "isolated mass." Citing the rural isolation noted above, supporters of the "isolated mass" argument saw miners as a unique group of workers—albeit sharing some similarities with loggers and seamen—whose unity, homogeneity, and strength of purpose predisposed them to frequent strikes, to class-conscious militancy, and to political radicalism.[11]

A second source of support for the idea that miners possess a special sense of class solidarity stems from the stereotype of the mining town as an "occupational community." This concept, which has a long history in sociological theory, was elaborated by Martin Bulmer in a 1975 article. Bulmer saw mining communities as uniquely bonded by overlapping ties of work, leisure, family, and neighborhood. Unlike workers in multioccupational urban areas, he argued, the inhabitants of mining towns and their family members interacted and bonded with each other not simply down the pit, but also after work in the same bars, sports clubs, churches, and schools. Hence they developed a special bond of solidarity that was reflected in their unions. Other sociologists and oral historians have elaborated on the same idea.[12]

This solidaristic collective image of miners' union as a model of industrial solidarity has been further reinforced by the stereotype of the individual miner as an "archetypal proletarian." In the 1930s, this view was often espoused by Marxist commentators.[13] In the hands of the miners' champions, this stereotype saw the miner as a defiantly class-conscious, quintessential wage earner who was leading the rest of the masses patiently by the hand toward some form of proletarian revolution. In the hands of his enemies, the stereotype has been used to characterize the miner as a violent, drunken, and socially backward misfit who threatened to subvert

10. Philip Taft, *The A.F. of L. in the Time of Gompers* (New York: Little Brown, 1954), 218.

11. Charles Kerr and Abram Siegel, "The Inter-Industry Propensity to Strike—An International Comparison," in *Industrial Conflict,* ed. A. Kornhauser, R. Budin and A. M. Ross (New York: McGraw-Hill, 1954), 189–212.

12. Martin Bulmer, "Sociological Models of the Mining Community," *Sociological Review* 23 (1975): 61–92. See also E. Thorpe, *Coalport: An Interpretation of Community in a Mining Town* (Durham: University of Durham, 1970); and C. Storm-Clark, "The Miners: A Test Case for Oral History," *Victorian Studies* 10 (1972): 358–74.

13. See, for example, Anna Rochester, *Labor and Coal* (New York: International Publishers, 1931).

society by his animal habits and underground ways. The latter view, rendered plausible by the miner's physical prowess, by his hidden workplace, and by his grimy features, has a long history in both European and American popular culture. In Scotland in the 1840s, for example, it was feared that the growing concentration of recently arrived Irish colliers in the rural areas of Lanarkshire would bring about a social explosion.[14]

In nineteenth-century America, this negative image was reinforced by the pitched battles—more fierce than any fought in England—that miners carried out with agents of the operators (often disguised as agents of the state) in such places as Kentucky, West Virginia, and Colorado.[15] On the other hand, credence was lent to the miner as plucky proletarian by the undoubted cruelty and cynicism with which the coal operators have always sought to exploit and manipulate him through lockouts, company housing, the importation of strike-breakers, and the political control of coal-county courts. Readers who see the company store as a potent symbol of this exploitation will take special interest in Price Fishback's revisionist interpretation of this institution (Chapter 8).

Anyone even remotely familiar with the realities of miners as human beings, and with the historic achievements of the UMWA in protecting its members from exploitation by the coal operators, will find far more truth in the positive aspects of this stereotype than they will in the negative one. No one who has read an objective account of a mining disaster, or of a prolonged mining strike, can fail to be moved by the special qualities of courage, sacrifice, and suffering such episodes entail. A good example is the famous Colorado Iron and Fuel strike—the so-called Ludlow Massacre strike of 1914—upon which Priscilla sheds new light (Chapter 14). In that chapter, Long also engages historian Price Fishback in an argument about violence in mining strikes that contains shades of the nineteenth-century middle-class view of miners as inherently violent. My own sympathies are with Long on this point.

And yet, in dealing with the image of the miner and his union as models of industrial solidarity, it is important to separate out myth from reality. A bucket of cold water was poured on the romantic exaggerations inherent in this concept by Royden Harrison and his fellow authors in a book published in England in 1975. It was called *Independent Collier: The Coal Miner as Archetypal Proletarian Revisited* (see note 8). This work demonstrated, not that miners were unconcerned with unionism or incapable of solidarity in a chosen cause, but that the community of colliers was composed of a wide range of workers, not all of whom saw eye to eye.

In mid-nineteenth-century America, small rural mining towns and their unions were frequently led by groups of native-born or skilled British immigrant miners whose high rates of literacy, pride in craft, and strong sense of personal worth

14. Alan Campbell, *The Lanarkshire Miners: A Social History of Their Trade Unions, 1775–1874* (Edinburgh: John Donald, 1979), chap. 8.
15. For a description of the coal-mine wars that took place in Harlan County, Kentucky, in the 1930s see John W. Hevener, *Which Side Are You On? The Harlan County Coal Miners, 1931–39* (Urbana: University of Illinois Press, 1978).

identified them, quite rightly, as respected members of the community. Yet their high levels of skill, and their role as petty contractors rather than as wage earners sometimes led these Anglo-Saxons to look down upon African-American miners, as well as upon recently arrived immigrants who found their way into the trade. Transferred into places like West Virginia, as Joe Trotter shows in his discussion of black miners (Chapter 11), this Anglo-American condescension could often be translated into racial exclusiveness in the pit village, and output competition underground.

Other valid criticisms of the archetypal proletarian argument have also been advanced. They include the recognition that many miners do not, and never have, lived in isolated rural enclaves. To the contrary, many lived in or near quite large cities, like East St. Louis. Pit villages were also found to have been divided not simply on racial lines, as in Alabama or West Virginia, but on lines of ethnicity and caste as well. Many of the UMWA's Protestant "Johnny Bull" founders, for example, at first either made fun of, or shunned the east European Catholic immigrant miners who entered the pits in the 1880s and 1890s.[16] In 1920s southern Illinois, temperance-minded Protestant miners treated their wine-drinking Italian fellow workers with contempt.[17] Nor were these differences merely social and cultural. Both in the southern and the midwestern mining states the racial and ethnic hierarchies that segregated blacks from whites, and Anglos from East Europeans above ground in the mine patch, were reproduced in occupational hierarchies below ground as well.

It can be said, with considerable truth, that these ethnic and racial differences were deliberately exploited by the coal operators, and that the UMWA, despite initial lapses, made a strong effort to overcome both racial and ethnic divisions among its members, if only to try and ensure harmony at the bargaining table. In Chapter 3 Perry Blatz describes the principled and successful effort that President John Mitchell made to incorporate the Slavic miners of the anthracite district of Pennsylvania into the UMWA in the early 1900s. In Chapter 13 Mildred Beik shows how admirably these efforts bore fruit in the bituminous mining town of Windber, Pennsylvania, a generation later. By the 1930s, she points out, not only did Slavic miners control the UMWA local there, they also engaged in a sophisticated social interaction with the local Catholic priests and businessmen so as to enhance and develop the union's strength. All in all it can be said that by 1930, outside of the Deep South, class differences between miners on the one hand and coal operators on the other were far more important than differences in race or ethnicity.

Nevertheless, if we examine other aspects of the UMWA's record, we see that by no means does all of it uphold the image of the union as a model of industrial solidarity. One problem has been bureaucratic manipulation from the international headquarters in Washington, and the undermining of local and district traditions of

16. See, for example, Frank J. Warne, *The Slav Invasion and The Mine Workers, A Study in Immigration* (Philadelphia: J. B. Lippincott, 1904).

17. Daniel J. Prosser, "Coal Towns in Egypt: Portrait of An Illinois Mining Region, 1890–1930" (Ph.D. diss., Northwestern University, 1973), chap. 4.

union democracy. This has been a consistent theme in the UMWA's internal history, at least in the period between 1919 and 1960, when John L. Lewis held office as president of the union. It was particularly bad in the post–World War I period, when Lewis suspended the charters of several midwestern UMWA districts and installed his own officers in their place.[18] The same process of riding roughshod over district traditions of autonomy and democracy continued on and off until the overthrow of President Boyle, Lewis's sidekick and successor, in 1969.[19] It was sometimes argued that bringing recalcitrant district unions into line was necessary in order to preserve the UMWA's united front against either the coal operators or the government, thereby preserving the union's overall unity. But such explanations usually shrouded less honorable motives.

A second, and related issue, concerns the corrupt power plays that have frequently attended both national and district elections in the UMWA. Examples range from President Lewis's stealing of the union's presidential election from District 2 radical John Brophy in 1926,[20] to President Tony Boyle's shameful murder of his opponent Jock Yablonsky in the late 1960s.[21] Morally speaking, this was the lowest point in the history of the union. A third has been the sweetheart deals that have frequently been negotiated behind the membership's back between leaders supposedly loyal to the UMWA, and leading coal operators. How class-conscious can a union be that permitted such a prostitution of labor's basic aims? A notorious example was the deal agreed to between President Frank Farrington of District 12, and the Peabody Coal Company in the late 1920s. Later on, such deals became regular practice, with President Boyle once more being the most notorious offender.[22] But Lewis himself was not immune from this practice, either. As David Clark shows (Chapter 19) it was only in the 1970s, under the leadership of President Arnold Miller and the Miners for Democracy Movement, that the UMWA was able to fully redeem its erstwhile reputation for union democracy and rank-and-file control.

None of these weaknesses, of course, are unique to the UMWA. They can, unfortunately, be found in the history of many other U.S trade unions, including those with socialist reputations like the International Ladies' Garment Workers' Union. But they do not fit the image of the UMWA as a model of industrial solidarity, either. These shortcomings conjure up, instead, an opposite model of American trade union development, one favored by conservative sociologists like Seymour Martin Lipset. This is the image of the American labor movement (to be distinguished in this respect from the European) as an arena of bureaucratic manipulation, financial corruption, and oligarchic rule.[23] Such shortcomings acquire even greater

18. Sylvia Kopald, *Rebellion in Labor Unions* (New York: International Publishers, 1920), passim.

19. Finley, *Corrupt Kingdom,* chaps. 10–11.

20. For Brophy's account of this strike, see Brophy, *Miner's Life,* chap. 15.

21. Finley, *Corrupt Kingdom,* 203–39.

22. Harold W. Perrigo, "Factional Strife in District No. 12, United Mine Workers of America, 1919–1933" (Ph.D. diss., University of Wisconsin, 1933), 231–32.

23. Seymour M. Lipset, "Trade Unionism and the American Social Order," in David Brody, *The American Labor Movement* (New York: Harper and Row, 1971), 7–29.

significance when we point out that President Lewis sought, in many ways success-fully, to transfer his oligarchic habits of governance from the UMWA to the CIO when he became president of that organization in 1936.[24]

III

One way to assess the relative validity of the solidaristic/militant versus the auto-cratic/bureaucratic interpretation of the UMWA's history would be to draw a sharp distinction between the sometimes corrupt leaders of the union, on the one hand, and the decent, democratic, and comradely character of the rank and file, on the other. There is much to be said for this approach. No one can deny that a powerful tradition of union democracy and rank-and-file governance has always existed within the UMWA. It stems, in turn, from an even older history of pit democracy that came out of the British miners' democratic traditions, which were transported here by the Scottish, English, and Irish founders of the UMWA in the 1870s and 1880s.[25] That tradition also derives from the governing practices of the Knights of Labor, and from the indigenous tradition of American democratic republicanism that can be seen at work among miners' unions as far back as the American Miners' Association during the period of the Civil War.[26]

It can be argued, too, that those leaders who have sought to deny the UMWA's democratic traditions or who have attempted to thrust an unpopular contract down the throats of the membership have usually had to face an angry rank and file who fought to restore democracy and responsible trade unionism.[27] Often, they have been successful. This struggle, for example (as historian Paul Clark again demonstrates in Chapter 19) was key to the success of the Miners for Democracy Movement, and to President Trumka's leadership of the UMWA in the late 1980s and early 1990s. Initially, at least, democratic governance and rank-and-file control also provided the main dynamic behind the Progressive Miners Association of Illinois in the early 1930s, as well as other democratic breakaway movements. The PMA originated in a rank-and-file revolt against the Lewis/Farrington machine in Illinois District 12, as Stephane Booth shows (Chapter 15). But at some point the painful question must still be asked: If the UMWA's rank and file has always stood for solidaristic and comradely values, why has it allowed so many shady characters to rise to the top of its union?

Another way to approach the question is to conduct a case-by-case study of the strengths and weaknesses present in the UMWA's record by breaking down its his-

24. Dubofsky and Van Tine, *John L. Lewis*, part 3.

25. Campbell, *Lanarkshire Miners*, chaps. 1–3.

26. Edward A. Wieck, *The American Miners Association* (New York: Russell Sage Foundation, 1940), chap. 6.

27. Kopald, *Rebellion*, chap. 2.

tory into its discrete periods and component parts. In Chapter 18, David Frank sheds comparative light on this approach by comparing the attitudes toward union governance and industrial democracy that were taken up by those Canadian and American miners' leaders, respectively, who struggled for control over Nova Scotia's miners' unions during the period of the First World War. At issue here were also two separate visions of the relationship between miners and the state. Could it be argued, on this basis, that the period from 1890 to 1919 was one of rank-and-file governance and democratic unionism in the UMWA's history; that the Lewis years between 1919 and 1960 were ones of growing autocracy, punctuated by periodic rank-and-file revolts; and that the 1970–84 period saw a climatic convulsion that finally (and irrevocably?) restored the forces of democracy and militancy to control over the UMWA? One might make such an argument. But it would be easy to poke holes in it on the ground of oversimplification.

If pursued in a scholarly manner such a periodistic approach would, however, respect history as a developmental process, and deal with the rise and decline of the UMWA as a sequential chronology in which its successes and failures could be judged in the context of the appropriate time and place. For example, it would help us to answer the hypothetical question of whether the union should be judged as harshly for tolerating racially biased hiring practices (hence abandoning its claims to be a model of industrial solidarity) in, say, the West Virginia coalfield in 1910, as it should be in the state of Illinois in 1970. The first time and place puts us in a racially divided state at the height of Jim Crow; the second, in a more liberal state at a more enlightened period of history.

But such an ad hoc approach does not provide us with an overall framework within which to judge the UMWA's achievements in a comparative and analytic context. Such a framework is also indispensable to making a considered historical judgment. In the next section I shall seek to provide such a framework by proposing four basic variables, or historical constraints, within which the UMWA was obliged to organize its members, govern itself, and relate both to the work process of mining and to the operators it bargained with. Introducing these variables does not mean that we should suspend judgment on the question of whether the UMWA was a model of industrial solidarity. They do mean, however, that answers to this question must be modfied in light of what the union and its leaders could reasonably be expected to do, and what they could not.

IV

The four variables that follow are not exclusive: they do not deal, for example, with such matters as coal-town culture. Nevertheless, I believe them the most important to take into account in assessing the role of the UMWA in U.S. labor history, as well as in the broader arena of American society. They should also help, rather than hinder, us in our search for an answer to the model of solidarity question.

In what follows I shall lay out each variable, explain its relationship to the history of the UMWA, and touch briefly on the way it illuminates the essays that follow. The four variables, which are deliberately rank-ordered in the sequence given, deal with the following issues: the nature of the coal market; the character of the labor force; changes that took place over time in mining technology; and the evolution that has occurred in relations between the UMWA and the state.

NATURE OF THE COAL MARKET

This was, as David Brody has pointed out in a recent essay, highly exceptional in American industry.[28] Its peculiarities had a profound effect in influencing both the pay levels and employment patterns of miners at their workplaces underground, and their ability to develop a trade union that could adequately take care of their interests.

Unlike other industrial products, the demand for coal during its heyday between 1870 and 1920—as virtually the sole source of fuel for factories, railroads, and household heating—was inelastic. That is to say, with the exception of seasonal changes for home heating, the demand for coal was determined more by the general level of business activity than it was by price. Demand went up rapidly during periods of economic prosperity, and fell heavily during periods of economic depression. The industry was also easy to enter: all that was required to build a primitive shaft mine in the early days was a mine sinker, plenty of timber, and a crude ventilation and drainage system. Hence despite spectacular overall growth in the demand for coal during the late nineteenth and early twentieth centuries, the normal condition of the industry was one of overcapacity, underemployment, and severe price competition between a plethora of small competing operators who opened and shut their mines in response to changes in seasonal demand. Often, indeed, unlike urban factory owners, these small coal operators preferred to keep their mines open even when they were running at a loss, rather than risk flooding and permanent damage to their physical plant.[29]

Competition was not so much between individual operators (which was kept in check by the efforts of individual fieldwide operators' associations), as it was between rival coalfields operating in a common market. In addition, save in the large "captive" mines owned by the steel industry in Pennsylvania and West Virginia, this state of overcapacity and competition—except in time of war—has persisted

28. David Brody, *In Labor's Cause, Main Themes in The History of the American Worker* (New York: Oxford University Press, 1993), 138–41.

29. For a description of the economics of the mining industry, and of the operators' economic interests, see Isadore Lubin, *Miners' Wages and The Cost of Coal* (New York: McGraw-Hill, 1924).

throughout much of the UMWA's history until quite recent times. In an industry where transferability of jobs was difficult, the prospects for high wages and stable employment were inherently bleak, unless its unstable and competitive nature could be controlled by some form of industrywide, or regionwide agreement.

This brief economic analysis already tells us much about the condition of the typical U.S. coal miner at the time when the UMWA first came into being in 1890. He was likely to be employed at periods of peak demand in the winter, but to be either underemployed or entirely unemployed during the summer. This pattern of underemployment necessitated a high tonnage rate of payment if he was to make ends meet. The UMWA sought to ensure that this state of affairs continued. But the labor-intensive nature of the industry, coupled with seasonal shutdowns in the pits, continued to make the collier susceptible both to abrupt changes in his wage levels and to extensive periods of unemployment. When unemployed in one area, he would either tramp or ride the rails to another coal-mining region, take another job, or cultivate chickens and pigs in his backyard. Thus, from its inception in 1890, the primary aim of the UMWA was to secure an interstate agreement with the operators that would bring about competitive equality between different regional coalfields, each of which had its own idiosyncratic coal seams, transportation networks, and urban markets.

The first effort the UMWA made to control the peculiar nature of the coal market, and to guarantee its members decent pay and conditions of work, resulted in the Central Competitive Field Agreement of 1898. This agreement governed tonnage rates and relations with employers in the four main midwestern coal-producing states up until the mid-1920s. Leaving aside President John Mitchell's anthracite breakthrough of 1902, as Perry Blatz shows (Chapter 3), making this interstate agreement stick constituted Mitchell's major achievement. As a result of it, most midwestern miners gained union recognition, the eight-hour day, and negotiated agreements over the dimensions of the coal screen, which determined what size of coal he was actually paid for. On the negative side, however, in order to ensure competitive equality between conditions in a wide variety of different coalfields, midwestern miners continued to put up with significant wage differentials between their earnings in different fields.

Did this system, which openly acknowledged the need to maintain significant wage differentials between miners' earnings in different states in order to maintain competitive equality between the operators, mean that the UMWA—in its first significant foray into collective bargaining—had sold the rank-and-file miners down the river? Did it mean, in particular, that President Mitchell tied the union to the interests of the coal operators in a class-collaborationist manner, thereby making it more difficult for the union to behave, and to be seen to behave, as a model of industrial solidarity?

The character of the annual meetings that took place between the UMWA's leaders and the representatives of the midwestern operators over the Central Competitive Field Agreement, and the outcome of the negotiations they conducted, certainly seemed as though they might support that view. Socialists in high-wage coal districts like Illinois District 12, which were sometimes forced to accept lower wage levels than they otherwise might in order to maintain the principle of competitive equality, frequently voiced their objections to the new system. These annual negotiating sessions were also treated by the union, as one speaker stated at the 1899 conference, "not as an arena where foe meets foe," but as a "friendly meeting-place of those who are interested for the benefit of all."[30] What were the leaders of a supposedly class-conscious union like the United Mine Workers doing using language like that?

In making up their minds on this matter, readers will certainly want to take into account the views that Craig Phelan puts forward in his discussion of John Mitchell's legacy to the UMWA in Chapter 4. Before condemning the UMWA on this issue, however, the reader should also take into consideration the evidence that John Laslett brings forward (Chapters 2 and 17), regarding the nineteenth-century miner's view of relations with employers. For years the British immigrant miners, who constituted a majority of the membership of the UMWA in its early years, took the position that friendly cooperation between coal miner and coal operator was a desirable, rather than an undesirable goal. This policy of compromise and cooperation in collective bargaining did not necessarily preclude either solidarity among the miners on their side of the bargaining table, or pursuing industrywide trade unionism. Besides, it can be argued, if the peculiar characteristics of the market for coal were to be brought under control, what realistic alternative did the UMWA have?

After the First World War, when nonunion fields like West Virginia began to assert a decisive influence in the national market and the Central Competitive Field system of bargaining broke down, John L. Lewis chose a different approach to the problem of market instability. He sought to replace the tonnage system of payment with a system of hourly or day rates, and to keep wages high by driving small inefficient operators out of business. In the then-weakened state of the UMWA, he failed abysmally, at least for a time. (In the 1920s, wages fell rather than rose, and more than half a million miners lost their jobs). Lewis faced a storm of criticism from his left-wing critics, to which—significantly for our theme—he responded by ruthlessly purging them from office.[31]

A second chance for Lewis came in the 1930s, however, when there was a friendly New Deal administration in power in Washington. By this time—against all his instincts, as well as his earlier political practice—Lewis realized that he needed the state to help him achieve his collective bargaining goals. Thus he embarked on a new course of action. Since that course meant invoking the political power of the federal government to counterbalance the economic power of the operators, I shall review it later in this chapter.

---

30. Quoted in Brody, *In Labor's Cause*, 140.
31. Dubofsky and Van Tine, 98–159.

CHARACTER OF THE LABOR FORCE

As John Laslett shows in Chapter 2, most of the men who founded the UMWA in 1890 were either native-born whites, or—more typically—immigrant pick miners from Great Britain. Here and there, a few hundred skilled miners from Belgium, France, and Germany were also to be found. These Anglo-Saxon miners were proud, literate, experienced men who saw themselves as petty contractors, not as mere wage earners. That was part of the reason why they found the philosophy of the Knights of Labor so attractive. In midwestern coal states like Ohio and Illinois, many of them also possessed homes and gardens of their own, carpets on the floor, and wives who did not work. They were paid by the tonnage of coal they raised in their daily shifts, not by the hour. In the early days, payment varied from about 70 to about 90 cents a ton. This method of payment allowed them both to control the level of their own daily output, and indirectly that of the operators also. Sometimes, in the early days, the individual pick miner might choose to work only three or four days a week, and spend the rest of his time away from the pit.

This labor system worked to the advantage of the Anglo-Saxon collier in the 1870–1900 period, when he constituted a majority of the labor force. But by the time the UMWA was founded in 1890 three developments had begun to undermine the miner's workplace independence. One was the invention of the coal-undercutting machine; the second, the beginnings of a massive influx into the industry of poor, unskilled peasants from Eastern and Southern Europe who had no experience of mining and who were willing to work for longer hours and less money. Third, the midwestern coal operators, anxious to break the pick miners' monopoly of skill, stepped up their habit of bringing in black miners from the South so as to break the white miners' strikes, and stall union growth. Brought in under contract, trainloads of Italians and Slavs first invaded Pennsylvania, then Ohio, Indiana, and Illinois, and then even parts of the South. The flood went on until 1924, when Congress cut off unlimited European immigration.[32]

Besides a wholly different culture, the ignorance the newly arriving Slavs, Italians and Greeks displayed about mining techniques seemed to threaten not simply the Anglo-Saxon miner's safety underground, and his monopoly of skill; their Catholic faith and peasant habits appeared alien to his whole way of life. Hence at first, he responded to their arrival with a mixture of condescension and contempt. In the 1890–1900 period large numbers of Anglo-Saxon pick miners actually left Pennsylvania and other eastern mining states, and moved west partly in order to escape the new and alien horde. Did the prejudice many of them showed also undermine what-

---

32. For a contemporary discussion of miners' attitudes toward the "new immigration" from Southern and Eastern Europe, see Peter Roberts, *Anthracite Coal Communities: A Study of the Demography, the Social, Educational and Moral Life of the Anthracite Regions* (Westport, Conn.: Greenwood, 1970), esp. chaps. 1–2.

ever pretensions the UMWA might have had to being a model of industrial solidarity?

On this matter, despite lingering prejudice in the more isolated coalfields, the answer is a decided no. By the turn of the century UMWA leaders in most districts, even though they favored immigration restriction as a matter of federal policy, recognized that they were powerless to prevent the operators from importing large numbers of Eastern and Southern Europeans. Although the UMWA tried to limit the frequency of accidents by raising the certification requirements for practicing miners, it switched rapidly—more rapidly than most other unions—from a policy of exclusion to one of integration and acceptance. Once they were in, contrary to the AFL's persistent nativist prejudices, John Mitchell found that these new immigrants were more, rather than less, willing to strike for higher wages and union recognition than their Anglo counterparts (both Perry Blatz and Craig Phelan refer to this point in Chapters 3 and 4). Over time the new immigrants also proved themselves to be just as loyal to the UMWA as any of its other members. Indeed, in the anthracite mining towns of eastern Pennsylvania during the celebrated hard-coal strike of 1902, social ostracism—a formidable instrument among the communal Slavs—fell just as heavily upon the wives of Slavic miners who allowed their husbands to go to work as it did upon the wives of Anglo-Saxon strikebreakers.[33]

Although the exact date by which these new European minorities achieved office at the district level of the UMWA is unclear, Mildred Beik shows effectively (Chapter 13) that by the mid-twentieth century Slavic officers and organizers already constitututed the core of union leadership in the bituminous mining town of Windber, Pennsylvania. Indeed it was natural, given the need for unity at the bargaining table, that in the multiethnic mining towns of this part of the country minority colliers should be elected to office. More surprising, but still more commendable (in view of its earlier enthusiasm for excluding the Chinese) was the way in which the miners of Wyoming District 15 came to accept Japanese miners into their ranks in 1907. Having initially rejected these "yellow miners," thereby playing into the hands of the operators (who would substitute cheap immigrant labor of any kind for expensive Anglo miners any day), District 15 reversed itself, and accepted the Japanese as comrades in their union.[34]

This did not mean, however, that the new arrivals were always accepted socially. Culturally speaking, barriers between the Anglo-Saxon colliers and these new ethnic and racial minorities took longer to break down. For some years after 1900 separate denominational churches, neighborhood ethnic bars, and immigrant benevolent associations continued to transform mining towns in the eastern states into community patchwork quilts.[35] Sometimes, after payday on a Saturday night when many miners

33. Donald L. Miller and Richard E. Sharpless, *The Kingdom of Coal: Work, Enterprise, and Ethnic Communities in the Mine Fields* (Philadelphia: University of Pennsylvania Press, 1985), 249.

34. Long, *Where the Sun Never Shines,* 250–51.

35. Roberts, *Anthracite Coal Communities,* chap. 6.

were flush with drink, fist fights would break out between dissidents among different minorities. But after about 1940, when the rise of the class-conscious CIO and the liberal policies of the New Deal had each had their homogenizing effect, miners of most nationalities got along with each other pretty well; they drank in the same bars, shopped in the same stores and rubbed shoulders on the same sports teams. By this time, too, many of the formerly labor aristocratic Scots, Welsh, and English miners had become mine superintendents and had moved up and out of the mines.

Why was the UMWA so quick to integrate these "new European immigrants," when other unions in the AFL considered most of them to be unorganizable? It was partly because of underground solidarity, the communal traditions of the mining village, and the pioneering role the UMWA had itself played in establishing industrial unionism. But it was also because the national leaders of the union, particularly President John Mitchell, recognized early on that not to organize them would threaten the Anglo miners' cherished traditions of workplace autonomy, and require them to submit to the operators' dictates regarding wage scales and hiring practices. After 1900, it became particularly important to organize the rapidly growing number of Slavic and Italian miners who had been brought in under contract to operate the rapidly proliferating mining machines. Regarding the acceptance of the "new Europeans," therefore, and later on even Japanese and Mexicans,[36] the answer to the model of solidarity question should be an unqualified yes.

Integrating African-American miners into the UMWA was slower and more painful. Oddly enough, it seemed more difficult to accomplish this task in the northern coal-mining states than it was in the southern ones. Ronald Lewis (Chapter 12) shows clearly the conflicting racial currents that flowed through the mines of the Deep South at the height of the Jim Crow period, as white and African-American miners struggled manfully to organize a common front against the operators. On the one hand, Lewis shows us the solidaristic imperative that drove black and white miners together to form the (initially unsuccessful) District 20 of Alabama. On the other, he recognizes how difficult it was for black and white miners alike to resist the tremendous community pressures that the coal operators were able to mobilize against the specter of "social equality" and racial miscegenation. It was the successful mobilization of these fears that caused the defeat of the 1908 strike in the Alabama coalfield. It was not a failure of UMWA policy, or racial tensions between black and white miners, as such.

Yet white pit bosses and even fellow miners could, and sometimes did, consign African-American colliers to dirtier and more dangerous workplaces than they would accept for themselves. Moreover, as hand loading gave way to mechanical loading in the 1930s and 1940s southern white colliers often held onto their higher paying, tonnage-based jobs, while consigning black miners to day-wage machine running, or pony driving slots. Or they would tacitly accept the persistence of a

36. For the acceptance of Mexicans into the UMWA, see Long, *Where the Sun Never Shines*, 253.

long-standing work hierarchy in which Anglo pick miners took the safest and most lucrative workplaces, Slavs and Italians got the second-best ones, and African-Americans were left with workrooms containing the stoniest or most gaseous seams. All this, despite an official UMWA policy that in most districts banned racial discrimination. In Chapter 11, Joe Trotter shows us how African-American miners responded to this racial discrimination by developing higher productivity rates than white miners, by moving to other towns in order to get better treatment, or by making an alliance with the barely less despised Italians.

But officially at least, the UMWA *did* struggle against racial exclusion almost from its founding, whereas most craft unions in the AFL did not. All in all, despite a bitter argument that recently broke out in an academic journal over Herbert Gutman's alleged romanticizing of the union's racial record in the north,[37] the UMWA in my view does not have a great deal to be ashamed of as regards interracial organizing. Certainly, it has built up a far better record over the years in this area than most other American trade unions. Thus on this matter the answer to our model of solidarity question should also be a cautious yes.

To mention women in the context of so masculine an occupation as mining— mining was perhaps the most masculine of all industrial occupations, with the possible exception of logging or seafaring—might seem startling. But it is precisely the masculinity of mining as a task that gives gender its relevance to our theme. It has long been recognized that the wives and daughters of colliers have played an important and courageous role on the picket line, or in discouraging (and sometimes even beating up) male scabs during strikes. Or they founded and led highly supportive women's auxiliary clubs. In Chapter 15, Stephane Booth describes the Women's Auxiliary of the Progressive Miners Association (a rival to Illinois District 12 of the UMWA) in the early 1930s. Marat Moore takes the analysis of women's role one step further in Chapter 20, with her intriguing oral histories of the women coal miners who went underground to dig coal from the 1960s on. Boosted by affirmative action laws and the civil rights movement of the period, female mining activists also played a critical role in helping to win the 1989 Pittston strike, even though it must be admitted that the male leaders of the UMWA resisted the employment of women underground for a very long time. James R. Green describes the important role of women at Pittston in Chapter 21.

However, aside from the courage and suffering of Mother Jones and the tent colony wives of Ludlow Massacre fame, which Patricia Long illuminates in Chapter 14, none of our authors takes much of a look at mining women inside the home. Someone familiar with recent gender studies should. Traditional accounts here point to the resiliency of miners' wives during the savage mine wars of the 1920s and

---

37. Herbert Hill, "Myth-Making as Labor History: Herbert Gutman and the United Mine Workers of America," *International Journal of Politics, Culture and Society* 2 (winter 1988): 132–200. For critics of Hill, and his reply to his critics, see *IJPCS* 2 (spring 1989): 361–403; 2 (summer 1989): 587–95.

1930s in Kentucky and West Virginia.[38] Or they describe the Easter fetes, church socials, and fund-raisers for widows held by Slavic miners' wives in Pennsylvania and Illinois.[39] But to my knowledge no American scholar has attempted to resolve the contradiction that seems to exist between the traditionally gendered (or even submissive) behavior that characterized the miner's wife in her domestic surroundings, on the one hand, and her brazen courage on the picket line, on the other. This divided form of behavior—which may have derived in part from traditional family mores among peasant women in Eastern Europe—was the way their aggressive, hard-drinking husbands liked it, one might say.

But such views as this may well insult both the miner and his wife. Surely it can be argued that the wife who handed her husband his slippers the minute he came home, or rubbed his aching back in the tin bathtub in front of the kitchen fire, did not simply do so out of affection or wifely duty. In caring for her husband's body, she also played a crucial role in servicing the physical machine that alone sustained her children and put food on her table. Historically speaking, most mining families knew this fact instinctively. Scholars seem not to, yet.

CHANGES IN TECHNOLOGY

I mentioned above that while the invention of the coal-cutting machine in the 1870s and its slow but increasing deployment after 1890 did undermine some of the pick miner's traditional skills, it did not seriously weaken the collier's control over his pace of work, his level of output, or his freedom from supervision. Nor did many of the other new technologies such as power drills and electric motors that were put to use in the period before the First World War.

To be sure, after 1910 a new caste of machine-cutters and other underground workers was created, some of whom were paid by the day instead of by the ton. (The UMWA insisted that the machine miner be paid at roughly the same rate as the pick miner, so that as pick miners began to use cutting machines themselves, they would not lose any appreciable income).[40] But in 1920 most colliers were still paid by the ton. They still controlled how many coal cars they filled each day. And they still ran their workplaces much as they pleased, often employing their own sons as underground helpers.

But, as Keith Dix shows (Chapter 7), the invention and installation of hand-loading machines in the 1920s and 1930s *did* radically weaken the grip the old-fashioned collier had for generations held over the mining process. By making it possible to

38. See, for example, John W. Hevener, *Which Side Are You On? The Harlan County Coal Miners, 1931–39* (Urbana: University of Illinois Press, 1978), 21–29.

39. Roberts, *Anthracite Coal Communities*, 207–22.

40. Keith Dix, *What's A Coal Miner To Do? The Mechanization of Coal Mining* (Pittsburgh: University of Pittsburgh Press, 1988), 108–9.

load coal automatically, hand-loading machines ended the traditional manner in which each individual miner loaded his own coal cars. The installation of the hand-loading machine also brought new supervisors down into the pit, and began for the first time to radically tip the balance of underground workplace control in favor of the operators. At a time of chronic union weakness in the post–World War I period, the introduction of the hand-loading machine also weakened the UMWA's bargaining position over pay scales. It encouraged Taylorite demands for improved efficiency. And it brought other pressures to bear upon what Carter Goodrich, in a famous book, once called "The Miner's Freedom."[41] In the 1940s and 1950s, the introduction of the continuous mining machine made things still worse.

It was in these circumstances that President John L. Lewis, building on John Mitchell's earlier endorsement of mining machines, made a fateful decision. After the post–World War I breakdown of the Central Competitive Field Agreement brought chaos to the coal market, Lewis sought to stabilize the industry and to recoup the fortunes of the UMWA by two related means. First, he proposed to replace the tonnage method of payment by a system of daily or hourly wages. Second, he sought to encourage the spread of coal-cutting machines. Because of the initially higher costs that these two changes would impose upon the employers, Lewis hoped that they would have two beneficial effects: (a) that they would drive the small and inefficient operators out of the industry; and (b) that they would create a national, instead of a statewide or regionwide, system of collective bargaining. In this way, he hoped to establish a uniform wage for all miners, thereby strengthening the union's bargaining position across the board. By driving the small, "dog-hole" operator out of business, Lewis also hoped that the UMWA could bring the chronic oversupply of coal back into balance with demand.[42]

President Lewis did not, as we stated earlier, succeed in achieving either of these two objectives during the 1920s. For the most part, this was not his own fault. His plan presupposed that the UMWA would remain large enough and strong enough to force the operators to move in the direction he wanted. In the years of rapid union growth that preceded World War I, this was not an unreasonable supposition. Given the dramatic decline that took place in the union's position during the course of the 1920s, however, which was due partly to the rise of oil and partly to competition from nonunion coalfields in the South and West, he failed in both of his aims. As a result, Lewis incurred the bitter enmity both of those district leaders who disagreed with him, and of radical elements in the rank and file. Half a million strong in 1922, by 1928 the UMWA's membership had fallen to less than 100,000, and its bargaining position vis-à-vis the operators had significantly declined.

But the issue for us, in the context of the model of industrial solidarity argument, is whether Lewis approached these issues in the right manner, and whether he took

41. Carter Goodrich, *The Miner's Freedom: A Study of the Working Life in a Changing Industry* (Boston: Marshall Jones, 1925).
42. Brody, *In Labor's Cause,* 152–57.

sufficiently into account the wishes of the rank and file. In making up his or her own mind on this point, the reader will find Alan Singer's views (Chapter 5) highly illuminating. The issue is a thorny one: on the one hand, it is insufficient to accuse Lewis of class collaborationism merely because he found it necessary to take into account the interests of the operators as well as those of the miners. Faced with falling coal prices—and hence with falling wages—as well as with a piecemeal bargaining system that could bring the UMWA no lasting rewards, it was probably inevitable that he should have sought to help the operators restructure the industry as a whole. The alternative (since the government stood aside) was strike action. But what might that have accomplished? Lewis had managed to preserve temporarily the immediate post–World War I wage level by a nationwide strike in 1922. But a repeat strike in the barren period of the late 1920s or early 1930s would almost certainly have failed.

On the other hand, Lewis had no clear mandate from the UMWA membership for his actions. He had come to the presidency of the union fortuitously in 1919; although he was elected in his own right in 1924 most commentators agree that he stole the 1926 presidential election from John Brophy of District 2. In that year Brophy was the candidate of the powerful minority of socialists, communists, and "Save the Union" progressives, who exerted considerable influence in states like Illinois and Pennsylvania in the period following the First World War. The logic of the industry's development may well have mandated that the regional method of collective bargaining that had hitherto prevailed (e.g., under the Central Competitive Field Agreement of 1898) be replaced with a national one. But as David Brody points out, while this fact may help explain Lewis's ruthless imposition of his policies over the heads of the various district leaders who disagreed with him in the 1920s, it by no means justifies it.[43] Alan Singer again has much to say on this point in Chapter 5.

The withdrawal of UMWA district charters from the Illinois, Kansas, and other state unions in the 1920s and the appointment of Lewis surrogates to office in several of them effectively ended internal democracy within the UMWA for several decades. As Stephane Booth shows (Chapter 15), by the late 1920s the situation in Illinois District 12 had degenerated into union civil war. If "industrial solidarity" is defined to mean governing the UMWA in a manner that represented the solidaristic interests of the majority of its members, then Lewis in this period can only be seen as an arrogant and insensitive oligarch.

As Dix also points out (Chapter 7), President Lewis's espousal of day wages to replace the tonnage rate, coupled with his open invitation to the operators to push mechanization to its limits, also ignored the economic interests of large numbers, perhaps a majority, of working miners. Lewis gave lip service to John Mitchell's earlier insistence that the miner share in the fruits of the higher productivity brought about by the installation of coal-cutting and hand-loading machines. But it was little

43. Ibid., 153.

more than lip service. Mechanization increased operator supervision and weakened the individual collier's control over his workplace and way of life. Daily or hourly wages, by dissociating payment from output, prevented miners from benefiting from increased productivity. The first development may have been inevitable; the second was not.

The key to John L. Lewis's trade union philosophy, like that of John Mitchell before him, lay in their espousal of free market economics. That is why President Lewis deliberately engineered the scuttling of proposals to nationalize the coal industry in 1923, even though the idea had been endorsed by the UMWA's own national convention. As a Republican (although not a very principled one) and an admirer—for a time at least—of Herbert Hoover, Lewis made his free market views very clear in his book *The Miners Fight For American Standards* (1924). "The policy of the United Mine Workers," he declared, "ought to have the support of every thinking businessman in the United States, because it proposes to allow natural economic laws free play in the production and distribution of coal."[44] By the late 1920s, with the UMWA in a shambles, those principles had led him near to disaster. However, by 1933, with a sympathetic New Deal administration in office, Lewis came to realize that he could not achieve his goals either for the UMWA or for the industrial unions of what in 1936 was to become the CIO, without the help of the state. Hence his stormy love affair with President Roosevelt between 1933 and 1940.

RELATIONS WITH THE STATE

In Chapters 2 and 17, John Laslett describes some of the ideological and cultural reasons why the leaders of the UMWA, unlike those of the Miners Federation of Great Britain, have always been suspicious of state power. His analysis could be supplemented by a more extensive consideration of American labor's overall traditions of voluntarism, as well by an account of why the UMWA's hostility toward state intervention in industry has been reinforced by the role of the courts in issuing injunctions during labor disputes. Fear and hatred of the role of the state militia in such disputes is another factor here.

In Chapter 14, Priscilla Long provides us with further insight into this aspect of the matter with her description of the brutal role the Colorado State Militia played in the 1914 Ludlow Massacre. In Chapter 6, Robert Zieger gives yet another twist to the antistate argument when he describes President John L. Lewis's disillusionment with the federal government after World War II, and his warnings about the incipient dangers of the military-industrial complex.

In his discussion of community-based miners' clinics in Chapter 10, George

---

44. Quoted in ibid., 151.

Goldstein also provides insights into the suspicious attitudes that many miners as well as mine operators took up toward legislatively determined care. For all of these reasons, there is plenty of evidence to show why the UMWA has tenaciously held onto its misgivings about permitting the federal government to engage itself too deeply in the affairs of the coal industry. We cannot examine all of that evidence here. By extension, however, it might be argued that if the model of industrial solidarity is defined to include the advocacy of mine nationalization, or still more political socialism, the UMWA has flunked the solidaristic test.

But to say this would be to throw the baby out with the bathwater. Maier B. Fox (Chapter 22) is right to point out the danger of confusing workplace militancy with political radicalism. If we limit our definition of industrial solidarity to militant forms of behavior that do not necessarily include socialist politics, then such issues as mine nationalization (even though it was espoused by a significant minority) can be left to one side. But this still leaves open various other lines of inquiry. For example, as Melvyn Dubofsky has shown in a recent book, historically, the UMWA's experience of state power has been as much positive as it has been negative.[45] On the negative side, one can cite the hostile use of labor injunctions by the courts, the use of violence by state militia to defeat mining strikes, and the recent reversal of many New Deal and Fair Deal labor laws to the benefit of the coal operators. On the positive side, one can cite the general benefits of twentieth-century labor legislation, which have helped miners along with other workers, as well as the large number of special safety laws that have been enacted as a result of the UMWA's own lobbying actitivities in coal-state legislatures across the years. While (again unlike the Miners Federation of Great Britain) the UMWA has always eschewed the idea of a separate labor party, rank-and-file miners have often used their votes to press for valuable social legislation.

If the last two paragraphs describe an attitude of ambivalence on the part of the UMWA in its relations with the state, they are meant to. In the early days many of the union's Anglo-Saxon founders voted Republican. In the 1930s, however, most members of the union did cross a political Rubicon of sorts. In the presidential election of 1932 (still more in the one of 1936), they switched their votes en masse to the Democratic Party. Most coal miners also enthusiastically endorsed the great bulk of the social legislation enacted by the New Deal. John L. Lewis himself made a major contribution to the passage of Section 7(a) of the National Industrial Recovery Act (NIRA). In addition, of course, he and other leaders of the UMWA like Len De Caux, Philip Murray, and (the now reconciled) John Brophy played a major role in developing the CIO, which was in turn committed to the interventionist role of President Roosevelt's first two administrations. The Communists, too, played a role. The UMWA was also at the center of efforts to develop Labor's Non-Partisan League, and to reelect President Roosevelt to office in 1936. Thus if "a model of

---

45. Melvyn Dubofsky, *The State and Labor in Modern America* (Chapel Hill: University of North Carolina Press, 1994), esp. chap. 4.

industrial solidarity" means helping the labor movement to organize millions of industrial workers, face down General Motors in the auto workers' sit-down strike or pulling in labor voters behind the Democratic Party in 1936, the UMWA of the mid-1930s unquestionably fits the bill. During this period, indeed, the UMWA— more than any other American union—helped fashion a labor movement that was more class-conscious than any that has existed in the United States either before or since.

But this class-consciousness did not mean favoring the nationalization of the coal mines (as most miners' unions were now doing in Europe); still less did it mean uncritically endorsing the collectivist thrust of the modern industrial state. It did not even mean, despite the labor-Democratic alliance of 1936, unconditional support for the Democratic Party. In 1937, outraged by the failure of President Roosevelt and the Democratic governor of Ohio to help the CIO organize "Little Steel," Lewis was already backing away from the Democrats. In Chapter 5, Alan Singer retells the story of Lewis's flirtation with the idea of a separate labor party in 1937– 40, but provides no evidence that it was anything more than a flirtation.

As with the Miners Federation of Great Britain (MFGB) in England, where the concentration of miners into specific geographical areas had by this time enabled them to elect more than fifty MPs to Parliament (thereby helping to transform the Labour Party into a party of government), by the mid-1930s the UMWA also possessed considerable political clout. With more than 600,000 members packed strategically into the mining constituencies of states like Illinois, Kentucky, Pennsylvania, West Virginia, Alabama, and Colorado, America's miners, along with their allies, could unquestionably have given a significant boost to the political fortunes of either the Socialist or Communist Party. Or, in conjunction with farmers and other disaffected elements, they could have pushed hard for a major realignment of national politics toward the Left. But despite mass unemployment, violent confrontations between labor and capital, and a willingness on Lewis's part to bring known Communists into the upper echelons of the CIO, the UMWA was unwilling to pose any real challenge to the existing two-party system. Had the CIO been led by a labor party sympathizer (as John Brophy of Pennsylvania had been in the 1920s), the situation might have turned out differently. But too many other factors, ranging from President Roosevelt's personal popularity to the ethnic voting traditions of particular groups of miners, and from the CIO's split from the AFL at a critical moment to the ideological flexibility of the existing two-party system, stood in the way. John Laslett demonstrates the relevance of some of these factors in his comparative essay on miners and labor politics (Chapter 17).

Instead, Lewis showed his true political colors—but not his best political judgment—when anger at Roosevelt caused him to switch his endorsement to presidential Republican candidate Wendell Wilkie in 1940. Although returning thereby to the Republican fold, Lewis failed abysmally to pull the CIO's voters along behind him. Besides making him look foolish, this misjudgment forced him, for a time, to relinquish the CIO presidency. But by demonstrating their loyalty to the Democrats, this episode also showed that the bulk of America's coal miners were equally unlikely to support a new, third party of labor. Very few of them actually voted either Socialist or Communist, either. Alan Singer grasps this point very well when he asserts (in Chapter 5) that in 1940: "Neither Senator Wheeler nor the idea of a third party held much appeal for American workers and the majority leadership of the CIO once Roosevelt declared himself a candidate for reelection."

The fact of the matter was that in the 1930s and 1940s, instead of seeking to capture state power in order to exercise it on behalf of a politically united working class, John L. Lewis and other leaders of the UMWA were unwilling to do more than to keep the federal government under cautious observation. They took an instrumental and corporatist view of the state, not a collectivist one. Having grown up in the voluntarist school of the AFL, the UMWA had by this time been rendered so suspicious of state power by years of court injunctions, by the role of the state militia, and by Lewis's own ringing declarations of faith in the free market system, that they would go no further. They flirted with the state, and they tried to get it on their side when they needed it. But they would not get permanently into bed with it.

For this decision, the UMWA paid a considerable price. During the 1930s, and at intervals afterward, Lewis and other UMWA leaders did occasionally manage to persuade Presidents Roosevelt and Truman to support legislation necessary for establishing the national method of collective bargaining that Lewis had first advocated in the 1920s. The major example of this was the 1937 Guffey-Vinson Act, which helped to stabilize the coal industry and created something like a national wage bargaining system under the aegis of the National Recovery Administration (NRA). But when World War II came along and the UMWA found itself, as in World War I, at loggerheads with the government over the union shop, over wage increases, as well as over wage uniformity in different coalfields, the organization quickly found itself out in the cold. Lewis did manage to force the U.S. government to come to terms with the UMWA's wage demands as a result of the defiant national coal strike of 1943. But both he and his union paid dearly for this victory when, fighting the government once again in 1946, he helped bring down upon the UMWA, and upon all of labor, the anti-union Taft-Hartley Act of 1947.[46]

How does this review of the four issues answer the model of industrial solidarity question? Ultimately the reader, having read through the essays in this collection, must puzzle out an answer for himself. For myself, I would suggest that the answer depends partly on how he (or she) interprets the historical evidence that follows in the subsequent chapters, and partly on what pair of spectacles the reader is wearing when he puts down this book. If he is a radical (or perhaps a romantic) who admires what the UMWA managed to do but believes that it might have achieved more along the lines of the archetypal proletarian thesis, he will probably answer that the UMWA provided no such model. Mining communities, he will argue, and the unions they produced, were possessed of a magnificent tradition of class-conscious solidar-

46. Brody, *In Labor's Cause,* 161–62.

ity that—if only the UMWA had been better led—could have helped produce a more radical, and a more politically independent American labor movement. That it did not do so was the fault, not of any lack of political will among the miners themselves, but of a cynical and corrupt national leadership.

If, on the other hand, the reader chooses to wear less rose-tinted spectacles, he may come to a different, but nevertheless historically more informed answer. The coal miners of America, and the unions they created, were indeed possessed of a magnificent legacy of struggle. But they grew to maturity in a society in which socialism was seen as un-American, in which the object of the overall labor movement was to shun the state as much as it was to embrace it, and in which the union's leaders have been as susceptible as Americans of other social classes to the temptations of political office and personal aggrandizement.

Given all of the constraints we have considered—most of which derived from the nature of American industrial society and from the peculiar nature of the coal market, not from personal weakness—my own answer to the question, Can the United Mine Workers of America be considered a model of industrial solidarity? is a regretful no. But it came as near to being such a model as any other American trade union ever has done, or perhaps is ever likely to.

PART ONE

FOUNDERS AND LEADERS OF THE UNITED MINE WORKERS IN ITS HEYDAY, 1890–1960

CHAPTER TWO

BRITISH IMMIGRANT COLLIERS, AND THE ORIGINS AND EARLY DEVELOPMENT OF THE UMWA, 1870–1912

JOHN H.M. LASLETT

The dominant role that immigrants from the British Isles played in the origins and early development of the United Mine Workers of America is inescapable. The prime movers behind the first important American miners' union to be established in the midwest, the American Miners' Association (1860), were Englishman Daniel Weaver and Welshman Thomas Lloyd.[1] When John Siney, the Irish-born miners' leader, attended the founding convention of the Workingmen's Benevolent Association in 1868, there were sixteen miners present: twelve English, three Irish, one Welshman, and two Americans.[2] At the time of the founding convention of the United Mine Workers of America, which took place in Columbus, Ohio, in January 1890, its first National Executive Board consisted of one Scotsman, one Irishman, three Englishmen, one African-American, and two miners whose places of birth were not revealed.[3]

1. Edward Wieck, *The American Miners Association: A Record of the Origin of Coal Miners Unions in the United States* (New York: Russell Sage Foundation, 1940), 26.
2. Edward Pinkowski, *John Siney, The Miners' Martyr* (Philadelphia: Sunshine Press, 1963), 15.
3. *First Annual Convention of the United Mine Workers of America* (Columbus, Ohio, 1890), 8.

In order to understand these pioneers better, and the contribution they made to the development of the UMWA, we shall consider here three sets of questions. The first concerns these early British miners as an immigrant group. Who were they, why did they come, and where did they settle? The second deals with the mining practices and trade union traditions they brought with them, and how these traditions impacted on the trade union philosophy of the UMWA. How much of the UMWA's early structure, collective bargaining philosophy, and political outlook was British in origin, and how much of it was American? What did industrial unionism mean to the American miners, and how did it differ from that of the Miners Federation of Great Britain (1889)? In order to answer these questions, some comparisons will be made with British practices, and with British trade union traditions. Third, why, around 1890, did the number of British immigrant miners begin to diminish, and then decline to a trickle in the period before the First World War? And what consequences did the decline of British influence have for the overall development of the UMWA?

The first set of questions is not difficult to answer. In general, the first generation of skilled English pick miners who came to the United States at the time of the Civil War—who, together with their successors, amounted to about 60,000 in all—came for the same reasons that other skilled British workers moved to the United States during the same period: in response to the voracious demand for skilled labor in America's exploding post–Civil War industries.[4] U.S. coal operators commissioned articles and advertisements in the British press; recruiting agents were sent to offer contracts and cheap passage; and on occasion American mine operators benefited from the fact that British miners' leaders advocated emigration as a solution to the problem of overproduction and low wages in the United Kingdom, particularly during periods of depression.[5]

The flow of British miners in the 1860s and 1870s (the decades of highest migration) did not only consist of settlers who moved here with their families. Many immigrant miners were young single men who traveled from mining camp to mining

4. A precise figure cannot be given because the basis of calculation changed over time in the official immigration statistics, and because the definition of "miner" in these figures was loose. Sometimes it included such groups as quarryman, and mine laborer, as well as miner, and sometimes it did not. The actual number was probably considerably higher than 60,000 because the official figures included winding engineers, blacksmiths, and other workers who habitually worked in the mines but who were classified differently. The estimate is based on U.S. Department of the Treasury, *Annual Reports of the Superintendent (later Commissioner General) of Immigrants, 1892–1914* (Washington, D.C.: GPO, 1914). An illuminating essay on skilled workers who emigrated to the United States from Britain in this period is Charlotte Erickson, "Who Were the English and Scottish Emigrants to the United States in the Late Nineteenth Century?" in *Population and Social Change,* ed. David Glass and R. Reveille (London: Edward Arnold, 1972), 347–82.

5. *National Labor Tribune* (February 1, 1890), 2; Peter Conley, *History of the West Virginia Coal Industry* (Charleston, W.Va.: Education Foundation, 1960), 79–80; Charlotte Erickson, "The Encouragement of Emigration by Trade Unions, 1850–1900," *Population Studies* 3, no. 3 (December 1949): 248–73.

camp in search of higher American wages on a seasonal basis. They would come out with cheap steerage tickets for what was called "a run in the summer season";[6] return to Britain for the sustained winter's work; then travel again the miners' circuit through Maryland, Pennsylvania, Ohio, and Illinois the following summer looking for the mining camp with the highest wages, and perhaps also for a place to settle. Fluctuations in the business cycle also affected the numbers who moved back and forth across the Atlantic. British miners would come over in good times, such as in the boom years of the later 1860s and the early and late 1880s, but the flow would be reversed when times were better in England than they were in the United States. Early in 1873, for example, rising wages in Britain drew back hundreds of recent emigrant colliers to their former homes in Durham, Yorkshire, Scotland, and South Wales.[7] These sojourning habits help explain the traditionally peripatetic habits of the American coal miner. More important for our purposes, the transatlantic immigrant networks they set going became conduits through which British influences over American mining practices and mining trade unionism were both modified and maintained.

Not all emigrant colliers came to America because of higher wages. Some came became they admired American republican and democratic institutions; others, especially those who had worked as farm laborers before being drawn into the British pits, were attracted by the prospect of acquiring cheap land.[8] In the early days, mines were shallower and discipline more lax in the small American mining camps than they had been in the English mining towns. Hence quite a few emigrant miners in the 1870s and 1880s sought to reproduce the relatively privileged craft position that they had earlier enjoyed in the British pits.[9]

Some good insights into the background and subsequent fortunes of these early British miners can be found in a survey that was taken of fifty-seven such men who migrated to the northern Illinois coalfield between 1865 and 1910.[10] In Britain, mining was a hereditary occupation even more than it was in the United States, so only

6. Rowland T. Berthoff, *British Immigrants in Industrial America, 1790–1950* (Cambridge: Harvard University Press, 1953), 52.

7. Ibid.

8. In 1867 Scots mine leader Alexander McDonald told a British Royal Commission on Trade Unions that "hundreds of the workmen in America . . . go out west and pre-empt a hundred and twenty acres of land. They build a cabin upon it and then, in some cases, they return to work. If the wages given by the employer are sufficient and they deem that they are better off working for him, they work. If, on the other hand, they find that they would be as well off living on their lands, they betake themselves to their lots." Quoted in Royden Harrison, ed., *Independent Collier: The Coalminer as Archetypal Proletarian Reconsidered* (New York: St. Martin's, 1978), 67.

9. On this point, see Laslett, *Nature's Noblemen: The Fortunes of the Independent Collier in Scotland and the American Midwest, 1855–1889* (Los Angeles: UCLA Institute of Industrial Relations, 1983), 14–16, 43–44.

10. Amy Zahl Gottlieb, "The Regulation of the Coal Mining Industry in Illinois, With Special Reference to the Influence of British Miners and British Precedents, 1870–1911" (Ph.D. diss., London School of Economics, 1975), app. 5.

eight out of the fifty-seven had fathers who had not also been miners. Most of them had migrated to the United States in their twenties, and almost all had begun their working lives in the pits at the age of seven, eight, or nine. As apprentices, they had worked their way up the underground employment ladder from trapper boys and pony drivers to skilled miners.[11] If they stayed in the pits, this was the identical route that most American-born miners were to follow until the era of machine mining began at the turn of the century. Evidence of prior trade union activity in Great Britain could be seen in the careers of fifteen out of the fifty-seven colliers.[12]

Three out of the sample of fifty-seven miners had been born in Ireland, two of whom had received training in Scotland before coming to the United States. This reflected a common practice whereby the sons of poor Irish peasants crossed the Irish sea to Liverpool or Glasgow to spend a few years in Lancashire or Lanarkshire before traversing the Atlantic to take jobs as all-round miners. A still larger number of Irish immigrants worked as canal and railroad builders in the United States before entering the American pits. But the most striking thing about the sample of 57 miners was their rapid rate of upward social mobility. Although many of them stayed in the industry, within twenty years of migrating to Illinois all 57 had found employment away from the coal face. Eleven of them had been appointed as mine inspectors; seven had become mine superintendents or managers; six had become owners of mining enterprises; and three had served on the Illinois State Bureau of Labor Statistics, where bills for mining statutes often originated. Of those who left mining, several became saloon- or other shop-owners; a few bought land. Three others, Samuel Drew, William Mooney, and David Ross studied law and were admitted to the bar by the Illinois Supreme Court.[13]

Tables 2.1 through 2.3 give a more balanced insight into the settlement patterns of British miners by covering the years 1880, 1890, and 1900 not only for Illinois, but for the states of Pennsylvania, West Virginia, and Kansas as well. Several things are noteworthy about these tables. Look first at the overwhelming dominance of British immigrants, including the Irish, in the foreign-born columns for both 1880 and 1890. Miners from Germany and Scandinavia, at 6.4% overall, were barely in the picture. Note, too, the increase from 20.2% to 23.9% of British-born miners in Kansas between 1880 and 1890, the only state to record such an increase. This confirms my earlier impressionistic remark about British miners moving west. Given

11. The word "apprentice" is used here advisedly, even though some scholars have challenged its use in relation to the coal industry on the ground that articles of apprenticeship were rarely signed and that physical strength was more important than cognitive skills. But the length of time required before a boy entering the pits was permitted to act as a full-fledged collier, and the training he underwent in different aspects of the craft of mining, suggests that something very close to an apprenticeship was undergone. See Henry Pelling, *Popular Politics and Society in Late Victorian Britain* (London: Macmillan, 1968), 47; David Bremner, *The Industries of Scotland* (Edinburgh: Adam and Charles Black, 1869), 15–16; and Alan Campbell, *The Lanarkshire Miners: A Social History of Their Trade Unions, 1775–1874* (Edinburgh: John Donald, 1979), 38–42.

12. Gottlieb, "Regulation," app. 5.

13. Ibid.

Table 2.1 Country of Birth of Miners in Pennsylvania, Illinois, West Virginia, and Kansas in 1880

	Pennsylvania		Illinois		West Virginia		Kansas	
	No.	%	No.	%	No.	%	No.	%
Native-Born	35,015	50.4	5,460	42.3	2,777	75.0	2,174	65.8
Foreign-Born	34,400	49.6	7,438	57.7	924	25.0	1,132	34.2
Gt. Britain	15,739	22.8	4,428	34.4	447	12.1	668	20.2
Ireland	11,224	16.1	1,202	9.2	274	7.4	120	3.6
Germany	3,926	5.7	1,069	8.3	159	4.3	91	2.8
Scandinavia	1,135	1.6	36	0.3	17	0.5	141	4.3
Canada	289	0.4	99	0.8	2	—	32	0.9
Others	2,037	2.9	604	4.7	25	0.7	80	2.4
Total	69,415	100.0	12,898	100.0	3,701	100.0	3,306	100.0

SOURCE: *Statistics of the Population of the United States at the Tenth Census, 1880* (Washington, D.C.: GPO, 1883), table 34, 808–54. These figures probably included "quarrymen" as well.

Table 2.2 Country of Birth of Miners in Pennsylvania, Illinois, West Virginia, and Kansas in 1890

	Pennsylvania		Illinois		West Virginia		Kansas	
	No.	%	No.	%	No.	%	No.	%
Native-Born	48,966	41.9	9,575	42.7	8,426	86.0	2,644	48.3
White	48,117	41.1	8,919	40.2	6,320	64.5	2,371	43.3
Native-Born Parents	23,062	19.7	4,744	21.3	5,523	56.4	1,730	31.6
Foreign-Born Parents	25,055	21.4	4,175	18.9	797	8.1	641	11.7
Black	849	0.8	556	2.5	2,106	21.5	273	5.0
Foreign-Born	67,790	58.1	12,720	57.3	1,375	14.0	2,831	51.3
Great Britain	25,783	22.2	4,837	21.8	740	7.6	1,307	23.9
Ireland	11,606	9.9	1,136	5.1	251	2.6	212	3.9
Germany	6,335	5.4	2,777	12.5	161	1.6	364	6.6
Scandinavia	1,934	1.7	700	3.2	2	—	309	5.6
Canada	277	0.2	85	0.3	11	0.1	28	0.5
Others	21,878	18.7	3,185	14.4	211	2.1	594	10.8
Total	116,756	100.0	22,295	100.0	9,801	100.0	5,475	100.0

SOURCE: *Eleventh Census, 1890, Report on Population*, part 11, table 116, 530–37.

British immigrant dominance in the industry in its early years, it may seem surprising to find that even in 1880, save in Illinois, they were outnumbered by native-born miners. However, the great majority of these native-born miners would have had British parents.

West Virginia native-born miners, at 75% of the total in 1880 and 86% in 1890, vastly outnumbered the immigrants in that state. This was because of the significant

Table 2.3 Country of Birth of Miners and Quarrymen in Pennsylvania, Illinois, West Virginia, and Kansas in 1900

	Pennsylvania		Illinois		West Virginia		Kansas	
	No.	%	No.	%	No.	%	No.	%
Native-Born	74,629	41.4	19,697	51.6	17,829	85.7	6,337	66.3
White	73,013	40.6	18,329	48.0	13,209	63.5	5,179	54.2
Native-Born Parents	36,297	20.2	9,778	25.6	12,028	57.8	3,768	40.5
Foreign-Born Parents	36,716	20.4	8,551	22.4	1,181	5.7	1,311	13.7
Black	1,616	0.8	1,368	3.6	4,620	22.2	1,158	12.1
Foreign-Born (Country of Birth of Foreign-Born and Foreign-Born Parents of Native-Born)	105,845	58.6	18,487	48.4	2,968	14.3	3,204	33.5
Great Britain	31,849	17.7	6,598	17.2	1,053	5.1	1,487	15.6
Ireland	22,958	12.7	2,679	7.0	520	2.5	1,487	5.1
Germany	12,236	6.8	6,151	16.1	368	1.8	683	7.2
Scandinavia	2,778	1.5	1,121	2.9	7	—	221	2.3
Canada	336	0.2	142	0.2	14	—	49	0.4
Austria-Hungary	40,076	22.2	2,709	5.4	915	4.4	354	3.7
Poland	10,999	6.1	1,422	3.7	220	1.1	47	0.5
Russia	5,356	3.0	1,241	3.2	275	1.3	13	—
Italy	8,972	5.0	2,915	7.6	554	2.7	458	5.1
Mixed Foreign Parentage	4,356	2.4	1,000	2.6	111	0.5	225	2.4
Others	2,683	1.5	1,046	2.7	113	0.5	506	5.3
Total	180,474	100.0	38,184	100.0	20,797	100.0	9,541	100.0

SOURCE: *Twelfth Census, 1900, Special Report on Occupations*, 220–28.

number of African-American miners in the area, which is disguised in the tables until 1900, when they are shown separately for the first time. In that year, they constituted 22.2% of the total. Few British colliers settled in states such as West Virginia or Alabama, partly out of racist feeling, and partly because wage levels were lower there than they were in the northern mining states. Note, finally, the increasing number of Austro-Hungarians and other Slavs in the pits as one moves up in time. They are put in the "Other" column in 1880 and 1890, but already in the latter year they constituted 18.7% of the total in Pennsylvania, and 14.4% in Illinois. By 1900 Austro-Hungarians (a polyglot name that would have included German-speaking Austrians and Bohemians, some of them already miners in their home country, as well as peasant Slovaks, Serbs, and Croats), at 40,076, constituted by far the largest group of foreigners among the miners in Pennsylvania.

The second set of questions concerns the transfer of British mining practices to the United States. Basically, two methods of mining prevailed in the United States in the late nineteenth century, both of which originated in Great Britain. One was the "room and pillar" method (more often called "pillar and stall" in the United

Kingdom). Essentially, this method consisted of driving side entries into the coal from the main passageway, and then cutting subsidiary openings into the side entries at frequent intervals, thus forming "stalls," "bords," or "rooms," in which miners worked either in pairs or singly. Such rooms varied in size from twelve to forty feet square. The other method of mining, called "longwall," involved advancing along all parts of the coal face simultaneously, roughly in a straight line.[14] Examples of both the "room and pillar" and the "longwall" systems can be seen in Diagrams 2.1 and 2.2.

"Room and pillar" methods were generally preferred in the United States, although the "longwall" system was introduced into the country in 1865 by the Scottish pit boss James Braidwood, in the northern Illinois mining town that bore his name.[15] Whichever system he worked under, therefore, in his early years in America the British immigrant miner would have utilized the same methods of cutting, blasting, and loading coal that he had used at home. Later on, so-called blasting off the solid, which obviated undercutting and was made possible by the invention of more

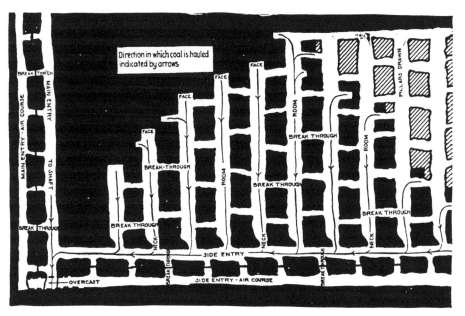

Diagram 2.1. Working methods in British and American mines in the late nineteenth century: room and pillar system. Keith Dix, *Work Relations in the Coal Industry: The Hand-Loading Era, 1880–1930* [Morgantown, W.Va., Institute for Labor Studies, 1977], 5.

14. B. R. Mitchell, *Economic Development of the British Coal Industry, 1800–1914* (Cambridge: Cambridge University Press, 1984), 71–74; Keith Dix, *Work Relations in the Coal Industry: The Hand-Loading Era, 1880–1920* (Morgantown, W.Va.: Institute for Labor Studies, West Virginia University, 1977), 4–6.

15. Berthoff, *British Immigrants,* 54.

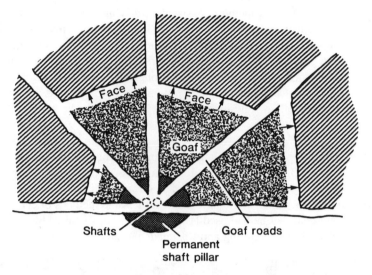

Diagram 2.2. Working methods in British and American mines in the late nineteenth century: longwall system. Roy Church, *The History of the British Coal Industry, 1830–1913: Victorian Pre-Eminence* [Oxford: Clarendon Press, 1986], 339.

powerful forms of dynamite, became widespread, although it was looked down upon by the older generation of British miners. Hence it is obvious that until the widespread introduction of coal-cutting machinery in the 1890s, the immigrant miner's skills were easily transferred from the pits of his homeland to those of the United States.[16]

Whether he worked under a "room and pillar" system or under a "longwall" one, until the 1920s—and in some areas, even thereafter—the Anglo-American miner also enjoyed much the same degree of workplace autonomy that the British miners had. Unlike the factory, where workers were concentrated and foreman/worker ratios were high, the widespread dispersion of workplaces made underground supervision of mine workers practically impossible. Longwall systems of mining, which concentrated larger bodies of men in one place, to some extent made supervision easier. Yet by making the extraction of coal dependent on the simultaneous presence and coordinated activity of thirty or forty men, the absence of two or

16. Carter Goodrich, in his classic study *The Miners' Freedom*, pointed to minor differences between the techniques used by miners from different regions of Great Britain when they first came to the United States. He notes with some amusement that at the Bell mine in Illinois a so-called Durham entry inside the pit "had been sheared (cut vertically) on the right-hand slot from the left while the Welshmen— whether they were left-handed or not—had sheared on the left and shot from the right." See Goodrich, *Miners' Freedom* (Boston: Marshal Jones, 1925), 108–9.

three of them could bring production to a halt in a manner not possible under the "room and pillar" method.[17]

Also crucial to the miner's famed workplace independence was his ability to leave the pit on his own initiative when he had hewed a sufficient tonnage of coal in any given day to satisfy his immediate earning needs. This practice, which was also brought over from the United Kingdom to the United States, originated in the British miner's policy of attempting to maintain a high level of wages by artificially limiting output.[18] Attempts to break this habit were at the forefront of the coal operator's efforts to discipline the miner for over seventy years between 1865 and 1925; and it is a sign of the continuity of mining practices between Britain and the United States that the coal-owners' struggle on this issue should have been conducted in almost identical ways on both sides of the Atlantic for this whole period of time. Rule 3 of the English Mines Inspection Act of 1855 sought to curb the miner's control over his hours of work by insisting that all colliers must "work at their appointed coal faces continuously, . . . and without interruption while the shift continues."[19] Sixty-five years later, an Ohio mining official reported to the 1923 U.S. Coal Commission that "in actual practice 60 to 70 percent [of the miners] do not observe the eight-hour rule." And "for these employees even the six-hour day is the exception and not the rule."[20]

It was arguments over control of the miners' traditional rights vis-à-vis the operators, therefore, as much as it was arguments over hours or wage levels, that first sparked the need for miners' unions on both sides of the Atlantic. This brings me to the issue of trade union philosophy and tactics. National miners' unions in both Britain and America came into being in much the same way. First came local groups of activists who called mass meetings to protest wage cuts or the encroachment of the operators on the collier's privileges; then countywide organizations with a rudimentary, if temporary, form of organization; then regional bodies with dues and some form of benefit system; and finally national trade unions, with a complex federal structure and a bureaucracy of their own. Such were the United Mine Workers of America, and the Miners Federation of Great Britain (which was established in 1889, only one year before its American counterpart). By 1912 the UMWA had 353,066 members concentrated mostly in Illinois, Pennsylvania, and the Midwest.

---

17. In 1924, one authority put it this way: "Successful long-wall mining depends on . . . a steady supply of labor, for even a short stoppage of operation may result in serious damage to the working area through the caving of the roof. In the pillar method this is less important." Isador Lubin, *Miners' Wages and the Cost of Coal* (New York: McGraw-Hill, 1924), 16.

18. Harrison, *Independent Collier*, 118–22.

19. Quoted in Laslett, *Nature's Noblemen*, 23.

20. "Evidence and Testimony Submitted to the U.S. Coal Commission by the Bituminous Operators' Special Committee," September 10, 1923. Quoted in Keith Dix, *What's A Miner To Do? The Mechanization of Coal Mining* (Pittsburgh: University of Pittsburgh Press, 1988), 13.

The MFGB was even stronger. In 1912, it contained 733,000 miners spread all over Great Britain.[21]

At first it appeared as if the policies of the organized miners in both Britain and America would follow a similar course. When Irish-born John Siney, Scottish-born John James, and other Anglo-Saxon unionists convened the first meeting of the Miners' National Association in Youngstown, Ohio, in October 1873, its constitution was modeled after that of Alexander McDonald's British union of the same name. So, too, were its principles: control over output; producers' and consumers' cooperatives; arbitration and conciliation of disputes; and the avoidance of strikes wherever possible.[22] In this period the latter policy was not based on pusillanimous kowtowing to the will of the coal operators. It was based, in the British case, on the mid-Victorian idea that mine-owner and miner (who at this point was a petty contractor, not a wage laborer) had a mutual responsibility for extracting wealth from the industry, and that disputes between the two sides could be satisfactorily resolved on a gentlemanly basis around the negotiating table. In the American case, the same belief was buttressed by notions of republican liberty.[23]

For some years, this ambivalent attitude toward strike action continued on both sides of the ocean. Some miners, believing that coal prices inevitably determined wages, upheld the idea of a sliding scale as a mechanism for regulating wages. Others espoused the Knights of Labor belief in a mutualist type of economy in which miners and small- and medium-sized operators, although not mining trusts, would continue to enjoy harmonious relations. Even the Declaration of Principles adopted by the first convention of the United Mine Workers, in January 1890, committed the union "to use all honorable means to maintain peace between ourselves and employers; adjusting all differences, so far as possible, by arbitration, and conciliation, that strikes may become unnecessary."[24] As the depression of the mid-1890s deepened, however, and wages fell steeply, it became increasingly apparent that a living wage could not be maintained without resorting to strike action. Hence rank-and-file miners in both Britain and America repudiated the mid-Victorian ideal of class harmony, and espoused instead a class-conflict—although not necessarily Marxist—model of labor relations in which strikes, along with other means of coerc-

---

21. There is no satisfactory single-volume history of either the UMWA or the MFGB. The MFGB's history during this period can be pieced together from R. Page Arnot's *The Miners: A History of the Miners Federation of Great Britain, 1889–1910* (London: George Allen and Unwin, 1949), and Roy Church, *The History of the British Coal Industry, 1830–1913: Victorian Pre-Eminence* vol. 3 (Oxford: Clarendon Press, 1986). That of the UMWA can be found in McAlister Coleman, *Men and Coal* (New York: Holt, Rinehart and Winston, 1949), and Priscilla Long, *Where the Sun Never Shines: A History of America's Bloody Coal Industry* (New York: Paragon House, 1989),

22. Andrew Roy, *A History of the Coal Miners of the United States* (Columbus, Ohio: J. L. Trauger, 1905), 156–60.

23. For a further elucidation of this mid-Victorian concept of mining trade unionism, see Laslett, *Nature's Noblemen*, chaps. 3–4.

24. *Constitution, United Mine Workers of America* (1890), 1.

ing the employers were seen as necessary tools for defending, and if possible improving, the miners' standard of living.

Although strikes were accepted as a legitimate weapon by the new generation of miners' leaders that came to power soon after the United Mine Workers was founded, the earlier preoccupation with arbitration and conciliation led to the elaboration of complex negotiating procedures for dealing with day-to-day disputes in both Britain and America. These procedures also had common roots, the most notable being the system of continuous collective bargaining, which appears to have originated in Durham in the 1870s. This system had two elements. The first was a joint committee system whereby grievances originating at the pit level were settled by representatives of the union and the employers via a hierarchy of officials appointed by both sides to deal with the matter, on an ongoing basis. The second element, which only operated up to the county level in Great Britain until the turn of the century but which covered the entire bituminous Central Competitive Field in the United States, involved an Interstate Joint Agreement for renegotiating the annual UMW wage scale.[25]

The Interstate Joint Agreement, which set wage rates for the Central Competitive Field consisting of Illinois, Indiana, Ohio, and western Pennsylvania, was first established at a conference of union leaders and representatives of mine operators' associations held in Columbus, Ohio, in February 1886. It broke down between 1889 and 1898 because of rivalry between the Knights of Labor and the National Federation of Miners and Mine Laborers, and also because the coal operators of southern Illinois and Indiana were unwilling to sacrifice the competitive advantage they enjoyed over the operators of other regions by joining the scheme. After being reestablished in 1898 following the first really successful UMW national strike the previous year, the Interstate Joint Agreement was renewed up into the 1920s.[26]

The Interstate Agreement was entered into by the miners and operators because each side recognized the destructive impact that unregulated competition was having on both wage levels and profit margins, at a time when too many operators had entered the industry, thereby causing a coal glut. The coal operators hoped to improve their profit margins by negotiating wage agreements with built-in differentials between coalfields so as to equalize their costs. The union entered into the Interstate Agreement because it hoped that limiting cut-throat competition between operators would enable them to press their wage demands with more hope of success—a hope that turned out to be justified.[27]

25. For a description of the Joint Committee system of negotiating in Great Britain, see Church, *History of the British Coal Industry*, 697–98, 731–34. For an analysis of the origins and development of the interstate joint conference that negotiated the annual UMW wage scale in the Midwest, see Arthur E. Suffern, *Conciliation and Arbitration in the Coal Industry of America* (Boston: Houghton Mifflin, 1915), passim.

26. Suffern, *Conciliation and Arbitration,* chap. 5.

27. One source states that the Interstate Agreement helped raise the wages of the bituminous miners from $270 a year in 1898 to $522 in 1903. See Michael Nash, *Conflict and Accommodation: Coal Miners, Steel Workers, and Socialism, 1890–1920* (Westport, Conn.: Greenwood, 1982), 90.

However, to be successful, such an agreement required the disciplining of union members so as to prevent wildcat strikes, and to reconcile dissatisfied miners to wage differentials between different regions. In turn, this set up a constant source of friction between union officials and rank-and-file members that became even more explosive in America than it did in Great Britain because the Joint Committees' agreements there covered a smaller geographical region. In 1910, for example, UMW District 12 President John H. Walker helped negotiate an agreement with the Illinois Coal Operators Association which gave foremen the right to dismiss any man who was absent from work without a valid medical excuse. Henry Kassenbein, a black delegate to the next District 12 convention, objected to the clause "as making all men, like my people used to be, slaves." Walker replied that the agreement was binding on all rank-and-file members, and that the protest would not keep the union from showing "that it respected a contract which it [had] . . . negotiated."[28] Later on, these disputes over the enforcement of contracts in the United States—unlike those in Great Britain—reached such heights that whole districts were for a time expelled from the UMWA when they refused to abide by the terms.[29]

In other respects, also, it had become clear by the turn of the century that, despite common ground on some issues, on other ones the philosophy of trade unionism espoused by the majority of miners in the UMWA had begun to diverge somewhat from that of the MFGB. By this I do not necessarily mean that the UMWA became more conservative than the MFGB. On the question of industrial unionism, for example, as we shall see in a moment, the UMWA in some respects took up a more advanced position than did the MFGB. I refer instead to the changing attitude of unions on both sides of the Atlantic toward the role of the state in industry. Both unions strongly supported the enactment of safety and other mining legislation, in the American case by state legislatures; in the British case by Parliament in London. Both unions also, albeit with some misgiving on the part of the Durham and Northumberland miners in England, supported the idea of a legislatively mandated eight-hour day. Once the mid-Victorian ideal of class harmony had been discredited in the 1870s and 1880s, however, the MFGB slowly but decisively abandoned its formerly voluntarist (i.e., neutral or even suspicious) position and embraced the idea of state intervention in the coal industry on a widespread scale to supplement the bargaining power of the union down the pit.[30] The UMWA, on the other hand, despite a theoretical committment to mine nationalization, was unwilling to go that far.

Two examples will suffice to make the point. One comes from the arena of collective bargaining; the other from the idea of a minimum wage. The English national coal strike of 1893 prompted the British government to enact the first Conciliation

28. Ibid., 92.

29. Note, for example, the expulsion of Kansas District 14 over the enforcement of an unpopular contract, as described in Melvyn Dubofsky and Warren Van Tine, *John L. Lewis: A Biography* (New York: Quadrangle, 1977), 113–19.

30. Harrison, *Independent Collier,* 157.

(Trades Disputes) Act in 1896. This act empowered the Board of Trade to establish conciliation boards to look into the causes of industrial disputes, bring warring employers and employees together under a neutral chairman, and appoint boards of conciliation to arbitrate disputes. This Conciliation Act was voluntary in its application; it only provided arbitration services to employers and unions that asked for its services. Nevertheless, between 1986 and 1910 out of 432 industrial disputes which it arbitrated, 54 were in coal mining.[31] The number might well have been higher had it not been for the Joint Committee grievance negotiating system within the MFGB that I described earlier.

When it came to appealing for outside help to settle a mining dispute that could not be solved by its internal grievance negotiating system, the UMWA took a very different tack. It is true that President Theodore Roosevelt intervened successfully in the 1902 anthracite strike, just as Prime Minister William Gladstone had done in the British national coal strike of 1893. But the main vehicle used to bring about a settlement of the 1902 U.S. anthracite strike was not a government-sponsored arbitration and conciliation service. It was the National Civic Federation. This was an ad hoc, joint committee of businessmen, labor leaders, and prominent citizens headed by Mark Hanna and Samuel Gompers that had no statutory powers at all.[32]

The dispute that took place in Britain over a legally enacted minimum wage for miners between 1908 and 1912 also reflected the greater willingness of the MFGB to invoke the power of the state to aid the miners when compared to the UMWA. As far as I have been able to discover, no proposals for a legal minimum wage for miners were put forward by the leaders of the UMWA during this period, not even by the powerful minority of socialists in such states as Pennsylvania or Illinois. Instead, the union's national leaders preferred to use collective bargaining and the threat of an annual strike to determine the level of wages. In Britain, on the other hand, the demand for a legally enacted minimum wage began to gather strength almost as soon as the late Victorian belief in the sliding scale—the idea that movements up and down in the price of coal should determine wage levels—had lost its hold. The immediate cause of the movement for a national minimum wage in Britain was the problem of "abnormal places." This referred to the inability of a miner who worked in old narrow seams, for example in South Wales, to raise as much coal in a day—and therefore earn as much money in a shift—as the miner who worked in the newer, wider seams of the Midlands.[33] But after the enactment of the Eight Hour Law in 1908, the demand for a minimum wage became the primary focus of the MFGB's political activity, reaching a climax in the 1912 national miners' strike and in the enactment of the Minimum Wage Act by Parliament soon after.[34]

31. Suffern, *Conciliation and Arbitration,* 283–85.

32. For the role of the N.C.F. in the 1902 Pennsylvania anthracite strike, see Margaret Green, *The National Civic Federation and the American Labor Movement, 1900–1925* (Westport, Conn.: Greenwood Press, 1973).

33. Church, *History of the British Coal Industry,* 741–42.

34. Ibid., 743–46.

The UMWA and the MFGB also developed different ideas about the nature and purposes of industrial unionism. After its founding in 1889, the MFGB did gradually absorb a range of workmen besides colliers who worked in or about the mines. These included enginemen, firemen, mine mechanics, and colliery clerks. Nevertheless large numbers of other workers associated with mining remained outside of the Miners Federation;[35] and the British union remained a federation of partially sovereign county organizations that lagged considerably behind the UMWA both in the breadth of its membership, and in its degree of central control. In the American union all locals, subdistricts, and districts were subject to the rulings of the International Executive Board. In theory no strikes involving the majority of workers in a district could be called without sanction of the board, either. By 1910, moreover, the UMWA contained about fifty additional kinds of workers, both above and beneath ground, besides those who actually cut the coal. This was a far larger number of trades than were included in the MFGB. In that year a resolution was proposed that would have enabled tradesmen who were not miners (coal-hoisting engineers, for example) to elect delegates of their own to the UMWA national convention. But it was voted down by a large majority.[36]

Why did the British and American miners' concepts of industrial unionism diverge? Part of the reason for the U.S. union's incorporation of a larger number of ancillary craftsmen was purely pragmatic. At the turn of the century jurisdictional disputes emerged between the UMWA and the Blacksmiths, the Hoisting Engineers, and several other craft unions whose members worked in the mines. When such craftsmen proposed to strike, they threatened to breach the UMWA's own contract by throwing the majority of underground workers in a mine out of work. The answer to the problem, declared the *United Mine Workers Journal* in November 1900, was for "all employees working in or around a mine . . . [to be brought] under the control of the one organization, with one agreement, applying to all and expiring at a given time."[37] This policy was adopted, resulting in the Scranton Declaration of December 1901, under which the AFL reluctantly acknowledged the right of the UMWA to organize all workers in and around the mines.[38]

But there were other reasons for the divergence. One was the legacy of the Knights of Labor, which had a far broader concept of working-class unity than any British trade union did at the time. Indeed, for a brief time in the mid-1880s the K of L established a number of branches among colliers in England.[39] Upon coming to America a number of British immigrant miners also joined National District As-

35. In 1920, non-MFGB British miners established the National Council of Colliery Workers Other Than Miners in order to maintain a separate existence. See Marion D. Savage, *Industrial Unionism in America* (New York: Ronald Press, 1922; repr. New York: Arno, 1971), 8–9. See also Church, *History of the British Coal Industry,* 713.

36. Savage, *Industrial Unionism,* 86–87.

37. *United Mine Workers Journal* (November 22, 1900): 6.

38. Philip Taft, *The A.F. of L. in the Time of Gompers* (New York: Little Brown, 1955), 325–26.

39. Fred Reid, *Keir Hardie, The Making of a Socialist* (London: Croom Helm, 1978), app. 2.

sembly 135, which was of the founding bodies of the UMWA.[40] Another reason for the greater stength of industrial unionism in the U.S. union derived from the earlier and more widespread introduction of coal-cutting machinery into the American mines. This development, while it alienated many British immigrant pick miners, blurred the distinction between skilled and unskilled underground workers, and created a growing cadre of semiskilled miners who shared a broader set of common assumptions about their trade.[41] Third, because of the larger size and more combined character of the big American mining companies, the need for unified action on the part of the various regional districts in UMW was more urgent than it was for the MFGB. At the 1910 UMWA convention a resolution was proposed by a number of Pennsylvania delegates pointing to the growth of such trusts, which "the present system of sectional trades unionism is incapable of combating."[42] It urged greater efforts on the part of the international office to lend support to strikes against large companies by the various districts.

Finally, important differences developed between the political policies adopted by the MFGB and the UMWA. As already stated, despite its desire to keep the federal government out of the collective bargaining process, the UMWA and its predecessor unions showed no hesitation in pressing state legislatures (and, later on, the federal government) for safety laws and other measures that became incorporated into the mining code. And at first, the political tactics it followed differed little from those that had earlier been adopted by the British miners' unions. In the 1880s and 1890s American miners' leaders (many of them of British origin), read avidly about the passage of safety legislation by the British Parliament; lobbied their state legislatures for the passage of similar measures; and, in certain states at least, even pressed to have their own members elected to state lawmaking bodies on the Democratic and Republican tickets. In Illinois, for example, between 1874 and 1910 eleven miners were elected to the State Assembly in Springfield.[43]

British coal miners were not inherently more radical in their politics than were U.S. ones. For example, most of them voted Liberal, not Labour, until World War I, and some even supported the Conservatives. But in December 1905, when fifty-one working-class MPs were elected to Parliament, quite of a few of them were miners. An even more important step was taken in May 1908, when the MFGB as a whole voted to affiliate with the Labour Party. Soon afterward the *United Mine Workers Journal* was replete with letters from radicals in the UMWA urging it to follow the British miners' example. "This election has special interest to organized labor in the United States," wrote one correspondent in February 1906, "which has not one Congressman where it could elect sixty, [and] not a Senator where it could have

40. For the influence of the Knights of Labor over the UMW, see Roy, *History of the Coal Miners,* chap. 21.
41. Savage, *Industrial Unionism,* 20.
42. *UMWJ* (January 27, 1910): 15.
43. Gottlieb, "Regulation," 90.

sixteen.''[44] At the 1909 convention of the UMWA, D. B. Robb of Ohio District 6 introduced a resolution urging the union to "encourage, in spirit and in fact, the promotion of a national labor party." The resolution was heavily defeated.[45]

The debate that took place on this 1909 resolution was interesting. It revealed why the UMWA was never willing to commit itself to a separate political party, even though the strong minority of socialists in the union frequently urged it to do so.[46] The reasons advanced by the union's national leaders for this opposition to independent political action were various. Some believed that partisan politics were a private matter that should not be taken up by the union as such; others, that politics were divisive, and that if the UMW officially endorsed any given set of candidates, it would tear the union apart. (Incidentally, this did not prevent quite a few UMWA local unions, especially in Illinois and Pennsylvania, from endorsing Socialist candidates, and even spending union money on their behalf.)[47] But the most frequent justification used by UMW officials to prevent the union from endorsing either the Socialist Party of America, or a separate labor party on British lines, stemmed from the fact that local and district officials had, over the years, been able to secure a great deal of mining legislation by twisting the arms of the representatives of one or another of the two major parties; if the union came out openly for a third party, it would lose all of the political capital it had built up with the Democrats and Republicans.[48]

We turn now to our third set of questions: Why did the number of British immigrant miners diminish after the mid-1880s? What were the consequences of this for the future development of the United Mine Workers? To some extent the decline was part of a general post-1885 shift in immigration patterns to the United States, away from the industrialized countries of Northern and Western Europe to the agricultural societies in the eastern and southern parts of the continent.[49] One result of this was that a somewhat larger proportion of British emigrant miners went to the coal-producing dominions of the British Empire than they did to the United States.

---

44. *UMWJ* (February 1, 1906): 4.

45. *Proceedings, Twentieth Annual Convention of the United Mine Workers of America* (Indianapolis, Ind., 1909), 402–17.

46. Not all of the radicals who were members of the Socialist Party of America supported the idea of a labor party, however. In the debate over Robb's 1909 resolution, for example, Adolph Germer of Illinois District 12 opposed it, not because he opposed independent political action, but because he wanted the miners to lend their support to the Socialist Party. See *Proceedings, Twentieth Annual Convention*, 407–8.

47. The Socialists in the UMWA were particularly strong in Illinois and Pennsylvania, and Socialist Party candidates sometimes did very well in local mining districts. For details, see Nash, *Conflict and Accommodation,* chaps. 3–4; Laslett, *Labor and the Left, A Study of Socialist and Radical Influences in the American Labor Movement, 1881–1924* (New York: Basic Books, 1970), chap. 6.

48. Laslett, *Labor and the Left,* 212.

49. For this shift, see any textbook on American immigration; e.g., Alan Kraut, *The Huddled Masses, The Immigrant in American Society, 1880–1921* (Arlington Heights, Ill.: Harlan Davidson, 1982), passim.

As far as the American coal industry was concerned, the two main reasons for decline were the increasing use of coal-cutting machines in the American pits; and the rapidly growing influx into the American mines of unskilled peasant workers from Italy, from Austria-Hungary, and from the western provinces of the Tsarist empire. The first of these developments rendered many of the pick-mining skills of the British miners obsolete, thereby undermining their attractiveness on the American labor market; the second brought alien ways of life to the mining towns, thereby undermining the cultural hegemony that Anglo-Saxon miners had hitherto enjoyed.

These two developments were interrelated: new developments in mining technology made more efficient coal-cutting machines available; the influx of Slavic migrants provided a new source of cheap labor, thereby cutting labor costs sufficiently to make it economic to run the machines. A number of myths became attached to the new immigrants: that most Italian and Slavic migrants deliberately entered into the mining industry as strike-breakers; that they were socially and culturally inferior to the Anglo-Saxons; that they were easily manipulated by the coal operators; and that they were difficult, if not impossible, to organize into trade unions.[50] The misleading character of these myths, at least as far as support for the UMWA was concerned, was quickly demonstrated by the courage and tenacity the Slavic miners displayed in the anthracite strikes of 1898 and 1902.[51]

Unfortunately, the cultural dimension of the myth concerning East European inferiority proved to be more long-lasting. It resulted partly from religious differences, partly from variations in behavior stemming from a peasant rather than an urban culture, and partly from differences in language, diet, dress, and other social customs. Many, if not most of the English-speaking miners were Protestants. If they were Scots, many would have been Presbyterians; if they were Welsh, they were likely to be Methodists. If they were Catholics, as many of the Irish miners were, they belonged to the Roman branch of the church. Most Slavic miners, on the other hand, were Greek or Russian Orthodox. Many of the Italians and Slavs were also either illiterate or semiliterate when they first came to America, and were used to a far lower standard of living. Densely packed into boardinghouses, they wore strange peasant garb, celebrated different ethnic festivals, and appeared overexcitable and swarthy in their appearance to the older generation of stolid, light-skinned Northern Europeans. Slavs and Italians also seemed to live by choice in their own separate neighborhoods.

But part of the cultural condescension of the Anglo miners must also be attributed to the arrogance and labor-aristocratic traditions of the ''Johnny Bull'' colliers themselves. By the time the UMWA was founded in 1890 they had enjoyed a monopoly of the skilled positions in the trade for more than a generation, and many of

50. For a contemporary account that displays these prejudices against the Slavs, see Frank J. Warne, *The Slav Invasion and the Mine Workers, A Study in Immigration* (Philadelphia: J. B. Lippincott, 1904).

51. Victor Greene, *The Slavic Community on Strike: Immigrant Labor in Pennsylvania Anthracite* (Notre Dame: Notre Dame University Press, 1968), 88–133.

them were determined to hang onto it. There is an unmistakable note of condescension, for example, in this 1904 account by Frank J. Warne of the differences between the two groups: "The Irish, English, Welsh, Scotch and German mine-workers, who entered the hard-coal industry before and for some time after the Civil War, had grown accustomed to a social life of some dignity and comfort by the time of the Slav's entrance into the industry. This English-speaking miner wanted a home, wife, and children. A picture of that home represented, usually, a neat two-story frame house, with a porch and yard attached. He wanted a carpet on the best room, pictures on the wall, and the house to be otherwise attractive. In that house he wanted none but his own immediate family."[52]

"In marked contrast to this," continued Warne, "was the mode of life of the Slav mine-worker. Escaping, as he was, from an agricultural environment which had barely supplied food, clothing and shelter, the Slav came single-handed, alone. Wife and children he had none, nor wished for them. . . . The Slav was content to live in a one-room hut, built by his own hands on a hill-side near the mine, of driftwood gathered at spare moments along the highway, and roofed with tin from discarded powder-cans; or he crowded into the poorer and cheaper living sections of the larger mining towns."[53] This supposed contrast is ironic: many of the English-speaking miners had also been single men living under primitive conditions when they first came to Pennsylvania a generation earlier. Nevertheless, as a result of the perceived threat to their jobs, after 1890 significant numbers of Anglo-Saxon miners either returned home to Britain, or moved further west to states such as Wyoming or Utah where their pick-mining skills were still in demand. Or they moved up and out of the pit altogether, either taking up a different occupation, or—more frequently— becoming supervisors or managers in the coal industry themselves.

The numerical impact of this change in the ethnic composition of the mine labor force can be seen by referring again to Table 2.3. It shows that by 1900 the combined total of Austro-Hungarians, Poles, and Russians working in the anthracite mines of Pennsylvania had reached 31.3%; in the Illinois bituminous mines the total stood at 12.3%. An even better sense of the cumulative impact of this changeover on an individual coal company can be obtained from Table 2.4, which documents changing employment patterns at the Reading Coal and Iron Company in Pennsylvania during the 1890s. As the decade unfolded there was a steady decline in the proportion of English, Welsh, Scots, and Irish miners working for the company, and a rapid increase in the number of "new immigrants." A 1910 visitor to the Pennsylvania anthracite region summarized the new occupational hierarchy at another local mine, that skilled Welsh pick miners had first worked in 1868, as follows: "Managers and superintendents, Welsh; foremen and bosses, Irish; contract miners, Poles

52. Frank J. Warne, *The Slav Invasion and the Mine Workers: A Study in Immigration* (Philadelphia: J. B. Lippincott, 1904), 5–6.
53. Ibid., 67–68.

Table 2.4 Ethnicity of Miners Employed by Reading (Pa.) Coal and Iron Company, 1890–1896

Nationality and Parentage	1890		1895		1896	
	No.	%	No.	%	No.	%
English	2,088	8.4	1,960	7.0	1,799	6.3
Welsh	1,282	5.2	1,112	4.0	1,037	3.7
Scots	210	0.9	223	0.8	168	0.6
Irish	6,887	27.8	6,450	23.0	6,025	21.3
German	3,709	15.0	3,471	12.4	3,207	11.3
"New Immigrants"	5,819	23.6	9,000	32.2	10,286	36.2
Native-Born	4,719	19.1	5,765	20.6	5,838	20.6

SOURCE: G. O. Virtue, "The Anthracite Mine Laborer," *Bulletin of the Department of Labor,* no. 13 (November 1897), 751.

and Lithuanians; and outside laborers, Slovaks, Ruthenians, and Italians.''[54] Similar patterns developed in other eastern mining states, as well.

Care must be taken in analyzing the impact these occupational changes had on the position of the British immigrant miner in the coal industry generally. It is not true, for example, that the introduction of coal-cutting machinery immediately caused all skilled Anglo workers to lose their jobs. For one thing, the introduction of the machines was gradual, and in some places not feasible at all due to narrow coal seams, or to the type of fuel mined. In Illinois, for example, although the overall number of coal-cutting machines rose from 241 in 1891 to 1,920 in 1917, in the latter year only 98 mines used machines exclusively, while 53 pits used both machinery and pick-swinging men.[55] The introduction of new machinery also created several new categories of skilled or semiskilled jobs, including shot-firer, timberman, driller and cutter (machine-operator), and loader. Quite a few of the older generation of Anglo-Saxon miners took over these new jobs, thereby temporarily retaining their position somewhere near the top of the occupational hierarchy. Under the UMW contract, many of the new jobs were quite well paid also, ranging in scale from $2.50 per day for the cutter to $1.75 for the loaders.[56]

Nevertheless, the long-term effect of these changes was to destroy the old job monopoly the British pick miner had once enjoyed in the North American labor market, and to undermine many of his skills. "The result of all these forces," concluded the Dillingham Immigration Commission in 1915, "is the displacement of the former miners and a deterioration of their conditions of employment."[57]

54. Quoted in Berthoff, *British Immigrants,* 56.

55. *Statistics of Coal Mining in Illinois: Reports of the State Inspector,* part 3 (Springfield, Ill.: H. W. Rocker, 1893), 495–96.

56. *Fifth Annual Report of the Illinois Bureau of Labor Statistics* (Springfield, Ill.: H. W. Rocker, 1887), lxv.

57. *Immigrants in Industries, Part 1: Bituminous Coal Mining. Reports of the Immigration Commission* (61st Congress, Second Series, Senate Doc. No. 633), 667.

What effect, finally, did this have on the British immigrant miner's position within the United Mine Workers of America? In the absence of industrywide data on the relationship between ethnicity and officeholding in the UMWA in this early period, this question is not easy to answer. For a number of years, the changeover from a union rank and file dominated by miners of Anglo-Saxon background to one (in the eastern mining states at least) in which the bulk of the miners came from Southern and Eastern Europe, seemed to make little difference to Anglo-American control of the major offices of the union. So far as I have been able to discover, no miner of East European background was elected to the International Executive Board until after the First World War.

Lower down the UMWA hierarchy, however, a mixed ethnic system of governance soon began to emerge. For example, in Pennsylvania two Slavs, Paul Pulaski and Adam Ryscavage, were elected to District 2's Executive Board in 1908.[58] Until the time of the First World War, this promotion of new immigrants to district office appears to have been somewhat rare. It was not until 1918 that an East European was elected to the Executive Board of Illinois District 12, even though by that time non-Anglos outnumbered Anglo-Saxon miners in the region. At the local union level, on the other hand, especially in areas where Italians, Slavs, and other immigrants from Southern and Eastern Europe constituted a large majority, they were by then strongly represented in positions of leadership, although it took some years before the changeover was complete. A list of officers of UMWA locals for the year 1920 in southeastern Ohio and northern West Virginia illustrates the point. Of 82 locals for which information was given, virtually all had one or more officers of the same ethnic background as the majority of the members of that local.[59]

A further point concerns the implications of this division between Anglo-Saxon leaders at the top and an increasingly diverse rank and file beneath it for the miners' famed reputation for industrial unionism and community solidarity. Since black miners played an important role in places like Alabama and West Virginia, the issue of how best to deal with an increasingly diverse membership included a racial as well as an ethnic component. Perhaps predictably, the ethnic problem was more readily resolved than the racial one. In the North, genuine racial tolerance was practiced by a minority of first-generation British and German immigrant miners who had earlier been influenced by abolitionism, or by internationalist traditions of socialist and Forty-Eighter thought. However, despised "Nigger Alleys" persisted not simply in the South but also in a number of midwestern mining states for many years after the UMWA was founded, and racial outbursts against black strike-breakers (like the one that occurred at Pana, Illinois, in 1898 in the middle of an otherwise liberal mining district) continued to blemish the UMWA's reputation.[60]

58. *UMWJ* (February 14, 1908), 3.

59. William Dennis, *Official Miners Service Record* (Indianapolis, Ind.: United Mine Workers of America, 1920), 18–33.

60. McAlister Coleman, *Men and Coal* (New York: Arno and The New York Times, 1969), 62–63.

As already indicated, however, despite the condescending attitude that many Anglo immigrant miners initially displayed toward incoming "new European" immigrants in the nativist nineties, the Anglo-Saxon leaders of the UMWA soon found it expedient not only to organize them into the union but also to let them elect their own share of local officers. If not done out of principle, this course was adopted in the interests both of mine safety and of presenting a united front to the local coal operators in grievance procedures and bargaining negotiations.

Besides, in isolated coal camps the miners' hall was often one of the most important social institutions in town, rivaled in importance only by the local churches or by the mine manager's residence. Sometimes, it became as much a gathering place for miners of different nationalities as it was a union headquarters. The larger UMWA locals established reading rooms for their members, held dances and sociables, or let out rooms on their upper floors to labor newspapers and ethnic benevolent societies. The more radical locals even sponsored cooperative stores. For example, in 1912 Staunton Local 575 in Illinois District 12 was housed in a "beautiful and sizeable Labor Temple."[61] Besides Sub-District 7's headquarters, the first floor housed a cooperative store containing groceries and dairy goods, where miners' wives of all nationalities shopped. There was also a separate shop selling coal, as well as mine clothes and equipment to the men.

UMWA officials of British origin were also aware of the need to maintain a reasonable degree of social harmony among the different ethnic groups of colliers in town in the interests of union solidarity. This was not only valuable in itself, but became indispensable during strikes, periods of unemployment or even on election day. Coal operators were quick to exploit ethnic or sectional rivalries between different elements in a local union when it came to adjudicating pit grievances, or to favor Anglos over Italian "hotheads" when it came to influencing coal-town elections. This gave such officials (or, at least, the best among them) a strong sense of social responsibility. As one aging local union secretary from Durham, England, put it in Scranton, Pennsylvania, in December 1911: "I an'nt never seen the place so teeming with foreigners this season in all my thirty years. These Hunkie chappies be a funny-looking lot to be sure, but we mun get along with 'em for the good of all."[62]

Despite its origins in a similar mining culture, therefore, and despite the profound influence that British immigrant colliers exerted over the founding and early history of the United Mine Workers of America, by 1912 the UMWA had begun to move in directions that differed in many ways from those of the MFGB. Many, if not most, of the first generation of English, Irish, Welsh, and Scotch colliers who had entered the industry in the 1870s and 1880s had by now either retired from the scene, or had moved up and out of the mines into managerial and supervisory positions. Their successors were more attuned to American traditions of trade unionism,

---

61. E. Colston Warne, *The Consumers Cooperative Movement in Illinois* (Chicago: University of Chicago Press, 1926), 263.

62. *UMWJ* (December 8, 1911), 4.

which differed in important respects from those of the British. The American miners remained just as class-conscious and militant down the pit as their English counterparts. They were also just as determined—if not more so—to preserve and extend their traditions of industrial unionism. However, most of the new generation of leaders who now led the UMWA were considerably more skeptical about the role of the state in industry than their British counterparts were.

Thus ended the era of British influence in the UMWA. In April 1913 the *Druid*, a newspaper that had circulated for years among the Welsh miners of Schuylkill County, Pennsylvania, pronounced a kind of epitaph on the period. Forty or fifty years before, the paper said, the "Welsh had control of the mines; outside and inside." Now the surviving old-timers complained of "being ousted by degrees by the foreign element which crowd out the country. Not enough Welshmen could . . . be found in the Pennsylvania bituminous mines to organize a prayer meeting," let alone a UMWA local.[63]

---

63. Quoted in Berthoff, *British Immigrants*, 64.

CHAPTER THREE

WORKPLACE MILITANCY AND UNIONIZATION
The UMWA and the Anthracite Mine Workers, 1890–1912

PERRY K. BLATZ

With an eye to the relative importance of the bituminous and anthracite coal industries in recent decades, historians have focused their attention on the former.[1] However, some one hundred years ago, the anthracite industry was of considerable importance, employing more Pennsylvanians than its bituminous counterpart.[2] During its first decade, while the United Mine Workers of America (UMWA) led two massive strikes in bituminous, the second of which resulted in the pathbreaking

---

1. For example, see Keith Dix, *What's a Coal Miner to Do? The Mechanization of Coal Mining* (Pittsburgh: University of Pittsburgh Press, 1988); Price Fishback, *Soft Coal, Hard Choices: The Economic Welfare of Bituminous Coal Miners, 1890–1930* (New York: Oxford University Press, 1992); and Joe William Trotter Jr., *Coal, Class, and Color: Blacks in Southern West Virginia, 1915–32* (Urbana: University of Illinois Press, 1990).

2. More Pennsylvanians worked in anthracite than in bituminous until 1906. See Pennsylvania, Department of Mines, *Report of the Department of Mines of Pennsylvania,* part 2, *Bituminous, 1906* (Harrisburg: Harrisburg Publishing, State Printer, 1907), 67; U.S. Department of Commerce, Bureau of the Census, *Historical Statistics of the United States: Colonial Times to 1970* (Washington, D.C.: GPO, 1975), 1:592–93.

trade agreement for the Central Competitive Field, the union failed in a number of attempts to organize the anthracite industry. In the struggle for unionization, anthracite mine workers and the UMWA confronted substantially greater challenges than those faced by workers in the Central Competitive Field. First, although much of the anthracite industry had been unionized in the late 1860s and early 1870s, after 1875 unions had little impact until the end of the 1890s. Second, not only were anthracite mine workers just as fragmented ethnically as bituminous workers; they were further fragmented by age, by the wider variety of jobs they performed, and by a staggering variation in wages, even for similar jobs. Third, the corporations that anthracite mine workers and the UMWA faced were generally larger than those in the Central Competitive Field and more hostile toward unions. While a contract with the UMWA offered bituminous operators a way to limit competition by stabilizing labor costs, the small number of major railroads that dominated the anthracite industry had already limited competition on their own. Only at the end of the 1890s did the union make significant progress, combining an organizing drive with a wave of workplace-related local disputes that gave workers the invaluable experience of victorious collective action. This militancy would provide the foundation for the well-known industrywide strikes of 1900 and 1902. The latter walkout, noted for President Theodore Roosevelt's even-handed intervention, resulted in an important, though limited union triumph which made certain that the anthracite mine workers would long have a vital place in the UMWA, and that the union would have a major role in the industry.

Throughout the 1890s, the *United Mine Workers Journal* commented regularly on the lack of organization in the anthracite fields. Its August 27, 1891, issue noted that the problems of anthracite mine workers were "of their own making," since they had failed to join the union. The March 2, 1893, *Journal* described conditions in the anthracite fields in an article that carried the following headline: "Direct—From the Heart of Anthracite Serfdom—Account of the Astonishing Condition of Hard Coal Miners—Fraud, Oppression, Thievery in Various Forms." Two months later (May 23, 1893) the *Journal* commented on a recent wage cut: "We had thought that the men in the anthracite field were already down to their lowest existing notch, but it appears that their vampire-like masters think they can stand just a little more tapping." Unfortunately, little had changed for the union or the workers nearly six years later, after a number of organizing campaigns. In the January 19, 1899 issue, the editor of the *Journal* wrote: "The present condition of the organized forces in . . . [anthracite] stands as a stumbling block to the betterment of their impoverished state, and strong efforts will be needed to bring the unorganized into line."

In the anthracite industry, glimmerings of union activity as early as the 1840s were followed by the organization of the Workingmen's Benevolent Association (WBA), which exercised considerable power from 1868 until its demise in 1875. The WBA played a central role in the passage of safety legislation and participated in some of the earliest uses of formal arbitration in America.[3] However, that union

3. Perry K. Blatz, "Ever-Shifting Ground: Work and Labor Relations in the Anthracite Coal Industry,

was swept from the anthracite fields after the unsuccessful "Long Strike" of 1875, and no organization of comparable influence arose to replace it. The Knights of Labor did have a presence in the anthracite industry, and in numbers at least, a rather impressive one. In 1877, nearly sixty local assemblies of the Knights were established, with more than twenty other new assemblies set up the following year. Many of those did not survive, however, until the next flurry of organization by the Knights in 1885, when nearly twenty assemblies were organized, or the following year, when forty-eight were established. These assemblies generally had thirty to forty members and often many more, so in some years there must have been more than 2,000 active Knights in the anthracite coal industry.[4] Still, the Knights took relatively little militant action, and their only attempt at an industrywide strike, in collaboration with the Amalgamated Association of Miners and Mine Laborers in the fall and winter of 1887–88, resulted in utter failure.[5]

The weakness of unions in the anthracite industry in the 1880s and early 1890s becomes clearer from a comparison with their role during the same period in the bituminous industry. Jon Amsden and Steven Brier have shown how unionization in the latter proceeded hand-in-hand with strike activity, presenting data from the listing of strikes by the United States Bureau of Labor for the years 1881 to 1894. Throughout this period in bituminous, a generally increasing percentage of strikes was called by a union, from 30% in 1881 to nearly 70% in 1894.[6] However, in the anthracite industry, there is no such gradual increase in these years. Only in 1887 were as much as 40% of the strikes called by a union, and, of the other years, only in 1888 did the percentage reach 30. In nine of these years, no strikes at all were called by a union. For the entire thirteen-and-a-half years, unions called a total of only 16% of the strikes in the anthracite industry.[7]

Still, anthracite mine workers did strike throughout this period, a total of 112 times if we accept the Bureau of Labor's count. All sorts of anthracite mine workers struck, including the young slate pickers, many of whom were not yet teenagers,

1868–1903" (Ph.D. diss., Princeton University, 1987), 50–82; Anthony F. C. Wallace, *St. Clair: A Nineteenth-Century Coal Town's Experience with a Disaster-Prone Industry* (Ithaca: Cornell University Press, 1988), 275–313. On labor disputes during the Civil War, see Grace Palladino, *Another Civil War: Labor, Capital, and the State in the Anthracite Regions of Pennsylvania, 1840–1868* (Urbana: University of Illinois Press, 1990).

4. These figures are calculated from data in Jonathan Garlock, comp., *Guide to the Local Assemblies of the Knights of Labor* (Westport, Conn.: Greenwood, 1982), 430–31, 434–49, 460–67, 472–75.

5. Blatz, "Ever-Shifting Ground," 108–16. Also see Harold W. Aurand, *From the Molly Maguires to the United Mine Workers: The Social Ecology of an Industrial Union, 1869–1897* (Philadelphia: Temple University Press, 1971), 121–30; and Victor R. Greene, *The Slavic Community on Strike: Immigrant Labor in Pennsylvania Anthracite* (Notre Dame: University of Notre Dame Press, 1968), 79–110.

6. Jon Amsden and Stephen Brier, "Coal Miners on Strike: The Transformation of Strike Demands and the Formation of a National Union," *Journal of Interdisciplinary History* 7 (spring 1977): 604–7. On the early years of the UMWA in bituminous and its predecessor organizations, see Maier B. Fox, *United We Stand: The United Mine Workers of America, 1890–1990* (Washington, D.C.: International Union, United Mine Workers of America, 1990), 12–50.

7. Perry K. Blatz, *Democratic Miners: Work and Labor Relations in the Anthracite Coal Industry, 1875–1925* (Albany: State University of New York Press, 1994), 40, 44.

separating slate from the coal in massive buildings called breakers located on the surface. The generally youthful mule drivers who transported coal underground would strike too, as of course would their elders, the miners who blasted and loaded the coal and the many other workers who performed a wide range of maintenance tasks in and around the mines. Slightly less than half of these strikes were either for an increase or against a reduction of wages, but many other walkouts occurred for a multitude of reasons tied to specific problems at the workplace. Several examples show not merely the militant spirit of some anthracite workers but also the many ways in which their bosses, taking advantage of the complexity inherent in coal mining, tried to take advantage of them. In May 1888, some 100 slate pickers struck for two days at a mine in Shamokin, but failed in their attempt to persuade their employer to reinstate a worker who had been discharged. During August of that year, twelve slate pickers at a mine in Kingston struck without success for two days to curtail the imposition of overtime, while mule drivers forced a mine in Parsons to close for three days in May 1894, but did not obtain their demand for the discharge of a foreman. Miners often struck over the severity of docking; that is, being penalized for loading what their bosses did not see as sufficiently clean coal. On occasion throughout this period miners struck, albeit unsuccessfully, to achieve thoroughgoing reform to end the system of payment by the car of coal, hoping to substitute payment by the ton. Workers also struck for such diverse reasons as to obtain their pay twice, rather than once each month, and to protest being required to pay for the oil and cotton they needed to keep their lamps burning. One small walkout casts discredit upon the workers. Some fifty laborers left their jobs in January 1889 in Shenandoah in a vain effort to persuade their employer to fire a number of foreigners.[8]

Grievances such as these illustrate the complex mix of problems that anthracite mine workers confronted at the workplace. But organizing in the 1890s would have to contend more generally with a major industrial depression, as well as a workforce of 100,000 to 150,000 divided by significant differences in ethnicity, skill, income, and age. Thanks in large part to Victor Greene's pioneering work, *The Slavic Community on Strike,* the best-known of these differences is the diversity of ethnic groups in anthracite. In a manner similar to what John Laslett has described for Illinois,[9] English and Welsh mining veterans established the mining industry of northeastern Pennsylvania, first dominating it numerically in the antebellum era, and later continuing to exert control from the supervisory ranks. But by the 1860s and 1870s, as more and more Irish had come to the anthracite fields, ethnic conflict

8. For brief descriptions of strikes, see U.S. Commissioner of Labor, *Third Annual Report of the Commissioner of Labor, 1887: Strikes and Lockouts* (Washington, D.C.: GPO, 1888), 488–95, 504–7, 532–35; and U.S. Bureau of Labor, *Tenth Annual Report of the Commissioner of Labor, 1894: Strikes and Lockouts* (Washington, D.C.: GPO, 1896), 1:1046–53, 1062–65, 1074–81, 1090–97, 1106–9, 1114–21, 1126–29. For total number of strikes in anthracite, see Blatz, *Democratic Miners,* 40, 44.

9. John H. M. Laslett, "British Immigrant Colliers and the Origins and the Early Development of the UMWA, 1880–1912," in this volume, Chapter 2.

between them and the English and Welsh flourished. It would play a major role in both the struggles of the WBA and the notorious deeds of the Molly Maguires.[10] Still, as that conflict continued to smolder, additional sources of ethnic division arose. In 1870, the establishment by both Poles and Lithuanians of their first parishes in northeastern Pennsylvania signaled the beginning of a building wave of immigration by Eastern and Southern Europeans.[11] While such immigrants made up about 5% of the anthracite workforce in 1880, by 1890 this figure exceeded 20%. Ten years later, the proportion of mine workers who had either immigrated from Eastern and Southern Europe or whose parents had done so was approaching one-half of the workforce.[12]

Of course, the numerous ethnic groups of the anthracite fields came together, at least physically, in and around the mines. But there they faced additional pressures in the workplace that tended to drive them apart. Coal mining may convey the impression of a relatively undifferentiated workforce, toiling away underground extracting and loading the coal. While this portrait holds some accuracy for the bituminous industry, it holds far less for anthracite. First, in anthracite less than 30% of the workers were miners, while in bituminous, nearly 80% were. Approximately 15% in anthracite were miner's laborers, loading coal for the miner who, in many places, only planted explosive charges. So, less than 50% of the workers in anthracite worked at mining or loading coal, and those two activities were frequently

10. See Wayne G. Broehl Jr., *The Molly Maguires* (New York: Vintage/Chelsea House, 1964); and Wallace, *St. Clair,* 101–83, 331–75.

11. Greene, *Slavic Community on Strike,* 35–38. On ethnic rivalry in general, also see Isaac A. Hourwich, *Immigration and Labor: The Economic Aspects of European Immigration to the United States* (New York: Putnam, 1912; repr. New York: Arno, 1969), 415–57; and Peter Roberts, *The Anthracite Coal Communities* (New York: Macmillan, 1904), 3–56.

12. The estimate for 1880 is from Roberts, *Anthracite Coal Communities,* 19. The estimate for 1890 is derived from a census that the largest producer, the Philadelphia and Reading Coal and Iron Company, made of its workers, in which it reported that some 23.6% were of Polish, Hungarian, or Italian "nationality or parentage." In its censuses of 1895 and 1896, this figure grew to 32.2% and 36.2% respectively. See U.S. Department of Labor, *Bulletin of the Department of Labor,* No. 13, "The Anthracite Mine Laborers," by G. O. Virtue (1897); 751. The estimate for 1900 is derived from several sources. Peter Roberts, in *The Anthracite Coal Industry* (New York: Macmillan, 1901), 105, stated that 25% to 30% of all mine workers over the age of sixteen were from Eastern or Southern Europe. This, of course, excluded the youngest workers in the industry, many of whom by this time might have been born in America, but whose parents were likely to be immigrants. However, in *Anthracite Coal Communities,* 19–20, Roberts estimated that approximately 50% of the mine workers or their parents were from Eastern and Southern Europe. This figure is given further credence by a survey of the "nationality of employés" of anthracite companies, made by the state in 1903. Of some 62,404 workers surveyed, or slightly more than 40% of the total workforce, 20.2% were reported as Polish, 9.6% were reported as Hungarians, 4.8% were reported as "Slavish," 4.6% were reported as Italians, 2.3% were reported as Russians, and less than .1% were reported as Greeks. So, approximately 41.5% of these employees were of Eastern and Southern European "nationality." This figure may not include the children of immigrants, who might have been reported as "Americans." See Pennsylvania, Secretary of Internal Affairs, *Annual Report,* Part 3, *Industrial Statistics* 31 (1903): 431–32. The figure for total number of employees is from *Historical Statistics of the United States,* 1:592.

performed separately.[13] Second, approximately one-third of the workers in anthracite were employed outside of the mines, while less than 10% were in bituminous. Since anthracite coal was used primarily to heat homes, a great deal of effort was directed toward ensuring the cleanliness of the product, and most of the workers on the surface either participated in cleaning the coal or maintaining equipment that did so. Third, while workers under sixteen comprised slightly more than 4% of all workers in soft coal, more than 17% of the anthracite labor force was under sixteen.[14]

Upon closer examination, even greater fragmentation appears in the workforce in the anthracite industry. In contrast to bituminous, more than half of the mine workers in anthracite were neither miners nor miner's laborers, but "company men." They worked for a daily wage as opposed to the miners, who were generally paid according to the amount of coal they mined, or the miner's laborers, who were usually paid by the miner in a separate transaction. The category of company men covered a wide variety of jobs, and most important, little uniformity existed in the industry over the rates to be paid for similar kinds of work. In 1888, the Pennsylvania Bureau of Industrial Statistics surveyed some forty-six mines to determine daily wage rates for company men in forty-three jobs in the mines and fifty-three on the surface. Although no mine reported wage rates for every job listed, nearly all reported rates for at least fifteen underground jobs and twenty above ground. Some mines reported rates for as many as twenty-five jobs below and thirty on the surface. A multiplicity of wage rates accompanied this multiplicity of jobs. For example, daily rates at the twenty-eight mines that reported rates for carpenters underground ranged from $1.50 to $2.50, and a total of eighteen different rates were listed. The forty-three mines that had "barn bosses," to care for the mules who still provided much of the motive power for mining, reported a total of nineteen different rates ranging from $1.20 to $2.77. At the forty-two mines that reported "prop-men," who fashioned timber to support the mining "roof," rates ranged from $1.00 to $2.66, with a total of eighteen different rates.[15]

Similarly extensive variation in wages can also be seen for miners. First, miners were paid in several different ways. Some were paid by the car of coal, with a variety of different rates and sizes of car, sometimes even at the same mine or at different mines of the same company. Others were paid by weight, a so-called miner's ton

13. U.S. Department of the Interior, Census Office, *Report on Mineral Industries in the United States at the Eleventh Census: 1890* (Washington, D.C.: GPO, 1892), 402, 406. For a discussion of the separation between mining and loading coal in the anthracite region, see *UMWJ* (November 8, 1900). In the bituminous industry, miners may have worked with partners, but they generally loaded their own coal. See John Brophy, *A Miner's Life,* ed. John O. O. Hall (Madison: University of Wisconsin Press, 1964), 43–49; and Keith Dix, *Work Relations in the Coal Industry: The Hand Loading Era, 1880–1930* (Morgantown: West Virginia University Press, 1977), 8–14.

14. *Report on Mineral Industries in the United States at the Eleventh Census: 1890,* 402, 406.

15. Calculated from data in Pennsylvania, Secretary of Internal Affairs, *Annual Report,* Part 3, *Industrial Statistics* 16 (1888); C2–C14.

that was far heavier than a standard ton to include a sizable allowance for impurities. Some miners were even paid by the yard; that is, the amount of distance they advanced the coal face in their room or chamber in the mine. Second, regardless of the method of payment, there was little similarity in rates from mine to mine, much less from one part of the anthracite fields to another. While much of this variation was tied to geological differences, the lack of anything approaching uniformity must have bewildered miners at the same time that it provided opportunities that bosses could exploit.[16] The UMWA frequently made accusations of favoritism and the use of bribery in hiring and job assignment as it organized in the 1890s.[17]

In 1888, the Pennsylvania Bureau of Industrial Statistics sought to answer the question, "What can miners earn who are industrious and able to work whenever employment is offered?" For forty-five mines it compiled the net annual earnings of the ten miners at each mine who earned the most and the ten who earned the least of those miners who worked steadily throughout the year. The miners who ranked at the top at each mine averaged earnings of $3.65 per day, or nearly $900 per year, while the miners who ranked at the bottom averaged earnings of only $1.72 per day or less than $400 for a full year of work. Generally, the miners in the top ten would earn from $2.50 to $4.00 a day, while those in the bottom ten would earn from $1.30 to $2.50 a day.[18]

Still, these data in no way convey the paramount problem faced by anthracite mine workers in the 1890s, one that has often plagued coal miners whether they dug hard or soft coal: underemployment. When confronted by an economic downturn, coal operators seldom laid off employees. Since a coal mine cost a great deal to open, an operator could not merely close it during a depressed period to await better times, because the mine would quickly be ruined without extensive daily maintenance. Facing these high overhead costs, most operators continued to produce some coal in order to have some income, even when prices were very low. Combined with the highly seasonal demand for anthracite as a home-heating fuel, this resulted in extensive overproduction and severe underemployment. During 1889, when anthracite mines overall averaged 194 full ten-hour days of operation, about one-quarter of them were in operation for fewer than 150 days. Some might lie idle for months to undergo extensive repairs and a number would be abandoned each year. The 1890s were especially difficult, as the anthracite mines averaged only 183.3 full ten-hour days of operation at the same time that the nation's manufacturing industries averaged 285 days annually in a decade in which the nation experienced depression from 1893 to 1897.[19]

16. Blatz, "Ever-Shifting Ground," 8–21.

17. Blatz, *Democratic Miners,* 51–52.

18. Calculated from data in *Industrial Statistics* 16 (1888): Bvi–B111; also see Blatz, *Democratic Miners,* 15–17.

19. For the overall process, see G. O. Virtue, "The Anthracite Combinations," *Quarterly Journal of Economics* 10 (April 1896): 318–19; and Hourwich, *Immigration and Labor,* 432–35. The data for 1889 is calculated from Pennsylvania, Secretary of Internal Affairs, *Annual Report,* Part 3, *Industrial Statistics*

The impact of such pervasive underemployment on workers and their families was described in poignant detail by the General Master Workman of the Knights of Labor, Terence V. Powderly. In February 1890, he wrote for the *New York World* about the difficult conditions facing anthracite mine workers. Powderly told the story of one Thomas Daley, who had come from Wales to work in the mines of the Delaware, Lackawanna, and Western Railroad (DL & W) near Scranton toward the close of 1888. His wife and five children joined him eight months later but, at the very time that his financial responsibilities grew, he found he had less of an opportunity to meet them. After his family arrived, Daley barely worked half-time; in December 1889, he worked only ten days. January 1890 was even worse—in that month he worked less than seven full days. His earnings for January totaled only $13.10 in an era in which less than $30 in monthly earnings imperiled a family's survival. Powderly told his readers: "Mr. Daley is not an intemperate man, he does not gamble, he is not addicted to any of the vices that reduce the incomes of other men, but he could not fatten his children on $13.10 a month." To add to Daley's burdens, his wife had died recently after she gave birth to the couple's sixth child. As Powderly put it: "The hopes which animated Thomas Daley's breast when he came to America but eighteen short months ago are dead ashes on his lonely, poverty-stricken hearth tonight."[20]

Powderly found other workers who told similar tales. "An English miner" had averaged only eight-and-a-half days of work per month from December 1888 to December 1889. Each month he brought home approximately twenty dollars; but, with less work in December and January, his earnings fell first to sixteen dollars and then to eleven dollars and a quarter. He told Powderly that he could scarcely afford to feed himself. Another miner said he had worked only a little over four days in January; for this he earned so little that he could not properly feed his wife and five girls. All of his children had become ill because they couldn't get enough to eat.[21]

Thus, the anthracite industry in the 1890s presented an especially formidable task of industrial organization. Anthracite mine workers performed many different kinds of work. From numerous ethnic groups, they ranged in age from ten or less to elderly men who returned to the breaker after they had become too weak to do any other work. In addition, workers performing the same task might earn very different wages from one mine to another. Still, this was only part of the challenge that the anthracite industry presented to the UMWA. Another essential ingredient of that challenge was the unbending opposition of the powerful railroad corporations that employed most

---

17 (1889): B4–B15; the data for the 1890s is calculated from *Historical Statistics of the United States,* 1:592–93.

20. *The New York World* (February 20, 1890). For an estimate of $320 as the minimum annual income on which a family of five in the anthracite region could survive in 1890, see Blatz, *Democratic Miners,* 25.

21. *The New York World* (February 25, 1890).

of the workers. Like most employers in the 1890s, they wanted nothing to do with unions.

Perhaps the central figure in eliminating unionism in the anthracite fields during the 1870s was Franklin B. Gowen, president of the Philadelphia and Reading Railroad. Through his control of freight rates, Gowen prevented operators who shipped over his line from making a separate deal with the union. As a member of the prosecuting team in several of the Molly Maguire trials, he insinuated to telling effect, despite a lack of evidence, that the protests of the WBA and the deeds of the Mollies were linked. Gowen's control of coal mining in the southern or Schuylkill field of the anthracite region is reflected in his firm's purchase of some 100,000 acres of coal land by 1874.[22] His effectiveness in driving unionism from the Reading's mines is seen in the following testimony of the general superintendent of the Reading's coal company, R. C. Luther, before the United States Industrial Commission in March 1900. When asked about the company's attitude toward the recognition of trade unions, he responded: "We have had so little opportunity to do that that I scarcely can tell you. We have no labor organizations, and have not had for a great many years, so we have not been called upon to take any steps in that direction at all."[23]

Similarly, corporate heads in the northern or Wyoming field were willing to go to practically any extreme to avoid dealing with a union. The leading railroads there, the DL & W and the Delaware and Hudson (D & H), decided in 1869 to pay their workers an increase of approximately 50% rather than subscribe to the WBA's call for an arrangement in which wages would be tied to the price of coal. That was the peak of the union's influence in that region, as well as the peak of wage rates, which soon returned to their former levels.[24] Attitudes did not change during the period from 1880 to 1900 when, for the most part, unions posed little threat. Union leaders were viewed, not as representatives of the workers, but as "outside agitators" whose efforts amounted to nothing more than meddling designed solely to enhance their own power. According to William R. Storrs, head of the coal department of the DL & W, unions were nothing more than sinister "secret organizations." In a revealing statement, Storrs showed his fear of labor organizations, a fear that had surely been intensified by the conspiratorial activities of the Molly Maguires and reinforced by the secrecy that characterized the Knights of Labor in its early years: "No one outside can tell what a secret organization will do—only the managers know. While they desire to be respectable and orderly the better to delude friends and foes, their purposes must be secured at any cost. Their followers do what they are told and rely

22. Aurand, *From the Molly Maguires,* 65–95; Blatz, "Ever-Shifting Ground," 60, 79, 85–86; Jules I. Bogen, *The Anthracite Railroads* (New York: Ronald Press, 1927), 51–54; Broehl, *The Molly Maguires,* 102–27, 169–73, 181–209, 294–340; Wallace, *St. Clair,* 331–61, 411–27.

23. U.S. Industrial Commission, *Reports of the Industrial Commission,* vol. 12, *Report of the Industrial Commission on the Relations and Conditions of Capital and Labor Employed in the Mining Industry* (Washington, D.C.: GPO, 1901), 146.

24. Blatz, "Ever-Shifting Ground," 55–56.

on what is promised.''[25] As employers saw it, unions sought to limit their freedom—their "freedom to control" employees.[26] For Storrs, in dealing with workers, "absolute silence, which they construe as strength, or bold decisive action should govern us—not discussion.''[27] Storrs's son, William H. Storrs, who succeeded his father, took a similar stance in 1897. Commenting on an early effort by the UMWA to organize some DL & W miners, he stated: "Agitators are making a strong effort to get all the men into a sort of a union. The demands they intend to make are for the purpose of calling attention to their organization, and if granted by us, or by others, will do more than anything else to swell their ranks.''[28] The company's antiunionism was only strengthened by a series of organizing successes by the UMWA. In the following response to union President John Mitchell's request in February 1902 that the companies meet with union representatives to negotiate wages and conditions, President William H. Truesdale of the DL & W offered no possibility that his firm would ever do so:

The policy and practice of this Company is, and always has been, to deal directly with all classes of its employes through committees or other representatives of them duly acredited [sic] as such and also in the employ of the Company, on all questions concerning wages, hours of service, and other conditions pertaining to their employment.

No good or convincing reason has ever been given, nor does the management of this Company conceive of any that can be, why the employes in or about its mines should ask to have their wage matters singled out and handled in the radically different way suggested, from that fixed by the Company in dealing with all other classes of its employes.

The situation and conditions vary so widely as respects the mining of anthracite coal in the different fields, the several districts of each field, in the different mines in each district, and in the numerous veins of coal in each mine, that it has been found necessary during the years of experience in mining anthracite coal, to establish a great variety of rates of wages, and allowances of different kinds, in order to adjust the wages equitably as between men working under these varying conditions.

It must be manifest therefore, to any one familiar with these conditions and the practice that has grown up under them, that it is entirely impracti-

25. W. R. Storrs to Samuel Sloan, February 6, 1888, Corporate Records of the Delaware, Lackawanna, and Western Railroad—Coal Department, Lackawanna Historical Society, Scranton, PA, hereafter cited as DL & W Records—Scranton.

26. See Rowland Berthoff, "The 'Freedom to Control' in American Business History," in A Festschrift for Frederick B. Artz, ed. David H. Pinkney and Theodore Ropp (Durham: Duke University Press, 1964), 158–80.

27. W. R. Storrs to Samuel Sloan, February 19, 1889, DL & W Records—Scranton.

28. W. H. Storrs to Samuel Sloan, October 15, 1897, DL & W Records—Scranton.

cable to adjust these wage questions in the anthracite regions in any general convention or mass meeting.[29]

The consistent refusal of the anthracite operators, from the 1870s through 1902, to deal with unions obviously constituted a fundamental challenge to the UMWA. Adding to that challenge, at about the same time that the union made its first important moves into the anthracite fields in 1897 and 1899, the corporations it faced had begun to succeed in limiting competition by apportioning the market and thus regulating the price of coal. While there had been some efforts along these lines in previous years, the resulting pools did not last long. Some of the railroads, in particular the Reading, had been in and out of bankruptcy on a number of occasions. However, by 1900, each of the railroads was in a reasonably strong condition, and some were experiencing especially good years. Through interlocking directorates and the calming influence of J. P. Morgan, the railroad companies who had engaged in cut-throat competition in coal sales and transportation for most of their history ushered in a lengthy period of price stability.[30]

Thus, the anthracite mine workers and the UMWA faced foes who were powerful and utterly opposed to unions. The anthracite operators lacked the incentive that their smaller, weaker counterparts in bituminous had for accepting unionization, namely that the union could play a major role in stabilizing the coal market by eliminating competition in wages. This was one of the keys to the UMWA's stunning achievement in the Central Competitive Field contract of 1898.[31] As early as the 1860s and 1870s in the anthracite industry, the WBA tried to assume such a role, seeking to impose discipline on a market dominated in the Schuylkill field by small, independent firms. However, Franklin B. Gowen preferred to impose his own discipline by purchasing those firms, while other corporate leaders were able to avoid dealing with the WBA. Those corporations had warred off and on in the 1870s, 1880s, and 1890s, but they came out of that latter depression decade stronger and more united.

Despite this array of challenges—a recent history of union weakness, a fragmented workforce, and staunch resistance from powerful corporations—the UMWA succeeded in organizing the anthracite fields between 1897 and the strike of 1902. In dealing with these challenges, the union had the all-important advantage of trying to organize workers who were disposed to be militant because of a growing realiza-

    29. William H. Truesdale to John Mitchell et al., February 18, 1902, Corporate Records of the Delaware, Lackawanna, and Western Railroad, George Arents Research Library, Syracuse University.
    30. Bogen, *Anthracite Railroad*, 54–72, 96–104, 122–39, 161–82, 197–202; Eliot Jones, *The Anthracite Coal Combination in the United States* (Cambridge: Harvard University Press, 1914), 41–97.
    31. Arthur E. Suffern, *The Coal Miners' Struggle for Industrial Status* (New York: Macmillan, 1926), 11–18, 31–72; Fox, *United We Stand*, 50–54. Also see David Brody, "Labor Relations in American Coal Mining: An Industry Perspective," unpublished paper, 2–4, 12–15. I thank David Brody for suggesting that I consider the impact of the changing competitive picture in anthracite on labor relations, especially in comparison with the bituminous industry.

tion of the unfairness of the workplace regime. Workers, more and more of whom were of Eastern and Southern European ethnicity, engaged in numerous localized job actions with no apparent prompting from the UMWA. Again and again, these walkouts provided organizers the opportunity they needed to add to the ranks of the union. More important, the success workers achieved in such actions would help convince other anthracite mine workers that their protests could have a similar outcome. Nevertheless, numerous instances of localized militancy could build into an ever more powerful wave only because the UMWA provided the indispensable organizational link that tied them together and gave them a larger purpose.

As it grew this rank-and-file militancy posed problems for union leaders, who hoped, despite numerous refusals to negotiate by the men who ran the corporations, to persuade them that the UMWA was a responsible, conservative organization with which they could deal effectively. Having helped bring some order out of chaos in the bituminous industry, UMWA officials thought that the anthracite operators would appreciate the order the union offered to bring to the wage picture in anthracite. However, the anthracite operators did not face the same harsh realities of competition that so concerned their bituminous counterparts. Furthermore, while the wage picture in anthracite was utterly chaotic, it had become so on an ad hoc basis that consistently worked to the advantage of the companies. They indeed had nothing to gain from dealing with the union, although the leaders of the UMWA were most reluctant to realize that. Thus, in responding to the wave of localized walkouts from 1897 through 1902, the union often sought to control and even discourage job actions by the rank and file.

The UMWA established its first locals in the southern or Schuylkill field in 1894 as a by-product of efforts to collect funds to support the massive bituminous strike of that year. However, this initial success did not last long. At the union's national convention in January 1897, the entire anthracite region, with some 150,000 workers, had only two votes, representing approximately 200 members in good standing. This decline caused the president of the union's sole anthracite district, an Ohio veteran of the bituminous industry named John Fahy, to abandon organizing for lobbying the state legislature in Harrisburg. There Fahy helped to secure passage of several pieces of legislation. The most notable law aimed at discouraging the employment of immigrants by requiring any employer who employed foreign-born males over the age of twenty-one to pay a tax of three cents per day per worker. Of course, the legislature conveniently allowed employers to deduct the tax directly from each employee's earnings. This law would benefit the union, but in a most peculiar way. After the tax was first deducted from workers' pay on Saturday, August 21, large numbers of immigrants from Eastern and Southern Europe struck at mines near Hazleton in the middle or Lehigh field. Fahy responded by returning to the anthracite region from Harrisburg to organize the strikers, who apparently were unaware of the union's nativist proclivities. The strike wave continued to spread in late August and early September, with workers demanding redress of a variety of grievances in addition to the recently enacted tax. But while Fahy organized numerous locals, he apparently made little effort to take control of the strikes, or at least he was unable to do so. He advised workers to stop marching en masse through the area to extend the walkout to mines that were still operating. But the marchers paid no attention to him.[32]

On September 10, 1897, when workers from the coal-patch town of Harwood marched to the neighboring patch of Lattimer, the marchers twice confronted the sheriff and his deputies. In the second confrontation, as the sheriff scuffled with several workers in an attempt to halt the march, the deputies fired directly into the crowd, killing nineteen and wounding perhaps fifty in what would become known as the Lattimer Massacre. Shortly thereafter the strike wave subsided, especially once the Pennsylvania National Guard arrived. By September 21, all of the affected mines had resumed production without any evidence of resistance by workers or substantial concessions by the companies. There is no evidence of Fahy trying to draw the workers of the various companies together to submit a unified set of demands, nor is there evidence of the workers trying to do so on their own. Still, this month of militancy had one tangible result—the organization of a new district of the UMWA, District 7. Despite the dominant role of immigrants from Eastern and Southern Europe in the walkouts that preceded the massacre, the district's president and secretary were of Irish and Welsh ethnicity, respectively.[33]

Thus, the walkouts in the Lehigh field in August and September 1897 provided the UMWA with the opportunity it needed to organize a good portion of that field, the smallest of the three in anthracite. However, throughout 1898 and into 1899, organizers remarked on their lack of success in maintaining the existing organization, much less building upon it.[34] This undoubtedly prompted the union to initiate a special organizing effort in the latter year, one that would finally give the UMWA a reasonably secure foothold in anthracite. The recent growth of the union resulting from its successful strike in bituminous in 1897 and the Central Competitive Field contract that followed gave the UMWA the strength necessary to conduct a broad-based campaign in a scarcely organized area like the anthracite fields. Still, that campaign could not have succeeded without the militant spirit wrought, not by the exhortations of union organizers, but by workers responding to the many inequities at the workplace by undertaking militant job actions and seeing them succeed.

In one particularly interesting local strike, which shows the complexity and job-centered character of so many of these walkouts, militant action clearly provided the opportunity for the UMWA to organize, as it had in the Lehigh field in the summer of 1897. On June 28, 1899, at the Dorrance mine in Wilkes-Barre, officials ordered miners, who worked in veins that generated large quantities of explosive

---

32. Blatz, *Democratic Miners,* 46–59.

33. Ibid., 59–60. The first president of District Seven was Thomas Duffy and the first secretary was Benjamin James. I have been unable to determine who was the first vice president of the district. Of course, the common practice of UMWA anthracite districts, at least from 1899, was to give the district vice presidency to someone of Eastern or Southern European ethnicity. See 75, 130, 180.

34. Ibid., 60–63.

gas, to stop using their usual source of illumination, the open-flame lamps they clipped to their caps. Instead they were to use the Wolf safety lamp, reputedly the best safety lamp available. This would decrease the likelihood of explosions, which not only took lives but also caused massive destruction to company property. The company maintained that using the Wolf lamp would cause the miners little or no additional labor or expense. Lamps would be provided without charge, filled with fuel, and cleaned each evening by the company.[35]

However, the miners pointed to several features of the Wolf lamp that would make their work more difficult. The lamp not only gave off less light than the cap lamp, but it was also rather heavy and had to be held, hooked to the belt, or hung in a chamber, so that its light seldom could be made to shine directly where a miner was working. Also, if the lamp's glass bonnet was broken, or the concentration of gas rose above 6%, the flame was extinguished automatically. The lamp had been designed with this feature to prevent both an explosion and tampering by mine workers. If they had to use a safety lamp, workers may have preferred an older style, whose flame required monitoring to determine the concentration of gas and could be drawn through the wire gauze surrounding it to light a fuse. With the Wolf lamp in use, miners would need to wait for another employee to come to their chambers in the mine to ignite the fuses. This would cause delay, thus decreasing the production of the miner who, of course, was paid by the amount of coal he sent to the surface. Furthermore, the weaker flame of the Wolf lamp, while far less likely to ignite gas, would provide less light and make it more difficult for a miner to spot dangerous conditions overhead. The strikers ended their walkout after two weeks, finally consenting to use the Wolf lamp. Still, in the wake of the dispute, the Dorrance mine, along with several others in the area where miners had left their jobs, was organized by the UMWA.[36]

Crucial to the union's success in this local strike and many others was its industrial structure. Regardless of the specific grievances of a particular group of workers that might bring an organizer to a mine, the union sought to organize all the workers at that mine on an industrial basis. In the demands it formulated at various mines, it sought to offer something to every category of worker, from miner to slate picker. Just as important, it held out the promise of a negotiated scale for entire companies and later for the whole industry to regularize wage rates and reduce the confusion, complexity, and inequity that dominated the lives of anthracite mine workers. For example, in late July 1899 grievances by miners over docking prompted a walkout by approximately 4,000 workers at the mines of the Susquehanna Coal Company, owned by the Pennsylvania Railroad. Still, since all categories of workers struck, their grievances were represented in the list of demands presented by the strikers, many of which they obtained after a strike of four-and-a-half months.[37]

---

35. *Wilkes-Barre Record* (June 29, 1899).

36. *Ibid.*

37. On the strike at the Susquehanna Coal Company, see Perry K. Blatz, "Local Leadership and Local Militancy: The Nanticoke Strike of 1899 and the Roots of Unionization in the Northern Anthracite

That strike, led by Thomas D. Nicholls, an employee of the Susquehanna Coal Company and president of the new district set up in 1899 for the northern field, District 1, was sanctioned by the UMWA and was the union's first important victory in the anthracite industry. That victory spurred organization in 1900 and, along ·with it, heightened local militancy. But many of the strikes that occurred were not sanctioned by union leaders, who wanted to show employers that they could control the workers. Benjamin James, first secretary of District 7 in the Lehigh field and the first anthracite mine worker to be elected to the UMWA's national executive board, expressed his uneasiness over the wave of strikes in March 1900. He advised the men of District 1 ''to adhere more closely to the laws of the organization.'' He noted: ''A number of strikes have occurred lately that were not approved of, or your troubles even brought to the attention of your District officers.'' James added that dealing with such strikes only distracted union officials from their other duties, and he admonished workers that the trend toward local strikes could only bring ''disgrace'' upon them.[38] In June, District President Nicholls discussed the large number of unsanctioned local strikes in a letter to John Mitchell, informing him that ''we have actually got to fight them [the men] and show them the folly of small strikes.'' He called for a convention of the three anthracite districts to consider an industrywide walkout.[39]

On one level, Nicholls was quite right in referring to ''the folly of small strikes.'' The mass of anthracite mine workers stood to gain far less in a series of small, local strikes as opposed to one for the entire industry. For example, as a result of the six-week industrywide strike in September and October 1900, the union won a wage increase of about 10% and many new members, so that at the end of 1900 more than 53,000 anthracite mine workers were officially enrolled, nearly six times the number reported just one year before.[40] Still, in looking at the many local strikes that occurred in the latter half of 1899 and throughout 1900, it seems quite likely that these walkouts built solidarity, community by community, in a way that made success possible in the industrywide strike. In fact, local militancy and union growth complemented one another, although union leaders were reluctant to admit it. Without the union, militant action would have been more difficult to undertake successfully; more important, any gains that resulted would have been limited to one mine or one company. Yet, by seeking to suppress local militancy, the union risked losing touch with the most significant concerns of the rank and file. Such militancy arose

Fields,'' *Pennsylvania History* 58 (October 1991): 278–97. The UMWA's industrial inclusivity was not a universal characteristic of miners' organizations; see Laslett's discussion of the Miners Federation of Great Britain in Chapter 2.

38. Blatz, *Democratic Miners,* 79–83; quotations from *UMWJ* (March 29, 1900). On Benjamin James see Blatz, ''Ever-Shifting Ground,'' 366, 372, 475–76; on Thomas Nicholls and District One, see Blatz, ''Local Leadership and Local Militancy,'' 283.

39. Thomas D. Nicholls to John Mitchell, June 9, 1900, John Mitchell Papers (microfilm edition), Catholic University of America, Washington. D.C.; hereafter cited as Mitchell Papers.

40. Blatz, *Democratic Miners,* 88–98.

from the day-to-day violation of the workers' instinctive sense of fairness through the impact of the utterly ad hoc morass of work rules and wages under which they labored. Their resulting feelings of outrage, however haphazardly expressed through overt protest, constituted nothing less than the primary impulse toward unionization.

While the strike of 1900 did not lead to recognition of the union by the corporations that operated the anthracite mines, union leaders hoped for progress in that direction, perhaps based on nothing more than their very different experience with employers in the bituminous industry. On a number of occasions, the *UMWJ* labeled the settlement, in which negotiations occurred entirely through intermediaries and the companies announced concessions at their mines simply by posting notices, as a "contract" or "agreement." Throughout the next year and a half leading to the industrywide strike of 1902, union leaders implored mine workers to avoid local walkouts, especially after President Mitchell was granted an informal audience with the president of the Erie Railroad, Eben B. Thomas, in March 1901. There, Thomas held out the possibility of some sort of recognition if the union could eliminate local strikes.[41]

Still, local leaders realized the value of militant action. As industrial unionists, they could turn the complex interdependency among various groups of workers in the mines to the advantage of the union. For example, the distribution of coal cars had long been a source of friction between miners and their bosses. In the distant reaches of coal mines this had always been difficult to coordinate; if miners did not receive cars promptly in which to load the coal they had blasted, they had little choice but to wait, seeing their earnings for the day drop with each passing minute.[42] Bosses usually gave priority in the distribution of cars to miners doing development work, that is, opening new areas in a mine, work for which miners would generally have a number of laborers and earn sizable sums of money. Union leaders had often deplored favoritism in car distribution and had demanded in the strike of 1900 that no miner should get more than his "legal share of cars," but this demand had received little attention.[43]

After the 1900 strike, there is no evidence of directives from district leaders ordering local unions to equalize the distribution of cars. But some locals tried to do so, relying on the militancy of the young drivers and runners who distributed the cars. For example, on several occasions during the fall of 1901 at the D & H's Jermyn mine, drivers refused to give miners performing development work all the cars that

41. For references to the "contract" or "agreement," see *UMWJ* (November 29, 1900, August 1, 1901, and September 5, 1901); for Mitchell's analysis, see Mitchell to William B. Wilson (March 26, 1901), Mitchell Papers.

42. For a fascinating discussion of this problem, see Hugh Archbald, *The Four-Hour Day in Coal: A Study of the Relation between the Engineering of the Organization of Work and the Discontent among the Workers in the Coal Mines* (New York: H. W. Wilson, 1922).

43. Blatz, "Ever-Shifting Ground," 450–51, 507; the quotation is from J. P. Gallagher, John T. Dempsey and George Hartline [*sic*] to the Operators of the Anthracite Coal Fields of Pennsylvania, August 16, 1900, Mitchell Papers.

they wanted. Consequently, the foreman discharged two drivers on December 12, and on the next day he asked other boys to replace them. They refused and were also fired, thereby idling a section of the mine. After a grievance committee met with the foreman, he agreed to reinstate the drivers if they would give the miners as many cars as they wanted. The drivers complied, but the local passed a resolution to expel from the union any miners who loaded more cars than their fellows. In its struggle to maintain discipline, the company closed the mine for a period. According to the foreman, Thomas R. Thomas, the D & H "wanted to control the men" and did not want "the Union to run the colliery."[44]

At some mines, the fear alone of militant action had an impact upon management. Patrick Mitchell, a miner at the Pennsylvania Coal Company's no. 14 mine in Pittston, was fined five dollars by the local for loading too many cars. At other times he received only a certain limited number of cars from the runners. When he complained to his foreman, he was told that the company did not wish to risk a strike by discharging the runners.[45]

The youthful drivers and runners, generally in their teens, seemed to be the most consistently militant mine workers. For example, employees of the DL & W's mines had from time to time expressed their dislike for a system initiated early in 1901 in which underground workers were required to check in and out of the mine. The company claimed that it had instituted this procedure to enable bosses to know who was underground in the event of an accident. However, the system also allowed the company to keep track of the actual amount of time spent underground by miners, who generally were free to leave their chambers and quit work when they pleased. Although it would seem that miners would be most likely to protest this innovation, the drivers took action instead. At the Hampton mine near Scranton drivers struck when the company refused their demand to abolish the check-in system. With the entire mine idle as a result, District President Nicholls, after considerable effort, managed to persuade the drivers to return several days later.[46]

In some disputes, there was little that national, district, or even local leaders could do to restrain workers. Workers at the Shamokin Coal Company's Natalie mine walked out for a short period when the company refused to discharge a superinten-

44. U.S. Anthracite Coal Strike Commission, "Proceedings of the Anthracite Coal Strike Commission, 1902–1903," 4919–22; hereafter cited as "Proceedings." The determination of the local union to restrict the number of cars loaded by those miners performing development work can be seen in another episode at this mine. In September 1901, two miners working as partners were informed by drivers and runners that they should load no more cars than other miners. They met with Henry Collins of District 1's executive board to explain their case, and he informed District President Nicholls that these men were doing necessary work that should be allowed to continue unhindered. Nicholls so informed the local, but in November these miners were told again that if they continued to load more cars than the chamber miners, they would be expelled from the union. When the miners met once more with Collins, he interceded on their behalf with Nicholls, but this time Nicholls told them they would have to settle the issue with the local; see 4951–58.

45. Ibid., 5438–41.

46. *UMWJ* (February 20, 1901).

dent who sold the employees tickets for a raffle from which he stood to benefit. Edward McKay of the national executive board, members of the executive board for District 9 (the new district created for the Schuylkill field), and even John Mitchell failed to dissuade the workers from striking.[47] At the Melville Coal Company's Lee mine near Nanticoke, workers walked off their jobs in October over a variety of grievances, including the firm's failure to pay wages promptly. The executive board of District 1 did not sanction the strike, and firemen, pumpmen, and other essential maintenance workers were included in the strike call, thus endangering the mine. The company appealed to the district and a member of the board advised the strikers to return to work and present their grievances to the company and the district officers. When the workers refused, District President Nicholls interceded. The president of the local admitted to Nicholls that he had little control over his men, but local and district officers finally persuaded the men to go back to work.[48]

Through the auspices of the National Civic Federation, UMWA leaders finally won the meeting they desired with the railroad executives. However, in meetings in March and April 1902, the executives offered no concessions, certainly not official recognition of the UMWA. They seemed perfectly willing to accept a strike, which Mitchell and a number of district leaders wanted to avoid. At a convention of the three anthracite districts in May, Mitchell did try to dissuade the workers' representatives from calling a strike, emphasizing how difficult it would be for the union to win. Nevertheless, the convention authorized a strike by a margin of 57% to 43%.[49]

The resulting five-and-a-half-month walkout is one of the best known in the history of American labor. The solidarity of the mine workers, which owed as much if not more to the spirit developed during militant action as to the leadership of John Mitchell and others, was undoubtedly a major reason that the railroad executives decided, under strong pressure from President Theodore Roosevelt, to accept arbitration from a presidential commission. After nearly five months of deliberations, the Anthracite Coal Strike Commission presented its award toward the end of March 1903. The mine workers received several important concessions: most notably, a wage increase of approximately 10% for miners and a reduction in the hours of work from ten to nine for most company men at no decrease in pay. Still, the union did not win official recognition nor any commitment to broad-ranging joint conferences, like those that had prevailed for several years in the Central Competitive Field, for the establishment of a union scale and contract. In fact, the employers argued for a number of years that the Coal Strike Commission had so effectively adjudicated issues that there was no need even to discuss change, especially since

47. *Engineering and Mining Journal* 72 (October 12, 1901): 473; McKay to Mitchell, September 25 and October 1, 1901, and Mitchell to McKay, October 2, 1901, Mitchell Papers. For the establishment of District 9, see Blatz, "Local Leadership and Local Militancy," 287–89.

48. *Proceedings of the Semi-Annual Convention of District One, United Mine Workers of America, January 13–17, 1902, Wilkes-Barre, PA,* 16–17, Michael J. Kosik Collection, Fred Lewis Pattee Library, Pennsylvania State University, University Park, Pennsylvania.

49. Blatz, *Democratic Miners,* 121–31.

the Commission had established an arbitration panel with representatives from labor and management to deal with disputes arising from the settlement.[50]

From 1903 to 1912, the operators would deal openly with UMWA district leaders at meetings of that panel (the Board of Conciliation) and would work with local union leaders to mediate disputes as they arose. But the operators strictly limited the scope of industrywide bargaining. In 1906 and again in 1909, extensive collective bargaining resulted in two disappointingly meager agreements that went little beyond retaining the terms offered by the Coal Strike Commission. Until 1912, the UMWA in anthracite was trapped in a kind of "twilight" status, accepting the modicum of security the operators extended to it. While the union's cautious conservatism ensured its survival, such an approach could not build or even maintain the support of the rank and file, increasingly dominated by Southern and Eastern European immigrants and their children, who composed well over half the workforce by 1912. From 1906 until 1912, the union struggled to keep one-sixth of the anthracite mine workers as members in good standing.[51]

Still, the UMWA remained the only viable vehicle for solidarity, especially since it retained its fundamentally democratic character. After a brief walkout in 1912, the union won the first substantive contract gains since the award of the Anthracite Coal Strike Commission: a wage increase of 10% and the right to establish grievance committees at each mine. The UMWA did not win the checkoff of union dues, but after 1912, it organized vigorously on an almost continual basis, thus transforming the "passive support" of the industry's workers it had retained for the past decade into active membership. For most of the rest of the 1910s and the 1920s, half or more of the industry's workers were members in good standing. From 1912, recent immigrants and their children would demand greater power in the leadership of the anthracite districts and would join insurgent movements when that power was not forthcoming. Their ever-expanding role in the union is best exemplified by the election of Italian-born Rinaldo Cappellini, onetime insurgent, to the presidency of the largest anthracite district in 1923. The union's solidarity in the 1920s is reflected in its strikes of 163 days in 1922 and 170 days in 1925, approximately the same length as the epochal 1902 walkout. But in that most difficult decade for unionism, those lengthy strikes were necessary just to maintain the status quo.[52]

50. Ibid., 131–40, 166–69.
51. Ibid., 171–215. For another view of the aftermath of the 1902 strike, see Joe Gowaskie, "John Mitchell and the Anthracite Mine Workers: Leadership Conservatism and Rank-and-File Militancy," *Labor History* 27 (winter 1985–86): 54–83.
52. Ibid., 215–260. The phrase "passive support" was used by UMWA Vice President Frank J. Hayes in January 1912 in discussing the condition of the UMWA in anthracite: "Our strength in this particular field is not measured altogether by our membership, but somewhat by the great public forces in sympathy with our cause and the passive support, at least, of practically all the mine workers in the region." See *UMWJ* (January 18, 1912).

On the strikes of the 1920s, see Harold K. Kanarek, "The Pennsylvania Anthracite Strike of 1922," *Pennsylvania Magazine of History and Biography* 93 (April 1975): 207–25, and "Disaster for Hard Coal: The Anthracite Strike of 1925–1926," *Labor History* 15 (winter 1974): 44–62; also see Blatz, *Democratic Miners,* 253–58.

While the accomplishments of the UMWA in the anthracite industry had a power-ful impact on the lives of mine workers, intractable grievances at the workplace continued to loom just as large, if not larger in the 1920s as at the turn of the century. The workforce remained fragmented, especially so because, compared to other industries, relatively little technological change occurred in the anthracite mines, particularly in the miner's work.[53] Many of the problems that sparked so much of the local militancy that characterized the union's first years in anthracite were never resolved by the UMWA. For example, workers never received a full reevaluation of wage rates or work rules through negotiation with the operators. Instead, they had to cope with the ad hoc procedures of the nonunion era, albeit modified in a variety of ways by the influence of the UMWA. In particular, the union's failure to win concessions on old issues like payment by the car, which the miners never trusted, or newer ones like the spread of subcontracting, would alienate a sizable number of the rank and file and make them willing insurgents. In District 1 in the 1920s, one insurgent regime toppled after another, culminating in a bitter battle over dual unionism that did not come to its own bloody conclusion until 1936.[54]

Although David Montgomery has characterized the sort of workplace militancy on which this essay focuses as having revolutionary potential, I see its roots in the day-to-day concerns of workers, rather than some larger vision of "workers' con-trol." Workers tended to view the anthracite walkouts described above instrumen-tally, as a way to obtain a fairer deal concerning the particular matter in dispute. For workers, such walkouts reflected their "job consciousness" rather than their poten-tial for revolutionary action.[55] However, bosses viewed workplace militancy quite differently, seeing strikes over work rules as the most dire sort of threat to their "freedom to control," their "right to manage," or, most fundamentally, their prop-erty rights. Thus demands for changes in work rules evoked the most vigorous oppo-sition from employers.[56] In the anthracite industry, workplace grievances, which

53. Here the difference between anthracite and bituminous is especially striking. See Dix, *What's A Coal Miner To Do?*

54. Blatz, *Democratic Miners,* 202–64. Also see Douglas Keith Monroe, "A Decade of Turmoil: John L. Lewis and the Anthracite Miners, 1926–1936" (Ph.D. diss., Georgetown University, 1976).

55. Of course, David Montgomery has developed the concept of "workers' control" in *The Fall of the House of Labor: The Workplace, the State, and American Labor Activism, 1865–1925* (New York: Cambridge University Press, 1987), 9–44, and in *Workers' Control in America: Studies in the History of Work, Technology, and Labor Struggles* (New York: Cambridge University Press, 1979), 3–5, 9–31, 91–112. For "job consciousness," see Selig Perlman in *A Theory of the Labor Movement,* repr. ed. (New York: Augustus A. Kelley, 1970), 7–8, 169.

56. Peter N. Stearns has commented on the failure of European unions at the turn of the century to deal effectively with workplace issues in *Lives of Labor: Work in a Maturing Industrial Society* (New York: Holmes and Meier, 1975), 322–25. David Brody has shown how American unions, during the years following World War II, largely restricted their efforts in collective bargaining to obtaining in-creases in wages and benefits. However, he also maintains that unions fought doggedly to retain certain advantages on the shopfloor. See Brody, "The Uses of Power I: Industrial Battleground," in *Workers in Industrial America: Essays in the Twentieth-Century Struggle* (New York: Oxford University Press,

provided the impetus for organization at the turn of the century, remained for decades the most difficult grievances to remedy. As those grievances continued to smolder, workers became increasingly likely to blame the union rather than the employer for their persistence. In the 1920s and 1930s in anthracite, this would lead to disillusionment with and insurgency against the union, rather than solidarity against capital.

1980), 181–98. Alvin W. Gouldner describes an episode in which negotiations ostensibly over wages masked a variety of concerns about the workplace in *Wildcat Strike* (Yellow Springs, Ohio: Antioch, 1954), 27–37. For the "freedom to control," see Berthoff, "The 'Freedom to Control' in American Business History," in *A Festschrift for Frederick B. Artz,* ed. David H. Pinkney and Theodore Ropp (Durham: Duke University Press, 1964), 158–80. For the "right to manage," see Howell John Harris, *The Right to Manage: Industrial Relations Policies of American Business in the 1940s* (Madison: University of Wisconsin Press, 1982), especially chaps. 2 and 5.

CHAPTER FOUR

JOHN MITCHELL AND THE POLITICS OF THE TRADE AGREEMENT, 1898–1917

CRAIG PHELAN

More than any other trade union notable, even more than AFL President Samuel Gompers, John Mitchell personified the American labor movement in the Progressive Era. Not only did he preside over the largest and most powerful union of the period, the United Mine Workers of America, but he engineered the only victory of labor against an industry bound by trusts before the 1930s. Indeed, his leadership of the anthracite mine workers in the strike of 1902 made him more famous and powerful than any of his predecessors could have dreamed. To the miners he was a demigod; to the working class as a whole, he was a hero, a champion of their rights; to progressive employers he was a straightforward, conservative man who had earned their respect; and to national politicians he was a power broker to be wooed and won over. He dealt with senators and robber barons nearly as an equal, counted the president among his friends, and strode like a giant in the industrial world. With an army of miners ready to act on his command, he symbolized the movement's new status.

Mitchell's leadership of the UMWA (1898–1908) was historically significant not only because of his fame or the concrete benefits he was able to win for the miners, but also for his development and propagation of a particular trade union philosophy based on the trade agreement. National collective bargaining—or the trade agreement, as it was called during the Progressive Era—had long been a goal of trade unionists. Yet far more than any labor leader before or since, Mitchell was the outspoken champion of the trade agreement as the basis for harmony between labor and capital. He perceived the growing proliferation of such agreements in the first years of the century as a movement that would soon sweep the country and lift industrial relations out of the dark ages of conflict and violence. In many ways his entire career was an attempt to sell this idea to those who remained skeptical. He imagined that he was riding the wave of history as more and more industries turned to the trade agreement, to which he was ideologically and emotionally wedded, as the ultimate solution to the labor problem.

Yet Mitchell and his message of peace were only shooting stars in the economic sky. As quickly as he rose to the lofty heights of power and prestige, he descended once again into obscurity. After 1904 increasing numbers of employers broke their collective bargaining agreements and resumed their long-standing war against trade unionism. An aggressive open-shop movement effectively stymied further labor advances and killed the dream of class harmony. While the majority of workers and their leaders recognized that the "honeymoon" was over and that new strategies and tactics were necessary to combat the growing antiunion offensive, Mitchell refused to abandon his conviction that a permanent and peaceful solution to the perennial "labor question" had been found. After 1908 Mitchell's insistence that the trade agreement held the key to industrial justice and class harmony left him increasingly isolated in labor circles. As we shall see, his faith in trade agreements, while founded in the economic reality of the soft-coal industry, ultimately served to strengthen the forces of reaction and cripple labor's efforts to take its place as a national force.

While Mitchell's reign was brief, an investigation of his life provides insight into some of the salient developments of the Progressive Era. One theme is the impact of national collective bargaining on the relationship between labor leaders and the rank and file. Success of the trade agreement depended on the existence of a highly centralized and bureaucratic union. Mitchell could be quite ruthless in asserting his authority and subduing his rivals, and he laid the foundations of a union in which rank-and-file sentiment would exercise limited influence. Equally important, the trade agreement meant that he would spend an ever-increasing amount of his time, both on the job and socially, with large-scale coal operators who purchased the labor he sold and national political figures concerned with economic affairs. His removal from the social and physical setting of mine workers had a profound impact on his attitudes. The more he hobnobbed with the wealthy and powerful, the more he adopted their attitudes and culture. Perhaps to a greater degree than any other labor leader, Mitchell underwent what the German sociologist Robert Michels described as "embourgeoisement."[1] By the time he stepped down as UMWA president, his

1. Robert Michels, *Political Parties*, trans. Eden and Ceder Paul (New York: Dover, 1959), 310–11.

speech, his clothing, his associations, and, to a remarkable degree, his outlook more closely resembled those of employers than the rank and file.

A second theme, related to the first, is the tendency of labor officials to grow increasingly cautious over time. Mitchell's career beautifully illustrates this trend. Once ensconced in power, once in a position to begin working to create a more ethical basis of industrial relations, Mitchell underwent a slow process of change from the aggressive and militant voice of oppressed miners to the conservative head of an established institution. The change did not happen all at once, nor did he fully realize the change had occurred, but gradually and irrevocably he underwent a metamorphosis from labor leader to labor bureaucrat. The term "labor leader" connotes a champion of the working class, a spokesperson and interpreter of its desires, a warrior for its collective aspirations. John Mitchell, however, eventually became the epitome of the labor bureaucrat, a person for whom the demands of the union as an institution, ultimately, shaped his decisions. Even as he built the apparatus necessary to bargain with employers at the national level, he fell victim to the iron law of oligarchy: championship of the cause became secondary to the preservation of the institution. More and more of his actions as president were aimed at protecting the union from destruction. And throughout his presidency, he displayed an unwillingness to take chances for fear of damaging the union under his control. How and why this metamorphosis occurred is fundamental to an understanding of Mitchell and other labor officials.

A third theme is the development of alliances between labor leaders, reform politicians, and progressive employers. Since the power of coal unionism rested on the trade agreement, it was natural for Mitchell to join hands with other powerful men to promote this mechanism of labor peace. The institutional expression of this desire was the National Civic Federation, a voluntary association of wealthy capitalists, trade unionists, and representatives of the public. The NCF represented the promise of the early Progressive years, when increasing numbers of experts became convinced that there were no irreconcilable differences between capital and labor, that industrial relations could soon be permanently established on an ethical and mutually advantageous basis, that employers and responsible unions could work together to create industrial peace and economic prosperity. While his political allies and the NCF assisted Mitchell in his efforts to extend the trade agreement to hard coal, their assistance came with strings attached. As we shall see, Mitchell was quite willing to allow these elites to intervene in the affairs of the union and dictate policy on important union matters.

John Mitchell was born on February 4, 1870, the child of Robert Mitchell, a Dublin-born Protestant who had come to America via Scotland, and his second wife, Martha Halley.[2] He was raised in Braidwood, a coal "boom" town, that was for a brief time

---

2. On Mitchell's youth see Craig Phelan, *Divided Loyalties: The Public and Private Life of John Mitchell* (Albany: State University of New York Press, 1994), chap. 1; Elsie Gluck, *John Mitchell, Miner: Labor's Bargain with the Gilded Age* (New York: John Day, 1929), 1–35.

the most important coal producer in northern Illinois. In numerous ways Mitchell's youth was similar to that of hundreds of thousands of nineteenth-century coal diggers. He had intimate knowledge of the daily grind of poverty and hunger, the horrendous working conditions and daily fear of death in the mines, the uncertainty of employment that forced him to adopt a "gypsy's life" and travel to Colorado twice before 1892, and the brutality of strikes and lockouts that cast the pall of outright starvation in the coal communities. The solidarity that bound those who shared these horrors was etched upon his soul.

Yet in some ways Mitchell's experience was even more unfortunate than that of most miners. By the age of six he had lost both of his natural parents, and he was left in the care of a stern, unloving stepmother who whipped him severely for minor transgressions. Because his labor was required to help maintain the fatherless family, he attended school only irregularly and quit altogether after five years. The paucity of his education and the consequent feeling of alienation from the other boys in town made Mitchell a pitiable character even by the heartwrenching standards of coal towns.

Perhaps it was his privation and unhappiness as a child that ignited the spark of ambition. Largely through his natural intelligence, his gift for conciliation, and his talent for inspiring confidence in his superiors, Mitchell ascended with remarkable speed through the hierarchy of the UMWA. By 1897 he had been elected to a seat on District 12's executive board, but he was still a relatively minor player at the district level of an impotent union. No one could predict that within two years he would emerge as the president of one of the nation's most powerful unions. In 1897 Mitchell rose like a phoenix out of the poverty-stricken prairie of Illinois.

The year began as inauspiciously as previous years for the miners and their union. The nearly bankrupt UMWA claimed less than 10,000 members, and in desperation the new president, Michael Ratchford, issued the call for a national suspension to begin July 4, 1897.[3] The response to the strike call shocked both union leaders and operators. Within days 150,000 diggers laid down their picks. The strike was almost completely effective in shutting off coal production in northern Illinois, Indiana, and Ohio. But in several important districts the strike was less than complete. Tens of thousands of miners continued to work in central Pennsylvania, West Virginia, and southern Illinois.

Ratchford ordered Mitchell to the southern section of Illinois. Since there were no funds for train fare, Mitchell walked from camp to camp, sleeping under the stars and eating whatever the miners would give him. His appeals on behalf of the union induced thousands of men to refrain from work. Although he never achieved a shutdown of the southern Illinois field, he was successful enough to attract the notice of

---

3. On the 1897 strike, see John E. George, "The Coal Miners' Strike of 1897," *Quarterly Journal of Economics* 12 (January 1898): 204–7; Andrew Roy, *A History of the Coal Miners of the United States* (Columbus, Ohio: J. L. Traeger, 1905), 356–58; Maier B. Fox, *United We Stand: The United Mine Workers of America* (Washington, D.C.: UMWA, 1990), 52; K. Austin Kerr, "Labor-Management Cooperation: An 1897 Case," *Pennsylvania Magazine of History and Biography* 49 (January 1975): 66–68.

Ratchford and other UMWA leaders.[4] The 1897 strike was one of labor's great struggles, and Mitchell believed he was part of history in the making. His central role as the organizer in southern Illinois and the national focus given the strike made the summer of 1897 memorable and fired him with enthusiasm for the cause of unionism. Although it ended in compromise, the 1897 strike marked the first national victory for the UMWA and led to the establishment of the interstate joint conference.

In January 1898 Mitchell was part of the UMWA delegation that met in Chicago with operators in joint conference. This was the first national joint conference held in more than a decade, and it signaled a new era in soft-coal industrial relations that would last, with occasional lapses, for nearly three decades. Since union attempts to organize West Virginia and other outlying districts had failed, the joint conference involved only the Central Competitive Field: western Pennsylvania, Ohio, Indiana, and Illinois. The basis of unity between capital and labor in soft coal was the mutual desire to maintain labor peace over an extended period. With the depression lifting, both sides hoped to benefit from the resurgence in coal demand. Labor peace meant higher profits for operators and higher wages for miners.[5]

While the bargaining sessions were often heated, operators ultimately agreed to most of the union demands. Miners won a wage increase, the checkoff of union dues, and the eight-hour day. Leading economists praised the new joint conference system in soft coal as a major step toward the solution of the "labor problem." It was an orderly, nonviolent, nongovernmental approach that promoted class harmony and cooperation. Numerous journalists, academics, and political leaders agreed and called for the adoption of this system by other industries. So, too, did young John Mitchell. He believed the coal accord should be "regarded as an epoch in the industrial movement of our country." During those eleven days in Chicago, representatives of capital and labor, "those two forces formerly so antagonistic," met and "agreed to apply reason and intelligence, instead of force and coercion, in the adjustment of wage differences."[6] Throughout his career, Mitchell continued to regard the trade agreement with the same reverence.

Mitchell's organizing activity in southern Illinois had helped contribute to the victory in 1897. It catapulted him from obscurity to the national vice presidency at

4. On Mitchell's activities in southern Illinois, see Marion Kinneman, "John Mitchell in Illinois," *Illinois State University Journal* 32 (September 1969): 29; Roy, *History of the Coal Miners,* 353; John H. Keiser, "John H. Walker: Labor Leader from Illinois," in *Essays in Illinois History,* ed. Donald Tingley (Carbondale: Southern Illinois University Press, 1968), 78; Gluck, *John Mitchell,* 29–30; McAlister Coleman, *Men and Coal* (New York: Farrar and Rinehart, 1943), 60.

5. For a discussion of the 1898 Interstate Joint Conference, see Fox, *United We Stand,* 53–54; John E. George, "The Settlement in the Coal Mining Industry," *Quarterly Journal of Economics* 12 (July 1898): 447–57; Arthur E. Suffern, *Conciliation and Arbitration in the Coal Industry of America* (New York: Houghton Mifflin, 1915), 154–55.

6. JM, "Labor Day Address," 1899, delivered in Hocking Valley, Ohio, John Mitchell Papers. Microfilm edition. Hereafter cited as JMP. For the impact of the Joint Conference on social and economic thought, see Kerr, "Labor-Management Cooperation," 60–71.

the January 1898 UMWA convention and set the stage for his rise to the presidency. In September 1898 Ratchford accepted President William McKinley's invitation to become a member of the newly created United States Industrial Commission. His duties were to begin October 20, when the first session of the commission was slated to open.[7] Yet Ratchford was deeply concerned about the future success of the organization that had grown so dramatically under his charge. He therefore took pains to make sure the most gifted man succeeded him. And in Ratchford's eyes, Mitchell was the obvious choice.

Exactly why Ratchford believed Mitchell was the best candidate is impossible to determine. There were certainly more experienced and knowledgeable men, most notably District 5 President Patrick Dolan and District 6 Secretary-Treasurer Tom L. Lewis. But Mitchell had demonstrated leadership qualities essential to the UMWA's success after the establishment of the interstate movement. In 1898 the union had embarked on a new course. After years of class warfare and confrontation, the goal was now to uphold peaceful contractual relations. This new course required new skills: soundness of judgment, deliberate and calculated rationality, willingness to compromise, and an ability to persuade the rank and file to live up to existing contracts rather than inspire them to fight. While Mitchell had not always succeeded in his efforts as vice president, he seemed to understand the new rules of the game at least as well as anyone else.

Ratchford's choice of Mitchell by no means guaranteed victory for the young man. There was no traditional pathway from the UMWA vice presidency to the presidency, and previous union chiefs gained office only after bitter and even ruthless infighting. But Ratchford, a wily veteran of intra-union battles, devised a means by which Mitchell's chances would be greatly improved. Rather than resign, he chose to remain official head of the union until the expiration of his term on April 1, 1899. And he installed Mitchell as ''acting president,'' a position not provided for in the union's constitution. This subversion of union law would greatly assist Mitchell in the January 1899 elections. As head of the administration Mitchell could take credit for all UMWA advances in 1898, and he had control of the internal mechanisms of power, such as the union's journal and the staff of organizers, to help defeat his enemies.[8]

When UMWA convention delegates gathered at the ''Old City Hall'' in Pittsburgh in January 1899, Ratchford all but guaranteed Mitchell's victory through his power to control debate and make committee appointments. The most important committee affecting union elections was the credentials committee, and Ratchford made certain it was packed with administration supporters. This committee examined the credentials of each delegate and decided, on the basis of how many members each delegate

7. JM to W. R. Russell, September 24, 1898, JMP.

8. In her discussion of Mitchell's assumption of the acting presidency, Gluck, *John Mitchell*, 48–49, implies that the subversion of the constitution was simply a practical consideration to avoid ''political wrangles.'' It should also be mentioned that once in office, Mitchell would demonstrate the same cavalier attitude toward constitutional questions.

represented, the number of votes each delegate possessed. Thus even though Ohio was considered the strongest district, few were surprised when this committee reported that Illinois delegates controlled 261 votes and Ohio just 154. Recognizing this meant his certain defeat, Tom L. Lewis bowed out of the presidential race on the second day of the convention, and Patrick Dolan withdrew soon after. With the removal of the opposition, the election itself was a mere formality. Mitchell received 571 of the 613 votes cast and at age twenty-eight, began his ten-year reign as president of the miners.[9]

The establishment of the Interstate Joint Agreement in 1898 made the UMWA a permanent force in the soft-coal fields. It was without a doubt the single most important reason for the success of Mitchell's presidency. But the Joint Agreement implied obligations as well as permanence. One principal obligation of the union was to expand its control beyond the boundaries of the Central Competitive Field and organize all miners. If the UMWA failed in its efforts to organize all coalfields, and to force all coal operators to pay union wages, CCF operators paying high union wages would be unable to compete for markets against nonunion operators in the South and such Appalachian fields as West Virginia. Such a situation would eventually force CCF operators to demand extensive wage cuts from the union. Mitchell recognized the threat of nonunion fields all too well.

In the union's need to expand, the Interstate Agreement itself proved invaluable as a selling point to both operators and miners. Mitchell and his corps of organizers could hold out the promise of high wages and the eight-hour day to entice nonunion miners to join the fold. Operators were told about the relative labor peace that had come to many of the midwestern coalfields as a result of the Interstate Agreement, a labor peace that meant steady production. Operators were also told about the CCF's establishment of uniform wage rates, which promised to eliminate much of the cutthroat competition among coal firms. With such a package to offer, it is hardly surprising that membership skyrocketed and the number of signed contracts with operators mushroomed after 1897. By January 1900 union membership stood at 93,000, a figure that did not include the thousands exonerated from paying dues because of strikes and lockouts. Hundreds of new locals had been formed, lapsed districts were revived in Iowa, Alabama, central Pennsylvania, and Kentucky, and new districts were created in Maryland, Kansas, Missouri, Michigan, Arkansas–Indian Territory, and the anthracite region of northeast Pennsylvania.[10]

Mitchell's incredible success in organizing the unorganized in 1898 and 1899 was not a simple matter or salesmanship, however. As acting president and then in his first year as president, he was often forced to flex union muscle. He engineered

    9. UMWA, *Proceedings of the Tenth Annual Convention,* 1899, 3–6, 37; Joseph M. Gowaskie, "John Mitchell: A Study in Leadership," (Ph.D. diss., Catholic University of America, 1968), 31–32; Gluck, *John Mitchell,* 52: JM to James O'Rourke, January 13, 1899, JMP.
    10. UMWA, *Proceedings of the Eleventh Annual Convention,* 1900, 17.

large-scale and militant organizing drives in central Pennsylvania and Arkansas that forced recalcitrant operators to submit to the growing power of the union. That this boy president proved such an able field general surprised many, including some of his own supporters.

The Interstate Joint Conference also necessitated a strong central leadership able to negotiate a national contract and enforce its terms. Before 1897, when miners and operators of a single state met to devise wage agreements, national officers were conspicuously weak, performing mostly administrative functions. Interstate bargaining, however, forced a high degree of coordination and collaboration between districts. Conflicting goals had to be balanced, and the demands of individual districts had to be subsumed under the interest of the national organization. Negotiating and enforcing national contracts required strong centralized control over constituent bodies. Only the president and the national board could be counted on to see the larger picture, to transcend local interests. Once attaining power, therefore, Mitchell naturally strove to subdue the power of locals and districts and centralize authority. There is no evidence that Mitchell, like his successor Tom L. Lewis, pursued centralization merely to enhance his personal power. For Mitchell, centralization was prerequisite to the proper functioning of the interstate agreement.

While the process of centralization was in many ways a natural result of the joint conference, there were those in the union who opposed this trend. Before 1897 the focus of power in the union had been the district, and a few district leaders proved unwilling to abdicate their authority voluntarily. Over the years, these officials had created their own fiefdoms, their own political machines and mechanisms of power. When Mitchell moved to impose national authority, these district leaders were thus able to entrench and resist quite effectively for some time.

In his campaign of centralization, Mitchell often employed questionable strategies and tactics. Rather than engage these leaders in the open forum of the convention to decide through democratic means who would control the use of organizers and strike funds, and what the proper relationship between district and national should now be, he engineered covert operations and rearguard actions involving subterfuge, duplicity, and intrigue. In his unsuccessful campaign to remove Patrick Dolan from the District 5 presidency, for instance, Mitchell misused national funds, used national organizers as personal spies and campaigners for himself and district favorites, and showed a propensity for ignoring constitutional restraints.[11] His machinations helped pave the way for the corruption and dictatorial control that infected significant elements of the UMWA's leadership for much of the century. Moreover, in his secret wars to undermine district autonomy, the young and inexperienced Mitchell made numerous mistakes. He placed his trust in incompetent insurgents, such as William Warner of District 5, whose bungling jeopardized his reputation. He built up opposition blocs but proved unable to control them. He exposed himself

---

11. On Mitchell's attempt to remove Dolan, see Phelan, *Divided Loyalties,* chap. 2; Gowaskie, "John Mitchell," 35–47.

to potentially damaging accusations. And his inexperience even permitted the rise of one of the most powerful district opponents, Tom L. Lewis, into the national vice presidency in January 1900, where his obstructionism continued unabated.

Despite Mitchell's clumsiness, by 1900 the process of centralization had stripped districts of much of their former power. By no means were all district leaders transformed into Mitchell boosters, but most found that continued obstruction was a futile and damaging policy. District leaders had become dependent on the national for strike funds and organizers, and they found that Mitchell had become so popular among the rank and file that public attacks on the new president threatened their own hold over the miners in their districts.

At the 1900 UMWA convention, Mitchell was ready to codify in union law the transference of authority from the district to the national organization. He had hand-picked members of the committee on the constitution and had named his friend Billy Ryan as chair. On the morning of January 30, the committee introduced eighteen amendments to the constitution, of which all but one passed. By far the most important amendments involved expanding the powers of the president. First, the president would be given the right, with the consent of the International Executive Board, to fill all vacancies occurring in the national office. This was a matter of closing the stable door after the horse ran off. Had he possessed this power in August 1899 when Vice President Tom Davis resigned, Mitchell easily could have replaced Davis with one of his own boosters. But because Mitchell lacked this power in 1899, and because he had not yet perfected his political control, Tom L. Lewis, his powerful District 6 opponent, was able to capture the vice presidency. Second, the president was empowered to appoint as many organizers and other workers as he believed were required. The number of organizers had risen dramatically in 1899, and he did not want limitations placed on his right to increase staff. Third, the president was empowered to attend in person, or send national organizers, to visit locals, district conventions, and "any other places in the districts . . . when convinced that such services are required." He now had explicit constitutional authority to send his organizers anywhere he wanted. Fourth, the president shall "decide all questions of dispute on constitutional grounds." After a close voice vote on the floor, Mitchell declared that all the proposed amendments had been adopted.[12] In one mighty chop, Mitchell had struck at the very roots of local and district sovereignty and had centralized authority in a way unthinkable a few years earlier.

His agenda was not yet complete. The constitution committee also moved to create a central defense fund. In 1898 miners had defeated the creation of a national strike fund through referendum vote. This time he avoided the pitfalls of such direct democracy by asking the convention to place authority in the hands of the president and executive board to levy assessments in support of those on strike. The amendment made each member's standing in the organization contingent upon prompt payment of the assessments. After a great deal of squabbling, this amendment also

12. UMWA, *Proceedings of the Eleventh Annual Convention*, 1900, 50–51.

narrowly passed by voice vote.[13] The creation of the defense fund was a major step toward centralized control. Only strikes approved by the president and the national board received strike funds, thus giving Mitchell incredible power to discourage wildcat strikes through the withholding of money.

Once the command structure of his union army had been duly empowered, Mitchell was prepared to wrest concessions from CCF operators. The interstate joint conference can be seen as a ritualized dance between two hostile powers. Shifting from joint discussions to scale committees to subscale committees, the two sides followed prescribed formulas as they sized each other up, using taunts, jokes, and statistics to measure the other side's war readiness and to determine the minimum price of peace. It was the most important human element in the bituminous coal industry, and its outcome determined whether or not there would be a strike, a wage increase, or a decrease. Only expert negotiators able to withstand marathon bargaining sessions could succeed. Despite his youth and inexperience, Mitchell demonstrated amazing skill as a negotiator. He came armed with an impressive arsenal of facts and arguments. Without a second's hesitation he could bring forth statistics on the tonnage of coal produced in each district, the price that coal brought on the market, the wages paid at present to each category of mine worker, differentials between pick and machine mining, and the costs of living for miners down to the price of beer. At the joint conference he was the aggressive and confident salesman with exclusive rights to a necessary product, mine labor.

At the 1900 joint conference, after days of verbal sparring, Mitchell heard what he wanted to hear, a compromise he could accept. The operators offered an advance of fourteen cents a ton for picked, screened coal, nine cents a ton for run of mine coal, and twenty cents a day for day laborers. Although there were many aspects of the agreement to which he objected, he believed he had received the best offer possible without resort to strike action.

He realized that his job was not finished with the signing of the accord with the operators. Indeed, in many ways his duties had just begun. First, he had to convince the miners that the advance was the best possible. To those miners who came expecting more than they received, Mitchell proved a capable pitchman, describing the contract in such glowing terms that one would hardly recognize it as the product of a compromise with which he was not completely satisfied. Second, he had to make certain, for the life of the contract, that operators abided by its terms. Addressing the operators, he warned, ''I will serve notice to the Operators now that when they go home unless they keep the agreement inviolate we will call the men out.'' Third, and most important, he had to control his own members and guarantee they would maintain absolute compliance with the terms of the agreement. ''Miners must not strike contrary to the laws of the organization,'' he insisted. ''I will serve notice on the Miners that unless they keep the laws of the organization we will suspend them

13. Ibid., 56, 65–67.

from the organization.''[14] Mitchell the negotiator had turned Mitchell the policeman, standing between labor and capital to maintain labor peace through coercion.

For Mitchell the Interstate Conference was the salvation of an industry in despair, beset with too much competition and declining prices. It represented the fruition of the dreams of Dan McLaughlin, that noble pioneer of coal unionism who had impacted his youth in Braidwood and shaped his ideals. Only by bargaining in good faith, and sharing whatever profits existed, did the industry have a chance to emerge ''out of the slough of despair in which it has wallowed for so many years.''[15] For Mitchell the Interstate Movement was no stopgap measure to prevent the worst abuses of capitalist exploitation. It was the harbinger of a free enterprise utopia on the not too distant horizon in which workers and owners shared profits equitably. As long as coal production expanded and prices continued to rise, many miners were willing to accept his solution to the labor problem.

Once relations with soft-coal operators were established on a sound basis, Mitchell turned his attention to hard coal, an industry all but ignored by the UMWA prior to his tenure. The anthracite strike of 1900 was a remarkable turning point in Mitchell's career.[16] Never was he more militant than during the organizing drive and strike call. At the start of the campaign, all signs pointed to union failure: the union had almost no organization in the hard-coal fields; the labor force seemed hopelessly divided by region, skill, ethnicity, and other factors; Mitchell and other union leaders were densely ignorant of the anthracite industry, which bore little resemblance to soft coal; and above all, hard-coal operators were powerful men, ruthless and sophisticated in their opposition to unions, who did not need to rely on union strength to ensure labor peace and the stability of trade. Despite the enormous odds, Mitchell spearheaded an aggressive drive to organize as many mine workers as possible, expending a great deal of money and resources. The drive met with only limited success. Then, over the cries of local officials that a strike would surely fail, Mitchell called the men out, initiating a labor-capital confrontation even greater than the soft-coal strike of 1897.

The resolution of the strike, however, foreshadowed Mitchell's conservative future. Bowing to political pressure, he accepted a limited settlement made in the interest of securing the reelection of the Republican administration of President William McKinley. The Republicans' desire for labor peace during the election year, not a lack of solidarity on the part of the strikers, led Mitchell to call a halt to the walk out just five weeks after it began. And even though the settlement addressed none of the mine workers' leading demands, even though strikers were prepared to

14. *Third Annual Joint Conference of Coal Miners and Operators of Illinois, Indiana, Ohio, and Pennsylvania* (Indianapolis: n.p., 1900), 141–42.

15. Ibid., 141; JM to Tom W. Davis, February 10, 1900, JMP.

16. On the 1900 anthracite strike, see Perry Blatz, *Labor Relations in the Anthracite Coal Industry, 1875–1910* (Albany: State University of New York Press, 1993), chap. 3; on Mitchell's role, see Phelan, *Divided Loyalties*, chap. 3.

remain out until a more complete victory was achieved, Mitchell demonstrated his mastery of the situation by convincing workers to accept the settlement and return to work.

The 1900 strike was also a proving ground in all aspects of strike management. Mitchell learned how to control his forces, how to unite the disparate elements under his command, how to prevent their actions from bringing down on the union the wrath of adverse public opinion. Equally important, he learned the complicated tactics of behind-the-scenes maneuvers, the give-and-take that goes on in corporate boardrooms, the political realities of industrial relations. Mitchell proved a quick study: he was able to translate his limited victory into significant union growth, secure for himself the friendship of some of the most important politicians in Washington, and win the approval of the mainstream press.

Adding to his oppressive burden of strike management was his belief that the mine workers in hard coal were a particularly volatile lot prone to irrational behavior. Never one to praise the virtues of the proletariat, Mitchell described the largely ethnic workforce in hard coal as even less sufferable than soft-coal miners. Confiding in his friend Billy Ryan, he wrote: "Of course, these miners are not like the men we know in the West; they remind me very much of a drove of cattle, ready to stampede when the least expected."[17] These were strange words indeed from a man soon to be all but deified by these "cattle." Needless to say, Mitchell never uttered such ethnic slurs in public. Indeed, throughout the organizing drive and strike, he proved remarkably sensitive to ethnic concerns. The UMWA under Mitchell was one of the few unions of the time that actively sought to enlist immigrants from Southern and Eastern Europe. He overcame the language barrier by hiring organizers conversant in the various tongues. He demonstrated his concern for the welfare of the various nationalities by visiting many of their enclaves in person. And he showed respect for their institutions by establishing close ties to their religious leaders, especially Bishop Michael Hoban of Scranton.[18] These actions made him immensely popular among the immigrants and helped ensure their participation in the strike, but his personal prejudices meant that the large number of immigrants would remain a constant source of worry.

Throughout the strike Mitchell's spirits were buoyed by the admiration strikers and their families heaped upon him. While he had no love of the rank and file, he was often moved by the affection they showed in return. Within a few weeks, he was already becoming the object of hero worship to the working people of the anthracite region. Exactly why this happened is a matter of conjecture. Some observers pointed to his success in bituminous coal, which held out the promise that he would bring that success with him. Others focused on his appearance and personality. To English-speaking miners he was regarded as a brother, one of their own kind; and

17. JM to W. D. Ryan, September 24, 1900, JMP.

18. Victor R. Greene, *The Slavic Community on Strike: Immigrant Labor in Pennsylvania* (Notre Dame: University of Notre Dame Press, 1968), 160–64.

to the foreign-born his somber and thoughtful visage, combined with his long western miner's coat and high collar, reminded them of their own priests. Still other observers pointed to his message of unity, his public declarations that miners must forgo ethnic antagonisms and join hands in the struggle. He was often credited with having uttered, "The coal you dig isn't Slavish or Polish or Irish coal, it's coal."[19]

While these factors were certainly noteworthy, they tend to show Mitchell's popularity more as a mystique. These factors suggest there was something peculiar in the makeup of working people in the anthracite region that made them especially prone to hero worship, or that there was something especially remarkable about Mitchell that made the rank and file tremble in awe. Nothing could be further from the truth. The admiration for Mitchell was neither mysterious nor unique. On the contrary, the strikers quite naturally looked to him, as strike leader and union president, as the champion of their demands and hopes for a better life. He had not created strike sentiment. He simply gave organization and direction to their protest through the strike and the union. Other strike leaders received the same adulation. John Siney, Dan McLaughlin, Chris Evans, William B. Wilson, and Mother Jones all had received hero treatment for their leadership of coal strikes.

When the strike ended with a 10% wage advance but without union recognition, all three participants—the union, the railroad presidents, and the workers themselves—were able to claim victory. The failure of the strike settlement to address fundamental grievances, and the adamant refusal of the operators to deal with the union, however, made it quite clear that the strike had resolved very little. The peace in anthracite proved fragile.

The most obvious victor in the anthracite strike of 1900 was John Mitchell himself. Within the UMWA, Mitchell now reigned supreme. His successful conduct of the strike crushed the remnants of power wielded by his leading internal opponents. He also won for himself the admiration and friendship of Republican party leader Mark Hanna. Indeed, the strike was more than a conflict between workers and employers; it also had been something of a personal test for Mitchell, a test prepared and administered by the powerful Ohio senator. Mitchell's ability to control the strikers, to get them to return to work before their grievances had been addressed, to prevent headline-making bloodshed—all helped ensure the labor peace necessary for a Republican presidential victory in the fall. Mitchell passed Hanna's test of trustworthiness with flying colors, and the two men quickly established a mutually beneficial relationship. Mitchell affectionately referred to Hanna as "the Captain," and he frequently corresponded with him and even visited him at his Cleveland

19. On Mitchell's popularity in anthracite, see contemporary observations in E. C. Morris, "John Mitchell, the Leader and the Man," *Independent* (December 25, 1902): 3073–78; Lincoln Steffens, "A Labor Leader of To-Day," *McClure's* (August 1902): 355–57; Frank Julian Warne, "John Mitchell, the Labor Leader and the Man," *Review of Reviews* (November 1902): 1044–49; Walter Weyl, "The Man the Miners Trust," *Outlook* (March 24, 1906), 657–62. There is no evidence in the Mitchell Papers or in any other source to indicate that Mitchell ever uttered these exact words.

home. Mitchell saw in Hanna a veritable mother lode of opportunity to obtain government patronage posts for his friends.

By 1901 Mitchell was no longer simply the president of the miners. Whether he liked the idea or not, his fame had made him a spokesperson for the entire labor movement. Therefore his attitudes on numerous issues took on new meaning. How should the labor movement respond to the growing numbers of immigrants and African-Americans in the nonfarm workforce? Should the craft union structure of the AFL be discarded in favor of industrial unionism to accommodate the rising tide of unskilled workers in mass-production industries? Should the AFL become more active in the political arena to combat its powerful foes? American workers eagerly awaited answers to these and other fundamental labor issues from the new star in the movement's galaxy, the militant hero of the hard-coal strike of 1900, John Mitchell.

For those working-class Americans who envisioned a bold transformation of the labor movement, Mitchell's views were disappointing. For those who regarded the AFL as the conservative bastion of native-born, white, male, skilled workers and were pressing for a more inclusive movement, Mitchell proved an obstacle rather than an ally. And for industrial union advocates and those demanding the formation of a third political party to advance labor's cause, Mitchell represented the status quo. Although he was the head of an industrial union with a positive record on the organization of immigrants and African-Americans, and although he was second vice president of the AFL, Mitchell failed to champion the cause of progressive reform within the national labor movement. To the great dismay of radicals and reformers, his conservative views on the salient labor questions of the day buttressed the cautious and increasingly outmoded policies of Gompers and the AFL Executive Council.

Indeed, in many ways Mitchell personified the conservative trade union leader of the Progressive Era. Radical opponents found him on the wrong side of every issue. His acceptance of industrial capitalism and pursuit of capital-labor harmony was a denial of the class struggle. His participation in the National Civic Federation, an organization controlled by monopoly capitalists, served only to ''chloroform'' the class-consciousness of working people. His outspoken condemnation of sympathy strikes and belief in the sanctity of contracts undermined labor solidarity.

Mitchell's stance toward African-Americans and immigrants reflected the racist and antiforeign attitudes he had learned as a youth. Despite the positive role immigrants had played in the 1900 hard-coal strike, despite the many accolades they had given him, Mitchell went on public record to say that immigrants did not make good unionists, and called for a law ''prohibiting immigration of foreigners to this country.''[20] Similarly, despite the fact that African-American miners were loyal to the union and held numerous positions of authority at the district and local level, he

---

20. *Report of the Industrial Commission on the Relations of Capital and Labor Employed in the Mining Industry* (Washington, D.C., 1901), 12:45–52.

condemned them with the same contempt he held for immigrants. While mentioning that the UMWA "does not make distinctions between classes," he found blacks lazy and a danger to the union because they were willing to accept a lower scale of wages.[21]

In comparison to other unions at this time, the UMWA had an outstanding record on organizing immigrants and African-Americans. The UMWA was one of the few unions to recruit immigrant and African-American workers actively and enroll them on an equal status with native-born, white members. Moreover, before union conventions and other labor gatherings, Mitchell never disparaged African-Americans or immigrants. Except for occasional public remarks, his views were largely personal ones. As far as can be discerned from his personal papers, although he certainly never encouraged the promotion of African-Americans or immigrants to powerful posts in his administration, he never denied union membership or advancement on the basis of race or ethnicity. As Mitchell's personal views indicate, however, union policy on race and ethnicity sprang from the nature of the industry, not the "progressive" outlook of its president.

Nor did he adopt a "progressive" stance on industrial unionism. In his attempt to make industrial unionism a reality in coal Mitchell never sought to join forces with those who saw it as an ideological issue. At the 1901 UMWA convention Mitchell pushed for passage of a resolution demanding an industrial charter to organize all workers in and around the mines. Delegates dutifully responded.[22] He then led the fight at the 1901 AFL convention to obtain an industrial charter. The thrust of his argument at the AFL convention was that the UMWA could only live up to its contracts with operators if it controlled the "outside" workers' right to strike. Gompers agreed, and the result was the adoption of the Scranton Declaration, granting an industrial union charter to the UMWA.[23] Mitchell's intent was hardly the radicalization of the AFL by promoting industrial unionism. In later years when socialists introduced resolutions in favor of industrial unionism, he stood by Gompers and the craft union heads of the AFL and helped defeat these efforts.

Radicals understood that Mitchell's conservative approach to these issues was not simply a result of his support of the trade agreement movement. Indeed, many radicals, such as UMWA socialists, were staunch supporters of the trade agreement themselves. Instead, radicals believed Mitchell had contaminated himself through constant socializing with the bourgeoisie. Fraternization with the enemy class stripped labor leaders of their working-class values, poisoned them with riches, perverted them with praise. Groups such as the NCF were conceived by powerful men to seduce labor leaders, fill their heads with false notions of class harmony, and thus "chloroform the labor movement into a more submissive mood."[24] Eugene Debs

21. Ibid.

22. UMWA, *Proceedings of the Twelfth Annual Convention*, 1901, 13, 90.

23. Philip Taft, *The A. F. of L. in the Time of Gompers* (New York: Harper, 1957), 194–98.

24. This was how Duncan McDonald, UMWA official and socialist, described the NCF at the 1911 AFL convention. Quoted in James Weinstein, *The Corporate Ideal in the Liberal State* (Boston: Beacon, 1968), 22.

condemned Mitchell and other established labor leaders for having succumbed to "the blandishment of the plutocrats."[25] Joseph Buchanon put the radical view best when he wrote in 1903 that "when the daily press and the employing class begin to praise a labor 'leader,' it is time for workingmen to keep an eye on him."[26]

In one sense, Buchanon and other radicals were right. Mitchell's conservatism did stem in part from constant hobnobbing with employers. And by 1901 he was certainly one labor leader earning the praise of both employers and the press who needed watching. The constant flattery and apparent respect he received from the nation's political and economic elite had indeed turned his head. By 1901 he had largely adopted the lifestyle of the bourgeoisie, wore tailor-made suits and gold jewelry, smoked expensive cigars and drank imported wine. He chose coal operators as his close friends and had almost no contact with the rank and file outside conventions and parades. He had substantial investments in coal mines and powder companies that represented clear conflicts of interest, and he had proven his willingness to "mine the miners" for personal profit on several occasions. If the radicals were correct, if capitalists had conspired to seduce labor leaders, then John Mitchell was a willing victim.

Yet the radicals' charge that Mitchell had abandoned the class struggle in return for wealth and privilege, while containing elements of truth, ultimately rings hollow. He had not "sold out" the class struggle. The truth was that Mitchell had never believed in class struggle. From the time he first learned about capital-labor relations from Dan McLaughlin, he had been committed to accommodation and harmony between employer and employee. Nor was his commitment to class harmony a pipe dream completely divorced from economic reality. The joint conference established in soft coal demonstrated to his satisfaction that miners and operators, once organized, could cooperate to each other's advantage, and he sincerely believed that trade agreements could be adopted in all industries to the benefit of both workers and employers. What separated Mitchell from his radical opponents who supported trade agreements was his conviction that national collective bargaining could transcend, rather than simply mitigate, class conflict.

Before the "era of trade agreements," Mitchell argued, when industrial relations were anarchic, the disputes between capital and labor resulted not from irreconcilable class differences but from sheer ignorance. Workers routinely exaggerated the profits of employers and thus believed, "frequently without cause, that they were being exploited." Capitalists, on the other hand, often had no knowledge of their workers' true standard of living, obtained misinformation from foremen, and out of their ignorance developed "a feeling of superiority over their workmen and their representatives." But now industrial relations had entered a more enlightened stage;

25. Quoted in Marc Karson, *American Labor Unions and Politics, 1900–1918* (Carbondale, Ill.: Southern Illinois University Press, 1958), 160–61.

26. Quoted in Warren Van Tine, *The Making of the Labor Bureaucrat: Union Leadership in the United States, 1870–1920* (Amherst: University of Massachusetts Press, 1973), 177.

the trade agreement imparted knowledge to both employer and employee. Through the Joint Conference, the veil of ignorance was "being lifted."[27]

If the hard-coal strike of 1900 won Mitchell a measure of national fame, the hard-coal strike of 1902 ensured his place in the pantheon of great labor leaders. His Herculean efforts on behalf of the 150,000 anthracite mine workers in a righteous but socially responsible war against the coal barons was the focus of national media attention for more than five months. His ability to control the strike field, and at the same time maneuver successfully on the complex terrain of national politics, earned for him the devotion of working people and the admiration of the press and political establishment. By the time the strike ended, Mitchell had become a national hero, a larger-than-life symbol of the collective aspirations of the dispossessed.

In his history of coal miners, Andrew Roy, a miners' union pioneer, wrote that the 1902 anthracite strike was "the best managed of any strike that ever occurred in the United States." He claimed "it was one of the most orderly strikes that ever occurred in any trade in any country of the world, and stamps John Mitchell as a peerless leader of men."[28] More recent historians have agreed that Mitchell's strike management in 1902 approached perfection.[29] And so it did. Taking into account the strike's duration, the number of strikers involved, the bitterness of feeling it engendered, Mitchell certainly deserved the homage he received at the time and since for his able control of 150,000 striking mine workers for more than five months.

Much of Mitchell's success stemmed from the results he had achieved in 1900. When the strike began, mine workers already regarded him a hero committed to their cause. Moreover, Mitchell's leadership style was attractive to the rank and file. There were far greater orators who could better stir the passions of men, but Mitchell cultivated an image that proved equally effective in commanding a loyal following. The image he presented to the strikers was one of kindness, courage, and sincere concern for their grievances, big and small. The donning of the priestlike garb was a conscious attempt to command the same reverence as their clerics. He kept in constant contact with his men, touring the region often and encouraging them to voice their opinions. The Hotel Hart in Hazleton where he stayed was always open to mine workers who wanted to give or receive advice or simply meet their leader.

27. John Mitchell, *Organized Labor; Its Problems, Purposes and Ideals* (Philadelphia: American Book and Bible House, 1903), p. 352.

28. Roy, *History of the Coal Miners,* 440.

29. See, for example, Selig Perlman, *A History of Trade Unionism in the United States* (New York: Macmillan, 1923), 177; Gluck, *John Mitchell,* chap. 6; Robert J. Cornell, *The Anthracite Coal Strike of 1902* (Washington, D.C.: Catholic University of America Press, 1957), 258–59; Gowaskie, "John Mitchell," 165–69, 189; Bruno Ramirez, *When Workers Fight: The Politics of Industrial Relations in the Progressive Era, 1898–1916* (Westport, Conn.: Greenwood, 1978), 40–41; Robert Wiebe, "The Anthracite Strike of 1902: A Record of Confusion," *Mississippi Valley Historical Review* 48 (September 1961): 240.

When talking to the men, he appealed not to their passion but to their reason. Breaker boys found him kind, and older mine workers who approached him found explanations rather than irrational oratory.

Mitchell's strongest rank-and-file support came from immigrant miners. These "cattle," as Mitchell called them in 1900, spoke of Mitchell as a god. According to one eyewitness, nearly every Slav in anthracite placed Mitchell's picture on the wall beside those of the saints.[30] One important reason for Mitchell's hold over the immigrants and rank and file in general was his careful recruitment of the Catholic clergy. Although not religious himself, Mitchell understood the important role played by priests and went to great pains to secure their support. He often received letters of support from priests and developed "an intimate acquaintance with several in this region."[31] His closest clerical friends were among the most important, Bishop Michael Hoban of Scranton and Father John J. Curran in Wilkes-Barre. Priests provided Mitchell with a valuable tool to keep the men in line.

Mitchell's ability to win over public sympathy contributed mightily to the ultimate outcome of the strike. According to Selig Perlman the anthracite strike of 1902 was the first time in American history a union had tied up a strategic industry for months "without being condemned as a revolutionary menace."[32] Yet Mitchell paid a heavy price to maintain the support of the public. Because he perceived a need to appear reasonable and flexible, he abandoned all hope of securing union recognition. While a trade agreement was not one of the stated demands of the strikers, it was well known that Mitchell hoped to achieve in hard coal the same joint conference method that existed in soft coal. In late August Abram Hewitt, ex-mayor of New York and member of the board of directors of the Erie Railroad, asserted that the real issue of the strike was not wages and hours but union recognition. Convinced the public would not endure a coal shortage for the sake of union recognition, Mitchell publicly declared that recognition of the UMWA "is not and never has been the paramount issue of the present strike." Mine workers were striking for living wages.[33] Mitchell's dedication to public sympathy was indeed an expensive proposition.

Jubilant reaction from all quarters greeted Mitchell's acceptance of President Roosevelt's arbitration proposal and the end of the strike. The majority of people in the labor movement or sympathetic to it hailed the settlement as a tremendous victory. Most mine workers in the anthracite region were both relieved and happy now that the ordeal was over and they could look forward to steady incomes. And once again Mitchell was worshiped as a deity. Banquets were held in his honor, and gifts were offered to the hero. Amidst the hurrahs, however, discordant voices could be heard. Within the UMWA, Mother Jones was the most vocal detractor. She believed

30. Cited in Greene, *Slavic Community on Strike,* 200.
31. JM to Father John Power, August 9, 1902, JMP.
32. Perlman, *History of Trade Unionism,* 177.
33. John Mitchell, "Dictation by the Unions," *Independent* (September 18, 1902), 2228.

the mine workers should have continued the strike until full recognition was achieved.[34] Socialists also assailed Mitchell's acceptance of the settlement. John Spargo, a socialist who had worked for the union during the strike, castigated Mitchell for succumbing to his "friendship with T. R."[35] One socialist paper called it "one of the worst fiascoes ever presented by an impotently led labor movement."[36]

Had Mitchell placed his trust in the fighting spirit of the mine workers, he might well have spurned the offer to arbitrate and battled to achieve full recognition. Yet unlike Jones and the socialists, Mitchell did not place his faith in the rank and file. He depended on the friendship of elites and public approval to advance the union cause. His visit to the White House, in particular, had added immensely to his prestige. His constant willingness to arbitrate had earned him the sympathy of the public. Having worked so diligently to cultivate public opinion and political alliances, he could not contemplate jeopardizing these bases of support by reneging on his promise to arbitrate. As he put it, "as we had struggled for the principle of arbitration, we would not be justified in refusing to accept it because victory was in our hands."[37]

By keeping his word and ending the strike, he helped gain a measure of legitimacy for organized labor at a time when trade unions were considered part of the radical fringe. By his ability to control the rank and file and his ability to avert a sympathy strike of soft-coal miners, he ingratiated himself with some of the most powerful people in the nation. His gentile demeanor, in contrast with the arrogance of the operators, encouraged Roosevelt to bring the weight of presidential power to bear against the coal barons. The only thing he did not achieve was a clear-cut victory for the anthracite mine workers. Indeed, the struggle was far from over.

Nothing better illustrated the emerging bureaucratic unionism of the Progressive years than John Mitchell's preparations for the Anthracite Coal Strike Commission. The terrain of capital-labor conflict in hard coal would no longer be the strike field, where there were too many risks involved for the union as an institution, but rather the conference room and the courtroom. Here political alliances and public pressure took the place of rank-and-file militancy. Here reasoned argument, backed by reams of facts and figures, took the place of pickets and rallies. The mine workers themselves were now important only for statistical purposes, and for the emotional impression their tales of woe might make on the public and the commissioners. Mitchell rented two floors of a house in Philadelphia and hired an army of labor's new mercenaries: investigators, economists, publicists, and secretaries. Above them stood Mitchell himself, the four-star general of bureaucratic unionism preparing for battle.

The artillery for this battle was information. Statistics on every conceivable as-

34. Mary Field Parton, ed., *Autobiography of Mother Jones* (Chicago: Kerr, 1925), 59–61.

35. Quoted in John H. M. Laslett, *Labor and the Left: A Study of Socialist and Radical Influences in the American Labor Movement, 1881–1924* (New York: Basic Books, 1970), 205.

36. *Social Democratic Herald,* January 31, 1903, quoted in Gowaskie, "John Mitchell," 195.

37. Mitchell, *Organized Labor,* 390.

pect of the industry had to be gathered and processed. Not simply wages and hours, but endless details on the costs of living, the costs of mining coal, production and distribution of coal, and profit levels were marshaled for the upcoming war of words. Mitchell was truly in his element. His success at the annual bituminous joint conferences testified to his expertise in this type of confrontation. Because the anthracite industry was far more complex in its detail than soft coal, Mitchell realized he needed more assistance than the union staff could supply. He therefore enlisted some of the best research talent available. The justice of the mine workers' case also earned for Mitchell the active support of one of the best-known social critics of the day, Henry Demarest Lloyd. Lloyd proved valuable, adding not only research skills but prestige and oratorical abilities. It was Lloyd's suggestion that Mitchell hire Clarence Darrow to head up the UMWA's legal defense team. Darrow had already achieved a measure of national acclaim for his defense of Eugene Debs during the Pullman strike in 1894.[38] These three men—Mitchell, Lloyd, and Darrow—were most responsible for representing the mine workers before the commission and the public. Among union supporters, they became known as the "miners' trinity."

The Anthracite Coal Strike Commission opened hearings on November 14 at Scranton, and for the next four months it commanded national attention. The press was there in force, and the eyes of the nation watched to see if Roosevelt's commission would mete out justice as he had promised. On the second day of the hearings Mitchell took the stand as Darrow's first witness. In clear and confident tones he articulated the union's demands and the reasons for their acceptance. He then stated his case for the extension of the trade agreement to hard coal. The trade agreement, he asserted, was the only effective means to establish employer-employee relations "on a just and permanent basis." It represented the only fair way to settle questions arising between workers and employers without resort to strikes and lockouts.[39]

Mitchell was cross-examined for four full days. Numerous attorneys for the operators challenged him, but it was Wayne MacVeagh, chief counsel for the Pennsylvania Coal Company, who took charge of the grilling. Mitchell withstood the test well, using his quick wit and debating skills to fend off his attackers and win over the reporters. For instance, when MacVeagh expressed concern that wage increases won by mine workers would lead to higher coal costs and thus fall on the "bowed backs of the poor," Mitchell suggested that operators need not raise coal prices. They might take the wage increase "out of their profits and so put it on the bowed backs of the rich."[40] His skillful performance on the witness stand won praise from all sides. Even MacVeagh was impressed, remarking at one point: "You are the best witness for yourself, Mr. Mitchell, that I have ever confronted."[41]

38. Irving Stone, *Clarence Darrow for the Defense* (New York: Doubleday, 1941), 141.

39. Anthracite Coal Strike Commission, *Report to the President on the Anthracite Coal Strike of May–October 1902* (Washington, D.C.: GPO, 1903), app. A, 39–41.

40. Caro Lloyd, *Henry Demarest Lloyd* (New York: Putnam, 1912), 210; see also Gowaskie, "John Mitchell," 186.

41. *Buffalo Courier,* November 18, 1902, cited in Cornell, *Anthracite Coal Strike,* 242 n.24.

The final summations presented radically contrasting social philosophies, but much more memorable than the words of either Darrow or George Baer, who spoke for the operators, was the action of Mitchell. Upon the conclusion of Baer's speech, he walked across the room and shook his hand.[42] After five months of industrial warfare that required presidential intervention to quell, after more than two hundred witnesses had testified to the horrific exploitation resulting from absolute corporate dominance in the industry, and after the coal barons had castigated him personally and disparaged his union as the root cause of the industry's problems, Mitchell professed no animosity. Mitchell never explained this action in print, but as were all his public actions and utterances, the handshake was quite obviously premeditated and calculated for its effect. It was pure theater, intending to symbolize, for the benefit of commission members, operators, and the public, that he was the kind of reasonable, conservative labor leader who deserved recognition. He had calculated that greater sympathy could be earned for the union, and greater prestige for himself, by a public turning of the cheek.

The findings of the commission, which were made public on March 21, 1903, consisted of a report and an award, the former being a theoretical discussion of general principles of capital-labor relations; the latter, specific recommendations bearing on the anthracite industry. In short, both the report and the award represented compromises between the position of the coal barons and the union. And both sides were thus able to claim victory. Because they had not been forced to recognize the UMWA, operators were quick to hail the award as a major triumph. Mitchell was also delighted. He had little to say regarding the report, with its contradictory endorsement of both the open shop and collective bargaining as the basis of industrial relations. But he applauded the wage gains and the hourly reduction contained in the award. And he chose to interpret the creation of the Board of Conciliation as a significant step toward a trade agreement for the industry. "While disclaiming the wish to compel the recognition of the United Mine Workers of America," he wrote, "the Commission in practice made that recognition inevitable."[43] The operators themselves did not agree with Mitchell's glowing assessment of the Board of Conciliation, and for many years they successfully blocked all union efforts to obtain more complete recognition.

In 1903 Mitchell stood at the apex of his prestige and power. His national fame equaled that of AFL president Samuel Gompers, and within his own union he was almost beyond reproach. Yet by early 1905, less than two years later, Mitchell's impervious armor was badly tarnished. Socialists had become emboldened and could denounce the UMWA president without fear of censure. A movement was underfoot to disallow Mitchell's participation in the NCF, a movement that would achieve its objective in 1911. Moreover, the rank and file was growing increasingly

42. Gluck, *John Mitchell*, 148.
43. Mitchell, *Organized Labor*, 394.

skeptical of their president. Policies that had once passed unnoticed became matters for acrimonious debate. Although Mitchell remained head of the union until 1908, the unquestioning support of the rank and file had vaporized.

A number of factors account for this dramatic reversal of fortune, but no one factor was more significant than the wage reduction of 1904. An economic downturn beginning in 1903 led operators to demand a 12% wage reduction at the January 1904 interstate joint conference. This proved the first real test of the union's commitment to the trade agreement. Since 1898, when the trade agreement in soft coal was first established, the nation had experienced general economic prosperity. Both profits and wages had risen in the industry. Now that the economy had soured, would the union live up to its pledge that wages must be tied to market conditions? And could Mitchell force union members to accept a wage cut without resort to a strike?

Despite NCF pressure, Mitchell was at first adamant that no reduction would be acceptable. And by March 4, just as newspapers began discussing the strong possibility of a bituminous strike when present contracts expired on April 1, the operators backed away from their original demand and now called for a 5½% slash and a two-year contract.[44] On March 6 the miners' representatives met in special convention, and to the surprise of many, Mitchell pressed for acceptance. What prompted Mitchell, one of the greatest labor statesmen of the day, to press vigorously for a two-year giveback he believed was not justified by market conditions? First, he was convinced the operators' offer was final and that there would indeed be a strike if the offer were rejected. Second, he believed a strike would not succeed, and he was duty-bound to protect the institution under his control from possible destruction. Third and most important, having presented himself to the public as the champion of the trade agreement, Mitchell could not endanger the Joint Conference in coal without destroying his own credibility. His fame and fortune were intimately tied to the success of the trade agreement, of basing labor-capital relations on the high level of rational argument rather than the strike. To strike now, when capitalists believed the market justified wage cuts, would demonstrate that he was at best a fair-weather friend of class harmony and at worst a hypocrite who failed to act on his own principles.[45] In a sense, Mitchell had become a victim of his own rhetoric.

Other miners were not bound by public pledges to uphold labor peace, and Mitchell encountered a great deal of opposition at the special miners' convention. Many delegates exhibited the class-consciousness their president abhorred. ''We will strike, if necessary until hell freezes over and not concede anything to the millionaires,'' one Illinois delegate fumed. Indeed, the entire Illinois delegation, representing as they did the most solidly organized district, stood united against the

44. *Seventh Annual Joint Conference of Coal Miners and Operators of Western Pennsylvania, Ohio, Indiana, and Illinois* (Indianapolis, 1904), 57–114.

45. UMWA, *Proceedings of the Special National Convention* (March 5–7, 1904), 28–29.

reduction.[46] While no delegate directly challenged Mitchell's leadership, several class-conscious delegates supported their opposition to the giveback with allusions to the elitist affectations of their president. Many resented Mitchell's tailored Prince Albert coat, his cane, and his derby. One Illinois socialist took particular note of the cane, commenting that a cane was a sure sign of a social climber. Some delegates began to question whether their president, who had adopted the dress of operators, might have adopted their outlook as well.[47]

Before the vote was taken, Mitchell told the delegates to regard the issue as a vote of confidence in his presidency and asked them to remove him from office if they disregarded his advice and elected to strike. Despite this plea, the miners' representatives voted against acceptance of the reduction.[48] At this point, the strike order should have been issued. Yet Mitchell had not exhausted his efforts to sidetrack the strike movement. He successfully maneuvered the convention to agree to a referendum vote of the entire soft-coal union membership. In the guise of democracy, he was in fact trying to subvert the special miners' convention by going over the heads of the delegates to the rank and file. The referendum was a convenient tool to be used only when representative conventions took actions contrary to the will of the union head.

The referendum afforded Mitchell the opportunity to apply all the coercive and persuasive power of the presidency against what appeared to be the majority sentiment of the miners. Indeed, the ballot itself revealed Mitchell's control. Attached to the ballot was a statement by Mitchell urging miners to accept the reduction. Unwilling to allow the weight of his arguments alone to sway the miners, he dispersed his flock of organizers throughout the coalfields to spread the no-strike gospel according to Mitchell. In his instructions to organizers, he was quite specific as to the arguments he believed would be the most effective.[49] He also made use of the union journal to affect the outcome of the referendum. Several days before the vote, the journal printed an article praising the Joint Conference and implying a vote against the reduction was tantamount to treason.[50]

When at last the votes were tabulated, 102,026 miners voted to accept the reduction and 67,951 had voted to reject it. Mitchell had achieved his victory. He took great pride in having sidetracked majority sentiment for a strike, and he believed the miners would come to recognize the wisdom of their action. Above all, he was proud that he had preserved the Interstate Joint Conference.[51]

Operators, the mainstream press, NCF leaders, and industrial relations scholars were all equally ecstatic that a strike had been averted, and they were quick to thank

46. Ibid., 2, 10.

47. Duncan McDonald, unpublished "Autobiography," 37, located in the Duncan McDonald Collection, Illinois State Historical Society. See also Gowaskie, "John Mitchell," 240 n. 14.

48. UMWA, *Proceedings of the Special National Convention* (March 5–7, 1904), 28, 33.

49. JM to John H. Walker, March 12, 1904, JMP.

50. *UMWJ* (March 10, 1904).

51. *NCF Monthly Review* (July 1904), 12.

the man most responsible for undermining strike sentiment. All joined in a chorus of praise for Mitchell's conservatism, his farsightedness, and his devotion to public welfare.[52] Indeed, everyone seemed pleased by the action except the miners themselves. Those who had opposed acceptance of the reduction remained bitter long after the decision. And many long-time supporters condemned Mitchell personally for his crusade to avoid strike action regardless of the consequences. In Spring Valley and elsewhere, miners turned Mitchell's picture to the wall. Others refused to speak to him. One man with whom Mitchell had labored in the mines addressed his old comrade as "Mr. Mitchell." When the wounded Mitchell asked for an explanation of this formality, the miner explained he had come to doubt a labor leader who dined with the captains of industry.[53]

Socialists also mercilessly attacked Mitchell's role in forcing the wage reduction. Indeed, the wage cut marked the decisive break between Mitchell and the socialists. Until 1904 he had maintained a cool but cordial relationship with socialists within the union and nationwide. Although Mitchell and the socialists disagreed on almost every major issue, socialists were careful to avoid making direct attacks against Mitchell's leadership before 1904. The wage gains secured between 1898 and 1903, the successful strikes and organizing drives, and Mitchell's own immense popularity made confrontational union politics a suicidal policy for the radicals. But the wage reduction gave socialists their first major issues to exploit, and they were quick to turn their guns on the conservative presidency of John Mitchell.

As he surveyed the national scene in 1906, Mitchell had reason for concern. With anti-unionism on the rise in the form of the National Association of Manufacturers, and with the growth of radical unionism in the form of the Industrial Workers of the World, he could not have been sanguine about the future. His dream of a republic transformed by universal acceptance of the trade agreement, once shared by so many influential labor leaders and industrialists, seemed less and less plausible. Even Ralph Easley and other NCF leaders, once they realized they could not compete with the NAM by making vague appeals to labor peace and economic justice, took a decidedly conservative turn. While they did not espouse opposition to unions and did not completely abandon the promotion of trade agreements, they did begin emphasizing other aspects of labor relations that were of little benefit to organized labor.

The one bright spot in this bleak picture was the state of the UMWA. In January 1906 the union topped the 300,000 mark of dues-paying members for the first time in its history. In the past year nearly 200 locals had been established, the treasury was strong, and the union had successfully checked unauthorized strikes. The price

52. See, for example, the editorials in the *Baltimore American* (March 18, 1904), *Springfield Daily Morning Sun* (March 23, 1904), clippings in JMP; see also the assessment in Ramirez, *When Workers Fight*, 80.

53. Gluck, *John Mitchell*, 164–65.

of both soft and hard coal had risen substantially since 1904, and there was every reason to expect continued prosperity. And for the first time, all three major wage agreements—anthracite, the Central Competitive Field, and the southwestern field—expired on the same date. This gave Mitchell an incalculable edge. If negotiations stalled, he could threaten a general strike of all miners without having to break existing contracts. For all these reasons, Mitchell believed the union was in a powerful position to renegotiate its contracts.

But at the 1906 Joint Conference, CCF operators once again claimed poverty. While a few were willing to restore the wage cut of 1904, the majority voted against a wage advance of any kind. Miners again were forced to hold a special convention to consider the possibility of a national strike. Meeting just two days before the April 1 deadline, the special convention buzzed with electric anticipation. All the chatter centered on union solidarity and the need for a national suspension. From the first words of his opening address, however, Mitchell preached the wisdom of separate settlements with the minority of operators willing to grant the 1903 scale. He argued that industrial strife in coal and the irreparable damage it would cause to the interstate movement would play into the hands of radicals on both the Left and Right who hoped to reintroduce open class warfare in America. Open-shoppers and Wobblies both stood ready to applaud the failure of the joint conference in the CCF, the most celebrated trade agreement of the Progressive Era. Were it to fail, were the miners and operators unable to hash out their disagreements peacefully through reason rather than force, the agents of class warfare would stand triumphant.[54] Mitchell's attempt to squelch rank-and-file strike sentiment in 1906, therefore, beautifully illustrated how his ideological commitment to the trade agreement served to undermine labor solidarity.

Mitchell's appeal for separate settlements did not go unchallenged. Numerous delegates rose to point out the pitfalls of such an approach and contend that a national strike was the only viable option. When the debate ended, Mitchell ordered a vote be taken on separate settlements, and a majority voted in the affirmative.[55] Mitchell had again snuffed the sentiment for a national strike. Only those miners employed by operators refusing to pay the 1903 scale were ordered to refrain from work beginning April 1. As they had in 1904, soft-coal miners exhibited once again their faith in the conservative judgment of John Mitchell.

On April 1, 1906, all soft coal miners without contracts guaranteeing a $5\frac{1}{2}\%$ increase struck. But the quick settlements Mitchell anticipated were not realized. Many strikes dragged on for months.[56] And once the smoke cleared, the disaster of separate settlements became evident. Because each district had been allowed to bargain individually, the settlements were far from uniform. While most miners

54. UMWA, *Minutes of the Special Convention* (March 15–30, 1906), 72–73.
55. Ibid., 87–92, JM to Mrs. John Mitchell, March 31, 1906, JMP.
56. *UMWJ* (June 14, 1906); UMWA, Minutes of the National Executive Board (June 4 and August 1, 1906); UMWA, *Proceedings of the Eighteenth Annual Convention,* (1907), 37–38.

obtained the wage increase, a significant number either settled for less or were forced to agree to unfavorable contract provisions.[57]

The true catastrophe of separate settlements was not the failure to gain wage increases for all miners but the damage done to the interstate movement. The future of the trade agreement in soft coal was now in jeopardy. When the 1906 contracts were about to expire in 1908, many CCF operators were unwilling to meet with UMWA officials in joint conference. Operators insisted on a continuation of the policy of separate settlements. In addition, district officials within the union also resisted a return to the interstate movement. Having assumed the role of negotiator, they were unwilling to transfer power back to the national. It was not until 1916 that the CCF was completely reestablished.[58] Ironically, while Mitchell had prevented class warfare in the coalfields in an effort to keep alive the most celebrated trade agreement in the nation, his policy of separate settlements had damaged the CCF more than a national strike could have.

More than at any time during his presidency, Mitchell felt the wrath of a disgruntled rank and file. Soft-coal miners had been prepared to initiate a national strike to secure their goals. Mitchell needed only to give the word. When he snuffed their militancy and failed to lead them in righteous conflict, miners openly criticized his leadership. Dissent quickly gave rise to factionalism, as Vice President Tom L. Lewis tried to capitalize on the fiasco and mount yet another bid to unseat him. Mitchell knew full well that Lewis was traveling throughout the mining districts condemning the separate settlement policy.[59]

The long negotiating process and the settlement of local strikes left him drained. There was no time for recuperation, however, for Mitchell was embroiled in equally tumultuous anthracite negotiations. The anthracite coal commission's award expired in 1906. But hard-coal talks proved every bit as frustrating as soft-coal negotiations. After months of effort, Mitchell could not secure a wage increase or union contract from the anti-union hard-coal operators. While anthracite workers displayed the same readiness to strike as their soft-coal brethren, Mitchell refused to lead them in battle for a third time in six years. When operators agreed to an extension of the anthracite commission's award for another three years, Mitchell undermined strike sentiment in northeast Pennsylvania and signed the accord.[60]

Mitchell emerged from anthracite negotiations with his reputation intact and remained for many years something of a demigod in the hard-coal region. Unlike John Siney, Mitchell never fell from grace in northeast Pennsylvania. Thus it was a paradox that after May 1906 mine workers began leaving the union. Anthracite member-

---

57. Fox, *United We Stand,* 80.

58. Ibid., 127–28; David J. McDonald and Edward A. Lynch, *Coal and Unionism: A History of the American Coal Miners' Unions* (Silver Spring, Md.: Lynald Books, 1939), 78–79.

59. JM to John Walker, August 27, 1906, JMP.

60. On the 1906 anthracite negotiations, see Joseph M. Gowaskie, ''John Mitchell and the Anthracite Mine Workers: Leadership Conservatism and Rank-and-File Militancy,'' *Labor History* 27 (winter 1985–86): 54–83.

ship fell from approximately 80,000 to 30,000 between May and December.[61] Hard-coal mine workers loved Mitchell because he was the first outsider to champion their cause, because he had fought alongside them in 1900 and 1902, and because he had taken the time to know them personally and understand their distress. There was an emotional bond between Mitchell and the men and boys of the region. There existed no such bond with the union, however. Without union recognition and the checkoff, mine workers could view the UMWA pragmatically, joining when necessary and leaving when dues became an economic burden. The union had failed to increase their wages in 1906, and now there was no chance of an industrywide strike, at least until the expiration of the award in 1909. Thus mine workers saw little point in remaining active in the union. When Mitchell retired in 1908, anthracite membership had dwindled to 23,000.[62] Mitchell had himself inspired hard-coal men and had fought for his own version of industrial justice. But in 1906 when he could not even offer them a small wage increase, the ranks were quickly depleted.

Mitchell fully understood the difficult tasks awaiting him in 1907. He needed to re-create unity within the UMWA. His growing number of detractors needed to be silenced. Faith had to be restored in his leadership abilities. The interstate movement needed to be revived. Each one of these jobs would tax his energies. Each one required a sophisticated exercise of both subtlety and power. Already weary from the lost campaigns of 1906, he approached the new year without enthusiasm.

In 1907 all the strains inherent in Mitchell's public life began to cripple his private world. His commitment to labor peace at a time when class war was gaining momentum, his loyalty to the NCF when the influence of that body was in descent, his adherence to the trade agreement as the solution for industrial relations when national collective bargaining was on the wane—all made his public posture increasingly difficult. The perceived need to continuously squelch rank-and-file militancy and the endless attempts to establish friendly relations with hostile employers had proven over the years an emotionally as well as physically draining experience. The constant intrusion of the press, the day-to-day grind of speeches and conventions, the tension of behind-the-scenes negotiations, the ever-present fear that one wrong word uttered or one bad decision made might impact negatively on hundreds of thousands of men and their dependents charged to his care—all took their toll on his psyche.

He sought escape through alcohol. He was plagued by insomnia and nagging physical ailments. In a desperate effort to find inner peace, he converted to Catholicism. He tried to forget his problems by focusing on stock market speculation, juggling his investments in a frenzy of compulsive activity. By the middle of the year Mitchell had descended into a nightmarish world of alcoholism, illness, and loneliness. This assortment of woes would rattle the sanity of any person. Yet Mitchell

---

61. Membership figures are located in JMP.
62. UMWA, *Proceedings of the Nineteenth Annual Convention* (1908), 26–29.

was especially ill-equipped to face his personal challenges. A man without close family ties, without intimate friendships, a solitary man whose entire adult life had been the labor movement, Mitchell lacked the emotional resources to sustain him through his crises.

In the midst of his inner turmoil he made a fateful decision. If the root cause of his maladies was the pressure of the UMWA presidency, the first step on the road to recovery was resignation. Mitchell announced his intention to retire in October 1907 and finally stepped down on April 1, 1908. His health slowly returned and his shattered personal life was soon on the mend. Still a relatively young man with expensive tastes and a large family to support, he could not simply retire. After weighing several job offers, he accepted a full-time position with the National Civic Federation.

Mitchell said farewell to his rank and file at the 1908 UMWA convention, and delegates responded with a magnificent display of affection for their outgoing president. Delegates from every district offered praise and gratitude for their leader. The committee on resolutions summed up the prevailing sentiment: "Resolved, that we appreciate, more than man can find words to express, the magnitude of his work and the brilliancy of his achievements in behalf of the downtrodden and oppressed wage workers in every sphere of toil." The resolution was carried unanimously.[63]

Other than celebrate Mitchell, the great task of the convention was to announce the new president. Balloting had taken place in November and December. The two principal candidates were Vice President Tom L. Lewis, the leading critic of Mitchell, and Secretary-Treasurer William B. Wilson, the top pro-administration man. Although too ill to take an active role in the campaign, from the very outset Mitchell pledged to support Wilson and promised to "line up my friends everywhere I can in your interest."[64] When the votes were tallied at the 1908 convention, Lewis had captured the presidency by a slim 2,000 vote majority out of 127,000 votes cast.[65] The election of Lewis was significant because it demonstrated that Mitchell had failed to build an effective political machine capable of surviving him. Over the years he had successfully dealt with internal opponents, controlled the union journal, and built up a cadre of loyal organizers. Had he not been so ill he might well have been able to engineer a Wilson victory. Yet once he announced his retirement, his loyal followers began leaving the flock. They threw their support behind the next most powerful man in the union, Tom L. Lewis, in the hope that Lewis might favor them the way Mitchell had.

In the spring and early summer of 1908, after he resigned his union post and before he took up his duties at NCF headquarters, Mitchell had time to battle his alcoholism and reacquaint himself with his family. He also found time to reflect upon the suc-

63. Ibid., 291–92.
64. JM to William B. Wilson, October 25, 1907, JMP.
65. UMWA, *Proceedings* (1908), 366.

cesses and failures of his UMWA presidency. How effectively had he dealt with the problems plaguing miners? How skillfully had he managed the union? What problems did he bequeath to his successors? Were there opportunities and avenues for the advancement of labor he failed to explore? These and other questions ran through his mind as he looked back over his ten-year reign. And on the whole, Mitchell was quite pleased with his accomplishments. "The organization, when I left it, was in better condition than ever before in its history," he wrote a friend.[66]

Mitchell's legacy is indeed an impressive one. He took command of a small union of 30,000 members that was in many ways weak. In 1898 the union lacked financial resources, a stable and effective bureaucratic structure, and a strong central authority. By 1908 the UMWA was the largest trade union in America. Its 300,000 members were welded together under a highly centralized and still largely democratic administrative authority. Considering the political, economic, and social conditions of the Progressive Era that made the very existence of trade unions precarious, the expansion and consolidation of the UMWA under Mitchell's leadership was truly remarkable. In the face of a hostile court system ready to issue injunctions on the whims of employers, pro-business politicians at all levels who challenged the legal right of unions to exist, and a public that often equated unionism with extremism and violence, Mitchell had erected a powerful and unified working-class organization.

In terms of concrete and immediate gains for miners, no one can deny Mitchell's accomplishments. In 1898 the coal industry was infamous for its low pay, long hours, and dangerous conditions. Under Mitchell's tenure, dramatic improvements were made in all three areas. Wages doubled for the soft-coal miners and rose significantly for hard-coal miners. Working hours had dropped from ten to eight in soft coal and ten to nine in hard coal. Mitchell was equally proud of his record on safety. At his retirement, the fatality rate in fully organized districts was 2.47 per thousand workers compared with 5.07 in partially organized districts and 9.49 where the UMWA was not present.[67] These were the figures Mitchell considered most important. He had helped improve the daily lives of miners. He had helped them achieve greater material comfort, more leisure, and increased peace of mind. For him the labor movement could serve no higher purpose.

Mitchell beamed with pride when he reflected on his ability to create a strong central authority and at the same time maintain a semblance of democracy within the union. His authority and popularity would have made it easy for him to squelch union democracy altogether and assume dictatorial control. Yet unlike his successors Tom L. Lewis and John L. Lewis, he was in some ways careful to uphold free speech and rank-and-file input. Socialists and other radicals were allowed to criticize his policies openly during conventions. Examples of this came at the 1905 convention when socialists mounted a lengthy attack on his handling of a failed Colorado strike

66. JM to F. E. Waite, July 2, 1908, JMP.
67. Fox, *United We Stand*, 205–6.

and at the 1908 convention when he gave "Big Bill" Haywood free rein to plea for syndicalism. Another action demonstrating concern for democracy was his expansion of the national executive board to include one delegate from each district to be chosen by that district.

In other ways, however, Mitchell foreshadowed the dictatorial methods of John L. Lewis. When union democracy stood in the way of a desired policy, Mitchell often cast it aside. His handling of internal enemies in his early years, notably Tom L. Lewis and Patrick Dolan, involved questionable covert schemes and, in the case of Dolan, a messy cover-up. He also could be quite devious when expecting opposition at national conventions. In 1902, for instance, he illegally delayed calling the special convention to consider a sympathy strike of soft-coal miners. And when he believed miners would press for a national strike at the 1906 convention, he instructed his allies in Illinois to purchase several thousand fake membership cards to increase their voting strength.[68] There were other, more subtle techniques of one-man control. He routinely sent organizers to already organized fields to campaign for his policies during referendums and his allies in district elections; he controlled the union journal, often denying access to his opponents, and used its pages to propagandize his own policies; and he jealously guarded his authority to make appointments to convention committees, thus guaranteeing that his policies would receive a favorable hearing. Mitchell was by no means dictatorial, but neither was he a staunch defender of democratic principles.

At the same time Mitchell shifted authority from the local and district levels to the national office, he often used district autonomy as an excuse for failure to act on important issues, especially the issue of racism. At national conventions he often spoke on the need for camaraderie between the races. At the 1904 convention, for instance, he secured a unanimous vote on the resolution that all AFL affiliates end discrimination. But his speeches had little impact on white coal miners in the South who insisted on segregated locals. In his tours of Southern states, he never challenged this practice for fear of sowing dissent among white miners. He never attempted to use his authority to outlaw segregation, and when he stepped down, the practice continued.[69]

Mitchell's legacy is marred by an even more notable failure. As the president of the largest industrial union in America, many expected him to play a leading role in shifting the AFL away from its narrow craft union base. At Mitchell's insistence, the AFL had in 1901 proved itself capable of making exceptions to craft jurisdictions. The so-called Scranton Declaration of that year awarded the UMWA an industrial charter. But Mitchell proved unwilling to fight for the principle of industrial unionism outside the coal industry. The primary reason for this failure was the absence of an industrial union movement of any significance before 1912 outside

68. See JM to W. D. Ryan, September 29, 1908, JMP.

69. On segregated locals, see Ronald L. Lewis, *Black Coal Miners in America: Race, Class, and Community Conflict, 1780–1980* (Lexington: University of Kentucky Press, 1987), 46.

the ranks of socialists. Mitchell was not about to ally himself with the left-wing element on this or any other issue.

Mitchell's ultimate contribution to the labor movement, however, went beyond concrete gains for miners or missed opportunities to crusade for industrial justice outside the coalfields. His lasting legacy was to provide a new model for union leadership. At a time when labor leaders were denounced as demagogues, radicals, and men of violence, he was able to cultivate a new image, one that has held sway in mainstream labor circles ever since. Through his words and actions he carefully crafted an image of himself as a responsible, respectable, trustworthy, cautious, conservative, and peaceful trade union leader. He became all things to all people. To the miners he was a leader who could be trusted to care for their interests, a fighter when necessary and a skillful negotiator capable of securing the most favorable contract; to employers he was a man who squelched unauthorized strikes, upheld the sanctity of contracts, and opposed radicalism; and to the general public he was the prince of moderation, a progressive who called for a measure of justice and not revolution, a man who stood ready to arbitrate any dispute. He had risen to fame as a result of class warfare in anthracite, but his image was that of a man of peace.

This pacifist image was often untenable and the chief victims were union solidarity and militancy. In 1906 and again in 1908, his commitment to labor peace led him to undermine widespread strike sentiment and adopt the disastrous policy of separate settlements, which pitted miner against miner. The fighting spirit and solidarity of the miners, the twin bases of union strength, were sacrificed time and again so that Mitchell could present himself and the union to employers and the public as acceptable and responsible. In hard coal this stance had led to mass desertion from the union's rolls, and in soft coal it placed the future of the interstate movement in doubt. Mitchell had accomplished a great deal for the miners, but upon his retirement in 1908 his successors were faced with enormous tasks.

Above all, Mitchell's career symbolized the promises and pitfalls for organized labor in the Progressive Era. With the return of prosperity at the turn of the century, progressive businessmen and politicians were prepared to accept conservative labor leaders as junior partners in the production process. As long as these labor leaders assisted capitalists by crushing unauthorized strikes, preventing sympathy strikes, and upholding collective bargaining agreements, they could expect a measure of legitimacy and acceptance unthinkable in earlier years. As long as these leaders helped rationalize industry by guaranteeing continued production and steady profits, capitalists would refrain from their perennial war against the organization of their workers. More clearly than any other labor leader, Mitchell recognized the opportunities for trade union advance in the Progressive Era, as well as the obligations such opportunities demanded. In a remarkably short time, he constructed the type of union Progressives desired, and he was rewarded with praise, influence, and acceptance. Quite naturally, he convinced himself that the strategy of peaceful coexistence heralded a new day in labor relations and would eventually establish industrial justice for all workers.

Unfortunately, the Progressive vision of cooperation between capital and organized labor died quickly. Employers soon found more expedient methods to rationalize industry, methods such as welfarism and scientific management, methods that could be implemented without the assistance of labor. The new antiunion offensive necessitated new and more aggressive strategies and tactics on the part of unions and their leaders. But Mitchell balked. He clung to the increasingly irrelevant dream of labor peace and capital-labor partnership as embodied in the declining National Civic Federation. Insisting that cooperation was still viable, he refused to unleash the force he had worked so hard to crush: worker militancy. By the time of his retirement from the UMWA, he had become an increasingly estranged and isolated voice for capital-labor harmony based on the trade agreement.

At the age of thirty-eight, Mitchell had abdicated his central role in the labor movement. And while he believed his new position in the National Civic Federation would allow him to exercise immense informal power on the industrial relations scene, he was soon disappointed with his own limited authority and the weakness of the NCF. His dream of championing a movement of workers, employers, and the public that would bring about industrial peace and economic justice died quickly. He stood by the NCF, however, and he continued to believe it was the only viable alternative to militant anti-unionism among employers and the rising tide of socialism among workers.

In 1911 Mitchell was aghast to find the NCF itself had become the target of radical unionists. Socialists in the UMWA joined hands with Tom L. Lewis to pass a resolution denouncing the NCF and forbidding any union member to associate with the organization. Mitchell was thus faced with the unpleasant choice of severing his ties with the NCF or facing expulsion from the UMWA. After days of soul-searching, Mitchell resigned from his job. He continued to remain active in the NCF, however, and in 1911 he assisted Gompers in a dramatic battle against AFL socialists over the issue of the NCF.

After 1911 Mitchell sank into relative obscurity. He continued to intervene in the affairs of the UMWA, working behind the scenes to lead an insurgent movement that overthrew Tom L. Lewis; he played a role in a religious crusade within the AFL called the Men and Religion movement; and he found employment first on the New York Workmen's Compensation Commission and later as chair of the Industrial Commission of New York. This work, too, he found unsatisfying, and in his later years personal problems once again mounted. He began to drink heavily and in 1919 he died of pneumonia at age forty-nine, a sick and largely forgotten man.

CHAPTER FIVE

"SOMETHING OF A MAN"
John L. Lewis, the UMWA, and the CIO, 1919–1943

ALAN   J.   SINGER

In November 1940, when John L. Lewis "retired" as president of the Congress of Industrial Organizations (CIO), he told delegates to the national convention in Atlantic City: "Your cheers do not enthuse me over much. And your curses discourage me not at all. You know when you first hired me I was something of a man, and when I leave you in a day or two, I will still in my own mind be something of a man." More than fifty years later, John L. Lewis's legacy to the American labor movement still remains as complex and as ambiguous as his proud claim to be "something of a man."[1]

Many factors contribute to the difficulties historians have in assessing the life and work of John L. Lewis. During the 1930s he was simultaneously United Mine Workers of America (UMWA) president, spokesman for industrial organization and America's emergent working class as head of the CIO, a political activist in the drive to institutionalize the New Deal, a Washington lobbyist on intimate terms with the denizens of its halls of power, a prosperous entrepreneur and banker, a co-

---

1. *United Mine Workers of America Journal* (December 1, 1940): 15.

worker of communists and a colleague of corporate executives. He was a man with few friends, but numerous subordinates, admirers, and enemies who left behind divergent accounts and evaluations of their experiences with Lewis. While extravagant of gesture and extroverted in his public life, his family and business affairs were intensely private matters. He carefully hid them from public scrutiny and left behind few written clues about his feelings or his sometimes inappropriate business dealings. Lewis was a man of apparent contradiction. He viewed ideas and words as political tools, chosen for particular circumstances, making it difficult to find consistency in action and belief during the two dozen years covered in this essay. Add to this Lewis's tendency to reinvent his past in an ongoing effort to create a mythic JOHN L. LEWIS, a tendency that was reinforced by both friendly and hostile commentators eager to use Lewis's life to illustrate their own political positions, and we are left with an exceedingly difficult man to understand or analyze. Finally, changes in the modern labor movement and its role in American society during the last half-century—changes that have been reflected in the movement to expand democracy in the United Mine Workers of America—have led to repeated reevaluations of John L. Lewis and the world he helped to create.[2]

The John L. Lewis saga begins in February 1880 in the coalfields of south-central Iowa about eighty miles from Des Moines. Though Lewis's father and grandfather were bituminous coal miners and he spent part of his teen years and early adulthood working in the mines, John L. Lewis sought other options for his life. He traveled extensively in the west from 1900 to 1905, and after returning to his hometown of Lucas, Iowa, he married, dabbled in municipal politics, and ran a grain and feed business. After a 1907 defeat in the town's mayoralty contest and the collapse of his business, Lewis and his extended family (including his adult brothers and his parents) relocated in Panama, Illinois, a company town in the central Illinois coalfields.[3]

In Panama, Illinois, Lewis, his father, and his brothers became involved in union activities and by 1910, the Lewis family had established a local union political machine. John L. Lewis was elected president of UMWA local 1475, one of the ten largest UMWA locals in Illinois. His brother Thomas Lewis was elected the local police magistrate, succeeded John as the president of the union local, and was later appointed a state mining inspector. His brother A. D. (Dennie) Lewis was elected financial secretary of the Panama local in 1916 and followed the success of his brothers to become commissioner of the Illinois State Mining Department. How-

2. There is little new "hard evidence" on the life of John L. Lewis that can be added to the masterly 600-page biography of John L. Lewis by Melvyn Dubofsky and Warren Van Tine: *John L. Lewis, A Biography* (New York: Quadrangle, 1977). They exhaustively pored over the existing UMWA, CIO, and personal sources and tore away at the veil of myth that has frequently been used either to demonize Lewis or to elevate him to heroic status. All succeeding work draws largely on theirs; see the Guide to Further Reading on John L. Lewis at the end of this chapter for footnote references not mentioned in the text.

3. Dubofsky and Van Tine, *Lewis*, 3–19; Singer, "Which Side," 97 n. 26; Alinsky, *John L. Lewis*, 18–19.

ever, the family's upward path was not without problems. At one point, Tom, Dennie, and their father were investigated for embezzling money from the local union and were forced to repay missing funds.

John L. was the most astute and successful of the Lewis brothers. He used his local union position to enter UMWA and American Federation of Labor (AFL) state and national politics. In 1909, he supported the statewide and national slates of John Walker and the district-autonomy forces in the UMWA election and he was rewarded with an appointment as an Illinois state lobbyist for mine safety. In 1910, Lewis helped the Walker group defeat T. L. Lewis (no relation) as union president. John L. Lewis also drew national attention for a spirited defense of Samuel Gompers against charges of racial discrimination. Once again, he was rewarded with rapid advancement: UMWA Secretary-Treasurer William Green, President John White, and John Walker all endorsed Lewis for appointment as a special AFL lobbyist.

In this new position, Lewis was able to expand his contacts among UMWA and AFL officials without becoming closely tied to any side in the UMWA's constant factional battles. He worked as an AFL representative in the 1912 Wilson presidential election campaign and in local UMWA organizing drives in Pennsylvania, Ohio, and West Virginia. During this period, Lewis made valuable contacts with business leaders and government officials. He developed a special relationship with nonunion financier and publisher Al Hamilton and Hamilton's agent, K. C. Adams. According to UMWA opponents in the 1920s, Hamilton helped enhance Lewis's reputation as an organizer of the unorganized. He arranged for Lewis to negotiate contracts with receptive mine operators and channeled payments to Lewis. In return, Lewis agreed not to organize selected mines and to provide contractual concessions to companies that Hamilton represented.[4]

When John White and John Walker battled for the UMWA presidency in 1915 and 1916, John L. Lewis sided with White and helped secure his reelection through a series of shady political maneuvers. These may have included forging a series of telegrams that Walker had supposedly sent to coal operators seeking their financial support for his campaign. Lewis's decision to support White assisted his rapid ascendancy up the UMWA hierarchy. In January 1917, he was appointed union statistician. Later he became business manager of the UMWA *Journal* (*UMWJ*) and was part of the labor delegation to the wartime coal-production committee. In 1917, when John White left the union to take a position in the Federal Fuel Administrator's office, Lewis was appointed UMWA vice president by the union's International Executive Board (IEB). When the new union president, Frank Hayes, was later incapacitated by bouts with alcoholism, Lewis became acting UMWA president. In 1920, John L. Lewis defeated Robert Harlan and was elected UMWA president in his own right.[5]

---

4. Dubofsky and Van Tine, *Lewis*, 20–42; John Brophy, *A Miner's Life*, ed. John O. P. Hall (Madison: University of Wisconsin Press, 1964), 134–37.

5. Dubofsky and Van Tine, *Lewis*, 20–42, esp. 31. There is a notarized affidavit of the charges

John L. Lewis's career advances from 1910 to 1920 were made possible by his own political astuteness, by the more or less constant political infighting between shifting alliances in the United Mine Workers union and by an emerging consensus among both International union officials and their District-autonomy opponents on the role of union officials. When John Mitchell was sworn in as acting union president in 1898, the UMWA office was seen as a temporary position. In February 1899, Mitchell promised miners at the District 12 convention: "When I have finished my term of office I shall return to Illinois and take my pick among you." However, this concept of union leadership quickly yielded to the idea that UMWA officers were professional and permanent labor leaders, different from ordinary miners, who because of their special ability had the right to special rewards. John Mitchell, who resigned from the UMWA in 1908 to work full-time for the National Civic Federation, and T. L. Lewis, his immediate successor as UMWA president, also initiated the pattern of either combining union office with private business initiatives or using union office as a stepping-stone to corporate executive positions. These practices greatly expanded when the First World War opened up new contacts between "professional" labor leaders, coal operators, and government regulators.[6]

Paralleling this change in the notion of union leadership was a virtual deification of the contract. During his tenure as UMWA president, John Mitchell repeatedly explained to rank-and-file miners that "if we expect the operators to carry out those provisions that are advantageous to us, we in turn, must carry out just as explicitly those provisions which are unfavorable to us." In 1914, UMWA President White advised the union that the "success of our movement depends largely, if not wholly, upon a rigid enforcement of all contracts that have been legally entered into. One of the worst evils with which our organization has to contend, and one that brings sharp criticism, is the local and unauthorized strike."[7]

The John L. Lewis who emerged as acting UMWA president in 1919 was a skilled political operative with a network of labor, corporate, and government ties, who had ascended to the top of the UMWA without a substantial political base of support within the union. He had been able to succeed through advantageous, though temporary alliances, and by not allowing loyalty or principles to interfere with political judgments. Lewis's considerable political skills were quickly put to the test as he attempted to hold onto the leadership of the UMWA in the turbulent years following

---

dated January 7, 1918, in the Elections File, UMWA Papers. Walker made similar charges at the 1921 UMWA convention, see *Proceedings*, 1921 UMWA Convention, 701; Coleman, *Men and Coal*, 91–92.

6. Singer, "Which Side," 45–49; Everling, "Tactics," 111; Warren Van Tine, *The Making of a Labor Bureaucrat, Union Leadership in the United States, 1870–1920*. (Amherst: University of Massachusetts Press, 1973), 44, 53; James O. Morris, "The Acquisitive Spirit of John Mitchell, UMWA President (1899–1908)." *Labor History* 20, no. 1 (winter 1979): 5–43; *UMWJ* (March 16, 1900): 7; *UMWJ* (June 4, 1908): 2; *UMWJ* (June 26, 1917). For a case study in transition from union official to corporate executive, see the story of Charles O'Neill, *National Cyclopedia of American Biography*, 37: 479.

7. Singer, "Which Side," 51–56; Van Tine, *Making of a Labor Bureaucrat*, 81; Louis Bloch, *Labor Agreements in Coal Mines*, (New York: Russell Sage, 1931), 307–8; Coleman, *Men and Coal*, 78–79; Everling, "Tactics," 79–80, 92.

the First World War. In the short term, Lewis had to face rank-and-file dissatisfaction caused by wartime inflation and a declining standard of living, opposition on the International Executive Board and in some of the major district offices from presidential claimants who saw Lewis as an outsider and usurper.

In spring 1919, John L. Lewis controlled the UMWA International offices, but he remained vulnerable. World War I had ended and rank-and-file miners were demanding a major wage increase. In March 1919, the International Executive Board recommended that the UMWA convention vote for a strike on November 1, 1919, and endorsed a militant platform calling for a 60% wage increase to alleviate the effects of wartime inflation on the miners; the nationalization of the coal mines as a long-term solution to mismanagement, unemployment and overproduction in the coal-fields; an organizing drive to unionize the remaining nonunion coalfields; and the formation of a new labor party to spearhead the struggle for the union's demands and the broader programmatic needs of America's working class.

Lewis did not believe that a 60% wage increase was likely and feared that a strike would threaten the wartime government, industry, and labor coalition that had helped the union expand in previously inaccessible fields and had propelled his own rise to power in the union. The *UMWJ*, which Lewis controlled, set a considerably more moderate tone than the IEB. On May 15, it told UMWA members that "if the miners cannot accept the promises of a department of the government and rely upon it to live up to those promises, then there is not much good in accepting the promise of anyone on the subject."[8]

But the radical IEB program more clearly addressed the aspirations of rank-and-file coal miners than Lewis's conservative/cooperative approach. During the spring and summer of 1919, wildcat strikes broke out in a number of coalfields. In Kansas, District 14 President Alexander Howat led a walkout against the continuing wartime wage freeze. In July 1919, a number of Illinois (District 12) locals struck without approval of either district or national officials. Lewis and District 12 President Frank Farrington tried to force the men back to work, accusing the strikers of "dual unionism" and blaming the insurgents for creating confusion among miners by violating the union's wartime "no-strike" pledge, which Lewis argued was still in force.[9]

The IEB-endorsed program and the growing rank-and-file restiveness placed John L. Lewis in an apparent "no-win" situation. Rank-and-file miners were ready to strike, but if the strike were successful, his opponents on the IEB could take credit for the initiative. If the strike failed, Lewis, as acting president, would be held responsible for the defeat. Lewis's position was made even less tenable when operators refused to negotiate, arguing that since the war had not formally ended, the

8. Singer, "Which Side," 81; *UMWJ* (May 15, 1919).

9. UMWA Circular (August 18, 1919), "To the Officers and members of District 12 from Acting President John L. Lewis," Frank Farrington File, UMWA-MA; *Proceedings*, 27th Consecutive, 4th Biennial, UMWA Convention, Cleveland, Ohio, 1919, 462–559, esp. 462, 484, 524, 549, and 559; Sylvia Kopald (Selekman), *Rebellion in Labor Unions* (New York: Boni and Liveright, 1924), 33, 69–70, 118, 122; Everling, "Tactics," 133; Singer, "Which Side," 105–8.

miners were bound by the "no-strike" pledge and their previous contract until April 1920. According to the *UMWJ*, the "operators were hoping for government intervention." Caught in this bind, Lewis remained silent at the UMWA's September convention while the IEB program was adopted.[10]

On October 25, President Woodrow Wilson declared that a coal strike would violate the Lever Act and the union's "no-strike" pledge; Attorney General Palmer moved to secure a restraining order against the UMWA and its leadership. However, rank-and-file miners were not deterred and they walked out on November 1. On November 8, a federal court injunction ordered the miners to return to work by November 11. Even though the union's membership rejected the operator and government claim that a binding contract remained in effect and the AFL promised strike support, John L. Lewis announced that he would not lead a strike against the government and canceled the strike order. Lewis, however, was not in control of rank-and-file union members and the miners refused to return to work. In December, President Wilson threatened to deploy 100,000 troops in an all-out push to reopen mines and a federal court threatened union officials with arrest and individual fines. Finally, the men returned to work after the IEB voted to accept a 14% wage increase with the provision that a federal investigatory commission would explore the justice of the miners' demands.[11]

At the UMWA's reconvened convention in January 1920, John L. Lewis justified his decision to honor the injunction and call off the strike. According to Lewis, "the United Mine Workers' organization . . . could not, if it so desired, defeat the government of the United States in a contest. And neither do I as a citizen, as a man, as a member of our union, desire to defeat the government of the United States." Lewis emphasized that his decision was not only patriotic; it was tactically correct. "We stand here today, not with a wrecked organization, but with a proud institution embracing hundreds of thousands of men, and still embodying their hopes and ideals, with the machinery of the organization in such a condition that it can go on and on in making such progress as might be possible." Despite spirited debate at the convention, the contract was overwhelmingly approved. When the federal investigatory commission later agreed to raise the wage increase from 14% to 27%, Lewis emerged as a UMWA hero and he was elected UMWA president over weakened opposition in the December 1920 union election.[12]

John L. Lewis had gambled and won during the 1919 strike, and somewhere during the next six months he decided to gamble again. He endorsed the same militant IEB program he had previously ignored and used it to launch an unsuccessful challenge to Samuel Gompers for the AFL presidency. Significantly, by the September 1921 UMWA convention, Lewis's support for the IEB program had dis-

10. *Proceedings* (1919), 841–49; Dubofsky and Van Tine, *Lewis*, 52–53; Singer, "Which Side," 83, 114; *UMWJ* (November 1, 1919): 3.

11. Singer, "Which Side," 84–88; Dubofsky and Van Tine, *Lewis*, 48–60.

12. *UMWJ* (January 1, 1920): 4–5; Dubofsky and Van Tine, *Lewis*, 59, 61–63; Singer, "Which Side," 88.

solved and he told the convention that "eminent authorities" had declared nationalization impractical in the American federal system of government.[13]

The results of the 1919 strike confirmed John L. Lewis's wartime experience in
the AFL and UMWA and his commitment to cooperation between labor and management under the auspices of the federal government. Lewis believed that with
continued government support, the UMWA and the Central Competitive Field operators could solve the problem of overproduction in the bituminous coal industry
through rational planning, increased mechanization, fair shipping rates, and a stable
unionized workforce. At U.S. Coal Commission hearings during this period, UMWA
representatives argued that the union would cooperate in the rationalization and
mechanization of the industry because "the countries, the industries, and even the
individual establishments where trade unionism is strongest are those in which machinery is applied earliest and to the largest extent."[14]

However, cooperation with a Republican government and capitalist entrepreneurs
required the explicit rejection of the demand to nationalize the mines or create a
labor political party. Even a campaign to organize the unorganized had to be rejected
because the logic of rationalization was that nonunion miners and operators had to
be driven out of the industry. In order for the UMWA to play the role that he conceived of for it in the industry, John L. Lewis, the union president, had to discipline
the rank and file. He spent the next decade battling against insurgents whose ranks
were continually fed by increasingly class-conscious miners who were experiencing
the collapse of the industry and the destruction of their way of life. Lewis's primary
weapons in this campaign were branding all dissidents as dual unionists and Communists and expelling them from the UMWA.

From 1919 through 1929, John L. Lewis ruthlessly suppressed rank-and-file dissent and dismembered district autonomy, using all the weapons available to him as
union president to ensure his unchallenged control over the UMWA. His attack on
Kansas (District 14) and Alexander Howat, its district president, became a model
for future campaigns to eliminate opposition and centralize authority. To break
Howat and his Kansas supporters, Lewis declared striking District 14 miners in
violation of a legal contract and created a "new" district office that ordered the
miners back to work. Miners who supported Howat were blacklisted by local operators and denied transfer cards by the union that would have allowed them to work
in other districts. Union miners from neighboring fields were recruited to work in
Kansas mines to undermine continued rank-and-file resistance; and the Lewis loyalists, in charge of the "new" district, cooperated with federal prohibition officers

13. *Proceedings*, 28th Consecutive, 5th Biennial, UMWA Convention, 1921, "Report of the President," 21; *Proceedings*, 1921, 91–92; Brophy, *Miner's*, claims that Lewis wanted to pigeonhole nationalization, 161–62; Dubofsky and Van Tine, *Lewis*, 73–75. The battle over nationalization is also
discussed in Alan Singer, "John Brophy's 'Miners' Program': Workers' Education in UMWA District 2
during the 1920s," *Labor Studies Journal* 13, no. 4 (winter 1988): 50–64.
14. UMWA, *Lewis*, 20.

who raided and harassed pro-Howat mining camps. Meanwhile, Howat and his allies were barred from holding future union office.[15]

Lewis also developed a network of organizers on the International payroll who were assigned to keep track of local and district opposition and to collect potentially damaging information on his opponents. When the network of organizers was insufficient, private security police were hired to keep track of dissidents. The "UMWA Master Alphabetical Files" are punctuated by reports from international organizers and official reports of the Committee on Organization detailing the activities of Lewis opponents and potential opponents. Much of the information in the "Anti-Communism" file was printed in pamphlet form to justify the attack on Lewis's opposition as part of a campaign to prevent Communist infiltration of the UMWA and the American labor movement. The pamphlet, titled "Attempt by Communists to Seize the American Labor Movement," blamed Communists for pushing the issue of nationalization of the mines and for pressing for a strike in 1922 in an effort to bankrupt the union.[16]

In 1922–23 and 1926–27, much of Lewis's effort to control rank-and-file and district opposition was directed against Central Pennsylvania and District 2 President John Brophy. When the UMWA struck at the expiration of its contract in March 1922, District 2 officials launched an independent drive to organize miners in neighboring Somerset County. Despite an enthusiastic response from local miners, the effort faltered when John L. Lewis signed a national contract with the coal operators in August 1922, that did not include the Somerset mines. Some District 2 locals threatened to remain on strike until Somerset was included in the agreement, but finally returned to work under pressure from the UMWA International office.[17]

As an outgrowth of the strike, a contingent of District 2 and Somerset County miners participated in a June 1923 Pittsburgh conference of the Progressive International Committee of the UMWA. The conference was called by left-wing miners from District 5 and 12 and trade union militants, including William Z. Foster and a group of American communists, to organize a committee of miners to work within

15. Domenico Gagliardo, *The Kansas Industrial Court* (Lawrence: University of Kansas Press, 1941), 135–45; Mary Heaton Vorse, "Ma and Mr. Davis," *Survey* (December 15, 1922); UMWA Circular (December 19, 1921), "To the Officers and Members of District 12, UMWA from John L. Lewis," Farrington File, UMWA-MA; Singer, "Which Side," 110–18; *Proceedings* (1921), 2:606–7, 614–28; Wickersham, "Oppositions," 71–75; Dubofsky and Van Tine, *Lewis*, 118.

16. *Congressional Record*, 68th Congress, 1st session, Document 14 (Washington, D.C. 1924); Singer, "Which Side," 189. The UMWA Anti-Communism file contained transcripts of meetings and reports on the movements of the opposition. Lewis used the same tactics against the UMWA opposition as operators used against the union.

17. Singer, "Which Side," 168, 177; *Proceedings* (1919), "Report of the Committee on Organization" (July 29, 1920), 66; Decision of the International by the International Executive Board (July 30, 1920), District 2 file, UMWA-MA; Brophy Papers; "Report of the Committee on Organization" (October 20, 1922), UMWA Papers; "Decision of the International Executive Board" (October 27, 1922), District 2 File, MWA-MA; Heber Blankenhorn, *The Strike For Union* (New York: H. W. Wilson, 1924), 3–83, 115–71; Singer, "Brophy," 50–64.

the UMWA to challenge Lewis and revive the union's 1919 program calling for nationalization of the coal mines, organization of the unorganized, and the formation of a labor party. Lewis's agents were present at the conference and forwarded him reports on its proceedings. His response was to declare the Progressive International Committee a "dual" organization and he instructed all districts and locals to expel any union member who had participated. Lewis also ruled that association with known Communists was proof of dual intentions and was sufficient grounds to bar people from membership in the UMWA.[18]

The Progressive Committee and its allies attempted to battle Lewis at the January 1924 UMWA convention. But even with support from district leaders hostile to Lewis, their demand that the union's International organizers be elected instead of appointed was defeated. An analysis of the vote tally shows both the depth of dissatisfaction with Lewis's conduct of union affairs and the difficulty any opposition group would have in unseating him as union president. Lewis's margin of victory depended on solid support from the anthracite field and "blue-sky" Kentucky, Tennessee, Alabama, and West Virginia locals. "Blue-sky" was the miners' term for a local with no working members, because only out-of-work miners ever saw the blue sky. Lewis's control over the "votes" from these nonfunctioning locals made it nearly impossible to defeat his supporters in any convention ballot or union election.[19]

In 1926, with the collapse of the 1924 Central Competitive Field contract and with union miners besieged by an open-shop campaign, John Brophy and his allies in District 2, with support from the remnants of the rank-and-file opposition movements in Illinois and western Pennsylvania, and with help from communist and noncommunist groups in the labor movement, organized a "Save the Union" slate to challenge Lewis for control of the union. The "Save the Union" slate campaigned on the 1919 IEB-endorsed program that the Progressives had attempted to revive in 1923. Lewis red-baited the ticket, and then declared himself the winner of an election marred by vote fraud that he may actually have lost.

In an appeal of the official results to the IEB, Brophy and the "Save the Union" slate charged: "Tens of thousands of votes have been added, subtracted or twisted about as best suited the desires or needs of the perpetrators. In fact the large amount of vote 'fixing' that has been done leads me to believe that the men now occupying the offices of International president, Vice-President and Secretary-Treasurer were not really elected and that the 'Save the Union' candidates were duly elected the

18. Circular, Action of the International Executive Board of the United Mine Workers of America on Dual Organizations (June 20, 1923), Anti-Communism File, UMWA papers; Singer, "Which Side," 169–74, 186–88; Action of the International Executive Board on Dual Organizations (June 20, 1923), Anti-Communist File, UMWA Papers; Alan Singer, "Communists and Coal Miners: Organizing Mine Workers During the 1920s," *Science and Society* (summer 1991): 132–57, esp. 139–43.

19. Singer, "Which Side," 191–92; *Proceedings*, 29th Consecutive, 6th Biennial, UMWA Convention (1924), 1:594, 617–22.

international officers of our union."[20] Brophy, who would later become the director of organization for the Committee for Industrial Organization, was eventually driven out of the union, his membership was suspended, and he was not readmitted until 1933.

While John L. Lewis battled rank-and-file dissidents and district autonomy advocates for control over the UMWA, he continued to advocate cooperation among the union, the industry, and the federal government to solve the problems created by overcapacity, mechanization, the development of new fuels and the shifting of coal production to nonunion regions. Lewis, who at this juncture conceived of himself as an industrial leader and a Republican, urged Secretary of Commerce Herbert Hoover to use his position in the Republican Party and the federal government to promote long-term labor-management peace in the industry. In 1924, with the assistance of Hoover, Lewis and the union negotiated the Jacksonville Accord, a three-year contract extension for the Central Competitive Field that maintained the industry's base wage at $7.50 per day. On March 1, 1924, the *UMWJ* declared that February 19, 1924, the day that the Jacksonville Accord was signed, "will go down in history as one of the red letter days." In a telegram to Lewis, Herbert Hoover issued unrestrained congratulations, praising "one of the most statesmenlike settlements in many years." In the Department of Commerce *Annual Report,* Hoover declared: "Through cooperation by the department with the unionized operators and with the leaders of the United Mine Workers, a long term agreement has been entered upon which insures industrial peace in the industry."[21]

In 1925, John L. Lewis expanded on his vision for the future of the industry in *The Miners' Fight for American Standards* (Indianapolis: Bell, 1925). In the book, which was actually written by UMWA economic advisor W. Jett Lauck and publicist K. C. Adams, Lewis proposed government-sponsored, union-endorsed, cartelization of the bituminous coal industry as the solution to excess capacity and overproduction and to ensure "American principles" in the coalfields and "American rights in the mines." He endorsed price-fixing and the distribution of markets among the large mechanized coal producers. Lewis believed that these policies would force nonunion mines in more marginal fields to close up while the unionized Central Competitive Field would survive this weeding-out process. Behind his argument was an unstated conclusion that any attempt to organize miners in the nonunion fields was self-defeating for the union and the industry.[22]

20. *Labor Unity* (June 15, 1927); "John Brophy Appeals to International Executive Board for Honesty and a Square Deal," Hapgood Papers, University of Indiana; Singer, "Communists," 143–45; Brophy, *Miner's,* 200–218.

21. *Illinois Miner* (April 5, 1942), 1; *New York Times* (April 20, 1924), sect. IX, p. 10; Singer, "Which Side," 192; Dubofsky and Van Tine, *Lewis,* 107–8; Dubofsky and Van Tine, *Labor Leaders,* 191; Zieger, *Republicans,* 229–53; *UMWJ* (March 1, 1924); U.S. Department of Commerce, Twelfth Annual Report (Washington, D.C., 1924), 13, cited in Zieger, *Republicans,* 232.

22. John L. Lewis, *The Miners' Fight for American Standards* (Indianapolis: Bell, 1925), 15, 41, 122–27, 180; Singer, 200–202; Dubofsky and Van Tine, *Lewis,* 106.

Lewis's plans relied on what he believed to be Herbert Hoover's support for "cooperative capitalism" and the union. However, although Hoover accepted the government's role as a mediator between labor and capital at the Jacksonville conference in order to promote industrial peace, he opposed labor's right to strike, and rejected government-sponsored cartelization; further, he was not committed to the long-term survival of either the Central Competitive Field or the UMWA. In March 1925, as the Jacksonville Accord unraveled, Hoover declared that he and other members of the Coolidge administration had neither encouraged a long-term agreement in the bituminous coal industry, nor provided the terms of the contract. He claimed that the negotiations were solely a matter between miners and the operators. In May 1926, Hoover testified before the House Committee on Interstate and Foreign Commerce against the passage of legislation to stabilize the bituminous coal industry. Hoover told the committee that "My own feeling is that it might be quite well to give these folks an opportunity to see whether they can set up some sort of machinery on their own."[23]

Despite his abandonment by Hoover and the Republicans, Lewis never attacked them publicly or broke off his relationship with them. In 1924, Lewis used the apparent success of the Jacksonville Accord to promote himself, with support from Harriman financial interests, as a potential Republican Party vice presidential candidate. He appears to have been offered, but rejected, the position of secretary of labor. Then, in 1928, with the union in decline, Lewis campaigned for Hoover for president, and in a change of heart, lobbied for the position of secretary of labor. While unemployed miners and their families were going hungry, Lewis told a radio audience that he was supporting Hoover because "we are in the midst of a new industrial revolution that has become the marvel of the civilized world. . . . The fundamental objective thus made possible is a constant gain in the living standards of people and the ultimate possibility of the elimination of poverty itself." However, Hoover did not want Lewis as his secretary of labor, and bypassed him twice.[24]

There is also some evidence in the UMWA Master Alphabetical files that during the 1920s, John L. Lewis was working both sides of the street in his relationship with bituminous coal operators. In November 1924, Lewis was offered a position as head of the Illinois Operators' Association and of a projected National Union Operators' Association. Ellis Searles, editor of the *UMWJ*, conducted cryptic correspondence with a group of operators but the negotiations fell through. In December

23. Zeiger, *Republicans*, 15, 64, 65, 116–227, 239–43; Ellis Searles, "Giving Stability to the Coal Industry," *Review of Reviews* (June 1922); 639–42; *New York Times* (April 24, 1924), sect. IX, p. 10; Coleman, *Men and Coal*, 125; "Mr. Hoover's Plan," *Literary Digest* (December 4, 1920): 12–13; Singer, "Which Side," 200–202.

24. K. C. Adams to John L. Lewis, March 31, 1924, and April 2, 1924, K. C. Adams File, UMWA Papers; Van Tine, *Making of a Labor Bureaucrat*, 180; Bernstein, *Lean Years*, 123, 334; Dubofsky and Van Tine, *Lewis*, 148–49, 172–73; Dan Smith to John L. Lewis, December 13, 1928, John L. Lewis to Dan Smith, December 16, 1928, Lewis file, UMWA Papers; "Hoover's Tonic Safest For Industry" (1928), UMWA Papers.

1925, a group of Illinois operators approached Lewis about his participation in a merger plan. He directed them to contact his brother A. D. Lewis, director of the Illinois Mine and Minerals Bureau. In addition, during the 1926 UMWA election campaign, the "Save the Union" ticket found a former general manager of Consolidation Coal's Kent, West Virginia, mines, who claimed that he was chairman of a committee that had raised a $100,000 slush fund for Lewis in 1922, in addition to a regular annual $100,000 payoff. In return, Lewis is alleged to have promised not to run an organizing drive in West Virginia.[25]

Despite Lewis's continuing efforts to nurture his relationships with both the operators and the Republican administrations during the 1920s, the UMWA was increasingly in jeopardy. From 1924 to 1926, northern unionized mines closed and coal companies shifted production to nonunion southern fields. With the expiration of the Jacksonville Accord in March 1927, the IEB was forced to abandon the Central Competitive Field as a bargaining unit and authorize individual districts to negotiate independent contracts. In December 1927 operators told Secretary of Labor Davis that there would be no joint conference: "So far as we are concerned that organization is entirely out of the picture." In March 1929, John L. Lewis delivered a "confidential and privileged address" to the union's Executive Board on conditions in the industry. He reported that, "with the waning and dissolution of our union in certain coal fields of America today, there is coming back into those coal fields the same injustices and the same evil practices that prevailed in the days of our boyhood. . . . Labor has always had these cycles in its history in our country, it has had its triumphs, and it has had its reverses, and it always will. Progress has come in cycles."[26]

However, John Brophy, whom Lewis had defeated in the disputed 1926 UMWA election, was not prepared to dismiss the condition of the union as simply the result of the "cycles of history." He wrote Oscar Ameringer, editor of the *Illinois Miner*: "Exposure of the character of the man and his treacherous work against the interests of the miners is necessary. . . . To defeat Lewis is of primary importance. Everything else is secondary. Until Lewis is disposed of there cannot be any rebuilding of the Miners' movement. . . . The miners of America cannot have confidence in the union as long as he is there. His presence in the Union is an insult to every honest man. . . . Resistance to one who has perverted the democratic principles of the union and

25. Singer, "Which Side," 227; J. W. Blower, Hisylvania Coal Company to Joseph Pursglove, November 6, 1924, Taplin to Joe (Pursglove), undated; Ellis Searles to Joseph Pursglove, November 7, 1924; Joseph Pursglove to John L. Lewis, November 18, 1924; November 24, 1924; undated; Pursglove File, UMWA-MA; John L. Lewis to A. D. Lewis, December 15, 1925, A. D. Lewis File, UMWA-MA; Albert Coyle to Powers Hapgood, August 4, 1926, Hapgood Papers.

26. Singer, "Which Side," 252–55; *Illinois Miner* (March 26, 1927, April 2, 1927); *Federated Press* (March 23, 1927); *American Appeal* (June 25, 1927); *New York Times* (December 10, 1927), 9 and (December 11, 1927), 28; Dubofsky and Van Tine, *Lewis*, 146–47; Report to the International Executive Board, March 13, 1929, IEB file, UMWA Papers.

almost destroyed it with his senseless policies is obedience to the miners' best interests.''[27]

During the 1920s, John L. Lewis secured absolute control over the UMWA's International union machinery, but it was a costly triumph. He had failed to develop an effective strategy to resist the open-shop forces of corporate America or that allowed the union to sustain its membership in an industry where productive capacity far exceeded the demand for coal. In 1929, the UMWA was a seriously depleted union, whose monthly membership in the bituminous coalfields had declined from an average of 384,617 miners in 1920 to approximately 86,000 miners in June 1929. On a more personal level, despite his political maneuvering and his relationships with coal operators and Republican Party leaders, John L. Lewis was unable to follow the example set by Mitchell, White, and other UMWA officials, and leave the union for a suitable position in government, the AFL hierarchy, or in the bituminous coal industry.[28]

From 1929 until 1933, as the Great Depression deepened and the UMWA and most of the American labor movement floundered, Lewis did not change his basic ideological position. John L. Lewis and the UMWA International office continued to battle against insurgent threats to their control over the union: the Communist-organized National Miners' Union, the reorganized UMWA and the Progressive Miners of America (both with roots in Illinois's District 12); and numerous small localized rank-and-file uprisings. Lewis also continued the union's unsuccessful lobbying effort to convince the Hoover administration to support plans to reorganize the industry.[29]

In the early years of the depression, Lewis hoped that increasing misery and economic dislocation would compel Hoover to adopt UMWA proposals for rationalizing the bituminous coal industry. In 1931, Lewis called on Congress to create an economic council to study and regulate the coal industry. He testified before the La Follette Committee that ''unless we recognize squarely and deal intelligently with these new forces and movements in modern industry and finance, our existing troubles will grow in volume and intensity, and . . . the future will be filled with recurrent disasters.'' In 1932, Lewis supported Herbert Hoover for reelection, even though the UMWA and the AFL made no official endorsements.[30]

After the election of Franklin D. Roosevelt as president, the miners and the American working class exploded in an electric surge of union organization. Class-conscious coal miners, who had been beaten down since 1919 by economic recession in the industry, open-shop operators, and by Lewis's often ruthless efforts to dominate the union, rose up to demand the right to unionize. In a few short months,

27. John Brophy to Oscar Ameringer, October 25, 1929, John Brophy Papers, Catholic University.

28. *Illinois Miner* (October 26, 1929), 8.

29. Bernstein, *Lean Years*, 368–76; See the *UMWJ* for this period, especially vol. 44, nos. 1–12 (January 1, 1933–May 15, 1933).

30. Address to LaFollette Committee, Senate Sub-Committee on Manufactures, Investigating National Economic Council, Friday, December 4, 1931, UMWA Papers; Brophy, *Miner's*, 235.

they rebuilt the UMWA. Irving Bernstein, in *Turbulent Years*, argued that the passage of Section 7(a) of the National Industrial Recovery Act on June 16, 1933, was the spark that rekindled the union movement. He credited John L. Lewis with anticipating the upsurge and committing the union's treasury and organizers to the drive. Lewis had a similar interpretation. On October 15, 1933, the *UMWJ* published an official union circular that explained: "Previous to the enactment of the National Industrial Recovery Act and for a period after its adoption, the United Mine Workers of America waged an intensive organizing campaign in the non-union and partially-organized bituminous coal fields of the country. This campaign of organization was successful beyond expectations. Local unions were established at every bituminous coal mine, embracing in membership all the mine workers employed in or about the mines."[31]

But the labor militancy of the 1930s was a general classwide phenomenon that predated the involvement of John L. Lewis. In 1931 and 1932, bituminous coal miners in the Appalachian region and the Central Competitive Field, began to reaffirm their heritage of rank-and-file militancy, often under the leadership of activists who had been driven out of the UMWA over the years for radicalism, dual unionism, involvement with leftist organizations, or for disagreeing with John L. Lewis. In 1931, Harlan, Kentucky, miners struck with support from the Communist-organized National Miners' Union (NMU). The NMU effort was directed by Thomas Myerscough, a former District 5 (Western Pennsylvania) miner who had been active in the creation of the Progressive International Committee of the UMWA in 1923. The NMU also led walkouts in western Pennsylvania and Ohio. These strikes were coordinated by Pat Toohey, a Pennsylvania coal miner who had worked with John Brophy in 1927 and 1928 in the Save the Union movement. From July until October, West Virginia miners struck under the leadership of Frank Keeney, a former UMWA district official who had broken with Lewis and left the union and the industry in 1924. During the summer of 1931, wildcat strikers walked out in southern Illinois, long a hotbed of UMWA rank-and-file dissidents, because they were dissatisfied with a contract negotiated by Lewis and Illinois operators.[32]

John L. Lewis, who had battled against the UMWA rank and file, understood the strength of the organizing surge. At some point in 1933, he decided to take advantage of it to rebuild the UMWA under his centralized control and to use it as a base of support to assert his leadership in labor and national politics. This was the first in a series of crucial judgments made by Lewis during the next few years. They included the decision to break with the AFL hierarchy and participate in the founding of the CIO in 1935, to endorse Franklin D. Roosevelt in the 1936 presidential election, to utilize former UMWA opponents and active Communists as CIO orga-

31. Bernstein, *Turbulent*, 41–43; *UMWJ* (October 15, 1933), 11.

32. Davis, *Prisoners*, 56–57; Zeiger, *American Workers*, 29; Bernstein, *Lean Years*, 374–84; Dubofsky and Van Tine, *Lewis*, 170–72; Art Shields, *On the Battle Lines, 1919–1939* (New York: International, 1986), 186–91.

nizers, to cooperate with rank-and-file left militants in the mass-production indus-tries, and to support the sit-down movement in the automobile industry in 1937. These decisions thrust John L. Lewis into the historical spotlight and they reflected what Lewis called his "strength . . . that I am able correctly to interpret the aims of my people," rather than a long-term strategy or ideological commitments.[33]

An examination of the *UMWJ* during the early months of 1933 suggests that at first, Lewis and the UMWA leadership did not grasp the possibilities involved in the rank-and-file upsurge. The *Journal* does not announce preparations by the interna-tional union for an organizing drive in the coalfields, even though notices from District 2 (Central Pennsylvania) and District 5 (Western Pennsylvania) report that rank-and-file miners in those districts were anxious to rebuild the union and UMWA Vice-President Philip Murray attended one of their rallies. On May 15, the *Journal*'s front-page cartoon attacked "communists" in District 12. It was not until the June 15 issue that the front-page cartoon signaled a shift in attention to rebuilding the union. In this cartoon, a locomotive labeled U.M.W. of A. is speeding down the "New Deal Track" with President Lewis at the throttle. As it speeds along, it pushes obstructionists and dual unionists out of its way. Tailing the UMWA is the National Recovery Act. This issue of the *Journal* was the first official recognition of the stirrings in the coal fields. An editorial on page 6 announced: "This union proposes to carry the gospel of trade unionism to every miner in America and give him an opportunity to join the United Mine Workers of America. This campaign is already in progress and has met with wonderful success. Tens of thousands of mine workers in various fields and districts have enrolled as members of the union, and more tens of thousands are following their lead. The country never before witnessed such an enthusiastic rush for union membership."[34]

On July 1, 1933, the organizing drive was finally the lead story in the UMWA's newspaper. The *Journal* reported: "A tidal wave of enthusiasm for the United Mine Workers of America is sweeping over the entire country, with the result that mine workers everywhere are joining the union by the tens of thousands. So tremendous is this ground-swell that it is almost impossible to keep track of it. In every coal mining field in America the campaign of organization is going forward by leaps and bounds never before witnessed" (3).

The reportage and the cartoons in the *Journal* suggest, therefore, that Lewis and the international union entered the picture after rank-and-file miners had already begun to organize themselves in response to the election of Roosevelt in November 1932, his inauguration in March 1933, and the early days of the New Deal. Reports from field organizers support this interpretation. On June 17, the day after the NIRA passed, John Cinque reported to the union that 80% of the Ohio miners had signed up as members. On June 19, Van Bittner reported that anti-union Logan County,

33. UMWA, *Lewis*, 250.

34. See *UMWJ* 44, nos. 1–14 (January 1, 1933–June 15, 1933), esp. *UMWJ* (February 1, 1933): 13; (April 1, 1933): 12; (May 1, 1933): 8; (May 15, 1933): 5; *UMWJ* (June 15, 1933): 1, 6.

West Virginia, was completely organized. Garfield Lewis wrote Philip Murray from anti-union Kentucky on June 22, 1933: "The people have been so starved out that they are flocking into the union by the thousands. . . . I organized 9 Locals Tuesday." On June 23, Sam Caddy reported that all of the substantial mines in Kentucky were organized. By the end of June, 128,000 new members had joined the union in the Pennsylvania bituminous coalfields. John Brophy concluded that the miners had "moved into the union en masse. . . . They organized themselves for all practical purposes." They had been union miners before and they wanted to be union miners again. Neither John L. Lewis nor the NIRA created this surge; it was the outpouring of pent-up rank-and-file desire for unionization. John L. Lewis's contribution was to see what was happening, understand its potential, and support it.[35]

During the summer of 1933, as miners poured back into the UMWA, Lewis cautioned them to wait while the union negotiated a new union contract for the CCF and the southern coalfields. At the same time, Lewis reestablished the union's infrastructure in reorganized fields utilizing provisional district offices to ensure his control. In September, with President Roosevelt's encouragement, the bituminous coal operators and the UMWA announced an agreement that covered more than 90% of the bituminous coal mined in the United States. The contract established an eight-hour day and forty-hour week in the coalfields and check-off, but did not provide for a union shop.

In January 1934, a little more than fourteen years after John L. Lewis had cancelled the post–World War I strike, a decision that advanced his control over the union while contributing to the UMWA's decadelong decline, he reported to the UMWA convention that "the United Mine Workers of America has substantially accomplished the task to which it has been dedicated . . . through the forty-four years of its history. It has at last succeeded in bringing into the fold . . . practically all the mine workers in our great North American continent."[36]

The organizing explosion in the coalfields paralleled similar explosions in the other mass-production industries. Art Preis in *Labor's Giant Step* (New York: Pioneer, 1964), his history of the first twenty years of the CIO, viewed rank-and-file worker unrest across the nation, rather than any one individual, as the impetus behind the formation of the CIO. Preis argued that three 1934 strikes, the Toledo Autolite strike, the Minneapolis Teamsters strike and the San Francisco longshoremen's strike, are of special importance. Each of the strikes grew rapidly after attempts were made to break them using local police and National Guard units, each had local leftist leadership not tied into the traditional union structures, each was unauthorized by the AFL, and each strike involved support from the unemployed and other workers in their communities. The AFL response to these organizing drives was not that different from Lewis's efforts to integrate newly organized coal miners into the UMWA's existing "provisional district" structure. The AFL at-

35. Bernstein, *Turbulent*, 41–45; Brophy, CIO files, UMWA Papers; Brophy, *Miner's*, 236.
36. Bernstein, *Turbulent*, 43–45; *UMWJ* (January 15, 1934 or February 1, 1934).

tempted to control the rank-and-file uprisings through the creation of "federal locals" that would enlist workers from the mass-production industries into the ranks
of organized labor with the eventual goal of redistributing them among the traditional craft unions. The advantage that the UMWA had over the AFL was that the
miners' union was already organized on an industrial basis.[37]

At the October 1933 AFL Convention, Charles Howard of the Typographical
Union, argued in favor of a new AFL policy to encourage independent industrial
unions in the mass-production industries. However, craft unionists in control of the
AFL doubted the feasibility of organizing permanent unions in the mass-production
industries and remained committed to existing craft jurisdictions. The debate over
the AFL's response to the labor upsurge in the mass-production industries continued
at the October 1934 annual convention, until a compromise report was worked out
that temporarily resolved the dispute. The AFL Executive Board was ordered to
grant charters to National or International Unions in automotive, cement, aluminum,
and other mass-production industries, while at the same time respecting the craft
jurisdictions of the federation's constituent unions. While the report was adopted
unanimously, John L. Lewis, who supported the formation of new industrial unions,
warned the convention that "we are going to have as many interpretations of these
resolutions as there are conflicting viewpoints on the committee" and that ultimately, a majority on the "Executive Council will interpret what it means." By the
time of the 1935 AFL convention in Atlantic City, John L. Lewis was convinced
that the compromise was not a victory for industrial unionism. He told the assembled unionists that "At San Francisco they seduced me with fair words. Now, of
course, having learned that I was seduced, I am enraged and I am ready to rend my
seducers limb from limb."[38]

At the conclusion of the 1935 convention, the Committee for Industrial Organization was born. While the events that transpired at the convention, especially the
"fight" between Lewis and Hutcheson, are well documented, the relationship between Lewis's intentions going into the convention and the results that came out of
it, are not so clear. John Brophy reported that during the summer of 1935, he met
with Philip Murray, Judge Warrum, the UMWA attorney, and Lewis to discuss strategy for pushing the issue of industrial unionism at the 1935 AFL Convention. Lewis
also met with steel workers to try to get them to press the issue at the convention.
But what did they actually plan? Was Lewis preparing a break with the AFL?[39]

At the convention, Lewis precipitated conflict with the AFL traditionalists by
attacking Matthew Woll's relationship with the National Civic Federation and the
American Federationist's policy of accepting advertising from nonunion business
interests. He also antagonized Hutcheson when he challenged the United Brother-

37. Preis, *Labor's Giant Step*, 19–31; Farrell Dobbs, *Teamster Rebellion* (New York: Monad, 1972);
Jeremy Brecher, *Strike!* (San Francisco: Straight Arrow, 1972), 150–66.

38. Bernstein, *Turbulent*, 356–58, 364–66, 386–87; *UMWJ* (December 15, 1935); 13–16; Preis,
Labor's Giant Step, 34–35, 42; Davis, *Prisoners*, 58–59; Dubofsky and Van Tine, *Lewis*, 211–21.

39. John Brophy, Columbia University Oral History Collection, 1957, 552–57.

hood of Carpenters leader's parliamentary ploy to quiet delegates from the Federal Locals, bringing on the exchange of "words" and fists. When he spoke at the convention, John L. Lewis criticized the AFL's reluctance to support industrial unions because it did not account for "the dreams or requirements of the workers themselves" or the "power of the adversaries of labor":

> Great combinations of capital have assembled great industrial plants, and they are strung across the borders of several states from the north to the south and from the west in such a manner that they have assembled to themselves tremendous power and influence, and they are almost 100 percent effective in opposing organization of the workers under the policies of the American Federation of Labor. . . . If you go in there with your craft union they will mow you down like the Italian machine guns mow down the Ethiopians in the war now going on in that country.[40]

But despite Lewis's staunch defense of the rights of industrial unionists at the convention, his electrifying fight with Hutcheson, and his customary eloquence, the call for industrial unionism was defeated 18,024 to 10,933. While state federations, city labor councils, and the new federated unions, lined up in support of industrial unionism, its advocates did not have the votes to reverse AFL policy.[41]

The *UMWJ* (November 1, 1935) report on the convention focused on the lost vote on industrial organization. The AFL convention "defeated every effort on the part of the progressive and liberal element in the ranks of organized labor to endorse and carry out the policy of organization along industrial lines, and decided to continue organization along craft lines." Significantly, it wasn't until midway through the article that the Lewis-Hutcheson battle was even mentioned:

> Much bitterness crept into the debate upon this proposition. The craft unions, who are in control of the Federation oiled up their steam roller for the purpose of flattening out the industrial union movement. In fact, the situation became so tense at one time that President Hutchinson, of the Carpenters Union, called President John L. Lewis a vile name, and Lewis socked Hutcheson on the snoot with a straight right hand punch that jarred Hutcheson's six foot four inches from head to foot. Two more wallops of the same kind by President Lewis ended Hutcheson's belligerency. (15)

The tone of the article suggests that crucial decisions were being made on the convention floor and behind the scenes in Atlantic City, and that there was not a preconceived strategy to break with the AFL and independently organize industrial workers. The way the fight is reported is significant. There is no screaming headline

40. *UMWJ* (December 15, 1935): 13–16.
41. Preis, *Labor's Giant Step*, 42; Bernstein, *Turbulent*, 386–97.

or claim of victory. Lewis may have relished the fight with Hutcheson and he certainly moved with it, but he didn't plan events to happen this way. Later, in retrospect, it became the "shot heard around the world"; but at the time the punch was thrown, no one knew what to make of it.

After the convention adjourned, however, John L. Lewis did move quickly to consolidate support for industrial organization. On Sunday, October 20, 1935, at a meeting with Philip Murray, Thomas Kennedy, and John Brophy of the UMWA, International Typographical Union President Charles Howard, ILGWU President David Dubinsky, Max Zaritsky of the Hat, Cap and Millinery Workers Union, Thomas McMahon of Textile and Sidney Hillman, president of the Amalgamated Clothing Workers Union (ACW), the CIO was born. On November 9, this initial group was joined by Harvey Fremming of Oil Fields, Gas Well and Refinery Workers and Thomas Brown of the Mine, Mill and Smelter Workers when they announced the founding of the American Federation of Labor's Committee for Industrial Organization at UMWA headquarters in Washington, D.C.[42]

But the *Journal* still hesitated in its coverage. In the November 15 issue, there is only a small notice of the formation of the Committee for Industrial Organization. It is not until December 1, when the *Journal* announced that Lewis had resigned as a vice president of the American Federation of Labor, that the *Journal* shifted its focus and emphasized the new developments. The paper reprinted a Lewis letter to William Green, reported on a Lewis press conference, and published editorials rallying miners to support the CIO. The editorial page declared: "The members of that committee are men widely experienced in the labor movement, and they believe they understand why these millions have not been brought into the labor movement. One principal reason is that the unorganized workers have not had an opportunity to join the kind of union they wish to join. . . . They want industrial unionism."[43]

In the next few issues, the *Journal* started to champion the CIO. This was not a surprising development since John L. Lewis was dependent on financial and organizational support from the UMWA and the miners to maintain the new committee. The December 15 *Journal* reprinted Lewis's statement in support of industrial unionism at the AFL convention and an introduction, written by John Brophy, to a pamphlet titled "Industrial Unionism, The Vital Problem of Organized Labor." In January, the *Journal* reprinted a letter from Brophy to William Green, calling on the AFL to take up the banner of industrial organization, and describing the "momentous opportunity" the AFL Executive Committee has if it takes "serious and immediate steps to promote union organization in the steel, automobile, rubber and a number of other mass production industries."[44]

Throughout 1936, the AFL and the CIO leaderships moved toward an apparently

    42. *UMWJ* (November 15, 1935): 9; Bernstein, *Turbulent*, 395–400, Preis, *Labor's Giant Step*, 43; Dubofsky and Van Tine, *Lewis*, 222–26.
    43. (November 15, 1935): 9; (December 1, 1935): 10.
    44. *UMWJ* (December 15, 1935): 13–16; and (January 15, 1936): 3.

inevitable and permanent split. On September 5, 1936, the ten CIO unions were suspended from the AFL pending a final ruling by the AFL convention. At that point, Lewis was apparently determined to finalize the break and establish the CIO as an independent labor federation with himself as its head. To embarrass William Green, who was still a member of the UMWA, Lewis charged him with conspiring against the union in his position as AFL president and he ordered him to appear at a trial before the UMWA International Executive Board on the same day the AFL convention was scheduled to begin. Green, not surprisingly, did not appear to defend himself against Lewis's charges and instead proceeded with the expulsions. They became official in January 1938. In October 1938, the Committee for Industrial Organization held its first convention and became the Congress for Industrial Organizations. John L. Lewis was elected its president.[45]

Did John L. Lewis—depicted from 1910 through the 1920s as an opportunist seeking personal economic and political advancement and as an autocrat committed to tight control over the rank and file, suppression of dissent and cooperation among union leaders, capital, and government—suddenly change into a radical class-based activist during the 1930s? Lewis argued that conditions in American society had changed and that he was responding to these changes. He reportedly told Powers Hapgood, a John Brophy ally during the 1920s who went to work for the CIO in the 1930s, that "[i]f I had adopted the policies you and your friends wanted me to adopt ten years ago, my union would have been smashed by the tremendous opposition it would have received. Today is different." Hapgood, who doubted that Lewis had changed significantly, nevertheless agreed to work with him. Hapgood defended his decision, claiming that Lewis's talents made him a capable and "practical fighter" for working people. He told fellow labor radicals:

> I saw John L. Lewis at that (1935 AFL) convention fighting for the very things that we in the opposition had long been contending for. What is more, I saw him fighting with an effectiveness that none of us could muster. I saw hundreds of his former enemies applaud him to the echo when he fought for modern ideas as few but he can fight. . . . [S]eeing him in action at Atlantic City and in talking with him at that time I realize now for the first time that he doesn't have to change to be of tremendous service to the modern labor movement.[46]

Lewis's role in the early CIO was also discussed by John Brophy in his oral history. Brophy, who bitterly fought against Lewis for years, believed that at the time of the founding of the CIO, Lewis "was concerned with organizing the workers

---

45. Bernstein, *Turbulent*, 399–431, 682–703; Dubofsky and Van Tine, *Lewis*, 222–28, 232–47. See also *UMWJ* (February 1, 1938): 3–4; (February 15, 1938): 5–7; (November 15, 1938): 3–4; (December 1, 1938): 3, 12–15.

46. Powers Hapgood, "The Necessity for Unity in the Coal Fields," Decataur, Illinois, *Sunday Herald and Review* (January 5, 1936), Hapgood Papers.

and the miners," even though the organization of the CIO "also fed Lewis' ego and strengthened his personality, because he thus became a person of some distinction as the union achieved success. . . . But there's no question in my mind that Lewis's aims in those early years of the C.I.O. were definitely tied to the good of the general labor movement, and the workers as a whole. . . . I think that he was stirred by the drama."[47]

From 1936 until 1943, the drama of the American labor movement stirred both John L. Lewis and the nation. Initially, Lewis and the CIO leadership established two priorities. The first was to support Roosevelt's 1936 reelection campaign, establishing both the political clout of organized labor and ensuring government support for CIO efforts in the mass-production industries. Other CIO leaders, especially Sidney Hillman of the ACW, were strong pro-Roosevelt New Dealers. For Lewis, who had been an active Republican, this was primarily a coalition of convenience.[48]

The CIO's second priority was a concerted campaign to unionize steel. This campaign would break open one of the major bastions of the open shop, demonstrate the power of industrial organization in an industry where AFL craft unionism had always failed, and serve as a model organizing campaign for the other mass-production industries. John L. Lewis wanted the steel industry targeted because its antiunion stand in its "captive" coal mines was a thorn in the side of the UMWA. Steel, rather than in auto or rubber where rank-and-file militants had established strong independent locals, also gave Lewis and the CIO an opportunity to create a centrally administered, disciplined, International union, modeled on the UMWA.[49]

Although John L. Lewis had supported Herbert Hoover in the 1932 presidential election, the Roosevelt administration's receptivity to UMWA input on Section 7(a) during the NIRA hearings, the successful rebuilding of the UMWA during the summer of 1933, and Roosevelt's support of UMWA efforts to organize U.S. Steel's "captive" mines, convinced Lewis to shift his support to Franklin D. Roosevelt in 1936. At the 1936 UMWA Convention, which unanimously endorsed Roosevelt for reelection, Lewis repeatedly praised "Roosevelt for what he has done for labor and the common people of the country." However, despite this endorsement, John L. Lewis was not willing to subordinate the CIO or his own political position to the Democratic Party and work within established Democratic Party committees under the direction of AFL officials. Instead, Lewis established an independent Labor's Non-Partisan League (LNPL), which he controlled, and which gave him and the CIO, a permanent political base for the future. In return for FDR's pledge to work for new pro-labor legislation, Lewis established a Washington office for the LNPL, set up a national pro-Roosevelt labor network, and channeled $600,000 in UMWA

47. Brophy, Columbia University Oral History Collection, 595–97; 606.

48. C. K. McFarland, "Coalition of Convenience: Lewis and Roosevelt, 1933–1940," *Labor History* 13, no. 3 (summer 1972): 400–414; Ross, "John L. Lewis," 160–90; Dubofsky and Van Tine, *Lewis*, 248–52; Bernstein, *Turbulent*, 448–50.

49. Lorin Lee Cary, "Institutionalized Conservatism in the Early C.I.O.: Adolph Germer, A Case Study," *Labor History* 13, no. 4 (fall 1972): 475–504.

funds to the Roosevelt campaign, the Democratic National Committee, and other New Deal candidates. On October 17, in a national radio address, Lewis personally urged American workers to vote for FDR: "He has succeeded so well in his task of rehabilitating America, that the industrialists and financiers have recovered sufficiently to fight him with malice and venom, defamation and prevarication. They have bought the Republican party with their gold. They seek to use it as a ruthless weapon to destroy the great champion of progress and reform." Later, Lewis also claimed that under his direction, the CIO delayed strikes until after the 1936 election was over.[50]

For these efforts, Lewis required a stiff price. In a 1937 New Year's Eve address, he demanded the active use of state power to defend labor's right to organize, notifying Roosevelt that "Labor will . . . expect the protection of the Federal Government in pursuit of its lawful objectives." The speech also represented a demand that Roosevelt recognize Lewis's personal position as the preeminent leader of American labor. But unfortunately, the 1936 reelection campaign turned out to be too successful to achieve Lewis's purpose. Roosevelt's margin of victory was so overwhelming (he polled over 60% of the popular vote and carried the electoral college by 523 to 8) that the role played by Lewis and the CIO appeared to be considerably less significant than Lewis claimed, a development that contributed to the eventual dissolution of the Lewis-Roosevelt alliance.[51]

In June 1936, while still in the early stages of the Roosevelt reelection campaign, Lewis and the CIO announced the start of its organizing drive in steel. The CIO pledged a $700,000 war chest to the newly established Steel Workers Organizing Committee (SWOC), most of it from the UMWA, began a labor newspaper for the industry, opened 35 regional offices, and assigned 433 full- and part-time field organizers to the task of unionizing the steel industry. It also decided, as an inducement to attract new union members as rapidly as possible, not to collect dues until after a first contract was successfully negotiated.[52]

Rank-and-file militants in other basic industries, particularly rubber and auto, were not content to wait for the CIO to organize steel before challenging employers in their industries. They were also not anxious to have Lewis and the other established labor leaders who headed the CIO dictate the structure and tactics for their unions. In November 1935, Goodyear Rubber workers in Akron, Ohio, sat down on the job to protest a wage cut. In January 1936, Firestone rubber workers sat down and stayed in the plant for several nights. From April to December 1936, there was a wave of sporadic and unpredictable sit-down activity in the rubber industry led by local leadership who refused to accept the authority of the CIO-affiliated national United Rubber Workers Union. As early as April 1, 1936, the *New Republic,* com-

---

50. Preis, *Labor's Giant Step*, 46; Dubofsky and Van Tine, *Lewis*, 194–97, 248–54; McFarland, "Coalition," 400–414; *UMWJ* (February 15, 1936): 5; *UMWJ* (November 1, 1936): 18.
   51. *UMWJ* (January 15, 1937).
   52. Preis, *Labor's Giant Step*, 51; Bernstein, *Turbulent*, 435–41, 448–57.

menting on the role of the CIO in the rubber industry, reported that "some observers on the scene felt that the Lewis group might well have been more militant and vigorous." In July, John L. Lewis assigned Allen Haywood of the UMWA to work with the union to establish rules, routinize grievance procedures, and tame the sit-down strikers. Lewis's use of Haywood, Van Bittner, and Adolph Germer as CIO field organizers to control rank-and-file dissent was a product of his continuing commitment to centrally organized, highly structured, "professionally" managed, labor unions.[53]

During this same hectic period, John L. Lewis tried to convince the United Auto Workers Union to join the CIO. In January 1936, he told Cleveland, Ohio, auto workers: "Because of my own personal interest in industrial unionism, as well as that of all members and officers of the United Mine Workers of America, we have followed your splendid course as brothers enlisted in the same cause." The UAW decided to join the CIO in July 1936. By November 13, 1936, auto workers were engaging in spontaneous sit-down strikes at Fisher Body No. 1 in Flint, Michigan. This was followed by sit-downs at Bendix in South Bend, Indiana, and at Midland Steel Products and Kelsey-Hayes in Detroit. On December 21, John L. Lewis sent a telegram to the head of General Motors demanding a collective bargaining agreement for its employees. When the company refused to negotiate, GM workers began to walk out. On December 30, workers in Fisher Body Plant 1 and 2 in Flint, Michigan, sat down and within three weeks, fifteen other GM plants were closed by strikes. Eventually, 140,000 of GMs 150,000 production workers were on strike and auto had replaced steel as the focal point of CIO organizing efforts.[54]

Lewis and the CIO had planned on an organizing drive in steel and support from Roosevelt to convince the steel companies to accept collective bargaining and grant union recognition, but the rubber and auto workers, using the sit-down strike as their major weapon, had rewritten the CIO's script. In 1937, J. Raymond Walsh, a former Harvard economist who became the CIO's research and educational director, concluded that, not only had the CIO leadership not planned the GM sit-down strike, but that initially "the CIO high command, preoccupied with the drive in steel, tried in vain to prevent the strike." It wasn't until January 3, 1937, days after the start of the sit-down, that the UAW formally authorized a corporationwide strike against GM. However, to John L. Lewis's credit, instead of trying to control the rank-and-file forces during those crucial weeks in the winter of 1936–37, he acted quickly to change the CIO's strategy. On December 31, 1936, Lewis announced that "the CIO

53. Preis, *Labor's Giant Step*, 45–46; Proceedings of the First Convention of the URW of A, September 13–21, 1936, 429–31, cited in Daniel Nelson, "Origins of the Sit-Down Era: Worker Militancy and Innovation in the Rubber Industry, 1934–38," *Labor History* 23, no. 2 (spring 1982): 219, and 198–225; Cary, "Institutionalized Conservatism," 491.

54. *UMWJ* (February 1, 1936): 9; Roger Keeran, *The Communist Party and the Auto Workers' Unions* (New York: International Publishers, 1980), 121–47; Preis, *Labor's Giant Step*, 52–53; Bernstein, *Turbulent*, 499–529; Sidney Fine, *Sit-Down: The General Motors Strike of 1936–37* (Ann Arbor: University of Michigan Press, 1969).

stands squarely behind these sit-downs." When William Knudsen of GM demanded evacuation of the plants, Lewis countered with a demand for a national contract.[55]

While Lewis actually had little to do with the day-to-day operation of the General Motors strike, it gave him and the CIO the national center stage its leadership sought. Lewis knew how to play the press, and according to Brophy, a decision was made "to emphasize Lewis's presence, and to center the activities around his personality, because he was very much in the public press at the time." With Lewis on the scene in Detroit, the *New York Times* worried that his leadership might "hasten, by violence, the process of taking from those who have and giving to those who have not." When GM reneged on a truce agreement, it was Lewis who announced that "GM was caught in a barefaced violation of the armistice and so evacuation of the plants was stopped. The men are not going to leave them." On January 21, Lewis publicly pressured President Roosevelt for support, declaring that during the election "the Administration asked labor for help to repel this attack and labor gave its help. The same economic royalists now have their fangs in labor. The workers of this country expect the administration to help workers in every legal way and to support the workers in General Motors plants." When FDR phoned John L. Lewis in an effort to persuade him to accept a one-month contract for the auto workers, Lewis demanded a six-month pact. When Michigan Governor Frank Murphy, pressed by GM to use the National Guard to eject the strikers, ordered Lewis "to do something about this," Lewis responded, "I did not ask these men to sit-down. I did not ask General Motors to turn off the heat. I did not have any part of either the sit-down strike or the attempt to freeze the men. Let General Motors talk to them." Finally, on February 11, 1937, after nearly six weeks of sit-ins, threats, bluffs, and negotiations, GM agreed to recognize the union and to sign a six-month pact with the UAW.

The steel pact, instead of being the benchmark CIO agreement, was the result of the General Motors accord. Lewis had been secretly negotiating with Myron Taylor of U.S. Steel for months. On March 2, SWOC signed a contract with Carnegie-Illinois, the largest U.S. Steel subsidy. The agreement granted the steel workers union recognition, a 10% wage increase, an eight-hour day and a forty-hour week, time and a half for overtime, vacations, and seniority. Within a week of the settlement, 20,000 new union members had joined SWOC and 30 steel companies had agreed to negotiate contracts. Within three months, 140 companies representing 75% of the steel industry had signed union contracts. The UMWJ declared the agreement with U.S. Steel a victory for the CIO and confirmation of Lewis's decision to split with the AFL and to organize based on the principle of industrial unionism. According to the *Journal,* the steel pact was also confirmation of Lewis's stand in favor of centralized union hierarchies headed by "professional" managers who had the experience to find a "logical solution."[56]

55. Preis, *Labor's Giant Step*, 54; *UMWJ* (February 1, 1937); Bernstein, *Turbulent*, 499–529.

56. Preis, *Labor's Giant Step*, 66; *UMWJ* (March 15, 1937): 6; Bernstein, *Turbulent*, 457–73; *UMWJ* (March 15, 1937): 6.

The last two months of 1936 and the first half of 1937 were marked by a string of outstanding CIO triumphs: the FDR reelection victory; the sit-down strike in auto and the ensuing settlement; a steel contract; passage of the Guffey-Vinson bill to provide for a greater federal role in the coal industry; a Senate inquiry on coal-operator abuses in nonunion Harlan County, Kentucky; and a Supreme Court decision upholding the Wagner Act. These were victories for both the CIO and for Lewis personally. On December 31, 1936, in a New Year's Eve radio address to the nation, John L. Lewis spoke with the American people as the leader of the CIO. In his speech, he spoke out for labor's right to bargain collectively and select representatives of its own choosing. Significantly, his message was militant but not radical, and his goal, "industrial democracy," was based on labor-management cooperation.

> Industrial democracy . . . means collective bargaining and fair industrial relations. . . . Employers talk about possible labor trouble interfering with continued expansion and progress of industry. . . . It would be more fitting and accurate to talk about "employer trouble"—that is something from which wage earners are suffering. . . . It is the refusal of employers to grant such reasonable conditions . . . that leads to widespread labor unrest. . . . The sit-down strike is the fruit of mis-management and bad policy towards labor. . . . Huge corporations . . . have no right in a political democracy to withhold the rights of a free people.

Lewis warned industry that after decades of management intransigence, there was a new reality of power in the United States. "The time has passed . . . when the workers can be either clubbed, gassed, or shot down with impunity." In the CIO, and in John L. Lewis, ordinary Americans had a new champion. Lewis proclaimed: "I solemnly warn the leaders of industry that labor will not tolerate such policies or tactics."[57]

John L. Lewis also maintained his belief that obedience to experienced union leadership, was the preferred, if not the only, road to labor's success. An April 15, 1937, editorial in the *UMWJ* reminded union members of their recent accomplishments and contained a veiled warning to rank-and-file coal miners that it would be a mistake for them to join the sit-down strike wave. "The United Mine Workers of America commands the respect and enjoys the confidence of the American public, because its record of forty-seven years of orderly procedure and adherence to contract has earned that respect and confidence" (8).

Conditions for the expansion of the CIO and of John L. Lewis's national political influence, which looked so promising at the beginning of May 1937, increasingly deteriorated over the next four years. A revival of anti-union open-shop forces spearheaded by the "Little Steel" companies, competition from a revived AFL, internal battles between communists and non-communists for influence in CIO unions, a

---

57. *UMWJ* (January 15, 1937): 3.

national economic reversal in 1937 and the rapid growth of Nazi Germany's power in Europe, combined to sweep Lewis and the organization of the mass-production industries off the national center stage. Most of these developments were beyond John L. Lewis's control, but strategic errors by Lewis and the CIO leadership, questionable political judgments by Lewis, disagreements about whether Communist organizers could be relied on or controlled and how to respond to Nazism, and the increasingly acrimonious relationship between Lewis and Roosevelt, combined to worsen a difficult situation. During this period, one of Lewis's underlying strengths, his fundamental conviction that he (and only he) understood and spoke for the miners and the American working class, betrayed him. Were John L. Lewis's decisions during this period the product of an enormous egotism or of self-serving cynicism? Or of insight into long-term political and economic developments that his contemporaries in the labor movement failed to understand? Whichever, his choices during this period contributed to his isolation from former allies and his political eclipse.

The first major CIO setback was in a drive to unionize the smaller steel companies, known collectively as "Little Steel." It was an important campaign for the CIO and the Steel Workers Organizing Committee (SWOC) for a number of reasons. The Little Steel companies owned nonunion "captive" mines that the UMWA wanted organized. Also, a defeat in "Little Steel" would not only stall the growing CIO momentum; it could threaten the U.S. Steel–SWOC agreement. Bethlehem Steel, Republic Steel, Youngstown Sheet and Tube, Inland Steel, and Weirton Steel were well prepared for the strike. They had stockpiled millions of dollars' worth of arms and ammunition in preparation for a war againt SWOC and the CIO. SWOC, led by UMWA Vice President Philip Murray, planned a traditional strike with mass picketing and counted on political support from New Deal Democratic governors and President Roosevelt. A decision was made not to use sit-down strike tactics, which might force elected officials who were being counted on as allies, to distance themselves from the strike. Further, despite its success in auto and rubber, the sit-down strike held potential dangers for SWOC because it shifted control of a strike away from the central union into the hands of the rank-and-file workers occupying the plants. SWOC was run by a centralized bureaucracy organized along the lines of the Lewis-controlled UMWA, a bureaucracy that was not anxious to empower radicals or interested in promoting internal union democracy.

Unfortunately for the steel workers, the leadership of SWOC and the CIO had miscalculated the strength of their political support. The Democratic governor of Ohio used National Guard units and state police to break local strikes. In Johnstown, Pennsylvania, martial law was declared and the steel plants were forcibly reopened. And in the most disturbing development, on Memorial Day, 10 strikers were massacred and 58 were wounded by Chicago police outside the Republic Steel plant. Three weeks after the Memorial Day massacre, President Roosevelt, in response to an appeal from the governor of Ohio, appointed a panel to mediate the dispute. But, after the steel companies rejected a proposed settlement, Roosevelt withdrew the federal government from the controversy. His public remarks at that time suggest the limited amount of support organized labor could actually expect from the Roosevelt administration. FDR told a press conference that a majority of the American people were saying to both parties in the "Little Steel" strike, a "plague on both your houses." The statement infuriated John L. Lewis and contributed to the eventual chasm between him and Roosevelt.[58]

The defeat of the strike in "Little Steel" was one in a series of setbacks for the CIO. The 1937–38 recession ended the economic recovery that had stimulated the growth of CIO unions. By February 1938, the CIO had been forced to suspend its organizing drives in the steel and textile industries. In auto, Henry Ford continued to resist unionization and his private army attacked UAW organizers at the Ford Motor Company's River Rouge plant. Conplicating the efforts to combat Ford, the UAW, which had started out as a coalition of independently based local unions, was weakened by continuing internal divisions. At the same time, a resurgent AFL with larger and better-organized affiliates than the CIO, challenged it in jurisdictional battles. The AFL scored a major victory when David Dubinsky, upset about the prospect of a permanent split in the labor movement and concerned with Lewis's ability to control "communists" who were working for the CIO, led the ILGWU back into the older labor organization.[59]

John L. Lewis responded to some of these setbacks in two important speeches in the summer and fall of 1937. While these speeches were addressed to American workers, they were also aimed at Franklin D. Roosevelt. In them, Lewis challenged Franklin D. Roosevelt to support labor, as labor had supported him; reminding Roosevelt that the "organized workers of America, free in their industrial life, conscious partners in production, secure in their homes and enjoying a decent standard of living will prove the finest bulwark against the intrusion of alien doctrines of government." These speeches are examples of Lewis at his oratorical best. He gives voice to the frustrations of the American working class and the pain and bitterness that arose out of the Memorial Day massacre. However, the speeches also pinpoint a continuing problem in Lewis's view of America and the world. Lewis feels compelled to deny the radicalism of the CIO and, once again, he has no alternative vision to offer working people besides his belief in a more responsive and cooperative capitalism.

In his Labor Day speech, Lewis protested industry's intense and backward resistance to unionization and collective bargaining and government callousness to the plight of workers. He charged: "Five of the corporations in the steel industry elected to resist collective bargaining and undertook to destroy the steel workers' union. These companies filled their plants with industrial spies, assembled depots of guns and gas bombs, established barricades, controlled their communities with armed

58. Preis, *Labor's Giant Step*, 66–72; Zieger, *American Workers*, 48–59; Dubofsky and Van Tine, *Lewis*, 313–15; 407–13; Bernstein, *Turbulent*, 485–97.

59. Zieger, *American Workers*, 55–59; Preis, *Labor's Giant Step*, 72–77; Dubofsky and Van Tine, *Lewis*, 312–23.

thugs, leased the police power of cities and mobilized the military power of a state to guard them against the intrusion of collective bargaining within their plants. . . . In Chicago, Mayor Kelly's police force was successful in killing ten strikers before they could escape the fury of police, shooting eight of them in the back."

Lewis was outraged because "the murder of these unarmed men has never been publicly rebuked by any authoritative officer of the state or federal government" and because the Roosevelt administration, instead of imposing sanctions against the political machine that controlled Chicago, continued to support it with federal patronage. He challenged FDR and the Democratic Party to respond to the needs of organized labor or else face the political consequences, declaring that "labor . . . cannot avoid the necessity of a political assay of the work and deeds of its so-called friends and its political beneficiaries. It must determine who are its friends in the arena of politics as elsewhere."

Lewis concluded with one of the most poignant and oft-quoted passages in the history of American labor. He warned Roosevelt: "Labor, like Israel, has many sorrows. Its women weep for their fallen and they lament for the future of the children of the race. It ill behooves one who has supped at labor's table and who has been sheltered in labor's house to curse with equal fervor and fine impartiality both labor and its adversaries when they become locked in deadly embrace."[60]

The second speech was John L. Lewis's address at the Atlantic City convention of the CIO where it became a permanent organization. After listing the CIO's accomplishments, especially the organizing drive in steel, Lewis challenged FDR to fulfill the promises he made during the 1936 campaign: "The president said . . . that one-third of all Americans were ill-housed, ill-nourished and underfed. . . . What has been done about it so far? Nothing. The last congress adjourned without even enacting that poor, halting wages and hours bill that finally emerged from the committee. . . . Americans cannot eat or live on platitudes or musical phrases—they want buying power—they want shorter hours. Give them buying power and shorter hours and they will improve their economic and their social status."[61]

Roosevelt responded to Lewis's Labor Day speech arguing that both sides had "made mistakes" in the "contest between capital and labor." But Lewis was not prepared to accept a policy of even-handedness. He believed that the CIO brought Roosevelt millions of votes in 1936 and that Roosevelt was reneging on his part of the deal. Lewis, whose "sense of self" was totally interwoven with his position as head of the UMWA and the CIO, was also responding to being personally slighted. Len De Caux, the editor of the CIO newsletter, believed that there was always a measure of personal competition between Lewis and Roosevelt. "Lewis loved to take on the big ones. In Roosevelt he took on the biggest, one who held himself champ in the same sport. Both liked the battle of wits, I'm sure to a point. That point was when either felt outsmarted, outbluffed, or betrayed politically. Then anger

60. *UMWJ* (September 15, 1937): 3.
61. *UMWJ* (November 1, 1937): 14–16.

followed.'' A *New York Times* columnist, discussing the exchange between Lewis and Roosevelt, commented that the two men ''must be considered definitely at 'outs.' ''[62]

Politically, John L. Lewis's biggest problem in the escalating competition with Roosevelt for the support of the American working class was the absence of a viable alternative party that he could use to challenge its loyalty to Roosevelt, the Democratic Party, and the New Deal. While he may have been toying with the idea of a third political party as early as February 1937, during the 1938 midterm election, Lewis had little choice but to contribute large sums of UMWA money to Democratic Party congressional campaigns in an effort to sustain the Labor–New Deal alliance. Later, Lewis used his position as head of the LNPL to sound out possible support for a new party among organizations like the National Farmers' Union, the National Negro Congress and the NAACP. However, their constituencies essentially supported Roosevelt, and whatever interest these groups had in a new party, was dependent on whether FDR sought a third term in 1940.[63]

Complicating the Lewis-FDR split was their disagreement over U.S. involvement in the intensifying European conflict. Lewis opposed Nazism because it was antagonistic to a free labor movement. But he also opposed American involvement in a potential new world war, arguing that war fever detracted from the need to invest in building American institutions. In a speech to an anti-Nazi rally organized by the Jewish Labor Committee in Madison Square Garden in 1937, Lewis told the audience ''that I know of only one means of insuring our safety. . . . [I]f the fate of Germany is to be averted from this nation we must and we shall secure a strong, well organized, disciplined and articulate labor movement.'' While Roosevelt was prepared to abandon the New Deal and to concentrate his efforts on making the United States an ''arsenal of Democracy,'' Lewis was more concerned with an internal threat generated by increasing poverty, political instability, and the archaic policies of open-shop employers.[64]

In the late 1930s, Lewis's opposition to American involvement in a new European war and his willingness to use his official position for personal financial benefit, also involved him in business and political activities that threatened his reputation and increased the tension between him and Roosevelt. Lewis used contacts with the Mexican labor movement and government to help William Rhodes Davis, a Texas entrepreneur, purchase oil for resale to Hitler's Germany. Later, Davis used his business relationship with Lewis to involve him in a German-initiated plan to en-

62. Dubofsky and Van Tine, *Lewis*, 323–25; Len De Caux, *Labor Radical: From the Wobblies to CIO* (Boston: Beacon, 1970), 293–95; *Newsweek* (September 13, 1937) and *New York Times* (September 12, 1937), cited in McFarland, ''Coalition,'' 407.

63. Ross, ''John L. Lewis,'' 160–61; McFarland, ''Coalition,'' 406–11; Preis, *Labor's Giant Step*, 78–81; Dubofsky and Van Tine, *Lewis*, 325–29, 340, 356; Bernstein, *Turbulent*, 699–703; Alinsky, *John L. Lewis*, 168–72.

64. *UMWJ* (April 1, 1937): 10; Ross, ''John L. Lewis,'' 162–63; Dubofsky and Van Tine, *Lewis*, 331–32.

courage the United States government to mediate between England and Germany. The Lewis-Davis connection may have been responsible for Lewis's final decision to break publicly with Roosevelt, and with Roosevelt's supporters in the CIO. Lewis appears to have been investigated by the FBI (including a wiretap on his phone) because of his dealings with Davis and Germany, an intrusion into his personal affairs that Lewis deeply resented. Davis also paid for Lewis's national radio broadcast endorsing Wendell Willkie for president in October 1940. John L. Lewis's relationship with Davis, like his earlier relationships with coal operators and financiers, was at the least, inappropriate. It appears to be another episode where good judgment on Lewis's part was overwhelmed by concern for his personal business interests and his sense of self-importance.[65]

Throughout 1940, Lewis searched for an acceptable alternative to Roosevelt's third-term presidential bid. At the January 1940, fiftieth anniversary UMWA convention, John L. Lewis charged that the "Democratic Party is in default to the American people" and that Roosevelt had "broken faith" with American workers. He introduced Senator Burton Wheeler, an isolationist, as a potential Democratic candidate for president.[66]

John L. Lewis also continued to explore the possibility of creating a third political party. In April 1940, he announced that "in the event that the Democratic party does not nominate a candidate for President, or adopt a platform, satisfactory to labor and the common people of this country, I shall . . . espouse and urge . . . the assembling of a great delegate convention, . . . to meet in some central city and present their views, crystallize their judgment into a program that each and every American can support."[67]

Whenever Lewis spoke out against the broken promises of the Roosevelt administration, he reminded his audience that "My own voice, my own words, would not be listened to in this country . . . unless the people of this country believed that I was speaking for you. . . . You tell me what to do, and with your strength I will carry on, and with your strength we will win." But, in this case, Lewis was not listening to the reaction of his constituency and he was not speaking for them. Neither Senator Wheeler nor the idea of a third party held much appeal for American workers and the majority of the leadership of the CIO once Roosevelt declared himself a candidate for reelection.[68]

Did John L. Lewis really think that Wendell Willkie would win the presidential election when he endorsed him in October 1940? Historians can only speculate about the answer. Lewis should have recognized the pattern of support for Roosevelt amongst the CIO unions and the coal miners in the UMWA. Perhaps his anger at Roosevelt had blinded him, and he was no longer able to see what the American

65. Dubofsky and Van Tine, *Lewis*, 331–32, 345–57; Ross, "John L. Lewis," 162–63.
66. Dubofsky and Van Tine, *Lewis*, 341–45; Preis, *Labor's Giant Step*, 79–81.
67. *UMWJ* (April 15, 1940): 3.
68. Ibid.

workers wanted. Maybe Lewis had experienced too many organizational and personal slights from Roosevelt and the Democrats, including Lewis's own unrealized political ambitions, for him to endorse Roosevelt or to remain silently in the background. It is also conceivable that Lewis, surrounded in his Washington, D.C., office by CIO and UMWA subordinates who were unable or unwilling to tell him what he did not want to hear, had simply grown isolated from the political reality in the country.

Another alternative worth considering is that Lewis really did understand what was happening in the country and that he made a calculated gamble. For a number of reasons, Lewis's unquestioned ability to speak for the CIO was already being eroded. Most of the new CIO unions had developed independent leadership. Longtime Lewis aides, men like Philip Murray and Van Bittner, whom he could generally count on to endorse his decisions, supported Roosevelt's reelection. Sidney Hillman and other top CIO and AFL officials clearly had more influence with the Roosevelt administration than Lewis had and Lewis must have realized that he had had no ability to redirect the nation away from preparation for war with Germany. Only Lewis's authority in the UMWA remained unquestioned and secure.

The same John L. Lewis who had manuevered his way into the UMWA presidency in 1919, had challenged Samuel Gompers for the presidency of the AFL in 1921, and had slugged William Hutcheson at the 1935 AFL convention, may have decided that it was time for another big political move. He had little more to lose if Roosevelt were elected; and if lightning struck, if American workers abandoned Roosevelt to support his call, if Wendell Willkie were elected president, John L. Lewis would be the kingmaker. He would finally have the position of influence and power he believed that he was entitled to and had been denied after the 1936 election.[69]

On October 25, 1940, Lewis delivered a radio address carried on the three hundred stations of the National Broadcasting Company, the Columbia Broadcasting Company, and the Mutual Broadcasting Company. In his speech, John L. Lewis denounced Roosevelt and the New Deal for "thoughtless and sadly executed experimentation" that had not solved the problems of the Great Depression and for unnecessarily "moving the nation towards war." Lewis expressed fear that if "President Roosevelt is re-established in office . . . , he will answer to no man, including Congress, for his executive acts, that may create a dictatorship in this land." He concluded that "the reelection of President Roosevelt for a third term would be a national evil of the first magnitude" because "he no longer hears the cries of the people." Lewis had no other choice but to reject Franklin D. Roosevelt and endorse Wendell Wilkie for president.

At that point in the speech, Lewis could have stopped. He had expressed his opposition to Roosevelt in the sharpest terms possible. But John L. Lewis decided

69. Alinsky, *John L. Lewis*, 185–91; Ross, "John L. Lewis," 161–203; McFarland, "Coalition," 411; Preis, *Labor's Giant Step*, 79–81; Dubofsky and Van Tine, *Lewis*, 339–64; Bernstein, *Turbulent*, 715–20.

to put all of his cards out on the table. He went one step further and announced his intention to resign as president of the CIO if Franklin D. Roosevelt was reelected president of the United States:

> It is obvious that President Roosevelt will not be re-elected for the third term, unless he has the overwhelming support of the men and women of labor. If he is, therefore, re-elected, it will mean that the members of the Congress of Industrial Organizations have rejected my advice and recommendation. I will accept the result as being the equivalent of a vote of no confidence, and will retire as President of the Congress of Industrial Organizations, at its convention in November. This action will save our great movement, composed of millions of men and women, from the embarrassment and handicap of my leadership during the ensuing reign of president Roosevelt. . . . Sustain me now, or repudiate me.[70]

With Roosevelt's reelection, the issue became, Would John L. Lewis really resign?

The December 1, 1940, issue of the *UMWJ* commenting on the third annual CIO convention, simply stated that "Mr. Lewis declared some time ago his intention to retire from the presidency of the CIO, and he carried out his plan." But John L. Lewis's contemporaries in the labor movement were not so certain about his intentions when the next CIO convention opened in November 1940.[71]

In his autobiography, John Brophy suggested that Lewis hoped to be "drafted" by the convention and forced to continue to serve as president of the CIO. Brophy believed that a draft failed to materialize because many in the CIO were relieved to be done with Lewis's "eccentricities" and to establish a more regular operation with Philip Murray as president. Lee Pressman, legal adviser for the CIO, believed that the "draft" Lewis forces were independent of Lewis himself, and that the main problem was that Philip Murray wanted Lewis to remain as president of the CIO. According to Pressman, Murray feared that if he accepted the CIO presidency, Lewis would use Murray's position as a vice president of the UMWA to control him. "Murray . . . knew that Lewis was putting him there as president, expecting him to act as an agent for Lewis." R. J. Thomas, president of the UAW, charged that during the convention he was pressured by UMWA representatives and CIO unionists to support a Lewis draft. Thomas reported that, "I told Lewis his goons were pushing me around and I wasn't going to tolerate it any longer. I said, 'I don't have to tolerate that Mr. Lewis, . . . I don't believe you know this is being done. I come to see you because I know you can stop it.' " According to Thomas, Lewis responded that he was not a candidate for CIO president and that he would stop the activities.[72]

70. *UMWJ* (November 1, 1940): 4–6.

71. *UMWJ* (December 1, 1940): 10–13; Bernstein, *Turbulent*, 723–25; Lichtenstein, *Labor's War*, 32.

72. Brophy, *Miner's*, 285; Lee Pressman, Columbia University Oral History, 1958, 198, 310; R. J. Thomas, Columbia University Oral History Collection, 1958, 190–91.

At the start of the CIO convention, John L. Lewis probably was undecided whether he should hold onto the CIO presidency or not. Lee Pressman, who was a close adviser to Lewis, described him as "the kind of man who could well say to himself, "I'll take my first step, or my second step, and what'll emerge, I don't know yet." If his behavior at prior UMWA, AFL, and CIO conventions can be used as a model, then Lewis went into this convention prepared for a "draft," but willing to make a pragmatic decision after evaluating the tenor of the major delegations.[73]

Three key developments shaped Lewis's final decision at the 1940 convention to give up the CIO presidency. The first was the response from R. J. Thomas, who had secured the presidency of the UAW with support from Lewis and the CIO. Lewis should have been able to count on Thomas's support, but he didn't receive it.

Second, was the deluge of letters that the *UMWJ* received protesting Lewis's endorsement of Willkie. The *UMWJ* (January 1, 1941) responded to the letters: "The Journal does not question the right of these brothers to write any kind of letters they please, nor the right to criticize their elected officers, nor is their sincerity in any way questioned. . . . But what the individuals and local unions who severely criticized President Lewis seem to have overlooked was that he had as much right to freedom of speech as they—the North American right to express his personal political views. And they were personal. Mr. Lewis made that perfectly clear." (9)"

That the *Journal* felt compelled to respond (I cannot find one other example during the entire period discussed in this essay when the *Journal*'s pages were opened up to the opinions of miners or union locals who disagreed with the official position of the union or its leadership), suggests that there was some concern that John L. Lewis's position in the UMWA might even have been in jeopardy.

Lewis's third problem was Sidney Hillman, Roosevelt's major CIO ally, who was ready to provide Lewis with whatever additional shove was necessary to push him out of the CIO presidency. At the convention, while Philip Murray wavered about accepting the presidency and the "draft" Lewis forces were waiting for their opportunity to act, Hillman outmaneuvered Lewis. He came to the podium and announced: "I regret that John L. Lewis will not be the leader of this organization. I know there is nothing else he can do and will do and will agree to do but what he believes to be the best for the organized labor movement. I have great respect for a man who in a crisis stands by his guns. . . . It is my considered judgment that when John L. Lewis steps down there must be a demand for Phil Murray."[74]

Yet, even though Lewis "decided" to give up his official title as president of the CIO, he was clearly not "retiring." In his speech to the convention, Lewis reasserted his claim to be the champion of America's dispossessed and his continuing leadership role in the American labor movement. He spoke out against reconciliation with the AFL and in traditional Lewis-fashion, he ridiculed the intelligence and

73. Pressman, Columbia University Oral History Collection, 105.
74. Bernstein, *Turbulent*, 721–26; Dubofsky and Van Tine, *Lewis*, 364–70.

"manhood" of "Old Lady Green" and those in the CIO who disagreed with him. "Explore the mind of Bill Green?" he asked rhetorically. "Why, Bill and I had offices next door to each other in the same corridor for ten years. I was a member of the same executive council that he was for one year. I have done a lot of exploring in Bill's mind and I give you my word there is nothing there."[75]

Following the 1940 CIO convention, increasing U.S. involvement in wartime preparations, and within a year, war itself, forced the nation and the labor movement to reevaluate possibilities and strategies for the future. For John L. Lewis, the nation's movement toward war meant increasing estrangement from Philip Murray and isolation from power in the CIO. Lewis, who resisted what he felt were FDR's unfairly restrictive labor policies until the point when war was formally declared, found himself threatened with marginalization in the labor movement, a position he was not prepared to accept. To counter it, he eventually reversed his earlier position and proposed that the CIO and AFL reopen merger negotiations. When this did not have the desired impact, Lewis led the UMWA in a nationwide coal strike that challenged organized labor's acceptance of junior partner status in the increasingly cooperative relationship between government bureaucracy and industrial capitalists.

Under Philip Murray's leadership, the CIO began to grow again in the beginning of 1941. A wartime economy, and with it the possibility of wartime profits, helped CIO unions recruit new members and secure contracts in previous bastions of the open shop. A March 1941 strike at Bethlehem Steel ended with victory in National Labor Relations Board (NLRB) elections at Bethlehem, Youngstown, and Republic. An April walkout at Ford's River Rouge plant also ended with victory in a NLRB vote. Lewis participated in this surge as president of the UMWA. In April and May, he led 400,000 bituminous coal miners on a strike that won a dollar-a-day wage increase, paid vacation time, and with support from the northern coal operators, ended the North-South wage differential.[76]

However, by June, deteriorating war news began to shift the balance of power in the CIO away from labor militancy toward increased support for the war effort. In June 1941, the UAW leadership under pressure from the federal government and with Philip Murray's acquiescence, supported the use of federal troops to suppress strikes by communist-led UAW union locals at the North American Aviation plant in California. A key in this changing equation were communist labor organizers, who had originally shared John L. Lewis's position that organized labor should take advantage of the wartime industrial boom to aggressively pursue trade union demands. However, after Germany invaded the Soviet Union on June 22, 1941, Communist militants changed their position and supported forces in the CIO endorsing a pro-war nondisruptive labor policy. In the fall of 1941, communist activists who had supported the UMWA strike in the spring, denounced John L. Lewis for leading

75. *UMWJ* (December 15, 1940): 10.

76. Zieger, *American Workers*, 62–69; Preis, *Labor's Giant Step*, 104–12; Dubofsky and Van Tine, *Lewis*, 390–94.

a strike of 45,000 miners working in the "captive mines." Murray and other UMWA officials active in the CIO, were put in an extremely awkward position by this strike, trapped between their support for Roosevelt's war-preparation policies and their organizational obligation to support the striking miners. Tension mounted between Lewis and Murray as Lewis questioned Murray's loyalty to the UMWA and Murray resented Lewis's interference with the CIO.[77]

The "captive mine" strike began September 14, 1941, was suspended for 30 days while the federal government's National Defense Mediation Board attempted to resolve the dispute, and then resumed on October 25. On September 1, the *Journal* declared: "The United Mine Workers will not accept the defeatist attitude of some weak-kneed union leaders." On October 1, it added that "President Lewis and his co-workers feel . . . that if there ever was a time in American history when it was imperative for labor to assume the aggressive and complete job of organizing American working men that time is now." Franklin Roosevelt disagreed and appealed to Lewis to cancel the strike because "in this crisis of our national life there must be uninterrupted production of coal." Lewis demanded that FDR put the same pressure on industry: "If you would use the power of the state to restrain me, as an agent of labor, then sir, I submit that you should use that same power to restrain my adversary in this issue, who is an agent of capital." Faced with a threat of military intervention in the mines, the UMWA stood its ground and Lewis responded: "If the soldiers come, the mineworkers will remain peacefully in their homes, conscious of the fact that bayonets in coal mines will not produce coal." The troops did not come and the strike continued intermittently during the month of November 1941. Finally, the Roosevelt administration agreed to appoint a three-member arbitration board that approved a union shop in the "captive mines" by a 2-1 vote. The board's decision was announced on Pearl Harbor Day, December 7, 1941.[78]

On December 16, following a formal declaration of war and a weeklong labor and industry conference in Washington, D.C., Philip Murray, John L. Lewis, and James Emspak of United Electrical, Radio, and Machine Workers of America (UE), representing the CIO, agreed to a "no-strike" pledge for the duration of the war. As part of the pact, the CIO, the AFL, and industrial representatives, agreed to act in conjunction with a National War Labor Board to mediate all disputes.[79]

The UMWA accepted the wartime "no-strike" pledge. In the *Journal* (January 1, 1942) an editor's note declared that "the President's [President Roosevelt's] letter represents a guarantee, . . . by which American labor can be assured of the preservation of its rights as prescribed under American law. Labor always has been willing to do its part in any hour of peril; now that we have an understandable labor code, by which labor can seek redress from managerial stupidity and arrogance, it be-

77. Pressman, Columbia University Oral History Collection, 201–3; 315; Zieger, *American Workers*, 71–74; Lichtenstein, *Labor's War*, 59–62; Preis, *Labor's Giant Step*, 127–31; Davis, *Prisoners*, 73–77.

78. *UMWJ* (September 1, 1941); Preis, *Labor's Giant Step*, 127–31; Lichtenstein, *Labor's War*, 69–70; Dubofsky and Van Tine, *Lewis*, 397–404.

79. Preis, *Labor's Giant Step*, 147–48; Zieger, *American Workers*, 74–76.

hooves labor leaders everywhere to conform to the tenets of the program and refrain from agitating or promoting any work stoppages whatsoever'' (3).

The "no-strike" pledge, which was signed by Murray and Lewis for the CIO and William Green, Matthew Woll, George Meany, and Daniel Tobin, for the AFL, may have suggested the possibility of long-term government-sponsored labor unity growing out of wartime cooperation between the two labor organizations and among their internal factions. But it proved to be a very ephemeral truce. Hopes for labor unity died with a nasty battle between Lewis and Murray. In January 1942, Lewis, who remained chair of the CIO's inactive peace committee despite his resignation as CIO president, wrote to William Green and Philip Murray, calling for a resumption of unity negotiations between the CIO and the AFL. Murray and the other members of the CIO Executive Board believed that Lewis was promoting a merger hoping that he would emerge as the head of a new unified labor federation. The CIO's official response to the letters was that Lewis was unauthorized to make the overture to the AFL and Murray requested that Lewis, who had resigned from the CIO Executive Board, attend a meeting to explain his actions. Lewis, who refused to appear before the board, answered that he had acted in accord with a 1939 CIO convention mandate and recommended that the Executive Board "call a special convention to take up the question." Neither Franklin Roosevelt nor Murray wanted Lewis to emerge as the leader of a new united federation. They circumvented his proposal with an alternative presidential initiative that established a Labor Victory Council designed to maintain the status quo between the AFL and CIO until the end of the war.[80]

The dispute between Lewis and Murray escalated from this point. UMWA District 50, whose secretary-treasurer was John L. Lewis's daughter Kathryn, had made organizing inroads in jurisdictions claimed by the UAW and the United Rubber Workers' union. When they protested to the CIO, District 50 demanded that Murray, still a UMWA vice president, answer charges before the UMWA International Executive Board that CIO and UAW officials had attacked the UMWA and John L. Lewis at a UAW Executive Board meeting and that the content of the attacks had been leaked to the press. The *Journal* called on Murray to respond to the accusations and printed statements by "outraged" UMWA personnel who were quitting CIO committees in protest against these "attacks."[81]

Philip Murray attempted to calm the UMWA assault on the CIO, writing that he was "[p]erfectly aware of the completely unassailable record of the UMWA. . . . There is no one who deplores more than I do inflammatory statements designed to discredit leaders of our union or cause disunity within the ranks of our organization." In an effort to prevent a split with the union he had worked for for his entire adult life, Murray made the requested appearance before the UMWA International

---

80. *UMWJ* (February 1, 1942): 3; Dubofsky and Van Tine, *Lewis*, 405–12; Preis, *Labor's Giant Step*, 125–32.

81. *UMWJ* (April 15, 1942): 4; Lichtenstein, *Labor's War*, 161–62.

Executive Board and praised Lewis's leadership role in the labor movement. But Lewis was not to be assuaged. Philip Murray's acceptance of the presidency of the United Steel Workers Union was declared a violation of the UMWA constitution, and "the international executive board declared the office of vice-president of the international union vacant." With Murray's banishment, the UMWA also lost Lewis lieutenants Allan Haywood, Van Bittner, Clint Golden, Pat Fagan, William Mitch, and David McDonald, who opted to remain with Murray and the CIO.[82]

The fight between Lewis and Murray precipitated the UMWA's withdrawal from the CIO. The UMWA IEB "[c]ondemned the actions and attitude of the Congress of Industrial Organizations against the UMWA as represented by its officials, employes [sic], agents and representatives," and "[a]uthorized the withholding of cash payments of per capita tax to CIO until such time as the CIO validated loans owed the UMWA totaling $1,665,000." On October 7, 1942, the UMWA Convention voted 2,867 to 5 to leave the CIO because it had reneged on loans from the UMWA and had slandered John L. Lewis's patriotism. Following this decision, the UMWA expanded its organizing budget for District 50 as a potential independent alternative to the CIO and it began to explore the possibility of reaffiliating with the AFL.[83]

As a result of organized labor's "no-strike pledge" and broad public support as the United States entered the war, there were only 2,968 strikes involving 840,000 workers in 1942, a steep decline from 4,288 strikes involving more than 2.3 million workers in 1941. The UMWA joined the rest of the labor movement in exhorting its members to aid the war effort and to set new production records. On July 15, 1942, the *Journal* declared: "We must produce more coal, we must buy more bonds, we must cooperate and do everything possible to contribute to victory for the Allied nations. Because this is a war for survival, we cannot, we must not at any time content ourselves with the thought that we may be doing our part; we must constantly strive to do more" (3).[84]

But the United Mine Workers of America, the American Federation of Labor, and the Congress of Industrial Organizations still had to grapple with the dilemma of whether it was possible to both support the war effort and at the same time defend, or perhaps even extend, the rights of unions and workers. After the initial exhilaration, rank-and-file workers, squeezed between wartime price inflation, government restrictions on wage increases, and "patriotic" business leaders, always willing to enforce limits on labor while they raked in guaranteed profits, began to ignore government officials and union leadership and challenge the "no-strike pledge." In 1943, there were 3,700 strikes involving nearly two million workers and three times

82. *UMWJ* (May 1, 1942): 5; Preis, *Labor's Giant Step*, 168–73; *UMWJ* (June 1, 1942): 9; Dubofsky and Van Tine, *Lewis*, 409–12.

83. *UMWJ* (July 15, 1942): 3; Preis, *Labor's Giant Step*, 169–73; Lichtenstein, *Labor's War*, 161–62; Dubofsky and Van Tine, *Lewis*, 412–14.

84. Zieger, *American Workers*, 85–90; United States Department of Commerce, Bureau of the Census. *Historical Statistics of the United States*, 93d Congress, 1st Session, House Document No. 93-78 (Part 1) D 970-985 (Washington, D.C.: 1975), 179.

the number of idle man-hours. In 1944, over 2 million workers participated in 5,000 strikes and in 1945, almost 3.5 million workers struck. This new rank-and-file upsurge gave John L. Lewis one more opportunity to become the leading figure in the American labor movement.[85]

In January 1942, President Roosevelt established the National War Labor Board, a twelve-member tripartite board equally divided between labor, government, and business representatives, to promote and review settlements between labor and industry under the parameters of the "no-strike" pledge. On July 16, 1942, the NWLB announced what came to be known as the "Little Steel Formula" in a case involving a wage settlement for half-a-million steel workers. Under this decision, wartime wage increases were limited to the rate of inflation from January 1941 through May 1942, which was approximately 15%. While labor protested that this locked most industrial workers into prewar Depression-era standards of living, the "Little Steel Formula" became the basis for all wartime wage settlements. For bituminous coal miners who had received a 16% increase in spring 1941, the NWLB decision meant a wage freeze for the duration of the war.

Despite increasing rank-and-file unhappiness with government regulatory policies, the AFL and CIO were committed to cooperation with government and industry for the duration of the war and their leaders refrained from publicly condemning NWLB decisions. John L. Lewis, while critical of a federal policy "that runs to the premise of rewarding and fattening industry and starving labor," was also trapped by an unwillingness to violate the UMWA's "no-strike pledge" and the political difficulties inherent in challenging government rulings during a time of war. However, a wildcat strike by 20,000 Pennsylvania anthracite miners in December 1942, created an opening for an effective UMWA challenge to the injustice of the "Little Steel Formula" and the incompetence of what the UMWA *Journal* characterized as the federal "burrocracy."[86]

The anthracite strike was initially precipitated by a 50% hike in UMWA dues and was led by anti-Lewis insurgents. In the past, John L. Lewis would have quickly moved to squash the opposition, declaring the strikers dual unionists or Communists and banishing their leaders from the union. But this time, while Lewis called for an end to the work stoppage and declared it an unauthorized strike because it violated the union's contract, he moderated the union's response to the dissidents. He held off threatening them with loss of UMWA membership for a month, publicly sympathized with the plight of their families, and did not attack them for either undermining the war effort or for breaking the "no-strike" pledge. The anthracite wildcat gave John L. Lewis the opportunity to gauge the willingness of rank-and-file workers to challenge the expanding wartime power of the federal government. It convinced him that with the expiration of the UMWA contract in March 1943, he would

85. Zieger, *American Workers*, 85–90; Preis, *Labor's Giant Step*, 161.

86. Zieger, *American Worker*, 87–96; Dubofsky and Van Tine, *Lewis*, 415–21; *UMWJ* (March 15, 1943): 18; (June 1, 1943): 17.

be able to lead the entire UMWA out on strike, reasserting the rights of organized labor and challenging Roosevelt, the NWLB, the coal operators, and the AFL and CIO, all with one grand gesture.[87]

In March 1943, the UMWA opened negotiations for a new bituminous coal contract with a frontal assault on operators "who smugly hope the government will chastise the mine worker for daring to make known the miserable facts of his existence" and on the NWLB and the Roosevelt administration for pursuing policies that "inflame the workers in industries who know that their rights are being withheld from them by this strange combination of government and industry." The union's basic demands, "portal to portal" pay and a $2-a-day raise were clearly in excess of the "Little Steel Formula." But, according to Lewis, the demands were justified because: "The coal miners of America are hungry. They are ill-fed and undernourished below the standards of their neighbors and other citizens. . . . I am quite sure that the Little Steel Formula has outlived its usefulness and it is not going to last too long. It can't last because it is so viciously unfair. It seeks to deny labor what the government gives to industry, namely, the cost of living plus a profit."[88]

For his aggressive stance, Lewis was ordered to appear before Senator Harry Truman's Senate War Investigating Committee and was vilified in the press. An editorial in the *New York Herald Tribune* demanded that "[t]he government of the United States . . . has got to do something about John L. Lewis." There is also evidence that under Roosevelt's orders, the Justice Department explored ways to indict Lewis.[89]

As the crisis in coal came to a head, the UMWA charged that the NWLB, not the UMWA, had violated the "no-strike" pledge. "Labor representatives did not agree to accept any set formula, nor arbitrary method, upon which mass production adjudication of labor controversies could be handled . . . did not agree to suspend nor waive labor's right to pursue and enjoy collective bargaining . . . did not agree to vest power in a tribunal to usurp and set aside the statutory labor laws of the nation and the separate states." The union also accused the NWLB of pursuing a vindictive policy specifically intended to crush the mine workers' union and "get Lewis."[90]

The operators' strategy, at this point, was to refuse negotiation of any new contract that would violate federal regulations. According to Charles O'Neill, a former UMWA official who represented District 2 operators: "We of course, rejected these on the grounds of the "Little Steel" formula. . . . It would have to be subject, in our

87. Dubofsky and Van Tine, *Lewis*, 421–40; Preis, *Labor's Giant Step*, 174–97; Lichtenstein, *Labor's War*, 157–60; *UMWJ* (January 15, 1943): 3; Zieger, *John L. Lewis*, 132–38; *UMWJ* (February 1, 1943): 5.

88. *UMWJ* (March 15, 1943): 9; Preis, *Labor's Giant Step*, 177; Dubofsky and Van Tine, *Lewis*, 421–24.

89. Dubofsky and Van Tine, *Lewis*, 417–19, 424–25; Zieger, *American Workers*, 94–96; Preis, *Labor's Giant Step*, 178–79, 193.

90. *UMWJ* (May 15, 1943): 3.

opinion, to the War Labor Board and its approval. So this demand for $2 a day has been rejected generally by the operators ever since the conference started.''[91]

Meanwhile, the NWLB's position was that it was obligated to enforce President Roosevelt's April 8, "Hold-the-Line," executive decree, placing wages under sweeping controls. Its representatives argued that ''a successful defiance of the War Labor Board by any employer or union, large or small, would endanger the continuance of the 'no strike, no walkout' war time labor policy." On May 1, 1943, the NWLB suspended hearings on the UMWA's wage demands because 60,000 miners were already out on strike. The board refused to consider ''any cases when strikes, walkouts or lockouts are in progress.''

The coal miners started to walk out in wildcat strikes in western Pennsylvania (District 5) and in Alabama on April 24. By April 28, 41,000 bituminous coal miners were out on strike. From April through November 1943, John L. Lewis led the UMWA in a series of brief strikes that challenged the authority of the NWLB and forced President Roosevelt to nationalize the mines to ensure wartime operation. Lewis realized that the general public would turn against the union, but he gambled that the miners would win support from disaffected workers in the mass-production industries, forcing the leaders of the AFL and the CIO to actively challenge the ''Little Steel Formula'' in order to maintain their legitimacy. A unified labor movement, under the leadership of John L. Lewis and the UMWA, would then be in a position to force the Roosevelt administration to abandon the NWLB, the "Little Steel Formula,'' and its exclusive wartime alliance with the industrial capitalists. Major wildcats did in fact sweep Detroit and Akron in conjunction with UMWA strikes.

The UMWA's strike plans were contingent on Lewis's unquestioned control over the UMWA rank and file. But in June, union discipline began to break down and an increasing number of striking miners refused to return to work. During the summer and early fall months, the strike was put in abeyance while the U.S. flag flew over the mines and the federal government, acting through the operating companies, maintained nominal control over the coalfields. Federal intervention gave John L. Lewis the opportunity to reestablish control over the union and to try to work the kind of negotiating and public relations magic that had helped the CIO secure contracts in auto and steel in 1937. Lewis targeted Secretary of the Interior and Solid Fuel's Administrator Harold Ickes, whom Roosevelt had placed in charge of the seized mines, and appealed to him to intervene in the negotiations between the operators and the union and to enforce a negotiated agreement over the head of the NWLB. However, Roosevelt denied Ickes authorization.

In October, the UMWA leadership began to lose control over the rank-and-file miners again. By October 16, there were approximately 90,000 illegal strikers. On November 1, the entire industry was closed down and Roosevelt seized the mines again. This time, he instructed Ickes to enter the negotiations. Perhaps because both

91. *UMWJ* (April 1, 1943): 3.

Lewis and Roosevelt feared that the strike was getting out of control, a settlement was reached and it was approved by the NWLB.[92]

The prolonged battle in the bituminous coalfields produced mixed results at best for John L. Lewis, the UMWA, and the American labor movement. While the government could not mine coal with bayonets, the strikes showed that it didn't have to. The overdevelopment of coal resources and the availability of alternative fuels that had plagued the industry and the union since the end of World War I, coupled with record production preceding the strikes, meant that the UMWA was not in a position to affect the war effort severely. This suggests that the media attention to Lewis and the attacks on his patriotism and the union's, were products of conservative political propaganda rather than of any actual threat to national security. A conservative political upswing was already apparent in the results of the 1942 congressional elections. The bituminous coal strikes made Lewis and the UMWA convenient targets, and gave the conservative forces the ability to override a Roosevelt veto and pass the Smith-Connally War Labor Disputes Act in June 1943. Among its provisions, the War Labor Disputes Act authorized the NWLB to make binding decisions in labor disputes, confirmed the president's wartime power to seize essential industries threatened by strikes, and established criminal penalties for strikers and union leaders.[93]

The militant UMWA response to the NWLB did have the desired effect of forcing the AFL and CIO into public vocal criticisms of the "Little Steel Formula" and wartime federal labor policies. However, too many fights had taken place between former coal miners William Green, Philip Murray, John L. Lewis, and their various assistants and associates, for labor unity under Lewis's leadership ever to be a real possibility. The merger of the AFL and CIO awaited the emergence of a new generation of top labor leaders somewhat distanced from these long-term bitter personal battles.

For the miners striving to make a living in the bituminous coalfields, the strikes also had mixed results. It is difficult to calculate what individual miners actually earned, factoring in travel, overtime, and expenses. *The New York Times* headline reported, "Coal Strike Called Off as Ickes Grants Lewis $1.50 a Day Rise in Pay," and this was echoed in most of the national press. But according to economist Colston W. Warne, the miner's average weekly wage only rose from $54.50 under the 1941 contract to $57.06, an increase of less than 5%. This was considerably less than the union's initial demands, and most of the raise resulted from a negotiated extension to the workday. To secure it, the miners had to pay the hefty price of alienation from the nation and continued isolation from the rest of the organized labor movement.[94]

92. Lichtenstein, *Labor's War*, 163–69; Preis, *Labor's Giant Step*, 180–90, 193–96; Dubofsky and Van Tine, *Lewis*, 427–36; Zieger, *American Workers*, 91; Zieger, *John L. Lewis*, 138–49.

93. Dubofsky and Van Tine, *Lewis* 432; Zieger, *American Workers*, 97–99.

94. Colston Warne, "Coal—The First Major Test of the Little Steel Formula," in Colston Warne et al., *Yearbook of American Labor*, vol. 1, *War Labor Policies* (New York, 1945), 298, cited in Dubofsky

Life magazine gave some real sense of that "price" in a photo essay on the Nanty Glo, Pennsylvania, coal miners. After reporting somewhat sympathetically on the living and working conditions faced by the miners and their families, the story attacked the strike whose "international significance . . . was not lost on the Axis": "On May Day, which for Lewis was showdown day, most miners stopped work, preferring to take orders from the president of the union than from the President of the U.S. As they confusedly obeyed Lewis, the miners did not realize that his disruptive tactics were serving only to turn the whole country against labor, start a congressional stampede for more stringent curbs on labor's rights."[95]

In evaluating the life of John L. Lewis and his impact on the UMWA, the CIO, and the American labor movement, it is useful to make three important distinctions; distinctions among John L. Lewis, the man with personal goals and ambitions; John L. Lewis the president of the United Mine Workers of America; and John L. Lewis, the leader and symbol of a broader American labor movement.

First, as an individual, John L. Lewis was committed to the possibilities inherent in the American capitalist system and viewed himself as a model Horatio Alger, entitled to the position and affluence he earned through intelligence, ruthlessness, and hard work. In 1928, while the United Mine Workers union and America's coal miners were suffering from a nearly decade long collapse of the industry, Lewis endorsed Herbert Hoover, the Republican candidate for president, with the claim: "We are in the midst of a new industrial revolution that has become the marvel of the civilized world. . . . The fundamental objective thus made possible is a constant gain in the living standards of people and the ultimate possibility of the elimination of poverty itself."[96]

In 1938, Lewis told coal miners attending the nation's biannual convention that the United Mine Workers "stands for the proposition that the heads of families shall have sufficient income to educate . . . these sons and daughters of our people, and they go forth when given that opportunity for education, they become scientists and great clergymen in the church, great lawyers, great statesmen, doing their part in the world of affairs." In the speech, Lewis took great pride that many former members of the UMWA had succeeded as businessmen.[97]

According to one contemporary commentator, Lewis's identification as a self-made man was an important element of his appeal to coal miners and other American workers. Louis Adamic believed that Lewis represented the "instinct and im-

and Van Tine, *Lewis*, 439; *UMWA* (June 1, 1943), 10; Lichtenstein, *Labor's War*, 157–60; Zieger, *American Workers*, 95–96; Preis, *Labor's Giant Step*, 177–79; Dubofsky and Van Tine, *Lewis*, 435–40; Wechsler, *Labor Baron*, 249–52.

95. "U.S. Takes Over the Coal Mines," *Life* 14, no. 19 (May 10, 1943): 25.

96. "Hoover's Tonic Safest For Industry" (1928), printed by the Republican State Executive Committee, Charleston, West Virginia, UMWA Papers.

97. United Mine Workers of America, *Proceedings of the 35th Convention* (Washington, D.C., 1938), 2:172; Dubofsky and Van Tine, *Labor Leaders*, 203.

pulse to improve themselves, to get on, to acquire the material symbols of well-being, power, and progress that are the chief contemporary elements of the American 'Dream.' ''[98]

John L. Lewis was always supremely confident in his own abilities, especially in his political judgment of the miners and of the American working class. This confidence was both the source of his genius and his Achilles' heel. It propelled him into action when others remained immobile and it at times blinded him to realities he did not want to see.

Lewis's speeches, reported on and reprinted in the *UMWJ* throughout this period, give a sense of how he worked. John L. Lewis was constantly on stage, using words as tools for achieving specific goals at particular times. It made little difference which of his advisers (speeches were generally written by UMWA economic adviser W. Jett Lauck or *Journal* editors Ellis Searles and K. C. Adams) wrote a particular speech. The speeches were not intended to reveal consistent ideology or to explore long-term strategy. Lewis's interest was short-term effect and his speeches were spiced with carefully chosen biblical allusions, Shakespearean references, and pungent insults that impressed and entertained his audiences and helped him make his points. The speeches show John L. Lewis as a politician, not a philosopher, as a labor union "entrepreneur," not a visionary leader with a broader conception of society. Lewis knew that he could always change his words and positions when it suited him. Perhaps that is one of the reasons that John Walker, Samuel Gompers, John Brophy, William Green, and Philip Murray, eventually grew to dislike him. John L. Lewis was a powerful orator and a powerful man, but too often, Lewis's primary loyalty, his broader purpose, appears to have been self-advancement, personal aggrandizement, and power.

Second, John L. Lewis rarely distinguished between himself as an individual and his position as president of the United Mine Workers of America. He claimed to understand and embody the collective will of the coal miners because "I am one of them." Lee Pressman recognized this quality in Lewis, commenting: "To contemplate him being aware of somebody else's power or influence over the organization that he had given birth to [in this case the CIO]—that's something you just don't contemplate. I mean, it would be like talking to him about the atmosphere on Mars."[99]

Throughout this period, John L. Lewis claimed that the requirements of leadership, the nature of the coal industry, and his personal identification with the miner, entitled him to rule his personal union with an iron hand. While he argued at UMWA conventions that "We have more democracy in the United Mine Workers of America than any other labor organization I know," Lewis's conception of democracy permitted him, as the president of the union, to deny autonomy to UMWA districts, to use International Union organizers to impose central decisions on the union's

98. Adamic, *My America*, 388.
99. UMWA, *Lewis*, 248. Pressman, Columbia University Oral History Collection, 170–71.

membership, to rig election results, and to suppress dissidents by branding them as Communists and barring them from the UMWA as dual unionists.[100]

Sometimes, as in the 1920s, Lewis's personal stubbornness in upholding a failing strategy and vindictiveness toward those who disagreed with him, contributed to the crippling of the union. Sometimes, as in the period from 1933 to 1943, Lewis's ability to understand the aspirations of coal miners and to personalize them, helped the union to grow and influenced the entire labor movement. But, even in these periods, Lewis's determination to control the entire structure of the union, saddled the UMWA with a corrupt and autocratic political machine that rank-and-file miners and democratic union leaders had to battle against for decades.[101]

Third, John L. Lewis was both the leader of, and the larger-than-life symbol of, the emerging American working class and industrial unionism during the turbulent years of the 1930s and early 1940s. Cecil Carnes subtitled his 1936 biography of Lewis, "Leader of Labor." James Wechsler called his 1944 biography, "Labor Baron." In *My America* (1938), Louis Adamic described the John L. Lewis that he saw:

> "Big" is one of the first words that tumble into any description of the exterior of John L. Lewis. He weighs in the vicinity of 230 pounds, but although in his late fifties, . . . he has little excess flesh about him. . . . Lewis' head is the most impressive affair I have ever seen on top of a man's neck. No photograph, drawing or painting of him that has come to my notice renders it entire justice. . . . The face holds just a hint of incongruity. Above the nose it is the face of a philosopher, a brooder; below, that of a fighter, a man of action. The two are not fused or integrated. The fighter dominates the brooder.[102]

This John L. Lewis dwarfed his contemporaries. In a public opinion poll conducted in 1942, 43 percent of the public interviewed could identify American Federation of Labor President William Green, 24 percent could identify Congress of Industrial Organization President Philip Murray, but 63 percent knew who John L. Lewis was. However, name recognition does not always translate into popularity. In a 1941 public opinion poll, five times as many people disapproved of Lewis as approved of him and a *Fortune* magazine article identified him as the nation's most common "bad-man symbol." John Brophy, who was the first director of the CIO, claims that the public's love-hate affair with Lewis was initially no accident, but was the result of a decision by the early CIO leadership to "emphasize Lewis'

100. UMWA, *Lewis*, 245. Lewis's treatment of union dissidents is described by John Brophy in *Miner's*, passim.

101. Finley, *Corrupt Kingdom*; Dubofsky and Van Tine, *Lewis*, 518–29; Brit Hume, *Death and the Mines* (New York: Grossman, 1971).

102. Adamic, *My America*, 385–86.

presence, and to center the activities around his personality, because he was very much in the public press at the time."[103]

But whatever the reason for the close identification of John L. Lewis and the labor movement during the 1930s and 1940s, it was real. For many miners, and for much of the general public, John L. Lewis *was* the UMWA (and the CIO). *Life* magazine captured that connection during the 1943 wartime bituminous coal miners' strike, when it reported on Nanty Glo, Pennsylvania, miners. *Life* interviewed Steve Mutzko, the head of one of the area's union locals, who explained: "No matter what the Government said, we have to follow Mr. Lewis." Coal miner Mabrey Evans, whose 21-year-old son was in the army, added, "If John Lewis says no work, then it's no work for me."[104]

As the symbol of the labor movement, John L. Lewis was the target for those who wanted it destroyed or humbled. But, if they believed that he could dictate to industrial workers in the CIO or the coal miners, they were mistaken. During the 1930s and 1940s, his impact expanded when he was able to express the long-pent-up aspirations of the American working class and helped to mobilize workers through the CIO, new industrial unions, and Labor's Non-Partisan League. However, as John L. Lewis painfully discovered in 1940 when he failed in a yearlong attempt to draw labor support away from FDR's third-term effort, he could not take American workers where they did not want to go.

John L. Lewis was at his best as a labor leader when he understood the demands, needs, and aspirations of American workers and when these coincided with his personal goals. From 1933 to 1937 and in 1943, rank-and-file coal miners and other American workers were stirred to action by the Great Depression, by political upheavals, by a sense of injustice and possibility, and by their own early labor union experiences. John L. Lewis did not create these upsurges nor could he control them. But Lewis did marshal his considerable talents to stimulate, direct, and channel them into permanent labor organizations. In these periods, Lewis articulated labor's demands and spoke for American workers, but coal miners and other workers were the force behind the hurricane.

John L. Lewis was at his worst when his personal goals and aspirations conflicted with the hopes and struggles of the people he was pledged to represent and when he stubbornly tried to force the miners and organized labor to bend to his will. The Lewis who championed the auto workers in Flint, Michigan, in January 1937, was the same man who blacklisted UMWA opponents as Communists and dual unionists throughout the 1920s and early 1930s, who negotiated sweetheart contracts with favored coal operators, and who supported Republican Party administrations while the UMWA was being decimated by open-shop forces. It was the same man who sabotaged coal strikes, who sacrificed large numbers of coal miners in 1919, 1922,

103. C. Wright Mills, *The New Men of Power* (New York: Harcourt, Brace, 1948), 44; Wechsler, *Labor Baron*, 1; Brophy, Columbia University Oral History Collection, 595–96.

104. "U.S. Takes Over the Coal Mines," *Life* 14, no. 19 (May 10, 1943): 23–29.

and 1924 to secure contracts that solidified his hold over the International machinery of the UMWA, who tried to lead organized labor into the Republican Party in 1940, and who split the CIO when other labor leaders were not prepared to follow his dictates.

There is an element of egotism in John L. Lewis's intense personification of his union and his belief that he and only he spoke for the miners, but it is a mistake just to dismiss this as ego. His equating of self and the miners, of Lewis and the UMWA (or the CIO) is at the root of his creativity, his insight, and of his blindness. It is what gave him his power and made him "something of a man."

GUIDE TO FURTHER READING ON JOHN L. LEWIS

Biographies

Alinsky, Saul. *John L. Lewis: An Unauthorized Biography*. New York: Vintage, 1970.

Carnes, Cecil. *John L. Lewis: Leader of Labor*. New York: Robert Speller, 1936.

Dubofsky, Melvyn, and Warren Van Tine. "John L. Lewis and the Triumph of Mass-Production Unionism." In *Labor Leaders in America*, edited by Melvyn Dubofsky and Warren Van Tine. Urbana: University of Illinois Press, 1987.

———, eds. *Labor Leaders in America*. Urbana: University of Illinois Press, 1987.

Fine, Sidney. "John L. Lewis Discusses the General Motors Sit-Down Strike: A Document." *Labor History* 15, no. 4 (fall 1974): 563.

McFarland, C. K. *Roosevelt, Lewis, and the New Deal, 1933–1940*. Fort Worth: Texas Christian University Press, 1970.

Ross, Hugh. "John L. Lewis and the Election of 1940." *Labor History* 17, no. 2 (spring 1976): 160–90.

Sulzberger, C. L. *Sit-Down with John L. Lewis*. New York: Random House. 1938.

Wechsler, James. *Labor Baron: A Portrait of John L. Lewis*. New York: William Morrow, 1944.

Zieger, Robert. *John L. Lewis, Labor Leader*. Boston: Twayne, 1988.

Historical Studies

Adamic, Louis. *My America*. New York: Harper and Bros., 1938.

Bernstein, Irving. *The Lean Years: A History of the American Worker, 1920–1933*. Baltimore: Penguin, 1960, 1966.

———. *Turbulent Years: A History of the American Worker, 1933–1941*. Boston: Houghton Mifflin, 1971.

Cochran, Bert. *Labor and Communism: The Conflict that Shaped American Unions*. Princeton: Princeton University Press, 1977.

Coleman, McAllister. *Men and Coal*. New York: Farrar and Rinehart, 1943.

Davis, Mike. *Prisoners of the American Dream: Politics and Economy in the History of the U.S. Working Class*. New York: Verso, 1986.

Everling, A. Clark. "Tactics Over Strategy in the United Mine Workers of America: Internal Politics and the Question of Nationalization of the Mines, 1908–1923." Ph.D. dissertation, Pennsylvania State University, 1976.

Finley, Joseph. *The Corrupt Kingdom: The Rise and Fall of the United Mine Workers*. New York: Simon and Schuster, 1972.

Lichtenstein, Nelson. *Labor's War at Home: The CIO in World War II*. Cambridge: Cambridge University Press, 1982.

Minton, Bruce, and John Stuart. *Men Who Lead Labor*. New York: Modern Age, 1937.

Preis, Art. *Labor's Giant Step: Twenty Years of the CIO*. New York: Pathfinder, 1964, 1972.

Singer, Alan. "Which Side Are You On? Ideological Conflict in the United Mine Workers of America, 1919–1928." Ph.D. dissertation, Rutgers University, 1982.

United Mine Workers of America. *John L. Lewis and the International, United Mine Workers of America: The Story from 1917 to 1952*. Edited by Rex Lauch. Washington, D.C., 1952.

Wickersham, Edward. "Opposition to the International Officers of the United Mine Workers of America, 1919–1933." Ph.D. dissertation, Cornell University, 1951.

Zieger, Robert. *American Workers, American Unions, 1920–1985*. Baltimore: Johns Hopkins University Press, 1986.

———. *Republicans and Labor, 1919–1929*. Lexington: University Press of Kentucky Press, 1969.

CHAPTER SIX

JOHN L. LEWIS AND THE LABOR MOVEMENT, 1940–1960

ROBERT H. ZIEGER

During the last twenty years of his leadership of the UMW, John L. Lewis was an active and often incisive critic of the mainstream labor movement. At the same time, however, his own increasingly feckless and authoritarian stewardship of the UMW undermined his credibility and detracted attention from his analysis of organized labor's dilemmas in the age of the national security state. Lewis's pronouncements about the labor movement's course were vivid and scathing, but, especially after World War II, the shrinkage of the UMW's membership and the union's increasingly scandalous internal affairs blunted their impact. Not until a new generation of labor activists and observers emerged in the 1960s and 1970s did the Lewis critique gain the serious attention it merited.[1]

It was in this period that the UMW's formal association with the House of Labor took on the form that prevailed until 1989. Following his October 1940 blockbuster

---

1. The definitive biography of Lewis is Melvyn Dubofsky and Warren Van Tine, *John L. Lewis: A Biography* (New York: Quadrangle, 1977). Some material in this paper is taken from a more recent work, Robert H. Zieger, *John L. Lewis: Labor Leader* (Boston: Twayne, 1988).

endorsement of Wendell Willkie, Lewis stepped down from the CIO presidency in December 1940 in favor of his long-term associate, Philip Murray. For the next two years, tensions between the UMW and the CIO tightened. In 1942, the UMW delivered a staggering bill of more than $1.6 million to the CIO, representing, Lewis claimed, loans advanced to the industrial union federation in its infancy. Amid UMW complaints that the CIO was not supporting mine workers' organizing initiatives launched through the recently revitalized District 50 and the United Construction Workers, the mine workers ceased payment of per capita tax to the CIO. UMW and CIO operatives struggled for control of state and local industrial union councils. In mid-1942, the UMW, which had launched the CIO seven years earlier, severed its relationship completely. Until 1989, with the exception of a brief reaffiliation with the AFL in 1946–47, the UMW remained outside the House of Labor.[2]

The UMW's breaks with the CIO in 1941–42 and the AFL in 1947 were not gentlemanly affairs. In each case, some of John L. Lewis's most scathing rhetoric and disdainful attacks on his fellow labor chiefs punctuated the separation. Thus, for example, Lewis accused the CIO of having betrayed the mine workers during the 1941 captive mine dispute. The CIO leadership, he snarled, was a bunch of "lap dogs and kept dogs and . . . yellow dogs." They were "miserable mediocrities."[3]

The UMW's departure from the AFL in December 1947 was equally acrimonious. At first, Lewis saw in the postwar AFL a bulwark against statist control of the labor movement, in contrast to what he believed was an irremediably compromised CIO. But the AFL's response to the anti-Communist affidavit mandated by the 1947 Taft-Hartley Act outraged the UMW chief and evoked his bitterest denunciations yet. When at its 1947 convention, the federation voted to amend its constitution as a means of partially side-stepping the affidavit's impact, Lewis accused his colleagues of "grovel[ing] on their bellies" to appease the government. They were a bunch of "fat and stately asses." Indeed, he told the convention "I don't think that the Federation has a head. I think its neck has just grown up and haired over." A terse notice of disaffiliation soon followed. And into the 1950s, he continued his public expressions of disdain, declaring in 1952 for example that both AFL and CIO leaders lacked "the courage of a long-eared jack rabbit."[4]

Beyond the barbed rhetoric, however, was a real, if not always fully articulated, critique of the path organized labor was taking in the age of the national security state. Although Lewis's many enemies attributed his maneuverings to unbounded ego, in reality his various moves both within the labor movement and with regard to the federal government reflected a legitimate alternate conception of the role of labor in modern society. From his opposition to American involvement in the international crisis of the late 1930s to his anti-Roosevelt announcement in 1940,

2. "United Mine Workers of America," *Labor Unions*, ed. Gary M. Fink (Westport, Conn.: Greenwood, 1977), 228–33; Dubofsky and Van Tine, *Lewis*, 364–70, 405–14, 456–58.

3. UMW, *Proceedings of the . . . Convention* (1942), 190–91.

4. Zieger, *Lewis*, 164–70; Dubofsky and Van Tine, *Lewis*, 474–75; American Federation of Labor, *Proceedings. . .* (1947), 486–92; UMW, *Proceedings. . .* (1952), 339.

Lewis warned presciently of the dangers to an independent labor movement of un-critical enlistment in the national security state's apparatus of mobilization, physical and moral. During World War II, he and the miners stood against the curtailment of the right to strike and the absorption of collective bargaining into an intricate state bureaucracy. After the war he repeatedly defied the government and felt the heavy hand of its retribution.[5]

For Lewis, these episodes of dissent were not idiosyncratic personal quarrels or battles confined to mine workers. He argued that laborites who willingly placed themselves under the government's guidance and direction, no matter how seem-ingly worthy the excuse, were paving the way for "a corporate state, wherein the activities of the people are regulated and constrained by a dictatorial government." In a 1945 magazine article, he asserted dramatically that "There Is No Labor Move-ment." Independent unionism, he charged, had become so corrupted by governmen-tal manipulation that it had virtually ceased to exist. Both the AFL and the CIO depended on government for union security provisions and for assistance in recruit-ing new members. Both enjoyed cozy relationships with the Democratic Party, which put them in unsavory alliance with the racists and states' righters who had chronically hamstrung liberal legislative initiatives. Under the excuse of wartime exigency, he believed, the organizations affiliated with the AFL and the CIO were little more than "political company unions." His objection to the Taft-Hartley affi-davit was not so much its anti-Communist intent—after all, the UMW had pioneered in barring party members from union participation—as its bald assumption that any governmental body had any right to dictate terms of membership or participation to a free union movement.[6]

In response to unionists who pled that signing the affidavit was necessary so that unions could avail themselves of the machinery of the National Labor Relations Board, Lewis voiced disdain. The refusal of union leaders to sign would isolate the board and render the government powerless to impose its standards on organized labor. Bypassing the Board would return industrial relations to the voluntary proc-esses that had existed before the 1935 Wagner Act—except that now there were powerful unions in place to assert workers' rights. According to Lewis, the repres-sive features of Taft-Hartley might be a blessing in disguise if vigorous labor leaders defied the government, reasserted the autonomy of their organizations, and appealed to the rank and file for legitimation and not to a Board dominated by eggheads, theorists, and political stooges.[7]

Indeed, the UMW's postwar experience deepened his hostility to the federal gov-ernment and to laborites who looked to it for sustenance. In 1946 and again in 1948,

5. For the wartime experience of the UMW, see Dubofsky and Van Tine, *Lewis*, 389–455; Zieger, *Lewis*, 132–49; and Nelson Lichtenstein, *Labor's War at Home: The CIO in World War II* (Cambridge: Cambridge University Press, 1982), 158–70.

6. John L. Lewis, "There Is No Labor Movement," *Colliers* (May 5, 1945): 63; Dubofsky and Van Tine, *Lewis*, 330–34, 339–70, 456–57, 474–75; Zieger, *Lewis*, 124–31.

7. Zieger, *Lewis*, 166–67; Dubofsky and Van Tine, *Lewis*, 474–75.

federal judges assessed enormous fines against the UMW and Lewis personally during strikes in which the union ignored back-to-work injunctions. These episodes brought Lewis into direct conflict with President Harry S. Truman, who most of the rest of the labor movement regarded as the savior of New Deal liberalism. As usual, Lewis had choice words for his adversary, calling Truman ''a malignant, scheming sort of an individual,'' who was ''dangerous to the United States.'' But, again as usual, verbal savagery reflected real issues: How far could a government go in bringing a private body, a union in this case, to heel? What price had the labor movement paid for the legal ''protections'' it had won in the 1930s? How could organized labor align itself with a Democratic Party whose leader was capable of such sledge-hammer attacks on the UMW, the mother of unions?[8]

John L. Lewis was not a theoretical man. His reading was largely confined to westerns, popular histories, daily newspapers, and labor documents. Yet his running critique of the federal government and his dismay with his fellow labor leaders were real and reflected, however episodically and intermittently, a genuine concern for the maintenance of a republican political order that he saw jeopardized by an expansive state, a militarized polity, and a tamed and subordinated labor movement. Before launching the CIO in the mid-1930s, Lewis and his chief advisor and speechwriter, W. Jett Lauck, had voiced these concerns repeatedly. Thus, in a 1935 statement that Lewis used as a basis for the public utterances that marked the launching of the CIO, Lauck had declared that ''our self-governing republic is at the cross-roads.'' The threat came not from Communists or even fascists but from plutocratic corporations and small cabals of eastern bankers, ''Kings of Money and Lords of Finance,'' who were perverting the Constitution, dominating political life, and thwarting the organization of working people, the only means of defeating the threat and revitalizing the republic. ''While organized labor is striving to endure its Valley Forge'' in the winter of the Great Depression, the ''insidious and menacing'' minions of finance capital were plotting a ''Tory Revolution.''[9]

The creation of the CIO had thwarted that ugly prospect. For a time, government had been on the side of the workers. But now the republic was once again in danger, this time from ''a vast centralized government and regulation by federal edict.'' And now the threat was the more insidious because the leadership of the labor movement was either too corrupted or too blind to see that they and their members were being used to aggrandize governmental power and that a labor movement that depended on men such as Truman, and governmental agencies such as the National Labor Relations Board was no labor movement at all. Only the UMW held out. But while it defied a meddlesome government, the William Greens and the Philip Murrays were invited to the White House ''and while there,'' Lewis sneered in 1948, ''they would sell out the labor movement and sell out their own Union for a lunch.''

8. Dubofsky and Van Tine, *Lewis*, 445–89; Zieger, Lewis, 161–64.

9. Lauck memo, October 9, 1935, W. Jett Lauck Papers, Alderman Library, University of Virginia, Box 40, Folder: 1934–5.

Increasingly, it became apparent to Lewis that the labor movement and workers more generally could not rely upon government either for institutional growth or protection or, in the conservative postwar period, for provision of social benefits.[10]

During the 1940s and early 1950s, Lewis and his mine workers coupled this critique of mainstream labor with organizing and collective bargaining initiatives designed to bypass the New Deal dispensation and perhaps to rebuild a new and genuinely autonomous labor movement. As early as the late 1930s, for example, Lewis began to carry organization into the construction trades, agriculture, and general manufacturing and services. Thus, the United Construction Workers Organizing Committee would challenge the racist, corrupt, and economically inefficient AFL building trades unions and bring industrial unionism to the nation's building sites and public projects. A revitalized District 50, reorganized under the leadership of Lewis's daughter Kathryn in 1941, quickly expanded from its original jurisdiction in coal derivatives, gas, and chemicals to general organizing among paper workers, farm-equipment workers, packinghouse workers, taxi drivers, and other industrial and service workers. The creation in 1942 of a District 50 unit for dairy farmers suggested expansion far beyond the traditional purview of organized labor. With the departure of the UMW from the CIO in 1942 and the bituminous strikes of 1943, which drew down upon it the hostility of government and the established union leadership alike, Lewis's critics feared that he would use these new organizations as a nucleus around which to build a new labor movement, challenging both the AFL and the CIO, along with the comfortable relations the two federations enjoyed with the Democratic Party and the federal government.[11]

The construction and dairy initiatives quickly died but District 50 proved more tenacious. Indeed, during the height of Lewis's and the UMW's defiance of the federal government in the 1943 strikes, established unions girded themselves for a major onslaught. Both AFL and CIO functionaries reported nervously on the appearance of Lewis's organizers at industrial sites throughout the East and Midwest. In Virginia, District 50 organizers used the UMW's reputation for militancy and the magic of the Lewis persona in a contest against both the AFL and CIO in the state's largest papermaking facility. In Illinois, CIO Farm Equipment Workers' leaders reported effective District 50 appeals in a large war-equipment plant in Springfield. In meatpacking, Lewis brought popular dissident organizers, impatient with the slow progress of the CIO Packinghouse Workers' union, into the District 50 fold to conduct organizing campaigns in the Chicago heartland of both AFL and CIO meatcutters' unions. From Ohio came a report of ''Bitter struggles with the forces of District 50'' and of a popular Lewis organizer recently discharged from the army running ''hog-wild'' through industrial districts there. The CIO, whose leaders knew firsthand the magnetic appeal of Lewis and the mystique of mine workers' militancy, took the District 50 initiatives seriously indeed. To Farm Equipment leaders, ''The

10. Lewis, ''There Is No Labor Movement,'' 63; Zieger, *Lewis*, 160–65.
11. Zieger, *Lewis*, 118–20; Dubofsky and Van Tine, *Lewis*, 449–50.

real motives of John L. Lewis are now laid bare. This is . . . part of planned strategy
to wreck the CIO." Philip Murray agreed, noting in May 1943, that only recently
Lewis had boasted to a UMW group that he was in the process of destroying the
CIO "and that it was only a question of time until he succeeded in taking away from
the . . . CIO some of its most important affiliates."[12]

In the end, District 50 failed to fulfill either Lewis's ambitions for it or the fears of
its rivals. Despite massive expenditures and a series of widely publicized organizing
initiatives, by the end of the war it could claim a membership of only about 50,000.
After the war, it continued to make progress, eventually reaching a peak of 200,000
members, mostly in chemicals, pulp and paper, and utilities. In the stabilized industrial environment of the late 1940s and 1950s, District 50, however, no longer
seemed to pose a dire threat to established unions, although on occasion the appearance of its organizers in trouble spots would set off the alarms and bring reminders
to established leaders of the unit's wartime reputation.[13]

In the mid-1950s, Lewis and the UMW were at the center of another, rather
bizarre, episode that for a time promised to challenge the two central labor federations. The death of Philip Murray in November 1952 launched a struggle for power
within the CIO. The election of United Auto Workers' President Walter P. Reuther
in December left powerful elements in the CIO dissatisfied, notably David J. Mc-
Donald, Murray's successor as head of the United Steelworkers. McDonald detested
Reuther on personal and ideological grounds and from the start maneuvered to undermine Reuther. Repeatedly, McDonald hinted that the USWA was on the verge of
abandoning the CIO, perhaps to establish a formal liaison with the UMW, the labor
organization that many steel workers, for both historical and geographical reasons,
regarded as their natural ally.

In the spring of 1954, Lewis and McDonald began a series of "secret," but
actually well-leaked, luncheon meetings. Soon joining them was Dave Beck, the
powerful chief of the Teamsters union, then engaged in sharp conflicts with the AFL
and its new leader, George Meany. Journalists began noting the arrival of a labor
leader on the scene by the name of "Lew McBeck," whose appearance perhaps
heralded a new labor federation that would combine the UMW's financial resources
and historic mystique with the Teamsters' aggressive organizing and strategic position and the steel workers' large membership of traditional blue-collar workers. The

12. Rick Halpern, manuscript in progress on United Packinghouse Workers of America, chap. 7 (in
Zieger's possession); Robert H. Zieger, "The Union Comes to Covington: Virginia Paper Workers Orga-
nize, 1934–1952," *Proceedings of the American Philosophical Society* (1982): 72–75; Grant Oakes and
Gerald Fielde to James B. Carey, July 6, 1943, Box 52, Folder FE; Alan Haywood to Grant Oakes,
August 6, 1943, Box 50, Folder FE-UAW; Anthony Esposito to Haywood, March 20, 1944, Box 58,
Folder Playthings; CIO Secretary-Treasurer Papers, Archives of Labor and Urban Affairs, Wayne State
University (ALUAWSU); Murray remarks, May 14, 1943, CIO Executive Board Minutes, ALUAWSU.

13. On District 50's intriguing career, see Donald G. Sofchalk, "International Union of District 50,
Allied and Technical Workers of the United States and Canada," in *Labor Unions*, ed. Gary M. Fink
(Westport, Conn.: Greenwood, 1977), 76–79.

three union sultans went so far as to issue joint press releases on economic and political issues and to print stationery emblazoned with the names of the three unions and without noting the affiliations of the steel workers (CIO) or Teamsters (AFL).

In the end, there was little chance that the three imperious union chiefs could actually work together for very long. The steel workers, for all their skepticism about the new Reuther regime, were too committed to the CIO ever to permit Mc-Donald to withdraw the USWA from it. For his part, McDonald hoped that his maneuvering might encourage the movement toward merger of the AFL and CIO, a process just then gathering steam. Beck and Lewis, however, both had reasons to deplore the impending merger: Beck, because a merged labor movement might insist on investigating the questionable financial affairs of the Teamsters union; Lewis, because a merged AFL and CIO would simply legitimate the general co-optation and lethargy of the postwar labor movement. Both Lewis and McDonald detested Reuther, whom they regarded as a socialist fakir, but mutual dislike of the red-headed UAW and CIO chief was an inadequate foundation on which to build a dynamic new labor federation. Indeed, the contrast between Lewis's magnificent role in creating the CIO in the mid-1930s and his participation in the floating of this ludicrous ''phantom federation'' twenty years later caused reporters, who once hung on his every word, now to smirk with amusement and to quote Karl Marx on tragedy and farce.[14]

Lewis did attempt on occasion to appeal directly to rank-and-file workers over the heads of their elected union leaderships in an effort perhaps to rekindle some of the dynamism and vigor of the early CIO. In a notable example, in June 1951 he agreed to appear at a mammoth celebration outside Detroit to mark the tenth anniversary of the birth of UAW Local 600. It was victory over Henry Ford in the spring of 1941 at River Rouge that marked the founding of this union, whose 60,000 members made it the largest local union in the world. Many UAW members regarded Lewis's assistance for their cause then as the key to cracking the notoriously anti-union power of Ford and they regarded him, and not current UAW president Walter Reuther, as ''the father of our union.''

From its inception, Local 600 had been a center of dissidence. Home of a large and well-led Communist contingent, the Rouge local had combined shopfloor militancy, radical politics, vigorous internal democracy, and stubborn opposition to Reuther's efforts to centralize and streamline the 1,500,000-member UAW. In 1951, Local 600's anti-Reuther leadership hoped to make the anniversary celebration a public display of displeasure with Reuther. Influential Communists in the local also sought to call to workers' attention the price that heavy military production in the midst of the Korean War was exacting on the Rouge's workforce in terms of speed-ups, deteriorating health and safety conditions, and poor national union leadership

---

14. On this episode, see Robert H. Zieger, ''Leadership and Bureaucracy in the Late CIO,'' *Labor History* 31, no. 3 (summer 1990): 256–60.

on the part of officers in thrall to the anti-Communist priorities of the Truman administration. The celebration, declared the local's anti-Reuther leaders, would not only commemorate an earlier victory; it would seek "to recapture the unity that prevailed among labor forces in 1941."

Lewis's acceptance of the invitation was in itself a provocation to Reuther. He arrived in Detroit on June 22 amid heavy press coverage and public interest. Local 600's Flying Squadron, sporting military-style caps and natty ties emblazoned with the local's logo, escorted him from the railroad station as the Local 600 band blared out "Solidarity Forever," the UAW anthem. At the open-air gathering the next day attended by 50,000 auto workers, their families, and well-wishers, Lewis lashed out at the compromised CIO and UAW leadership, accusing them of truckling to the Truman administration by participating in wartime labor relations machinery that disadvantaged their own members. He called for a renewed commitment to extend organization, pledging massive UMW financial contributions. "John Lewis wants nothing," he declared in response to reports that District 50 representatives were trying to detach the Rouge local from the UAW. Surveying the huge and enthusiastic gathering, Lewis observed that the UAW leadership had attempted to dissuade the auto workers from attending. In a pointed reference to Reuther, he remarked that "it appears that the best way to have a successful celebration is to have some pseudo-intellectual nitwit boycott it."

The Local 600 celebration and Lewis's incendiary remarks made little lasting impact. Reuther's UAW opponents hoped that the spectacular affair would signal a return to the militancy and enthusiasm of the early CIO. "Your presence," one dissident told Lewis, "and your talk provided us with renewed faith . . . the rank and file . . . is teeming with renewed faith in their Union in anticipation of better things to come." But it soon became clear that the seventy-one-year-old Lewis, while enjoying the opportunity to beard Reuther in his den and once again to command a mass meeting, had no intention of reliving the tumultous days of the 1930s. Recounting the episode to his new friend, industrialist Cyrus Eaton, Lewis deflated the lasting importance of the event, which had quickly faded from public attention. At least, he remarked, "there were more than a few chuckles involved."[15]

Although none of these organizational initiatives bore much fruit, UMW collective bargaining strategy in the immediate postwar period did for a time forcefully project an alternative to the path that other unions pursued. The epic strikes that occurred almost annually in the late 1940s secured for the union a unique and seemingly envious position. The UAW and the steelworkers had to content themselves with gaining medical insurance and company-administered pension benefits. In the protracted 1946 bituminous strike, however, the UMW gained a regular basis for

---

15. Discussion of this episode is based on Robert H. Zieger, "Showdown at the Rouge," *History Today* 40 (January 1990): 49–56. It, in turn, was based largely on the author's examination in July 1987, of unorganized material examined in the United Mine Workers Papers, then located in an Alexandria, Virginia, storage facility.

employer-funded and, eventually, union-administered pension and medical care plans. Faced with an aging labor force ravaged by the illnesses and injuries common to coal mining, the UMW eventually constructed regional hospitals throughout Appalachia. At first at least, UMW benefit levels and medical services were superior to those enjoyed by auto and steel workers. Moreover, by controlling the funds and administration of the medical and pension programs, the UMW seemingly had taken a major step toward building a more autonomous union, dependent neither on government nor employers, a union whose members drew sustenance on an ongoing basis directly from the union and not through some remote pension board or doctor-controlled insurance company. The innovative contracts negotiated with the Bituminous Coal Operators' Association in the late 1940s and early 1950s made Lewis an even more heroic figure among rank-and-file miners than he had been. ''God bless the day John L. Lewis was born,'' said the first recipient of a UMW pension check.[16] And certainly Lewis and UMW officers lost few opportunities to boast of the superiority of their contracts and the munificence of these benefits in contrast to the more limited and restricted entitlements that the UAW, the USWA, and other industrial unions were winning for their memberships.[17]

The one area in which the postwar UMW did not initiate a direct challenge to organized labor's mainstream was in the political arena. From the mid-1930s through the early 1940s, Lewis had hinted at a political realignment that would bring all popular forces—farmers, workers, blacks, the elderly, peace activists, and idealistic young people—together into a mass, democratic organization, perhaps even a new political party. His break with Roosevelt in 1940 was, in his view, a warning to labor of the dangers of tying itself to a national security state that, he believed, inevitably followed the priorities of international bankers, British colonialists, and power-obsessed politicians.

Yet even before the end of the war, the UMW's political profile, apart from its legendary showdowns with Truman, began to lower. Roosevelt and Truman were anathema to Lewis but in 1944 and 1948 large numbers of mine workers nonetheless voted for them. Increasingly, Lewis threw his political weight into the statewide politics of the Appalachian mining states, largely avoiding national commitments. The Democrats were flawed, and certainly neither Lewis nor any of his associates would have any truck with the Communist-tinted Progressive Party of 1948, which attempted to rally the kinds of progressive forces to which Lewis had earlier appealed. He remained on good terms with selected Republicans, thus maintaining a tinge of his partisan loyalties of the 1920s, but the postwar GOP, proud incubator of the Taft-Hartley Act, offered no political home either. In general, Lewis and his UMW cohorts could do little other than cast unenthusiastic ballots for selected Dem-

16. Quoted in Brit Hume, *Death and the Mines: Rebellion and Murder in the United Mine Workers* (New York: Grossman, 1971), 30.

17. The UMW's postwar bargaining initiatives are described in Dubofsky and Van Tine, *Lewis*, 458–68, 477–81, 484–89, and 498–500. See also Zieger, 156–61, 171–73.

ocrats while using their lobbying abilities and coal-state leverage to shape legislation increasingly designed not so much to protect and advance the direct interests of coal miners as to shore up a sagging coal industry, on whose production tonnage the royalties for the UMW's expensive health and pension plans were based.[18]

In the final analysis, several factors combined to blunt the impact of Lewis's and the UMW's critique of the post-1940 path of organized labor. The postwar shrink-age of soft-coal production and hence of UMW membership both drastically dimin-ished the numerical weight and strategic importance of American labor's historic shock troops, the UMW, and cut deeply into the tonnage-based royalties that fi-nanced the health and retirement programs. Lewis did nothing to groom a new generation of able leaders or to work with leftist and reform-minded activists who shared much of his criticism of the postwar labor movement, thus forestalling any possibility of giving substance and continuity to his vision. The increasing authori-tarianism and ineptitude with which the UMW and its pension and health funds were administered discredited Lewis and made the UMW an embarrassment to orga-nized labor, suffering as it did in the 1950s from public exposure of the lack of democracy and abundance of corruption that characterized some unions. Moreover, the ability of the mainstream labor movement to bring home the bacon to its mem-bership in both the political and collective bargaining arenas robbed the Lewis cri-tique of much of its force.[19]

Indeed, for all the perceptiveness of Lewis's criticisms of the labor movement, he remained so intimately bound to the Kingdom of Coal that in a fundamental sense he lacked sympathy for and understanding of mass-production, service, white-col-lar, and other workers who constituted the overwhelming mass of organized labor's actual and potential constituency. True, during the magnificent decade after the mid-1930s he had transcended the parochialism of traditional coal mining and had spo-ken and acted with eloquence, authority, and brilliance. The creation of the CIO and the permanent establishment of industrial unionism stood as a testament to his enormous gifts, his uncanny sense of timing, and his boldness and decisiveness. Yet the CIO phase of his life lasted but seven years, aborted on the verge of the CIO's

18. John Gaventa, *Power and Powerlessness: Quiesence and Rebellion in an Appalachian Valley* (Urbana: University of Illinois Press, 1980); Harry M. Caudill, *Night Comes to the Cumberland: A Biography of a Depressed Area* (Boston: Little, Brown, 1963).

19. Dubofsky and Van Tine, *Lewis*, 491–529; Zieger, *Lewis*, 170–84. There is a substantial literature chronicling the pathologies of the UMW during the last decade of Lewis's stewardship. See, for example, Hume, *Death and the Mines*; Trevor Ambrister, *Act of Vengeance: The Yablonsky Murders and Their Solution* (New York: Dutton/Saturday Review Press, 1975); Joseph Finley, *The Corrupt Kingdom: The Rise and Fall of the United Mine Workers* (New York: Simon and Schuster, 1972); Gaventa, *Power and Powerlessness*; Caudill, *Night Comes to the Cumberland*; Stuart Brown, *A Man Named Tony: The True Story of the Yablonski Murders* (New York: Norton, 1976); and Paul Clark, *The Miners' Fight for Democ-racy: Arnold Miller and the Reform of the United Mine Workers* (Ithaca, N.Y.: ILR Press, 1981), 4–23. David Brody, "Market Unionism in America: The Case of Coal," in David Brody, *In Labor's Cause: Main Themes on the History of the American Worker* (NY: Oxford University Press, 1993), 164–69, analyzes the decline of unionized coal production in the 1950s and 1960s.

greatest expansion in favor of renewed commitment to the problems and exigencies of the coal miners. Standing alone in battles against government from 1943 to 1950 further deepened this isolation, but it was the sharp drop-off of the soft-coal industry in the 1950s that both undercut UMW influence in the world of labor and intensified Lewis's focus on the industry itself. Thus, through the 1950s collective bargaining in bituminous coal, once an annual cockpit of bitter conflict, became increasingly congenial, as Lewis and the UMW accommodated the coal operators even to the point of ignoring obvious violations of the tonnage-royalty provisions of the master contract.

Over the years, the Lewis mystique had been compelling to masses of industrial workers. Certainly this was true on the icy streets of Akron and Flint in 1936 and 1937 and in the grimy steel towns of Pennsylvania, Illinois, and Ohio. During the war, the defiance of Lewis and the UMW had stirred dissatisfied auto, steel, munitions, and other industrial workers, unhappy with the antiworker operation of the "no strike" pledge and the government's wage restraint policies. Thus, Auto Workers' president R. J. Thomas warned his CIO colleagues in 1943 that the sentiment in the overcrowded, speeded-up war plants of Detroit was that "John Lewis has the right program; he is at least out fighting for the workers and is doing something for them." And, of course, even after the war, despite the UMW's loss of panache and Lewis's increasingly isolated position, reminders of his old charisma remained, as witnessed by the massed Auto Workers who shouted "You Tell 'em, John," during his 1951 bout of Reuther-bashing at the Rouge.[20]

But Lewis's immersion in the mining industry always limited his ability to respond to this broad constituency. Coming as he did out of the solidaristic traditions of coal mining, Lewis had an unreflective sense of worker loyalty that did not, finally, resonate among other industrial workers. Auto, steel, electrical, and other mass-production workers were, to an extent impossible in the remote and self-contained mining locales, integrated into a sophisticated complex of competing ethnic, political, and cultural loyalties. These mainly semiskilled workers, and even more so the masses of clerks, salespersons, and office workers, many of them women, were worlds apart from the manly, dangerous milieu of the rugged coal miner. Although he often invoked the cause of the industrial masses, too frequently Lewis displayed contempt for the actual workers who toiled in the offices, factories, and workshops. During World War II, even as war workers thrilled at the UMW's defiance of government, Lewis coupled his claims for the miners with disdainful remarks about the abilities and contributions of other industrial workers. In 1944 he contrasted the high wages of the "morons in the Southern shipyards" with those of his heroic miners. In 1945, he lashed out at CIO defense workers who struck their plants "for causes shameless in their essential triviality."[21]

20. R. J. Thomas remarks, May 14, 1943, CIO Executive Board Special Meeting (ALUAWSU); Zieger, "Showdown at the Rouge."

21. Zieger, *Lewis*, 132–49; quotations are from 148–49.

Lewis was also vulnerable as a would-be leader of a revitalized labor movement because of his actual conduct of UMW affairs. Since the 1920s, he had remorselessly persecuted his critics, using UMW publications and resources to build a powerful machine dedicated to maintaining his control. He had placed once-autonomous UMW districts into receivership and kept them in that condition, using them to provide his cronies and relatives with jobs. He had stifled union democracy, and with the appointment of William Anthony ("Tony") Boyle in 1948 as his administrative assistant, the UMW plunged ever deeper into violence, corruption, and internal repression. Thus, for example, in 1951 Reuther supporters did not fail to point out the irony of John L. Lewis presuming to come to Detroit to lecture the UAW on how to conduct union affairs. In a response to Lewis's harsh speech, the UAW issued a detailed attack on Lewis's recent record as a labor leader. To be sure, Lewis was "once a great labor leader," but in recent years he had become "an embittered, petulant and argumentative minor public figure," the UAW declared. Already, the vaunted UMW pension and welfare funds were showing signs of mismanagement and underfunding.

The Reuther rejoinder saved its most biting criticism, however, for Lewis's role as leader of the UMW. How could UAW dissidents, in the name of union democracy, embrace a man who ruled his own union with an iron hand, and had done so for thirty years? The UMW chief would simply not tolerate the kind of meeting that Local 600 had staged: dissenters in the mine workers had been harassed, ridiculed, deprived of their livelihoods, and even physically brutalized by Lewis's henchmen throughout his entire reign. Moreover, the UAW spokesmen pointed out, the contrast between the abstemious Reuther, who received a salary of $11,000 as president of the 1,500,000-member UAW, and the extravagant Lewis, whose salary of $50,000 and whose virtually unlimited expense account were legendary, could hardly be greater.[22]

Thus it was that, whatever the acuteness of his critique of the postwar labor movement and of its relationship to the national security state, Lewis and the UMW were too vulnerable on too many counts to have his analysis taken seriously. Yet in the 1960s and 1970s—ironically, at a time when the Lewis legacy of authoritarianism and neglect were coming to a grisly climax—a new generation of historians began to reexamine and offer more positive assessments of Lewis's stance in the 1940s and early 1950s. Rejecting earlier notions of industrial pluralism and countervailing power, scholars such as Paul Koistinen, Nelson Lichtenstein, Katherine Stone, Christopher Tomlins, and James Green found much in Lewis's contemporary critiques to buttress their view of the New Deal order as skewed against workers and of the CIO-led labor movement of the 1940s and 1950s as hopelessly bureaucratic and increasingly unresponsive to rank-and-file workers. They assailed the "Barren Marriage of Organized Labor to the Democratic Party" and castigated mainstream labor leaders who permitted a Communism-obsessed government to co-opt them

22. Zieger, "Showdown at the Rouge," 54–55.

into corrupt and bloody foreign adventures benefiting only governmental elites and corporate interests. They assailed the system of legal regulation of labor relations established under the Wagner Act, pointing to its enmeshment of workers in endless strands of red tape that deprived them of any hope of real empowerment on the shopfloor.[23]

A good deal of this historical and legal scholarship invoked Lewis's scathing critiques of the post–New Deal labor movement and its relationship to government. Of all the labor leaders of that era, Lewis seemed the most articulate, the most militant, and the least compromised by false ideological or political considerations. Lewis, of course, died in 1969, just as this emerging critique of the New Deal system was taking off. No doubt he would have found the Marxist analysis that undergirds much of it distasteful and the implicit political agenda of its most vocal spokespersons unacceptable. For their part, even those who found sustenance in Lewis's bold actions in defiance of government and his vivid words of disdain for mainstream laborites drew back quickly from the sordid Lewis record of union governance. But the rediscovery of the Lewis critique has helped historians to gain new perspective on labor's role in the World War II–cold war era, as witnessed most perceptively in the outstanding biography of Lewis by Melvyn Dubofsky and Warren Van Tine, published in 1977. Lewis's words and actions did raise important questions about the relationship of organized labor to the emerging national security state, and his critique of the Roosevelt and Truman administrations did underscore the tenuous and insecure nature of the gains industrial workers had achieved in the 1930s. Lewis's warnings about the dangers to organized labor—and to free society generally—in becoming an appendage to the military-political machine were shrewd and even prescient. Those who see a need in the unsettled present to redefine organized labor's relationship to the state, the legal order, and the political system could do worse than to ponder them.

23. Lichtenstein, *Labor's War at Home*; Paul A. C. Koistinen, "Mobilizing the World War II Economy: Labor and the Industrial-Military Alliance," *Pacific Historical Review* 42 (November 1973): 443–78; Katherine Van Wezel Stone, "The Post-War Paradigm in American Labor Law," *Yale Law Journal* 90, no. 7 (June 1981): 1509–80; James Green, *The World of the Worker* (New York: Hill and Wang, 1980); Christopher Tomlins, *The State and the Unions: Labor Relations, Law, and the Organized Labor Movement in America, 1880–1960* (Cambridge: Cambridge University Press, 1985); Mike Davis, "The Barren Marriage of American Labour and the Democratic Party," *New Left Review* 124 (November–December 1980): 434–84.

PART TWO

WORK HABITS, MINERS' HEALTH, AND COAL COMPANY PATERNALISM

CHAPTER SEVEN

MECHANIZATION, WORKPLACE CONTROL, AND THE END OF THE HAND-LOADING ERA*

KEITH DIX

THE MINER'S FREEDOM

The very fact that the knowledge of the mining process belonged to the body of miners at work in their respective rooms and that this knowledge was passed on through an informal apprenticeship system gave miners a considerable amount of control over their job. Carter Goodrich, in his 1925 book *The Miner's Freedom*, pointed out that "the miner does in practice pick up his trade almost entirely from his buddy or his neighbors and hardly at all from his boss."[1] In addition, the miner developed a proprietary interest in his room and rarely was transferred until it had been worked out. Even if a miner was absent from work for a considerable time, his room was ordinarily held for him. Further, the hand-loading coal miner worked without supervision, being almost an independent contractor.

---

*Portions of this chapter reprinted from Keith Dix, *What's A Coal Miner To Do? The Mechanization of Coal Mining,* by permission of the University of Pittsburgh Press. Copyright © 1988 by University of Pittsburgh Press.

    1. Carter Goodrich, *The Miner's Freedom* (Boston: Marshall Jones, 1925), 37.

One of the most powerful features of the miner's control of the production process was his freedom to leave the workplace whenever he decided to do so. According to the 1922 U.S. Coal Commission, the reasons generally given for leaving the mine before its official closing time were that the miner got "cleaned up" or that he had earned enough for the day. A miner also might leave his work if empty cars were unavailable for loading, if his shots misfired, if his tools broke, or if other factors left him without sufficient coal to load. The point is, he was free to do so. Even where the eight-hour day was established under a union contract, the tonnage men still retained the right—by virtue of management's inability to change it—to leave the mine when they pleased. One Ohio mining official reported to the Coal Commission that "in actual practice 60 percent to 70 percent [of the loaders] do not observe the eight-hour rule." And "for these employees even the six-hour day is the exception and not the rule."[2]

When the industry was faced with an economic crisis in the 1920s, this lack of industrial discipline became increasingly incompatible with management's need to plan, to coordinate, and to control the labor process for maximum productivity. L. E. Young, vice president of the Pittsburgh Coal Company, reported on an industry survey made in 1929, confirming the contradiction between the miner's freedom to leave his workplace and a rational labor process: "The one point which is stressed most by the [owners] is the difficulty of operating a coal mine economically when the daily output is contingent upon the whims of the coal loader who works when, as long, and as hard as he pleases."[3] It is not surprising that the establishment of a standard workday became an integral part of the movement for increased productivity that brought about an end to the hand-loading era.

One of the most important characteristics of work relations in the early period of coal mining was the lack of direct and continuous supervision of the workforce. Unlike the factory, where workers are concentrated and foreman/worker ratios are high, the widespread dispersion of workplaces under the room-and-pillar mining system and the industry practice of hiring only one inside foreman for each mine made close supervision of mine workers practically impossible. The long distances between workplaces meant that a single mine foreman had only minimal daily contact with the miners. Although by 1915 some state safety laws required that mine foremen visit each workplace at least once a day, it is doubtful that such laws were

2. *Comparative Efficiency of Labor in the Bituminous Coal Industry Under Union and Non-Union Operation.* Evidence and testimony submitted to the U.S. Coal Commission by the Bituminous Operators' Special Committee, September 10, 1923, West Virginia Collection, West Virginia University Library, 154. It is worth noting that in the shaft mines coming and going to the workplace was not so easy as in the drift mines. The mechanical means for entry and exit—the cage or man trip—was located on the surface under management's supervision, and miners who wanted to leave the mine early would have to wait until the coal had all been "caged." Over the years, as coal production came increasingly from shaft mines, it became more difficult for workers to leave the mine at will; consequently their workday became more regimented and disciplined.

3. American Mining Congress, *1929 Yearbook on Coal Mine Mechanization* (Washington, D.C.), 7.

routinely followed. Instead, management continued to depend on the skill and individual initiative of the miner, a fact that gave the miner a freedom and an independence found in only a few other industrial settings.

Alternatives to Direct Supervision

Given this lack of supervision in the early days, payment by the ton evolved as the only reward system that could assure that mine workers would put forth a reasonable effort to load coal. Tonnage rates were determined by competitive market forces or, where the mines were organized, by collective bargaining. However, the history of the industry is replete with evidence that mine owners, while relying on piece-rate payments, continually tried to increase their profit levels by various manipulations and abuses of the system. For example, the practice of short weighing became so common in the industry that one of the first demands of miners when they formed unions was for a checkweighman to assure them an honest weight for the coal they sent to the surface. Dockage, an arbitrary reduction in payment because of impurities loaded with the coal, was another abuse of the piece-rate system that provided management with a partial control of the miner's efforts. Howard B. Lee, former West Virginia attorney general, reported that operators admitted it was their policy "to dock considerable [*sic*] more than the waste in their cars . . . to punish the miner and make him more careful in the future."[4]

A modification of the piece-rate system came with the practice, common in some nonunion mines in West Virginia, of making payment by the car rather than by the ton. Increase in the size of cars and nonpayment for improperly loaded cars were frequent complaints of miners under this system. The introduction of screens, which allowed only lump coal to pass onto the scales, was yet another management effort to get greater production and profits out of the tonnage system.

Mine owners also tried to maintain their profitability by the use of an elaborate system of off-the-job control mechanisms. Because of the isolated nature of most mining operations, miners were usually dependent on the company to provide housing, stores, and recreation. This provided an opportunity for direct economic exploitation, which frequently was seized. There is evidence that some companies made greater profits from their company-run stores than they did from their mining operations.[5] Intimidation and physical violence from company-hired armed guards and spies were other forms of control common in many coalfields, especially during the nonunion era.[6]

4. H. B. Lee, *Bloodletting in Appalachia* (Morgantown: West Virginia University Press, 1969), 188.

5. See Richard A. Simon, "The Development of Underdevelopment: The Coal Industry and Its Effect on the West Virginia Economy, 1880–1930" (Ph.D. diss., University of Pittsburgh, 1978), 210–12.

6. These tactics constitute an important chapter in the history of this industry, but the story has been told numerous times through state and federal investigations, independent journalistic exposés, and eyewitness accounts. See, for example, U.S. Coal Commission, *Report, Part 1: Principal Findings and*

Looking back on the early hand-loading period, it seems that these forms of exploitation and control of miners off the job were substitutes for management's lack of control over miners on the job. But this contrast is too sharp. Management did exercise control over certain aspects of the job and working conditions. For example, the power of the mine foreman to hire whomever he pleased was more or less an unchallenged right that gave management the opportunity to show favoritism or to honor blacklists of union supporters. More important, the mine foreman's authority to discharge workers and evict them from company-owned houses gave significant disciplinary power to mine management. During periods of recession in coal markets when jobs were scarce, such discipline was quite effective. The power of the foreman in nonunion mines to assign workplaces, to determine the distribution of empty mine cars, and to establish rates of pay for so-called dead work gave him influence over the miners' earnings.

Mine workers were not, however, without their own defenses against these practices. From the very early years in the industry, when mine management attempted to alter the terms and conditions of employment or to impose arbitrary disciplinary actions, miners frequently resisted such interference—even before union organization came to the coalfields—by a concerted refusal to work. There are numerous reports of local strikes resulting from management's attempt to increase productivity and to effect greater profits at the miners' expense.[7] These local job actions were a corollary to, if not dependent upon, the control that workers in the mines exercised at the point of production. Before the coal industry could take its place among the technologically advanced industries of the twentieth century, this control, rooted as it was in the hand-loading system, had to be broken or at least severely limited.

The End of Hand Loading

The principal motivation of the early inventors of mine machinery was to develop an individual machine for each of the separate tasks embodied in the age-old miners' craft. As early as the 1890s, some inventors were working on ideas that would incorporate all the tasks into one machine, but these precursors of the modern-day continuous mining machines were not commercially successful until the late 1940s. Therefore, the technology that evolved prior to successful continuous mining sys-

Recommendations (Washington, D.C.: GPO, 1925), 153–82; Homer Morris, *The Plight of the Bituminous Coal Miner* (Philadelphia: University of Pennsylvania Press, 1934), 85–97; and *Report of the West Virginia Mining Investigation Commission,* August 28, 1912 (Charleston, W.Va., and Senate Committee on Interstate Commerce; *Conditions in the Coal Fields of Pennsylvania, West Virginia, and Ohio,* 70th Congress, 1st sess. (Washington, D.C.: GPO, 1928).

7. Mine workers' resistance to these abuses has been analyzed by Jon Amsden and Steve Brier in "Coal Miners on Strike: The Transformation of Strike Demands and the Formation of the National Union," *Journal of Interdisciplinary History* (spring 1977), 583–616.

tems included separate machines for undercutting, drilling, and loading, all linked to the surface by various forms of mechanized transportation.[8]

By 1920, 61% of all underground coal was mined with an undercutting machine.[9] Some coal was "shot from the solid"; that is, it was blasted without being undercut. But this practice generally was deplored by those concerned for the miner's safety because it involved using an excessive amount of powder to break the coal.

The second task for the skilled miner of an earlier day was to drill one or more shot holes for the blasting powder. Long, hand-held breast augers, resembling in design the carpenter's brace and bit, were used for this purpose until air-powered, and later electrically driven, drills were developed. Installation of compressed-air-powered drills for use in bituminous mines began as early as 1890, and in 1911 electrically propelled augers, including types that were mountable on cutting machines, were placed on the market. Mine owners' interest in power drilling did not advance very fast, however, even after one-man portable machines were developed. Hand augers were most common in the industry until mechanical loading made it economically feasible to mechanize the whole mining cycle. As late as 1936 only 27.2% of all underground coal was produced from working places in which the shot holes were drilled by mechanical drills.[10]

Paralleling the improvements available for undercutting and drilling were improvements in explosives and methods of blasting. The U.S. Bureau of Mines, established in 1910, very early began testing various types of explosives and made known to the industry its approval of certain "permissible" explosives, which were safer and more efficient than the traditional black powder. In the 1920s, some mines began switching from chemical explosives to methods using mechanical force, such as hydraulic pressure, compressed air, and the heaving action of carbon dioxide, the latter being called the Cardox system.[11]

Along with, and in many cases preceding, the changes taking place at the face were major changes in coal haulage from the face to the surface. Mules, horses, and ponies had been the traditional source of transportation until the electric motor proved to be much more efficient. The original wooden rails were replaced with steel rails, while larger cars and more powerful locomotives made it possible to speed mine cars filled with coal to the surface and return them quickly to the loading

8. The mechanized system of mining described herein continued in use long after the introduction of the continuous mining machine in 1948. It came to be known as the conventional mining system and as late as 1970 accounted for 46% of all coal mined underground. U.S. Bureau of Mines, *Minerals Yearbook, 1970* (Washington, D.C.: GPO), 342.

9. Keith Dix, *Work Relations in the Coal Industry: The Hand-Loading Era, 1880–1930* (Morgantown: West Virginia University Press, 1977), 20.

10. Willard E. Hotchkiss et al., *Mechanization, Employment and Output Per Man in Bituminous Coal Mining* (Philadelphia: Works Project Administration, 1939), 2:20. This document is the single best source on the development of early mine mechanization.

11. Ibid., 23.

machines. Conveyor systems were also being installed during the 1920s and 1930s, and in 1938 one manufacturer marketed a truck mounted on rubber tires powered by a small electric storage battery that delivered coal from the loading machine to the main hauling system. This shuttle car proved to be an important link in the search for an integrated transportation system, which would help the mine owner realize the full potential of mechanical loading.

Each new technological development increased productivity, but the labor process itself remained largely unchanged until the advent of the loading machine. After the introduction of the cutting machine, for example, miners still worked alone or with a partner in separated and rather isolated rooms. They still set their own pace of production (with an upper limit set by the amount of coal cut by the cutting machine), and they continued to be paid according to the amount of coal they loaded. The tonnage payment system was so accepted in the industry that the cutting machine operator and his helper were also paid in this manner. Electric drills, better blasting powder, improved ventilation, and more efficient mine haulage all worked to increase output per man-hour, but taken together they had little impact on the organization of work underground. It was the introduction of the hand-loading machine that made the critical difference.

The Arrival of the Loading Machine

Wylie Erwin started working at age sixteen in a large southern West Virginia mine in 1938, just one year before the mine installed its first mechanical loading machine.[12] Erwin recalled that the first machine used at his mine was called a Clarkson loader: "We knew it was coming," he said, "but we didn't know it was going to be as quick as it was." Although rumors were flying, the company gave no advance notice to the hand loaders that their jobs were being eliminated. "The day they put the loading machine on our section, the coal loaders went in to work but the boss was already there and he said that the men not on his list could pick up their tools and leave. And the men walked out of the mines," Erwin recalled. Fortunately, for these miners, there was an upswing in the coal trade, so other jobs were available. "The biggest majority of the men fired just laughed it off 'cause at that time you could—if you really wanted to work—you could go anywhere and get a job. There was a lot of work."

Of the men left on the job to run the new machinery, few liked loading coal mechanically. For one thing, it was hazardous work. Erwin said that "when you had hand loading, your faces stayed clean. You didn't have accumulation of dust because the coal loader was responsible. You could eat off the bottom, it was so clean." With the loading machine "you couldn't hear and you couldn't see." Erwin ran a gathering motor—called a pull 'n place—for the first loading machine in his mine and remembered that it was so dusty that "you would have to reach out and feel to

12. Interview, March 15, 1982, at Eccles, West Virginia.

tell when your car was full. They had a man standing there with a water hose, but that was just like pouring water in this creek out here as high as it is.''[13]

Along with speeding up the pace of production, there was pressure to keep the machine running at all times. Erwin remembered well the new work schedule after the switch to mechanical loading:

> They had a timekeeper on each section. He would sit right there and clock you, to see how long it would take to load the car and switch it out. And if you wasn't fast enough, son, you didn't have a job. He came in with an old dollar watch and sat down—that's all he done, he sat right there. He'd sit there and you were supposed to come in, hit the machine, load the car, switch out, and be back to that machine in three minutes. He would put down every second that machine wasn't running. A lot of times you would wreck and if you were too long putting that car back on [the track] they'd get another brakeman who could put the cars on. You worked under a strain and you worked hard because you know a man sitting there has a watch on you, and you knew what they could do with you.

Wylie Erwin pointed out that when it came to the actual loading of coal, the machine failed in one important way. The machine loaded not only the coal but all the slate and other unwanted material shot from the face. The skilled hand-loader had always prided himself on sending clean coal to the surface, which he did by picking out the impurities and setting them aside before loading his coal. And some hand-loaders believed that their skill in mining clean coal would protect their jobs against competition from the machines. George Korson in his book *Coal Dust on the Fiddle* recorded an interesting song in this connection, ''The Coal Loading Machine.''

Chorus
Tell me, what will a coal miner do?
Tell me, what will a coal miner do?
When he goes down in the mine,
Joy loaders he will find.
Tell me, what will a coal miner do?

Stanza
Miners' poor pocketbooks are growing lean,
Miners' poor pocketbooks are growing lean,
They can't make a dollar at all,
Here is where we place the fault:
Place it all on that coal loading machine.

13. Ibid.

> Now boys, I think I have a scheme,
> And I'm sure that it's neither rude nor mean.
> We will pick our bone and refuse,
> Then we'll know our coal is clean,
> Then we'll outdo the coal loading machine.[14]

A coalfield poem written in Kentucky expressed the hope that the Joy machines would be short lived because they could not mine clean coal.

> Here is to Old Joy a wonderful machine,
> That loads more coal than any we've seen.
>
> Ten men cut off with nothing to do,
> Their places needed for another Joy crew.
>
> Fifty cars a day is the goal they have set,
> With coal and slate together they will get it, I bet.
>
> The bosses all smile to see Joy at work,
> And keep him well oiled, he never will shirk.
>
> He tears up the bottom, tears up the track,
> And never gets tired for he has a steel back.
>
> He loads lots of coal and very cheap too,
> But when offered for sale the dirt won't do.
>
> We hope they will dock him the next day at work,
> And cut him off for loading so much dirt.
>
> We will pick out a spot with plenty of room
> Where Joy can rest till the day of doom.[15]

For the coal operator, the solution to the problem of dirty, machine-loaded coal was simple, if not costly. Wylie Erwin pointed out that the company for which he worked found it necessary to build a facility on the surface for cleaning impurities from the coal. And this is precisely what happened throughout the coalfields in the wake of the mechanization movement. Elaborate cleaning and preparation plants began to dot the hillsides as hand loading disappeared.

   Mike Murphy, a West Virginia coal miner, was a hand-loader for nine years until his mine converted to mechanical loading in the early 1940s. He remembers that earlier the company had brought in a Joy 7BU to load some slate from a roof fall, but, he noted, "when it first came there a factory man came to teach somebody to

14. George Korson, *Coal Dust on the Fiddle* (Philadelphia: University of Pennsylvania Press, 1943), 138–39. This song was recorded in 1940 in Welch, West Virginia.
   15. Ibid., 141.

operate it, a bunch of the foreign born, a bunch of coal loaders ran the man out. They chased him down the road. They did, yes sir, 'cause it was going to take their jobs. They ran him down the road with clubs and everything else. It was a Joy Manufacturing Company representative. I suspect if they had caught him they would have killed him. He was taking their jobs. That one machine, it would take a lot of jobs.''[16] Murphy made his own adjustment to the loading machine by quitting face work and applying for a maintenance mechanic's position, a job he held until he retired. Admittedly, he was making good money as a hand-loader; his father, also a loader, told him he was ''crazy to trade that for a mechanics job which only paid $7.14 a day.'' It was not an easy decision because ''hand-loading is an awfully nice job, you don't have any boss. If you load a couple of cars and want to go home, just go home. You can come back the next day and clean it up.'' But he ''saw what was coming'' and decided to try for the mechanic's job. Others, like his father, who had loaded by hand all their lives did not make the adjustment so easily. ''There weren't too many of the hand loaders who got into machinery. A lot of them just quit coal mining. Quite a few left and went to other places where they were still loading coal by hand. That's all they knew, was hand loading. They went to what they call 'dog holes' over in Preston County [West Virginia]''[17]

Murphy made the important observation that it was the hand-loaders who stood to lose the most from mechanical loading. The day men, or ''company men,'' already were paid a daily rate and ''it didn't make any difference to them about the machines.'' At the time the mine changed over to mechanical loading, ''the hourly people just about equaled the piecework people.'' Sabotage was one way some miners responded, Murphy admitted. As a mechanic he was called in when a piece of machinery broke down.

> I remember one time especially. A man called in and said that he didn't have any lights on one side of his loading machine. They had two lights on the loading head and two on the discharge boom on each side. Well, what happened is that this guy had ripped one of his lights off by letting a car hit it, a guy pushed a car up and it took the light and blew the fuses. A boss sent me in to fix it up. I put a new fuse in and hooked the wire together where the light used to be [so the other lights would work]. Well, that made the operator mad: ''By God, I'll show you what I'll do.'' And he ran that thing against the rib and tore off the left front light. That used to go on a lot, tearing stuff up.[18]

With mechanical loading, the mine was reorganized. ''When we went to mechanical sections, the bosses went down from 120 men to 22 men,'' Murphy remembered.

16. Interview, October 12, 1979, at Mannington, West Virginia.
17. Ibid.
18. Ibid.

And under the new system, the section bosses were on a sort of piecework system. "He's required to get all the coal he can, and lots of times they take short circuits. They'll tell a man to do something without regard to safety," Murphy explained. Even with the reorganization of work into small crews, each with its own boss, the mine workers retained substantial control over the pace of production. The section bosses who didn't get any production "were the ones that the men didn't like. If he's arrogant, if he thinks he's a lot better than they are and lets them know it, they show him who's boss by cutting his production."

When asked how the company went about selecting persons to run the loading machines, Murphy said "that was something the company didn't know what to do about it." The factory men came in to oversee the assembly of the machine, which had to be taken into the mine in pieces and then put together before they could demonstrate its operation. At that time the company had a policy of giving a man ninety days to learn how to run the loader but, Murphy said, "I told my boss that's too much time. If a guy can't learn to run it in one day, he's never going to learn to run it. It wasn't that difficult to run." The union took the position that "the oldest man was entitled to the job but if he didn't want it the next one would get it," although apparently that was not enfoced.[19]

Job Safety and the Loading Machine

Putting large machines to work in constricted areas was, in itself, a hazardous thing to do, and many lost-time accidents occurred when miners were pinned against the rib or knocked in the head by the boom of a loading machine. Machines were rarely engineered with the operator's safety in mind—miners' feet and hands were not protected from open gears, chains, conveyors, and other moving parts. Compounding the problem of men and machinery working together in a confined area was an inadequate lighting system, made even worse by increasing levels of machine-created dust. Since the loading machine needed more work room than hand-loaders, when production pressures were great, the temptation was to neglect roof-control procedures, especially near the face, where a majority of roof-fall accidents occurred. Mining engineers argued that the more rapid rate of mining with mechanical loaders made it possible to mine out a room and retreat before the roof had a chance to settle and fall, so that the new technology should reduce roof-fall accidents. While that may have been an advantage of the system, in many coalfields the more rapid rate of mining liberated more methane gas, which combined with higher dust levels to create conditions conductive to major disasters. And the use of electricity to power the new machinery increased the likelihood that such disasters would occur. Indeed, the very pace of production under the new system became a source of mine accidents, as speed and continuous operations were necessary to make the more capital-intensive methods economically feasible. Finally, the higher levels of dust

19. Ibid.

associated with mechanical mining created a new occupational disease—coal miners' pneumoconiosis, or black lung.

It is not necessary to review the whole history of mine safety in the period from the early 1920s to the 1940s, although that is an interesting history in itself. In this discussion of the impact of mechanization on safety, some observations of a more general nature are appropriate. Underlying most safety work in the period—the coal executive's comments above notwithstanding—was a general belief that mining was inherently dangerous and could never be made as safe as other industries. Even the miners' union reflected this view. "Coal mining will never be a safe occupation. Secrets of Mother Nature are not all known and the unexpected will always happen," the *UMWJ* asserted in 1932.[20]

One frequently expressed belief of the operators was that miners tended to be a careless lot of workers. Others believed that miners actually liked to take chances. In fact, one operator was convinced that taking chances was basic to human nature so he reasoned that he could reduce mine accidents by giving miners an alternative gambling method. He offered door prizes at monthly safety meetings, believing that if his workers were given an opportunity to take chances outside the mine they would be less likely to do so when they got underground. Finally, the view was expressed by some in the mining literature that miners were basically stubborn and would refuse to obey orders, even if these were safety orders aimed at their own protection.

Given these notions about human behavior, it is not surprising that the focus of company safety measures emphasized more the role of the individual worker rather than the importance of improving working conditions. It was necessary to persuade, educate, cajole, and even discipline the mine worker to work safely for his own benefit, many coal operators reasoned. A wide variety of programs evolved during the period: "safety first" campaigns, safety awards such as those given by the Joseph A. Holmes Safety Association, safety bonuses for foremen and for miners, safety contests, safety education programs, and safety meetings.[21] The program at the Pennsylvania Coal and Coke Corporation reflects quite clearly this predisposition on the part of mine management to see individual carelessness as the principal cause of accidents.

> It was realized from the first that to be successful one had to reach the individual and make him a responsible person in this safety movement. With

20. *UMWJ* (January 15, 1932), 6.
21. See, for example, the awards given in 1932, *UMWJ* (May 1, 1932): 14. See *Mining Congress Journal* (December 1927): 922, for a description of the Holmes Safety Association. See also J. J. Sellers, "Safety Bonuses," *1937 Yearbook on Coal Mine Mechanization* (Washington, D.C.: American Mining Congress, 1938), 319–25; F. S. Lenhart, "Promotion of Safety Education Through Meetings," *1934 Yearbook on Coal Mechanization* (Washington, D.C.: American Mining Congress, 1934), 239–40; and John Lyons, "Safety Training for Employees," *1938 Yearbook on Coal Mechanization* (Washington, D.C.: American Mining Congress, 1938), 300–303.

this in mind, a small book of rules was devised, containing abstracts from the state mine laws and additional company safety rulings. These were distributed to each employee with the distinct understanding that they must be read until each one had a good knowledge of what his particular job required in the way of safeguarding himself and his fellow workman. The rules were also discussed at the various meetings, and in addition the foreman and assitants were instructed to ask each workman, on making their periodic inspections, to answer some simple safety questions. Naturally, some of the men thought the whole thing was just another stunt and treated it lightly, if at all, so disciplinary measures had to be used, varying according to the accident infraction of state mine laws or company rulings. Such infractions are becoming less every day.[22]

The safety record for coal mining generally improved during the period from 1930 to 1948. The number of fatal accidents per million man-hours of exposure at work fell from 2.39 in 1930 to 1.35 in 1948. Similarly, the number of nonfatal accidents dropped from 83.75 per million man-hours at the beginning of the period to 56.28 at the end of the period. There is a serious problem, however, in using these injury rates for establishing long-term trends. The bureau had admitted in 1949 it had so much difficulty in obtaining accurate data on the number of hours worked, especially in the early part of the period when workdays were of irregular length and time clocks were rarely used, that it makes the results "so undependable as to be almost fantastic. . . . Comparing these calculated or estimated figures of the past with the more nearly accurate data of the present is the acme of folly if there is a really sincere desire to obtain factual data as to the progress of safety in coal mines."[23]

The bureau apparently had no problem in obtaining accurate data on the number of fatal coal-mine accidents, but nonfatal accident reporting was an entirely different matter. Some companies did a good job of reporting all accidents, but others neglected to report accidents unless compensation payments were made or a hospital visit was recorded. "This is believed to be one of the many reasons for the wide fluctuations in nonfatal injury records and in data on a man-hour of exposure basis," the bureau reported.[24] Further, the nonfatal injury rates are combined rates, including underground mining, surface operations, and strip mining. The fatal accident rates in combination will yield a long-term downward trend as employment shifts from underground mining to the relatively safer strip mining. The measure also suffers from the fact that all lost-time accidents are recorded as single accidents regardless of their severity; that is, all accidents are recorded as single accidents

22. A. L. Hunt, "Successful Accident Prevention," *1933 Yearbook on Coal Mine Mechanization* (Washington, D.C.: American Mining Congress, 1933), 217.

23. U.S. Bureau of Mines, "Safety in the Mining Industry," Information Circular 7485 (Washington, D.C.: GPO, 1949), 15.

24. Ibid.

regardless of the number of days of work actually lost. (In the mid-1940s, the bureau made an effort to correct this deficiency by publishing an index of severity, but no long-term trends are available for evaluating the impact of mechanical loading.)

These statistical problems aside, a comparison of the trends of injury rates and the progress of mechanical loading does not, unfortunately, suggest a very close relation, one way or the other. For example, the early 1930s experienced a drop in mine accidents, but the rate of technological change was nearly constant, and in 1932 and 1933 technology actually dropped. After 1935, when the percentage of mechanically loaded coal began to increase quite rapidly, the fatality rate held steady and even increased in several of the years. It was only after 1942, when the industry was 45.2% mechanized, that the fatality rate began a perceptible and consistent decline.

The Bureau of Mines, which usually took the position that mechanical loading was more dangerous than hand-loading, credited the 1941 Federal Coal Mine Inspections and Investigations Act with effecting the improvement in the industry's safety record during the 1940s. In a review of the transition period to mechanical loading; the bureau pointed out that the general trend of fatality rates was upward during the nine-year period from 1933 to 1941, but in 1942 when federal mine inspections got under way ''the trend was reversed, and the downward trend has been generally maintained since 1942 despite the unfavorable factors and influence during the war years.''[25] Furthermore, the bureau reported, ''in 1942, the trend in nonfatal accident rates started abruptly downward to a level never obtained previously and the favorable trend is being maintained.'' While this assessment may have been self-serving, it does point out that the bureau was not in agreement with those industry spokesmen who were saying at the time that mechanization alone would improve mine safety. In fact, in several of its published reports the bureau went on record with the opposite view: that mine mechanization introduced new health and safety hazards to the workplace.

In a paper presented to the 1930 annual meeting of the International Association of Industrial Accident Boards and Commissions, Daniel Harrington, chief safety engineer of the U.S. Bureau of Mines, addressed the issue of miners' safety under mechanical loading. Although the process was in its infancy at that time and sufficient data was not available for definite conclusions, Harrington told his audience that when the new technology is installed and operated ''with reasonable safeguarding of the mine and its workers,'' it could give good results in safety. But, he emphasized, ''there seems to be a decided tendency to take it for granted that mechanized loading is automatically safe; hence safety is given little or no consideration in the installation or in the operation of these newer methods and there is much reason to believe that safety has been lessened rather than enhanced by them. This is indicated to a certain extent by the fact that the latest complete figures on death rates per

25. *U.S. Bureau of Mines, Report of Health and Safety Division, Fiscal Year 1949* Information Circular 7562 (Washington, D.C.: GPO, 1950), 44.

million man-hours of exposure show that these rates have increased in the two most highly mechanized coal-mining states, Illinois and Wyoming.''[26] Focusing on roof-fall accidents, the primary cause of coal-mining fatalities, Harrington said, ''It is significant that this increase in fatalities from fall of roof and coal during the period 1924–1928 took place in those activities in mines most directly affected by the new mechanized loading systems, hence there is good reason for the inference that the influence of the new systems was in the direction of increasing the hazards from falls of roof and coal.''[27]

THE UNION AND MECHANIZATION

The United Mine Workers' policies and programs relating to the question of mechanization of mining and, more specifically, the question of the use of the loading machine evolved within and was shaped by, these economic realities. As we trace the evolution of the UMWA's policy toward mechanization, however, it is important to keep in mind that job control and local union control could slow the introduction of labor-saving machinery, affect the type of new machinery introduced, and even prevent its introduction altogether.

The story essentially begins with the administration of President John Mitchell, which lasted from 1898 to 1908. As union leader, Mitchell was a very popular individual, with widespread support for most of his policies and programs. He did, however, come under attack on many occasions by the socialists within the union, who disliked his conservative policies, his business unionism, and his propensity to socialize with industrialists, financiers, and national political figures.[28] Mitchell could not deny many of the charges made against him by his critics, but defended his conservative policies and tactics as being more appropriate for solving the problems of the day than the idealism of the socialists. Mitchell promoted the use of conciliation and arbitration for settling industrial disputes. He hoped to establish harmonious relations between employers and employees, asserting that cooperation, rather than conflict, best served the interests of workers. Above all, he believed in the sanctity of the labor agreement, treating it almost as a religious covenant. He

26. U.S. Bureau of Labor Statistics, *Proceedings of the Seventeenth Annual Meeting of the International Association of Industrial Accident Boards and Commissions,* Bulletin 536 (Washington, D.C.: 1931), 186.

27. Ibid., 197–98.

28. For a good account of John Mitchell's contribution to the development of the UMWA and its policies, see J. M. Gowaskie, ''John Mitchell: A Study in Leadership'' (Ph.D. diss., Catholic University of America, 1968). A less scholarly treatment of the Mitchell years can be found in David J. McDonald and Edward A. Lynch, *Coal and Unionism* (New York: Farrar and Rinehart, 1943), 58–80. An explanation of the union's internal structure and bargaining structure that evolved in the Central Competitive Field during Mitchell's tenure can be found in Frank J. Warne, *The Union Movement Among Coal-Mine Workers,* U.S. Department of Labor Bulletin 51 (Washington, D.C.: GPO, 1904), 380–414.

opposed wildcat strikes and sympathy strikes, and although on occasion he found it necessary to authorize a strike against an employer who had failed to live up to an agreement, he did so under pressure from competing operators who continued to pay the agreed scale. Mitchell joined the National Civic Federation, an organization of the top business leaders in the country, and he kept the union out of state and national politics even to the point of prohibiting political discussion in the *UMWJ*.[29]

On the question of machinery in the mines, Mitchell also expressed a very conservative trade union philosophy, and one that influenced the thinking of John White and John L. Lewis, who followed him into the UMWA presidency. Mitchell made this philosophy public in a book he published in 1903, *Organized Labor, Its Problems, Purposes and Ideals and the Present and Future of American Wage Earners*.[30] In a chapter titled "The Right of the Machine," the UMWA president defended the trade union movement against the business community criticism that organized labor generally obstructed mechanization. While there may have been opposition in the past to machinery, Mitchell wrote, "at the present time all but a small minority of workmen are converted to the view that machinery is a necessity, to which it is foolish and unwise, if not impossible, to offer permanent resistance." He then claimed that trade unions (and presumably he was referring to his own union) "have consciously adopted the policy of encouraging inventions and the use of machinery."[31]

Mitchell was well aware of the employment impact of mechanization and the dehumanizing effect of machines that deskilled traditional craft jobs. In describing the machine impact, he wrote that "in hundreds of thousands of cases the machine drove the man from his work and in many instances substituted for patiently and painfully acquired skill the services of an untrained laborer, of a little boy or girl."[32] Where the worker retained his or her job, Mitchell understood that skilled workers "lost their positions and their only asset, their knowledge of a trade." As a skilled miner himself, Mitchell described what it meant for the worker to lose control over his tools and his job: "The old tool of the workers, like the sword of the soldier or the pen of the scholar, had been their friend, their assistant, their very own, but this new machine was a terrible, soulless monster, to which they were chained, to which they were subject, and over which they had no manner of control."[33]

Yet with all of this concern for the negative impact of technology, Mitchell still counseled against trade union resistance. Obstructing the introduction of machinery in one plant or mine would be "to send the new machines into non-union establishments, and by means of competition of the new with the old, of the better with the worse methods of production gradually to lower and reduce the union scale," Mitch-

29. Arthur C. Everling, "Tactics Over Strategy in the United Mine Workers of America," (Ph.D. diss., Pennsylvania State University, 1976), 18.

30. (Philadelphia, America Book and Bible House, 1903).

31. Ibid., 247 and 253.

32. Ibid., 248.

33. Ibid.

ell wrote.[34] It is not clear what his position would have been if the whole industry had been organized and under union contract. Since this situation did not exist in Mitchell's day, and would not exist in the coal industry for at least thirty years to come, Mitchell cannot be faulted for not dealing with a hypothetical situation.

Even if outright resistance was unacceptable to Mitchell, he did state firmly that the union should retain control of the workplace. "While there can be no doubt that the sudden introduction of machines often works great hardship to working men, the method of securing redress is not by fighting the machine but by obtaining control of it."[35] By obtaining control, Mitchell meant that the union must fight to keep collective bargaining rights and to retain jurisdiction over any new jobs created in the process of mechanization. Writing as if he represented the views of all organized labor, Mitchell said that "what the trade unionist desires is not the prohibition of machinery but its regulation. . . . The unionist demands first that machinery be introduced in such a way as to give the least possible damage to the workman, and second, that the introduction of machinery shall rebound to the direct and immediate advantage of the workman, as well as to the direct and immediate advantage of the employer." Mitchell believed that mechanization had to take place in a union setting: "Where trade unions do not exist, employers with the worst and oldest machinery and the most antiquated methods manage to eke out a precarious existence by underpaying and starving their workmen, but where trade unionism is able to enforce a definite maximum wage, these less skillful and less adequately equipped manufacturers must either introduce the modern appliances or go to the wall."

Mitchell was not faced with a crisis in coal; on the contrary, it was a growth industry during his tenure as president. But Mitchell did not understand the dynamics of market competition, and he believed that trade unions, if they stuck to the narrow goal of better wages, hours, and working conditions, could promote the interest of workers and industrialists alike. He viewed the employment relationship as a cooperative one in which factors such as mechanization, which benefited the employer, could serve to benefit the employee as well. In his book, he did not deal with the private and social costs of unemployment resulting from technological change, however.[36] That problem, it seems, was beyond the scope of Mitchell's business unionism. His influence on the evolution of UMWA policy toward machinery was nonetheless important.

The machine question does not appear to have been a burning issue at the collective bargaining table during Mitchell's time. True, the question of the differential in wages between machine miners (i.e., loaders who followed the machine) and pick miners continued to be a matter of contention between the union and the operators. Mitchell did not offer his readers an economic analysis of the role of labor-saving

---

34. Ibid., 252.
35. Ibid., 249.
36. He believed in negotiating shorter hours, which would spread the available work around and thereby reduce layoffs.

machinery in the coal industry, but he did promote the idea, later developed by John L. Lewis, that modernization through mechanization was necessary for the healthy growth and development of any industry. Mitchell was probably motivated to discuss the question of machinery and to develop a positive policy toward it by contemporary critics of unionism who argued that the labor movement was restricting the nation's output.[37] Whatever the motivation, Mitchell can be credited with initiating a national UMWA policy toward mechanization that remained influential for many years to come.

New Machinery and the 1920 Bituminous Coal Mining Convention

The question of mechanization was also brought before the 1920 Bituminous Coal commission (the commission that set national coal policy after World War I) by the operators. In item 6 of a seven-point program, the operators asked.

> That the commission in its award provide for the introduction of devices or machinery which may serve to reduce the cost of coal and consequently the cost to the public for which there is no scale of wages in the then-existing contract.[38]

At this late date, more than forty years after undercutting machines were first introduced, the operators were still faced with opposition by miners to the use of undercutting machines. By 1920, 60.7% of all coal was undercut mechanically, but the refusal of locals and subdistricts to negotiate machine rates continued to be such an obstacle that the mine owners sought support from this presidential tribunal. The majority report cited it as a serious problem: "It is recognized by the commission that the introduction of machinery and devices can be prevented by the mine workers by failure to agree upon the rates, terms, and conditions under which the machinery and devices are to be used." The majority report then made lengthy recommendations pertaining to the mechanization question, as follows:

> 4. That pending the joint district agreement between the miners and operators covering a fair schedule of rates for piecework or tonnage operation of any new device or machinery, the right of the operator to introduce and operate any such new device or machinery shall not be questioned, and his selection of such men as he may desire to conduct tests with or operate such device or machinery shall not be in any way interfered with or obstructed by

37. See U.S. Commissioner of Labor, *Special Report on Regulation and Restriction of Output* (Washington, D.C.: GPO, 1914), 383–481.

38. U.S. Bituminous Coal Commission, *Majority and Minority Reports* (Washington, D.C.: GPO, 1920), 14 and 18.

the miners or their representatives, provided the wages offered are at least equal to the established scale rates for similar labor.

The operator shall be privileged to pay in excess of the established scale rates of pay without such excess pay being considered as establishing a permanent condition for the operation of said device or machine.

After the device or machine shall have passed the experimental stage and is in shape to be introduced as a regular component part of the production of coal, then for the purpose of determining a permanent scale of rates (such rates to continue until the joint scale conference above referred to fixes a scale) for operating such device or machine, the mine workers may have a representative present for a reasonable time to witness its operation, after which a schedule of rates shall be determined by mutual agreement, which scale shall be concluded within 60 days after a fair test has been made.

The test will disclose the labor-saving in the cost of producing coal, out of which labor-saving the mine worker shall receive the equivalent of the contract rates for the class of work displaced, plus a fair proportion of the labor-saving effected.

In like manner new or untried systems of mining; for instance, long wall, retreating long wall, or the panel system may be introduced by the operator for the purpose of conservation, increasing production, the lessening of cost, or in the interest of safety without his right to make such change being abridged: Provided, however, that for this class of work the mine worker shall in the same manner receive the equivalent of the contract rates for the class of work displaced, plus a fair proportion of the labor-saving effected.[39]

A close reading of this statement, with which the operators' representative concurred, reveals that the mine owners may not have been so much concerned with the cutting machine as they were with entirely new types of mining machinery and mining systems. It will be remembered that developmental work on mechanical loading machines had been going on in the years immediately prior to the war and continued, notably at the Jeffrey Company, during the war. And at the time the commission was holding its hearings, it was no secret that the Pittsburgh Coal Company, the nation's largest, was having success with four Joy loading machines, which had been installed in one of its mines on an experimental basis.[40] The statement did not specify any particular type of mining equipment but referred simply to a "device or machine." A detailed plan was proposed, however, for establishing wage rates for operators of new machinery. It is interesting to note that the commission proposed a floor under wages so that mine workers affected by new machinery would receive "the equivalent of the contract rates for the class of work displaced." Although the amount was not specified, the operators also agreed in principle that

39. Ibid.
40. See chap. 2 of Dix, *What's A Coal Miner To Do?*

the mine workers on new machinery should receive "a fair proportion of the labor-saving effected." Since the operators proposed a parallel set of principles in the event of the introduction of new mining systems such as long-wall mining, it seems quite clear that the stage was being set in anticipation of major technological developments in the industry.

The union's position, as expressed in John White's minority report, was to reject outright the extended discussion on the issue in the majority report and to propose quite briefly the following substitute:

> Labor-saving machinery: The operators have the right to install labor-saving machinery at any time, and such machine work not now covered by this agreement shall be governed by such scale as the miners' and operators' representatives may determine.[41]

If this was the union's policy toward mechanization, it was little more than a policy of expediency, to allow the problems associated with mechanization to be solved at the local and district levels. The policy—or nonpolicy—did reflect the reality of local control and the reality of the internal structure of the union, which at that time had not been sufficiently centralized to weaken the authority of its subordinate units and the power of the rank and file.

In his report, White reiterated the UMWA's position on the machine question, namely that "the United Mine Workers have always been favorable to and have never opposed the introduction of machinery or labor-saving machinery in the operation of the mines."[42] He went on to cite the increase in the number of machines in unionized territory and then tried to demonstrate the savings operators had realized upon installing machinery. In all cases, he was referring to the cutting machine and seems quite oblivious to the fact that the operators, as suggested in the majority report, had something else in mind. Nor did he respond to the operators' suggestion that when new machinery is installed a union representative would be permitted for a "reasonable time to witness its operation," so that a scale could be negotiated. Why the union failed at this point even to consider a constructive policy toward mechanization is not known. It may have been that White was unaware of the potential threat to jobs and working conditions of the new loading machines, or it may have been, as suggested above, that a hands-off policy was the only realistic one the international union officers could take at that particular time.

When the Bituminous Coal Commission reported its findings in March 1920, it awarded a twenty-four-cent advance in scale to both pick miners and to those who loaded after an undercutting machine. A dollar-a-day advance was recommended for day workers, and when these awards were later incorporated into the Central Competitive Field and outlying districts' agreements, miners' wages were at record

41. U.S. Bituminous Coal Commission, *Reports,* 105.
42. Ibid.

high levels. The central Pennsylvania wage agreement, for example, established the following basic rates:[43]

Per Ton Scale
Pick mining $1.14
Machine loading $0.77

Inside Day-Wage Scale
Motorman $6.10
Spragger $6.00
Tracklayer $6.00
Tracklayer helper $5.77
Timberman $6.00
Timberman helper $5.77
Inside day laborer $5.77

It is somewhat confusing for this labor agreement to specify a "machine loading," rate, because it did not mean that a rate was established for a loading machine operator. The term machine loader, in common use at the time, was the designation for the miner who loaded coal that had been undercut by a cutting machine.

The general terms and conditions of earlier agreements were carried forward in the CCF agreement and in the various district and subdistrict agreements made in 1920. The much-disliked penalty clause was carried forward without change, and the traditional work rules negotiated over the years were also to be found in the new agreement. Mechanization was dealt with in mixed fashion; some agreements ignored it entirely, while others made passing reference to the Bituminous Coal Commission's report. The CCF and the Illinois agreements made no mention of the issue, and the absence in the central Pennsylvania agreement of any mention of it prompted one coal trade journal to note, quite prophetically, "If anybody thinks up a thing that will dig and load the coal without human energy they will have to start non-union, for there is no provision for this sort of thing in the Central Pennsylvania contract."[44]

In a few other agreements, such as the one negotiated in northern West Virginia, the contract introduced the mechanization issue by the following language:

The majority report of the Bituminous Coal Commission regarding the introduction of new machinery is adopted. The joint boards will agree upon a commission for making any necessary tests.[45]

43. *Coal Trade Bulletin* (May 15, 1920): 140.
44. Ibid.
45. Ibid. (May 1, 1920): 140.

In Harlan County, Kentucky, the question was more directly addressed in that the contract gave the operators unilateral authority to install machinery:

> The right of an operator to change from pick to machine basis, or from machine to pick basis, or change the type of machinery or appliance for any purpose, when he desires to do so, shall not be questioned.[46]

And in the George's Creek field of Maryland, the 1920 miners' contract contained this provision:

> The operators have the right to install labor-saving machinery at any time and such machine work not now covered by agreement shall be governed by such rates as the miners' and operators' representatives may determine.[47]

Within a few weeks after the signing of the 1920 agreements, opposition to its terms developed across the coalfields. The day men in particular were dissatisfied with the $1.00 increase they received and, later in the summer, led a series of unauthorized strikes in Illinois and Indiana. Under pressure from these strikes, the operators, who at the time were enjoying a temporary improvement in coal markets, met with the union and renegotiated day wages. The operators conceded an increase of an additional $1.50, bringing the daily rate up to $7.50. Ironically, the renegotiated contracts continued the penalty clause, although it had been largely ignored during the 1920 strike period.[48]

By the time these contracts expired in the spring of 1922, the operators were experiencing serious financial problems resulting from declining sales and falling coal prices. The industry's overexpansion in capacity was compounded by a national recession in 1922, and many operators let it be known in negotiations that they would demand wage reductions instead of agreeing to wage increases. To support their hardship claim, the operators published data showing that wages in some non-union fields were as much as 56% lower than the union scale. And they claimed further that, if wage concessions were not made, union mines would lose markets for their product and miners would lose jobs. Other operators took an even harder line when they announced that they were absolutely unwilling to meet with the national union for any purpose but were willing to negotiate at the district level. Others said that they would bargain with their own employees on a mine-by-mine basis.[49] Miners were thus caught in a contradiction not of their own making. When

---

46. Ibid. (September 18, 1920): 215.
47. Ibid. (January 1, 1921): 75.
48. *Monthly Labor Review* (November 1922): 4.
49. Union leaders believed that the operators' strategy was inspired by the nationwide open-shop drive of the 1920s—called the American plan—which was aimed at destroying collective bargaining. There seemed to be some basis for their belief, when the operators began demanding abolition of the union dues checkoff system, which had been in effect in the Central Competitive Field for many years; ibid., 11.

it came to wages and other economic considerations, they needed a strong national union that could speak for them with one voice; they needed union solidarity to prevent wage reductions that would follow from local bargaining as operators played one local against another. At the same time, it was important to maintain the control that they had through their local unions and pit committees in order to protect basic job rights and working conditions.

Local Agreements and Workers' Control

At the district, subdistrict, and local levels of the union, labor agreements also were negotiated for a one-year term. These agreements continued the tonnage rates and the basic wage of $7.50 a day that had been won in 1920. In addition, these agreements carried forward the negotiated work rules and other terms found in prior agreements. A year later, the 1923 agreements were extended without significant modification in what became known as the Jacksonville agreement. If little new appeared in the labor contracts at this time, they were no less important in the history of collective bargaining in the industry, because they marked the beginning of the end of an era for coal miners. The agreements of the hand-loading period came under increasing pressure as management moved to mechanize the mines, to increase discipline of the workforce, and to extend management's rights and prerogatives. A review of two subdistrict agreements made in this period will establish an appreciation for why some miners a decade later lamented their loss of job rights and why they petitioned their union at that time to seek a restoration of the worker's control they once enjoyed.

The 1923 subdistrict agreement between the UMWA and the operators of the Hocking District of Ohio is a good example of a typical contract in the early period before the introduction of mechanical loading.[50] Mining rates were established at $1.12 per ton, run-of-the-mine, and the day rate for most inside jobs was $7.50. An eight-hour-day provision for day or company men was continued from earlier agreements, and eleven unpaid holidays were set aside. Under the terms of the agreement, the operators were bound to provide a "square turn" (i.e., an opportunity for each miner to receive an equal number of empty mine cars), while the miners agreed to mine clean coal and "produce their coal in such a way as not to increase the percentage of fine coal." Many other details were included in the contract, such as payment for slate removal, establishment of a standard room width, rules governing work on idle days, and the conditions under which call-in pay was to be awarded. The settlement of disputes was left to an informal arrangement under which a matter would be taken up by the mine superintendent and the mine committee. There were no restrictions on the rights of the mine committee and, most interestingly, there was no provision for grievance arbitration. Although the standard no-strike and pen-

---

50. U.S. Bureau of Labor Statistics, *Hours and Earnings in Bituminous Coal Mining, 1922, 1923, and 1926,* Bulletin 454 (Washington, D.C.: GPO, 1924), 11–20.

alty clause inserted in all coal labor agreements since 1917 was included in the Hocking Valley contract, it is likely that grievances not settled in the informal procedure in fact resulted in a local work stoppage.

The Hocking Valley contract is noteworthy as much for what was left out of it as for what it contained. There was no discipline and discharge provision nor was there any form of a management's rights or management prerogatives clause. It is clear from this contract that workers exercised considerable control over the labor process, so much so that the mechanization issue was not even mentioned. There was not even a reference to the 1920 Bituminous Coal Commission report and its recommendations on technology. And all this was happening in the shadow of the Columbus plant of the Jeffrey Manufacturing Company, the world's largest producer of mining machinery.

In northern West Virginia, a coalfield organized only a few years earlier, a labor agreement was signed in the spring of 1923 similar in many ways to the Hocking District agreement, although it also differed in important ways.[51] The similarities related to wages, holidays, and basic work rules relating to hand-loading coal, while the differences suggested new trends in labor-management relations in the industry. For example, a well-defined grievance procedure contained an arbitration provision for "a final and binding award." That this new procedure was intended to serve as a substitute for local strikes is implied in the arbitration clause, which stated that "in all cases all parties involved must continue at work pending the investigation and adjustment" of grievances. And "if any employee . . . refuses to work because of any grievance . . . [he] will be subject to dismissal without recourse at the option of the company." The mine committee, which "shall consist of three men, all of whom shall be American citizens," was responsible only for the adjustment of disputes "that the mine boss and miner or miners have tried but are unable to adjust." It was specified that the mine committee "shall have no other authority or exercise any other control, nor in any way interfere with the operation of the mine." There was the further admonition that "the mine committee shall under no circumstances go around the mine for any cause whatsoever unless called upon by the mine foreman or by the miner or dayman who may have a grievance that he can not settle with the mine boss, and then only to investigate that grievance with the parties involved." Unlike the Ohio agreement, the northern West Virginia contract included an Irregular Work section aimed at disciplining individual miners who absented themselves from work for two days or more "unless through sickness."

For those who have worked under or who have knowledge of modern wage contracts in the coal industry, this 1923 agreement will sound quite familiar. One important difference, however, should be pointed out. There was no allowance, either implicit or explicit, for the introduction of new technology. New machinery might have been introduced under a management's rights clause, but none existed at that

---

51. Boris Emmet, *Labor Relations in the Fairmont, West Virginia, Bituminous Coal Field,* U.S. Bureau of Labor Statistics, Bulletin 361 (Washington, D.C.: GPO, 1924), 11–20.

time. The closest thing to it was a provision under the Hire and Discharge section, which read as follows: "The operator or his superintendent or mine foreman shall be respected in the management of the mine and the direction of the working force."[52] Nor did the contract contain any reference to the use of machinery. Even the clause appearing in the 1920 Fairmont, West Virginia, agreement, which said, "The majority report of the Bituminous Coal Commission regarding the introduction of new machinery is adopted," was missing from the 1923 contract.

While it is purely conjecture, it is reasonable to conclude that the operators wanted to drop the commission's recommendations suggesting that wage rates for machinery operators be negotiated locally. After introducing a new arc-wall cutting machine in 1920, the Fairmont coal operators consulted with union officials to establish a wage scale, as recommended. But it took almost two years before agreement could be reached and the machinery installed.[53] The operators were convinced that their workers, acting through their local union representatives, were simply trying to stall or halt completely the use of labor-saving equipment. A summary of this situation by the U.S. Bureau of Labor Statistics at the time tended to support the operators' contentions:

> The many obstacles interposed by the workers to the introduction of labor-saving machinery result indirectly in restriction of output. The United Mine Workers of America is on record as favoring the introduction of labor-saving machinery. Actually, however, when a labor-saving machine is to be introduced there are violent objections on the part of the men. These objections express themselves very often in a demand for rates which, if paid, would eliminate all saving brought about by the new machine, thus causing a distinct loss to the extent of the additional investment. The Arc-Wall case is typical of the situation.[54]

The 1922 U.S. Coal Commission

Public concern with the coal industry went beyond the inconveniences brought about by the lengthy 1922 strike. There was growing evidence at this time that the industry was moving rapidly toward economic disaster. For example, in its 1923 annual report, the U.S. Department of the Interior summarized conditions in the following manner: "The salient features of 1923 and the years immediately preceding may be summarized in a word. The number of employees and the output per man have been increasing and with them the potential capacity. The demand has been stationary or even declining. The average time worked has therefore been de-

52. Ibid., 15.
53. Ibid., 33.
54. Ibid., 35.

creasing, and with it prices have tended to fall.''[55] Both the 1922 strike and the general state of the industry prompted President Warren Harding to recommend to Congress that a special investigating commission be established to study the industry and make suggestions for its economic reorganization. In asking Congress to deal in this manner with the pending industrial crisis in coal, the president said, ''I am speaking now on behalf of mine workers, mine operators, and the American public. It [a commission] will bring protection to all and point the way to continuity of production and the better functioning of the industry in the future.[56] Following this presidential request, Congress set up in October 1922 the U.S. Coal Commission and charged it with the duty of investigating all phases of production, transportation, and distribution of coal and ''all organized or other relationships among operators and miners with a view to recommending remedial legislation.[57] (It was not the first, nor would it be the last, time that a president and Congress responded to a crisis in coal by appointing a fact-finding commission.)

Some statistics on the industry in the early 1920s will indicate the seriousness of the problem confronting the new commission. High wartime prices and special market conditions in the immediate post–World War I period stimulated expansion of production in existing mines and encouraged the opening of many new mines. Full-time mining capacity, which had grown by 82 million tons in the five years from 1913 to 1918, increased by 254 million tons in the five years from 1918 to 1923. The number of operating mines increased from 8,319 in 1918 to 9,331 in 1923.[58] Never before had the nation been in a position to mine so much coal. Unfortunately, however, this potential was not matched by an increase in demand for the fuel. On the contrary, the demand for coal was experiencing a decline, because competing fuels such as oil and natural gas were taking over traditional coal markets.

In addition, technological improvements in the utilization of coal, such as the development of the by-products of coke process and the redesign of steam locomotives, reduced demand. When the average number of days worked in the industry dropped from a wartime high of 249 days to 179 days in 1923, it was an early-warning sign for miners and operators. The downward trend in prices, from $3.75 a ton on the average in 1920 to $2.68 a ton in 1923, also indicated that the quantity of coal produced exceeded the demand. And when coal prices and number of days worked failed to rise with an upswing in the national economy in 1923, it became quite clear to everyone that there probably were ''too many mines and too many miners'' for the industry's well-being. In this economic context, the U.S. Coal Commission was directed to formulate long-run policies for stabilizing the industry.

Although the UMWA progressives, such as District 2 President John Brophy, hoped the commission would make recommendations that would support their pro-

55. U.S. Bureau of Mines, *Mineral Resources of the United States, 1923,* part 2 (Washington, D.C.: GPO, 1926), 516.
56. Ibid., 22.
57. Ibid.
58. Ibid.

gram for nationalizing the mines, John L. Lewis apparently expected very little from it. There were no union representatives on the seven-member board, as there had been on the 1920 commission, and while most of the members might have been considered neutral in their attitudes toward the labor movement, more than one was considered to be anti-union.[59] After eleven months of study, the commission published its findings that detailed the extent of the irregularity of operations, the over-expansion of the industry, and the destructiveness of the industry's competitive market structure. The deplorable conditions under which many miners lived and worked, especially in the nonunion fields, was documented along with many other aspects of the industry, such as collective bargaining relations, structures of the UMWA and the operators' associations, management practices, engineering problems, and railroad rate structures. While the study still stands as the most thorough one ever made of the industry, the final recommendations of the commission were quite disappointing to both the operators and the union. Labeled "vague, platitudinous, and occasionally even meaningless," by one scholar, the recommendations were frequently contradictory.[60] And as might be expected, "such trivial recommendations received the fate they deserved from operators, union and government, absolute neglect."

The commission's study of underground mine management is important to this review of the union's mechanization policies because it demonstrated that the technology for mechanical loading was scientifically well advanced and economically viable. Several mines that had been using mechanical loading equipment for a few years were examined and contrasted with hand-loading mines. The conclusion was that the cost of mining a ton of coal could be reduced by as much as 30% by using the new technology.[61] While noting that a decrease in human labor for any given production level would follow, the commission pointed out that, with the use of a machine-loader, many of the duties that the hand loader traditionally performed passed over to day men, or company men. A division of labor and specialization of tasks followed from efficient use of the technology: "Such work as timbering, laying track in rooms, cleaning up after the loader, and removing rock or slate, is necessarily done entirely by men who can be specifically trained for it. Furthermore, these men work in a small area and under constant supervision of the foremen, which is impracticable where individuals are scattered in work places widely apart. Consequently they can be more effectively employed and at correspondingly lower unit costs."[62]

After detailing the advantages to be gained from mechanical loading, the commission's report dealt with the problems associated with the transition. It was pointed

59. Melvyn Dubofsky and Warren Van Tine, *John L. Lewis,* 89–90.

60. Dubofsky and Van Tine, *John L. Lewis,* 91.

61. U.S. Coal Commission, *Report, Part 11, Bituminous Coal—Detailed Labor and Engineering Studies* (Washington, D.C.: GPO, 1925), 1905.

62. Ibid., 1913.

out, for example, that loading machines were not adaptable to thin seams of coal and that machine loading might not be so profitable where considerable slate was found mixed with the coal. Significantly, the commission claimed that the union itself was an obstacle to the introduction of machinery: "A handicap in the development of loading machines has been not merely the overcoming of mechanical and physical difficulties but also the opposition of the union, which has opposed their introduction or has attempted to attain so high a rate of pay for operating the machines as to invalidate a large part of their value from the economical standpoint."[63]

The operators, in a brief submitted to the commission, also charged that, while the UMWA claimed to support mechanization, its wage and other policies at the local level tended to restrict the use of new equipment. They noted that introduction of labor-saving devices is specifically permitted in almost all joint agreements but "while they do not object to the installation of the machines, as such, they do adopt a number of methods to make the installation of machines unprofitable to the operator and to prevent him from cutting down his force of laborers."[64] The central Pennsylvania operators offered specific examples of the union's opposition to introduction of labor-saving machinery and expressed the view that finding the ways and means for mechanizing the industry was the single most important question facing the U.S. Coal Commission. These operators summarized their feelings about the UMWA's mechanization policy in the following manner: "It is our opinion that if the United Mine Workers controlled the mining industry 100 percent, there would never be another machine introduced in the mining industry. It is only by the force of economic pressure, due to the introduction of labor-saving machinery in nonunion fields, that they are finally accepted in the union districts of the United States at this time."[65]

The UMWA's response to these charges of obstructing technological change came in the form of a letter written to the commission reaffirming a position taken publicly by former union president John White. In bold letters for emphasis the union wrote to the commission:

THIS UNION NEVER HAS OPPOSED THE INTRODUCTION OF ANY KIND OF SAFETY OR LABOR SAVING MACHINERY, METHODS OR DEVICES WHERE IT IS PROVED THAT SUCH MACHINERY, METHODS OR DEVICES MAKE FOR THE SAFE AND THE MORE EFFICIENT PRODUCTION OF COAL. WHAT THE UNION DOES INSIST UPON IS THAT WHEN SUCH SAFETY OR LABOR SAVING MACHINERY, METHODS OR DEVICES ARE INSTALLED THEY SHALL BE OPERATED BY UNION MINERS; AND THAT THE MINERS SHALL HAVE

63. Ibid., 1916.
64. U.S. Coal Commission, "Comparative Efficiency of Labor in the Bituminous Coal Industry Under Union and Non-Union Operation," 182.
65. Bituminous Operators' Special Committee, *Briefs and Other Communication Submitted to the United States Coal Commission by the Bituminous Operators* (1923): 4:59–60 (microfilm, West Virginia Collection, West Virginia Library).

SOMETHING TO SAY ABOUT THE RATE OF WAGES THEY ARE TO RECEIVE FOR SUCH WORK.[66]

This appears to be the only input the union made to the commission on this issue. However, it published a short pamphlet titled *The United Mine Workers and The United States Coal Commission,* in which it answered many of the commission findings. And the pages of the *UMWJ* were used to respond to others of the commission's recommendations. But the letter quoted above seems to be the only response it made to the charges of obstructionism.

Based on its perception of the importance of bituminous coal to the nation's economic welfare, the U.S. Coal Commission's final report urged two reforms for the industry, both to be conducted under "fishbowl" conditions of public fact-finding and supervision. The first recommendation called for a readjustment of railroad freight rates "to express the true relation of cost to service." The goal of this reform was to eliminate the discriminatory rate differentials that made it possible for southern Appalachian coals to compete with Illinois, Indiana, and Ohio coals for the Great Lakes trade. The second reform the commission proposed was the consolidation of mining companies by "removing the existing legal barriers to such an economic arrangement." In calling for a relaxation of the antitrust laws, the commission asserted that "the consolidation grouping, or pooling of bituminous mining operations should not only be permitted but encouraged, with a view to insuring more steady production, less speculative prices, better living conditions, more regular employment, and lower costs."[67] The necessary protection of the public interest could be assured, the commission asserted, by requiring federal supervision of the financial structure of any coal consolidation, in much the same way that transportation legislation required supervision of railroad mergers.

Although the UMWA tended to belittle the findings and the recommendation of the U.S. Coal Commission, both the freight rate proposal and the consolidation plan were important parts of John L. Lewis's scheme for rationalizing the industry. And the idea of allowing "grouping or pooling" of mining interests formed the basis of the union's stabilization proposals that were later incorporated into the New Deal industrial recovery programs of the early 1930s. The progressives in the union were disappointed that the commission failed to support the idea of nationalization of the mines but welcomed the recommendations of federal fact-finding and public involvement in reviewing the industry's performance.

By way of assessment, it can be said that President Harding's special investigating commission had little or no direct impact on legislation affecting the coal industry. Its report, which enthusiastically supported the introduction of mechanization and

66. Quoted in United Mine Workers of America, *The United Mine Workers and the United States Coal Commission* (Indianapolis, Ind., n.d.), 28.

67. U.S. Coal Commission, *Report, Part 1, Principal Findings and Recommendations* (Washington, D.C.: GPO, 1925), 28.

scientific management for the more rational production of coal, and its program for the consolidation of capital to increase control over the market both tended simply to justify what was already taking place in the industry in the mid-1920s.

Lewis's Response to Mechanization

As discussed earlier, Lewis's predecessors had adopted a general policy of supporting mine mechanization. Lewis not only favored the use of new technology but believed that it was the key to long-run stabilization of the whole industry. The Lewis stabilization program was outlined in his keynote address to the 1924 UMWA convention, was promoted in interviews in various newspapers and trade journals, and was featured in his 1924 book *The Miners' Fight for American Standards* (Indianapolis, Ind.: Bell). Although ghost-written by the men Lewis hired as consultants, speechwriters, and union publicists,[68] this book clearly reflected John L. Lewis's basic political and economic values. Writing as if he spoke for all union members and as if the nationalization movement within the UMWA was insignificant, Lewis rejected government control of the industry and supported "the operation of natural economic laws to bring about a permanent improvement."[69] He claimed that "the policy of the United Mine Workers of America at this time is neither new nor revolutionary. It does not command the admiration of visionaries and Utopians. It ought to have the support of every thinking business man in the United States, because it proposes to allow natural economic laws free play in the production and distribution of coal."[70]

The Lewis program, sometimes referred to as his Jacksonville program, was based on the belief that if the union could hold the line on wages, the operators in the union fields would be forced to install loading machines and would, in so doing, be able to lower their costs of production and thereby drive out of business the less efficient and, presumably, nonunion operators. By this process, industry capacity would be brought into proper relation to consumer demand. Lewis also argued that freight rates charged by the railroads should be adjusted to remove the existing unfair advantages enjoyed by many nonunion operators, notably those in West Virginia and points south. Stabilization of the industry also depended on extending union protection to all coal miners, Lewis argued. "Every car of non-union coal at present represents an intrusion into the general industrial system of a malignant influence; because this coal could not be produced and sold, as it is now, without the denial of American rights in the mines from whence it comes and without an uneconomic system of railroad favoritism to boost it to market," he claimed.[71]

Considerations of wage levels and wage structures played an important role in

68. Dubofsky and Van Tine, *John L. Lewis,* 137.
69. Lewis, *Miners' Fight,* 15.
70. Ibid.
71. Ibid., 180.

John L. Lewis's program for economic recovery of the industry in the 1920s, not to mention survival of the union and solidification of his own power and prestige in the labor movement.[72] It is interesting to note that Lewis urged that the tonnage payment system be abolished in favor of a time payment system. His argument rested on the notion that a uniform daily wage would make labor costs per unit of output higher for the less efficient (i.e., low productivity) mines and would force them from the industry. He also argued that elimination of piecework in the mines would help eliminate the source of many local disputes and would reduce local strikes. Also built into the traditional wage system were payments for various forms of dead work, which routinely created conflict and disagreement. A straight daily wage would, for Lewis, improve industrial relations in the industry: "It is Utopian to expect that such local conflicts can be entirely eliminated as long as piecework prevails and men are men."[73]

A second dimension to the Lewis wage-mechanization program for the industry was the elimination of regional wage differences, which tended, he felt, to keep too many mines, most notably the nonunion ones, in operation when they should be shut down. Over the years, Lewis kept steadfastly to his wage policy, and as he gained increasing control over the administration of the union, his policy became the union's policy. "The union's current [wage] strategy is easy to describe," one scholar observed in 1955. It has remained essentially unchanged since Lewis first tried to justify the Jacksonville scale: "By raising wage rates (and labor costs per ton) and by eliminating regional wage-rate differentials, heavy pressure to mechanize will be brought to bear on all firms, especially the relatively high-cost operations. . . . The increased use of machines will enable the union to exact even higher wage rates or shorter hours or both. Higher wage rates, in brief, encourage mechanization, which permits still higher wage rates."[74]

Lewis was, however, forced temporarily to abandon his no-backward-step, high-wage policy when an incipient mutiny among the membership in Illinois and Ohio threatened his control of the union. He had reasoned that, in his refusal to make wage concessions, the large coal operators would be forced to introduce labor-saving equipment and otherwise modernize their operations, while the smaller firms, which could not afford to mechanize, would be forced to shut down. He believed that technology, with the aid of the union's wage policy, would save the industry. It might have worked if, first, the union could have organized the whole industry and

72. The reader is referred to the following sources for accounts of the challenges to Lewis during the late 1920s, some of which revolved around the no-backward-step policy: Edward Dean Wickersham, "Opposition to the International Officers of the United Mine Workers of America: 1919–1933" (Ph.D. diss., Cornell University, 1951); Jack Richard Foster, "Union on Trial: The United Mine Workers of America, District 11 of Indiana, 1930–1940 (Ph.D. diss., Ball State University, 1967); and Stanley Miller, "The United Mine Workers of America: A Study on How Trade Union Policy Relates to Technological Change" (Ph.D. diss., University of Wisconsin, 1957).

73. Lewis, *Miners' Fight,* 98.

74. Morton S. Baratz, *The Union and the Coal Industry* (New Haven: Yale University Press, 1955), 72.

imposed a uniform wage and, second, if Lewis had been able to neutralize local control so that a national wage scale for machine-operators could have been negotiated and limitations on the use of machinery eliminated. Lewis was unable to do either during the 1920s. In response to rank-and-file pressure in parts of the Central Competitive Field, where coal markets and jobs were being lost to nonunion coal, Lewis reluctantly agreed to let district unions negotiate their own wage scales without reference to the Jacksonville scale. Further, Lewis relaxed his long-standing opposition to federal government involvement in the industry's affairs when, in the summer of 1928, the UMWA testified for and strongly supported passage of the Watson bill, a piece of legislation that would have exempted coal operators from antitrust laws so they could fix prices and that would have promoted industry collective bargaining. Lewis hoped at that point that the government could save the coal industry and his union.

Objections to the Lewis Plan

Mechanization was at the center of John L. Lewis's 1925 plan to stabilize the coal industry. A key element of this mechanization policy was the conversion of the traditional tonnage payment system to a daily or hourly wage rate. But on this question of a new payment system, it soon became clear that Lewis did not represent the views of all miners, especially after they realized that day wages involved more than just a new way of calculating their income; it involved a new way of doing things in the mines.

Lewis failed to address, either in his book or in response to his critics on the union's convention floor, the concealed issues behind the payment question. It is interesting to note that the industry itself was not so certain that a day wage was the only system to use with the installation of loading machines. One industry spokesman argued in 1924 that a tonnage payment system is better "because, by that method of compensation, the machines are most likely to be worked nearer to their full capacity and . . . the attendant work around a loader will be more expeditiously done."[75] But another, who clearly understood the changes the loading machines would bring to the labor process, argued that day wages were better for several reasons: "Loading machines are going to force mine operators to assume full responsibility for what goes on at the face . . . [which] means men working at the face are going to be under more direct supervision." Mines could be made to function more like Henry Ford's automobile factories, with close supervision and a daily wage, one mine superintendent claimed.

The day-wage system had the obvious advantage for the mine owners of limiting the returns to the mine workers who operated the new machinery, but it had the disadvantage of requiring greater supervision. After a local machine-loading scale was negotiated and several loaders were installed in a large Illinois mine in the

75. *Coal Age* (August 21, 1924): 261.

summer of 1924, one trade journal summed up the problem very succinctly: "The job that now confronts that coal company and every other company that adopts machine loading in Illinois is the ever-present job of getting a full day's work out of men paid on that basis."[76] Several plans were suggested by various industry people for sharing the gains from productivity increases with the workers. Most of these plans involved a combination day wage, or minimum wage, and a bonus or incentive program for production beyond a fixed standard.[77] Lewis showed no interest in any of these gain-sharing plans, preferring instead to rely on periodical wage negotiations to share in productivity increases.

At the 1927 UMWA convention, a delegate from the Belleville, Illinois, region made an eloquent appeal to the union policymaking body for a return to the tonnage payment system with mechanical loaders. His arguments on the convention floor were well thought out and were based on two years' experience with the new technology. He explained that the reason he and his fellow workers were opposed to the day wage was that it "gives the boss the right to direct every move." In other words, he said, "You have a boss looking down your shirt collar all day long."

In referring to the trade journal *Coal Age* and its advocacy of scientific management in the mines, the delegate claimed that the flat day wage "will factoryize the mine. . . . They want to make a Ford plant out of every coal mine."[78] Anticipating what was in store for miners, the delegate said emphatically, "we don't want a day-wage scale because in our opinion based on our experience, a flat day-wage scale will eventually mean a haven for efficiency experts and straw jacks and an underground hell for coal miners." Finally, the Illinois miner told the convention that he and his fellow workers objected to the day wage because it excluded miners from participation in the productivity gains created by the loading machines. But, he urged, "if we were put on a tonnage rate and the capacity of that machine is increased, our wages are going to automatically increase with the capacity of the machine." In concluding his appeal to the convention, the delegate offered a resolution that said, in essence, that the only way that miners could safeguard their "independence and prevent the factoryizing of our mines" was to "demand a tonnage rate for all cutting, loading and shooting of coal, and no day-wage scale be tolerated under any condition."

Response to this appeal came from three individuals: William Mitch, president of Indiana's District 11 and a staunch Lewis supporter; John Brophy, president of District 2 in central Pennsylvania and a long-time opponent of Lewis; and Lewis himself. Mitch said that several mines in Indiana had installed loading machines and were operating on a day-wage scale. He admitted that within his district there

76. *Coal Trade Bulletin* (August 1, 1924), 186.

77. See various issues of the then newly organized trade journal, *Coal Mine Mechanization,* esp. November 1924 and February 1925. It is interesting to note that incentive plans were reintroduced to the industry in the National Bituminous Coal Wage Agreement of 1978, and continued in the 1981 agreement.

78. *UMWA Proceedings, 1927 Convention,* 442–45.

was a "vast difference of opinion as to what should be done" on the pay question, but he also said that he thought that the decisions should be made by the union officers whose job it is to negotiate the contract.[79] He doubted that tonnage rates were feasible, because "when you go into the problem of fixing a tonnage rate you have got a tremendous problem . . . because we have found that there are too many opinions as to what should be done." But, he told the delegates, "I think you will all agree with me when I say that the officials of this organization, the men whom you pay, are certainly going to do the very best that they can for you."

If Mitch managed to divert attention away from the issue by trying to get the delegates to defer to their union leaders, John Brophy avoided the issue altogether when he rose to speak immediately after Mitch. Instead, Brophy launched an attack on Lewis's failure to organize the nonunion fields.[80] True, Lewis had been unable to expand the union's jurisdiction into hostile coalfields, but in his failure to respond to the mechanization questions raised by the Illinois delegate, Brophy missed an important opportunity to demonstrate his concern for a problem facing rank-and-file miners throughout the industry.

Lewis then took the floor and turned the situation to his advantage. "May the Lord save us from our alleged friends," he said. In referring to Brophy's attack, which Lewis went to great lengths to answer, he lamented that "it is an astounding situation that men who profess themselves to be leaders in our great movement should come upon the floor of our council chamber and give utterance to sentiments and to statements, every word of which brings joy to the sworn enemies of our movement and our people."[81]

Lewis's response to the "very pertinent discussion" by the delegate from Illinois was to say that the question would be discussed at the next Joint Interstate Conference "to the fullest possible degree consistent with our ability to secure consideration of it from the operators." That was it. There was no further discussion of the question of tonnage rates versus day rates on loading machines, although Lewis did use the opportunity to repeat his own position on the use of labor-saving machinery in general, a position the delegates had no doubt heard many times. He said "we stand for the encouragement of the installation of labor-saving devices and improved machinery in the mines. . . . We only ask that all of the benefits of that improved machinery be not taken by the operator entirely to himself."[82] That ended debate on the pay question, and the Lewis policy of bargaining for a day wage for machine operators became, in the years to follow, the official union policy.[83]

79. Ibid., 445–47.
80. Ibid., 447–51.
81. Ibid., 452.
82. Ibid., 457.
83. One of the ways Lewis controlled debate on substantive issues and determined union policy was by effective use of the committee system during UMWA conventions. The hundreds of resolutions submitted by local unions on a wide range of concerns were routinely disposed of by assigning them to various standing committees made up of Lewis appointees. Those related to wages, hours, and working

Lewis's diversion of convention debate on the issue did not, however, end rank-and-file support for the tonnage payment system, nor did it lessen rank-and-file concern over the impact that labor-saving machinery was having, and would have, on their jobs. Each year from 1927 until well into the 1940s, many local union resolutions were referred to the Scale Committee, under Lewis's control, which in turn ignored them.

By the end of the 1940s, however, Lewis's proposals for accepting hand-loading and other measures to rationalize the coal industry, even though they caused much hardship and unemployment for miners in small and inefficient mines in various parts of the country, had been generally accepted.

In some respects mechanization in coal was similar to the modernization process that undermined other hand skills during the period under review. In the battle for workplace control, the pick miner had an initial advantage over the urban artisan because of the difficulty of supervising his underground work. Ultimately, however, more jobs were lost to mechanization in the coal industry than they were in any other occupation. This was due partly to the introduction of coal-cutting and hand-loading machines. But it was also due to overcapacity, to underemployment, and to the failure of the UMWA to back up its demands for sharing the profits that flowed from the new equipment with any concrete plans for doing so.[84]

---

conditions were sent to the Scale Committee, which in turn offered substitute resolutions to the convention delegates. Through this process, local union resolutions expressing real issues facing the working miner rarely got to the convention floor, the above-mentioned resolution from Belleville, Illinois, being an exception. Usually, the Scale Committee offered a single substitute motion for the hundreds of resolutions submitted to local unions. Because of this weeding-out process, a review of local union resolutions over the years reflects substantive workplace issues more accurately than does debate on the convention floor. It is true that many resolutions sent in by locals were simply copied from standard resolutions sent out by Lewis, but others provide a rich source of information concerning changes in the labor process and new management practices. These resolutions, which were printed in the *Proceedings,* also provided a means for locals to communicate with each other in an increasingly centralized union.

84. The last two paragraphs were added to the text by the editor, at the request of the author.

CHAPTER EIGHT

THE MINER'S WORK ENVIRONMENT
Safety and Company Towns in the Early 1900s*

PRICE V. FISHBACK

When most workers are asked about the features of their job, they talk about wages, hours of work, and the intensity of the work. Most workers have never dealt with two features of employment experienced by coal miners in the early 1900s. First, coal mining was among the most dangerous jobs ever devised. Second, a large number of miners worked in isolated areas where the company also owned the housing and the store. Accurate pictures of these facets of mining are important to help us understand how these unique features affected the miners' lives.

---

*The material in this chapter summarizes the previously published work listed below. The interested reader can find more details on sources and statistical analyses in those works. Parts of the work in this chapter are adapted with the permission of Oxford University Press from chapters 7, 8, and 9 in *Soft Coal, Hard Choices: The Economic Welfare of Bituminous Coal Miners, 1890–1930* by Price V. Fishback. © 1993 by Oxford University Press. Reprinted by permission. Material on company housing is reprinted with the permission of Oxford University Press and the *Journal of Law, Economics, and Organization*, from Price V. Fishback, "The Economics of Company Housing: Theoretical and Historical

SAFETY IN THE MINES

Mining coal was among the riskiest activities a worker could find. Tons of rock often shifted overhead with only timbers for propping. Encompassed by darkness with limited lighting, the miners worked with explosives, sometimes in mines with ignitable gases. Cars heavily laden with coal were pulled through the mines and could crush men who were not careful. Fatalities per million man-hours in coal mining more than quadrupled the levels seen in any other major industry. This section responds to a series of questions about the dangers in the mines. How great was the danger? What steps did miners and employers take to reduce the risk of accidents? To what extent did workers demand wage premiums to accept more danger? How much did the United Mine Workers enhance safety in the mines? Were state mine-safety laws effective at reducing accident rates? And what impact did the introduction of workers' compensation have on the safety decisions of workers and employers?

In the early 1900s coal mining was nearly four times as dangerous as it is today. Prior to the drop in employment in the late 1920s, between 1500 and 2000 miners were killed in U.S. coal mines each year. The carnage translates to a fatality rate of 3 to 4 deaths for every thousand miners who worked a full year. Accidents permanently disabled another 5 to 6 miners per thousand, while 150 to 200 miners per thousand were injured badly enough to miss at least one day of work.[1]

The vast majority of deaths occurred one at a time, receiving attention mostly from family and friends before joining the long roll of fatalities in state mining reports. The typical accident occurred in the miner's room when the roof fell or explosives misfired. Operators paid the miners by the ton of coal produced and gave them a great deal of independence. The miner therefore explicitly saw the trade-off between income and safety while he made nearly all of the accident-prevention decisions within his own workplace. He decided how often to timber the roof to prevent roof falls, and how large a blast to use in dislodging the coal.

Perspectives from the Coal Fields," *Journal of Law, Economics, and Organization* 8 (spring 1992): 346–65. © 1992 by Oxford University Press. All rights reserved. Material on company stores is reprinted with the permission of the Economic History Association and Cambridge University Press from Price V. Fishback, "Did Miners 'Owe Their Souls to the Company Store'? Theory and Evidence from the Early 1900s," *Journal of Economic History* 46 (December 1986): 1011–29. © 1986 by the Economic History Association. All rights reserved. Material on safety is reprinted with the permission of Academic Press, from Price V. Fishback, "Workplace Safety During the Progressive Era: Fatal Accidents in Bituminous Coal Mining, 1912–1923." *Explorations in Economic History* 23 (July 1986): 269–98. © 1986 by Academic Press. All rights reserved. Some material on changes in liability rules is reprinted with the permission of the University of Chicago Press from Price V. Fishback, "Liability Rules and Accident Prevention in the Workplace: Empirical Evidence from the Early Twentieth Century." *Journal of Legal Studies* 16 (June 1987): 305–28. © 1987 by the University of Chicago. All rights reserved.

1. Miners also faced the spector of black-lung disease, which is covered in Chapter 9.

Early in the period the miner constructed his own explosives with powder and squib—a waxlike fuse—inside the mine. Accidents occurred when a miner overloaded the explosives or "walked back on the shot." The miner generally lit the squib and quickly crawled around the nearest corner, hoping to avoid a spray of coal in the behind. Sometimes there was no explosion. Most miners then quit for the day. Others, after a seemingly interminable wait, walked back to check on the explosives just as the fuse began to work. Improvements in fuses and standardized explosives helped eliminate some of these problems.

Outside the rooms the loaders and miners had much less control over their accident environment. Miners and loaders were at times killed by runaway cars, when clothes were caught in cars, or when they fell off the "mantrip," the car transporting miners through the mine. Faulty car brakes or tracks caused some accidents, while careless driving led to others. In the early days of mine electrification, electric wires that provided power to the cars and for lighting were left bare in some mines. Miners sitting in a mantrip sometimes accidently brushed these wires and were killed.

The most publicized accidents were mine fires and gas and dust explosions. For example, the Monongah, West Virginia, disaster of 1908 killed 362 miners, and twin explosions killed 117 at the Lick Branch mine in Switchback, West Virginia. Even the most careful miners were killed in the disasters, as the miscalculations of a single individual in the mine sometimes caused accidents that killed large numbers of people, regardless of their skill. A fire boss may have missed the presence of flammable gases in the mine, an individual miner may have set off too large an explosive and caused a chain reaction with the coal dust in the air, or mine management may not have "dusted" the mine with fine rock to keep coal dust down and minimize the spread of mine fires.

The division of safety tasks between miners and operators typically assigned responsibilities to the person who could prevent the accident at lower cost. While the miner was the primary preventer of accidents in his own room, the operator was primarily responsible for providing safety in the common areas of the mine and in situations where there were economies of scale. This led management to take responsibility for ventilation, mine gas inspections, watering of coal dust to prevent the spread of mine fires and explosions, and provision of precut timbers to use as roof props.

In several ways the operators' and miners' safety responsibilities overlapped. State laws and many mines' safety rules assigned the mine foreman the role of safety supervisor. On visits to a workplace, the foreman often examined the mine roof and could force the workman to make his workplace safe before he resumed mining. Yet the foreman visited at most once a day, leaving the miner alone to make nearly all the decisions about safety in his workplace. The operator also provided the large capital equipment, such as track and motors for haulage and cutting machines. Both the operator's choice of safety features on such equipment and the worker's care in handling it determined the probability of equipment-related accidents.

Unfortunately, both miners and operators at times ignored or relaxed safety pre-cautions. State mine inspectors complained that miners at times inadequately tim-bered their workplaces, rode illegally on mine cars, brought too much powder into the mine, overcharged their shots, and ignored many of the rules for "shooting off the solid," blasting the coal without making an undercut at the base of the wall. Similarly, coal operators failed at times to provide enough mine timbers, to meet state requirements with respect to ventilation, to train new miners in proper mining techniques, or to supervise the miners adequately.

So why did the miners undertake such dangerous tasks? Dangerous work paid better. Miners received higher hourly wages than in other industries in part because they did more dangerous jobs. Within the coal industry, workers in the more danger-ous jobs inside the mines received wages up to 14% higher than similarly skilled workers outside the mines. During the decade 1910–1919, miners received higher wages in states that did not have workers' compensation, in part because they re-ceived much lower postaccident compensation on average under the negligence lia-bility system.

A statistical study of the miners' willingness to supply labor to employers, shows that miners demanded higher wages to work at more dangerous mines. Coal workers who were willing to accept an added risk of one death for every 10 million man-hours worked for a wage increase of 6.3 cents (in 1992 dollars) per hour. When this information is translated into a value-of-life calculation, it implies a value of life of $630,000 (in 1992 dollars).[2] Other estimates of labor supply imply values of life of $250,000 and $840,000 (in 1992 dollars). The estimates are similar to the range of $590,000 to $1,090,000 (in 1992 dollars) estimated by Thaler and Rosen for danger-ous jobs in the late 1960s, but lower than more recent estimates in the millions of dollars by Kip Viscusi.[3] The lowest estimate of 250,000 (in 1992 dollars) is approximately equal to the present value of the lifetime earnings of a coal miner in the 1920s.[4]

2. See Fishback, *Soft Coal, Hard Choices*, 108–11, 242–47. The $630,000 figure was calculated in the following way. The increase in wage of 6.3 cents is equal to the value of life (V) multiplied by the increase in the probability of a fatal accident (1/10,000,000). Dividing both sides by 1/10,000,000 implies that the value the miner placed on the life was

$$V = 1.5 \text{ cents} \times 10,000,000 = \$150,000.$$

The calculations are translated into 1992 dollars to give people a better sense of the magnitudes that we are talking about. The price level (measured by the Consumer Price Index) has risen approximately tenfold from the period 1913–1923 to 1992, such that ten cents purchased the same amount of goods in 1913–1923 as one dollar purchases in 1992. The numbers here look different from those reported in the original source because the calculations there are measured in 1967 dollars.

3. See Richard Thaler and Sherwin Rosen, "The Value of Saving a Life: Evidence from the Labor Market," in *Household Production and Consumption*, ed. N. E. Terleckyz, Studies in Income and Wealth 40, National Bureau of Economic Research (New York: Columbia University Press, 1975), 281–82; W. Kip Viscusi, *Fatal Tradeoffs: Public & Private Responsibilities for Risk* (New York: Oxford Univer-sity Press), 34–59.

4. Miners in 1920 earned roughly $8,383 in 1992 dollars each year. Assuming a real interest rate of 2% and a working life of fifty years, the present value of that stream of earnings is $263,430 in 1967 dollars.

The miners' ability to increase their wages and rewards for accepting accident risk were enhanced by membership in the United Mine Workers of America. A statistical analysis of wage rates during the period from 1912 to 1923 implies that if a state's workforce shifted from completely nonunion to fully union, hourly earnings would have risen between 6.3 and 10.1%. Unfortunately, the UMWA did not have the same effect on lowering accident rates. Statistical examination of accident rates across states during the period from 1912 to 1923 shows little evidence that the presence of the UMWA lowered accident rates.[5] William Graebner suggests that mine safety was a secondary goal of the UMWA in the early 1900s. Most of its energies were devoted to establishing the union more firmly by organizing drives in nonunion states, where expansions in coal production threatened the strength of the union. The UMWA seemed ambivalent toward mine safety legislation. It sought certification of miners to reduce the number of inexperienced workmen, but this may have been an attempt to obtain more control over the labor supply. In fact, results later in this chapter show that accident rates were no lower and possibly higher in the states where state boards certified miners. Union pit committees might have promoted safety by providing a grievance mechanism that protected workers from dismissal when they complained of unsafe conditions. Graebner notes, however, that few of the grievances adjudicated by pit committees were related to safety. Miners were less likely to use the grievance mechanism to protest unsafe conditions than to seek reinstatement of a miner fired for violating safety provisions in the contract.[6]

Despite the UMWA's ambivalence, Progressive Era reformers pinned their hopes for improvements on mine safety on government regulation at the federal and state levels. The major federal agency for mine safety, the U.S. Bureau of Mines, was established in 1910. Graebner describes the overall impact of the bureau on mine safety as disappointing, primarily because the bureau shifted its main focus away from coal-mining safety and toward promotion of western metal mines within three years of its beginning. The bureau had no coercive power, so it became an informational agency. It conducted experiments to discover better safety techniques, sent out thousands of circulars and papers to publicize better mine-safety techniques, and tested mining equipment against noncompulsory safety standards (59).

The states were the primary regulators of mine safety. Nearly every coal-mining state had passed some form of coal mining regulation by 1900, but the regulations were often incomplete and vaguely worded. According to Graebner, the best safety statutes in 1900 were found in Pennsylvania and Illinois, while West Virginia's laws ranked among the worst (72). Between 1905 and 1915, most states revised and updated their mining codes in response to public outcry over a series of major mine explosions, killing 1700 miners from 1907 to 1909. Most states eventually expanded the codes to require state licensing of foremen, although only three directly licensed

5. See Fishback, *Soft Coal, Hard Choices*, 94–98, 242–47.

6. William Graebner, *Coal-Mining Safety in the Progressive Period* (Lexington: University of Kentucky Press, 1985), 3, 28, 127, and 130–35.

miners. Nearly every state code established means of enforcing the law: budgets for state mine inspectors, fines, guidelines for closing mines for violations, and minimum requirements for inspectors to prevent pure patronage appointments. Most laws required between one and six mine inspections per year, but the actual number of inspections per mine rarely met the required minimum. Small inspection budgets meant low pay for an already inadequate number of inspectors.

When the mine inspector discovered violations, his enforcement options often were limited. In most states for most offenses, a court order was required before the inspector could close the mine. Some inspectors complained that they got little support from the courts and in some cases direct opposition. State inspectors faced additional incentives to turn a blind eye to violations. Most were poorly paid with few chances for advancement within the bureaucratic hierarchy. Many had left mine management jobs and did not wish to jeopardize a return to such jobs. Aside from individual incentives, Graebner argues that the department's zeal for enforcing costly safety regulations was often dampened by the substantial coal price competition among mines across state lines. Imposing costly safety improvements with uncertain effects on safety could put a state's mines at a disadvantage when competing with mines in states without such requirements. Mine operators, directly and through the state legislature, pressured the inspectors not to put their mines at a cost disadvantage.

The problems with enforcing the law led Graebner and Lewis-Beck and Alford to believe that state safety regulations were a Progressive Era disappointment.[7] A statistical analysis of the fatal accident rate record across states between 1903 and 1930 suggest that in most cases they were correct. The only clauses of state laws that lowered accident rates in a statistically identifiable way were laws preventing coal miners from riding on mine cars, laws requiring that miners use only specific forms of prepackaged explosives, and laws requiring extra visits to each workplace by the mine foreman. On the other hand, laws requiring the licensing of miners and/ or foreman, and a variety of other laws about other aspects of the mine had no effect on accident rates.[8]

Most of the laws had little impact for a combination of reasons. First, many of these laws may have just codified practices followed by most mines already. Many mines, whether regulated or not, had daily inspections by fire bosses, provided mine timbers, and insulated electric wires. The laws preventing riding of coal cars and requiring use of permissible explosives probably had impact because they changed behavior in a major way. Second, the laws may not have been enforced very effectively. The average state mining department spent $10.90 (in 1992 dollars) on mine inspections for every thousand tons of coal produced. The statistical analysis shows

    7. Michael Lewis-Beck and John Alford, "Can Government Regulate Safety? The Coal Mine Example," *American Political Science Review* 74 (1980): 745–56; Graebner, *Coal-Mining Safety*, 10.
    8. The statistical work discussed in the section on safety is found in Fishback, *Soft Coal, Hard Choices*, 114–18, 242–47.

that increased expenditures on inspections would have lowered small-scale and roof-fall incident rates. Doubling the average mine inspection budget to $21.80 (in 1992 dollars) per thousand tons of coal would have saved an extra life for every 3,535 men working an average work-year.

The U.S. Bureau of Mines also had no statistically significant impact on mine safety. Lewis-Beck and Alford find that federal government intervention first lowered coal mining accident rates after 1941 when U.S. Bureau of Mines inspectors were allowed to inspect mines although without coercive power. Accident rates were nearly halved from their 1930s level when appropriations for coal mine inspections and investigations by the bureau reached approximately $32.90 (in 1992 dollars) per mine worker in 1949. Accident rates then fluctuated around a constant trend for two decades, despite additional increases in appropriation, rising to $272 (in 1992 dollars) per mine worker in 1969. The plateau ended with the passage of the stringent Coal Mine Health and Safety Act of 1969. The added costs of halving accident rates again were substantially higher than they were in the 1940s. The level of appropriations required rose to $725 (in 1992 dollars) per miner in 1972 before stabilizing at $574 (in 1992 dollars) per mine worker by 1975. There were additional costs to society in the form of compliance costs, as coal mining productivity, holding accident rates constant, fell significantly.[9]

The level of mine safety was also determined in part by the assignment of liability for workplace accidents through the legal system. In the late 1800s, before workers' compensation, liability for workplace accidents was based on common-law standards of negligence. If a worker was injured on the job, he could go to court and demand compensation from his employer. Under the common law, however, the employer was not expected to pay the injured worker's costs from the accident unless the employer had failed to exercise "due care."[10] The employer could also avoid compensating injured workers if he could successfully argue any of three legal defenses: assumption of risk by the worker, contributory negligence, and the fellow-servant doctrine. Under the assumption-of-risk defense, the worker had to show that his or her accident was not caused by factors ordinary for coal mining. Thus, employers were not required to compensate many of the miners killed in roof falls because such risks were known and accepted when miners took the job. Under the contributory negligence defense, the worker could not collect if he might have avoided the accident by exercising due care himself. Under the fellow-servant doctrine, an injured worker was not compensated if the accident had been caused by the actions of another worker.

Although employer-liability legislation modified the employers' defenses in many coal states by 1900, the major revolution in liability took place when workers'

9. See Hal Sider, "Safety and Productivity in Underground Coal Mining," *Review of Economics and Statistics* 65 (May 1983): 225–33.

10. Due care meant that the employer offered and enforced reasonable safety rules, posted warnings of dangers, hired enough qualified workers to handle the job, and provided the customary tools for the job.

compensation laws were introduced permanently in the 1910s. Every coal-mining state except Arkansas had enacted a law by 1930. Under workers' compensation law, the employer was obligated to pay employees or their heirs a set amount for any accident "arising out of or in the course of employment." The government limits on compensation typically meant that the worker received medical treatment for his injuries but was paid for lost working time at a rate two-thirds or less of his normal daily pay.

The change from negligence liability to workers' compensation caused an increase in the percentage of accident victims compensated, as well as an increase in the amount that each compensated victim received. Prior to workers' compensation, between 30 and 70% of victims of fatal and severe accidents received some form of compensation, mostly in out-of-court settlements.[11] The average amount paid to the families of fatal accident victims was typically equal to about one year's income. In contrast, under workers' compensation, employers were expected to compensate workers for all accidents "arising out of employment," and the average payment to the heirs of fatal accident victims jumped to about two to three times the miners' average annual income. Even with the increase in compensation, it is clear that workers' compensation was not designed to fully replace the miner's income.

Reformers cited workers' compensation as a substantial victory for workers, primarily because of the large-scale increase in the direct payments to accident victims. The shift to workers' compensation, however, led to changes in labor markets and accident prevention that diminished the gain from the new laws. A recent study of wage rates in the coal industry shows that the coal wage rates fell in response to workers' compensation by enough to offset the expected gain in postaccident compensation for workers.[12] Thus, coal workers essentially paid for higher postaccident payments with a decline in their wages. An analysis of accident rates shows that the shift to workers' compensation was associated with an unexpected increase in accident rates of approximately 28 percent.[13] This rise came despite the adoption by employers of safety measures, like first-aid teams and more safety training, that led to lower insurance premiums.

The employers' increased efforts were either cosmetic or insufficient to resolve a major accident problem. The rise in accident compensation created a "moral hazard" problem for accidents in each miner's workplace. Since loaders and pick miners were paid by the ton of coal, they always were aware that the road to higher

11. Under negligence liability, the costs of using the legal system were high. Delays of two to five years between the date of the accident and a decision were common, and the complexity of determining negligence led to great uncertainty about the final decisions. The delays and uncertainty were avoided by settling nearly all of the negligence cases out of court, generally within six months of the accident. As a result, nearly 90% of all fatal accident cases were settled without the courts.

12. See Price Fishback and Shawn Kantor, "Did Workers' Gain from the Passage of Workers' Compensation Laws," *Quarterly Journal of Economics* (August 1995), 713–42.

13. See Fishback, "Liability Rules," and *Soft Coal, Hard Choices*, 118–26.

earnings meant working a little faster and taking more risks. All too often, a roof fall injured or sometimes killed a miner who tried to finish loading the car before he set new props for the roof. Under negligence liability, the miner had extra incentive to work more slowly and safely because if he was injured in a roof fall, he probably would receive no compensation. Under workers' compensation he was freer to take risks because he received a much higher level of postaccident compensation, while the odds of an accident still remained low.

The resulting rise in risk-taking led to more accidents like roof falls. The problem was that roof falls were the types of accidents that employers could not prevent at low cost. Effective prevention required constant attention to changing natural conditions, which meant hiring large numbers of supervisors to check the rooms constantly with the added cost of hindering the miner's treasured independence. Rather than take these costly steps, the employers chose instead to pay the extra damages.

The move to workers' compensation did not raise accident rates in every industry. Machinery accidents in manufacturing fell with the introduction of workers' compensation because manufacturers could limit moral hazard at much lower cost than mine operators could. Supervisors could monitor the workers' use of machinery more easily in manufacturing. Instead of tramping long distances through a mine to visit sixty men in a day, the manufacturing foreman could probably meet with sixty men in two hours. Further, manufacturers could limit machinery accidents by redesigning the machines or the entire shopfloor, while coal employers had far less effective measures available for controlling the natural conditions of the mines.

In sum, while coal mining was a dangerous job, miners demanded higher wages to accept the higher accident risk, although their demands may have only been partially met. The UMWA helped miners increase their rewards for accepting accident risk, but had relatively little impact on the level of accident risk. Government attempts at regulation, with a few exceptions, were generally disappointing, partly because the regulations just codified existing practices and partly because the laws were poorly enforced. The introduction of workers' compensation laws increased the amount of postaccident compensation miners received but this gain was offset by a reduction in wages and an increase in accident rates.

THE COMPANY TOWN

One of the most fascinating aspects of the miners' environment was the company town, where the employer owned the housing and the store. Company towns were found in less settled regions where mines were in more remote locations. In the coalfields of Southern Appalachia circa 1920 (West Virginia, eastern Kentucky, Tennessee, Virginia, Maryland, and Alabama) and in the Rocky Mountains, roughly 65 to 80% of the coal miners lived in company towns. In the Midwest (Illinois, Indiana,

Kansas, Missouri, and Iowa), where prior development in agriculture and industry had led to self-governing towns and cities with ample transportation connections, less than 20% of the workers were housed in company towns. In Pennsylvania and Ohio, where there were mixtures of already settled areas and some isolated areas, more than 50% and roughly 25%, respectively, of the miners lived in company towns.[14]

The quality of life varied widely across towns. Some towns were no better than squalid pits with coal dust covering every surface, trash strewn about, and a pervasive stench in the air. At the other extreme were the "model towns," which offered decent housing, donated funds to the schools, built YMCAs, and generally tried to attract miners with families. The quality of the towns can be attributed in large part to the costs faced by the coal companies. In a statistical study of the U.S. Coal Commission's ratings of sanitation and the quality of life in company towns around 1920, Dieter Lauszus and I found that towns with larger populations generally were nicer because they could take advantage of economies of scale in building sanitation works and providing recreation services. Older towns generally had worse community and sanitation ratings, as they tended to rely on the technologies that they installed when they first built the town. Finally, company towns blessed with more space and less mountainous terrain, generally took advantage of the location to offer better services. Although many have the impression that conditions in independent towns were better than in company towns, comparisons of sanitation in the two types of towns suggest that company towns and independent towns of the same size offered sanitation services of similar quality.[15]

The common view is that employers established company towns to exploit a monopoly on store goods and housing. The story seems plausible at first because in many towns there was only one store and the company owned all the housing. However, the monopoly story does not withstand more careful scrutiny. There were limits on the company's ability to charge high store prices. In a number of company towns there were independent stores nearby that provided some competition. More important, the miners themselves could impose limits through their use of voice and exit. In a number of areas the UMWA counteracted the bargaining power of local employers. Even in nonunion areas, the miners had other options because they were not stuck in one place. In fact, nonunion coal miners displayed some of the highest rates of turnover of any group in America. This should not be surprising because the vast majority of miners had to migrate to the coalfields in the first place and thus

14. The sections on company housing are based on Fishback, *Soft Coal, Hard Choices*, chapters 3, 8, and 9; and Fishback, "The Economics of Company Housing."

15. The Coal Commission surveyed more than seven hundred company towns and scores of independent coal towns in the early 1920s. See Price V. Fishback and Dieter Lauszus, "The Quality of Services in Company Towns: Sanitation in Coal Towns During the 1920s," *Journal of Economic History* 49 (March 1989): 125–44, and Fishback, *Soft Coal, Hard Choices*, 161–66, for specific details on the statistical analysis.

had no strong ties to a particular mine. Further, most of the miners were renting housing and thus could avoid the costs of selling a house.[16]

There were thousands of coal mines in the United States competing for labor, and within any region there were often hundreds of mines. The mines in company towns competed in regional labor markets not only with other company towns but also with mines around independent towns and employers in other industries. When the miners chose among mines, they considered not only the wages and safety, but also the town's reputation for quality of housing, rents, and store prices. In such an environment if a company tried to raise rents or store prices too high, they were forced to pay higher wages or faced the risk of losing miners. In the Fishback-Lauszus study of the Coal Commission's sanitation ratings, we discovered that miners demanded an increase in monthly wages of a dollar for every dollar increase in monthly house rents. Further, we discovered that miners demanded wage increases on the order of 3.4 to 17% higher if they moved from towns with sanitary sewage control and clean indoor flush toilets to towns with unprotected outdoor privies.[17] Companies may have had more success in charging higher store prices, in part because miners found it harder to compare store prices on the wide range of goods they bought across mines.

In general the miners' use of exit and voice kept rents low. In Leifur Magnusson's survey of more than 200 employers providing housing (64 were coal employers) during the second decade of this century, he found that the rents of company housing appeared reasonable, with no attempt to overcharge the tenants. The U.S. Coal Commission found in the early 1920s that rents for company-owned houses were lower than for all others, as were charges for fuel, light, and water. The rents in West Virginia company towns were substantially lower than the rents in Charleston, West Virginia, in the 1920s, but Charleston homes and apartments had more modern conveniences. Finally, an analysis of the companies' rates of return on housing in the Magnusson sample shows that the rents generally covered the costs of maintaining the housing and gave employers a normal rate of return on their investment (i.e., the same return they would have gotten from investing in other businesses).[18] As shown below in the section on company stores, store prices in many regions were similarly low.

The regional labor markets did not work perfectly. Miners faced some costs of moving from town to town, so that they didn't move in response to small changes in prices. Conditions also worsened during coal busts, especially in the late 1920s

---

16. For more details on the miners' mobility, see chapter 3 of Fishback, *Soft Coal, Hard Choices.*

17. See Fishback and Lauszus, "Quality of Services."

18. See Leifur Magnusson, "Housing by Employers in the United States," *Bureau of Labor Statistics Bulletin No. 263* (Washington, D.C.: GPO, 1920), 49; U.S. Coal Commission, "The Bituminous Mine Workers and Their Homes," *Report of the U.S. Coal Commission*, part 3, 68th Congress, 2d Session (Washington, D.C.: GPO, 1925), 1437, 1519, 1533; and Price V. Fishback, "The Economics of Company Housing: Historical Perspectives from the Coal Fields," *Journal of Law, Economics, and Organization* 8 (April 1992): 349–52.

and early 1930s. In general, the competition among employers across mines and across industries meant that workers found coal mining to be a reasonable alternative to jobs in other industries. When the demand for coal stagnated and conditions in the industry worsened during the 1920s and 1930s, however, large numbers of workers left coal mining for other industries.

Why Did Companies Own Housing?

Since employers were not very successful at exploiting local monopolies in the company town, we need to look elsewhere for explanations of the monopolies' existence. Many union leaders and labor historians describe company towns as a means of busting unions and limiting collective action.[19] The companies themselves argued that the company town was a necessity because no one else would have provided housing or stores. Each view offers some insight into the nature of the company town, but the most compelling view focuses on the isolation of the towns and the nature of bargaining between miners and employers.

The companies and many contemporary observers claimed that company housing was necessary because the coal mines were located in isolated and sparsely settled regions. Claims of necessity are misleading because they imply no alternative to company housing. Independent investors or the miners themselves might have provided housing, but few did. Thus we need to explore the key elements that made it more economical for the employer than for an independent investor to provide housing.

Contemporaries were right to emphasize the isolation of the mine and prior lack of settlement around it, but many failed to clarify why the isolation was so important. Isolation forced all investments in housing to be strongly intertwined with the success of the mine. The interconnection gave the coal employer several cost advantages and other incentives for building and owning the housing that an independent did not have. The employer's costs of discovering and surveying housing sites were generally lower because he had already investigated the area for mining purposes. The success of the housing investment was also determined by effective forecasting of the fluctuations in the coal industry. The employer had two advantages there. First, since he produced coal, he already forecasted coal fluctuations. Second, he decided the number and type of workers he expected to house. The independent, on the other hand, not only had to forecast coal fluctuations but also the employer's response to them.

Employer ownership of housing (and stores) also avoided bargaining problems arising when someone else built the housing and tried to exploit a local monopoly on housing. The small number of houses in most towns, the short life of the mine, and the start-up costs of building in an isolated area made it hard to attract more than

19. For example, see David Corbin, *Life, Work, and Rebellion in the Coal Fields: The Southern West Virginia Miners, 1880–1922* (Urbana: University of Illinois Press, 1981).

one or two independents to build housing or start stores. An independent builder or storeowner was therefore in a position to exploit a local monopoly position and charge high rents and store prices. The independent only worried about the local market because he did not have to worry about hiring miners in the regional labor market. The employer saw this as trouble because high rents and store prices forced him to pay higher wages purely to compensate miners so that they could pay the independent's monopoly prices.

Rather than dealing with an independent, another alternative was for the miners to own the housing themselves. Some argue that economies of scale in home building and the inability to obtain credit were obstacles to the miners owning their own homes.[20] Such obstacles were easily overcome. Given economies of scale, the employer could build the homes and then sell them to miners. Further, the miners' lack of credit could have been overcome by establishing rent-to-own plans. A more important obstacle to the ownership of homes by the miners was the strong ties of housing to the mine in an isolated region. Since the employer had the larger investment in the area, the strong ties created incentives for both miners and employers to have the employer own the housing.

The worker's demand for home ownership diminished when there was only one employer within commuting range. A home-owning worker in an isolated mining town could only find work at that one mine. If the employer cut wages, the home-owning worker faced the choice of working at the mine or being unemployed. The worker might have sold his house, but buyers would offer a lower price because there was only one employer. The transactions costs of buying and selling houses also inhibited the home-owning miner's mobility. Such mobility was useful to the miner because he could maintain his earnings by moving to other mines when the mine where he worked shut down. The greatest risk facing the home-owning miner was the possibility of a capital loss on his house. He most wanted to leave when the mine closed and the value of his house was at its lowest. The risk of a capital loss on housing in a coal-mining town was greater than in most urban areas, because the value of housing was so dependent on the success of the mine in a risky industry. The typical miner, with relatively small wealth, had less opportunity than the typical employer to diversify and limit the impact of capital losses on his wealth holdings.

The U.S. Immigration Commission noted that the miners' lack of home ownership was also a function of company policy.[21] Although the company potentially had monopsony power over home-owning miners, miner-owned housing limited the mine employers' flexibility in replacing workers when they banded together and struck. As discussed below, when striking miners owned the housing near the mine,

20. For example, see Stuart Brandes, *American Welfare Capitalism, 1880–1940* (Chicago: University of Chicago Press, 1976), 43.

21. U.S. Immigration Commission, *Report on Immigrants in Industries, Part I: Bituminous Coal Mining* (Washington, D.C.: GPO, 1911), 2:206. The Immigration Commission performed an extremely large survey of the working and living conditions of immigrants and native workers between 1907 and 1909.

the mine owners' costs of housing replacement workers rose substantially, enhancing the striker's bargaining position.

Very few coal employers sold housing to their workers. In the case where miners purchased company homes, the purchases most often came when the region became more settled, or when companies sold the housing cheaply when the mine closed down. A number of oral histories have discovered that miners near the end of their working lives purchased company houses in these close-out sales. In general, it appears that most working miners who purchased housing or lots bought farms or houses in independent towns.[22]

Many labor historians see company housing as a valuable control for the operator against agitators, complaints, and strikes.[23] There are two elements of housing leases that can be seen as anticollective action devices. First, since the company town was on private property, the companies had the right to prevent trespassers. Second, most housing leases were contingent on employment. When the worker separated from the firm, his housing lease was also terminated.

Anti-unionism and worker control clearly played a role in the clauses that allowed the companies to prevent trespassing by anybody aside from miners and their immediate families. Companies may have inserted the clauses to eliminate gambling and forms of criminal activity, as they claimed. However, there were a number of instances where the clauses were used to keep union organizers and other "agitators" off company property.

In one sense, making housing contingent on employment was a device to control workers and prevent collective action. The clause raised the expected costs of complaining if a miner thought he might be fired. If the worker was fired, he not only incurred the costs of finding a new job but also the costs of finding new housing. But how much was the cost raised? Given that the mine was the only source of employment nearby, if the worker was fired, he had to move anyway to find employment. Most of the cost incurred therefore resulted from the location of the mine in an isolated area. The employment contingency clause raised the cost of being fired because the time horizon for leaving the house was shorter than in a standard housing lease. Typical landlord-tenant leases in West Virginia in 1920 gave tenants two to four weeks' notice. The typical mine house lease provided for five days' notice, although if the worker's employment was terminated, the company could put him out immediately. The true cost of the shortened notice was the difference in the cost of moving within five days as opposed to within two weeks.

The employment-contingency clause became most important during strikes. At some stage during a strike, companies sought to restart production. Long-term housing leases enhanced the striking workers' bargaining position. When strikers occupied mine housing, the company could not hire strike-breakers without establishing

22. For example, see James T. Laing, "The Negro Miner in West Virginia" (Ph.D. diss.: Ohio State University), 292–300.

23. See Brandes, *American Welfare Capitalism*, and Corbin, *Life, Work, and Rebellion*, 122–23.

new quarters, and strikers could more effectively use moral suasion and/or intimidation to prevent workers from returning to work. With leases contingent on employment, the companies could evict striking workers with little notice.[24] In addition to eliminating the bargaining advantage of the striking workers, the evictions imposed additional costs of finding and moving to new housing away from the mine. In major disputes strikers moved into tent colonies off company property. The evictions at times backfired by angering the miners, further convincing them that they were right to strike. Clearly, evictions were emotional events and missteps on either side sometimes brought fierce and violent responses.

In examining the employment contingency of housing leases, the anticollective action and the isolation arguments are strongly intertwined from the employers' point of view. Under either argument, the employer sought to avoid giving the miners or their union an enhanced bargaining position. The arguments differ in that the isolation argument recognizes that workers also had incentives to rent rather than own in isolated mining towns. By renting and remaining mobile the worker avoided making the employer the only buyer of his labor as well as investing in housing with significant risk of capital losses.

Was the desire to limit collective action the decisive determinant of company ownership of housing? Probably not. Miners' attempts to use collective action were ubiquitous throughout the coal industry, so companies seeking to limit the miners' bargaining power would have tried to use company housing everywhere. Yet the U.S. Coal Commission in the early 1920s found that large numbers of miners did not live in company houses. Company housing was highly correlated with the isolation of the mine and lack of prior settlement in the area. Further, the decline of company housing coincided with increased density of settlement and better trans-

24. More evidence is needed to investigate the extent of evictions without notice. In the U.S. Coal Commission reports from the early 1920s, the coal operators claimed to have been considerably more tolerant and slower to evict than was commonly believed. Corbin in *Life, Work, and Rebellion* (9–10) displays an eviction notice giving more than a month's notice, but on the other hand he shows another one that just said "I want my house." He then claims that in southern West Virginia "notification was exceptional; the coal companies usually sent mine guards to the miner's house and without warning dumped him, his family, and the furniture onto the company road," citing the Paint Creek–Cabin Creek strike of 1912–1913. Yet this is a misleading picture of the evictions in the Paint Creek strike. The Paint Creek strike began on April 19, 1912. The first eviction notices were not issued until May 8, 1912 and the notices gave ten days (longer than the contractual three days) to move out. The Paint Creek Colliery offered to deliver the household goods on railroad cars and prepay transport charges to any point in the union field of West Virginia or to store the household goods and then ship them prepaid to the place selected by the owner. Although many miners distrusted the companies' intentions, some took advantage of the offer. The company did not evict anybody until June 25, 1912, after a series of shootouts. The Paint Creek–Cabin Creek strike itself was not the norm because it was an extraordinarily violent confrontation with egregious actions by all parties. It is not clear that Corbin's description of evictions was commonplace during normal operations, or necessarily commonplace during all strikes. Evictions were more common during long strikes, but most strikes were settled peacefully within a week or two. However, the incidents in major strikes do show that the contingent clauses of the housing leases were used by the companies. For more detail about the sources here see Fishback, *Soft Coal, Hard Choices*, 155.

portation. The decisive factor seems to be the effect of greater isolation on the workers' demands to own housing and the independents' costs of building it. Company towns were more common in more isolated areas because the miners themselves sought to avoid owning housing in a one-employer setting in an uncertain industry. In more settled areas, the miners sought to own their own housing and independents faced no cost disadvantage, overcoming any desire by the company to maintain a company town.

Were Prices Exorbitant at the Company Store?

The company store is one of the most reviled and misunderstood of economic institutions. Nicknames, like the "pluck me" and more obscene versions, seem to point to exploitation. Songs, stories, and serious scholars claim that company stores charged exorbitant prices, miners were forced to purchase at the store because they were paid in scrip, and many miners "owed their soul" to the company store. The remainder of the chapter investigates these claims.[25]

The most common charge against the company store was that company store prices were "substantially higher, sometimes three times higher than at the local trade stores."[26] Because pricing practices varied across stores and across goods within stores, scattered evidence on a few prices at a few stores can be highly misleading when used to describe the price differentials faced by most miners. The evidence brought forth by the major Senate investigations of violent conflict in the mining regions is especially problematic. Evidence was gathered only through testimony in hearings before the Senate subcommittee. Testimony was often emotional, the evidence provided was adversarial, and miners offered contradictory testimony. Given the evidence presented, these investigating committees could hardly reach accurate conclusions about the norm for company store prices.

An effective investigation of store prices requires systematic collection of evidence, budget studies to determine weights for a price index, and widespread coverage of the mining fields. The investigation that best meets these requirements was performed by the U.S. Coal Commission in December 1922. By analyzing store purchases and interviewing miners' families, the commission determined the average miner's consumption bundle. Prices of food items in the bundle were collected in December 1922 from coal company stores and independent stores in the mining and manufacturing districts in Table 8.1. The commission held other conditions of demand constant by comparing goods of the same quality and by comparing stores in areas where incomes and tastes of the workers were similar to those of miners.

The results show that in six of the ten comparisons the stores in mining districts charged less than stores in nearby manufacturing districts. The price differentials were lowest in the unionized Ohio, Illinois, and Barnesboro, Pennsylvania, districts.

25. This section is based on material in Fishback, "Did Miners 'Owe Their Souls?' "
26. Corbin in *Life, Work, and Rebellion* (10) offers one of many examples of this view.

Table 8.1 Price Comparisons of Stores in Coal Areas with Stores in Manufacturing Areas of Nearby Cities, December 1922

Coal District	Nearby City	Price Difference (%)	Type of District
New River District, W.Va.	Charleston, W.Va.	11.9%	Nonunion
Kanawha District, W.Va.	Charleston, W.Va.	4.9	Mixed
Alabama District	Birmingham, Ala.	0.0	Nonunion
Connellsville Region, Pa.	Uniontown and Connellsville, Pa.	− 0.5	Nonunion
Westmoreland District, Pa.	Greensburg, Pa.	5.4	Nonunion
Barnesboro Region, Pa.	Pittsburgh, Pa.	− 5.0	Union
Belmont County, Ohio	Zanesville, Ohio, and Wheeling, W.Va.	− 2.2	Union
Central and Southern Illinois	Springfield, Ill.	− 2.0	Union
Southern Ohio	Zanesville, Ohio, and Wheeling, W.Va.	− 1.0	Union
Windber District, Pa.	Pittsburgh, Pa.	− 1.8	Nonunion

SOURCE: Reprinted from Price V. Fishback, ''Did Miners 'Owe Their Souls to the Company Store'? Theory and Evidence from the Early 1900s,'' *Journal of Economic History* 46 (December 1986): 1017, with the permission of Cambridge University Press and the Economic History Association. © The Economic History Association. All rights reserved. Original source: United States Coal Commission, *Report,* 68th Cong., 2d Sess. (Washington, D.C., 1925), 1457.

NOTE: The prices in the coal districts include both company stores and independent stores in the mining regions. The Ohio, Illinois, Windber, Pa., and Barnesboro, Pa., districts there were few company stores. In Pennsylvania, company-owned stores were illegal, but stores in mining areas were often affiliated with the mines indirectly. The price differential in percentage terms shows the percentage by which the prices at coal district stores exceed the prices in stores in the manufacturing district in the nearby city listed. The New River district was traditionally nonunion but was unionized briefly from 1918 to 1921.

Several factors led to the lower prices. The unionized workers had the greatest bargaining power in these areas, there were very few company stores, and the mines were located in established farming communities where food could be purchased relatively cheaply. The low-price Windber district of Pennsylvania also had the advantage of a location in established farm communities with lower prices. The nonunion districts in Alabama; Connellsville, Pennsylvania; and Westmoreland, Pennsylvania, show a range of prices between 0.5% below and 5.4% above the prices in nearby manufacturing towns. Even though company stores were illegal in Pennsylvania, the law was not very effectively enforced. Quite a few of the stores were owned and operated by the principal owners of the mine, made use of scrip, and were considered by the miners to be company-controlled. It may be that the law against company stores limited the ability of these storeowners to raise prices, but there is also evidence that these stores faced a substantial amount of competition from independent stores.

The largest differential appears between store prices in the West Virginia districts and Charleston, West Virginia. The differentials in the two southern West Virginia districts, the Kanawha district near Charleston and the more isolated New River district, merit further discussion. Since the UMWA often cited West Virginia as the site of the worst abuses, price differentials there should establish an upper boundary for price differences between company and independent stores in general.

The price differentials between the two districts and Charleston suggest that store prices and wages were higher in more isolated districts. Up to half of the price differential between the New River district and Charleston may be attributed to higher transportation costs. Further, the 6.6% difference in prices between the New River and Kanawha districts was offset partially by differences in wages. Average earnings per day listed on the payroll in the New River district were about 2.8% higher than in the Kanawha district in 1921.

The Coal Commission also compared company store prices with prices at nearby independent stores within the Alabama, New River, and Kanawha districts. Again, these comparisons hold the quality of goods, and incomes and tastes of consumers constant. In both West Virginia mining districts, the company stores charged roughly 4% more for food; in Alabama they charged 7% more. These differences represent a high estimate of the monopoly profit from the company stores' more convenient locations within mining towns. By examining the range of prices, one can see how scattered evidence can be misleading. On many foods the highest price at company stores was double the lowest price at independent stores. On those same foods, however, the highest price at independent stores was double the lowest price at company stores.

Of course, the Coal Commission evidence may not accurately depict the situation throughout the period from 1880 through World War II. As the number of mines expanded through the 1900s and 1910s, competition among mines probably increased. Evidence from comprehensive but less quantitative field investigations by the Immigration Commission in 1908 and 1909 portrays conditions similar to those found by the Coal Commission. In its general conclusion the Immigration Commission stated that "in isolated communities . . . it has been charged that the prices at the store were too high and that stock of an inferior quality was carried. In the majority of cases, however, the reverse is true, the employee being able to secure from the company store as good, if not better, articles for the same or a less price than would be charged by an independent store." In Alabama "a careful investigation of prices in several of these commissaries, as compared with market prices in workingmen's districts in Birmingham, reveals very slight differences." In West Virginia, "prices varied at different stores and in some isolated communities are excessive. In many locales there are independent stores in nearby towns and in stores so located they usually meet the prices of competitors. Many companies offer better quality at the same or lower prices. Stocks at company stores in many instances are larger, more varied, and of better quality." Investigators in Pennsylvania found that "many company stores handle first-class goods throughout and charge prices no higher than in the best-managed town and city stores," but at the other extreme were stores "marketing poor-quality merchandise and charging higher prices for the same brand as elsewhere." In sum the Immigration Commission's impressions suggest that at most company stores the prices were similar and sometimes even lower than those at nearby independent stores. Store prices were higher at more isolated mines. But the Immigration Commission pointed out that "in many of these isolated communities it costs more to get provisions laid down at the stores because of their inconvenient location, and this accounts, at least in part for the higher prices."[27]

Evidence collected from an earlier period also shows similar patterns. In 1885 the Illinois State Bureau of Labor Statistics Bureau enumerated "all the stores in the State, operated by mine owners or their representatives, for the use of their employees." Since Illinois was a more settled region, only 75 mines, or roughly one-fourth of the major mines in Illinois were equipped with company stores. Of the 75 stores, 48 faced direct competition from independents, while 27 were without local competition. To illustrate the typical situation in the larger fields, the bureau reported the statements of a miner "familiar with the facts" about thirteen mines. During a period when travel was more costly, the role of local competition was important. At nine mines the companies clearly faced local competition, of which seven had the same or lower prices as the competition, with two charging prices a little bit higher. At three mines with no local competition, the company store prices were somewhat higher to higher than at nearby towns. One mine appeared to meet the prices of a store 1.5 miles away, but charged higher prices than at a larger town 5 miles away. The principle of compensating differences also seemed to be at work. After examining wages, powder fees, rents, seams sizes, and other components of the miners' earnings and expenses, the bureau noted: "Wide as the differences in all these details seem, they in some cases offset each other so as to make the average condition in one place about as good as another."[28]

The range of store prices apparently widened as coal demand plunged during the Great Depression. Homer Lawrence Morris of the American Friends Service Committee presented price comparisons from an independent investigation in 1932. Two price lists comparing a company store to a nearby independent selected "at random" showed company store prices that were typically double those at nearby chain stores. At the other extreme, Consolidation Coal Company, which owned numerous mines in Kentucky and West Virginia, charged prices similar to those the Salvation Army paid in purchasing large lots from independent storekeepers.[29] With numerous operations failing and others working sporadically at a loss, the companies may have tried to use the store to offset their losses. But owning the store was

27. U.S. Immigration Commission, *Immigrants in Mining*, 2:95, 199, 201, 204, 213; 1:327.

28. Illinois State Bureau of Labor Statistics, *Statistics of Coal in Illinois* (1885), xxii–xxix.

29. Homer Lawrence Morris, *The Plight of the Bituminous Miner* (Philadelphia: University of Pennsylvania Press, 1934), 166–69.

not necessarily a good hedge against coal losses. At the Stonega mines in Virginia, where the sale price of coal fell from 7.5% more than the cost of production in 1929 to 12.4% less in 1933, net store profits also fell from 8 to −1% of sales.[30]

Generally, it appears that in normal or tight labor markets, company store prices were sometimes similar to and sometimes higher than prices at nearby independent stores. The drastic claims sometimes seen in labor histories are not supported by the evidence. Company stores faced two types of competition. Where there were independent stores nearby, the companies were generally forced to meet their prices. The stores in isolated towns were able to charge higher prices, but the high prices partly reflected higher costs of transporting goods to the town, and the wages in the towns may also have been higher. The overall employment package therefore may look less exploitative than store prices alone. During severe downturns, as in the Depression, the range of prices appears to have broadened. In sum, even had the miners been forced to purchase at the store, it appears that in most cases the miners' market power in union districts and the competition among mines for labor in non-union districts limited the degree to which high store prices were used to lower real incomes.

Did Miners Owe Their Souls to the Company Store?

Company stores were charged with maintaining a monopoly by three techniques: forcing miners to buy at the store, issuing scrip, or imposing debt peonage (i.e., keeping miners constantly in debt to the store). Reported cases of forced buying included delivery of unwanted goods to the miner's door, threats of dismissal for not buying at the store, and placement of recalcitrants in the worst workplaces. Yet these practices were not universal, and were more common in earlier periods. In their 1885 study of company stores the Illinois Bureau of Labor Statistics received 34 replies to a questionnaire on company stores from lodges of the Miners' Protective Association. There were no company stores at 17 of the lodges. Of the 17 lodges at mines with company stores, 10 reported no compulsion was used, in 2 cases companies openly demanded the miners trade at the store, and in 5 cases it was understood. In another sample of stores discussed by a miner "familiar with the facts," seven of eleven stores faced with competition expected their miners to trade at the store, although most of the companies charged prices that were the same as at other stores. The bureau noted that there was "rarely any open solicitation of trade, or threat made for failure to trade, but the employee who does not [trade] is regarded as an undesirable man to retain." In later years the compulsion to buy lessened. The Immigration Commission reported that Alabama and Virginia miners in 1908 were not forced to buy at the company store, although several cases of coerced buying

30. From Comparative Statements of Annual Store Reports, 1911–1947, in Boxes 253–255. Stonega Coke and Coal Collection, Series II, within the Westmoreland Coal Collection at the Hagley Museum and Library, Wilmington, Delaware.

were found in Pennsylvania. The Coal Commission in 1925 reported that "the system of openly forcing employees to buy at commissaries is said to be no longer in practice." They noted that attempts to solicit trade by an energetic store manager might be misconstrued as coercion and lead to ill feelings toward the company when not proposed congenially. Some abuses did occur. Some companies tried to keep peddlers and nearby independents from delivering goods. Other companies allowed peddlers but carefully checked that they transacted only their stated purpose.[31]

The most frequently misunderstood practice of the company store was the issuance of scrip to the miners. Despite claims that miners were paid almost entirely in scrip, miners were paid in cash monthly or every two weeks. Scrip was an advance on wages due the following payday, which was negotiable at full value at the company store. Given that periodic paydays were and still are an institutional feature of employment, scrip was a convenience that offered the miner the opportunity to draw his wages as he earned them. Relatively few firms today provide the service of advances on payday in any form.

The U.S. Immigration Commission survey of the coalfields in 1907–9 described scrip as a convenience in some parts of its report, but they also suggest that the practice made store "patronage practically compulsory," because only scrip was available between infrequent paydays. The extent to which scrip raised the percentage of miners' earnings spent at the store may have been small. Given the small differences in the prices of company stores and nearby independents, the fact that scrip prices and case prices at the company store were the same, and the company store's more convenient location, miners might have spent similar amounts at the store had they been paid entirely in cash. Any compulsion through scrip was lessened further with the shift toward biweekly paydays, which were almost universal by the early 1920s. By then, the Coal Commission, which also recognized scrip as a convenience, was criticizing issuance of scrip for relieving the miner's wife of all responsibility for planning a household budget, allowing her to avoid close examination of goods and prices, and dulling her sense of the value of money. They recommended a switch to a pure cash system, in essence, to give the miners the "responsibility of adults."[32] One wonders how the miners would have responded to the removal of this service, if this were the reason given.

Debt peonage at the mines was unusual. It certainly is not implied merely by the existence of scrip. Debt peonage could only have existed if the miner owed the company money on payday. Even then it cannot be confirmed without greater knowledge of the circumstances of the loan. The Immigration Commission and the Coal Commission suggested that scrip was rarely extended beyond the amount due the employee on payday. The coal companies saw little reason to give miners scrip

31. Illinois Bureau of Labor Statistics, *Coal Report*, 1885, xxvi; U.S. Coal Commission, "Bituminous Workers," 1462–63; U.S. Immigration Commission, *Immigrants in Mining*, 1:95, 326, and 2:204, 212–13.

32. U.S. Immigration Commission, *Immigrants in Mining*, 1:95, 326–37, and 2:66, 199, 212, 213. U.S. Coal Commission, "Bituminous Coal Workers," 1462.

in excess of what they had earned because there was always the risk that the miner would leave without repaying the scrip or working off the debt. The companies allowed miners to incur debts in three ways. To keep a skeletal workforce when the mine was not working, rent and fixed charges often were allowed to accumulate; at some mines in severe downturns these charges were waived. To attract workers from distant locations, the company advanced the cost of transportation to the mine. Finally, the company loaned funds to better workers to purchase durable goods like furniture, automobiles, and later, houses and washing machines. Debt peonage was not the primary motivation for these loans because the possibility that miners would repudiate their debts was enhanced by the lack of attachment to the mines of workers owing transport costs, and the adversarial attitudes that developed during strikes.[33]

Evidence from government reports and archival sources shows that miners received a significant proportion of their earnings in cash, that these proportions varied widely for individual miners, and that relatively few miners were in debt. Studies of various payrolls show that the percentages paid in cash ranged widely from mine to mine and over time. The Immigration Commission found percentages of 51 and 62 at "representative" mines in West Virginia in 1910. Representative companies in Pennsylvania, where the Immigration Commission's descriptions of stores were harshest, paid 60 to 80% of their payroll in cash on payday. After 1924, the Stonega mines in Virginia typically paid out 50 to 70% of their payrolls in cash despite sharp drops in income during the Depression that might cause miners to rely more on scrip prior to payday.[34] It should be noted that these are percentages in cash after the families had paid for rent, some food expenses, and a variety of other expenses. Most people, even today, would be left with approximately the same percentage in cash on payday after paying their housing and other bills.

At least part of the cash income on payday was used for savings. Stories of immigrants saving to send money home, to bring their families to America, or to return and buy property in their native land are legion. A number of black and white migrants from the South used West Virginia as a way station, where they earned enough to move north. Others saved enough to purchase farms or homes in nearby towns. Finally, miners saved during booms and spent their savings during downturns and stikes. Mining families in the Kanawha district accumulated savings during the coal boom in the late teens but ran them down during the 1921 downturn and the strike year of 1922. Morris gives examples of miners who accumulated savings during the 1920s but, like most workers, saw them dissipate quickly during the Great Depression.[35] The miners may have suffered more than most workers during the 1930s because opportunities to save were limited while the coal industry stagnated during most of the 1920s.

33. U.S. Immigration Commission, *Immigrants in Mining*, 1:95, 326, and 2:204, 212–13; U.S. Coal Commission, "Bituminous Coal Workers," 1517–22, 1536–37, 1438; Laing, "Negro Miner," 297–98.

34. See tables in Fishback, *Soft Coal, Hard Choices*, 143–47.

35. U.S. Coal Commission, "Bituminous Workers and Homes," 1454–58, 1534; Morris, *Plight of Bituminus Miner*, 169–72.

Studies of payrolls also show that there was a wide divergence in the cash percentage received by individuals at each mine, ranging from receiving all their pay in cash to receiving it all in scrip. The Immigration Commission found that immigrants drew much higher percentages of their earnings in cash than did native white and black miners, in part because a greater percentage of native workers had families. Given that so many miners received different percentages of their earnings in cash, it seems obvious that miners were a widely diverse group who had varying demands for store goods and savings. Enough miners bought small amounts at the stores that we cannot say that the companies forced everybody to spend a minimum percentage of the earnings at the store. In fact, the range of cash percentages was broad enough that it seems that variations in the miners' own demands and not specific company policies better explain how much each miner would spend at the store.

The miners of the early 1900s clearly led rough lives. Compared with today, mining was several times more dangerous, wages were substantially lower, and the housing was substantially worse. A modern worker thrust back into that environment would be horrified, but mining in the early 1900s must be discussed in the context of the times. A semiskilled or unskilled worker choosing among jobs in the early 1900s saw coal mining as a means of obtaining high hourly earnings, although at the risk of a more dangerous job and of living in an isolated area. After weighing all the good and the bad, coal mining seemed like a reasonable alternative to farming and manufacturing jobs.

Much of the discussion here is a hardheaded look at the material conditions provided miners in company towns. There were towns that were terrible places to live and where employers tried to exploit the miners at every turn. However, such towns were not the norm. Miners were able to prevent exploitation through two avenues, by collective action and by moving to new areas. Most miners avoided the worst towns and lived in places where company store prices were not exorbitant and where conditions were comparable or not much worse than conditions in manufacturing areas.

The negative image of the company town stems in part from nonmaterial factors. In a larger city, workers might have become angered with their employer over working conditions, their landlord over rent, the local merchant for price gouging, and the local politician for lousy garbage or police service. Thus, the workers' dissatisfactions were diffused over several independent entities. In the company town, the employer was landlord, merchant, and politician rolled into one. The employer therefore became the focal point of discontent over any and all aspects of life. Further, since the company town was private property, employers could prevent trespassers and maintain political control over the town. Workers feared the abuse of this power and the violation of their personal freedom. When these fears were realized in some situations where miners struck for higher wages or better conditions, violence erupted. In consequence, all aspects of the company town, material and nonmaterial, stood indicted.

CHAPTER NINE

THE ROLE OF THE UNITED MINE WORKERS IN THE PREVENTION OF WORK-RELATED RESPIRATORY DISEASE, 1890–1968

ALAN DERICKSON

At its founding in 1890, the United Mine Workers of America proclaimed as a fundamental aim "the introduction of any and all well defined and established appliances for the preservation of life, health and limbs of all mine employees."[1] Despite this straightforward declaration of principle, the campaign to eradicate occupational illness followed a circuitous path. Throughout the early and middle decades of the twentieth century, the UMWA found itself with more than one objective regarding the widespread problem of respiratory disease. It had to respond to the needs of members already disabled by dust disease as well as to the needs of members at risk. Given its limited economic and political leverage, the miners' organization faced a perennial dilemma. Throughout the period that ended in 1968, it resolved this dilemma by giving priority to the goal of compensation over that of prevention. Yet at the same time, the UMWA also did make some noteworthy pioneering efforts to introduce disease-prevention measures.

---

1. National Progressive Union of Miners and Mine Laborers and National Trade Assembly 135, Knights of Labor, *Proceedings of Joint Convention . . . , 1890* (n.p., n.d.), 17 (quotation), 17–18.

* * *

Coal-mine dust posed a threat to the health of underground workers as early as 1890. Even before the mechanization of extractive operations, routine tasks frequently raised sizable amounts of respirable dust. "Another evil too commonly met with in coal-mines is the cloud of dust with which the air is loaded," warned Henry C. Sheafer, a local observer of the burgeoning anthracite industry, in 1879. In Sheafer's view, "every fresh stroke of the pick or the hammer, every shovelful of coal moved, every fall of a dislodged mass causes a fresh cloud of dust." Of course, for those processes where mechanization had already taken hold, air contamination worsened. Regarding conditions inside the breakers where hard coal was crushed by machinery and then sorted by hand, Sheafer contended that "[t]he wonder is not that men die of clogged-up lungs, but that they manage to exist so long in an atmosphere which seems to contain at least fifty per cent of solid matter."[2]

By the turn of the century, coal workers' pneumoconiosis and such dust-related conditions as emphysema and chronic bronchitis had appeared in the United States. At the widely publicized hearings of the federal Anthracite Coal Strike Commission in 1902–3, for example, the UMWA called a series of medical witnesses to attest to the causes, severity, and prevalence of breathing problems in the hard-coal labor force. From years of practice in Scranton, Dr. John O'Malley saw "miners' asthma" as the result of "inhalation of great quantities of coal dust and powder smoke and vitiated air." In postmortem examinations of veteran miners, O'Malley found "thorough saturation of the lung tissue by these fine coal dust particles." In the bituminous districts, there was also a dawning of recognition that long exposure to mine dust often brought respiratory impairment.[3]

By the 1910s, effective methods of dust control were available and well understood. Then as now, the basic principles were to suppress dust at the point of generation or, where this was infeasible, to remove dust particles from the working environment as soon as possible after they were generated. In practice, engineering controls meant wet methods of dust abatement or mechanical ventilation. Before the turn of the century, many mines had installed powerful fans to move large volumes

2. Henry C. Sheafer, "Hygiene of Coal-Mines," in *On Hygiene and Public Health*, ed. Albert H. Buck (New York: William Wood, 1879), 245 (quotations), 229–30, 245–47; Keith Dix, *Work Relations in the Coal Industry: The Hand-Loading Era, 1880–1930* (Morgantown: Institute for Labor Studies, West Virginia University, 1977), 14–29.

3. U.S. Anthracite Coal Strike Commission, "Proceedings," 7:911 (O'Malley quotation), 912 (O'Malley quotation), 911–15, 921–25, 942–45, 952, 8:962–67, 984, 987–90, Michael J. Kosik Collection (Historical Collections and Labor Archives, Pattee Library, Pennsylvania State University, University Park), box 1; *UMWJ* (March 15, 1906): 3; (May 30, 1907): 1; (January 19, 1911): 12; (February 16, 1911): 7; (February 22, 1912): 6; (June 13, 1912): 4; U.S. Industrial Commission, *Report*, vol. 12, *On the Relations and Conditions of Capital and Labor Employed in the Mining Industry* (Washington, D.C.: GPO, 1901), 130; Andrew Roy, *A History of Coal Miners of the United States*, 3d ed. (Columbus, Ohio: J. L. Trauger, 1907), 450; Alan Derickson, "The United Mine Workers of America and the Recognition of Occupational Respiratory Diseases, 1902–1968," *American Journal of Public Health* 81 (June 1991): 782–84.

of air through their workings. By the early 1890s, mechanical ventilation was widespread in the western Maryland coalfield, for instance. By the 1910s, North American operators were learning of British techniques of killing dust by use of water and other fluids.[4]

Early on, the union called for implementation of these advances. In an editorial in 1912, the *United Mine Workers Journal* asserted that for every miner killed by a so-called accident, "at least ten die from ten to thirty years before their time, on account of poisonous gases and coal dust in the air they breathe." The editorial argued that miners' asthma and other occupational diseases "could almost be eradicated if the mine management would only use the well-known methods for keeping air up to the working faces, [and] for sprinkling the dust on the roadways and in the gob." The primary obstacle to progress was also well known, in the journal's view. Management avoided dust control because it "requires expense."[5]

Focused on issues like wages and union recognition, the UMWA made relatively little effort to negotiate more healthful working conditions. In 1905, representatives of Local 941 in Burnett, Indiana, who believed that "[t]he conditions of the mines are undermining the health of ourselves and thousands of our fellow workers," urged the international convention that "no agreement be made until measures have been mutually adopted by the two contracting parties to protect the men." The convention did not, however, follow through with the policy sought by this local. To be sure, some collective bargaining agreements at the district level mandated increased ventilation. But prior to 1930 the contracts covering the Central Competitive Field did nothing to curb the dust hazard.[6]

Throughout the early twentieth century, the miners' union tended to treat the issue instrumentally. The UMWA started down this path at its inception. The very first goal set forth in its founding constitution was "[t]o secure an earning fully compatible with the dangers of our calling and the labor performed." In the 1902 battle in anthracite, the union made no demands for dust abatement. Instead, Districts 1, 7, and 9 criticized working conditions in order to help justify pay increases and the eight-hour day. In preparing the bargaining agenda at the 1912 international convention, the Scale Committee held that "lung-befouling" dust warranted both a

4. Katherine A. Harvey, *The Best-Dressed Miners: Life and Labor in the Maryland Coal Region, 1835–1910* (Ithaca: Cornell University Press, 1969), 43–45; *Coal Age* (September 26, 1914): 513; (August 26, 1916): 336; (February 11, 1926): 219; (January 1948): 79; J. J. Forbes and Alden H. Emery, "Sources of Dust in Coal Mines," *Transactions of the American Institute of Mining and Metallurgical Engineers* 75 (1927): 654–55.

5. *UMWJ* (June 13, 1912): 4 (quotations); (December 28, 1911): 4.

6. UMWA, *Minutes of the Sixteenth Annual Convention, 1905* (Indianapolis: Cheltenham Press, 1905), 172; Thomas Kennedy to John B. Andrews, November 18, 1937, American Association for Labor Legislation Papers (Labor-Management Documentation Center, Catherwood Library, Cornell University), microfilm reel 57; William Graebner, *Coal-Mining Safety in the Progressive Period: The Political Economy of Reform* (Lexington: University Press of Kentucky, 1976), 130–31.

raise in wages and a reduction in hours of work, to seven hours a day in bituminous mines and to eight hours in anthracite.[7]

The UMWA looked primarily to government intervention to bring about an improved working environment. As early as 1891, William B. Wilson was lobbying Pennsylvania legislators for more stringent standards for underground air circulation. Wilson, who himself eventually developed pneumoconiosis, advocated a ventilation minimum of 200 cubic feet of air per employee per minute in order to prevent both explosions and miners' asthma. The 1893 session of the state legislature passed a law requiring 100 cubic feet of air. That the measure applied only to "gassy" mines in which methane created a risk of explosion indicated that public policy in the nation's leading coal-producing state had not yet begun to address directly the issue of occupational disease. The UMWA continued to voice its concerns regarding dust disease. When, for example, a representative of Pennsylvania's organized bituminous workers testified in 1909 on behalf of a bill providing for 250 cubic feet of air per employee per minute, he decried the large number of cases of miners' asthma. The UMWA also agitated for stricter enforcement of state ventilation requirements.[8]

As it did throughout the period under consideration, the union in the first decades of the century spent more energy in efforts to provide for current victims of respiratory disease than it did to prevent future victimization. The growing number of permanently disabled members, together with the death benefits paid to the families of asthma fatalities by local and district benefit funds, made it impossible for the UMWA to take the long view. When, for example, a long-standing member of Local 1157 begged District 1 for aid in 1915, the district convention was placed in an uncomfortable position. One convention delegate soberly predicted that "if we begin to make donations to such appeals[,] it will be only a short time until they come in here by the hundreds." By rejecting this plea, District 1 left itself with an unfulfilled obligation to help disabled members, who were struggling to stay out of the poorhouse.[9]

7. National Protective Union and National Trades Assembly 135, *Proceedings, 1890*, 17; UMWA, *Proceedings of the Twenty-Third Annual Convention, 1912*, 2 vols. (Indianapolis: Cheltenham Press, 1912), 1:587 (quotation), 587–88; Anthracite Strike Commission, "Proceedings," 2:13–14, Kosik Collection, box 1; UMWA, *Proceedings of the Twenty-Eighth Consecutive and Fifth Biennial Convention, 1921*, 3 vols. (Indianapolis: Bookwalter-Ball-Greathouse Printing, 1921), 3:29–30, 89–90, 365, 419–20.

8. Roy, *History of Coal Miners*, 285–87; Alexander Trachtenberg, *The History of Legislation for the Protection of Coal Miners in Pennsylvania, 1824–1915* (New York: International Publishers, 1942), 174–76; District 1, UMWA, *Proceedings of the Fifth Annual Convention, 1903* (Scranton: Sanders Printing, n.d.), 41, 97; idem, *Proceedings of the Sixth Annual Convention, 1904* (Scranton: Sanders Printing, n.d.), 10, 59; *UMWJ* (May 25, 1911): 2; John A. Garcia, "State Coal Mining Laws Concerning Ventilation," *Transactions of the American Institute of Mining and Metallurgical Engineers* 74 (1927): 417.

9. District 1, UMWA, *Proceedings of the Sixteenth Consecutive and First Biennial Convention, 1915* (Scranton: Sanders Printing, n.d.), 93 (quotation), 92–95; *Illinois Miner* [Springfield] (December 13, 1924): 3; (January 24, 1925): 3. On former coal workers with lung disease in almshouses, see Anthracite Strike Commission, "Proceedings," 7:911–13, 944–45, 8:984, Kosik Collection, box 1.

The union worked its way toward a welfare policy by trial and error. In 1903 the Pennsylvania legislature passed, as a concession to the UMWA, an act to "provide a Miners' Home or Homes for old, crippled and helpless employes of the coal mines." The law restricted admissions to indigent ex-miners who had reached the age of sixty but granted an exception for those afflicted by "what is commonly called 'miner's asthma.' " Employees, through payroll deductions, and employers, through an assessment on tonnage produced, were to finance the institution. Building on this model, the UMWA international convention of the following year resolved to support legislation to erect homes for old and disabled miners in all coal states, under similar financial arrangements.[10]

While Pennsylvania miners worked out the details of their plan for self-assessment during 1904, International President Mitchell visited Europe. There he observed the activism of miners' unions on behalf of protective legislation. Mitchell took these lessons to the 1905 joint convention of the three anthracite districts, where he opposed a plan for operators to pay one mill per ton and coal workers to pay five cents per month to fund a long-term care facility. "I am as much concerned for the welfare of the old or superannuated miners as any one here," he maintained, "but I am not willing that the miners shall build their own poorhouses; I am not willing that the State of Pennsylvania or the various counties within it shall be relieved of the burden of caring for miners as well as they care for other citizens." Mitchell then posed a progressive alternative: "What we ought to do is to ask the Legislature of Pennsylvania to make provision as is done in the countries of Europe to pay pensions, not only to aged and crippled miners, but to the wornout veterans of industry, no matter where they are employed." The convention delegates voted to kill the home.[11] In 1909, the international convention unanimously decided to advocate old-age pension legislation. Following through on this declaration, William B. Wilson, now a Democratic congressional representative, introduced the first federal old-age pension bill later that year.[12]

Besides such broad-gauge endeavors to support all its aging members, the UMWA mounted a campaign specifically to aid victims of work-induced chronic respiratory disease, through the workers' compensation system. Rationalistic reformers like John Andrews of the American Association for Labor Legislation (AALL) looked to social insurance as a panacea: the financial burden of experience-based compensation insurance premiums would ineluctably drive employers to eliminate hazards from the workplace. In this formulation, prevention of occupational disease became nothing more than good business sense. In September 1913, the

10. Pennsylvania, *Laws, 1903* (n.p., 1903), 248 (quotation), 249 (quotation), 248–50; *UMWJ* (October 5, 1905): 2, 5; UMWA, *Minutes of the Fifteenth Annual Convention, 1904* (Indianapolis: Cheltenham Press, 1904), 140.

11. *UMWJ* (December 21, 1905): 1, 4 (quotations); UMWA, *Minutes, 1905*, 27, 29.

12. UMWA, *Proceedings of the Twentieth Annual Convention, 1909*, 2 vols. (Indianapolis: Cheltenham Press, 1909), 1:373; *UMWJ* (December 9, 1909): 7; UMWA, *Proceedings of the Twenty-First Annual Convention, 1910* (Indianapolis: Cheltenham Press, 1910), 529–31.

United Mine Workers Journal reported on Andrews's advocacy of compensation for work-induced illnesses, in a speech in which he named miners' asthma as an object of concern.[13]

Pragmatic unionists, however, approached the subject of social insurance with trepidation. No UMWA representative appears to have espoused the argument that workers' compensation would necessitate disease prevention. Instead, at the AALL annual meeting in 1914, both Mitchell and Van Bittner, president of District 5 in western Pennsylvania, expressed fears that enactment of social insurance legislation would lead to mass firings. Bittner stated the matter plainly: "I say that 65 per cent or 67 per cent of the men who work in the mines of this state over ten years have miners' asthma, and under existing conditions it would be a crime to compel these men to undergo a physical examination and then discharge them, simply because they could not stand the test, in order that the employers may not have to pay them compensation." The unpleasant prospect that social insurance would serve in practice not to prevent disease but rather to prevent the continued employment of all those with any signs of respiratory impairment qualified UMWA enthusiasm for compensation from the second decade of this century on.[14]

Nonetheless, various district affiliates forged ahead with attempts to include miners' asthma within state workers' compensation plans. Indignation at the injustice of excluding from compensation illnesses that were fully as work-induced as mine injuries apparently outweighed apprehension over the possibility of preemptive discharge. Only one month after the passage of the Pennsylvania Workmen's Compensation Act of 1915, in fact before the law even took effect, Thomas Kennedy, who had begun his career picking slate in an anthracite breaker, called for coverage for occupational diseases. The following year, Kennedy's District 7 and nearby District 9 officially endorsed a proposal that miners' asthma and other occupational disorders be made compensable. At the same time, District 10 in Washington also raised the issue, in tandem with that of old-age pension legislation. The western miners responded to the weeding out of elderly employees by attempting to widen the state's safety net: broken-down old miners who were denied compensation benefits would presumably qualify for a public pension. Neither Washington nor Pennsylvania legislators responded favorably to these demands.[15]

Another workers' compensation campaign took place in the 1920s in Illinois,

---

13. *UMWJ* (September 11, 1913): 1; John B. Andrews, "Compensation for Work Diseases," *Survey*, n.d.; repr. *UMWJ* (July 3, 1913): 2.

14. Van Bittner, "General Discussion," *American Labor Legislation Review* 5 (March 1915): 30; John Mitchell, ibid., 22.

15. District 1, UMWA, *Proceedings, 1915*, 79; *UMWJ* (October 5, 1916): 7; District 9, UMWA, *Proceedings of the Seventeenth Annual Convention, 1916* (Shenandoah, Pa.: Herald Print, n.d.), 64, 248; UMWA, *Proceedings of the Twenty-Fifth Consecutive and Second Biennial Convention, 1916*, 2 vols. (Indianapolis: Bookwalter-Ball Printing, 1916), 1:482; District 10, UMWA, *Proceedings of the Twelfth Consecutive and Third Biennial Convention, 1918* (Seattle, Wash.: n.p., n.d.), 44–45, 51.

where organized coal miners had often played an active part in politics.[16] The president of the state labor federation, UMWA leader John Walker, lobbied for an occupational disease amendment drafted by District 12. Walker embraced the proposal not only because he was, like Kennedy, a member of the AALL. He had also watched his own father's deterioration over the course of thirty years, ending in his death in December 1926. He recounted these autopsy findings: ''[H]is heart, stomach, liver and all his organs were in good condition, [with] no sign of aterial [sic] hardening, but his lungs were caked with coal dust, baked as hard as a board and black as a shoe.'' Such intimate knowledge of the problem did not, however, enable Walker to prevail in the legislative sessions of 1927 and 1929.[17]

Although district organizations naturally took the lead in state-level political work, the union as a whole did address the occupational disease problem. The UMWA went on record in favor of extending workers' compensation to victims of miners' asthma at its 1924 international convention. Ten years later, the general convention called for compensation for all occupational disorders. Despite this policy statement and despite consistent support of this universalistic position by progressive reformers, UMWA activists in practice generally limited their compensation demands to miners' pneumoconiosis and a few other common conditions, like rheumatism and bursitis. Workers' compensation reform from the 1930s through the 1960s thus became largely a struggle to add miners' respiratory disease to a list of compensable disorders or to begin such a schedule where none existed. The UMW abandoned the broader approach because of the strong opposition of mine operators, who were terrified of the idea of covering all work-induced conditions.[18]

In Pennsylvania, the Great Depression forced the issue of compensation to the forefront. The anthracite organizations had continued to press for compensation coverage for miners' asthma throughout the twenties.[19] A crisis of destitution in coal-mining communities after 1930 intensified demands for social insurance. In re-

16. John H. Keiser, ''John H. Walker: Labor Leader from Illinois,'' in *Essays in Illinois History*, ed. Keiser (Carbondale: Southern Illinois University Press, 1968), 75–100; John H. M. Laslett, ''Swan Song or New Social Movement?: Socialism and Illinois District 12, United Mine Workers of America, 1919– 1926,'' in *Socialism in the Heartland: The Midwestern Experience, 1900–1925*, ed. Donald T. Critchlow (Notre Dame: University of Notre Dame Press, 1986), 167–214.

17. [John H. Walker] to John Steele, January 5, 1926 [sic, 1927], John H. Walker Papers (Illinois Historical Survey Library, University of Illinois, Urbana), folder 234; *Illinois Miner* (August 23, 1924): 3, 5; *Illinois State Federation of Labor Weekly News Letter* (January 8, 1927): 1–2; (January 29, 1927): 1; [Walker] to Subcommittee . . . Working Out Agreed Amendments to the Workmen's Compensation Act, January 14, 1929, Walker Papers, folder 775.

18. UMWA, *Proceedings of the Twenty-Ninth Consecutive and Sixth Biennial Convention, 1924*, 3 vols. (Indianapolis: Bookwalter-Ball-Greathouse Printing, 1924), 2:568; UMWA, *Proceedings of the Thirty-Third Constitutional Convention, 1934*, 2 vols. (n.p., n.d.), 1:303.

19. *UMWJ* (October 15, 1924): 5; District 1, UMWA, *Report of Proceedings of the Twenty-Second Consecutive and Seventh Biennial Convention, 1927* (Scranton: Sanders Printing, n.d.), 67, 99, 205, 210; District 9, UMWA, *Report of Proceedings of the Twenty-Third Successive Constitutional and Sixth Biennial Convention, 1928* (Mahanoy City, Pa.: Record-American Print, n.d.), 129.

sponse, in 1932 Governor Gifford Pinchot appointed the Commission on Compensation for Occupational Disease to make "a careful, impartial, and scientific study to determine what form of legislation is most desirable and most practicable." As the sole labor official on the commission, Thomas Kennedy represented the UMWA and all Pennsylvania unions.[20]

As expected, Kennedy pressed for compensation for miners' asthma. From a survey of seventy-eight physicians, who had under their care more than 40,000 anthracite workers, the commissioners learned that 23% of hard-coal workers were disabled by miners' asthma. The commission had no choice but to recommend compensation for this disorder. However, at the bottom of a deep depression, with low-cost mining developing south of the Ohio River, Pennsylvania policymakers backed away from the legislative implications of their own recommendation. The commission's report in March 1933 lamented the "lack of any precise information as to the exact nature and the prevalence of this disease" and sought further investigation.[21]

By early 1934, the U.S. Public Health Service (PHS) had begun a major study of miners' asthma in Pennsylvania's anthracite fields. Within months, the federal investigators examined 2,711 working miners and found exactly the same prevalence as had the state commission's less rigorous poll of coal-town doctors. After the final report of this inquiry was published in 1935, the next session of the state legislature passed an amendment to the workers' compensation law to cover chronic dust-induced respiratory disease in the coal industry. The UMWA had achieved its twenty-year-old political objective.[22]

But the victory was hollow. The Public Health Service had taken it upon itself not just to estimate the frequency of a given disease but also to redefine that disease. Federal epidemiologists shrunk the broad conception of miners' asthma down to a much narrower condition, which they labeled "anthraco-silicosis." Indeed, the compensation law of 1937 referred only to this new construction and left miners' asthma noncompensable. In the name of scientific rigor, the PHS discounted all self-

20. Gifford Pinchot, "Address," May 12, 1932, Gifford Pinchot Papers (Manuscript Division, Library of Congress), box 823, folder: 5–12–32, Penna. Safety Conference, Dept. of Labor & Industry, SN; District 7, UMWA, *Report of Proceedings of the Twenty-Fifth Consecutive and Ninth Biennial Convention, 1930* (Hazleton, Pa.: Anthracite Miner, n.d.), 40, 86–87, 251; Districts 1, 7, and 9, UMWA, *Verbatim Report, Reconvened Tri-District Convention, 1930* (Hazleton, Pa.: Anthracite Miner, n.d.), 7; Steve Nelson, James R. Barrett, and Rob Ruck, *Steve Nelson: American Radical* (Pittsburgh: University of Pittsburgh Press, 1981), 94–124; *Labor and Industry* (October 1932): 7.

21. Pennsylvania, Commission on Compensation for Occupational Disease, *Occupational Disease Compensation: A Report* (Harrisburg, Pa.: n.p., 1933), 26–27 (quotation), and passim; Thomas Kennedy to John B. Andrews, October 24, 1932, AALL Papers, reel 48; Andrews to A. Estelle Lauder, November 1, 1932, ibid.; Alice Hamilton to Andrews, February 24, 1933, ibid., reel 49; A. J. Lanza to R. R. Sayers, December 12, 1932, Records of the U.S. Bureau of Mines (Washington National Records Center, National Archives, Suitland, Md.), RG 70, General Correspondence, 1910–50, box 1584, file 437.4.

22. Charlotte E. Carr to Gifford Pinchot, May 17, 1933, Pinchot Papers, box 2266, folder: Labor and Industry, . . . Occupational Disease; U.S. Public Health Service, *Anthraco-Silicosis among Hard Coal Miners*, Bulletin 221 (Washington, D.C.: GPO, 1936); Pennsylvania, *Laws, 1937*, 2 vols. (Harrisburg, Pa.: n.p., 1937), 2:2714–19.

reports and other information on shortness of breath, pain, and disability. The key diagnostic criterion became X-ray evidence, a very poor indicator of loss of lung function. Moreover, the only radiological image deemed worthy of compensation was the pattern of shadows cast by silicosis, the chronic disorder caused by rock dust containing free silica. To be sure, the air in almost all coal mines contained some silica, but seldom enough to bring on silicosis. Instead, the vast majority of anthracite and bituminous miners breathed a mixture of coal dust, rock dust, and other airborne hazards, with coal particles by far the principal environmental air contaminant. Federal epidemiologists thus effectively doomed the lion's share of coal workers' compensation claims.

Further predisposition against the majority of disease victims came from the way in which the federal study was designed. By limiting the scope of investigation to the much smaller anthracite segment of the industry and by ignoring the larger bituminous workforce in the central and western parts of the state, the PHS created the presumption that soft-coal miners were not at risk of pneumoconiosis. Deployment of the term "anthraco-silicosis" served to underscore the notion that the disease was confined to anthracite areas only. A superficial follow-up study in the bituminous mines of Utah reinforced this misconception. By the early forties, federal expertise, under the auspices of the liberal New Deal, had contained coal workers' respiratory disorders within the narrowest bounds and had effectively trivialized the issue.[23]

Coal operators across the country attacked the vagueness of the concept of miners' asthma and substituted anthraco-silicosis or simply silicosis in its place. Legislation enacted in West Virginia and other coal states granted compensation only for pure silicosis. (Some states made no changes whatsoever in their compensation statutes during this period.) These narrow laws gave very few of the growing number of disabled ex-miners any relief. Understandably, by the 1940s, the UMWA had become disillusioned with the workers' compensation system.[24]

As the inadequacies of the social insurance approach became clearer, the need for preventive action became more imperative. The pace of technological change accelerated in the twenties and thirties. Diffusion of mechanical loading devices and other power equipment led to substantially higher concentrations of dust underground. "The use of labor-saving machinery is detrimental to the health of all miners," exclaimed one local in 1938, which considered the air in the mines "not fit to

23. U.S. Public Health Service, *Soft Coal Miners Health and Working Environment*, Public Health Bulletin 270 (Washington, D.C.: GPO, 1941); B. G. Clarke and C. E. Moffet, "Silicosis in Soft Coal Miners," *Journal of Industrial Hygiene and Toxicology* 23 (May 1941): 176–86.

24. West Virginia, *Acts and Resolutions, 1935* (n.p., n.d.), 345–58; Ohio, *Legislative Acts, 1937–38* (Columbus: F. J. Heer, 1938), 268–72, 475–76; Kentucky, *Acts, 1944* (Frankfort, Ky.: State Journal, n.d.), 144–55; Utah, *Laws, 1941* (Kaysville, Utah: Inland Printing, 1941), 79–87; Emery R. Hayhurst to John B. Andrews, September 27, 1937, AALL Papers, reel 56; UMWA, *Proceedings of the Thirty-Ninth Convention, 1946*, 2 vols. (n.p., n.d.), 1:101; *UMWJ* (May 15, 1945): 8–9; (March 15, 1946): 5, 23; (May 1, 1946): 20; (May 15, 1946): 16.

be breathed by any living being.''[25] In response to the dust and many other problems unleashed by increased mechanization, the UMWA set up an engineering department at the international headquarters. In 1940, the head of this department, Walter Polakov, declared the union's intention to address the human consequences of industrialization through diverse methods. At this critical juncture, the union appeared ready to reopen the issue of dust control, either through collective bargaining or state regulation. Without question, the UMWA had an opportunity to demand that a small fraction of the proceeds flowing from greatly increased productivity be applied to improved ventilation or wet methods of dust suppression.[26] The union could have accepted mechanization (as it always had) but insisted that the dust raised in the process be kept out of workers' lungs.[27]

Mine Workers' leaders did not aggressively pursue engineering controls of the dust hazard, however. Once again, pressing welfare considerations took priority over more far-sighted interest in primary prevention of disease. By the mid-1940s, John L. Lewis and other union leaders had begun to argue that the prevalence of respiratory disease, together with a host of other work-related afflictions, necessitated the creation of private health and welfare funds. The *United Mine Workers Journal* conveyed the sense of urgency surrounding this demand in an editorial in May 1946: ''The inhumane treatment of the past—leaving coal miners human wrecks . . . , suffering from silicosis and asthma, [leaving] widows and orphans, all upon the junk pile of human wreckage to feed as best they can upon the crumbs of public charity—must be brought to an end.'' Benefit plans financed solely by a royalty on each ton of coal mined were, among other things, a way to shift to employers the economic burden imposed by occupational diseases.[28] Unfortunately, unlike the workers' compensation approach, in which premium rates reflected changes in working conditions, the royalty approach was insensitive to hazard-prevention initiatives and thus gave individual mine owners no incentive to clean up the workplace. With the establishment of collectively bargained welfare funds in the late 1940s, the

25. UMWA, *Proceedings of the Thirty-Fifth Constitutional Convention, 1938*, 2 vols. (n.p., n.d.), 2:236 (quotations), 236–37; U.S. Bureau of Mines, *Some Preliminary Data on Methods for Controlling the Dust Hazards in Mechanical Mining*, Information Circular 7151 (Washington, D.C.: Bureau of Mines, 1941), 2–4; Keith Dix, *What's a Miner to Do? The Mechanization of Coal Mining* (Pittsburgh: University of Pittsburgh Press, 1988), passim, esp. 84, 93, 104–5; *UMWJ* (November 1, 1940): 10.

26. *UMWJ* (January 15, 1940): 25; (July 15, 1937): 10; (November 1, 1940): 10; UMWA, *Proceedings, 1940*, 1:74–77; U.S. Senate, Committee on Education and Labor, *Prevention of Industrial Conditions Hazardous to the Health of Employees: Hearings . . . on S. 3461*, 76th Congress, 3d session, 1940 (Washington, D.C.: GPO, 1940), 69–70.

27. Dix, *What's a Coal Miner to Do?*, 126–214; Melvyn Dubofsky and Warren Van Tine, *John L. Lewis: A Biography* (New York: Quadrangle, 1977), 494, 505; UMWA, *Minutes of the Twelfth Annual Convention, 1901* (Indianapolis: Hollenbeck, n.d.), 46–47; UMWA, *Minutes, 1904*, 32; *UMWJ* (May 1, 1949): 3.

28. *UMWJ* (May 1, 1946): 10 (quotation); (March 15, 1946): 6; (April 15, 1946): 17; Districts 1, 7, and 9, UMWA, *Proceedings of Tri-District Convention, 1946* (Washington, D.C.: [UMWA], n.d.), 10; Dubofsky and Van Tine, *John L. Lewis*, 376.

UMWA looked primarily to private arrangements to take care of victims of respiratory disorders.[29]

On their own terms, the miners' benefit plans succeeded admirably. The bituminous fund dramatically improved health services for miners and their families. In contrast to company doctors who did not diagnose chronic respiratory disease as work-inflicted, the UMWA Welfare and Retirement Fund spent untold millions of dollars to identify and treat these disorders during the period from the late 1940s through the late 1960s. Though far less efficacious than primary prevention, this initiative did deliver symptomatic relief in many cases. Shortly after its founding in 1946, the Anthracite Health and Welfare Fund set up a program of therapy and medical research with Jefferson Medical College of Philadelphia. In the interval 1947–68, this program served more than 2,000 hard-coal workers. In addition, union-won pensions enabled a great many breathless miners to retire and thus end their exposure to mine dust. Taken together, these programs represented a substantial venture into secondary prevention by virtue of their contributions to limiting disability.[30]

Moreover, a few members of the medical staff of the bituminous fund quietly maneuvered to continue the drive for workers' compensation. Beginning in the 1930s, British advances in pathology, radiology, and epidemiology had led to reconceptualization of the distinctive miners' dust-induced respiratory disorder as coal workers' pneumoconiosis (CWP). British researchers confirmed that this disease arose in the absence of exposure to silica and that it differed from silicosis in its radiographic appearance and in other ways as well. Most important, clarification of the nature of CWP had led directly and immediately to the granting of thousands of workers' compensation claims in Britain, from 1943 on. Compensation, in turn, had induced mine owners to take measures to curtail respirable dust. With the expectation that recognition of CWP in North America would set in motion the same dy-

29. UMWA and U.S. Coal Mines Administrator, *National Bituminous Wage Agreement*, May 29, 1946 (Washington, D.C.: UMWA, [1946]); Anthracite Coal Strike Commission et al., *Award of the Anthracite Coal Strike Commission, Subsequent Agreements, and Resolutions of Board of Conciliation* (Hazleton, Pa.: Anthracite Board of Conciliation, 1953), 129–30.

30. Janet E. Ploss, "A History of the Medical Care Program of the United Mine Workers of America Welfare and Retirement Fund" (Master's thesis, Johns Hopkins University, 1981); U.S. Department of the Interior, Coal Mines Administration, *A Medical Survey of the Bituminous-Coal Industry* (Washington, D.C.: GPO, 1947), 91–193, esp. 113–14; Lorin E. Kerr, "UMWA Looks at Coal Workers' Pneumoconiosis," *Journal of Occupational Medicine* 12 (September 1970): 359; idem, interview by author, tape recording, Chevy Chase, Md., June 26, 1989 (tape in author's possession); UMWA, *Proceedings of the Forty-Fifth Consecutive Constitutional Convention, 1968*, 2 vols. (Washington, D.C.: UMWA, n.d.), 1:177; *UMWJ* (June 1, 1947): 7; (December 1, 1947): 12; (March 15, 1949): 13; (December 15, 1955): 13; Maier B. Fox, *United We Stand: The United Mine Workers of America, 1890–1990* ([Washington, D.C.]: UMWA, 1990), 413–17, 449–53. On the concept of secondary prevention, see John M. Last, "Scope and Methods of Prevention," in *Maxcy-Rosenau-Last Public Health and Preventive Medicine*, 13th ed., ed. Last and Robert B. Wallace (Norwalk, Conn.: Appleton and Lange, 1992), 4–5.

namics of reform, medical activists at the Welfare and Retirement Fund attempted to publicize the British scientific discoveries.[31]

This small cohort of progressives faced steep obstacles. Both the basic structure of the bituminous fund and its particular financial arrangements served to inhibit advocacy on behalf of victims of occupational disease. Under the provisions of the agreement of March 5, 1950, the fund was a joint trust. The three trustees consisted of one union representative (Lewis), one management representative (Charles Owens in the early 1950s), and one neutral trustee agreed upon by the others. From 1950 on, this key position was held by Josephine Roche, who also directed the fund's operations. A former coal operator herself, Roche knew that many mine owners remained opposed to the mere existence of a jointly governed benefit plan. Hence, in her mediating role, she made clear that the fund should avoid the most controversial facets of the occupational disease problem. Staff members were not to testify in damage suits or in workers' compensation claims proceedings. They were not to lobby for compensation bills. Contrary to the policy of the anthracite fund, the resources of the soft-coal fund were not to be used to support research into occupational lung disease.[32]

Despite these strictures, some at the fund found ways to work toward reform. The first real chance to emulate British public policy came in Alabama. Dust-induced disease appears to have been quite prevalent in the 1940s among workers in the bituminous field surrounding Birmingham. At this time, Alabama's workers' compensation law covered no occupational respiratory diseases at all. This state of affairs perfectly suited the coal operators, the most prominent of which was the Tennessee Coal, Iron and Railroad Company (TCI), a subsidiary of U.S. Steel Corporation. According to UMWA attorney William E. Mitch, physicians in the Birmingham area "for all practical purposes denied the existence of coal workers' pneumoconiosis." TCI routinely conducted pre-employment examinations on prospective employees and periodic reexaminations on active employees; those screened were not informed if they had pneumoconiosis.[33]

31. Jethro Gough, "Pneumonoconiosis in Coal Trimmers," *Journal of Pathology and Bacteriology* 51 (September 1940): 277–85; Charles M. Fletcher et al., "The Classification of Radiographic Appearances in Coal-Miners' Pneumoconiosis," *Journal of the Faculty of Radiologists* 1 (July 1949): 40–60; A. G. Heppleston, "The Essential Lesion of Pneumokoniosis in Welsh Coal Workers," *Journal of Pathology and Bacteriology* 59 (July 1947): 453–60; Great Britain, Medical Research Council, *Chronic Pulmonary Disease in South Wales Coalminers*, 3 vols. (London: HMSO, 1942, 1943, 1945); Andrew Meiklejohn, "History of Lung Diseases of Coal Miners in Great Britain: Part III, 1920–1952," *British Journal of Industrial Medicine* 9 (July 1952): 208–20; Kerr, interview; Derickson, "United Mine Workers and Recognition of Diseases," 786.

32. Leslie Falk, interview by author, tape recording, Montpelier, Vt., July 12, 1991 (tape in author's possession); Kerr, interview; Allen Koplin, interview by author, tape recording, New York, September 29, 1990 (tape in author's possession); Murray Hunter, interview by author, tape recording, Ann Arbor, Mich., February 15, 1992 (tape in author's possession).

33. William E. Mitch, letter to author, November 1, 1989 (letter in author's possession); UMWA,

In the immediate postwar years, this web of control unraveled. Dr. Louis Friedman, a specialist in pulmonary medicine new to Birmingham, began to diagnose cases of what he came to term "pneumoconiosis in soft-coal workers." In an attempt to legitimate radiographic images other than the distinctive pattern exhibited by silicosis, Friedman developed his own scheme for classifying X-rays.[34] In the absence of workers' compensation coverage, victims of pneumoconiosis in Alabama were free to sue their former employers at common law. In the late 1940s, UMWA District 20 sponsored a large number of suits. With Friedman as their expert witness, plaintiffs began to win cases, and receive awards of a few thousand dollars or more. Friedman based his assessment of patients on a thorough workup that included both X-rays and tests of pulmonary function. Such an elaborate evaluation was dauntingly expensive to a sick (usually unemployed) former miner who had no assurance that he would ultimately recover any damages from his former employer. Fortunately for pneumoconiotics in this difficult circumstance, the UMWA Welfare and Retirement Fund paid Friedman for his services in preparing for lawsuits.[35]

Faced with a mounting wave of litigation, mine owners sought to contain costs. District 20 and the operators came to an agreement on an amendment to the state workers' compensation statute. This proposal sailed through the Alabama legislature and became law in June 1951. By extending benefits to "occupational pneumoconiosis," the statute covered a variety of respiratory maladies beyond silicosis. Although it unquestionably expanded miners' access to compensation benefits, the reform did, however, stop short of specifically identifying and thereby legitimating CWP as a discrete entity.[36] Under the revised compensation law, Alabama operators took steps to reduce dust concentrations in their workings. Ventilation improved markedly. Wet methods of dust suppression came into wider and more refined use. Though no panacea, especially for employees of small mines that could not afford hazard-control technology, social-insurance legislation did bring some amelioration in working conditions.[37]

Proceedings, 1944, 2:90; Koplin, interview; William Mitch to Josephine Roche and Warren F. Draper, November 2, 1951, UMWA Archives (International Headquarters, Washington, D.C.), President's Office Files, Correspondence with Districts, folder: District 20 Correspondence, 1951.

34. Louis L. Friedman, "Pneumoconiosis in Soft-Coal Workers," n.d. [1951], Louis L. Friedman personal papers (photocopy in author's possession); idem, "X-Ray and Pathologic Features of Soft Coal Miners' Pneumoconiosis," in *Symposium on Coal Miners' Pneumoconiosis Held under the Auspices of the Golden Clinic . . . , 1952* (n.p., n.d.), 26–37; idem, "Significant Case of Pneumoconiosis in a Soft-Coal Worker," *Archives of Internal Medicine* 95 (February 1955): 328–32; Koplin, interview.

35. William Mitch to Josephine Roche and Warren F. Draper, November 2, 1951, UMWA Archives, President's Office Files, Correspondence with Districts, folder: District 20 Correspondence, 1951; Koplin, interview.

36. Alabama, *Laws, 1951*, 2 vols. (Montgomery, Ala.: Brown Printing, 1951), 1:427–33; William E. Mitch, November 1, 1989; H. Ellsworth Steele, "Negro and White Miners under Alabama's Pneumoconiosis Law," *Industrial Medicine and Surgery* 31 (September 1962): 383; Koplin, interview.

37. J. A. Hagy, "Ventilation and Dust Control with Continuous Miners," *Coal Age* (July 1956): 56–59.

None of the leaders of the UMWA seized on the breakthrough by District 20. At the international convention in 1952, the officers' lengthy reports made no mention of this advance in protective legislation. The *United Mine Workers Journal* made only passing reference to the enactment of the Alabama law. Overall, the Lewis regime did virtually nothing to promote respiratory disease compensation based on the Alabama model, a glaring failure of leadership.[38]

Physicians at the fund did all they could to fill the leadership void. Beginning in 1952, the union's health specialists tried to persuade public health officials to undertake epidemiological research to determine the magnitude of the CWP problem. Authoritative determination of the immensity of this phenomenon would, it was hoped, help build a mandate for ameliorative measures. Unable to overcome the inertia of the U.S. Public Health Service, the fund's office in Pittsburgh convinced the Pennsylvania Department of Health to make a prevalence survey.[39] With the assistance of UMWA locals, the state screened more than 16,000 soft-coal miners during the years 1959–61. Of the working miners aged forty-five through sixty-four in the study, 23% had signs of pneumoconiosis on X-ray. Among retirees, more than one-third displayed radiological evidence of dust disease.[40]

These findings gave impetus to a renewed drive for social insurance reform. In 1965, Pennsylvania legislators responded to union demands to shed the anthraco-silicosis straitjacket. In granting benefits for coal workers' pneumoconiosis, the amended Occupational Disease Act explicitly withdrew the requirement of exposure to silica dust. Virginia made similar changes in its compensation statute in 1968. That same year, the international union convention declared its determination to "make all possible efforts to get the state compensation laws amended to include any chest ailment or disease that may be contracted while working in or around a mine."[41]

By this time, however, the uncompensated masses of disabled coal workers had largely given up hope that the UMWA's top officials would solve their problems.

38. *UMWJ* (September 15, 1951): 13; William Mitch to Josephine Roche and Warren F. Draper, November 2, 1951, UMWA Archives, President's Office Files, Correspondence with Districts, folder: District 20 Correspondence, 1951; Koplin, interview.

39. Lorin E. Kerr to Warren F. Draper, September 27, 1954, UMWA Health and Retirement Fund Archives (West Virginia and Regional History Collection, West Virginia University Library, Morgantown), ser. III, subser.: Health Care Delivery, box 12, folder: Pneumoconiosis Consultants; Kerr to Draper and Staff, October 8, 1954, ibid.; Leslie A. Falk to Draper, March 5, 1957, ibid., box 11, folder: Pneumoconiosis Conferences; Falk to Draper, June 20, 1957, ibid., box 14, folder: Pneumoconiosis Research; Kerr, interview; Falk, interview.

40. Jan Lieben to Allen Croyle, July 23, 1959, UMWA District 2 Collection (Special Collections, Stapleton Library, Indiana University of Pennsylvania, Indiana, Pa.), box 144, folder: Chest X-Rays; Jan Lieben and W. Wayne McBride, "Pneumoconiosis in Pennsylvania's Bituminous Mining Industry," *Journal of the American Medical Association* 183 (January 19, 1963): 176–79.

41. UMWA, *Proceedings, 1968,* 1:432 (quotation), 432–33, 462; District 1, UMWA, *Proceedings of the Sixth Quadrennial Constitutional Convention, 1965* (Wilkes-Barre, Pa.: n.p., n.d.), 73–78, 154–56, 226–27; Pennsylvania, *Laws, 1965,* 2 vols. (Harrisburg: n.p., 1965), 1:695–704; Virginia, *Acts and Joint Resolutions, 1968* (Richmond: Commonwealth of Virginia, 1968), 348–49; *UMWJ* (May 1, 1968): 7.

Especially in West Virginia, rank-and-file miners were exasperated with the sluggish unresponsiveness of international and district officers not only to long-festering demands for financial assistance for the disabled but also to growing demands for primary prevention for those at risk. From this perspective, the Boyle administration's decision to pursue compensation reform was seen as too little, too late. In January 1969, the formation of the West Virginia Black Lung Association marked the beginning of a new phase in the struggle for healthful working conditions.[42]

Founded to address problems peculiar to work in one of the most hazardous of all industries, the UMWA certainly did more than any other agency to deal with the plague of occupational disease among coal miners in the period 1890–1968. The union early on demanded legislation mandating proper ventilation of the underground environment. Moreover, by midcentury, a cohort of activists on the staff of the union's bituminous welfare fund had come to advocate workers' compensation not merely as a mechanism for reassigning the health and welfare costs of producing coal but also as a lever for instigating dust control measures.

Nonetheless, the union was continually diverted from the straightforward pursuit of disease prevention. The impoverishment and humiliation of large numbers of elderly miners disabled by dust disease forced the UMWA to address income-maintenance and related health concerns. Given its limited resources and the difficult competitive position of the coal industry, the miners' organization generally could not press this welfare agenda and the amelioration of working conditions at the same time. Only with the passage of the Federal Coal Mine Health and Safety Act of 1969, which set precise limits on permissible dust levels in mines, did most U.S. coal workers win effective protection against the threat of pneumoconiosis.[43]

42. Craig Robinson, interview by author, tape recording, Scarbro, W.Va., June 4, 1993 (tape in author's possession); Donald L. Rasmussen, interview by author, tape recording, Beckley, W.Va., July 26, 1991 (tape in author's possession); Brit Hume, *Death and the Mines: Rebellion and Murder in the United Mine Workers* (New York: Grossman, 1971), passim; Curtis Seltzer, *Fire in the Hole: Miners and Managers in the American Coal Industry* (Lexington: University Press of Kentucky, 1985), 85–107; Barbara Ellen Smith, *Digging Our Own Graves: Coal Miners and the Struggle over Black Lung Disease* (Philadelphia: Temple University Press, 1987), 75–200; Bennett M. Judkins, *We Offer Ourselves as Evidence: Toward Workers' Control of Occupational Health* (New York: Greenwood, 1986), 63–107.

43. United States, *Statutes at Large . . . , 1969* (Washington, D.C.: GPO, 1970), 83:760–65.

CHAPTER TEN

THE RISE AND DECLINE OF THE UMWA HEALTH AND RETIREMENT FUNDS PROGRAM, 1946–1995

GEORGE S. GOLDSTEIN

The United Mine Workers of America Health and Retirement Funds program in the U.S. coal industry has been unique in the history of the American labor movement.[1] Particularly the Funds' medical care delivery program is widely considered to have been, in its heyday in the 1950s and 1960s, one of the most pioneering and innovative in the United States.

The Funds' program, through both its pension and medical care elements, has made enormous contributions throughout its history to the welfare of the coal miners and their families and communities, who historically had been among the country's most neglected constituencies.[2]

Yet in spite of its contributions, the program in the 1970s entered a period of decline and failure in several major respects. Subsequently, following the election

1. Research for the essay has been supported by grants from The Henry J. Kaiser Foundation, The Group Health Association of America, The Kaiser Foundation Health Plan, and the Caldwell B. Esselstyn Foundation.

2. This neglect was described in the famous "Boone Report": *A Medical Survey of the Bituminous-Coal Industry*, Report of the Coal Mines Administration (Washington, D.C., 1947).

of newly effective union leadership in the early 1980s, the program was significantly renewed in its development from the mid-1980s into the 1990s. The reasons for the failure and the subsequent course of events, lie in a number of interrelated factors in the development of the coal industry itself, in the changes in its union leadership, and in its union-management relationships during the 1970s into the 1990s.

Some three decades after its founding in 1946, the Fund[3] program came upon profound organizational and financial crises that culminated in dramatic changes under the terms of the 1978 coal industry labor-management contract. That contract, although leaving the pension program essentially the same, reduced the medical benefits by instituting for the first time cost-sharing for both miners and pensioners. The 1978 contract also completed the dismantling of the medical program that had begun in the early 1970s. During the period from about 1973 to 1978, the effective delivery system built by the Fund in the previous thirty years was in effect abandoned by the weak UMWA leadership of President Arnold Miller as a result of his misguided choice of Fund leaders. These actions led to the disintegration of the delivery system built earlier by the Fund. Partial renewal of the program had to await new union and Funds leadership under new UMWA President Richard Trumka in the 1980s.

In the process of dismantling the delivery system in the 1970s, the methods of delivery and of payment for medical care in the industry retrogressed, in contrast to the positive movement occurring in many other industries and elsewhere in medical care organization in the country.

In fact, with the implementation of the 1978 contract, it became no longer appropriate to describe the UMWA Health and Retirement Funds as "the" medical care program in the coal industry. In the thirty-two years from its origin in 1946, the Fund had provided or arranged both for comprehensive health care and for pensions for all working coal miners and retirees. The 1978 contract, however, removed from the union-based Funds' program responsibility for the medical care for all *working* coal miners and for pensioners who retired in 1976 or later. That responsibility was returned instead to the individual coal companies, where it had historically mostly resided. Each company thereafter contracted separately with an insurance company.

Thus, the main tasks of the UMWA Funds since 1978 have been financing and servicing pensions and payment for medical care delivery for the "1950 Plan retirees," servicing pensions for the much smaller group of 1974 Plan retirees, as well as health care for some 1974 retirees. The 1950 retirees are currently a sizable but

---

3. The initial title of the miners' program, as established in the 1946 and 1947 contracts, was the "UMWA Welfare and Retirement Fund." However, in the 1974 contract, major structural and administrative changes were made. The single UMWA Welfare and Retirement Fund trust was replaced with four trusts named collectively the "UMWA Health and Retirement Funds." In this paper, the initial title, Welfare and Retirement Fund, or the singular word "Fund," is used for references to the program prior to 1974; and the current title, Health and Retirement Funds, or the plural "Funds," for references to the program after 1974.

naturally shrinking group that will slowly disappear altogether as those "1950 Plan retirees" gradually die.[4]

Thus, since 1978 a large and growing portion of medical care in the coal industry has been provided outside the UMWA Funds structure; that is, through individual insurance company contracts. For example, in the 1977 Funds fiscal year, it was responsible for a total of 813,000 beneficiaries (working miners, pensioners, and dependents), with total outlays of $567 million on health care and pensions. In its next fiscal year, after the 1978 contract, the total number of Funds beneficiaries was reduced by three-quarters (73%), to 218,000, and expenditures were cut by 28%, to $409 million. Further, in that same one-year period from fiscal 1977 to fiscal 1978, the shift of working miners to insurance company contracts with the operators meant that the number of Funds' health cards was reduced by 60%, from 299,852 to 120,605, while the number of pensions remained stable at about 86,000.[5]

With these developments, the responsibilities and role of the Funds declined significantly. The Funds remained a union-based program for retirees. But health care for working miners became a company-based program. Medical care delivery in the coal industry moved sharply away from the organized industrywide system built up by the Funds in its first three decades after 1946.

In contrast, for the United States as a whole since the 1960s, pressures in the health care industry itself and from government, corporate, and union sources, were increasingly moving events toward greater organization and rationalization of medical care financing and delivery.[6]

The health care industry has been moving rapidly, especially in the 1980s and 1990s, toward "managed care," that is, more highly organized and controlled forms

4. The "1950 Plan retirees" are those inactive coal miners who retired during or before 1975, under the provisions of the 1950 Plan (deriving from the 1950 coal industry labor-management contract). Responsibility for their medical care was left to the Funds. But those who retired in or after 1976, did so under the 1974 Plan (deriving from the 1974 contract). Their medical care was also, under the 1978 labor/management contract, turned over to the responsibility of the individual coal company contracts with insurance companies. Thus, the Funds' responsibility for medical care was restricted to a finite, decreasing group of pensioners. This changed, in the 1980s and 1990s, when the Funds became responsible for the health care of increasingly more 1974 retirees whose former employers went out of business or quit the BCOA and stopped payments into the Funds. See my discussion of the 1992 Coal Act, above.

5. The amounts of insurance company expenditures on health care for working miners and 1974 retirees are not available. However, in January 1994, in a sharply reduced total coal industry labor force, there were about 40,000 working miners and 30,000 1974 retirees under the insurance company health care contracts. The Funds had at that time about 105,000 beneficiaries, who on average were much older, so the bulk of expenditures for health care and pensions in the coal industry was in 1994 still provided under the Health and Retirement Funds, though these relationships will shift over time. UMWA Funds, *1978 Annual Report,* 8.

6. "There have . . . been enormous improvements in many aspects of American health services over the last several decades . . . as a result of social pressures to organize and rationalize both the financing and delivery of health care." This concept, introduced by Roemer, has had enormous significance in the history of the development of the health care industry. See Milton I. Roemer, *Social Medicine, The Advance of Organized Health Services in America* (New York: Springer, 1978), ix.

of delivery and financing of care. In the UMWA these trends did occur for retirees, in the partial Funds renewal under Trumka in the 1980s. But for the bulk of the coal industry, that is, for working miners and dependents, the direction of change after 1978 has moved back toward the kind of delivery and financing system much of the health care industry elsewhere is moving away from: the fragmentation of the fee-for-service system based on cash indemnity insurance company contracts.

Several interesting questions flow from this overall view of the miners' welfare program. From what sources did the unique UMWA program originate? In what respects was the medical program pioneering and innovative in the 1950s and 1960s? What led the program in some thirty years from a unique historical role, to decline and "failure"? In what sense, given its contributions and character, did it fail? What were the factors that led to partial renewal of the program? What was the nature of that renewal?

FROM WHAT SOURCES DID THE UNIQUE UMWA PROGRAM ORIGINATE?

The unique nature of the coal miners' health and welfare program emerged in the late 1940s and early 1950s from the gradual merging of two sets of ideas: first, what John L. Lewis wanted in a general health and welfare program for the miners; and second, the mix of ideas held by the Fund staff put together in the first years of the program. That staff, under the leadership of Lewis and Josephine Roche, his friend and lieutenant for the program, crafted and implemented the medical program.

These two sets of ideas combined to determine the nature of the program during a four-year struggle for control between Lewis and the operators. That struggle extended from May 1946, when the federal government returned the mines taken over immediately after World War II, to May 1950, when Lewis and the operators signed a contract giving Lewis complete control of the program.

A key fact in the struggle was that the 1946 and 1947 contracts, which technically established the Fund program, said nothing about what the nature of the program was to be.[7] Rather, they simply said there would be a program, and set up a financing

7. The 1946 contract section, which originally established a health and welfare program simply said: "There is hereby provided a health and welfare program in broad outline . . . to consist of three parts . . . : (a) *A Welfare and Retirement Fund* . . . managed by three [tripartite] trustees . . . to be used for making payments to miners . . . with respect to (i) wage loss . . . from sickness, permanent disability, death, or retirement, and (ii) other related welfare purposes, as determined by the trustees subject to the stated purposes of the fund . . . ; (b) *A Medical and Hospital Fund* . . . to be administered by trustees appointed by the UMW . . . [and] accumulated from the wage deductions . . . authorized by the Union and its members . . . to provide, or to arrange for the availability of medical, hospital, and related services for the miners and their dependents . . . [to] be used for the indicated purposes at the discretion of the trustees . . . ; (c) *Coordination of the Welfare and Retirement Fund and the Medical and Hospital Fund*

mechanism and a skeleton administrative structure. Determination of the substance of the program was left for later to the three trustees (one each for the UMWA, the operators, and the public) to be appointed to run the program. Thus, when the 1950 contract appointed Lewis's longtime friend and consultant on health care, Josephine Roche, as "neutral" public trustee, this gave Lewis an automatic 2 to 1 majority vote. Then Lewis and the staff he and Roche had assembled were able to build the program they wanted.

Lewis's Concepts of a "Social Welfare Program" for Miners

Historically, up to 1945 Lewis had shown little interest in welfare plans and health programs, in spite of frequent pressure over the years from district offices, local unions, and rank and file. The main reasons for this were his basically conservative social outlook, his constant and close involvement with "the most fundamental organizational and economic problems" of the union,[8] and his preoccupation with such other important labor matters as organization of the CIO.

But by 1945, conditions had changed significantly. The UMWA had increased its influence as a result of the large and increased demand for coal during World War II, and the members had lost confidence that the 1935 Social Security Act would provide satisfactory benefits. These changed conditions brought increasingly greater pressures from districts, locals, and rank and file on the UMWA leadership to provide a benefit system of its own.

Thus, in 1945, "With his genius for organization, Lewis saw a dramatic role for himself and his union as implementers of a new approach . . . called 'private social security.' "[9] From this approach came the origin of the first seriously intended demand that the operators finance a health and welfare plan. "Lewis . . . [wanted] to transfer a larger share of the coal industry's war-stimulated profits to the men who worked in the mines."[10] That demand, however, had to wait until 1946, when the federal government temporarily took over running the mines.

Lewis had long believed that the health and welfare needs of coal miners should

---

... necessary for the effective operation of each fund." From the "Agreement between the Secretary of the Interior, acting as Coal Mines Administrator . . . and the United Mine Workers of America, May 29, 1946." (Copy in the possession of the author, but filed as part of the I. Falk Papers, Manuscripts and Archives, Yale University Library, MSS Group 1039).

The 1947 contract combined the two funds into the one Welfare and Retirement Fund, eliminated miners' checkoff wage deductions, and provided for tripartite Trustees. The 1947 contract also said nothing about the nature and substance of the Welfare and Retirement Fund programs.

8. Raymond Munts, *Bargaining for Health* (Madison: University of Wisconsin Press, 1967), 31.

9. Munts, *Bargaining for Health,* 32.

10. Melvyn Dubofsky and Warren Van Tine, *John L. Lewis, a Biography* (New York: Quadrangle, 1977), 454.

be provided as part of a nongovernmental, industry-supported ''private social security system'' that would be responsible for ''maintaining'' workers, just as capital is
''maintained.'' ''The coal industry rather than the government,'' Lewis said,
''should take over the problems of welfare and retirement.''[11] The editor of *U.S.
News and World Report* put it this way: ''Mr. Lewis wants industry to include in
the price of its products the expense of social insurance.''[12]

What Lewis had in mind as social insurance, or a welfare progam for coal miners,
was described in 1945 by Welly Hopkins, the UMW's general counsel, in a ''Brief
Outline of a Miners' Health and Welfare Program,'' dated May 10, 1946.[13] This
''Brief Outline'' was used by the union in the negotiations for the 1946 contract
agreement between the UMWA and the government that first established the Fund.

The ''Brief Outline'' included an extremely broad social insurance spectrum:
retirement, disability, and unemployment income; death benefits; health, medical
care, and hospitalization benefits; vocational rehabilitation; care of orphans and neglected children; homes for the aged and infirm; and general welfare, including
vacations, convalescence care, scholarships, emergency relief, etc.

What was in fact negotiated between Lewis and the government in 1946 was
much narrower (see note 7). Presumably the government preferred to leave the substantive nature of the program to the union and operators to work out after the mines
were returned to private ownership.

What happened over the next four years, until the 1950 contract, was the struggle
between Lewis and the operators to determine how the program would work, what
its substantive nature would be, and who would control it.

Lewis had won from the government only what he was unable to win from the
operators; namely, establishment of the program and its financing mechanism.

The Ideas of the Fund Staff

The second set of ideas in which the Fund medical program found its roots came
from among the leaders of the Funds' own staff.

The most important of these leaders were Josephine Roche, the long-term director
(1948–71), who was Lewis's confidant and key agent in running the Fund; Warren
Draper, the first executive medical officer (1948–68), who as top medical administrator had a major impact on the program's establishment and implementation; and

11. Munts, *Bargaining for Health,* 30–32.
12. *US News and World Report* (November 1948): 23–24.
13. This ''Brief Outline of a Miners' Health and Welfare Program,'' dated May 10, 1946, surfaced as
a Social Security Administration staff document. It was prepared by the UMWA's attorney, Welly Hopkins, for Arthur Altmeyer, Director of the U.S. Social Security Board, who with his Director of Social
Security's Bureau of Research and Statistics, I. S. Falk, was working with Lewis and the UMWA negotiation team. (In Manuscripts and Archives, Yale University Library, I. Falk Papers, MSS Group 1039.)

a group of progressive medical care theoretician/practitioners in both the central Washington office of the Fund and a number of its regional offices. This group reflected the ideological legacy of the influential Committee on the Costs of Medical Care (CCMC) of the late 1920s and early 1930s, a self-created committee of top leaders in health delivery and financing.[14] The legacy of the CCMC emphasized the concepts and the goals of nonprofit, regionalized, prepaid group practice.

One of the most important members of this group was Lorin Kerr, a physician with a Quaker background and long involvement in public health affairs. Dr. Kerr was deputy executive medical officer of the Fund under Dr. Draper for many years, and later became longtime director of the UMWA Department of Occupational Health.

In 1947, Dr. Kerr was still working at the Public Health Service (PHS), the federal agency generally responsible for public health matters. He represented the Service in meetings concerned with the health program then being developed by the UMW Welfare and Retirement Fund. At that time the PHS was apparently a major locus of discussion on that subject. In a memo dated August 4, 1947, the PHS produced "A suggested health program for the bituminous coal mining communities."

Dr. Kerr wrote that memo and another shortly thereafter. These memos first spelled out the concepts that became the basis for both the program substance and the organizational structure of the Fund medical program, just as the Lewis/Hopkins May 10, 1946, "Brief Outline" did for the welfare program as a whole.[15]

Thus it can be said that the combination of the Lewis/Hopkins Brief Outline and the Kerr/PHS Memos provided the conceptual genesis of the entire UMWA Welfare and Retirement Fund program.

The Fund medical program was seen by the medical care progressives in the Fund leadership as a private-industry-supported substitute for a national health program, which had become politically and legislatively impossible in the post–World War II years. Inadvertently, therefore, their ideas and Lewis's own concept of a "private social security system" dovetailed. The progressives' concept got much support also from Josephine Roche, whose background was heavily influenced by the ideas of both the New Deal and the CCMC.

14. My comments on the Committee on the Costs of Medical Care depend heavily on I. S. Falk, "Some Lessons from the Fifty Years Since the CCMC Final Report, 1932," *Journal of Public Health Policy* (June 1983): 135–61.

The CCMC was self-created in 1927 by a group of influential leaders in medicine, dentistry, public health, hospital, and other institutional management people in the field of health care. It was supported by eight private foundations, including such as the Carnegie, the Josiah Macy, Jr., the Milbank Memorial Fund, the Rockefeller, and The Twentieth Century Fund. Its initial chairman was Dr. Ray Lyman Wilbur, who was president of Stanford University at the time, and had been AMA president in 1923.

15. Copies of these two memos and information about their preparation were given to the author by Dr Kerr during taped interviews at his home in Chevy Chase, Maryland, on September 8 and 9, 1987, January 13, 1988, and March 16, 1988.

The Influence of the CCMC

The Committee on the Cost of Medical Care (CCMC) was established in 1927 to study the conditions and problems of health care delivery in the country at that time. The centerpiece of its 1932 recommendations for the future of medical care was a system of nonprofit prepaid group practices organized on a local and regionalized basis. These concepts were among the significant factors that underlay the mix of ideologies in the UMWA Fund medical program.

Moreover, they were the first national-level recommendations in the United States expressing the ideas of managing in an organized system the delivery, financing, and access to quality health care by means of prepaid group practice.

When President Roosevelt was forced to exclude from the 1935 Social Security Act the CCMC's recommendation for a national health program, an open field was left for private insurance to meet the growing demands for health insurance. The demands in the coal industry were a part of that development.

But a key difference there, and one major element of the pioneering, innovative nature of the miners' program, was that while most unions in the late 1930s and postwar period were purchasing commercial insurance or Blue Cross/Blue Shield, the miners instead built their own program.

Similarly, early prepaid group practice medical programs, typified by the Kaiser Plan, were also partially a consequence of the CCMC ideas and of the failure of a national health progam to develop. Thus, the miners' program and the prepaid group practice movement came partially out of the same milieu.

Josephine Roche, a key figure in the UMWA Funds program, was very much part of these historical developments. As chief of the Public Health Service she was a main figure in the Roosevelt administration effort in the 1930s for a national health program.[16]

Although that drive had failed by the end of the 1930s, spending on health care and the need for insurance continued to increase rapidly. This was reflected in the fact that wartime wage and price controls permitted improved fringe benefits but not wage increases. So this was the atmosphere, coming out of the history of the 1930s and the World War II period, in which the UMWA Fund program got its start.

Given this history, Lewis's 1947 choice of Josephine Roche as his consultant and key lieutenant for developing the UMWA welfare program, may appear contradictory. But she had been a close friend of his since 1927, when she took over her father's coal mines and called in the UMWA to organize those mines. So his choice came in spite of the contrast between his own oft-expressed antipathy to government provision of services for people, and her heavy involvement in the New Deal drive during the 1930s to enact a national health program.

---

16. Bess Furman, *A Profile of the United States Public Health Service, 1798–1948*; U.S. Dept of HEW, NIH, NLM, DHEW Publication No.(NIH)73–369, 386.

THE 1950 UMWA/BCOA CONTRACT: WATERSHED FOR THE FUND PROGRAM

At the time the Fund program[17] was established in 1946–47, there was little precedent available in the field of medical care management that would provide either the theoretical or the practical precedents needed on which to base both the contract provisions and the early implementation of the program. Thus the social welfare concepts expressed in the 1946 Lewis/Hopkins "Brief Outline" and the 1947 Kerr/PHS Memos were historically pathbreaking, and were significant elements as well, of the pioneering and innovative nature of the Fund program.

However, these aspects of the program did not begin to have their full effect for four years, until the 1950 contract was signed and the operators stopped obstructing the Fund. They apparently had determined in this period of high postwar profits not to risk a strike, but did show their disapproval of the Fund program by fighting full implementation of it through Taft-Hartley court actions and operator-trustee obstructionism.

Thus, after some purposeful delaying tactics they finally signed the 1947 contract accepting the Fund. They apparently felt they could not repudiate what the government had initiated while running the mines, even though it was later shoved down their throats.

This contract was conceptually precedent-setting. It merged the separate retirement fund and the medical/hospital fund of the 1946 contract into one Welfare and Retirement Fund, and also eliminated the historical practice of making deductions from miners' wages to provide for medical care. It thus completed the transformation from the longtime company doctor "checkoff" system to a union-based Fund medical program. The contract also finally accepted the concept of tripartite control of the Fund; that is, control by three trustees, one each from union and management, and one jointly selected to represent the public.

In the 1948 negotiations, conservative former Republican Senator Styles Bridges became the long-awaited third, neutral trustee. Lewis's proposed $100 monthly pension was accepted, and Josephine Roche was appointed director of the Fund.

The operators' trustee tried to delay these moves with Taft-Hartley court action, but lost a key issue when the court ruled that only two of the three trustees were necessary for Fund action. The operators were then constrained to sign the 1948 contract, Roche started as director, and Lewis presented the first $100 pension check to a retired miner in a justifiably celebratory ceremony.

Soon, however, the industry's immediate postwar prosperity began to wane, as the growing competition of oil, gas, and nonunion coal production resulted in de-

17. For many details of the chronology of the history, I have made much use of "A History of the Medical Care Program of the United Mine Workers of America Welfare and Retirement Fund," by Janet E. Ploss, an excellent thesis for the M.S. degree at the School of Hygiene and Public Health of the Johns Hopkins University, 1981.

clining output and much unemployment. This factor, plus adoption in early 1949 of an excessively expensive and hence financially unsupportable medical program, in the face of huge unmet medical needs of the miners and widespread abuse by the fee-for-service delivery system, led to a rapid draining of the Fund's resources. The Fund was forced to shut off benefits, and so the miners again struck.

Thus, a continuously difficult set of postwar problems came to a head, creating an atmosphere in the industry conducive to the establishment of the widely heralded 1950 contract compromise.

This contract represented a major turning point in the history of the industry. It has been much reported that a secret agreement between George Love of Consolidation Coal and John Lewis lay behind that contract. Although there is no hard, factual evidence of that, the effect is the same whether or not there was an explicit agreement.

Love is reputed to have persuaded the operators that the long-term economic health of the industry depended on their acceptance of several concepts: rationalizing industry control, which led shortly to formation of the Bituminous Coal Operators Association (BCOA); widespread mechanization of the mines; concentration of production, driving out small operators; accommodation between the operators and the union, to end the costs to both of the postwar and longtime conflicts in the industry; and keeping the government out of industry affairs.

This approach dovetailed well with the thinking of Lewis. He had long foreseen and accepted the inevitability of extensive mechanization and its consequent—if unfortunate—creation of mass unemployment. He was willing to accept fewer miners with higher wages and better conditions, to ignore the unemployed, and to live with concentration in the industry and the consequent power of the big operators. And he agreed fully on the desirability of keeping the government out.

Historians generally concur that the 1950 contract agreement was a compromise that gave Lewis control of the Fund programs through appointment of his friend Roche as the third, "neutral" trustee (in place of former Senator Bridges), in return for his not obstructing extensive mechanization and concentration in the industry.

Historically, this was the atmosphere of compromise in which the Fund pension and medical programs got their start, after the four-year struggle between 1946 and 1950.

FUND ACHIEVEMENTS DURING THE TURBULENT 1946–1950 PERIOD OF ITS ESTABLISHMENT

In spite of the constant turbulence in the industry during the early period of the Fund's establishment, there were a number of major Fund achievements. Not the least of these was the eightfold increase in the royalty paid by the operators to support the Fund, from five cents per ton in 1946 to forty cents in 1952.

An early priority for the Fund was to locate and rehabilitate an estimated 50,000 paraplegics. These were injured miners, many of whom had lain immobilized in bed for years as a result of mine injuries. During 1947 and 1948, thousands of these men were transported to the country's leading rehabilitation centers and restored to a significant degree of functioning health and human dignity.

Moreover, the effort laid a basis for three important elements of permanent Fund policy: the concept of total rehabilitation of injured miners; the combining of Fund services with outside resources; and the development of a Fund outreach role.

A third achievement during this period was the early staffing and planning of the medical program. Shortly after Josephine Roche became director, Warren Draper was appointed executive medical officer. From 1948 to 1968, Dr. Draper, a man of great vision who quickly understood the needs of coal miners, played an extremely significant role in planning, developing, and directing the administrative structure of the Fund medical program.

Roche and Draper recruited staff with backgrounds in public health and preventive medicine in the military and the Public Health Service, and especially in the farm-labor programs of the New Deal Farm Security Administration, where a poor rural population with problems similar to those of the coal miners was served. Many of the staff hired had been working in the Roosevelt New Deal and in World War II and were looking for a forum to put their ideas and experience to work.

In addition, they put into effect operating principles and a long-term administrative structure of ten Area Medical Offices (AMOs), which worked superbly until changes became necessary in the 1970s as a result of changes in the industry, the UMWA, and the Fund itself.

As the program progressed into the 1950s, some major differences in philosophical approach developed among the physician Area Medical administrators in three policy areas.

First, some AMOs concentrated on developing cooperative relations with the fee-for-service system, while others emphasized the more adversarial method of developing "participating" lists of physicians and hospitals, utilizing more heavily those who would cooperate on quality and cost controls. Second, the more progressive administrators, rather than simply getting miners into the medical mainstream, emphasized instead developing a better alternative delivery system, including Fund support for establishing nonprofit community clinics with salaried medical groups. Third, there were different emphases on the use of a consumer (miner and community) role in program policy development, where such Fund-supported clinic facilities developed.

While absorbed with building its initial administrative structure and operating staff, the Fund was forced again, in the early to mid-1950s, to reduce services significantly in the constant struggle to keep costs within revenues. The impact of these limitations, when added to the already existing hostility of much of the traditional delivery system, precipitated many controversies in the following years, occasionally reaching the courts, between the Fund and organized medicine in many communities.

DEVELOPMENT OF THE PIONEERING, INNOVATIVE NATURE OF THE PROGRAM

The Fund medical program built in the 1950s and 1960s has come to be viewed as unique among union programs in two major respects. First, rather than simply buying care in the market, the Fund decided to develop its own program, adopting overt goals of improving the comprehensiveness, accessibility, quality, and cost of care for its members. During those early years, most other unions were concerned only with bargaining for money to purchase care and other benefits on the existing market, limiting their aims to buying on better economic terms.

Second, it was soon recognized that to attain the Fund's goals, two policies would be necessary: to impose an industrywide structure of quality and cost controls on the traditional fee-for-service delivery system; and to provide care directly through an alternative system of clinics and hospitals in the areas of greatest concentration of miners, the Appalachian coalfields.

On the latter issue, early Fund staff meetings in 1951 and 1952 discussed the policy implications of the 1947 Kerr/Public Health Service Memos and their ''Suggested health program for the bituminous coal mining communities.'' It was concluded that the cost of the kind of total program proposed in those memos, of hospitals and clinics for mining communities, was beyond the resources of the Fund. Instead, decisions were made only to construct ten hospitals in southern Appalachia, where the need for greater accessibility was the most pressing, and to leave development of the clinics envisioned to the preferences, efforts, and resources of the AMOs,[18] as they sought to meet the needs of the miners in their areas.

The historical significance and uniqueness of the program in these two major respects is widely recognized. As early as 1958, Joseph W. Garbarino noted this in his classic 1960 study of union bargaining for medical care, *Health Plans and Collective Bargaining*. He discussed the failure of most national unions to exploit their potential to become an ''organized consumer . . . in the demand for medical care.'' He then pointed out that ''the principal exception . . . (was) the United Mine Workers Welfare and Retirement Fund. The UMW Fund has encouraged the entrance of new

18. Information on these early Fund staff meetings in 1951 and 1952 was given to the author in taped interviews by John Newdorp, M.D., and Lorin E. Kerr, M.D., key Fund employees at the time, who attended the meetings. The author interviewed Dr. Newdorp on November 13, 1987, at his home in Oakton, Virginia, and Dr. Kerr on September 9, 1987, and January 13, 1988, at his home in Chevy Chase, Maryland. The information was corroborated by Harold J. Mayers, also then a key Fund employee, on December 8 and 9, 1987, in interviews with the author at Mr. Mayers' home in Washington, D.C.

doctors into its area of operations, has aided the development of group practice clinics . . . has built ten hospitals . . . and has attempted to control the abuse of benefits."[19]

Several aspects of the Fund effort to build an alternative delivery system were significant. While adoption of general program goals was policy from the start, the Fund never did adopt an *overt* policy of building an alternative system as such. Rather, that policy materialized out of the practical process of meeting the health care needs of coal-miner families, while at the same time attempting to enhance accessibility and control over both quality and cost.

Further, the effort involved much conflict within the Fund leadership. The minority group of progressives, who had broad service-oriented goals, envisaged building, wherever the concentration of beneficiaries would allow, a delivery system of non-profit, group practice clinics and hospitals using salaried staffs, cost reimbursement prepayment, and strong consumer involvement. Where the concentration of miners was too thin, or where political factors required, the program would depend on the traditional fee-for-service delivery system, but with strong quality and cost controls superimposed.

In contrast, however, most Fund and union leaders lacked such a strong progressive vision. Instead, they mostly accepted the traditional delivery system, aimed mainly at getting the miners into the medical care mainstream, and supported clinic development selectively and sporadically.

Finally, the effort to build an alternative delivery system took place within an antagonistic framework of community attitudes in many areas, where union-related hospitals and clinics were viewed with suspicion. This was a major factor created by active opposition from organized medicine and its community allies in those areas, such as most local politicians and businessmen.

In sum, there developed during the 1950s and 1960s the growth of a two-pronged system for meeting miners' needs: one prong imposing quality and cost controls in the traditional fee-for-service world; and the second, building the Fund's own delivery system of hospitals and community clinics.

To develop the latter, the Fund supported a number of independent, community clinic organizations, and constructed a network of hospitals in the Appalachian coal country, which had the poorest and least accessible existing medical facilities.

The Independent Community Clinic Organizations Supported by the Fund

Over the history of the Fund program, three types of clinic organizations developed. The differences among them depended mainly on their origin. First, there was a

19. Garbarino pointed to a rapid growth in the 1940s and 1950s of an organized consumer role via union collective bargaining, in the demand for medical care; see his *Health Plans and Collective Bargaining* (Berkeley and Los Angeles: University of California Press, 1960). But most unions' business

group of eight organizations, with some twenty ambulatory clinic centers, which were organized independently in the early to mid-1950s. Next came a group of six, with some twelve ambulatory centers, which were established in 1963–64 when the salaried staffs of the ten miners' memorial hospitals were organized on their own after the hospitals were sold. Third, there was a group of seven smaller organizations with one ambulatory site each, which started after 1973 during the Arnold Miller UMWA presidency.

The eight organized in the early 1950s were large, multispecialty groups of mostly social-service-oriented physicians working on salary in a nonprofit framework. A corporation with a consumer (coal miner/community) board owned the facilities.

The group of six organizations (started when the Fund sold the hospitals) were also large multispecialty medical groups working with a community board. Many of the physicians in these groups, however, were more conservative, less service-oriented; thus the groups tended to play a stronger role, akin to that of the medical staff in the typical nonprofit community hospital.

The seven clinic organizations that started after 1973 were mostly quite small centers in more isolated mining areas, established in response to community demands for primary care resources. Reflecting their origin, they had consumer boards with strong local union and district UMWA input, and tended to attract physicians oriented more toward service to people than toward technical/professional or financial aims.

The clinics were financed by a mix of revenue sources. Much of these revenues came from a Fund retainer intended to match that percentage of a clinic's total costs equal to the percentage of services going to Fund beneficiaries, varying in a range of about 25–75%. However, though so intended, the retainer was often negotiated, for a variety of reasons, to exceed the percent of services going to Fund beneficiaries. In fact, the retainer sometimes served a deficit financing role. The retainer was supplemented by fees from community users who were not Fund beneficiaries, and in some cases by various federal or state programs.

The clinic organizations, although strongly supported by the Fund progressives, never served more than a minority of beneficiaries, for a variety of reasons. The majority of union and Fund leaders in both Washington and several AMOs expressed only minimal support of the clinics to rank-and-file UMWA members. This was on both ideological grounds—opposition to building a separate delivery system as opposed to getting miners into mainstream medicine—and because they were seen as being too expensive, without compensatory gains for the Fund.

The progressives expected the clinic organizations to provide higher quality, less expensive care than that available in the communities, when their lower utilization

---

went to commercial insurance and to Blue Cross/Blue Shield. Thus, he said, although the union negotiation role has tremendous potential, nevertheless, "on the national level, this potential has remained relatively unexploited" (31).

and hospitalization rates, and hence consequent Fund savings, were added to the equation. These Fund savings, however, were never demonstrated, were always a much debated question among the Fund's leaders, and were especially disputed later by both the coal operators and the Fund's fiscal conservatives in Washington who saw the clinics as too expensive.

The Miners' Memorial Hospital Association

The second element in the Fund's own delivery system was the network of hospitals built in more isolated sectors of Appalachia. The Fund was acutely aware of the minimal and inferior facilities in the mostly small, for-profit, doctor-owned hospitals that existed in these areas. But it was prevented by the medical establishment from obtaining federal money made available elsewhere under the Hill-Burton Act for hospital construction. Thus, with its own money, the Fund built ten hospitals in southern Appalachia that opened in June 1956. These hospitals provided at their peak some 1000 beds and 170 physicians functioning in a prepaid framework in several salaried group practices based in the hospitals.

These hospitals played a brief but important role in the Fund's delivery system. It lasted until the early 1960s, when coal-industry mechanization, declining output, unemployment, and declining average miner age in some areas brought general underutilization and increased nonpaying use. In 1964 the Fund was forced to sell them to the state/federal supported Appalachian Regional Hospitals, Inc. (ARHI), to be operated thereafter as general community hospitals.

This sale symbolically marked the end of the era of Fund major policy developments during its heyday in the 1950s and 60s. The 1970s brought major changes in the industry, the beginning of the Arnold Miller administration for the union, and wrenching financial and organizational problems for the Fund.

THE ROLE OF FUND POLICIES IN EVENTS LEADING UP TO THE 1974 UMWA/BCOA CONTRACT

During the relatively stable conditions in the mining industry in the 1950s and 1960s, a number of Fund policies and actions contributed to the mounting rank-and-file union discontent which ultimately led to the Miners for Democracy (MFD) movement, and to the election in December 1972 of Arnold Miller as UMWA president. The relative contribution of Fund policies to these developments, though significant, was secondary to general union affairs. The decay of the UMWA and the rank-and-file revolt of the late 1960s must be laid largely to Lewis's long-standing

repression of democracy, financial manipulation, and collaboration with the operators.[20]

In spite of this legacy, however, the Fund and its contributions to the welfare of
miners must be viewed as one of Lewis's major works. The Fund did originate in
his ideas and received his major support over the years in contract negotiations.

During this period, however, when the Fund medical program reached the height
of its reputation, certain effects of the pension and medical program were factors
contributing to the miners' disaffection with the union.

For example, Lewis's decision in 1946 to establish a pay-as-you-go pension program, instead of trying to force the industry to bear the higher long-term costs of a
more stable funded pension, as other unions did (and as the UMWA itself did from
the mid-1970s on) meant inevitable cuts in miners' pensions, forced at times by the
industry's fortunes.

Another controversial Fund policy in that period was opposed by a probable majority of miners because of its impact on individual "free choice" of provider. This
was the policy that aimed at establishing quality and cost controls by restricting
Fund payments for hospitalization, surgery, and ambulatory care physician visits
only to those providers whom the Fund included on its "participating" list.

But of greatest historical significance for the Fund program was the exclusion of
some groups, or classes of beneficiaries, from certain benefits. For example in 1961,
in a period of much unemployment due to mechanization, the Fund adopted two
new rules aimed at cutting costs, rules that did so at the expense of unemployed or
older miners. Although the Fund saw these kinds of rules as unavoidable in order to
cut costs, beneficiaries viewed them as discriminatory. In 1969 this led a group to
bring the Blankenship lawsuit against the Fund, a case that was argued and won by
Harry Huge, a young, non-UMW lawyer who thereafter became a champion and
favorite of the MFD and Arnold Miller.

Huge argued breach of the trustees' duties because they kept the Fund's reserves
in noninterest-bearing accounts at the UMWA's Bank. He saw this as an illegal
union/bank conspiracy to use Fund money for their own benefit, instead of adding
legitimate interest earnings to the Fund's revenue flows usable for providing benefits.

The court upheld the Blankenship lawsuit in April 1971, and removed UMW
President Boyle and Josephine Roche as Fund trustees, and Roche as Fund director.
The court also ordered the Fund to accept as beneficiaries many previously excluded
pensioners, disabled miners, widows, and unemployed, estimated variously from
17,000 to 25,000. Obviously this contributed to the Fund's increasing financial problems.

When the Miller administration took control of the UMWA in January 1973, with
the Blankenship decision already decided, it saw the issues of eligibility determination and the inadequacy of pensions as the major Fund problems. In fact, however,

20. Dubofsky and Van Tine, *John L. Lewis,* 526–29.

both were more union negotiation matters than they were internal problems of Fund functioning.

The real underlying Fund problems were financial. They reflected the union's success (or rather lack of success) in bargaining for enough money from the operators to meet the ever-escalating costs of the Fund's medical care and pension programs. This problem originated in Lewis's policy of bargaining for a generous package of welfare benefits, but leaving until later the fight for money to pay for it. Given the cyclical as well as the declining competitive status of the bituminous coal industry, the UMWA was on a constant collision course with the operators to provide enough money to meet the ever-increasing costs of the expanding Fund programs.

Neither Miller nor his soon-to-be-appointed Fund leadership understood these underlying, interrelated issues. Instead, they saw the basic problems of the Fund as being administrative and managerial.

In August 1973, Harry Huge was appointed UMWA Fund trustee in place of Miller, and shortly thereafter a decision was made that the Fund's major need was for modernization and automation of its administrative processes. In February 1974, the trustees hired Martin Danzinger as director of the Fund to accomplish that modernization. Danziger, a former federal Justice Department attorney general and administrator, had no experience with union welfare programs.

Huge and Danziger felt that the Fund's problems were internal and administrative and lay with the existing personnel and systems. They considered the Fund staff to be largely incompetent and untrustworthy, that its systems needed to be dismantled, and that new systems needed to be put in place that would be run like any other business, on standard managerial principles. Thus, all that was needed to solve the Fund's financial problems was computerized efficiency and better management.

This was the conceptual framework within which the new Huge/Danziger Fund leadership started. They believed traditional fee-for-service to be just as good, more efficient, and cheaper than the existing medical care program with its excessive retainers and expensive clinics.

Their approach to the Fund's financial problems was very similar to that of the operators. As a result, in 1978 they ended up helping the operators to attain their ultimate objective, which was first formulated in 1974. That objective was to replace the Fund's industrywide, union-based medical program with a company-based system of individual coal company contracts with insurance companies to provide traditional fee-for-service medical coverage.

The Huge/Danziger views partially reflected their lack of a union orientation, and their view of the Fund as serving both management and labor equally, rather than as a union program. They assumed no conflict of interest between miners on the one hand and either physicians and hospitals, or operators on the other. This was ironical, since the new Funds leadership was supposed to represent the complaints that President Miller, the MFD, and the rank-and-file miners had earlier taken up against just such attitudes.

The Huge/Danziger reorganization, however, did have some positive aspects. These included decentralization of processing applications for benefits, better eligibility controls, uniform standards in the AMOs, and greater miner accessibility to an increased number of smaller Fund offices. But a crucial negative was the failure of the new centralized computer systems to pay medical bills faster, more efficiently, and cheaper, as had been claimed for them when first installed.

Impact on the Fund of the 1974 Contract

The UMWA entered new contract negotiations with the BCOA in 1974 with high hopes because industry profits were at record levels, and were expected to continue so because of the oil crisis.

The union's bargaining objectives for the Fund were straightforward: much improved pensions, and a sizable increase in the royalty necessary to sustain improved benefits and the increasing costs of the pension and medical care benefits the miners had come to expect. To get the needed money would require either a major fight or compensatory concessions by the UMWA in other areas the operators would see as being in their long-run interests. The latter is what occurred.

The operators had much broader objectives. After almost twenty-four years of Lewis and the union running the Fund, they were taking a new look, had become concerned about its costs, and now wanted to reverse the 1950 compromise and return to the historical practice of the miners' looking to them for health care, not to a union program.

But with profits at record levels, they were reluctant to face a strike, and instead determined to make concessions in the 1974 negotiations. They sensed correctly that both the UMWA rank and file and the Miller leadership had lukewarm support for, and therefore might be persuaded to give up, the Fund medical program as such. For years this had been the operators' already formulated, but so far unspoken goal. So they agreed to an expensive package of increases in 1974, anticipating the realization of their true goal in 1978.

Miller's passive stance played a key role in these developments. By giving his support to Harry Huge, he unwittingly gave tremendous influence to the Huge/Danziger views, which facilitated the purposes of the operators. These views, based in their uncritical acceptance of fee-for-service medicine and a Taft-Hartley view of the Fund as a neutral organization, led them to obscure the real underlying causes of the Fund's financial problems, behind real but lesser issues of administrative efficiency.

In addition to these basic policy matters, the 1974 contract made major structural changes affecting the long-term functioning of the Fund. To meet the requirements of the 1974 federal "Employees Retirement Income Security Act" (ERISA), the contract created four Funds in place of the single 1950 UMWA Welfare and Retirement Fund, and henceforth the program became the plural UMWA Health and Retirement Funds (the Funds).

Exacerbation of the Funds' Financial Crisis after the 1974 Contract

The high costs of the 1974 contract concessions caused many individual coal operators to adopt workforce practices that led to numerous local "wildcat" strikes. The BCOA blamed these strikes for the Funds' 1975–77 financial crisis. Though Miller initially questioned this, he and the Funds leadership eventually agreed.

Actually, a number of factors besides the strikes caused the inadequacy of Funds revenues. These included declining demand for coal, especially in the steel and electric power industries, the impact of continued expansion of western nonunion coal, sharply increasing health costs, an increase in the number of Funds beneficiaries due to the Blankenship decision, and increased benefits.

By mid-1977, the Funds' financial crisis forced it to cut benefits by imposing the first deductibles and co-payments (partial payment of fees by miners) in the medical program's thirty-year history, thereby causing the miners for the first time to bear part of the cost of the program.

Moreover, the Fund ended its long-standing policy of retainers, and instead instituted fee-for-service payments. Here, Huge and Danziger argued that the end of the excessive retainers would reduce Funds costs but would make no legitimate cash flow difference to individual physicians or to the clinics because, they said, an appropriate retainer was simply an advance of the same amount that would have been paid on a fee basis.

This Huge/Danziger belief in the inconsequential medical care functions of the retainer mechanism and the system of clinic organizations, helped lay the basis for the success in 1978 of the operators' campaign to end the Funds as a union-based medical program, and to replace it with a company-based program. That result was also brought about by the lack of understanding on the part of the Miller administration of the medical consequences for the miners if the operators were allowed to put health care insurance for working miners back onto a fee-for-service basis.

The interesting question is why key UMWA and Funds people accepted the operators' assessment. Huge and Danziger's basic beliefs explained their position. Miller, who was highly influenced by Huge, took the path of least resistance. And among rank and file miners and union leadership other than Miller and Huge, there was a mix of attitudes. Many union people considered the strikes that had been taking place to be senseless. In their view, the wildcats depleted not only the Funds' revenues but also the union's and the miners' personal funds as they faced a possible year-end strike when the contract expired. There was also much frustration with the Miller/Huge leadership, and many miners blamed the Funds' financial crisis on abuse of the Funds by doctors and hospitals, on the Funds' failure to police its systems, and on Funds mismanagement. Few on the union side, however, understood the full complexity of the causes of the financial crisis.

IMPACT ON THE CLINICS OF
THE FUND CUTBACK

A major consequence of the 1977 Funds cutback was its impact on the clinic programs. This was viewed, however, with considerably less alarm by the union and most miners than was the imposition of deductibles and co-payments.

The clinic administrators and the Funds' progressives argued that the end of retainers would force conversion from practice patterns based on a retainer type of prepayment, to practices characteristic of fee-for-service piecework. Under the former, the clinics' physicians, who were paid salaries based on training and experience instead of on the number of patients treated, were able to control the volume of visits for high-quality ambulatory care, for reduced hospitalization and surgical rates, and for greater emphasis on prevention and health education.

Though expensive in the short run, these methods meant better health for beneficiaries and lower long-run costs for the Funds, which reaped the benefits of the clinics' cost-saving methods in return for providing cost-based retainers to the clinics.

The cancellation of retainers and return to fee-for-service broke this symbiotic relationship, which had been intended as permanent by the designers of the clinic system.

Under the reestablished fee-for-service/insurance company payment system, the savings created by the clinics' lower utilization and surgical rates would be reaped instead by insurance companies, while the clinics remained burdened by their higher outpatient costs. To live with market-established fees, the clinics would have to utilize higher-volume market methods of practice, which they initially were not willing to consider.

Huge and Danziger pointed out that no evidence had ever been produced supporting the clinics' argument that their methods had ever produced long-run net savings for the Funds. This was mostly true, because the Funds never did the necessary studies or provided money for the clinics to do so. One small corroborating study done by one clinic was generally ignored.

Huge/Danziger argued further that the clinics were able to provide the same type of care to the non-Funds community only because their excessive retainers forced the Funds to ''subsidize'' the general community. This argument had been made for some years by the operators and frequently by the Roche leadership of the Fund.

The clinics' leadership did not deny this allegation totally, arguing that both savings for the Funds and some "subsidization" of the community occurred. They argued that in any case, any such benefit to mining communities generally beyond services to miners themselves, could be viewed as a necessary Funds cost to keep the clinics available to the coal miners.

The Clinics' Financial Self-Defense

The reactions of the clinic organizations to these draconian 1977 Funds cutbacks varied among the clinics and over time, depending on the nature of each clinic. Generally, most lost physicians. A few of the smaller and weaker primary care organizations were either forced to close or to allow greater volume of visits. Some of the larger multispecialty clinics were taken over by their medical groups, who then emphasized greater volume and higher revenue-producing surgical specialties, and developed greater dependence on private insurance payments. Two of these tried to transform themselves into HMOs, failed, and were taken over by their medical groups, with the same changes in practice patterns.

Clearly, the 1977 cancellation of retainers, reinstitution of fee-for-service, and imposition of cost-sharing for the miners were intended to reduce Funds health expenditures by targeting the beneficiaries and the system of clinics that had initially been designed to serve them as an alternative to fee-for-service medicine. This approach aimed to eliminate perceived clinic inefficiencies and community subsidization, both of which were viewed as supported by excessive retainers, and instead, to develop managerial efficiency for the clinics and to reduce miners' overutilization by cost-sharing.

These events represented the final loss of the ideological battle the Fund progressives and the clinics had fought in Fund circles for years. Because the union historically had failed to inform and educate the miners about the nature of the Fund health care program, few understood the value of that program as it differed from the traditional system. Therefore they did not understand the impact of the Huge/Danziger measures. The UMWA and most of its members were concerned more about the reduced scope of benefits because of the new deductibles and co-payments, than they were about the threats to the continued existence of the clinics and to the Funds medical program as such. Nor did they understand the consequences of transforming the industrywide, union-based Funds medical program into a coal-company-based insurance-type program.

The main exception to this were those very few miners who had had an opportunity to gain insight by virtue of their service on the boards of the clinic organizations.

These general attitudes of most miners were to be of tremendous significance in the outcome of the upcoming 1977–78 contract negotiations. In effect, they meant that the union was now finally willing to give up the Funds medical program and accept insurance company coverage for working miners.

Ideologically, the clinic system and the retainer method of payment were important elements of the pioneering nature of the Fund medical program: they have been seen as a quite early forerunner of the kind of managed care alternative to fee-for-service that became common later in nonprofit managed care programs throughout the United States as a whole in the 1980s and 1990s. The Huge/Danziger measures thus were contrary to the trend of managed care developments that became dominant later in the health care industry generally.

THE 1978 UMWA-BCOA CONTRACT

In order to enhance control over their workforce, a major objective of the operators in the 1977–78 contract negotiations was to replace the Funds medical program with company-based commercial health insurance for working miners, who would then look to the operators for their health care.[21]

The operators were in a strong bargaining position with respect to that objective because Huge, chair of the union bargaining committee on health and pension matters, also favored such a system, for the reasons that were discussed earlier. Further, the Funds financial crisis, which had come to a head in mid-1977, provided an ideal backdrop for the operators to attain their objective. They were able to put forward commercial health insurance as a financially more stable type of coverage than that of the frequently troubled Funds. Thus, the operators viewed the 1977–78 negotiations as the most important since 1950 and possibly in the history of the industry.[22]

The UMWA's initial major objectives for the Fund medical program in these 1977–78 negotiations, were to regain the pre-1977 full medical coverage without deductibles and co-payments, and to oppose replacement of the Fund medical program. For a number of reasons, both of those objectives were soon abandoned.

Most important was the fact that underlying support for the Fund medical program as such, by both miners and the Union hierarchy, was lukewarm at best. They were more interested instead, in the reduced cost sharing and in the greater ease of access to care, which they thought would be provided by insurance company payments. A majority of miners seemed to prefer the promised free choice of provider and guaranteed scope of benefits under insurance company contracts, instead of their historical experience with the Funds' periodic restrictions of benefits and limitations on choice by regular use of provider "participating" lists.

21. This effect of commercial insurance contracts for health coverage for working miners was argued specifically by Roger Haynes, a top executive of Consolidation Coal Co., during a tour of several Pittsburgh Area Clinics and personal visits with their administrative leadership, including the author, then executive director of the Bellaire Clinic, the Medical Foundation of Bellaire, Ohio.

Haynes also commented to the author that replacing the Fund medical program was more important than any possible future cost increases that might be associated with return to a fee-for-service insurance company program.

22. Ploss, "History," 223; Ploss quotes Joseph Brennan, president of the BCOA, without citing a source.

Moreover, the miners in these negotiations appeared to be more interested in the need to protect the local right to strike than they were in resolving the Funds' problems.

With respect to the Funds, Miller's passive role was again key, for he placed great reliance on Huge's arguments, which became determining. In spite of much union dissatisfaction with Huge's role as trustee, Miller had appointed him chair of the benefits committee, and there he argued in favor of cost sharing for all beneficiaries, and for insurance company contracts for working miners, as other unions had.

RENEWAL OF UMWA MILITANCY AND OF PART OF THE FUNDS PROGRAM IN THE 1980S

With the signing of the 1978 contract, the BCOA operators attained their major goal of replacing the union-based Funds medical care program with operator-controlled insurance company contracts for the health care of working miners. As of 1995 this arrangement remained in place, and was a key part of the industry benefits program.

The 1978 contract was in fact a second major watershed, that was equal to the 1950 contract in historical significance for the coal industry. The Funds' program had experienced a turnaround in the third of a century from its 1946 establishment by Lewis and the federal government, through its pioneering period of the 1950s and 1960s as a union-based program, to the reversal in 1978 back to a fee-for-service, company-based program for working miners. The latter development capped the decline of the program, a decline that had begun in the early 1970s.

In the 1980s, however, events were again to move the Funds back in a more positive direction. The late 1960s MFD ferment, which had elected Arnold Miller in 1972, continued, and elected Richard Trumka president in 1982. Trumka represented a new breed of UMWA leader. Many of these men were well educated, but had deep union roots. They brought a new, responsible militancy to the running of the UMWA near the end of its first century. Most had been activists in the MFD and appreciated Miller's contributions, but also saw his failings.[23]

By 1985, the impact of the new Trumka union leadership had led, among other things, to a renewal of the Funds vitality and a partial renewal of its program. Two new union Funds trustees (of the now five total trustees) were appointed, both of whom were skilled and experienced in union health and pension matters.

But this renewal of the Funds program was only partial. The 1978 return of working miners to the insurance company, fee-for-service world of medicine, where there

---

23. Maier B. Fox, *United We Stand: The United Mine Workers of America, 1890–1990* (Washington, D.C.: International Union, United Mine Workers of America, 1990), 514.

was then little organized cost management and quality assurance, remained unchanged. So in 1995, working miners remained outside the influence of the Funds.

This nearly 75% reduction in the Funds' beneficiary responsibilities, when coupled with the return of the Funds-supported clinics and hospitals to the fee-for-service world, brought the crippling of the initially pioneering Fund program of the 1950s that constituted the core of its failure.

In 1985, however, the new Funds leadership did reestablish an effective program of cost management and quality assurance measures for retirees. Such a program had been essentially missing from the entire Funds program during the Huge/Danziger regime in the 1970s.

Further, a central element of this new 1985 cost management program was significantly broadened, when in 1990 the Funds contracted with the federal Health Care Financing Administration (HCFA) to adopt a Medicare demonstration program for coal-miner retirees. The Funds took on responsibility for Medicare Part B services on behalf of its 87,500 Medicare-eligible beneficiaries, who were 86% of total Funds beneficiaries at that time. The key element in this program was that the Funds accepted from Medicare a risk-based capitation, that is, a per person payment for the Part B services for those retirees who enrolled in the new program. The Funds was at risk for that capitation payment because it was fixed periodically in advance and was to be paid at the agreed-upon level regardless of the actual quantity of services used. In this way, payment of providers for Medicare Part B services became the responsibility of the Funds.

Such risk-based contracts with Medicare are not uncommon today with HMOs. But in 1990 this was a major innovation for the Funds and its beneficiaries. The practice of enrolling beneficiaries, with the beneficiary choosing a primary care physician and expecting to be locked into that choice for a specified period of time, had previously been precluded under the Fund, by the union-management agreement that established the Fund program in 1946–50.

This new arrangement was considered by both Medicare and the Funds to be programmatically and financially successful. However, in spite of these successes of the mid-1980s and early 1990s, by the latter part of the 1980s the Funds was nevertheless facing serious deficits in both the 1950 and 1974 health trusts, although the pension trusts were fully funded by employer contributions.

The reason for these deficits was that after 1978 conditions in the industry had deteriorated rapidly. During the 1980s, coal-industry discipline and cohesiveness, represented so well for so long by the BCOA, began to fall apart. Many BCOA companies either went out of business, or simply stopped paying into the Funds and dropped out of the BCOA. By 1991 and 1992 the health trusts were approaching bankruptcy.

Under their UMWA contract, the BCOA was responsible for the bulk of costs of the Funds programs. In 1992 this meant the costs of pensions and health care for the 1950 Plan retirees and some 1974 Plan retirees. But by this time only 25% of these retirees were from BCOA member companies, while 60% had worked for companies that had gone out of business. These were the "orphan miners," so-called because no one appeared clearly responsible for them. And the remaining 15% were retirees of companies still in business but not paying into the Funds.[24]

These were the conditions that underlay the near bankruptcy of the health trusts in 1992, with the BCOA no longer able to discipline the industry. The resulting threat to the retirees' health benefits led to West Virginia Senator Rockefeller's Congressional proposal, supported by both the UMWA and the BCOA, to develop a formula for the industry to bail the Funds out. Rockefeller's proposal became the Coal Act of 1992,[25] a law based on the theory that the obligation for the health care of coal-miner retirees had initially been made as part of an industrywide agreement, and should continue to be shouldered on a similarly wide basis. However, the law did not intend that the responsibility be borne only by those coal companies that were then members of the BCOA. Nor did it intend that *all* companies in the industry be so responsible. Instead, the formula that resulted from the act specifically assigns responsibility and the cost for coal-miner retirees' health care to the retirees' former employers if still in business, or to companies who took over the properties of employers who went out of business, or to companies currently or formerly signatory to the BCOA agreement, or to their related companies, regardless of what business those companies were in at the time.

Thus, the 1992 Coal Act mandated sufficient contributions from coal companies to prevent deficits in the 1950 and 1974 health trusts. It also made the two into one combined trust, and authorized certain other future transfers to the combined trust, for health benefits for retirees, from the overfunded 1950 pension trust and from other industry sources.[26] So the Coal Act has apparently stabilized the Funds financially, at least for industry conditions of the 1990s.

Further, the act also mandated major programmatic measures for the Funds, requiring that it adopt "rigorous cost containment measures . . . [by use of] a managed care program . . . to provide benefits on a prepaid risk basis . . . [using] health maintenance organizations [and the like]."[27] In fact, the act "authorizes (or mandates) the Funds to channel (enroll) beneficiaries to networks of providers, (also) something that had previously been precluded . . . under the labor agreement in effect."[28]

24. *Pittsburgh Post Gazette* (December 20, 1991), quoting Richard Trumka, UMWA president, and Joseph Brennan, BCOA president.

25. *Funds 1992 Annual Report,* 11.

26. *Greater Pittsburgh Newspaper* (August 13, 1992).

27. *Congressional Record* (Senate, October 8, 1992); a combined note: partially from the House/Senate Conference Report, with respect to Section 9703 of the Coal Act, S17604; and from the comments of Senator Rockefeller, with respect to Section 9703(b) of the Coal Act, S17634.

28. *Proposal for a Medicare Part A and B Risk Sharing Demonstration,* for The Health Care Financing Administration (HCFA), U.S. Dept. of Health and Human Services, by The United Mine Workers of America Health and Retirement Funds, January 6, 1995, Abstract, 1.

In response to this 1992 mandate, and to the established success of the Funds' previous assumption in 1990 of responsibility for Medicare Part B services, the Funds and HCFA agreed to expand their joint program to a five-year demonstration beginning July 1995, to include both Parts A and B on a risk-based, capitated basis.[29]

However, this mandated expansion of the Medicare program presented a major problem. Networks of providers were not available in many areas, especially rural areas. Because a large portion of Funds retirees live in rural areas, implementation of a program emphasizing such networks will necessitate the development of many more such networks, to maximize accessibility for as large a portion of the retirees as possible.

Thus, in the first two years of the proposed program (July 1995 to July 1997), the Funds plans to extend its assumption of risk to include both Parts A and B "only in those geographic areas where it is able to contract with (existing) or build networks. Only starting in year 3" will the program cover all areas, including those "that lack sufficient concentration of beneficiaries to warrant network arrangements."[30]

Where provider networks do already exist, some retirees have already been enrolled under the earlier, 1990 program covering Medicare Part B services only. For those retirees, the Funds will accept risk for both Parts A and B.

Where networks do not yet exist and cannot be built in this initial period, enrollment will be delayed. But during this two-year period, the Funds and HCFA plan major joint efforts to build additional provider networks. However, the Funds expectation is that ultimately, because of the geographical scatter of the retirees and the fact that a large portion live in rural areas, the long-term potential will be for networks to be accessible to no more than one-half of the beneficiaries. For the other half, the Funds plans instead to develop as many partial elements of managed care as possible.

It is noteworthy that development of this Funds/HCFA program in the early to mid-1990s came at a time when an explosion of Medicare costs was anticipated on the national level, as the U.S. population aged and as medical care cost increases continued to exceed general inflation significantly. Thus, the Funds/HCFA Medicare demonstration can be viewed as one early example of the use of managed care programs to attempt to control this explosion. Once again, the UMWA Funds' medical care program led the way in an innovative development of national significance.

The willingness of the UMWA and HCFA to develop this joint Medicare program was based on two shared aims: first, to implement a variety of geriatric-oriented programs to assure the quality of care, and to reduce the use of high-cost inpatient services, and thus to improve the health of the elderly and frail Funds population; and second, to work out an innovative approach to developing provider networks

29. Ibid., Abstract, 1.
30. Ibid.

that would be useful for Funds' needs, but would also have broad applicability as a model of managed care for geriatric populations in many rural areas.

Thus, the impact of the 1992 Coal Act on the UMWA Health and Retirement Funds program, which had begun with federal intervention in 1946, has been to rescue the system with federal intervention in 1992. During this almost half-century, health care for *working* miners was returned to the market for fee-for-service medicine, where organized quality and cost controls are minimal or nonexistent. In contrast, the Funds reestablished such control systems in 1985, and broadened them in 1990 and again in 1995 with respect to its joint program with Medicare, for its mostly retiree beneficiaries.

Thus, the wheel of the Funds history took another significant turn: from its 1946 establishment with the help of the federal government, through the 1978 contract reversal, the Funds finished the near half-century with implementation of an innovative new managed care program, again with the help of the federal government.

In summary, given the experience of the U.S. health care industry in the 1980s and 1990s, it seems a safe prediction that all the changes resulting from, and since the 1978 contract, will result in better quality care and lower costs for Funds retiree beneficiaries, but the opposite for working miners (and probably for the coal industry as a whole).

In any case, it is ironic and noteworthy that such a path for the Funds' history came after the historical groundswell of the Miners for Democracy, which for a short period cast Arnold Miller into the UMWA presidency. His weak leadership temporarily placed the ideas of his staff in a position to determine industry policy, serving the purpose of the coal operators to transform the union-based Fund medical program into a company-based program for working miners.

But the impact of the new Trumka leadership in the UMWA has, for retirees, countered that effect on working miners, and seems likely to produce a positive long-term effect on the cost and quality of health care in the coal industry as a whole.

PART THREE

STRIKES, MINORITIES, AND THE ROLE OF FEMALE ACTIVISTS

CHAPTER ELEVEN

BLACK MINERS IN WEST VIRGINIA
Class and Community Responses to Workplace Discrimination, 1920–1930*

JOE W. TROTTER JR.

Our knowledge of urban black workers has increased considerably over the past several decades, but the rise of a black industrial proletariat was not limited to cities.[1] Large numbers of southern blacks migrated to the coalfields of Kentucky, Tennessee, Virginia, and West Virginia. Although they entered rural settings, they performed industrial work and mirrored the larger transformation of the African-American working class. Thus, a focus on the experiences of black coal miners in southern West Virginia between World War I and the early years of the Great Depression has broader significance. It not only reveals the dynamics of class and racial inequality in the bituminous labor force and the black miners' response, but,

*I thank the University of Illinois Press for permission to reprint portions of my book *Coal, Class, and Color: Blacks in Southern West Virginia, 1915–45* (Urbana, 1990). Portions of this essay have also appeared in Robert H. Zieger, ed., *Organized Labor in the Twentieth-Century South* (Knoxville: University of Tennessee Press, 1991).

1. For a recent review of this literature, see Joe William Trotter Jr., "African American Workers: New Directions in U.S. Labor Historiography," *Labor History* 35, no. 4 (fall 1994): 495–523.

perhaps most important, the comparative dimensions of proletarianization in different regions of the nation.

During the 1920s, like most of their white counterparts, African-Americans entered the West Virginia mines primarily as unskilled coal loaders. As before the war, they worked mainly in underground positions, called "inside labor," as opposed to doing outside or surface work. In 1921, and again in 1927, the West Virginia Bureau of Negro Welfare and Statistics (BNWS) reported that more than 90 percent of black miners worked as manual coal loaders or as common day laborers. The percentage of black laborers declined during the Great Depression. Yet, according to James T. Laing's survey of twenty coal-mining operations—covering McDowell, Mercer, Fayette, Raleigh, Kanawha, and Logan Counties—75% of black miners still worked in these positions in 1932 (Tables 11.1, 11.2, and 11.3).[2]

Coal loading was the most common, difficult, and hazardous inside job and thus was more readily available. Yet blacks often preferred it because it paid more than other manual labor jobs and "provided the least supervision with the greatest amount of personal freedom in work hours." As one black miner recalled, because coal loaders were paid by the ton, they could increase their wages simply by increasing their output.[3] On the other hand, while the average wage rates for coal loading were higher than most outside jobs, like other inside work, it was subject to greater seasonal fluctuations and presented greater health hazards.

Although coal loading was classified as unskilled work, it did require care and skill. For the novice especially, the apparently simple act of loading coal into a waiting train car could not be taken for granted. Watt Teal's father taught him important techniques for preserving his health as well as his life such as carefully pacing his work. As Watt Teal concluded: "There is a little art to it."[4]

Table 11.1   Black Coal Miners in West Virginia by Job Classification, 1921

	Number	%
Loaders	2,876	44.4
Inside and outside men (mainly common laborers)	3,376	52.1
Motormen	182	2.8
Skilled mechanics (mainly undercutting machine)	36	0.5
Foremen and other bosses	7	0.1
Officers and welfare workers	6	0.1
Total	6,483	100.0

SOURCE: West Virginia Bureau of Negro Welfare and Statistics, *Biennial Report, 1921–22* (Charleston, W.Va.), 57–58.

2. James T. Laing, "The Negro Miner in West Virginia" (Ph.D. diss., Ohio State University, 1933), 195.
3. Laing, "The Negro Miner," 416–22 and chap. 5; interview with North Dickerson, July 28, 1983. Unless otherwise stated, all interviews were conducted by the author and are in his possession.
4. Interview with Watt B. Teal, July 27, 1983; Laing, "The Negro Miner," chap. 5. For general

Table 11.2   Black Coal Miners in West Virginia by Job
Classification, 1927

	Number	%
Day laborer[s]	2,233	29.4
Coal loaders	4,674	61.4
Drivers	125	1.6
Brakemen	34	0.4
Trappers	10	0.1
Motormen	321	4.2
Machine-operators	215	2.8
Carpenters	8	0.1
Fireboss	1	—
Total	7,621	100.0

SOURCE: West Virginia Bureau of Negro Welfare and Statistics, *Biennial Report, 1927–28* (Charleston, W.Va.), 17–19.
NOTE: Table sample was 7,621.

Table 11.3   Mining Occupations by Race and Ethnicity in Twenty Coal Operations of Five
Southern West Virginia Counties, 1932

Occupation	American-Born Blacks		Immigrants		Whites	
	Number	%	Number	%	Number	%
Coal loaders	1,410	76,8	626	87.6	1,329	52.7
Machinemen	36	1.9	18	2.5	172	6.5
Motormen	85	4.6	16	2.2	199	7.6
Brakemen	128	6.9	7	0.9	169	6.4
Trackmen	109	5.9	36	5.0	177	6.7
Tipplemen	24	1.3	6	0.8	293	11.2
Other	43	2.3	5	0.7	224	8.5
Totals	1,835	100.0	714	100.0	2,613	100.0

SOURCE: James T. Laing, "The Negro Miner in West Virginia" (Ph.D. diss., Ohio State University, 1933), 195.
NOTE: The table included the following counties: McDowell, Mercer, Raleigh, Fayette, Kanawha, and possibly Logan.

Coal loading involved much more than merely pacing the work, though. It took over an hour of preparation before the miner could lift his first shovel of coal. The miner deployed an impressive range of knowledge and skills: the techniques of dynamiting coal, including knowledge of various gases and the principles of ventila-

---

insight into the miner's work, see Carter G. Goodrich, *The Miner's Freedom* (1925; repr., New York: Arno, 1971); and Keith Dix, *Work Relations in the Coal Industry: The Handloading Era, 1880–1930* (Morgantown: West Virginia University Press, 1977), chaps. 1 and 2.

tion; the establishment of roof supports to prevent dangerous cave-ins; and the persistent canvassing of mines for potential hazards. Referring to the training he received from his brother, Salem Wooten recalled: "The first thing he taught me was . . . my safety, how to set props and posts. Wood posts were set up to keep the slate and rocks from caving in on you . . . safety first."[5]

Coal loading was not the only job that blacks entered. Small numbers of them worked in skilled positions as machine operators, brakemen, and motormen. In its 1921–22 report, the BNWS proudly announced its success, although modest, in placing "three machine men, two motormen . . . [as well as] 57 coal loaders and company men." Labor advertisements sometimes specified the broad range of jobs available to African-Americans: "Coal Miners, Coke Oven Men, Day Laborers, Contract Men and Helpers, Motormen, Track Layers. Machine Runners, Mule Drivers, Power Plant Men, and other good jobs to offer around the mines." According to statewide data, the number of black motormen and machinemen (or mechanics) increased nearly 50%, from 218 in 1921 to 536 in 1927 (see Tables 11.1 and 11.2). Although their numbers declined thereafter, some blacks retained their foothold in skilled positions through the 1920s, with machine running being the most lucrative. Between 1926 and 1929, for example, Roy Todd and his brothers worked as machine-operators at the Island Creek Coal Company, at Holden, Logan County. On this job, Roy Todd recalled, he made enough money to buy a new car, bank $100 monthly, pay his regular expenses, and still have "money left over."[6]

However skillful black coal loaders may have become, coal loading took its toll on their health. Some men literally broke themselves down loading coal. Pink Henderson painfully recalled: "My daddy got so he couldn't load coal. He tried to get company work [light labor, often on the outside], but the doctor turned him down, because he couldn't do nothing. He done broke his self down. . . . My brothers done the same thing. They used to be the heavy loaders." Moreover, all coal loaders, black and white, careful and careless, were subject to the inherent dangers of coal mining such as black-lung disease, then commonly called "miners' asthma," a slow killer of miners caused by constant inhalation of coal dust. Explosions were the most publicized and dramatic cause of miners' deaths, but roof and coal falls were the largest and most consistent killer (Tables 11.4 and 11.5). All coal miners and their families had to learn how to live with the fear of death, although few fully succeeded. As one black miner and his wife recalled, reminiscent of Booker T.

5. Interviews with Salem Wooten, 25 July 1983, Charles T. Harris, 18 July 1983, and Leonard Davis, 28 July 1983.

6. West Virginia Bureau of Negro Welfare and Statistics (WVBNWS), *Biennial Report, 1921–22*, 59; "Safety First," "Go North," "Wanted," and "Employment Office," in Box 2, Folder 13/25, Record Group No. 174, U.S. Department of Labor; "Wanted: Sullivan Machine Men," *Logan Banner* (June 8, 1923); interviews with Roy Todd, July 18, 1983, and William M. Beasley, July 26, 1983. See also Dix, *Work Relations in the Coal Industry*, chap. 1; Laing, "The Negro Miner," 264–65; and Price V. Fishback, "Employment Conditions in the Coal Industry" (Ph.D. diss., University of Washington, 1983), chap. 6.

Table 11.4 Two Selected Fatal Accident-Types by Race and Ethnicity, West Virginia, 1917–27

	Roof and Coal Falls		Mine Cars	
	Number	%	Number	%
1917				
Blacks	41	18.9	14	27.5
Foreign-born whites	73	33.4	14	27.5
American-born whites	104	47.7	23	45.0
Total	218	100.0	51	100.0
1921				
Blacks	45	23.0	12	22.7
Foreign-born whites	52	26.5	11	20.7
American-born whites	99	50.5	30	56.6
Total	196	100.0	53	100.0
1925				
Blacks	67	18.8	24	23.6
Foreign-born whites	90	25.1	13	12.7
American-born whites	201	56.1	65	63.7
Total	358	100.0	102	100.0
1927				
Blacks	59	22.1	19	23.8
Foreign-born whites	60	22.3	8	10.0
American-born whites	149	55.6	53	66.2
Total	268	100.0	80	100.0

SOURCE: West Virginia Department of Mines, *Annual Reports, 1917*, 228, *1921*, 346, *1925*, 238, and *1927*, 207.

Washington's experience in the early prewar years: "That fear is always there. That fear was there all the time, because . . . you may see [each other] in the morning and never [see each other] any more in the flesh."[7]

As African-Americans abandoned southern life and labor for work in the coal-

7. Interview with Pink Henderson, July 15, 1983; Fishback, "Employment Conditions," 182–229; Ronald D. Eller, *Miners, Millhands, and Mountaineers: Industrialization of the Appalachian South, 1880–1930* (Knoxville: University of Tennessee Press, 1982), 178–82; interview with Walter and Margaret Moorman, July 14, 1983. For reports of black casualties, see "Six Miners Killed in Explosion at Carswell," *Bluefield Daily Telegraph* (July 19, 1919); "Gary (Among the Colored People)" (December 11, 1923; January 2, 1924), "Compensation for Six Injured Miners" (December 10, 1923), "Russel Dodson Killed Monday by Slate Fall" (July 14, 1925), and "Walter McNeil Hurt in Mine (July 22,

Table 11.5 Fatal and Nonfatal Mine Accidents by Race and Ethnicity, West Virginia, 1917–27

	Fatal		Nonfatal	
	Number	%	Number	%
Blacks	74	18.8	176	17.8
Foreign-born whites	115	29.2	237	23.8
American-born whites	205	52.0	580	58.4
Total	394	100.0	993	100.0
1919				
Blacks	72	20.9	137	16.3
Foreign-born whites	86	28.8[a]	203	24.3
American-born whites	188	54.3	500	59.0
Total	346	100.0	842	100.0
1925				
Blacks	128	18.7	645	19.1
Foreign-born whites	138	20.1	617	18.1
American-born whites	420	61.2	2,132	62.8
Total	686	100.0	3,394	100.0
1927				
Blacks	168	28.5	644	18.8
Foreign-born whites	96	16.3	554	16.0
American-born whites	326	55.2	2,245	65.2
Total	590	100.0	3,443	100.0

SOURCE: West Virginia Department of Mines, *Annual Reports, 1917–27* (Charleston, W.Va.).
[a]Includes three unknowns.

fields, the foregoing evidence suggests, their rural and semirural work culture gradually gave way to the imperatives of industrial capitalism. New skills, work habits, and occupational hazards moved increasingly to the fore, gradually supplanting their older rural work patterns and rhythms of "alternating periods of light and intensive labor." With the dramatic expansion of their numbers during World War I and the 1920s, black miners increasingly accepted southern West Virginia as a permanent place to live and labor.[8]

1925), all in the *Welch Daily News*; "Negro Miner is Killed at Thorpe" (June 12, 1929), "Colored Miner Killed Friday in Slate Fall" (March 5, 1930), "McDowell County Continues Out in Front in Mine Fatalities" (July 24, 1929), "Negro Miner Electrocuted in Tidewater Mines" (October 9, 1929), and "Hemphill Colored Miner Killed in Mining Accident" (January 8, 1930), all in the *McDowell Recorder*.

    8. For a discussion of these processes in the urban-industrial context, see Peter Gottlieb, *Making Their Own Way: Southern Blacks' Migration to Pittsburgh, 1916–30* (Urbana: University of Illinois

The working lives of black women also underwent change in southern West Virginia, but it was less dramatic. Along with their regular domestic tasks, working-class black women nearly universally tended gardens. Although the men and boys cleared and broke the ground, women and children planted, cultivated, harvested, and canned the produce: corn, beans, cabbage, and collard and turnip greens. The family's diet was supplemented by a few hogs, chickens, and sometimes a cow.[9] Gardening not only nourished the family, but also symbolized links with their rural past and soon became deeply entrenched in the region's economic and cultural traditions. Not yet eleven years old, while confined to a local hospital bed, a young black female penned her first verse, illuminating the role of the black women in the life of the coalfields:

> When I get [to be] an old lady,
> I tell you what I'll do,
> I'll patch my apron, make my dress
> And hoe the garden too.[10]

Although black women maintained gardens and worked mainly in the home, when compared to their white counterparts, they had a higher rate of wage-earning domestic service employment. Based on state-level data, in 1920, when 19.8% of black women were gainfully employed, only 10.8% of American-born white women, 15.5% of American-born white women of foreign or mixed parentage, and merely 8.2% of immigrant women were so employed. Recalling her mother's experience during the 1920s, Margaret Moorman opined, "No matter how poor white people are, they can always find a little change to hire a black woman in their home, and [my mother] did that, she would work occasionally for some of the bosses."[11] When Mary Davis's husband lost a leg in a mining accident during the 1920s, she

Press, 1987); James R. Grossman, *The Land of Hope: Chicago, Black Southerners, and the Great Migration* (Chicago: University of Chicago Press, 1989); Earl Lewis, *In Their Own Interests: Race, Class, and Power in Twentieth-Century Norfolk, Virginia* (Berkeley and Los Angeles: University of California Press, 1991); and Joe William Trotter Jr., *Black Milwaukee: The Making of an Industrial Proletariat, 1915–45* (Urbana: University of Illinois Press, 1985).

9. Interviews with Lawrence Boling, July 18, 1983, Andrew Campbell, July 19, 1983, William M. Beasley, July 26, 1983, and Charles T. Harris, July 18, 1983; "Annual Garden Inspection at Gary Plants," (July 17 and 23, 1925), "Annual Inspection of Yards and Gardens: Consolidation Cola Company" (July 27, 1925), all in *Welch Daily News*; Agricultural Extension Service, *Annual Reports, 1921–32*, especially "Negro Work" and "Extension Work with Negroes" (Morgantown, W.Va.); "The Annual Garden and Yard Contest Complete Success," *New River Company Employees' Magazine* 3, no. 1 (September 1925): 3–4, and 2, no. 2 (October 1924): 8–9; "55 Individual Awards Made Today in Yard and Garden Contests," *McDowell Recorder* (July 31, 1929).

10. The Peters Sisters, *War Poems* (Beckley, W.Va., 1919), 7.

11. WVBNWS, *Biennial Report, 1923–24*, 25–28; interview with Walter and Margaret Moorman, July 14, 1983; Women's Bureau, U.S. Department of Labor, *Home Environment and Employment Opportunities for Women in Coal Mine Workers' Families* (Washington, D.C., 1925), 47; interviews with Thornton Wright, July 27, 1983, and Andrew Campbell, July 19, 1983; "Goes South on Vacation," March 5, 1915, and Giatto Rapidly Progressing," May 29, 1915, in *McDowell Times*.

opened a boardinghouse restaurant, serving black miners in the area. She rented an eight-room facility, where her family of nine boys and seven girls resided. To supplement Mary's restaurant activities, the family purchased a mule and cultivated a relatively large hillside plot behind the restaurant. In addition to a variety of vegetable crops, the family raised several hogs, chickens, and cows.[12]

Part and parcel of the material services that black coal miners' wives provided their families were indispensable emotional encouragement and support. Even if exaggerated, the obituaries of black women suggest their successful interweaving of material and spiritual roles. The 1916 obituary of Maggie E. Matney, wife of a black miner and a teacher by training, testified: "Her aim in life was the comfort and happiness of her home. She worked day and night to have these conditions exist there. It was indeed a place where each absent member longed to be. . . . [She planned] minutely the cost and use of every item that entered the family's budget."[13]

Matney's teacher's training must have enabled her to systematize her parental role. Yet working-class black women placed a high value on children and family; some sought to adopt children when they could not have their own. In 1928, for example, a black woman in the coal town of Hiawatha, McDowell County, wrote to W. E. B. Du Bois seeking his aid in adopting a child: "I would love for you all to look out for a girl are [sic] a boy [w]ho have not got a good home. . . . We have not got children and we would be so glad to. . . . They would really have a good home." When one black woman married a coal miner who had recently lost his wife and had two sons, she dreaded the task of stepmothering, until one day she overheard one of her stepsons say to the other, "There is a dusty seat in Heaven waiting for a good stepmother and I believe Mrs. Lulu will get it; for she is a good step-mother."[14]

Family and gender relations in the black coal-mining community were by no means unproblematic, though. The son of one miner who remarried following the death of his first wife recalled that his stepmother "was very antagonistic toward her three stepsons." As tension built between the children and the stepmother, one of the sons left home at an early age, he said, "in order to avoid the conflict between us." When it came to defining gender roles, working-class black men endorsed the home as woman's proper and special sphere. In an ad for a wife, one black miner sought a woman who could "cook, iron, feed his children and hogs, milk his cows, patch his pants, darn his socks, sew buttons on his shirt and in a general way attend to the domestic duties of his palatial home." Working-class black men were acutely aware of their own tremendous labor value in the coalfields, as well as the small ratio of black female wage earners. Unfortunately, this awareness, in part, often

---

12. Interview with Leonard Davis, July 28, 1983.

13. Obituaries, *McDowell Times*, 1915–18, especially January 28, 1916 and August 13, 1915.

14. Susie Norwell to W. E. B. Du Bois, January 10, 1928; Du Bois to Norwell, May 16, 1928, reel no. 27, W. E. B. Du Bois Papers, Library of Congress; Minnie Holly Barnes, *Holl's Hurdles* (Radford, Va.: Commonwealth Press, 1980), 24–27; interviews with Thornton Wright, July 27, 1983, Walter and Margaret Moorman, July 14, 1983, Lester and Ellen Phillips, July 20, 1983, Watt Teal, July 27, 1983, and Leonard Davis, July 28, 1983.

led black miners to undervalue the black woman's contributions to the household economy. "My mother never hit a lick at a snake," exclaimed one second-genera-tion miner when asked if his mother worked outside the home.[15] Nonetheless, in the hostile racial environment of southern West Virginia, black men and women pooled their resources in the interest of group survival and development.

Although African-American coal-mining families gained a significant foothold in the coal industry, not all blacks who entered the coalfields were equally committed to coal-mining life. Some of the men were actually gamblers, pimps, and bootleg-gers, reminiscent of John Hardy of prewar fame. Middle-class black leaders attacked these men as "Jonahs" and "kid-glove dudes," who moved into the coalfields, exploited the miners, and then often moved on.[16] Other black men, like European immigrants, used coal mining as a means of making money to buy land and farms in other parts of the South. The 1921–22 report of the BNWS noted that some black miners continued to work, sacrifice, and save in order "to buy a farm 'down home,' pay the indebtedness upon one already purchased or, after getting a 'little money ahead,' return to the old home." The 1923–24 report observed that several hundred blacks in the mines of McDowell, Mercer, and Mingo Counties either owned farms in Virginia and North Carolina or else had relatives who did. In order to curtail the temporary, and often seasonal, pattern of black migration and work in the mines, the BNWS accelerated its campaign for the permanent resettlement of blacks on available West Virginia farmland.[17]

If some black workers entered the region on a temporary or seasonal basis, shift-ing back and forth between southern farmwork and mine labor, it was the upswings and downswings of the business cycle that kept most black miners on the move. Although there was an early postwar economic depression in the coal economy, it was the onslaught of the Great Depression that revealed in sharp relief the precarious footing of the black coal-mining proletariat. In December 1930, the black columnist S. R. Anderson of Bluefield reported that "more hunger and need" existed among Bluefield's black population "than is generally known. It is going to be intensified

15. Reginald Millner, "Conversations with the 'Ole Man': The Life and Times of a Black Appala-chian Coal Miner," *Goldenseal* 5 (January–March 1979): 58–64; "Looking for a Helpmate," *McDowell Times* (November 19, 1915); "Among Our Colored People," *New River Company Employees' Magazine* 2, no. 3 (November 1924): 11–12; interviews with Charles T. Harris, July 18, 1983, and Walter and Margaret Moorman, July 14, 1983.

16. "Idlers Between Ages of Eighteen and Sixty will be Forced to Work," *McDowell Recorder*, (May 25, 1917); T. Edward Hill, "Loafters and Jonahs," *McDowell Times* (May 25, 1917); "Dig Coal or Dig Trenches is the Word to the Miner," *Raleigh Register* (July 12, 1917).

17. "How a Coal Miner Can Save Money," *McDowell Times* (February 19, 1915); Laing, "The Negro Miner," chaps. 2, 3, and 4. Also see "Local Items," *McDowell Times* (March 26, 1915); WVBNWS, *Biennial Reports, 1921–22*, 5–11, 38–41, *1923–24*, 8–10, 39–45; "Kimball (Colored News)," *Welch Daily News* (January 28, 1924); "Among Our Colored," in various issues of the *New River Company Employees' Magazine* (1924–30); "Agricultural Extension Work in Mining Towns," in Agricultural Extension Service, *Annual Reports, 1921–26*.

during the hard months of January and February.''[18] In the economic downturn that followed, the region's black miners dropped from 19,648 in 1929 to 18,503 in 1931, though the percentage of blacks in the labor force fluctuated only slightly, hovering between 26 and 27%. Black miners desperately struggled to maintain their foothold in the coal-mining region. Their desperation is vividly recorded in the ''Hawk's Nest Tragedy'' of Fayette County.

In 1930 the Union Carbide Corporation commissioned the construction firm of Rinehart and Dennis of Charlottesville, Virginia, to dig the Hawk's Nest Tunnel, in order to channel water from the New River to Union Carbide's hydroelectric plant near the Gauley Bridge. As local historian Mark Rowh noted, ''Construction of the tunnel would mean hundreds of jobs, and many saw it as a godsend. Unfortunately, it would prove the opposite.''[19]

Requiring extensive drilling through nearly four miles of deadly silica rock, in some areas approaching 100%, the project claimed the lives of an estimated five hundred men by its completion in 1935. African-Americans were disproportionately hired for the project, and they were the chief victims. They made up 65% of the project's labor force and 75% of the inside tunnel crew. According to P. H. Faulconer, president of Rinehart and Dennis, ''In the 30 months from the start of driving to the end of 1932, a total of 65 deaths of all workmen, both outside and inside the tunnel occurred, six whites and fifty-nine colored.''[20] The Depression was not only a period of extensive unemployment, but, as the Hawk's Nest calamity demonstrates, also a time of extraordinary labor exploitation.

If unemployment pressed some men into the lethal Hawk's Nest project, it also required substantial sacrifice from black women. Pink Henderson recalled that while he worked on a variety of temporary jobs during the early depression years, his wife ''canned a lot of stuff,'' kept two or three hogs, raised chickens, and made clothing for the family. In 1930 the U.S. Census Bureau reported that 57.6% of black families in West Virginia were composed of three persons or less, compared to 37.5% for immigrant families and 40.8% for American-born white ones; but the difference in household size was offset by the larger number of boarders taken in by black families. During the late 1920s and early 1930s, for example, Mary Davis not only enabled her own family to survive hard times, but also aided the families of unemployed coal miners with her boardinghouse restaurant. ''We were pretty fortunate,'' her son later recalled, ''and helped a lot of people.''[21]

Black coal miners and their families, the foregoing evidence suggests, were inex-

18. S. R. Anderson, ''News of the Colored People,'' *Bluefield Daily Telegraph* (December 28, 1930); WVBNWS, *Biennial Reports, 1929–32*, 12–14.

19. Martin Cherniack, *The Hawk's Nest Incident: America's Worst Industrial Disaster* (New Haven: Yale University Press, 1986), 18–19, 89–91; Mark Rowh, ''The Hawk's Nest Tragedy: Fifty Years Later,'' *Goldenseal* 7, no. 1 (1981): 31–32.

20. Cherniack, *The Hawk's Nest Incident*, 18–19, 90–91; Rowh, ''The Hawk's Nest Tragedy,'' 31–32.

21. Interviews with Pink Henderson, July 15, 1983, and Leonard Davis, July 3, 1983; U.S. Bureau of the Census, *Fifteenth Census of the United States, 1930* (Washington, D.C., 1933), 6:1428.

tricably involved in the larger proletarianization process. As in the prewar years, through their southern kin and friendship networks, black coal miners played a crucial role in organizing their own migration to the region, facilitating their own entrance into the industrial labor force and, to a substantial degree, shaping their own experiences under the onslaught of industrial capitalism.

As the bituminous coal industry entered the post–World War I era, however, racial and ethnic competition increased. African-Americans found it increasingly difficult to retain their positions in the industry, especially in the few supervisory and skilled positions they had earlier managed to acquire. As manual loaders, they also faced growing discrimination in the assignment of workplaces, a factor that made it hard to keep pace with the production and wage levels of their white counterparts. For the most disagreeable tasks, employers sought blacks in preference to immigrants and American-born whites. The discriminatory policies of employers, however, were repeatedly reinforced by the racial attitudes and behavior of white workers and the state. Operating on the narrow middle ground between these hostile forces, black coal miners eventually developed strategies for combating them.

After the war, black representation among supervisory personnel dropped sharply. Black foremen, for example, increasingly lost ground during the postwar era. In the 1916–20 period, nearly 10% of the supervisory personnel killed or seriously injured were black men. Over the next five years no black fatalities or injuries were reported in this category, indicating a drastic dropoff in the numbers of blacks holding supervisory positions. As early as 1916, attorney W. H. Harris, a *McDowell Times* columnist, complained, "it has been the practice not to employ Colored men as bosses in the mines. This has been . . . a sort of unwritten law as it were—no matter how capable or efficient they were.[22]

In its 1921–22 survey of black miners, the West Virginia BNWS recorded only seven black foremen and other bosses in the entire state. A similar survey in 1927 produced "only one fire boss." "In late years, many or all of these places were filled by native whites and foreigners," wrote the teacher and political activist Memphis T. Garrison in 1926.[23] Under the impact of the Depression, sociologist James T. Laing found, only eleven blacks were in positions that, even by the most liberal stretch of the term, could be called positions of authority. Two of the eleven were assistant mine foremen; five worked as stable bosses in mines that still used mules; and the remainder held a miscellaneous set of jobs, including foreman over a slate dump, boss mule driver, and head of a "negro rock gang." In practice, employers modified their traditional position that "a Negro is a very good boss among his own color." One contemporary observer noted an emerging pattern when he remarked

22. "Exceptional Opportunities . . . At Olga Shaft, Coalwood, W.Va., *McDowell Times* (September 8, 1916); Price V. Fishback, "Employment Conditions in the Coal Industry" (Ph.D. diss., University of Washington, 1983), 284–85.

23. WVBNWS, *Biennial Reports, 1921–22*, 58–59 and *1927–28*, 15–17; newspaper clipping, *Welch Daily News* (September 21, 1926), in U. G. Carter Papers (West Virginia Collection, West Virginia University).

that "even foreigners are given these positions in preference to native Colored men."[24]

The discriminatory attitudes and practices of state officials reinforced black exclusion from supervisory jobs. To meet the new standards that had been set on the eve of World War I, West Virginia University expanded its mining extension classes for the training of white foremen. During the war years, enrollments reached over 4,500, accelerated during the 1920s, and by 1930 had climbed to over 20,000. These classes not only trained whites for managerial and supervisory positions but also heightened the racial stratification of the mine labor force. Only in the late 1930s did blacks receive similar classes, and then on a segregated and inadequate basis.[25] In the war and postwar years, as in the prewar era, caste restrictions continued to limit the occupational mobility of black workers.

If blacks found it nearly impossible to gain supervisory jobs, they found it somewhat less difficult to secure positions as machine operators and motormen. The employment of blacks in unskilled and semiskilled jobs was highly sensitive to the specific labor demands of the bituminous coal industry. During the coal strikes of the early 1920s, for example, company officials hired growing numbers of black machine operators and frequently praised them for their efficient labor. In 1921–22, according to the BNWS, employers of skilled black workers stated that "they are as efficient, more loyal, as regular and take a greater personal interest in their work and in the success of the business than workers of other races." Likewise during the economic upswing of the mid-1920s, the bureau enthusiastically reported: "Not only has the Negro made for himself a permanent place as miner and laborer about the mines, but he is being sought . . . by mine owners to fill positions requiring skill and training."[26]

Although some blacks gained skilled positions, their path was nonetheless difficult. During the war years, for example, a Logan County engineer informed operators that "where ever one finds a Colored motorman having a white brakeman or machineman a white helper, he may be sure that there is more or less friction between the two. . . . A white man doesn't care to have a Colored for his buddy." Black workers found it especially difficult to secure jobs as mainline motormen, workers who transported loaded coal cars from underground working areas to the surface. In the mines of Hemphill and Coalwood, McDowell County, Pink Henderson bitterly recalled, during the 1920s "the mine foremen wouldn't let the black[s] . . . run the motor. . . . A white man ran the motor." When the foreman assigned blacks to motormen jobs, he was careful to specify that they were "running the motor extra," as a temporary expedient, thus preserving for whites a proprietary

24. James T. Laing, "The Negro Miner in West Virginia," 182–83, 213; "Exceptional Opportunities . . . At Olga Shaft, Coalwood, W.Va.," *McDowell Times* (September 8, 1916).

25. Homer L. Morris, *The Plight of the Bituminous Coal Miner* (Philadelphia: University of Pennsylvania Press, 1934), 297–98; Fishback, "Employment Conditions," 308–9; West Virginia State College Mining Extension Service, *Annual Report, 1942–43,* in U. G. Carter Papers.

26. WVBNWS, *Biennial Reports, 1921–22,* 86–87, and *1923–24,* 36–37.

right to the job.[27] Another black motorman agreed: "When a white man came there and wanted the job then . . . you had to get down. . . . A black man had to get down and let the white run."[28]

Highlighting the exclusion of blacks from jobs on the mainline motor was their employment as brakemen and mule drivers. Among skilled and semiskilled jobs, blacks gained their strongest foothold in the dangerous brakeman job, which paralleled the hazardous coupling job on the old railroad cars. They worked behind white motormen but continually complained that white men "would not brake behind a black motorman." Although the use of draft animals steadily declined with the rise of mechanization, some southern West Virginia mines continued to use mules in the underground transportation of coal. During the 1920s, Oscar Davis and later his son Leonard drove mules at the New River and Pocahontas Consolidated Coal Company in McDowell County.[29] Disproportionately black, the mule drivers worked between the individual working places and the mainline rails, where the "mainline motor," usually operated by white men, pulled the cars to the tipple, the outside preparation and shipment facilities. According to the accident reports of the State Bureau of Mines, between 1916 and 1925 African-Americans accounted for over 35 percent of the state's 124 fatal and serious nonfatal accidents involving mule drivers.[30] Gradually, however, the "gathering motors" replaced the mules. The introduction of the gathering motor, which was ancillary to the "mainline motor," provided increasing opportunities for blacks after World War I.

As the coal industry entered the depression years of the late 1920s, white resistance to employment of blacks as skilled workers grew more vocal. Employers increasingly asserted that "the negro is not much good with machinery." At times, according to Laing, "the tone of the employer seemed to imply. . . . a coal cutting machine is a machine—hence, of course, he is no good." At the same time, white workers increased their resistance to the employment of blacks as machinist helpers, men who had privileged entrée into machinist jobs. When asked if his black helper was a good worker, one machinist replied, "Yes, he will do his work and half of mine if I want him to." He added that he never "gets familiar" and "keeps his place." The same machinist nonetheless expressed his preference for a white helper, and, as blacks lost such jobs, those who remained worked under reluctant and blatantly exploitative white bosses.[31] While racism indeed shaped the white workers'

27. C. F. Fuetter, "Mixed Labor in Coal Mining," *Coal Age* 10 (July 22, 1916): 137, quoted in Ronald L. Lewis, *Black Coal Miners in America: Race, Class, and Community Conflict, 1780–1980* (Lexington: University Press of Kentucky, 1987), 144–45; interview with Pink Henderson, July 15, 1983.

28. "Memorandum, Willie Parker," Straight Numerical Files, No. 182363, U.S. Department of Justice Records, RG 60, National Archives, Washington, D.C.; interviews with Pink Henderson, July 15, 1983, and Charles T. Harris, July 18, 1983; Laing, "The Negro Miner," 242.

29. "Memorandum, Willie Parker, SNF 182363, RG 60, National Archives; interviews with Leonard Davis, July 28, 1983, and Roy Todd, July 18, 1983.

30. Fishback, "Employment Conditions," 284–85; Laing, "The Negro Miner," 191, 242, 249–50.

31. Laing, "The Negro Miner," 234–36.

responses toward blacks, white machinists desired white helpers not because blacks were "lazy," inefficient, or uncooperative, but because they were apparently the opposite and were thus perceived as a threat during a period of increasing mechanization and subsequent economic decline.[32]

In the aftermath of World War I, as racial discrimination excluded blacks from important skilled, semiskilled, and supervisory positions, it blocked their progress in unskilled jobs as well. As coal loaders paid by the ton, blacks faced increasing discrimination in the assignment of work places. To be sure, black coal loaders shared a variety of debilitating working conditions with their white counterparts. Low wages, hazardous conditions, and hard work characterized the experiences of all miners regardless of ethnicity or race. Yet, according to the testimonies of black miners, racism intensified the impact of such conditions on them. "A lot of those mines had unwritten policies. The blacks would work a certain section of the mines. The [American] whites would work a certain section. The Italians and the foreigners would work a certain section," recalled Leonard Davis. Describing his father's experience during the 1920s and later his own, Davis also said, "At times . . . in certain conditions blacks would have a good place to load coal. But mostly they were given places where there was a lot of rock, water, and some days you worked until you moved the rock. You didn't make a penny because they weren't paying for moving rock then. You didn't make anything."[33]

During the mid-1920s, black miners repeatedly complained of poor working conditions. The seams they worked were characterized by excessive rock, water, low coal content, and bad air. They sometimes loaded three to four cars of rock before reaching the "good" coal. From the mid-1920s through the early 1930s, Roy Todd recalled, black miners lost a lot of time and money through "dead work." If there was a rock fall in your area, he said, "you had to clean it up for nothing." The cleanup sometimes took two or three days.[34] Although many observers emphasized the water-free nature of West Virginia mines, in fact work in excessive water was a common problem. Some men loaded coal in hip boots. Even where water was no problem, black men were disproportionately assigned low seams. They frequently worked in seams as low as two or three feet, loading coal on their knees. "I like it high. . . . I don't like it low," one black miner exclaimed. "You got to crawl in there."[35] Although they used pads when loading low coal, some men developed calluses on their knees that "looked like they had two knee caps." According to Lawrence Boling, poor ventilation also hampered the black coal loader's progress: "Sometimes the circulation of air or no air would be so bad you'd have to wait sometimes up to two hours before you could get back in there to load any coal. I

32. "Looking Back with Columbus Avery," *Goldenseal* 8, no. 1 (spring 1982): 32–40.

33. Interview with Leonard Davis, July 28, 1983; Laing, "The Negro Miner," 225–28.

34. Interviews with Walter E. Moorman and Margaret Moorman, July 14, 1983, and Roy Todd, July 18, 1983.

35. Interviews with Andrew Campbell, July 19, 1983, Pink Henderson, July 15, 1983, and Henry L. Phillips and Ellen Phillips, July 20, 1983.

have been sick and dizzy off of that smoke many times. . . . That deadly poison is there. . . . It would knock you out too, make you weak as water."[36]

Compounding the problems of bad air, low coal seams, and water were the difficulties of unmechanized mines. While few mines used pick mining exclusively, traditional methods persisted in portions of mines where use of machines was difficult and unprofitable. During the late 1920s, in one of the few mines relying upon pick methods, black miners outnumbered the combined total of immigrants and American-born white workers. In such cases the coal was undercut and loaded by hand, thus employing the traditional skill of pick and shovel mining. Recalling his father's employment as an occasional pick and shovel miner, one black miner said, "My dad would tell me many times that I was [a]sleep when he went to work and [a]sleep when he came back." Another black miner, Willis Martin of Gary, McDowell County, recalled, "We used to go to work so early in the morning and come home so late that on Sunday morning you'd see a little baby start to crying when he saw the strange man in the house."[37]

While these conditions indeed characterized the experiences of all miners to some extent, racism undoubtedly intensified their impact on blacks. Surveys of employer attitudes and practices during the late 1920s confirm the role of racism in shaping the coal loader's experience. "The best points of the colored coal loader are that he will work in wet places and in entries where the air is bad with less complaint than the white man," claimed an employer in the Kanawha–New River field. Another employer declared that "in this low coal I would rather have a negro than any other loader."[38]

Reflecting the immigrants' ability to outbid blacks for the better working areas, one employer exclaimed that "if they [immigrants] do not get the best places in the mine they will not work. . . . That is one thing about the colored man—he will work anywhere." Like American-born whites, immigrants in competition with black workers increasingly adopted anti-black attitudes and practices. According to blacks, some of them exceeded "native whites in this respect." When one immigrant foreman lost his job, black miners rejoiced, one of them stating, "I just can't stand being Jim-crowed by one of those fellows."[39]

Few workers of either race worked in the less hazardous outside positions, relatively safe from the dangers of explosions, coal dust, poisonous gases, and slate falls. Yet, even more than inside labor, the racial stratification of outside labor increased during World War I and its aftermath. Blacks dominated jobs in the coke yards, the hot, difficult, and most disagreeable of the outside positions, while whites dominated the less demanding phases of outside work, such as the preparation and

36. Interviews with North Dickerson, July 28, 1983, and Lawrence Boling, July 18, 1983.
37. Interview with Leonard Davis, July 28, 1983; Laing, "The Negro Miner," 189; Matt Witt and Earl Dolter, "Before I'd Be a Slave," in *In Our Blood: Four Coal Mining Families*, ed. Matt Witt (New Market, Tenn.: Highlander Research Center, 1979), 23–47.
38. Laing, "The Negro Miner," 225–28.
39. Ibid., 225–28, 474.

shipment of coal. In 1910, blacks had made up 47% of the state's coke workers, but in southern West Virginia during World War I and the 1920s, blacks constituted 65–80% of all coke workers, with immigrants and American-born whites making up only 20–35%.[40]

Racial discrimination gained concrete expression in the lower average earnings of black miners. During the economic downturn of the late 1920s, the racial wage gap widened. In 1929, the payrolls of three coal companies revealed an average semimonthly wage of $118.30, with the earnings of whites, both immigrant and American, exceeding those of blacks by nearly $20.[41] No doubt racial discrimination exacted a similar toll on the earnings of black miners throughout the postwar period. Despite the debilitating effects of class and racial inequality, black miners took a hand in shaping their own experience. They developed strategies designed to vitiate the effects of various discriminatory practices that white employers, workers, and the state devised to subordinate them. These strategies included high levels of productivity in the face of white worker competition, solidarity with white workers in the face of capitalist exploitation of all workers, and a growing alliance with black elites in the face of persistent patterns of racial inequality. Thus at times their actions appear contradictory and at cross-purposes with each other. Yet, within the highly volatile class and racial environment of southern West Virginia, the black coal miners' responses in fact had an underlying coherence and logic. As time passed and evidence of white hostility persisted, black miners placed increasing emphasis on racial solidarity with black elites as their primary strategy.[42]

In their competitive encounter with white workers, black miners targeted job performance as one of their most telling mechanisms of survival. Seeking to secure their jobs, black miners resolved to provide cooperative, efficient, and productive labor. During his career, one black miner set a record for hand loading. He loaded 90,000 tons of coal, an amount equal to a seventeen-mile-long train of 1,750 cars, each containing fifty tons.[43] More ordinary black coal miners also related with pride the number of tons they loaded in a day or week, and ultimately over a lifetime. Lawrence Boling later offered crucial insight into the black miner's contributions to the coal industry, the use of productivity as a strategy of survival, and the black miner's mentality, when he stated: "As far as I am concerned back in those days,

40. Joe W. Trotter Jr., *Coal Class, and Color: Blacks in Southern West Virginia, 1915–32* (Urbana: University of Illinois Press, 1990), chaps. 3, 4.

41. Laing, "The Negro Miner," 222–24; Fishback, "Employment Conditions," 169.

42. For the debate on the role of race and class in the coalfields, see Herbert Hill, "Myth-Making as Labor History: Herbert Gutman and the United Mine Workers of America," *International Journal of Politics, Culture and Society* 2, no. 2 (winter 1988): 132–200, and Stephen Brier, "In Defense of Gutman: The Union's Case," *International Journal of Politics, Culture and Society* 2, no. 3 (spring 1989): 383–95.

43. Interviews with Roy Todd, July 18, 1983, and Charles T. Harris, July 18, 1983; Lewis, *Black Coal Miners in America,* 179–80, citing *Color: A Tip Top World Magazine* 4 (February 1948): 13; "Among Our Colored People," *New River Company Employees' Magazine* (April 1928): 8 (West Virginia Collection, West Virginia University).

the black miner was the backbone of the mines. . . . I am proud of my life. . . . I may have worked hard. It was honest.''[44]

Up through the job hierarchy, black miners exhibited a similar resolve to perform well. At the Weyanoke Coal Company, Charles T. Harris transformed the dangerous brakeman job into a status symbol, as well as a mechanism of survival. ''I liked the brakeman best . . . because the guys . . . would get together in the pool rooms . . . to see who was the best brakeman and [to] show of[]f. . . . In fact I done it mostly for a name. . . . They said that I was one of the best brakemen . . . and they called me 'Speed Harris.' '' Harris even developed a joke around his job, which captured the inter- and even intraracial competition in the coal-mining labor force: ''I said, very few colored people can do what I do but no white at all.''[45]

In the face of white competition, black machine-cutters and motormen also worked to improve their productivity. In the early 1920s, William Beasley alternated between jobs as a motorman and machine-cutter. Later in the decade, using an old standard Goodman machine, he set a record on the undercutting machine, cutting twenty-eight places in eight hours. At times, coal operators used the performance of black men to raise standards for white workers. The general manager of a large company in McDowell County said, ''We try to standardize our work as much as possible. One day one of the groups of [white] coal cutters at a certain mine decided that five places were all that any one man could cut in a day. I went to one of my Negro cutters and told him to go down to that place and we would give [him] all the places he wanted and a $100 [bill] besides. That night this Negro cut 25 places. We standardized at seven.''[46]

Black miners not only worked to increase tonnage; they aimed to do so with minimal damage to their health. Even as they pushed to increase output, they sought to avoid lost-time accidents. Like whites, black miners participated in company-sponsored safety contests. Through such contests, but most of all through day-to-day attention to their own safety, black miners honed their survival and safety skills. Roy Todd later recalled that he worked in the mines ''47 years without a lost time accident.'' Another black miner recalled that his father worked in the mines ''51 years and he never had a lost time accident.''[47] After more than fifty years of coal mining, Charles Harris recalled that his father ''never was what you might say sick and he didn't have no bad back, and he didn't have no beat up hands. . . . That's right. I am telling you the truth now.'' No doubt Harris exaggerated this claim, but it nonetheless suggests insight into the black miners' attention to their own health

44. Interview with Lawrence Boling, July 18, 1983.

45. Interview with Charles T. Harris, July 18, 1983.

46. Interviews with William M. Beasley, July 26, 1983, and Roy Todd, July 18, 1983; Laing, ''The Negro Miner,'' 264–65.

47. Interview with Roy Todd, July 18, 1983; ''First Aid Contest at Gary'' (June 4, 1915), and ''Working Hard to Stop Accidents,'' (August 4, 1916), both in *McDowell Times*: ''Pocahontas Wins Safety Meet . . . New River Pocahontas Consolidated Teams of Berwind Jones First Place Among Colored Division,'' *McDowell Recorder* (August 22, 1929).

and safety. Other black men simply refused to work in the most dangerous places, reflecting the constant tension in the black miners' effort to provide productive labor while simultaneously protecting their lives and health. Columbus Avery said, "I'd go in to a place in the morning and inspect it. If it was bad, I wouldn't have anything to do with it. I never was hurt. I just wouldn't go into a dangerous place. They could fire me if they wanted to, but I wouldn't risk my life on a bad tap."[48]

Refusal to work in dangerous places was an aspect of the chronic transience of southern West Virginia's black coal miners. "They fired me at Pidgeon Creek once because I refused to go into a place I thought was dangerous," Avery said. Like their white counterparts, in efforts to improve working conditions, increase wages, and gain greater recognition of their humanity, black miners frequently moved between one mine and another within the region. They regularly traveled through southern West Virginia and farms in other parts of the South. Gradually, they made their way to the mines and steel mills of northern West Virginia, Pennsylvania, and Ohio. "I moved once ten times in ten years. I was high tempered. I would not take nothing off of anyone. I had a lot of pride," Northern Dickerson recalled. Another black miner said, "I would always be looking for the best job and the most money."[49]

Much of the black miners' geographic mobility was involuntary, generated by cyclical swings in the coal economy. Moreover, even during good times, coal operators and their supervisory personnel were often arbitrary and callous in their hiring and firing decisions. As Walter Moorman recalled, when miners complained about pay, one foreman retorted, "Don't grumble and stay, grumble and be on your way." In good and bad times, many black miners took this advice. When one mine foreman told a black brakeman that he had other brakemen tied up outside "with a paper string, if it rain[s] they'll come in," the brakeman reached upon the motor board, got his lunch bag, said "you get em," and quit.[50]

Roy Todd's travels typified the geographical mobility of black miners. In 1919, he took his first job at the No. 1 mine of the McGregor Coal Company at Slagle, Logan County. He worked there for one year before moving to Island Creek Coal Company at nearby Holden. Beginning at the firm's No. 1 mine, Todd soon moved to No. 8, before going to Trace Hollow for six months, working as a brace carrier on a company-constructed high school building. During the mid-1920s, he worked at several mines in McDowell County, including those of the Carswell Coal Company and the Houston Collier Company at Kimball. During the late 1920s and early 1930s, Todd spent short periods mining in Washington, Pennsylvania, the Fairmont

48. Interview with Charles T. Harris, July 18, 1983; "Looking Back with Columbus Avery," 32–40; Reginald Millner, "Conversations with the 'Ole Man': The Life and Times of a Black Appalachian Coal Miner," *Goldenseal* 5, no. 1 (January–March 1979): 58–64.

49. Interview with Charles T. Harris, July 18, 1983; interviews with North E. Dickerson, July 28, 1983, and William M. Beasley, July 26, 1983.

50. Interviews with Walter E. Moorman and Margaret Moorman, July 14, 1983, and Charles T. Harris, July 18, 1983.

District of northern West Virginia, and Lance and Wheelwright, Kentucky.[51] Thus, Todd, in common with other black miners, traveled widely, not only from company to company but from mine to mine within the same company, always seeking better seams and safer conditions throughout the multistate eastern bituminous region.

In response to the intrinsic hazards of coal mining, black coal miners sometimes developed close bonds with white miners, especially during crises surrounding such catastrophes as explosions. Echoing the sentiments of many, one black miner exclaimed that "when that mine [explosion or accident] come everybody seem like they were brothers. . . . If one man got killed it throwed a gloom over the whole mine." Even under ordinary circumstances, black and white miners slowly developed bonds across racial and ethnic lines. Such ties were apparently most prominent among blacks and immigrants of Italian origins, whom blacks called "Tallies." Pink Henderson recalled that a "certain bunch of whites would not work with a black man," but immigrants and blacks got along "pretty well." Lawrence Boling recalled, "They seemed like they'd rather be with the blacks than with the whites." While black coal miners made few comparable remarks about their relationship with American-born white miners, some suggested that blacks got along better with the West Virginia "mountain whites" than with white workers who migrated into the coalfields from Mississippi and other Deep South states.[52]

However uneven the relationship between black and white coal miners, union struggles brought about a substantial degree of interracial solidarity among the southern West Virginia coal miners. During World War I, districts 17 and 29 of the United Mine Workers of America (UMWA) expanded dramatically, covering the Kanawha–New River and Williamson-Logan coalfields, including Kanawha, Fayette, Logan, and Mingo Counties. District 17, the larger of the two, increased its membership from 7,000 in early 1917 to over 17,000 within a few months. By the war's end, it claimed over 50,000 members. Union membership in District 29—covering the southernmost Pocahontas and Winding Gulf fields, including McDowell, Mercer, and Raleigh Counties—increased during the period from fewer than 1,000 to 6,000. Black coal miners were prominent among the rank and file, frequently held office in local unions, served on the executive boards of districts 17 and 29, worked as district organizers, and served as delegates to the biennial meetings of the national body.[53]

Because of language barriers, immigrants sometimes deferred to black leadership.

51. Interview with Roy Todd, July 18, 1983.
52. Interviews with Charles T. Harris, July 18, 1983, Roy Todd, July 18, 1983, Pink Henderson, July 15, 1983, North Dickerson, July 28, 1983, and Lawrence Boling, July 18, 1983.
53. For membership statistics on UMWA districts 17 and 29, see David A. Corbin, *Life, Work, and Rebellion in the Coal Fields: The Southern West Virginia Miners, 1889–1922* (Urbana: University of Illinois Press, 1981), 76–77, 184. "Delegate [Frank] Ingham," in *Proceedings of the 28th Consecutive and 5th Biennial Convention of the United Mine Workers of America, Indianapolis, Indiana, 20 Sept. to 5 Oct. 1921*, vol. 1 (Indianapolis: Bookwalter-Ball-Greathouse, 1922), 173; Records of Districts 17 and 29, UMWA Papers, UMWA Archives, Washington, D.C.

At the 1921 meeting of the national body, for example, black delegate Frank Ingham of Mingo County eloquently addressed the gathering on conditions in his area: "I will first say that I am happy to be permitted to speak, not for myself but for Mingo county. . . . The real truth has never been told of Mingo county. It cannot be told. The language has not been coined to express the agonies the miners of Mingo county are enduring today. The world is under the impression that martial law exists there. That is not true. What exists in Mingo is partial law, because it is only brought to bear upon the miners that have joined the union." Even T. Edward Hill, the staunch anti-union director of the Bureau of Negro Welfare and Statistics, confirmed the positive character of interracial unionism in the area: "Negro members of the Executive Board . . . were elected in conventions in which white miner delegates outnumbered negroes more than five to one. The Negro union miners . . . are as staunch and faithful supporters of their organization as any other class of workers."[54]

George Edmunds of Iowa, a black international organizer, played a key role in helping to unionize black miners in southern West Virginia. In 1916 Edmunds wrote to West Virginia comrades, expressing intimate knowledge of conditions in the region: "I know so many of you, brothers. We have had some good times and hard times together. On Paint Creek and Cabin Creeks; from Gauley to the Ohio River, I have passed and repassed among you and . . . I always did my best for you and your cause." On one occasion, Edmunds addressed "a large and enthusiastic gathering" at Bancroft, West Virginia, where miners from several other mining towns in the Kanawha–New River district had gathered. On another occasion, he helped to organize a "rousing meeting" at Winnifrede, also located in the Kanawha–New River area. In the early postwar years, Edmunds continued to appear among the slate of speakers at the UMWA membership drives in the region.[55]

The immediate postwar years produced the most dramatic expression of working-class solidarity, culminating in the coal strike of 1921 and the "Armed March" of miners on Logan and Mingo counties. When coal companies denied workers the right of collective bargaining, armed conflict erupted in Logan and Mingo counties between more than 5,000 union miners on one hand and over 1,200 local law enforcement officers, strike-breakers, and company-employed detectives on the other. The conflict killed more than one hundred men and led to the declaration of martial law on three different occasions, once in 1920 and twice in 1921. Only the intervention of federal troops ended the brutal warfare. Before the conflict ended, however,

54. T. Edward Hill, "The Coal Strike and Negro Miners in West Virginia" (c. 1922), in "Early Surveys . . . ," Series 6, Box 89, National Urban League Papers, Library of Congress; WVBNWS, *Biennial Reports, 1923–24*, 22–24; *1925–26*, 131. For insight into black and white occupancy of the UMWA tent colonies of striking miners, see Box 2, Folders 9, 10, Van Amberg Bittner Papers, West Virginia Collection, West Virginia University.

55. "From Iowa: A Word to the West Virginia Miners," *UMWJ* (June 1, 1916); G. H. Edmunds, "West Virginia on Tap," (April 11, 1917); "District 29 Holds a Splendid Special Convention" (February 1, 1919); and "Assignment of Speakers for 1921 Labor Day" (September 1, 1921), all in ibid.

many black coal miners had demonstrated solidarity with their white brothers. The march on Logan and Mingo counties included an estimated 2,000 black miners, mainly union men from the Kanawha–New River field. The movement eventually attracted black adherents in the violently anti-union strongholds of Mingo, Logan, and McDowell Counties as well.[56]

In their violent confrontation with capital, black and white miners developed reciprocal loyalties. Their commitment to each other was sometimes demonstrated in dramatic ways. When law officers and Baldwin-Felts guards dispersed a meeting of union men at Roderfield, McDowell County (leaving four dead and four wounded), black miner R. B. Page organized a contingent of seventy-five men and marched to help his union brothers. Although the police thwarted his plans, his actions were a testament to the interracial character of the mine workers' struggle. At the height of class warfare, according to the *Charleston Gazette*, "One of the [white] deputies who was killed was John Gore. He was scouting through the woods near Blair [Mountain] and encountered a Negro scout. The negro [*sic*] opened fire on Gore and the latter fired in return. The negro was killed." When a white miner "came upon Gore who was bending over the body of the negro searching for identification marks," he shot the officer "through the heart." In an enthusiastic letter to the *United Mine Workers Journal*, a white miner summed up the interracial character of the miners' struggle in southern West Virginia: "I call it a darn solid mass of different colors and tribes, blended together, woven, bound, interlocked, tongued and grooved and glued together in one body."[57]

Given before a U.S. Senate investigation committee, headed by Senator William S. Kenyon of Iowa, the most potent evidence of black participation in the "Mingo War" was the testimony of black coal miners themselves. Black miners stood firmly with white workers and their testimonies reflect the complicated blending of class and racial consciousness. Black men also suffered a large, perhaps disproportionate, share of the violent reprisals from law enforcement officers and private Baldwin-Felts guards. For his union activities, Frank Ingham lost his job and house on several occasions. A veteran miner of fourteen years, in the early postwar years Ingham resisted efforts to divide workers along racial lines. The superintendent at his Mingo County mine fired Ingham when the black miner urged his fellow workers to ignore the company's promise to reward them for abandoning their white co-workers. "He

---

56. Daniel P. Jordan, "The Mingo War: Labor Violence in the Southern West Virginia Coal Fields, 1919–1922," in *Essays in Southern Labor History*, ed. Gary M. Fink and Merl E. Reed (Westport, Conn.: Greenwood, 1977), 102–43; Corbin, *Life, Work, and Rebellion in the Coal Fields*, 195–224; Hill, "The Coal Strike and Negro Miners in West Virginia, *Charleston Gazette* (September 1, 1921), and "Confessed Murderer of John Gore is Given Life Sentence," *Logan Banner* (October 19, 1923); Witt and Dolter, "Before I'd Be a Slave," 23–47. Heber Blankenhorn, "Marching Through West Virginia," *Nation* 113 (September 1921): 289, estimates 2,000 blacks among the 8,000 marchers.

57. See *Charleston Gazette* (September 1, 1921), and "Confessed Murderer of John Gore is Given Life Sentence," *Logan Banner* (October 1, 1923). "From Silush, W.Va.," *UMWJ* (September 1921).

told me to get out when I told the colored people not to take the white people's places,'' Ingham told the senators.[58]

Nor was dismissal and eviction Ingham's only punishment. Arrested several times by both federal and local authorities, he was brutally beaten and denied visiting privileges. On one occasion, he testified, a local officer suggested that ''what we ought to do with [Ingham] is not take him to jail; but to riddle his body with bullets.'' At midnight, law officers removed him from jail, stole his money and belongings, took him to an isolated spot, and beat him nearly to death. Federal and state authorities were no less brutal. Ingham said that Major Thomas Davis of the West Virginia National Guard denied him visitors and informed his wife, relatives, and friends that ''the next nigger that came over and asked him anything about me that he would put them in [jail] as well.'' Through it all, however, Ingham emphasized his working-class activities as the fundamental cause of attacks upon him. Even following his brutal beating, he testified, saying ''They asked me what I had been in the hands of the mob for and I told them because I belonged to the Union.''[59]

Still, basic to Ingham's support of the union was his commitment to his race. When he joined the union and resisted the use of black strike-breakers, he revealed consciousness of both class and race. Of his decision to oppose efforts to divide black and white mine workers, he declared, ''I did not think that would be a very safe thing to do, from the fact that it would terminate in a race riot, and I would not like to see my people in anything like that, because they were outnumbered so far as Mingo County'' was concerned. Ingham said further, ''My motive in advising the people was, I am a pioneer colored man in that creek. Before that they had been denied the privilege of working in these mines, and since they have got well established in there, many of them had found employment there. I did not want them to make enemies of the white race by taking their places.''[60]

Other black miners confirmed Ingham's commitment to working-class solidarity within the framework of black unity. George Echols, a union miner, local UMWA officer, and striker said, ''The United [Mine] Workers of America have privileges which are guaranteed by the United States, we have rights to protect us, both black and white, but they [operators and law officers] do not regard those rights at all. They take those privileges away from us. Now we are asking you to give them back to us. Let us be free men. Let us stand equal.''[61] Born in slavery, Echols articulated a distinctive African-American perspective. ''I was raised a slave,'' Echols related. ''My master and my mistress called me and I answered, and I know the time when I was a slave, and I feel just like we feel now.'' The remarks of another black miner, J. H. Reed, likewise expressed the blending of class and racial consciousness. Reed linked his arrest, incarceration, and mistreatment to his activities both as a union

58. Testimony of Frank Ingham, *West Virginia Coal Fields: Hearings Before the Committee on Education, U.S. Senate*, vol. 1 (Washington, D.C.: GPO, 1921), 26–38.
    59. Ibid.
    60. Ibid.
    61. Testimonies of George Echols and J. H. Reed, both in *West Virginia Coal Fields*, 469–82.

man and a black: "The thing here is that a man here is the same as being in slavery."[62]

Still, in West Virginia as elsewhere, working-class solidarity was a highly precarious affair. To be sure, white miners drew inspiration from black bondage, using the symbolism of slavery to help buttress the mine workers' case against the operators. Later, one white miner even put the issue in verse. "The boss said stand up boys— And drive away your fears / You are sentenced to slavery—for many long years."[63] Yet the white miners' own heritage of racism placed critical limits on their ability to identify with black workers.

White workers and employers coalesced to a substantial, even fundamental, degree around notions of black inferiority.[64] In its contract with employees, under a provision on workmanship and methods, the Carbon Fuel Company stipulated that "The miner shall load his coal in every case free from shale, bone, *niggerhead* [i.e., worthless coal] and *other impurities*" (my italics).[65] When the *United Mine Workers Journal* reprinted a racist joke from the operators' *Coal Age*, the racial consensus between operators and coal miners was made even more explicit: "Sambo, a negro [mule] driver . . . was able to gather his trips without speaking to his mule. . . . Mose, another driver [presumably black] . . . went to Sambo for help and asked Sambo what was needed to teach such tricks. Sambo said all that was necessary was to know more than the mule."[66] Further highlighting the white racial consensus were distasteful and often vicious stereotypes of black women.[67]

Cross-class white unity helped to engender a growing bond between workers and black elites. The activities of the Bureau of Negro Welfare and Statistics, the black press (especially the *McDowell Times*), and the McDowell County Colored Republican Organization (MCCRO), all evidenced aspects of the growing black worker– black elite alliance. Through the strike-breaking activities of T. Edward Hill of the BNWS, for example, some blacks gained jobs during the massive coal strikes of the early 1920s. The bureau proudly claimed credit for deterring more than one hundred black miners from joining the "Armed March." Under Hill's leadership, the BNWS nonetheless pursued its strike-breaking function with care, seeking to avoid racial violence. As an added measure of protection for black workers, Hill, with some success, advocated the use of small, interracial contingents of strike-breakers. "The coal companies that are bringing in workers are having them sent in bunches of not

62. Ibid.
63. "Agreement Between Carbon Fuel Company and Its Employees," 1923–25, in "Kanawha/Coal River," Mining Community Schedule-A, Box 28, U.S. Coal Commission Records, Record Group 68, National Archives.
64. Ibid.
65. "Easy," *UMWJ* (January 15, 1925).
66. "Agreement Between Carbon Fuel Company and Its Employees," 1923–25, in "Kanawha/Coal River," Mining Community Schedule-A, Box 28, U.S. Coal Commission Records.
67. WVBNWS, *Biennial Reports, 1921–22*, 54–60; "The Coal Strike and Negro Miners in West Virginia" (c. 1922), in "Early Surveys . . . ," Series 6, Box 89, National Urban League Papers.

more than 25 and in all crowds brought in to date there have been whites as well as negroes,'' he reported in 1922.[68]

Hill not only tried to avoid racial violence in the short run; he also sought long-run job security for the black miner. Keenly aware of the traditional dismissal of blacks after strikes, Hill attempted to pry protective agreements from owners. In a letter to the local secretaries of the Coal Operators' Association and the president of the West Virginia Coal Association, Hill wrote that it would be ''manifestly unfair to use negro miners in this crisis and then displace them when workers of other races are available.''[69] In the coal strikes of 1921–22, Hill secured an agreement from owners and managers, ''that, however the strike is settled, the negro miners now being employed'' would be retained; or, if they voluntarily left their jobs or were ''discharged for cause,'' their places would be filled by other blacks. In case operators could not secure other blacks to take the vacant places, the State Bureau of Negro Welfare and Statistics would ''be requested to supply qualified Negroes.'' M. S. Bradley, president of the West Virginia Coal Association, Hill reported, promised to ''lend his personal assistance in seeing that justice is done.'' The secretaries of the Kanawha and New River Coal Operators' Association endorsed the agreement. Hill believed the operators would keep their word and, until the Great Depression, most of them did.[70]

Such economic concessions, however, were purchased at a substantial price. They were achieved not only at the expense of interracial working-class unity, but at the expense of greater racial pride and self-assertion. Although based upon the interplay of concrete class and racial interests, the relationship between blacks and coal operators was mediated through the increasing rhetoric of welfare capitalism, conditioned by the operators' paternalistic and racist notions of black dependency. In a 1920 advertisement titled ''Discrimination Against the Negro,'' the Logan County coal operators hoped to convince blacks that they, not the United Mine Workers of America, were best suited to protect the interest of black workers. ''Colored miners in the Williamson field who have been induced to become members of the United Mine Workers,'' the operators lamented, ''were doubtless not informed about the discrimination practiced against their race in the unionized fields.''[71]

The following year the same operators sponsored a pamphlet directly toward the black workers. Again the owners informed blacks that only the company had their best interest at heart. ''First,'' the *UMWJ* warned black miners, ''when they open

68. WVBNWS, *Biennial Report, 1921–22,* 54–60; ''The Coal Strike and Negro Miners in West Virginia.''

69. Ibid.

70. ''Discrimination Against the Negro,'' *Bluefield Daily Telegraph* (June 20, 1920).

71. ''Negro Tricked into Logan County . . . ,'' *UMWJ* (June 15, 1921), includes extensive excerpts from the operators' pamphlet directed toward black workers; testimony of Langdon Bell, director of the Red Jacket Consolidated Coal Company, *Conditions in the Coal Fields of Pennsylvania, West Virginia, and Ohio: Hearings Before the Committee on Interstate Commerce* (Washington, D.C.: GPO, 1928), 1838–41.

up a new mine they think of the things that will lead you and your children to the better land. . . . So we can plainly see how kind and true the operators are to the colored people in the Logan fields." As late as 1928, before the U.S. Senate's coal investigation committee, a local coal operator testified that "The negro is not responsible for his position in America. It is the duty of the white man to treat him with justice, mercy, and compassion. . . . I do believe in providing the negroes with every economic and industrial [as opposed to social] opportunity possible."[72]

The black press supported the operators' portrait of themselves as just and paternalistic employers. In doing so, they also adopted aspects of a larger progressive tradition, which urged corporate America to take a more humane interest in the welfare of its workers. In a detailed description of the Carter Coal Company, the popular *Times* columnist W. H. Harris presented a telling contrast between what he called the old and new captains of industry: "The old time captain of industry was ob[sessed] with just one idea to get as much labor as possible for the smallest amount of money. . . . In late years the industrial captains have found that . . . the best investment is an intelligent, satisfied class of employees."[73] During the 1920s, the popular Bluefield columnist S. R. Anderson reiterated the same theme in his recurring column "News of Colored People," printed in the white *Bluefield Daily Telegraph*. On one occasion, Anderson reinforced the idea of welfare capitalism "as an expression of the human element in corporate interest upon which we may rely as a 'savor of life unto life' against the wreck of radicalism in labor and corporate insanity."[74] In exchange for employment, housing, credit at the company, store, and a gradually expanding variety of recreational and social welfare programs, employers expected deference from all workers, but especially from blacks.

Under the energetic editorship of M. T. Whittico, the paternalistic theme was a recurring feature of the *McDowell Times*. Describing the miners as "children" and the operators as "parents," the *Times* sometimes took the paternalistic theme to extremes. A *Times* columnist describing R. D. Patterson, general manager of the Weyanoke Coal Company, declared, "He is a father to every man, woman and child on his work—a kind but not overly indulgent one. He gets results because his men believe in him." Moreover, the columnist concluded, Patterson's personality, ideas, and way of doing things permeated the entire fabric of coal camp life. "If you will

72. W. H. Harris, "Exceptional Opportunities . . . ," *McDowell Times* (September 8, 1916). See also Agricultural Extension Service, *Annual Report, 1923* (Morgantown, W.Va.), 98–110.

73. S. R. Anderson, "News of Colored People," *Bluefield Daily Telegraph* (September 2, 9, 22, and 23, 1920; November 15, 1924; and January 1, 1925).

74. Ralph W. White, "Weyanoke: The Eldorado of the Coal Fields in its Section of State" (July 13, 1917); "Lynwin Coal Company: Offering Great Extra Inducements" (May 11, 1917); "Lynwin Coal Company: Offering Great Opportunities for Money" (May 4, 1917); "Sycamore C. Company: Located in Mingo County, W.Va.: Doing Good Work" (July 23, 1915); "The Coal Miners Provided For" (February 26, 1915); Lawson Blenkinsopp, "The Colored Miner 'Don'ts' for Safety First" (January 15, 1915); "Improved Conditions in the Winding Gulf Fields" (September 17, 1917), all in *McDowell Times*. See also S. R. Anderson, "News of Colored People," *Bluefield Daily Telegraph* (September 23, 1920); and Yvonne S. Farley, "Homecoming," *Goldenseal* 5, no. 4 (October–December 1979): 7–16.

stop to watch him a little, you will see Patterson reflected in everything on that works. . . . Chamelion-like, he has caused everything about him to become Patter-sonized.'' ''On the Winding Gulf,'' another columnist explained, ''the men say that Mr. Tams,'' a company official, ''is the working man's 'daddy.' ''[75] Such language helped to perpetuate notions of racial subordination and superordination, suggesting critical limits to the benefits to coal miners of their alliance with black elites. Yet black editors, columnists, and other community leaders no doubt exaggerated mana-gerial benevolence as a means of eliciting, as well as describing, the desired corpo-rate behavior.

At times, elite leadership was a good deal more assertive. Under the leadership of the McDowell County Colored Republican Organization during World War I and its aftermath African-Americans escalated their demands for representation in the state bureaucracy. Dominated by the region's small black elite, the civil rights strug-gle gave rise to a more urgent articulation of black demands, with greater attention to the needs of the black proletariat at work and at home, that is, in the larger community life of coal-mining towns.

In their efforts to move up in the bituminous coal industry, black miners perceived a great deal of value in the growing political alliance between black workers and black elites. It not only promised jobs for highly trained black miners in the state bureaucracy but also offered hope for the future training of black workers in the changing bituminous coal industry. Thus, in 1927, for example, the State Depart-ment of Mines appointed a black miner to the position of safety director. A former fire boss in the mines of McDowell County and a graduate of West Virginia State College, the new black appointee, Osborne Black, was responsible for instructing black miners in mine safety procedures. Mining experts soon came to regard Black as an effective official.[76]

Upon Black's death nearly two years later, the MCCRO passed a resolution ''Pay-ing a tribute of respect'' to the miner, who was also an active member of the strong-est black political organization in the region. The MCCRO also urged the State Department of Mines to replace the deceased safety director with another African-American miner, which it did. Upon John Patterson's appointment to the post, a contemporary student of black miners noted that ''so far as is known, he is the only Negro safety director in the world.'' Patterson had prepared for the position by taking correspondence courses from Pennsylvania State University. Moreover, be-fore passing his state mine safety examination and receiving appointment to the

75. U. G. Carter, ''Public Address'' and ''Speech to New River Colored Mining Institute, Fayette County,'' in Box 1, Folder 8, Carter Papers; ''McDowell County Colored Republican Organization,'' *McDowell Recorder* (October 23, 1920); Fishback, ''Employment Conditions,'' 231 n. 9; Lewis, *Black Coal Miners in America*, 223 n. 18; and Laing, ''The Negro Miners,'' 180–82.

76. Carter, ''Public Address'' and ''Speech,'' Box 1, Folder 8, Carter Papers; *McDowell Recorder* (October 23, 1929); Fishback, ''Employment Conditions,'' 231 n. 9; Lewis, *Black Coal Miners in America*, 223 n. 18; Laing, ''The Negro Miners,'' 180–82.

state job, Patterson had also worked for several years as "a practical miner" and a mine foreman in Raleigh County.[77]

As suggested by the career of John Patterson, some black miners benefited from their alliance with black business and professional people. Yet, black miners were by no means silent partners. They were highly conscious of the working-class basis of the bourgeois class's livelihood and even regarded it with a measure of suspicion, resentment, and distrust. One black miner recalled, for example, that a prominent black attorney gave "more favors to whites" than to blacks. During the early depression years, in one coal town black miners complained that the local branch of the NAACP did little to combat racial discrimination in the distribution of relief benefits. They also severely criticized the black attorney who headed the organization: "Why he's a rich man—he don't worry none about us people up here. . . . He don't care about us po' folks."[78]

Between World War I and the Great Depression, black coal miners in southern West Virginia developed a variety of responses to racial inequality in the workplace: high productivity in the face of white worker competition; solidarity with white workers in the face of capitalist exploitation; and, most important, a growing alliance with black elites in the face of persistent patterns of racial discrimination. Yet, although racial discrimination undercut the black miners' position in southern West Virginia, compared to black miners further north and south, black miners in the Mountain State secured a firm position in the bituminous coal industry. Black coal miners in the North remained few in number and highly dispersed, as employers recruited South, Central, and Eastern European immigrants. Between 1900 and 1930, black miners in the northern coalfields of Illinois, Indiana, Iowa, Ohio, and Pennsylvania never exceeded 3% of the total. Small numbers also made it impossible for African-Americans to wage the socioeconomic and political struggles that blacks waged in southern West Virginia.

White workers also developed strong labor unions in the northern fields, a development that reinforced the exclusion of blacks from mines in the region. In order to defeat the demands of white workers for higher pay and better working conditions, northern coal operators gradually employed black workers (some as strike-breakers). From the outset, white workers resisted the use of black labor. As historian Ronald Lewis notes, not only were African-Americans considered "scabs, they were *black* scabs, and the white miners displayed at least as much hostility to their color as to their status as strikebreakers."[79] On April 10, 1899, in Pana and Virden, Illinois, seven persons lost their lives and fourteen were wounded in a confrontation between black strike-breakers and white unionists. With little support from state and local authorities, the coal company accepted defeat and deported black strike-

77. For documentation of the following comparative discussion, see Trotter, *Coal, Class, and Color*, chap. 11, especially notes 9–11.

78. Laing, "The Negro Miner," 462, 487.

79. Lewis, *Black Coal Miners in America*, 81.

breakers from the area. Still, the number of black miners in the northern fields slowly increased from just over 5,000 in 1900 to nearly 11,000 during the 1920s. Paradoxically, given their precarious position within a union stronghold, black miners in the northern region soon joined white workers and spearheaded a vigorous tradition of interracial unionism. Indeed, black labor leaders from these northern fields later aided the UMWA's campaign to organize black and white miners in southern West Virginia and elsewhere. As discussed above, George Edmunds of Iowa was one of these, but the most renowned of these international black organizers was Richard L. Davis of Ohio.

If blacks were largely excluded from northern mines, they dominated the labor force in the Birmingham district of Alabama. Yet a variety of forces weakened their position in the Deep South and made them more vulnerable to the exploitative dimensions of industrial capitalism than their counterparts in southern West Virginia. They faced the abusive contract and convict labor systems, a program of political disfranchisement (reinforced by a vicious pattern of racial violence, including lynchings and race riots), and a racial wage scale, which placed black earnings distinctly below those of whites for the same work.

Despite the exceedingly hostile environment for interracial solidarity in the Alabama coalfields, black and white miners developed a degree of class unity. Beginning with the United Mine Workers of Alabama in the late 1880s and early 1890s, and, continuing with the southern campaign of the UMWA during the late 1890s and early 1900s, black and white miners joined together and fought the exploitative practices of Alabama coal companies, particularly the Tennessee Coal, Iron, and Railroad Company, which became a subsidiary of U. S. Steel in 1907. The UMW of Alabama and the UMWA developed policies that aimed to organize black and white workers across racial lines. Although local autonomy dictated the growth of separate black and white unions, Alabama District 20 nonetheless reserved the district vice presidency and three of the seven executive board slots for African-Americans. Under the leadership of the UMWA, black and white miners launched vigorous strikes in 1904, 1908, and 1920–21. In each case, however, partly because rank-and-file white miners had difficulty surmounting their own racism, coal companies appealed to white fears of racial equality and successfully mobilized private and public power against the union and defeated the strikes.

Conditions in the Deep South coalfields helped to drive many Alabama miners to southern West Virginia. Although they occupied the lowest position in the bituminous labor force, in the Mountain State black miners gained comparatively greater opportunities than their counterparts further north and south. They gained a solid footing in the coal-mining labor force, received equal pay for equal work, were allowed to vote, confronted fewer lynchings and incidents of mob violence, and waged a vigorous and largely successful political struggle for recognition of their human and civil rights.

CHAPTER TWELVE

COAL MINERS AND THE SOCIAL EQUALITY WEDGE IN ALABAMA, 1880–1908

RONALD L. LEWIS

The bituminous coal industry was one of the keystones in the New South edifice, but the natural tensions between modern industrial capitalism and the South's traditional social norms and customs soon became the source of internal conflict. At the vortex of this conflict was the African-American worker. Ironically, at the very time that blacks were being disfranchised and segregated and slavery was being modified into the caste system of Jim Crow, blacks found increasing economic opportunities in the South's expanding industrial base. Whether African-Americans could best improve their economic position through competition or cooperation with white-dominated industrial unions, however, raised serious questions in the minds of both races about class and caste relations. Few southern workers labored under the burden of this racial question so directly as the coal miners.

Development of the Alabama coalfield was phenomenal. Many coal and steel communities sprang up during the 1880s and 1890s in Jefferson, Walker, and Bibb counties, but Birmingham was the largest, its population growing from zero in 1870 to 132,685 in 1910. Jefferson County contained 12,345 people in 1870 and grew to 226,000 by 1910, and for the first time large numbers of foreign-born and black workers came into the area. In 1880, 42% of the district's 389 miners were black, but by 1910 blacks were about 55% of 18,000 miners. Of the white miners, 73% were native-born and 27% were either foreign-born or had foreign-born parents.[1]

This new mix of people created questions not only of industrial relations but of race relations as well. Mine operators employed so many blacks because they represented a known and plentiful supply of manpower in a labor-scarce, labor-intensive industry. Also the operators depended on traditional racial divisions to inhibit any movement among the workers to unionize. When the miners did begin to organize, therefore, the union had to enlist those workers found on the job or fail. In Alabama the majority of that group was black. Even though there was formidable resistance among white miners against belonging to the same union as blacks for fear that it implied "social equality," most of them soon realized that the only question worthy of consideration was raised in a prominent Alabama labor paper: "Will organized labor admit the black man, not only thereby benefiting him, but adding strength to the organization?"[2]

The roots of biracial unionism in the Alabama coalfield reached back into the 1870s when economic reform was sought through the National Greenback–Labor Party. The party was founded in February 1878 with the merger of the National Greenback Party, which had been created by farmers to promote monetary reform, and various workers' parties that had sprouted following the railroad strike of 1877.[3] Since the new party took a relatively progressive position on the race issue and the Republicans had all but abandoned them, many black workers could support the Greenback-Laborites.

Few industrial centers in the South boasted more Greenback clubs than the coal towns of Alabama, and blacks probably constituted the largest number of members in the district. The key black organizer of colored National clubs was a coal miner from Jefferson Mines, Willis J. Thomas, who was strongly supported by whites in the local movement. Thomas found his stride quickly as an organizer and soon had established an additional sixteen clubs in the county.[4] The Jefferson County Nationals opposed both the straight-out Democratic racists and the paternalistic Bourbon racists as well, arguing for working-class solidarity over race consciousness. As a white miner who signed himself "Dawson" observed: "We who are compelled to work side by side with [the Negro] must drop our prejudice and bigotry. This is the

1. Herbert Gutman, "The Negro and the United Mine Workers of America: The Career and Letters of Richard L. Davis and Something of Their Meaning, 1890–1900," in *The Negro and the American Labor Movement*, ed. Julius Jacobson (Garden City, N.Y., 1968), 70–71; Paul B. Worthman, "Black Workers and Labor Unions in Birmingham, Alabama, 1897–1904," *Labor History* 10 (summer 1969): 377–79; Carl V. Harris, *Political Power in Birmingham, 1871–1921* (Knoxville, Tenn., 1977), 32.

2. *Birmingham Labor Advocate* (June 30, 1900).

3. Philip S. Foner and Ronald L. Lewis, eds., *The Black Worker: A Documentary History from Colonial Times to the Present*, vol. 2, *The Era of the National Labor Union* (Philadelphia, 1978), 242; Gutman, "Black Miners and the Greenback-Labor Party," 506–8.

4. *National Labor Tribune* (June 29, July 6, August 3, 10, 17, 1878).

lever that's keeping labor in bondage to capital.''[5] In fact, Dawson urged the county organization to put Thomas forward as a candidate for public office in the 1880 general elections. If Thomas was elected, Dawson declared, 1880 would be the year ''when bigots and fanatics will have to fall to the rear and let men of brave hearts come to the front.'' He urged his fellow workers to cast aside their prejudices, for ''God made all of us.''[6] The party dissolved before Thomas could make his bid for elective office, however, because the workers demanded more radical reforms, such as government ownership of the railroads and other public facilities, than the farmers were prepared to support.[7] Unionism was still practically nonexistent in the coalfields of Alabama, but it was men like these who joined the first real union to enter the field.[8]

Almost immediately after the collapse of the National Greenback–Labor party, the first local assemblies of the Noble Order of the Knights of Labor Trades Assembly No. 135 were established in the Birmingham district at Helena, Jefferson, Pratt, New Castle, and Warrior.[9] Although the order was founded in 1869, the Knights made little headway in the Alabama field during the first decade of its existence. Class-conscious miners supported the Knights, but the coal operators effectively exploited the order's constitutional provision against racial discrimination by smearing it with a radical brush.[10]

Another biracial union that emerged during a series of strikes in the late 1880s and early 1890s was the United Mine Workers of Alabama. This shadowy organization seems to have become visible with each strike of this period and receded again once the battle had been lost. In each effort, however, thousands of black and white miners struck the companies together, even though they uniformly failed to prevent the importation of black strike-breakers from the farms. All of these skirmishes were only rehearsals for the UMW of Alabama's major battle in the spring of 1894 over a long list of grievances.[11] When the UMW of Alabama failed in its attempts to negotiate with the operators, approximately six thousand black and white miners walked out of the pits.[12]

Tennessee Coal and Iron was the largest producer in the district, so the union

5. Ibid. (April 26, 1878).

6. Ibid. (August 16, 1879).

7. Foner and Lewis, eds., *The Black Worker*, 2:242.

8. Some individuals, such as W. J. Thomas, were members of the Miners' National Association. *National Labor Tribune* (February 8, 1879).

9. Holman Head, ''The Development of the Labor Movement in Alabama Prior to 1900'' (M.A. thesis, University of Alabama, 1955), 85–86.

10. Foner and Lewis, *The Black Worker*, vol. 3, *The Era of the Knights of Labor* (Philadelphia, 1978), 72; *Alabama Sentinel* (August 4, 1881; August 13, 1887); Head, ''Labor Movement in Alabama,'' 56.

11. *Birmingham Labor Advocate* (May 10, July 4, November 8, December 6, 13, 20, 1890; January 10, 21, 24, February 21, 1891); Ward and Rogers, *Labor Revolt in Alabama*, 31–34; Head, ''Labor Movement in Alabama,'' 91–95; *Engineering and Mining Journal* 50 (December 13, 1890): 696; *Birmingham Labor Advocate* (October 21, 1893).

12. *Birmingham Labor Advocate* (April 14, 1894); Ward and Rogers, *Labor Revolt in Alabama*, 61.

focused its energies on that company. TCI officials reportedly were dumbstruck when the black miners at Johns joined the strike. According to one miner, the company had always assumed that because only blacks were employed at Johns, the company "could do anything they liked with them. They had found out their mistake and it has dawned upon their somewhat clouded vision that the colored men down here are just as wide awake to their own interests as the white men are. Company officials quickly dispatched a railroad car of beer and whiskey to dampen the strike fever at Johns, but when this ploy failed, TCI Vice President Henry F. DeBardeleben imported several hundred black strike-breakers to take the strikers' places.[13] DeBardeleben also enticed nonunion blacks to move to his Blue Creek mines by direct appeals to race-consciousness and the desire for security: "This is a rare chance for all first-class colored miners to have a permanent home. . . . This can be a colored man's colony. Colored miners, come along; let us see if you can have an Eden of your own or not. [Blacks have an opportunity to] manage their social and domestic affairs by themselves, in such a way as to command respect of the people at large. . . . As he, the negro, prospers, we can expect to grow rich, and we should go hand in hand."[14] Poor black farmers responded to DeBardeleben's offer, and by May 6, the Blue Creek mines were in operation with an exclusively black force. Still convinced that black miners were more tractable workers than whites, the operator soon installed an all-black workforce at the previously white stronghold at Pratt Mines as well.[15]

The decision to fill the mines specifically with nonunion blacks was an obvious attempt to divide the strikers along racial lines. As the *Birmingham Age-Herald*, a pro-company sheet, threatened: "Any serious and protracted struggle by white mine labor in the South will inevitably lead to its permanent displacement by Negroes from the plantations."[16] This strategy did not work as well as expected, however, for their common grievances had bound the union men of both races together in a remarkable unity of purpose. Many whites were surprised that so few blacks abandoned the cause. Fear that they would be killed by whites, Pinkerton undercover agent Thomas N. Vallens reported, secured their union loyalty.[17] Certainly coercion was a factor, but the black strikers were as determined a set of unionists as the whites. Many of them agreed with a black striker from Coalburg who was incensed by the constant references to the scabs as Negroes. He reported to the *Labor Tribune* that "all the blacklegs working [at Pratt Mines] were not 'niggers' from the color of their skins at least."[18]

13. *Birmingham Labor Advocate* (April 21, May 5, 1894).

14. *Birmingham News* (April 20, 1894).

15. *UMWJ* (June 7, 1894); Ward and Rogers, *Labor Revolt in Alabama*, 73–74; Richard A. Straw, " 'This Is Not a Strike, It Is Simply a Revolution': Birmingham Miners Struggle for Power, 1894–1908" (Ph.D. diss., University of Missouri, 1980), 16–17.

16. *Birmingham Age-Herald* (June 12, 1894).

17. Thomas Vallens to Thomas G. Jones, June 9, 1894, Thomas G. Jones Papers, Alabama Department of Archives and History, Montgomery, Ala. (hereafter ADAH).

18. *Birmingham Labor Advocate* (June 9, 1894).

Most of the African-American scabs were new to mining, for established black miners left the pits with the whites. When approximately four thousand miners assembled at a Birmingham demonstration, at least half of them were blacks carrying signs, some of which declared: "We the Colored Miners of Alabama, Stand with Our White Brothers."[19] In fact, the most arresting feature about this strike was the stubborn determination of the black miners. T. N. Vallens reported to the governor that "most of the men now at work are negroes, and the negro strikers are very bitter against them and threaten them at every opportunity and have done some acts of violence to intimidate them."[20] Another agent reported that there were "a great many negro strikers living at Pratt City and the most of them stand by the white strikers."[21]

Following a pattern common to strikes in the coal industry, the likelihood that miners would permanently lose their jobs to imported scabs soon produced violence. On the night of May 6, fifty men put Price's Mines at Horse Creek out of production by dynamiting the machinery.[22] In addition to offering a reward of four hundred dollars for information leading to the conviction of the dynamiters, Governor Thomas Goode Jones secured the services of Lieutenant James B. Erwin, a U.S. Army officer on duty with the Alabama troops, and several Pinkerton detectives to work among the miners as undercover agents. The most prominent operatives in this clandestine enterprise were T. N. Vallens, J. H. Foley, and two men identified only as "E.W." and "J.M.P." Their reports to the governor make for interesting reading but produced little of the incriminating evidence desired.[23]

Some of the violence and bloodshed resulted because TCI employed black labor agents for recruiting strike-breakers. For example, on the morning of May 17, a gunshot was fired into the Pratt City home of Chat Holman. Pinkerton detective "J.H.F." reported only one shot was fired through the window over the bed occupied by Holman. The buckshot was aimed upward, and evidently the gunman only intended to scare Holman. Three men were seen running away from the scene, and while the detective did not know whether the men were black or white, they did run toward the "negro settlement."[24] Holman himself was quickly spirited off to the TCI furnaces for safekeeping when a "mob of 600 gathered to vent their feelings in threatening language such as 'shoot him,' 'hang him' etc. and threw rocks and mud."[25]

19. *Birmingham Age-Herald* (April 24, 1894); *Birmingham Labor Advocate* (April 28, 1894). Undercover agent "T.N.V." reported that the "larger portion" were black. Vallens to Jones, April 23, 1894, Jones Papers, ADAH.

20. Vallens to Jones, May 8, 1894, Jones Papers, ADAH.

21. "J.H.F." to Jones, June 5, 1894, ibid.

22. *Birmingham Age-Herald* (May 8, 1894).

23. See various Pinkerton reports in the file, and James B. Erwin to Jones, May 17, 1894, Jones Papers, ADAH; Ward and Rogers, *Labor Revolt in Alabama*, 78.

24. "J.H.F." report, May 17, 1894. See also, Vallens to Jones, May 17, 1894, Jones Papers, ADAH.

25. Erwin to Jones, May 17, 1894, ibid.

On the morning of May 20, the first strike-related murder occurred when a black man, Walter Glover, was gunned down at his home in the same town. Before the strike, Glover worked at TCI's coke ovens in Pratt City, but he had been "black-legging" at the company's No. 5 slope during the strike. At about 2:30 A.M. three men knocked on the door, claiming to be officers of the law and asking to see Glover. Upon seeing that the men were not police, he tried to close the door but was struck by several shots fired through the door. As he lay on the floor, two more shots were fired point blank into his body. Two of those arrested for the murder, Jerry Hillery and Con Sullivan, were white, and the third, John Driver, was black. The trial of Sullivan and Driver (Hillery was released) occurred a few days later before a sympathetic justice of the peace, and both men were discharged even though the evidence against them was strong.[26]

Citing Glover's murder and roving bands of armed strikers, Governor Jones ordered state troops into the mine district on May 24 to protect the nonunion men.[27] Once the troops were on duty, company officials were even less willing to negotiate with the strikers. Incidents generally were isolated, however, and could not be controlled by the militia. Therefore, Governor Jones relieved them from active duty on July 16. No sooner had they left for home when the superintendent at Pratt Mines sent an urgent telegram to the county sheriff: "Send deputies and troops. Strikers are killing my negroes at Slope No. 3."[28] As the black strike-breakers emerged from the mine entry, a rain of bullets greeted them from ambush, leaving three blacklegs and one company guard dead.[29] Seventy-nine black and white strikers were arrested on charges of murder, and warrants were served for the arrest of twenty-five others, although only fourteen were ever tried.[30]

The strike of 1894 was lost before it began. The operators, assisted by the power of the state, were simply too powerful for the union to overcome, and strike-breakers and convict labor provided sufficient manpower to keep the mines in production. The companies did not succeed in destroying biracial unionism, but the miners had not yet achieved the depth of class unity required to shut down an entire field, which was necessary to win in Alabama. Whites too frequently engendered resentment among blacks by their failure to distinguish between black scabs and black loyalists. Moreover, the diversity of the new ethnic mix among the whites was also inhibitive. Pinkerton agent J. H. Foley was probably correct in his assessment that there were

26. Vallens to Jones, May 20, 1894, and "J.H.F." reports, May 20 and 25, 1894, ibid.

27. "J.H.F." report, May 24, 1894, ibid.; *Birmingham Age-Herald* (May 26, 1894).

28. Quoted in Ward and Rogers, *Labor Revolt in Alabama*, 110.

29. *Birmingham Age-Herald* (July 17, 1894); *Birmingham Labor Advocate* (July 21, 1894); *Warrior Index* (July 20, 1894); "Proceedings of a Conference between Members of the Executive Board of the Mine Workers of Alabama and Gov. Thomas G. Jones, July 19, 1894," copy in Philip Taft Research Notes, Birmingham Public Library Archives, Birmingham, Ala. TCI official James Bowron claimed that six were killed. See his unpublished "Autobiography," 1:354, Bowron Papers, University of Alabama, Tuscaloosa, Ala.

30. *Birmingham Age Herald* (July 19, August 2, 17, 1894).

a large number of Negro strikers living at Pratt City and most of them stood by the white strikers. However, according to the black miners who talked with Foley, the white strikers at Pratt City were "too mixed up" and would not trust one another.[31]

Following its final loss in the strike of 1894, the United Mine Workers of Alabama dissolved forever. Many of the strikers were able to regain their old jobs, but a large number of them, particularly the foreigners, migrated to other fields where they did not have to compete with that seemingly endless pool of destitute black farm laborers. Even though race relations steadily deteriorated in Alabama during this period, with blacks formally losing the franchise in 1901, it is important to remember that, despite its weaknesses, the UMW of Alabama followed a policy of organizing *all* miners, black and white, and represented a distinctive exception to the rest of institutional life in the state.

The same must be said of the United Mine Workers of America, the national union that would eventually succeed in organizing most of the nation's coalfields, including Alabama's. Although their names were similar, no official connection existed between the UMWA and the UMW of Alabama. The UMWA was founded in Columbus, Ohio, on January 25, 1890, but it made no real attempt to organize in the South until the latter part of the decade. Even more than their predecessors, UMWA officials recognized that racial and ethnic discrimination were the major obstacles that had to be conquered if the union were to succeed.[32] This judgment applied throughout American coalfields, but nowhere was race so serious an obstacle for the UMWA as in Alabama.

Herbert Gutman, a pioneer of the "New Labor History," was one of the first post–civil rights movement historians to explore the interplay between race and class in the United Mine Workers of America in a widely read essay, "The Negro and the United Mine Workers of America: The Career and Letters of Richard L. Davis and Something of Their Meaning, 1890–1900." This long essay was first published in *The Negro and the American Labor Movement*, edited by Julius Jacobson, and subsequently republished in a collection of Gutman's essays, *Work, Culture and Society in Industrializing America.*[33] Three years after Gutman's death in 1985, the *International Journal of Politics, Culture and Society* published an extended critique by Herbert Hill challenging Gutman's thesis.[34] Hill's observations on the centrality of race in working-class history, sparked a scholarly exchange in the journal's next number and provides an excellent framework for understanding the con-

31. "J.H.F." to Jones, June 5, 1894, Jones Papers, ADAH.

32. *UMWJ* (December 9, 1897).

33. Herbert G. Gutman, "The Negro and the United Mine Workers of America: The Career and Letters of Richard L. Davis, and Something of Their Meaning, 1890–1900," in *The Negro and the American Labor Movement*, ed. Julius Jacobson (New York, 1968), 49–127; Herbert G. Gutman, *Work, Culture and Society in Industrializing America* (New York, 1977), 120–208.

34. Herbert Hill, "Myth-Making as Labor History: Herbert Gutman and the United Mine Workers of America," *International Journal of Politics, Culture and Society* 2 (winter 1988): 132–200.

flicting roles of race and class confronted by the UMWA in its early campaign to organize Alabama miners.[35]

Richard L. Davis was an African-American coal miner in the southeastern Ohio coalfield who served as an organizer for the UMWA, and was the first black member of the UMWA National Executive Board. During the 1890s, the formative decades of the union, Davis engaged in a sharp exchange over the race-class issue in a series of open letters printed in the union's official organ, the *UMWJ*, until his premature death in 1900. In these letters Gutman found a window on the "local world" of coal miners that provided a glimpse of early tentative steps toward interracial cooperation in a major American union.[36]

Prior to Gutman's article on Davis, the issues of race and class were viewed from a national perspective, and historians generally portrayed black workers as strikebreakers on the one hand or victims of racist attacks on the other. This discourse on race and class suggested to Gutman that there was a more complex interplay between race and class if the "local world" of workers was examined more closely.[37] According to Gutman, African-Americans not only were welcomed into the UMWA, they also played an active role in the union as members, organizers, and even as local and district officers. In Gutman's words, "the UMW functioned as a viable, integrated trade union and quite possibly ranked as the most thoroughly integrated voluntary association in the United States of 1900."[38] The UMWA, therefore, provided a remarkable example of interracial class solidarity that prompted one black miner, O. H. Underwood, to declare in 1899 that "the United Mine Workers has done more to erase the word white from the Constitution than the Fourteenth Amendment."[39]

One of the major reasons for this extraordinarily progressive stance, Gutman hypothesized, is found in the social attitudes of its earliest leaders. In fact, Gutman wrote, "the early local and especially national leaders of the union deeply believed in the principle of human solidarity and in a kind of evangelical egalitarianism," which prompted them to form an integrated union at a time when segregation was solidifying into a rigid legal system (83). This is the dominant theme of Gutman's essay, but one that nearly every commentator believes at the very least overstates the case, and the point that bore the brunt of Herbert Hill's biting critique. Hill charged that Gutman's assertion reflected a general problem with the "New Labor History" in denying "the central role of race and the reduction of race conscious-

---

35. Steven Shulman, Nell Irvin Painter, David Roediger, Martin Glaberman, Francille Rusan Wilson, Stephen Brier, Irving Bernstein, and Albert Fried, "Labor, Race and the Gutman Thesis: Responses to Herbert Hill," *International Journal of Politics, Culture and Society* 2 (spring 1989): 361–403. For Herbert Hill's "Rejoinder" in the same journal, see 2 (summer 1989): 587–95.

36. Stephen Brier, in "Labor, Race and the Gutman Thesis," 384.

37. Nell Irvin Painter, 368, and Stephen Brier, 384–85, "Labor, Race and the Gutman Thesis."

38. Gutman, "Richard L. Davis," in *The Negro and the American Labor Movement*, ed. Jacobson, 114–15.

39. Ibid., 115.

The founding generation of the United Mine Workers, like this Scots-born miner shown emerging from the shaft with his old-fashioned carbide headlamp and lunch bucket under his arm, were mostly skilled pick miners from Great Britain.

John Mitchell, UMWA president from 1898 to 1908, engaged President Theodore Roosevelt in the settlement of the 1902 anthracite strike. A Scots-Irishman by background, he became a hero to thousands of southern and eastern European immigrant miners who helped to win the strike and make the UMWA a force to be reckoned with.

President John L. Lewis, whose iron will and mellifluous radio voice became synonymous with the UMWA's tradition of solidarity, is shown here in two poses. At left, he emerges from a pit shaft where a serious accident has just occurred. Below, he is shown as president of the CIO (right) with Philip Murray, president of the United Steel Workers. The two men are leaving a meeting in Washington, D.C., in December 1937, where they tried—unsuccessfully—to negotiate a treaty of peace with William Green, president of the AFL.

Stages in the mechanization of mining. In the first two (this page), a coal car is loaded by hand, and then passes over a scale where its contents are credited to the paycheck of the individual miner by a union-appointed checkweighman. On the opposite page above, a horse prepares to pull a loaded car from a mine. Below, a continuous mining machine at work. Introduced in the 1930s and 1940s, these machines cut and loaded coal in a single operation. The continuous mining machine greatly increased productivity, but it also made the skilled pick miner redundant.

Life in the coal camp. Above, miners' homes at River Seam Coal Company camp in Booth, West Virginia. Lower left, miner Major Fountain and his children in front of their home in Readville, Ohio, which he rents from the company for five dollars per month. Lower right, miner Dave Grubbs in the kitchen of his home in Scuddy, Kentucky, which he rents for eleven dollars per month for his family of seven.

Symbols of company power. Above, the company store, at which miners were often forced to shop in order to redeem their scrip. Below, miners and their families being ejected from coal company housing during a strike.

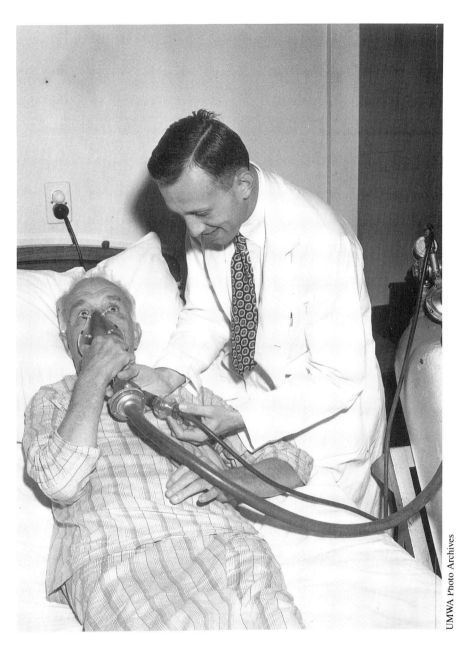

The career of a miner was often cut short either by injury or death in an accident, or, more insidiously, by the effects of pneumoconiosis or other respiratory diseases. On the opposite page above, one miner tries to free another killed in an accident. Below, miners are demonstrating in favor of a federal black lung law. Above, John Flannery, who worked in the Pennsylvania anthracite field for forty-five years, has his lungs tested in a Philadelphia hospital.

UMWA Photo Archives

Marat Moore

Although black miners might join with white miners above ground to have their picture taken, they were frequently segregated underground, or relegated to secondary tasks such as pony driving. Above, miners in Gary, West Virginia, in the early 1900s. Below, black and white miners mixing on terms of equality in Alabama in the late 1980s, after many years of segregation and second-class status.

Above, an English-language class provided for Slavic and Italian-speaking miners. These two ethnic groups predominated in both the bituminous and the anthracite fields in Pennsylvania from the 1880s until the 1940s. Below, breaker boys, who started work at the age of ten or even earlier picking slate and stones from the coal. They came from the same ethnic groups as their fathers.

The wives of immigrant miners made an essential contribution, both to the family economy and to the effectiveness of the UMWA during strikes. They are shown here (above) gathering fuel for their kitchen stoves from a dump during an 1898 anthracite strike in Hazleton, Pennsylvania, and (below) providing shelter for their families during a strike like the Colorado Fuel and Iron struggle in Ludlow, Colorado.

Because coal was essential to the running of the industry, the dominion government in Canada was just as likely to intervene in strikes there as it was in the United States. Above, a Scottish regiment is shown guarding a mine in British Columbia in 1912. Below, state militia unload munitions and supplies in southern Colorado as they prepare to help company guards break the UMWA strike in Ludlow.

Appalachia Information

After John L. Lewis retired in 1960, the UMWA went through a period of internal corruption and membership decline, culminating in the murder of Joseph ''Jock'' Yablonsky, by Lewis's hand-picked successor, Tony Boyle, on December 31, 1969. Boyle was convicted, and he was succeeded by Arnold Miller (center) of the Miners for Democracy Movement.

Marat Moore

One of the spin-offs of the civil rights movement of the 1960s and 1970s was the Coal Employment Project, a women's pressure group demanding the right for women to work underground. Here a multi-ethnic group of women are about to descend into the pit.

UMWA Photo Archives

One of the culminating events of the movement for renewal in the UMWA was the Pittston strike and boycott of 1989, when community activists, supporters from other unions, and members of the public, using up-to-date protest tactics, helped the UMWA win a major victory.

In 1982, coal miners elected a new leadership team—Richard L. Trumka (center) of Pennsylvania as president, Cecil E. Roberts (right) of West Virginia as vice president, and John J. Banovic (left) of Illinois as secretary-treasurer. Here the three men pose under a portrait of John L. Lewis at the UMWA headquarters.

ness to class consciousness." As a result, Hill claims, the Gutman approach tends "to permit questions of class to subsume racial issues" because it is based on a perspective that ignores racism as a system of domination, as it ignores the role of racist ideology in the working class itself.[40] Gutman had in fact, according to Hill, "created a myth about the history of the United Mine Workers of America—a myth woven of skewed and partial evidence" (141). Citing multiple examples from the same letters as evidence, Hill argued that the UMWA was, in fact, racist, and Gutman had helped to perpetuate a myth that distorted history and reinforced "traditional patterns of racial subordination" (132).

But if the failure of the New Labor History is its inability to confront the ideology of race-consciousness within the white working class, and therefore, as Hill puts it, "the failure to develop an acceptable theory of the relation of race to class" (135), it is equally true that historians of race have failed to develop a theory that recognized the significance of class-consciousness among the black and white workers. Although Hill claims otherwise, a fair reading of Gutman's essay reveals a recognition of the interrelationship between race and class issues among coal miners. Hill's "race first" polemic on the other hand recognizes no role whatever for the class interests of black and white miners. If Gutman does not pay enough attention to race, Hill ignores class altogether. Martin Glaberman suggests in his assessment of this issue that "neither concept can stand alone. Class needs to be modified by race; race needs to be modified by class. This is true not only in the relations between white and black workers . . . but also to understand the reality within black or white communities."[41]

What is clear from this exchange is the reflexive tendency of even sophisticated historians to essentialize race and class into mutually exclusive categories, or to rank them on an ideological hierarchy. And yet, the UMWA may well have been the most integrated voluntary association in America in 1900, as Gutman argues, and still have been influenced, even dominated, by racism and racists as Hill contends. It is safe to say that all American institutions operated in the context of racist ideology at the turn of the century. The pertinent issues are, therefore, to what degree did they act on their racist attitudes, and what were the causal forces that shaped variations in a less than uniform pattern of race relations? Who among union leaders and miners, black and white, were progressive and who were conservative on the race-class issue, and how are the differences explained? Ambiguity permeates much of the workers' world, then and now, and race relations within the working class are better understood within even a simple race-class matrix than with the black or white/freedom or oppression models now employed. Miners lived with the ambiguities of self-interest generated by working together underground, and separated topside by social and cultural imperatives. Coal miners have always shared a common, occupationally distinctive identity; nevertheless their local world was only a seg-

40. Hill, "Myth-Making as Labor History," 132.
41. Martin Glaberman in "Labor, Race and the Gutman Thesis," 376.

ment of a larger political reality. In Alabama, black and white miners, and the UMWA leadership, discovered that even though they achieved a remarkable interracial class solidarity, when their cause challenged the segregationist norms of society, the state would smash that cause on the anvil of racism. Curiously, neither Gutman nor Hill consider the critical role of the state in the "local world" of black and white workers. This is a grave mistake, and one that is readily apparent in the Alabama coalfield. The money and effort expended by the UMWA leadership to organize the black and white miners of Alabama into a biracial union, despite the predictable failures, illustrates the heroic proportions of the union's commitment if not the purity of its leadership's motives.

Even before the UMWA entered the state, the union's official organ, the *UMWJ*, was denouncing racial prejudice in the South as utterly "preposterous in the face of present day civilization" and calling on Alabama miners to "act like rational beings whose common interest it is to get from their capitalistic masters a share of their labor" (October 5, 1893).

Alabama miners generally were aware that failure would be inevitable if the racial divisions in their ranks were not surmounted. Consequently, blacks became an integral part of the UMWA's organization in Alabama (District 20). By 1902, 65% of the eighteen thousand miners in the state had been organized into the union, more than half of them African-Americans.[42] The most racially sensitive issue confronting UMWA District 20 was not whether blacks should be organized but rather how much power they should wield within the union. A compromise formula was developed that reserved the district vice presidency and three of seven seats on the executive board for blacks. Two slates then were presented to the membership, one black and one white. This formula ensured a racially mixed leadership but guaranteed that whites would retain control of the organization.[43] More than a simple question of minority white dominance was involved in this arrangement, for members of both races recognized the political dangers inherent in a black-dominated union. L. B. Evans, a white delegate to the 1904 district convention, for example, argued against popular election of all officials on the same slate because it would produce "race troubles" and maintained that the election of a black president in Alabama would mean the "destruction of the organization in the South." Realizing that Evans was correct, most blacks present agreed with a black delegate who asserted that Negroes would vote against such a plan "even though with it negroes would probably capture all the offices in the district organization."[44]

42. Sterling D. Spero and Abram L. Harris, *The Black Worker* (1931; repr. New York, 1972), 357–58.
43. Head, "Labor Movement in Alabama," 83; Worthman, "Black Workers and Labor Unions in Birmingham," 387; *Birmingham Labor Advocate* (May 21, December 17, 1894; February 11, July 15, 1899; June 23, 1900; March 6, May 11, July 2, 1901; June 28, 1902; June 20, August 12, December 19, 1903; June 13, 1904; June 17, 1905; June 28, 1906); *Birmingham News* (December 8, 10, 13, 1900; December 11, 12, 1902; December 15–20, 1903); *Wichita Searchlight* (June 8, 1901).
44. Straw, "This Is Not a Strike," 239.

Black delegates to the District 20 convention reflected the numerical and racial composition of their locals. As delegates they were not merely passive observers but active participants who agreed or differed with whites on specific issues according to their own free will. Even UMWA President John Mitchell, who attended the District 20 convention in 1900, could not persuade black delegates to vote for two resolutions he supported, one of which called on the delegates to support a proposal of the Birmingham Trades Council that miners patronize only union workmen. Silas Brooks, vice president of District 20 from 1898 to 1900, objected strongly because the council discriminated against African-Americans, and he persuaded the convention to reject the resolution.[45]

Benjamin L. Greer succeeded Brooks as district vice-president, serving from 1902 to 1908.[46] The year before Greer left office, he attended the UMWA national convention and was nominated to serve as a delegate to the International Miners Congress in London, although he lost in the balloting. Greer also voiced his opposition to racial discrimination at the national convention. When a resolution was introduced calling for the UMWA to recognize the cards of other unions if the skill was applicable to the UMWA's jurisdiction, Greer opposed it on the grounds that some of these trade unions barred blacks. "If I were a blacksmith, no matter how loyal I might be to the United Mine Workers' Organization, I could not take a card into the Blacksmith's Union. I understand that a man of my race cannot belong to that union," Greer argued. "We do not want to accept their cards . . . when a part of our membership could not be taken into their union on transfer cards." Greer reminded the delegates that "these questions are being discussed among the people of my race, and we should not do anything here that will keep them out of our organization."[47]

The UMWA's policy of incorporating blacks into the life of the organization naturally caused political difficulties in segregated Alabama, but the state organization resisted these pressures. At the 1901 district convention in Birmingham, for example, owners of the hall refused to permit access to the union when they discovered that it was to be an integrated affair. But the UMWA district president, William Kirkpatrick, declared that the Negro could not be eliminated; "he is a member of our organization and when we are told that we can not use the hall because of this fact then we are insulted as an organization." The miners denounced the owners, voted to hold the meeting in Bessemer, and advised all locals to boycott the city

45. *Birmingham Labor Advocate* (February 12, 1898; June 23, 30, 1900); *Birmingham News* (June 22, 25, 1900); Worthman, "Black Workers and Labor Unions in Birmingham," 391. Shortly after this convention the Birmingham Trades Council began to accept black delegates from the UMWA and several black unions. From 1900 to 1903 the council accepted black representatives. In 1903 Birmingham black trade unions merged with the Bessemer Negro Central Labor Council to form the Colored Central Labor Council with twenty member unions (Worthman, "Black Workers," 391).

46. *Bessemer Journal* (June 22, 1908).

47. UMWA, *Proceedings of the 18th Annual Convention, 1907*, 255.

merchants until they received an apology. Birmingham merchants quickly apologized for the "misunderstanding" rather than lose the business.[48]

Even though national and district conventions were integrated affairs, enough local autonomy existed in the UMWA to make it difficult, if not impossible, for the national, or even the district organization, to control the racial composition or politics of union locals. Segregated locals were less common in the North, but in the South racial imperatives intruded much more forcefully into local union affairs. African-Americans may have been rankled by this fact, but they had come to expect it. In fact, most blacks had considerably more race-consciousness than class-consciousness, the former having received much more reinforcement than the latter. Actually, segregated locals allowed blacks to exercise more direct control over their own internal affairs, and many of them preferred this arrangement. In several cases, integrated locals voluntarily split so that each race could control its own local. At Warner Mines, for example, about five hundred miners were employed in 1901, half black, half white. Both races belonged to the same union local, but blacks withdrew and two separate locals grew out of the division. "I will say right now," wrote one disapproving white miner, "that by separating the locals in that way in Alabama we will lose ground."[49] A black correspondent from Warner Mines disagreed, claiming that since they had withdrawn from the white local, "the colored local U.M.W. of A. here is getting along 'tip top.' "[50] Most locals were segregated from their inception. Integration would have courted political disaster by appearing to accept the social equality of the races. UMWA District 20 carefully balanced equal rights and full participation for its black members against the outward signs of white supremacy. Miners were organized "on business principles for the material advancement of labor," editorialized the *Birmingham Labor Advocate*, the official organ of District 20. Consequently, the editorial continued, no racial friction existed in the organization. The only circumstance that might produce that kind of animosity was "when social equality is expected or sought; and to the credit of the colored man can it be said that those worthy of having in the movement do not seek or expect this unobtainable boon."[51]

Miners recognized, therefore, that the social equality issue presented their primary antagonists with a powerful wedge that might be used to split the union's membership or to cleave away public support in times of labor disputes. The coal companies had plenty of incentive to employ this weapon against the UMWA because segregation provided them with significant competitive advantages in the marketplace. Labor costs were substantially reduced by several direct forms of discrimination against black miners, the most blatant of which was the racially based

48. Worthman, "Black Workers and Labor Unions in Birmingham," 401; *Birmingham News* (July 3, 1901).

49. *UMWJ* (September 5, 1901).

50. *Birmingham Labor Advocate* (December 14, 1901, February 11, 1899); *UMWJ* (April 6, 1899).

51. *Birmingham Labor Advocate* (April 27, 1901; see also March 12, 1898; November 20, 1908); *UMWJ* (December 12, 1901).

wage scale, which paid blacks less than whites for the same work. Operators also used wider screens for coal mined by blacks than for that mined by whites. This method was slightly less direct but effectively reduced the tonnage blacks were credited for mining nonetheless. Moreover, operators paid whites but not blacks for "dead work," such as cleaning up or preparing a section of the mine for production. A more complex differential resulted through the contract labor system, which categorized miners as either contractors or laborers. Contractors were paid more, and normally they were white; the laborers they employed in a working section were black. This was a southern variation of the traditional European system, which had been transplanted to America. The UMWA had succeeded in demolishing the system in the northern fields by the turn of the century, but it was still in widespread use in the nonunion mines of the South well beyond that date. These pay differentials were so common in Alabama that operators gave little thought to them, but the UMWA committed itself to their destruction.[52]

Occupational discrimination also reduced the earnings of blacks. The range of occupations in the coal industry was narrow, but the seasonal nature of mining rendered some occupations more lucrative than others over the course of the work-year. Jobs such as maintenance and repair or operating machines provided steady employment and were less responsive to the aggravated cyclical patterns that plagued the industry. The job hierarchy actually reflected the stratification of social prestige ascribed to the ethnic/racial groups at work in the Alabama mines. Native whites and Northern European immigrants (mainly from the British Isles) held the higher-paying and higher-status occupations, such as machine-operator and other skilled positions. Below this select group were the Southern European immigrants, and below them the multitude of blacks in the unskilled occupations, such as coal loading and pick mining. The net effect of this distribution was to place the burden of seasonal employment disproportionately on the poorest and lowest-status groups. Recent white immigrants might hope to rise in the hierarchy, but blacks could not.[53]

Average income figures, therefore, demonstrate the influences of discriminatory mechanisms as well as status stratification in the labor force, with native whites at the top, recent immigrants in the lower or middling range, and blacks at the very bottom. In 1909, for example, native-born white miners earned $2.15 per day, and whites with foreign-born fathers earned $2.03, but blacks earned only $1.85 per day, 14% less than native whites and 9% less than whites with foreign-born fathers.[54]

---

52. *UMWJ* (December 16, 1897; February 10, 1898); UMWA, *Proceedings of the Tenth Annual Convention, 1899*, 19; Paul David Richards, "Racism in the Southern Coal Industry, 1890–1910" (M.A. thesis, University of Wisconsin, 1969), 42–43; John Mitchell's testimony in U.S. House, *Report of the Industrial Commission on The Relations and Conditions of Capital and Labor* (Washington, D.C., 1901), 12:51–52.

53. Richards, "Racism in the Southern Coal Industry," 48; U.S. Senate, *Immigrants in Industries*, Part 1, 2:173–74, 176.

54. U.S. Senate, *Immigrants in Industries*, Part 1, 2:171, 181, App. 2, 10–11; Richards, "Racism in the Southern Coal Industry," 45, 70–72.

The black and white population of the rural South provided the coal operators with a differentiated labor reserve. The standard of living was so low that both groups were attracted to mining, but rural blacks were so poor, and their job opportunities so restricted, that significantly lower wages could recruit them into the pits. That situation did not remain static, however. Upon becoming assimilated into the mine force, blacks increasingly identified their economic interests with those of their brothers of the picks and sought to adjust the racial pay discrepancy to the standard in the trade.[55]

The economic ties that bound the operators to the caste system are further illuminated by the South's expanding share of the national coal markets as the costs of production declined in the South and increased in the North. Among southern states, Alabama led this trend, reducing its labor costs as a percentage of the whole from 82.3% in 1889, to 65.4% in 1909. In the northern fields, however, where the UMWA consolidated its strength, labor costs remained the same at from 81 to 82.3% during this period.[56] The major factors enabling this downward trend in southern labor costs were the operators' success in keeping out the union and their exploitation of African-American miners. The southern coal operators' profits, therefore, became inseparable from black subordination, and the coal companies brutally suppressed all attempts to create a biracial unionism that promoted the economic, if not social, equality of blacks.

The tension produced by the companies' determination to preserve the economic advantages it derived from the caste system, and the UMWA's mission to transform its black and white members into a biracial organization unified by class principles, inevitably generated an all-out conflict over whose will would prevail. That battle came in the strike of 1908.

The steel companies operated 60% of the coal mines in Alabama. The largest, TCI, tolerated the union as long as it remained a quasi-fraternal order that posed no serious threat to the company's control over its workforce. When the UMWA began to demand recognition as the miners' sole bargaining agent, however, TCI officials decided that the union must be destroyed before it became a powerful challenger. Several tactical skirmishes quickly occurred, followed by a short strike of 1902 and an arbitration of grievances in 1903.[57] The first real test between the UMWA and TCI came in 1904. According to a TCI spokesman, the company was losing authority over employees, and that control had to be restored "or all hope of permanent, successful competition with the products of other districts must be abandoned."[58]

55. *Birmingham Labor Advocate* (October 1, 1898; August 19, 1899).

56. Bureau of the Census, *Thirteenth Census of the United States Taken in the Year 1910, Mines and Quarries, 1909*, 40:208; *Bureau of the Census, Special Reports, Mines and Quarries, 1902*, 681, 685, 686, 689, 694, 697, 698, and 702.

57. Spero and Harris, *The Black Worker*, 357; *Birmingham Age-Herald* (July 1, 12, September 26, 30, October 4, 10, 16, 1902); Fuller, "History of TCI," 329–30.

58. Don Bacon, in the *Wall Street Journal* (May 16, 1905).

Therefore, a majority of the largest operators in the district followed the lead of TCI in refusing to renegotiate their contracts with the UMWA.

The short strike of 1904 was over within a few months as the miners were overwhelmed by immigrants imported directly from Ellis Island, blacks from the farms, and convict labor.[59] Nevertheless, five thousand of the nine thousand strikers were blacks, and the walkout again revealed that solidarity between black and white miners which seems so remarkable in the Deep South. Even though the company president predicted that 80% of the Negroes would return to work in less than one month, very few of the black unionists deserted the union.[60] Those African-Americans who entered the pits came primarily from the plantations, not from the mines. The UMWA grimly accepted defeat, but District 20 leaders expressed no reservations about the steadfastness of the black strikers. As the district president observed to the delegates at the 1905 convention, blacks had proven "their loyalty in this strike, ha[d] suffered many things for the good of the order, and ha[d] deemed it not a disgrace to be put in jail for the sake of the union."[61]

The struggle was reopened in 1908 in what would be the last major confrontation between the operators and the union for more than a decade. Once again the black and white union miners of District 20 would demonstrate that same unity that gave the operators cause for anguish, and the outcome of the contest was shaped more by southern racism than by racial schisms within the UMWA. The UMWA organizational drive was a phenomenal success. During the peak of the strike in August, eighteen thousand men belonged to the union, and more than half of them were African-Americans. Many of the strikers had entered the Birmingham district as scabs in 1894 and 1904 but subsequently had joined the union. Even at Blue Creek, the all-black scab colony established by DeBardeleben during the 1894 strike organized a 500-man local and carried their tools out of the mine.[62] As in 1904, the UMWA poured money into the district to support the miners and their families, emptying its treasury of approximately $400,000 in two months by supplying an estimated fifteen thousand people with one meal a day. Most of the operators evicted the strikers from their company homes, and by the end of August, seventy thousand people—strikers and their families—were living in UMWA tent camps.[63]

Even though the UMWA was successful in organizing the field, the strike, like its predecessors, was doomed even before it began. The coal industry was suffering from one of its periodic cyclical downturns, and the nation's economy had not yet recovered from the severe recession of 1907. As a consequence, the demand for coal

59. Congress, *Immigrants in Industries, Bituminous Coal*, 2:142, 197–98, 215; Fuller, "History of TCI," 278.

60. *Birmingham Age-Herald* (July 21, 30, August 9, September 11, 14, 1904); *Engineering and Mining Journal* 78 (October 13, 1904): 610, and 78 (December 1, 1904): 889; *Birmingham Labor Advocate* (October 1, 1904); *UMWJ* (June 2, 1904).

61. UMWA, *Proceedings of the 8th Annual Convention, District 20, 1905*, 29.

62. *Birmingham Daily Ledger* (July 13, 23, 1908); *Birmingham News* (July 13, 14, 1908).

63. *Birmingham News* (July 31, 1908); *Birmingham Daily Ledger* (August 24, 1908).

remained low, and unemployment was high. It was the large pool of unemployed workers outside of the district and that ever-dependable supply of convicts that destroyed any real chance for the union's success. The strikers' only hope was to prevent the importation of strike-breakers.[64] The companies understood this just as well as the strikers did, and in less than a week after the walkout, company agents were busy in Kentucky, Tennessee, West Virginia, Georgia, Missouri, and the cities of New Orleans and St. Louis, recruiting three to four thousand scabs for the Alabama field.[65] Union men usually met each trainload of strike-breakers at the railroad depot and pleaded with them not to assist the operators in breaking the strike. Some, especially those who were not informed of the strike by their recruiters, heeded the call. At Pratt City, for example, 75% of the imported men either left or joined the union. Fifty-five scabs at Wylam left the pits, marched into town, and to the cheers of the unionists joined the UMWA.[66]

Their inability to "talk out" most of the scabs and the companies' determination to replace the established miners with new men radicalized many of the younger miners. Older, calmer heads lost control to the firebrands, who, out of desperation, resorted to violence. The most dramatic cases involved the ambush of scab trains. On July 17, for example, a coachload of black strike-breakers and thirty company guards bound for Adamsville mines was fired upon by strikers as it approached Jefferson tunnel. In what was described as the "most exciting battle since the Civil War," a thousand shots were exchanged between strikers and company guards. The slope above the tunnel was "literally swarmed with armed men, constantly firing from behind rocks and trees" before the train could steam into the safety of the tunnel.[67] Major G. B. Seals of the Alabama National Guard subsequently described how an advance guard discovered "negroes ambushed near an old mill" waiting for the train. The major believed that these were only a "sample" of the black strikers, who, he said, were "armed to the teeth and seem to be directed by white men, although the negroes are everywhere in predominance."[68]

In one of the "most cunning ambushes ever arranged," strikers attacked another trainload of scabs near Blocton early on the morning of August 8. The engineer saw crossties piled on the track. Scarcely had he applied the brakes when "volley after volley of hot lead was poured into the side of the car" from the surrounding hill-

64. *Engineering and Mining Journal* 86 (August 15, 1908): 335–36, 351–52, and see 86 (August 22, 1908): 396.

65. Straw, "This Is Not a Strike," 120; *Engineering and Mining Journal* 86 (August 22, 1908): 396; *Birmingham Daily Ledger* (July 14, August 5, 29, 1908); *Birmingham News* (August 5, 1908); *Birmingham Age-Herald* (August 28, 1908).

66. *Birmingham Daily Ledger* (August 14, 1908); *Birmingham News* (August 14, 1908).

67. *Birmingham Age-Herald* (July 18, 29, 1908). See also *National Labor Tribune* (July 23, 1900); *Bessemer Journal* (July 27, 1908); *New York Times* (July 18, 1908). The press reports are confused on the details. I have used the *Age-Herald* account.

68. *Birmingham Age-Herald* (July 19, 29, 1908). The *Birmingham Labor Advocate* (August 7, 1908), disingenuously suggested that the ambush at Jefferson tunnel was a hoax, and that there "were no miners near the scene."

sides, killing three men and wounding eleven more. Others would have died had the conductor not had the presence of mind to press the throttle forward ramming the train headlong through the barrier. Eventually, a total of thirty people were arrested during the ensuing roundup: thirteen black men, one black woman, and the remainder Slavs (who, incidentally, had been imported as scabs in 1904).[69]

The almost daily incidents of violence that continued to occur even though Governor Comer ordered out units of the National Guard reveal the depth of hostility between the opposing parties. For example, at Johns a black striker was "shot to pieces," and two deputies were wounded in one clash; at Sayreton a black scab died from poisoned whiskey; and at Blossburg a black labor agent was found dead, his body tied to a log and set afire. There were many house and shaft bombings, and in one case, a black striker was lynched by two deputies who had placed him under arrest.[70]

Herbert Gutman has argued that in post–Civil War America, the industrial way of life took root in the cities more easily than in the small single-industry towns because the "social environs of the large American city . . . was more often hostile toward workers than was that in smaller industrial towns." The urban middle class extended little or no sympathy to the working class, but in small towns local conditions often hampered the employers' decision-making power, and the "social structure of small towns and the ideology of the residents shaped the behavior of those employers who reached outside their local environment in order to win industrial disputes."[71] The urban aspect of Gutman's assessment certainly holds true for Birmingham, where the coal and iron companies exercised their power with the solid support of the middle class.[72] But the mineral district was larger than Birmingham proper, and corporate tentacles reached out into the city's industrial satellite towns. Gutman's analysis of the small-town middle class is applicable for coal towns in the northern fields, but it needs some adjustment when applied to the Alabama coalfield.[73] Prior to the rise of coal and steel in the Birmingham district, the small towns were farm centers. Since most of the coal towns were created and controlled by the companies, they lacked the political infrastructure for the clash of old agrarian values and new bourgeois industrial values that British historian E. P. Thompson found in England and Gutman observed in the cities and the independent coal towns of the North. Since these single-industry towns were creatures of the companies,

69. *Birmingham Age-Herald* (August 10, 1908); *Birmingham News* (August 10, 1908). See also *Bessemer Journal* (August 21, 1908); *New York Times* (August 10, 1908).

70. *Birmingham Labor Advocate* (July 21, August 7, 1908); *Birmingham Age-Herald* (July 29, 30, August 4, 5, 18, 1908; and for examples of house bombings, see July 23, August 1, 2, 4, 5, 1908).

71. Herbert G. Gutman, "The Workers' Search for Power," in *The Gilded Age*, ed. H. Wayne Morgan (Syracuse, N.Y., 1970), 40–41, 47.

72. For a different point of view, see Wiener, *Social Origins of the New South*, part 3 in particular.

73. For an assessment of coal towns in the northern fields of Illinois and Ohio, see Ronald L. Lewis, *Black Coal Miners in America: Race, Class, and Community Conflict, 1780–1980* (Lexington: University Press of Kentucky, 1987), 79–118.

industrial conflict occurred along the sharp line separating the interests of the miners and their employers. The nonemployer middle class, both black and white, played a significant role in the outcome of this conflict because invariably they supported the companies against the union.

The 1908 strike revealed the depth of middle-class antipathy toward the miners' struggle. The rejection of the union was just as strong among blacks as it was among whites; middle-class Negroes feared any alteration in the caste system which they could not control. Booker T. Washington frequently spoke before Alabama industrialists, and his message was nearly always the same: the presence of blacks freed capital "from the tyranny and despotism that prevents you from employing whom you please."[74] Men such as the Reverend P. Colfax Rameau, black editor of the *Southern Industrial-Fraternal Review*, praised TCI for its generosity toward blacks and applauded the failure of "unionism to dictate" labor policy to the coal companies.[75] This conservative approach to capital-labor relations by the black middle class was succinctly articulated by Grand Master Henry Claxton Binford before the annual meeting of the Alabama Ancient Free and Accepted Colored Masons on August 18, 1908. Five hundred delegates, representing twelve thousand black Masons, listened with enthusiasm as Binford declared that he had warned black miners not to join the union. Miners who were dissatisfied with their working conditions had only one alternative: to quit. They had no right to prevent others from going to work, and he advised them against membership in the UMWA, which, he declared, was "not fit to live and should be put down by the strong arm of the law."[76]

Similarly the Reverend William McGill, editor of the black weekly, *Hot Shots*, opposed black affiliation with the UMWA and took the position that black miners' interests were best served by cooperation with those companies that hired them. Following the defeat of the miners in 1908, *Hot Shots* urged other blacks to apply for jobs vacated by the strikers and those with jobs to "hold fast to what they have." Mine management at such companies as TCI had treated black workers fairly, and blacks should demonstrate their appreciation by remaining loyal to the company. Preaching solid middle-class values, McGill urged the black miner to "work hard, earn his wages and then spend them judiciously," for to do otherwise "disgraces the race."[77]

The desperation-spawned violence only further aggravated the anxieties of Birmingham's white middle class, which expressed its fears differently from middle-class blacks. White businessmen formed a committee of citizens to organize a mass indignation rally and to muster public support for Governor Comer's forceful tactics in dealing with the strikers.[78] Meeting at the Bijou Theater in Birmingham on August 12, the group drew up a petition calling for mandatory arbitration that garnered

74. Woodward, *Origins*, 358.
75. Spero and Harris, *Black Worker*, 363–64.
76. *Birmingham Age-Herald* (August 19, 1908).
77. *Birmingham Hot Shots* (October 24, 1908, and see December 19, 1908).
78. *Birmingham Age-Herald* (August 10, 1908).

approximately twenty thousand signatures.[79] At the mass meeting, speaker after speaker simultaneously condemned violence, on the one hand, and advocated lynching those who broke the law, on the other. Every speaker favored protecting the strike-breakers, company property, and the employers' right to a free hand in dealing with their workers.[80] When a local union president was arrested, community leaders held a meeting to consider the deportation of all UMWA officials.

Only the reform farmers of the district, those who had experience in cooperating with labor during the Populist insurgency against the Bourbons, and organized labor in Birmingham demonstrated any sympathy for the miners' cause. Farmers provided food, and several allowed their land to be used for tent colonies. District 20 President John R. Kennemer received a resolution from the Farmers' Union of St. Clair County, which declared that since capitalism was "trying to enslave the poor miners," the farmers pledged their "hearty support and cooperation to them in any way that will assist them in their struggle."[81] A few days later the Farmers' Union of Lewisburg sponsored a barbecue for the strikers' benefit, and three thousand miners attended the feast to hear speeches condemning the companies and Sheriff Higdon's "dirty deputies." Blacks were not invited to the affair, but a group of them assembled on a hillside to hear the speeches.[82]

The farmers' support was hardly sufficient to swing the balance of power to the advantage of the miners, however. When the sentiments of the middle-class community became clear in early August, Governor Comer issued an official proclamation declaring that the "whole powers of the state will be exerted for the protection of everybody who desired to work."[83] With the governor and the middle class on their side, all the operators needed to crush the union by state force was a politically justifiable reason for doing so. That justification was readily available in the union's biracialism. The banner of "nigger domination" was, therefore, unfurled and hoisted aloft to guide the faithful into righteous battle.[84]

The white populace had become more and more concerned with the racial implications of the 1908 strike. The chief articulator of this concern was Frank V. Evans, an influential correspondent of the *Birmingham Age-Herald*. Evans had attended a union rally of about five hundred black and white strikers at Dora and became alarmed at what he perceived as a potential threat to the caste system. Indeed, Evans believed that conditions had reached a grave state when black leaders could "address assemblies of white women and children as social equals" on the "delicate matters of social status." Such a sight brought back visions of Radical Reconstruction, and when a black strike-leader embraced a white speaker in the presence of

79. Ibid. (August 13, 1908).
80. *Birmingham Labor Advocate* (August 14, 1908).
81. *UMWJ* (August 20, 1908).
82. *Birmingham Age-Herald* (August 23, 1908).
83. Ibid. (August 11, 1908).
84. *UMWJ* (September 10, October 1, 22, 1908).

white women, Evans thought to himself, "Has it again come to this?"[85] Evans claimed that the white UMWA leaders were as dangerous as the Radicals had been, for they were "daily instilling to the minds of the blacks ideas of social equality, which if they do take root soon will result in a worse condition than even now exists—a condition of bloodshed and absolute annihilation." No reasonable man could doubt for a moment that the blacks were vital to southern development, Evans asserted, but only so long as the "social line" between the races was strictly drawn. UMWA leaders were doing everything in their power to obliterate this line, however, by promoting "close social affiliation" and by encouraging black speakers to tell black miners that they were "as good as white men."[86]

Many whites agreed with Evans when he insisted that the race question was the most important issue in the 1908 strike. A county sheriff informed one crowd of miners that "this is a white man's country and there will be no nigger domination here." On the editorial page of the *Age-Herald*, J. V. Allen of Birmingham wrote that if the UMWA leaders and their black co-conspirators had invaded southern Alabama instead of Jefferson County, "nothing further would be needed but the coroner." In a thinly veiled call for lynch law, Allen argued that the time had passed for reasonableness toward those "who have brought shame and disgrace" upon the district. The UMWA's worst sin was its "attempt to overturn our social status and break down barriers sacred to the whole south." In another editorial, Dolly Dalrymple issued a public plea for a return to southern traditions and the day when blacks were like her mammy, who "knew where she belonged." To her it was "absolutely inconceivable" that any organization would "deliberately set about to upset the primary social laws of our beloved South," as did the UMWA. "When I hear of white miners eating side by side with black men; of womens' auxiliaries where white and black women meet on a equal footing, my heart swells to the bursting point." It was enough to prick the pride of any decent southerner, she complained, to see such infamies as "black men addressing white men as brother!" Another letter to the editor of the *Age-Herald* declared that "this social equality movement among United Mine Workers must be stopped at once."[87]

The *Birmingham Labor Advocate* editors understood the far-reaching implications of the strike far better than the UMWA national officers and attempted to defuse the social equality charges. Putting the best face on black and white unity, the *Labor Advocate* declared that white miners associated with blacks because the operators forced them to. Outside of the mines, however, whites associated with blacks on matters pertaining to their work and the union but nothing more. "There is not at present and never was and can never be social equality between the whites and blacks in this state." The only equality miners were after was "equal pay for

85. *Birmingham Age-Herald* (August 8, 1908).
86. Ibid. (August 22, 25, 1908).
87. Ibid. (August 27, 8, 25, 30, 24, 1908); *UMWJ* (August 13, 1908).

equal work.''[88] Being southerners, and not especially progressive on the race issue, the editors realized that race-baiting provided the operators with a powerful weapon against the UMWA.

By the end of August, Governor Comer had decided that it was time to bring the strike to an end, and he issued orders to cut down the miners' tent camps. District President Kennemer consulted with the union's legal counsel regarding a restraining order but was advised that it would be impossible to obtain. ''Who could you get to issue a restraining order in Birmingham? No judge would issue it,'' the attorney declared. Playing for time, Kennemer scheduled a conference with the governor before the order was implemented. Governor Comer informed Kennemer that he had already made up his mind on the matter and declared, ''You know what it means to have eight or nine thousand niggers idle in the State of Alabama, and I am not going to stand for it.'' Meanwhile, UMWA President Tom Lewis, Vice President White, Secretary William D. Ryan, and executive board member William R. Fairley arrived in Birmingham. In another conference with Comer, they received the same scolding, and the governor reiterated that he would ''not allow eight or ten thousand niggers out of employment living in tents.'' If the strike was not brought to an end, Comer informed the union officials, he would have legislation passed that would permit the arrest of every striking miner on charges of vagrancy.[89] The union officials realized that Comer was perfectly capable of gaining such a measure, for the state legislators were ''outraged at the attempts to establish social equality between white and black miners.''[90] President Lewis proposed that the union would transport every African-American striker out of Alabama, making it a white man's strike, but the governor rejected the plan.[91] Accordingly, the tent colonies were cut down by the militia, and the miners dispersed to fend for themselves as best they could.

That the union was dealing with a race problem, rather than an industrial dispute like those the national officials were accustomed to in the North, was driven home when UMWA Vice President White was visited by a committee of Birmingham citizens, who plainly informed him that the strike should be called off because it violated the region's social customs regarding racial equality. ''No matter how much merit there may be in the miners' cause,'' the committee argued, ''you cannot change the opinion of the people in this country that you are violating one of the principles the South holds near and dear.'' Before southerners would accept social equality of the Negro, they would ''make Springfield, Illinois look like six cents,'' referring to the race riot which had occurred in that northern city just a few days earlier. White claimed that much of this white fear had been aroused by the *Bir-*

88. *Birmingham Labor Advocate* (August 28, 1908); *Birmingham Age-Herald* (August 26, 1908); Richard A. Straw, ''The Collapse of Biracial Unionism: The Alabama Coal Strike of 1908,'' *Alabama Historical Quarterly* 37 (summer 1975): 92–114.

89. UMWA, *Proceedings of the 20th Annual Convention, 1909*, 865. See also *Birmingham Age-Herald* (August 25, 1908).

90. *Birmingham Age-Herald* (August 25, 1908).

91. UMWA, *Proceedings of the 20th Annual Convention, 1909*, 865–66.

mingham Age-Herald. "In all my experiences I never read such articles" as those in that paper, White later declared.[92]

The UMWA found itself in an awkward position, wishing to conduct a strike over industrial questions but confronted with social issues with which it was unable to contend. As White reported at the 1909 UMWA convention, when the union completely tied up the companies, the operators "went to the old closet and brought out the ghastly spectre of racial hatred and held it before the people of Alabama." In fact, White asserted, racial tensions were so high, "a small boy could have started a riot in the streets of Birmingham towards the close of that struggle that would have caused countless numbers of innocent people to lose their lives." Under such intense pressure, the UMWA Executive Board decided it could no longer persist and ordered an end to the strike on August 31, 1908.[93]

Manipulation of white racist attitudes by the press and the industrial elite rendered a UMWA victory impossible. Fearing a downturn in the economic life of the district, the public cried out for binding arbitration of the dispute. Since the operators had determined to crush the union, however, they unfurled the tattered banner of social equality to align public support behind them and against their union foes. "Nobody can deny that the late strike was won from an industrial standpoint," District President Kennemer lamented in 1909, but it had been lost because of the race issue. The large number of blacks in the union was not a reason to terminate the struggle in Alabama, however. Indeed, Kennemer asserted, "there are no better strikers in the history of the United Mine Workers in any district than the colored men of Alabama. They struck, and struck hard, they fought for their rights and fought manfully."[94]

It is important to note that the race issue was not sparked by the importation of black scabs. In fact, the race of the strike-breakers received little mention in the local press. The attention of the entire white power structure, and the white populace generally, was focused on black strikers who were violating social norms by assuming a militant stance within a biracial working-class organization. When the companies attempted to bring in trainloads of scabs to run the mines, a confrontation resulted that would have been edifying to those northern miners who believed the terms *strike-breakers* and *blacks* to be synonymous. Trainload after trainload of black and white imports were fired upon by the predominantly black striking miners. The exact racial composition of the imports remains uncertain, but considering the racial climate in Alabama, the situation was potentially explosive no matter what

92. Ibid., 873, 871. See also *UMWJ* (September 3, 1908); *National Labor Tribune* (September 10, 1908).

93. UMWA, *Proceedings of the 20th Annual Convention, 1909*, 872, 868–69. This order caused some grumbling among delegates at the 1909 convention, and was labeled a "sellout" by President Lewis's enemies in the organization. It was also perceived that way by militant miners who wanted to continue the struggle against any odds. See *Proceedings*, 864, 874–76; *National Labor Tribune* (November 5, 1908). For further explanation of the reasoning behind the order, see *Birmingham Labor Advocate* (September 4, 25, 1908).

94. UMWA, *Proceedings of the 20th Annual Convention, 1909*, 864.

the ratio; in either case black men were challenging the social order by resorting to arms against the white power structure. Furthermore, that these black unionists were "conspiring" with white unionists presented the explosive possibility of a class uprising in a region organized by caste and controlled by a small elite. The new industrial and social relations that were finally hammered into place in the Birmingham mineral district grew out of a struggle between unionists and nonunionists, and the latter won. The racial aspects of this power struggle did not concern the exclusion of black strike-breakers so much as the continued control of blacks already within the established caste system. The white power structure won that one, too.[95]

95. Many documents relating to the 1908 strike have been reproduced in Foner and Lewis, *The Black Worker*, vol. 5, *The Black Worker from 1900 to 1919* (Philadelphia, 1980), 156–98.

CHAPTER THIRTEEN

THE UMWA AND NEW IMMIGRANT MINERS IN PENNSYLVANIA BITUMINOUS
The Case of Windber

MILDRED A. BEIK

"The coal you dig isn't Slavish or Polish or Irish coal, it's coal."[1] With these words in the early 1900s, UMWA President John Mitchell launched what eventually became a successful drive to organize the anthracite miners of Pennsylvania. The miners' leader was responding to a major problem—ethnic division—that had impeded unionization in coalfields everywhere. English-speaking miners had been reacting with nativist prejudice, if not hostile actions, to what one contemporary writer called the "Slav Invasion."[2] In attacking nativism and ethnic prejudice, Mitchell was adhering to his union's constitution, which welcomed members "regardless of race, creed, or national origin," but his call for solidarity also reflected the reality of the entrance of massive numbers of Hungarians, Slovaks, Poles, Italians, and others into the workforce and the union.[3]

1. Elsie Glück, *John Mitchell* (New York: John Day, 1929; repr. New York: AMS, 1971), 72.
2. Frank Julian Warne, *The Slav Invasion and the Mine Workers: A Study in Immigration* (Philadelphia: J. B. Lippincott Company, 1904).
3. For a history of the early United Mine Workers, see Chris Evans, *History of the United Mine Workers of America*, 2 vols. (Indianapolis, Ind.: n.p., 1918–21). The best book on Slavic miners in

The purpose of this essay is to examine the interrelationship between Slavic and other foreign-born miners, on one hand, and the UMWA, on the other hand, in one important Pennsylvania bituminous coal town during the nonunion era of the town's history from its founding in 1897 until the 1930s. As McAlister Coleman pointed out fifty years ago, it is not possible to study the history of coal miners—even nonunion ones—without bringing in the UMWA because "whether or not they belonged to the U.M.W.A., the influence of that organization upon the life and fortune of every mine worker has been so preponderant as to make its story the bulk of any adequate chronicle of American coal mining."[4] Such is the case with the immigrant miners of Windber, Pennsylvania, an important industrial town located in Somerset County, considered a bastion of the open shop throughout the early century.

Certain problems inevitably arise when immigrant workers and their communities are the subjects of study and when the problems posed by ethnic divisions in organizing a class-based union are highlighted. The biggest danger is that the choice of subject automatically causes ethnic differences and ethnicity itself to assume more importance than may be warranted. Consequently, my aim is to explore the relationship between these foreign-born miners and the UMWA but without neglecting other important considerations or the larger context in which ethnic miners and their families lived.

The argument is that the Slavic and other foreign-born miners of Windber, Pennsylvania, had had a meaningful interaction with the UMWA throughout the nonunion era of the town's history and that successful unionization, made possible only by passage of section 7(a) of the National Industrial Recovery Act in 1933, fulfilled the hopes and aspirations held by many immigrant and American miners throughout the early century. Ethnic divisions within the local working classes were not unimportant. The coal company had sought to "divide and conquer" the various nationalities as a part of its anti-union policies, and ethnic diversity did present a host of practical problems for class-conscious unionists. Ultimately, however, it was the great disparity between the coal corporation's economic, legal, and political power vis-à-vis that of working people and organized labor—not ethnic divisions—that explains the company's ability to fend off unionization until the New Deal.

BACKGROUND

The Berwind-White Coal Mining Company, founder of Windber, was not a small or local concern but a modern business corporation with important interlocking ties to J. P. Morgan, the Pennsylvania Railroad, and many other national financial and

---

anthracite is Victor R. Greene, *The Slavic Community on Strike: Immigrant Labor in Pennsylvania Anthracite* (Notre Dame: University of Notre Dame, 1968).

    4. McAlister Coleman, *Men and Coal*, with a foreword by John Chamberlain (New York: Farrar and Rinehart, 1943), xix.

industrial interests. When the company's president, Edward J. Berwind, died in 1936, the *New York Times* stated that he was the world's largest individual owner of bituminous coal lands and on the board of directors of fifty leading U.S. corporations. Although the Berwinds had other mines and financial interests, the mines located in Windber were the basis on which the company's large fortune was ultimately built. Windber coal fueled the transatlantic steamship trade in a time when steamships were the way to travel. It also supplied the Interborough Rapid Transit subway system of New York City (on whose board E. J. Berwind sat, arousing fierce controversies), as well as the U.S. Navy. By any standard of judgment—tonnage statistics, the value of the coal produced, the national prominence of the coal corporation—Windber-area coal stands out as of unusual industrial importance in the nation.[5]

"Operations in the mines of Community A [Windber] were begun with immigrant labor, and the general expansion of the mining industry and the development of the locality have been due principally to immigration from Europe," reported the U. S. Congress's Dillingham Immigration Commission, which had selected Windber as one of two Pennsylvania bituminous towns to use as a case study for its landmark *Immigrants in Industries* series, published in 1911. The immigrants who came to mine coal in the Windber area at the turn of the century were remarkable for their great ethnic diversity. In 1910 four nationalities—Slovaks, Magyars, Poles, and Italians—comprised the bulk, or 84%, of the local foreign-born population, but at least 25 different nationalities were represented in a population that totaled about 10,000. Moreover, the number of foreign-born people was unusually large, even for bigger, more populated, industrial towns. According to the U.S. census of 1910, the foreign-born constituted 45% of the population of the Windber area. By contrast, only 17% of the inhabitants of Somerset County and 19% of the residents of the state of Pennsylvania had been born in foreign countries. Windber's rise and prominence as an industrial center had coincided with the height of immigration from Southern and Eastern Europe on which it was dependent for its labor force.[6]

The company had established autocratic control at the workplace and in the community at the town's founding in 1897. Since the rural area's population was sparse and no town had existed before the opening of the mines, the company did not have to contend with any preexisting powers—independent authorities, business groups, political competition, or an organized labor movement—as it established the basic

5. *New York Times*, August 19, 1935, 1; and *Dictionary of American Biography*, 1958 ed., s.v. "Berwind, Edward Julius," 11:37–38.

6. U. S. Immigration Commission, *Reports of the Immigration Commission*, vol. 6, *Immigrants in Industries*, pt. 1, *Bituminous Coal Industry* (Washington, D.C.: GPO, 1911; repr. New York: Arno and New York Times, 1970), 509, 479; and Department of Commerce, Bureau of the Census, *Thirteenth Census of the United States Taken in the Year 1910*, vol. 3: *Population; Reports by States, with Statistics for Counties, Cities and Other Civil Divisions* (Washington, D.C.: GPO, 1913), 563, 582.

structures of a company town. From the outset, it enjoyed a monopolistic ownership of land and resources, and miners who settled there were directly or indirectly dependent upon it for jobs, housing, and other necessities.

The borough's name, "Windber," an anagram of "Berwind," accurately reflected the pervasive influence that the Berwinds, as absentee owners, exercised from afar. The company's monopoly of jobs, land, and housing was rapidly supplemented by a compulsory company-store system and control of basic utilities and industries, as shown in Table 13.1. Outside competition, which would have led to a diversification of industry, was as systematically excluded from the town as were union organizers who sought to provide the masses of miners with a democratic collective voice for their grievances. Berwind-White enforced its virulent open-shop policy through discharges, blacklists, an espionage and police system, and control of local organizations. Its political domination of the borough guaranteed its position. When that position was threatened, company officials could expect help from local, state, and federal governments, which authorized additional gunmen, antilabor injunctions, wholesale forcible evictions, and contingents of the state police who served as strike-breakers. The nativism of American society and the relative lack of power of immigrant workers was fully revealed during the strike of 1906, when the company successfully blamed a violent massacre committed by its own hired gunmen on ignorant foreign-born strikers. Hastily dispatched strike-breaking state troopers occupied the town for one full year.

Table 13.1 Interlocking Directorates: Berwind-White Officials and Windber's Key Industries, 1897–1900

Business	Edward J. Berwind, Pres., New York	Harry A. Berwind, Sec., Philadelphia	William A. Crist, Gen. Mgr., Windber	Thomas Fisher, Gen. Supt., Windber	Frederick McOwen, Treas., Philadelphia	James S. Cunningham, Supt., Windber	Edward L. Myers, Philadelphia
Eureka Supply Co., Ltd.		X	X	X	X		X
Windber National Bank	X		X			X	
Windber Electric Company		X	X	X		X	X
Paint Township Water and Power Company			X			X	X
Windber Publishing Company			X			X	
Windber Park Association			X			X	

SOURCES: Somerset County Courthouse, *Books of Deeds*, 90:371–72, 97: 333–35, 99:152–54, 106:565–67; and J. L. Fehr, comp., *Windber-Scalp Level and Vicinity: Eureka Mines, Berwind-White Coal Mining Co. Operators* (Windber, Pa.: Windber Publishing, December 1900), 4, 7.

Immigrant miners and their families had to contest domination in all these areas in order to achieve greater control of their lives at the workplace and in the community. They succeeded in establishing ephemeral UMWA locals on three separate occasions, in 1899, 1906, and 1922. They defied ethnic stereotypes when they took part in significant protracted national strikes for unionization in 1906 and 1922 and a noteworthy but short-lived one in 1927. Their actions on behalf of unionization were all the more remarkable in that the UMWA's cautious conservative national leadership in 1906 and 1922 had, however reluctantly, accepted national strike settlements that excluded Windber and other newly organized miners.

THE ETHNIC "PROBLEM": THREE DIFFERENT PERSPECTIVES

Windber's polyglot ethnic population posed different problems and possibilities for the three major interested parties who had a stake in maintaining or changing the status quo in Windber throughout the nonunion era. Each approached the "problem" of ethnic division from radically different perspectives.

The Company

From Berwind-White's perspective, the ethnic "problem" was twofold: first, there was the problem of recruiting and retaining a stable immigrant workforce; second, there was the problem of keeping those workers divided, docile, and unorganized. The company instituted a variety of ethnic-related policies to help achieve these twin goals.

Berwind-White welcomed immigrants from Southern and Eastern Europe because it needed men to work its new mines in the Windber area and because a plentiful source of labor—new immigrants—had begun to come to the United States during this period. But the company had to compete for these new immigrants in a contested labor market. Bituminous mining was a fiercely competitive business, and other industries, notably steel, also hired unskilled labor. To attract and retain new immigrants, the coal company adopted a wide variety of mechanisms over time. Its initial transfer of men from its other mines and its placement of want ads in American newspapers proved insufficient for its manpower needs. As a result, it quickly turned to its vast corporate contacts and relied on steamship agents, immigrant bankers, and ethnic labor contractors, all of whom were important suppliers of labor in the early part of the century. Local ethnic leaders simultaneously served as intermediaries for new arrivals in the country and as de facto or authorized agents for Berwind-White. When needed, the coal corporation also sent a representative noted for his diverse linguistic talents to New York and other ports to meet incoming ships and persuade men to come to Windber. This individual occasionally "raided" other mining towns, too. Once foreign-born miners had settled in the Windber area, they themselves became active, if sometimes unintentional, agents of recruitment through letters and dollars sent to friends and relatives abroad.[7]

In trying to attract immigrant miners, Berwind-White had all the advantages of an autocratic employer that had established its own company town. Because of its monopoly of resources, it could simultaneously promise impoverished recent European arrivals jobs, housing, and credit from the company store for food, mining clothes, tools, and powder. The disadvantages to the miners often became evident only later when the compulsory store system and other company deductions kept them and their families in chronic debt and perpetually bound them to the company.[8]

The Dillingham Commission, however, found only one reason—steady employment—for miners to go to Windber rather than somewhere else. Berwind-White's markets enabled it to provide steady work, which helped to disguise the fact that its wages and working conditions were inferior to those in unionized mines. By controlling information, conducting public relations campaigns, and granting occasional well-publicized pay raises designed to offset union initiatives, the company even hoped to attract immigrants from South Fork or other unionized towns. Many of these efforts were unsuccessful. Immigrants had minds of their own, and out-migration from Windber was significant throughout the town's history. According to the Commission, the company's relative low wages, general lack of unionization, and specific grievances such as the requirement that miners push cars themselves, caused men to leave area mines during prosperous times when other jobs were plentiful. On the other hand, miners poured into the area for work during times of general depression.[9]

In order to solve its long-term problem of recruiting and retaining a stable immigrant workforce, Berwind-White resorted to another device: the promotion of segregated ethnic institutions and enclaves. By 1898 and 1899, new immigrant nationalities were already acting independently to found their own fraternal societies for insurance, mutual aid, and other purposes. By the time of the 1906 strike, for example, Slovak and Italian miners were taking necessary steps to carve out their own immigrant churches from the existing territorial one, which included Roman Catholics of all nationalities. Windber's polyglot immigrants, unhappy with priests who could not communicate in any language comprehensible to them, were motivated by a democratic desire to use their own languages and culture, not by any desire to isolate themselves from contact with other peoples. With relatively mini-

7. Industrial Relations Commission, *Final Report and Testimony Submitted to Congress by the U. S. Commission on Industrial Relations Created by the Act of August 23, 1912* (Washington, D.C.: GPO, 1916), 8:7596–97, 7749. I am indebted to Sewell Oldham, Berwind-White engineer, for his recollections about the traveling labor agent.

8. John Toth [pseud.], interview by author, tape recording, Windber, Pa., September 30, 1986.

9. Immigration Commission, 6:476, 477, 529.

mal conflict, they had founded, by 1923, five Roman Catholic parishes—one each for the Slovaks, Italians, Hungarians, Poles, and English-speaking populations.[10]

These autonomous movements to form ethnic community institutions gave Berwind-White a valuable tool with which to recruit immigrant miners as well as a means to keep them divided. In most cases, it donated lands—on its own restrictive terms—for emerging churches and needed cemeteries. It would tolerate no independence, however, and as landowner and sole employer, it was in a position to dictate terms. Consequently, deeds conveying land to churches and other organizations not only contained clauses that granted mineral rights to the company in perpetuity but included other restrictions that guaranteed the company perpetual control over use of those institutions. Churches could be used "for church purposes only"; cemeteries for "cemetery purposes only." Such restrictions guaranteed that no unions or other independent organizations could ever legally hold meetings in such places. The Altoona Diocese and the Slovak National Hall Association were two of the organizations that came into immediate conflict with the company over deed restrictions, while many churches secured partial removal of such restrictions only in the 1970s and 1980s.[11]

Miners reported that the company also sought to control ethnic institutions through placement of board members, subsidies to halls, and threats to fire dissidents. Controlling ethnic institutions was part of a general autocratic system of control in which bartenders reported potential troublemakers who had criticized the company, and in which postal officials reported on individuals who corresponded with the union. Ethnic leaders—contractors, bankers, foremen, priests—were expected to uphold company rule. One miner described how an ethnic contractor sought to ensure company loyalty: "The Polish people had a great leader in Stiney Roden. He was like a godfather to the Polish people. Now he received slush money from Berwind-White all the time, and he'd treat all the members in the Polish Club. They followed his rule, what he wanted, what Berwind wanted, and they followed him, and they believed in him. So they [the company] kept those people separated that way."[12]

By World War I, the company was widely using the newly created ethnic institutions in its advertisements for miners in foreign-language newspapers. A typical ad from 1920 in Hungarian papers, including *Dongó, Szabadság, Amerikai Magyar Népszava,* and *Magyar Bányászlap,* advertised Windber as a Hungarian mining town. Not only could former European peasants keep gardens, cows, pigs, and geese, but they could also speak their own languages in their own churches, schools, and other institutions. Some ads even cited specific priests or ministers who would

10. A detailed description of these and other events occurs in Mildred A. Beik, *The Miners of Windber: The Struggles of New Immigrants for Unionization, 1890s–1930s* (Penn State Press, 1996). See also Mildred A. Beik, "The Miners of Windber: Class, Ethnicity, and the Labor Movement in a Pennsylvania Coal Town, 1890s-1930s" (Ph.D. diss., Northern Illinois University, 1989), 220–73.

11. Ibid.

12. Joseph Zahurak, interview by author, tape recording, Windber, Pa., October 7, 1986.

confirm the company's claims about wages and working conditions. Similar ads, adapted to their respective constituencies, appeared in Slovak, Polish, Lithuanian, and Italian papers throughout the United States. To Berwind-White, Windber was not an American town but a Hungarian, Polish, Italian or other town, depending on which ethnic group was being recruited. "Americanization," even of the anti-union corporate type, was the antithesis of the company's labor policies and open-shop strategy.[13]

Berwind-White did many other things to try to keep its immigrant workers satisfied within the context of an autocratic company town. A progressive newspaper editor in 1903 and an investigator from the U.S. Department of Labor in 1919 both independently charged that the company curried favor with the foreign-born, often at the expense of American-born miners, political freedom, and civil liberties, in order to control them. The editor claimed, for example, that the company liberally allowed immigrant miners to take days off for foreign holidays, but routinely refused to let American citizens leave work a little early in order to vote on election days. In 1903, it was the company's arbitrary discharge of a number of English-speaking miners for leaving work early to inform a family that their friend—a fellow miner— had just been killed that had prompted him to help lead a major UMWA organizing drive.[14]

Berwind-White had still further means by which it sought to divide its workers. Following a technique widely used in the steel industry, it "judiciously mixed" the nationalities in the workplace. As the Dillingham Commission reported, the motivation for coal companies to distribute work to ethnic gangs so that no one nationality could predominate was an anti-union device, a means of preventing any single ethnic group from becoming the potential leader of an organizing drive. The company also established a number of ethnic occupational clusters and hierarchies. Italians predominated on the tipples, and Norwegians and Swedes in the car shop. However, the fundamental dividing line at work, as in the community-at-large, was between the Americans and Northern Europeans, on the one hand, and the Southern and Eastern European immigrants, on the other hand.[15]

It is not surprising that Americans and Northern Europeans occupied the vast majority of managerial and skilled company jobs. Without a single exception in the census of 1910, they monopolized Berwind-White's entire force of engineers, weighmasters, surveyors, car inspectors, and bookkeepers. At the same time South-

13. A convenient "Scrapbook" of these newspapers is located at the Windber Museum, Windber, Pa.

14. *Windber Journal* (October 29, 1903); and Frederick G. Davis, "FINAL REPORT Re Citizens' Association vs. Berwind White Coal Mining Company, Windber, Pa.," February 18, 1919, UMWA, District 2, UMWA Records, 1–3. I saw District 2, UMWA Records in District 2's office in Ebensburg, Pa. Since then, they have been transferred to Indiana University of Pennsylvania.

15. Immigration Commission, 6:546; Bureau of the Census, Manuscript Schedules, 13th Census 1910: Pennsylvania (Washington, D.C.: Bureau of the Census, 1910: Washington, D.C.: National Archives, 1978), microfilm rolls, 1324, 1420, 1421; and Pennsylvania, Department of Mines, *Report of the Department of Mines of Pennsylvania* (Harrisburg: State Printer, 1915–20), annual reports, 1914–18.

ern and Eastern Europeans occupied only a small number of the mines' managerial jobs, in sharp contrast to their numerical preponderance in the less skilled mining occupations and in the overall labor force. In fact, their proportional share of these positions was exactly the reverse of their share in the unskilled jobs. While they made up 90% of the miners in 1910, they were only 10% of those listed as mining foremen and assistant foremen. Table 13.2 contrasts the ethnic composition of the men employed in the two types of occupations.

It would be wrong, however, to conclude that the small number of Southern and Eastern European individuals who occupied managerial mining positions were unimportant. In fact, the reverse is true. These strategic elevated positions gave a handful or two of key ethnic men a stature, prominence, and power that extended far beyond their small numbers. Along with some others, these ethnic men played a crucial role in maintaining the Berwind system of authoritarian control at the workplace, and in Windber's various stratified ethnic communities.[16]

The company also used housing policy, which was secondary to hiring policy, to segregate workers. Given the labor turnover, availability of company houses at particular times, and the preferences of the immigrants themselves, this effort was necessarily limited. But Berwind-White did succeed in imposing mandatory segregation to keep American miners isolated from the new immigrants. If English-speaking and immigrant miners ever overcame ethnic suspicions, language barriers, and cultural differences, the company feared that the chances for unionization would grow. For that reason, it used railroad tracks to arbitrarily divide an enclave of English-speaking miners from an enclave of new immigrants near mine 35.[17]

Nativism was another useful tool to keep workers divided, provided it did not go

Table 13.2 Miners and Foremen, Berwind-White Mines, Windber, 1910

	Miners	Foremen
Americans	7%	56%
Northern Europeans	3	34
Southern and Eastern Europeans	90	10
	100%	100%

SOURCES: Pennsylvania, Department of Mines, Report of the Department of Mines of Pennsylvania, Part 2, Bituminous 1910, Harrisburg 1911, pp. 310, 902; and Bureau of Census, Manuscript Schedules, 13th Census 1910. Pennsylvania, Washington, D.C., 1910; Washington, D.C., 1978, microfilm; rolls, 1324, 1420, 1421.

16. This argument is developed in Mildred A. Beik, "The Competition for Ethnic Community Leadership in a Pennsylvania Bituminous Coal Town, 1890s-1930s" in *Sozialgeschichte des Bergbaus im 19. und 20. Jahrhundert: Beiträge des Internationalen Kongresses zur Bergbaugeschichte Bochum, Bundesrepublik Deutschland, 3.–7. September 1989* [Toward a social history of mining in the 19th and 20th centuries], ed. Klaus Tenfelde (Munich: C. H. Beck, 1992), 223–41.

17. Immigration Commission, 6:499, 511.

too far. Despite the handful of ethnic leaders, mining officials were predominantly American-born, and in the early century Windber supported a large chapter of the nativist Patriotic Order of the Sons of America, while the Ku Klux Klan was active there in the 1920s. Until the 1930s or 1940s, all major governmental institutions, including the town council, the police, and the fire department, were composed exclusively of the American-born or Northern Europeans. The company needed immigrant labor but benefited from those activities of the American middle class that were designed to reinforce the existing class/ethnic hierarchy and keep "Hunkies," "Polacks," and "spaghetti eaters" in their place. Also, as events in 1906 showed, the nativism of the larger society could be a potent weapon to use against the labor movement when the company's immigrant workforce organized.[18]

When he testified before the Industrial Relations Commission, Edward J. Berwind himself revealed his underlying condescension, if not nativist attitude, toward the new immigrants his company hired. He needed these people, but, he suggested, they were inferior to American workers. They lacked discipline, drank too much, overindulged in holidays and funerals. He said he tolerated their vices to keep them satisfied, but he would never allow them to have a union because unions were useful only where skilled American labor prevailed. After all, he maintained, immigrant workers were naive and easily misled. He concluded: "It [unionization] is harmful, especially where the classes of people are not such as to be intelligent and understand your languages altogether and are not educated up to a higher standard." Immigrant workers were better off with the company than with union troublemakers because, in his words, "it is very hard to communicate with them [immigrants] and to make them see what their best interest is."[19]

The Union

Whenever Windber's Slavic and other new immigrant miners spoke of "the union" in the early century or throughout the nonunion era, they were, more often than not, referring to District 2 of the UMWA. It was District 2 rather than the national organization that habitually took the lead in trying to organize Berwind-White miners from the outside from the 1890s to the 1930s. Not only were the area's unionized miners closer to the local situation, but they also had an immediate vested interest in the outcome. As a bastion of the open shop, Somerset County and its largest metropolis—Windber—threatened the status and well-being of all organized miners throughout the region.[20]

For the union, for District 2, then, the ethnic "problem" in Windber was primarily a practical one of reaching the foreign-born, communicating with them, and convincing them of the advantages of unionization. Indeed, the union might have

18. Beik, "Miners of Windber," 21–23, 342–60, 569–71.
19. Industrial Relations Commission, 8:7584, 7588, 7590–92.
20. Beik, "Miners of Windber," 456–95.

defined its "problem" with English-speaking miners in the same way. But since Windber's first mines were not opened until the late 1890s and 90% or more of the mining workforce was of new immigrant origin and foreign-speaking from the outset, Windber's experience differed in important respects from that of older, more settled, mining areas where previous generations of English, Welsh, Irish, and other Anglo miners had lived and worked.

The arrival of Slavs and other new immigrants into these older, established mining areas in the 1890s often precipitated interethnic tensions that were worsened by the depression. In some regions, English-speaking miners reportedly responded to the depression and "Slav invasion" by moving to the Midwest. Victor Greene has documented the efforts of Pennsylvania's English-speaking anthracite miners and union leaders to pass nativist, discriminatory legislation against new immigrants at the state level. By 1893, the problem of ethnic prejudice was so serious that President John McBride and other national UMWA leaders felt compelled to denounce a "new" tendency to "divide mine workers on the question of nationality and religion" because it posed a serious threat to the organization, thereby benefitting the coal operators and enemies of labor.[21]

Berwind-White's reliance on new immigrant labor and the composition of its workforce, however, meant that nativism—and the struggle against it—took different shapes in Windber than they took in many of these older mining regions. The Dillingham Commission had reported accurately that the major dividing line in the community was simultaneously a class/ethnic/religious one. It was the dominant American-born/Protestant middle classes—those who had migrated to Windber to manage the local mines, operate many of the businesses, run the town, and teach the schools—who originated and sustained numerous but limited discriminatory practices against the new immigrants. In Windber, it was these groups—not the small number of American-born or English-speaking miners, prejudiced or not— who were the mainstay of the local Patriotic Order of the Sons of America, temperance and sabbatarian movements, and Ku Klux Klan.[22]

District 2 had to try to organize a predominantly foreign-born workforce in Windber in the context of widespread nativism that pervaded the surrounding region and the state. Somerset County's belated industrial development had brought disruptive social changes that contributed to such movements. By 1900, outsiders often viewed Windber as a town of foreigners who had brought with them unwelcome change, including Catholicism, violence, and drink, into a county that had been overwhelmingly rural, American-born, white, and Protestant until then. In 1906, Berwind-White was able to mobilize these "outside" nativist sentiments to help

21. Victor R. Greene, "A Study in Slavs, Strikes, and Unions: The Anthracite Strike of 1897," *Pennsylvania History* 31 (April 1964): 199–215; and Evans, 2:257.

22. Immigration Commission, 6:499, 528; and Beik, "Miners of Windber," 66–67, 135–44, 342–60.

defeat the stereotypical knife-wielding, foreign-born, strikers, who had been seen as stereotypically docile before the strike.[23]

In trying to organize Slavic and other new immigrants, District 2's English-speaking officers faced obvious cultural and linguistic handicaps but were nevertheless committed to pluralistic, ethnic-friendly, yet class-based policies. In 1890, the district was fortunate in having inherited progressive leadership and inclusive tactics from its immediate regional predecessor, the Knights of Labor. In October 1891, District 2 President James White took an anti-Catholic, anti-immigrant editorial from the *Houtzdale Observer* as the basis for subsequent attacks on local coal operators for their policy of encouraging and exploiting national and religious prejudices for their own benefit. He refused to blame immigrants for problems that were inherent in the industrial economy. Meanwhile, District 2's Thomas W. Davis suggested that English-speaking miners should set the example for foreign-speaking ones (who, he maintained, would join the UMWA if the organization were stable). When the district organization began to rebuild in 1897 after debacle in 1894, its new officers continued to pursue inclusive, culturally pluralistic, policies. Having recognized the changing composition of the mining workforce, it immediately asked the national for more foreign-speaking organizers, dollars, and literature. At a convention held in Altoona on April 5, 1898, delegates passed a measure providing for a foreign-speaking representative on its executive board. From time to time, upon winning the eight-hour day, for instance, District 2 printed up foreign-language circulars for distribution, and in certain years the *United Mine Workers Journal* ran several pages in foreign languages.[24]

In his memoirs John Brophy, District 2 president from 1916 to 1926, indicated that he naturally found it easier to organize his own countrymen, who spoke English and had had some prior experience with trade unions, but he never once suggested that new immigrants were unorganizable.[25] That interethnic class organization was a desirable goal was a matter of principle, but it was also a necessity, if the immigrant miners of Windber and many other places were to unionize. The real problems were practical in nature, and resources were limited. The district never had enough foreign-speaking organizers or literature to meet the need.

District 2 had far more serious problems than linguistic limitations to overcome

23. See an especially nativist and inaccurate account of a company massacre in Windber during the strike of 1906 in *Somerset County Democrat* (April 18, 1906).

24. Dan Lennon, "An Important Mass Meeting at Houtzdale, Pennsylvania," *United Mine Workers Journal* [hereafter *UMWJ*], (October 15, 1891): 1; Thomas W. Davis, "Return of Davis," *UMWJ* (April 21, 1892): 1; Thomas W. Davis, "The Campaign," *UMWJ* (April 28, 1892): 5; "Proceedings of Convention," *UMWJ* (April 14, 1898): 1; James W. Killduff, "Killduff," *UMWJ* (July 7, 1898): 1; and Patrick Gilday, "Important Circular," *UMWJ* (October 22, 1903): 7. The limits of District 2's racially inclusive policies became evident in 1901, when leaders rallied to support renewal of the Chinese Exclusion Act. See "Matters in District 2," *UMWJ* (December 5, 1901).

25. John Brophy, *A Miner's Life*, ed. John O. P. Hall (Madison: University of Wisconsin Press, 1964), 12, 73.

in organizing Windber's new immigrants. It had to confront an autocratic company-town situation in which the Bill of Rights and the U.S. Constitution were ignored or violated for all its citizens. Windber was not at all geographically isolated, but the company maintained a surveillance system at entry points to keep union outsiders from making contact with local miners. Its reputation in 1922 was such that District 2 leaders referred to it and all of Somerset County as "Siberia," and when they made plans to try to get miners there to join the national strike effort, they decided to have organizers "invade" the county from all four directions at once. There was positively no hope that the unionizers could do their work unmolested. Consequently, they were instructed to get as far into the county as they could before being attacked or jailed by agents sympathetic to the coal companies, and then to make as much of a public disturbance as possible so that word of the union initiative would spread.[26]

From 1899 on, outside organizers complained about spies hounding their footsteps, preventing meetings, harrassing them. On June 29, 1899, an incredulous veteran organizer, William Warner, reported that "the circumstances at Windber cannot be described." Even public officials, such as New York City's prestigious Hylan Committee, which came to investigate conditions in Windber during the 1922 strike, found its members the object of company surveillance and harrassment. A 1922 strike leader described the situation UMWA organizers faced:

> These organizers didn't dare come in here with their own car. You could not come in on the streetcar, the Johnstown Traction Company, because if they got on the streetcar in Johnstown, the Traction Company conductor would stop in Moxham and go to the dispatcher. He would call the General Office that a stranger is on the streetcar. They all knew these people. . . .
>
> When the car arrived in Windber, the Berwind's Coal and Iron police was there. As soon as they [the organizers] got off, they wanted to know who they were, where they was from, what their business is. And when they found out, they told them: "If you know what's good for you, you'll get back on the streetcar and get back out of here." They wasn't allowed in here. They had to get out.[27]

26. Ibid., 182; and John Brophy, "The Reminiscences of John Brophy" (Transcript, Oral History Research Office, Columbia University, New York, 1957; New York: Columbia University, 1972, microfilm), 423–25.

27. William Warner to T. W. Davis, June 29, 1899, in the John Mitchell Papers, Department of Archives and Manuscripts, Catholic University of America, Washington, D.C. (Glen Rock, N.J.: Microfilming Corporation of America, 1974), series I, reel 1; David Hirshfield, New York City, Committee on Labor Conditions of the Berwind-White Company's Coal Mines in Somerset and Other Counties, Pennsylvania, *Statement of Facts and Summary of Committee Appointed by Honorable John F. Hylan, Mayor of the City of New York, to Investigate the Labor Conditions in Somerset and Other Counties, Pennsylvania* (New York: M. B. Brown, December 1922), 8–9; and Zahurak, interview, October 7, 1986.

Organizers' reports suggest that foreign-speaking unionists were often more successful in reaching their constituencies than their better known English-speaking counterparts because they were less conspicuous to English-speaking company guards and officials. On July 5, 1917, organizer Pat Egan complained that "the English-speaking men are very hard to do anything with as the spotters are onto me and follow me wherever I go." Foreign-speaking unionists also had their own reliable contacts within Windber's ethnic communities. At the suggestion of a Windber miner, District 2 officials corresponded with local unionists during the important post–World War I period by sending unmarked mail to a sympathethic officer of the Slovak Club. In 1922, Joseph Foster, District 2's Hungarian-speaking organizer (a former Windber resident who then lived in Nanty-Glo), coordinated district strike efforts with the help of his brother, a local miner, and his other Windber contacts.[28]

From 1899 on, organizers from outside the area reported that Slavic and other foreign-born miners in Windber had shown interest in the union. The problem was not one of getting them involved in organizing at key moments or of interesting them in intraethnic class cooperation. The real problems were much more concrete. Given the company's control over local halls, where could interested unionists of any ethnic background meet together unmolested? Who would be prevailed upon to speak on the union's behalf? When District 2 officers did succeed in holding meetings, usually in the fields of sympathetic farmers, during the nonunion era, the new-formed locals respected cultural and linguistic differences. Meetings were always long because representatives from the various ethnic groups had to take turns making speeches in their respective languages. In 1906 and 1922, the two main organizing campaigns during our period, Windber-area miners democratically elected officers that reflected the multiethnic composition of their locals' membership.[29]

In recruiting union members in Windber, District 2 officials had other more serious problems to contend with than those posed by ethnic differences. Persuading men of the value of unionism and of the comparative advantages of unionized wages, working conditions, and other freedoms was no abstract matter. The union had to be strong enough to provide a viable alternative to—and some protection from—the existing autocratic Berwind regime. It had to provide hope, and break down fear. Because repression and insecurity were a way of life, the officials had to convince rank-and-file miners that their efforts had a reasonable chance for success. From the 1899 drive on, individual foreign-born and American miners who had attended union meetings or otherwise expressed an interest in unionization in Windber had been summarily discharged. Moreover, those who engaged in strikes not only faced a loss of their jobs but armed intimidation, eviction from their houses, the ending of credit at the company stores, and the denial of medical services. To

28. P[at] H. Egan, Johnstown, to John Brophy, Clearfield, July 5, 1917, UMWA, District 2, UMWA Records; Edward J. Robinson, Windber, to John Brophy, Clearfield, May 13, 1918, UMWA, District 2, UMWA Records; and Heber Blankenhorn, *The Strike for Union* (New York: H. W. Wilson, 1924; repr. New York: Arno and New York Times, 1969), 52.

29. Beik, "Miners of Windber," 423; and Zahurak, interview, October 7, 1986.

help American- and foreign-born miners overcome fear of such reprisals, the union had to manifest some degree of strength and power. It had to be able to provide at least minimal financial assistance to strikers' families. Miners in other places may have been able to establish a union without a prolonged strike, but Windber miners knew that that was never a realistic option for them. In discussing the early 1930s, one miner paraphrased Berwind-White's ruthless opposition to unionism in this way: ''The Berwinds said we'll sign the union contract when grass grows on the railroad tracks. We'd have never had the union if it wasn't for Franklin Delano Roosevelt.''[30]

Thus it was not ethnic divisions nor the unwillingness of immigrant miners to organize, but the autocratic nature of the company's control that delayed the unionization process in Windber. Windber's miners would need outside help, and the UMWA's relative lack of power vis-à-vis the local coal companies was one of the biggest obstacles the union faced in organizing new immigrants. Both John L. Lewis and John Mitchell were reluctant to jeopardize the welfare and resources of the established organization in a full-scale national commitment to organize Windber and Somerset County. To avoid a confrontation with Berwind-White in the early century, Mitchell had tried—and failed—to get E. J. Berwind into the National Civic Federation. From 1919 to 1922 Lewis repeatedly cited the power and resources of Berwind-White and adjacent nonunion employers in the coal and steel industries as a reason for not undertaking a Somerset County drive. Conservative national union leaders thus defended strike settlements in 1906 and 1922 that had left Windber miners out in the cold and caused dissension in the district. In both cases, District 2 bore the bulk of the outside financial and moral burden of trying to support Windber miners in their prolonged local strikes for unionization.[31]

The relative weakness of organized labor, the problem of scarce resources, hostile governments, intra-union rivalries, dissensions between the district and national unions over policy, the national strike settlements of 1906 and 1922, hurt the local union's chances for success. During the national strikes of those key years, Berwind-White had ammunition beyond ethnic divisions for charging that the men should return to work because the union cause was hopeless.

The Foreign-Born Miners of Windber

For Windber's Slavic and other foreign-born miners, the ethnic ''problem'' was intimately connected to the larger class-related problem of how to achieve greater control over their everyday lives at the workplace and in the community. Immigrants from Southern and Eastern Europe were neither the stereotypical conservative, docile, hardy but willing sufferers who would endure any measure of capitalistic exploi-

30. Joseph J. Novak, interview by author, tape recording, Windber, Pa, May 19, 1985.

31. Beik, ''Miners of Windber,'' 334–36, 456–95. See, for example, John L. Lewis, Indianapolis, to John Brophy, Clearfield, April 15, 1918, UMWA, District 2, UMWA Records.

tation or any standard of living for the sake of a steady job, nor were they the contrasting stereotypical radical upstarts, lawless rioters, incipient anarchists or ready-made unionists. Windber's miners were pragmatic, rational, thoughtful. From day to day, they worked to expand their sphere of freedom at work and in the larger community, while realistically weighing their chances for successful unionization and acting with other nationalities to achieve that goal at key historical moments.

New immigrant miners and their families protested against company dominance in their daily lives in many ways. Throughout the nonunion era many ordinary people tried to bypass the dreaded company-store monopoly by buying food and other necessities elsewhere. Large numbers of immigrants or their children also migrated to other places. Rather than become strike-breakers, they returned to Europe in 1906 and moved to union mines in 1922. Some who became citizens dared to vote their consciences instead of supporting Berwind-White's candidates. The masses of ethnic workers formed their own ethnic institutions and communities with the hope of attaining more independence.[32]

Such efforts by ordinary people to achieve greater independence within the authoritarian context of the company town were repeatedly frustrated. From the 1890s until the 1930s, it became clear in one way or another to class-conscious ethnic miners that the real problem they faced in achieving greater economic and political freedom was not ethnic differences but company domination, which existed everywhere, even in their own stratified ethnic communities. They turned for help to the United Mine Workers, the only ethnic-friendly, class-based institution that could possibly fulfill these hopes in the coalfields. No other viable alternative existed.

To unionize in Windber, class-conscious ethnic miners had to face all sorts of external obstacles—a powerful wealthy corporation with vast resources and connections, hostile state and federal governments, widespread nativism—but they also had to confront those spies and ethnic leaders who collaborated with the company and represented its interests, not those of working-class miners. Seizing control of their own ethnic institutions and disposing of those ethnic stalwarts who upheld company rule would be necessary. Given the varied composition of the workforce, no single ethnic group could hope to succeed alone. Ethnic miners had to reach out and make contact with other interested miners from other nationalities. They had to find some way of meeting and acting together.

Ethnic divisions were muted by the class experience in Windber. The grievances that concerned miners at the workplace—wages, honest weights, pay for deadwork, the length of the workday, and most of all, democratic representation and grievance procedures—cut across ethnic lines, and these grievances remained remarkably constant throughout the nonunion period. As early as 1899, for instance, Windber miners were complaining about the issue of honest weights. In 1906, the Slovak and Hungarian leaders of the strike charged that the company habitually cheated the

32. For protests by miners and business people against the company store, see Beik, "Miners of Windber," 382–96.

men by not giving them full credit for the tons they loaded. The issue was a catalyst that brought large numbers of new immigrants into the union fold. When permanent organization was finally effected in 1933, one of the first acts of the new UMWA locals was to elect their own checkweighmen to ensure that company weights would be honest.[33]

Accidents did not respect ethnic boundaries either. The new immigrants, who had comprised 90% of the miners in 1910, made up the bulk of mining fatalities for the period from 1900 to 1918, when state reports listed the ethnicity of those killed. Of the 232 men killed in Windber mines during this period, 83% were Southern and Eastern Europeans, 12% were Americans, and 5% were Northern Europeans. When tragedy occurred, miners and their families were on their own in the early century. Until a state workman's compensation law forced it to do so in 1915, Berwind-White had assumed no financial responsibility whatsoever for deaths or injuries, regardless of who was at fault. Even then, miners reported that the company's attitude changed little: "If a man was killed, it didn't mean much. Ah, another Hunky'll come over and take his place. That's how serious they took anybody getting killed or hurt."[34]

Other class experiences muted ethnic divisions in the community. Regardless of nationality, miners and their families were required to shop at the company store or risk losing their jobs and houses. Foremen or other company bosses told them how to vote at the polls. No church or organization was exempt from Berwind-White's control. When six Slovak and Russian fraternal societies tried to found an independent common hall in which to meet in 1914, founding members faced a long series of threats, intimidations, and persecutions, which resulted in ongoing internal conflict over the company's attempts to control the movement. Such early struggles against the company were educational. It is not accidental that, in 1933, the newly organized UMWA Local 6186 held its first meetings in Slovak Hall, the first hall to contest Berwind-White's authority and open its doors to the union.[35]

While Berwind-White had promoted segregated ethnic enclaves in order to divide its workers, immigrant miners and their families had sought to establish independent ethnic institutions for reasons of their own. They wanted to use their own languages, but they had not sought to isolate themselves in self-contained enclaves, and having their own institutions did not preclude broad-based intraclass cooperation. The frag-

33. Ibid., 174, 418–20; George Dubik [pseud.], interview by author, tape recording, Windber, Pa., September 29, 1984; Joseph Foster, "Why Are the Windber Miners Out?" in Blankenhorn, 254–59; and UMWA Local 6186, Windber, Pa., Minutes, Meetings, September 21, 1933.

34. Calculations were based on information on accidents in Windber mines in Pennsylvania, Department of Internal Affairs, Bureau of Mines, *Report of the Bureau of Mines of the Department of Internal Affairs of Pennsylvania* (Harrisburg: State Printer, 1901–3), annual reports, 1900–1902; and Pennsylvania, Department of Mines, *Report of the Department of Mines of Pennsylvania* (Harrisburg: State Printer, 1904–19), annual reports, 1903–18. See also Mike Jankosky [pseud.], interview by author, tape recording, Windber, Pa., February 24, 1984.

35. Slovenská Národná Budova, "Zápisnica," Meetings, April 5, 1914–28, June 1914, passim, July 14, 1922, Slovak Hall, Windber, Pa.; and Novak, interview, May 19, 1985.

menting impact of the creation of five Roman Catholic national parishes out of one territorial one was somewhat muted by other considerations. The secessions had been relatively peaceful and friendly, in sharp contrast to the town's one really bitter religious division, which occurred in the 1930s *within* a single nationality: the Carpatho-Rusyns. Moreover, many families had fond memories of having attended more than one church. In large families it was common for children of different ages to have been baptized in different churches, as immigrant churches were established. The major religious division in the community-at-large, the distinction between Protestants and Catholics, remained. Catholics of all sorts had in common the threat posed by the KKK and nativist Protestant-based organizations.[36]

Housing segregation was not as rigid as terms such as "Little Italy" or "the Polish sector" suggest either. Certainly there were sections or streets in which one nationality predominated, especially near the center of town. However, census records show that none of these areas was entirely homogeneous. Then, too, a great variety of nationalities resided as neighbors in the outlying populous mining camps. Miners walked to work and wanted to live near their workplaces. They necessarily came into contact with one another. Women of various nationalities met at the company store or outside water pumps.

For many new immigrants, the experience of ethnic diversity that they encountered in Windber was not entirely new. Various nationalities and religious groups had coexisted in the Carpathian Mountains and adjacent regions from which many Windber immigrants had originally emigrated in the early century. Although nationalistic antagonisms had permeated the upper classes of Austro-Hungarian society and the Hungarian government had mandated Slovaks learn Hungarian, contemporary Emily Balch, an economist, activist, and pioneer of immigration studies, reported that she had found an absence of ethnic hostility in this part of Europe at the village level. Balch noted: "The peasants of both races [Hungarian and Slovak] are profoundly unconscious of any reason for hating one another, regard one another as friends, and intermarry freely."[37] In many cases, it was the experience of having become a foreigner in the United States that brought a consciousness of ethnic identity and nationalism. But by then, if not before, in Windber at least, immigrant miners had to confront the fact that they were not only "ethnic" but "working" people.

Many of Windber's new immigrants had had little or no formal education but could nevertheless speak a variety of languages that they had learned in Europe, Windber, or elsewhere. The sons and daughters of miners, some of whom were store clerks and order girls for the company stores, had to know numerous languages to do their jobs. Miners who held positions that required them to move about the mines in the course of their jobs often came into contact with other nationalities and

36. Beik, "Miners of Windber," 220–49.
37. Emily Greene Balch, *Our Slavic Fellow Citizens* (New York: Charities Publication Committee, 1910; repr., New York: Arno and New York Times, 1969), 112.

learned some of their languages. A local leader of the 1922 strike, a Slovak who could speak several languages, claimed that spraggers and motormen were the catalysts of the strike:

> The haulage men of Berwind-White—I mean mine motormen and spraggers—were in contact with all the miners in the mine because they always ordered their cars, the amount of empty cars that they wanted or the loads that they pulled out. . . . The haulage men got together in 1922 to get it organized to come out on strike. We avoided informers, made sure they didn't contact them so they don't know anything about it.[38]

New immigrant miners took part in every major organizing initiative that ever occurred in Windber during the nonunion era. Relatively little is known about the local union's composition in 1899, but the Dillingham Commission reported that Slovaks and Hungarians had led the strike of 1906 and been the most active participants in it. Slovaks themselves reported that the local UMWA initiative received great support when Slovaks with prior union experience in the anthracite region migrated to Windber in the years preceding the strike. They had carried the union message with them. Their previous experience with coal companies and the union may also have led to the Slovak church's relative independence from Berwind-White. The church's founders were unique in having insisted on purchasing a lot from an independent party instead of obtaining a free land donation—with restrictions—from the company.[39]

Miners were migratory people in general. Immigrant miners were all the more so. Thus they had a basis for comparing wages and working conditions and living conditions. New immigrants may have initially expected to work only for short stints in the United States in order to save money and buy homes or land upon their return to Europe, but this goal did not make them passive victims or poor union recruits. Many Windber immigrants returned to Europe during the strike of 1906 rather than become strike-breakers. Nor were miners as isolated as their geographical locations sometimes suggested. They traveled back and forth to Europe, visited other cities, and rarely resided in only one mining town. They communicated with friends and relatives who lived in other places, and many subscribed to a foreign-language newspaper or two.

These newspapers were an important means of communication, and during strikes, individual ethnic miners used them to ensure strike success. For example, on April 6, 1906, Martin Smolko, a local miner, wrote a letter to the editor of the national Slovak newspaper, *Slovák v Amerike*, to inform his countrymen about the Windber strike. Ethnic newspapers generally covered the coal strike in some depth

38. Zahurak, interview, October 7, 1986.

39. Ibid., Immigration Commission, 6:500; *Windber Era* (July 20, 1905); and SS. Cyril and Methodius Parish, *Golden Jubilee SS. Cyril and Methodius Parish, Windber, Pennsylvania, 1906–1956* (Windber: SS. Cyril and Methodius Parish, 1956).

because so many of their readership were participants in it or affected by it. Smolko reported that Windber miners were seeking union recognition from the company. He explained that miners had awakened from their sleep and that they were now actively fighting to end enslavement and be respected as free people. After warning fellow Slovaks that agents were trying to recruit miners to break the strike, he appealed to his brothers to stay away and stand up like brave Slovak countrymen should do. Then he concluded his letter by quoting a familiar slogan: "All for one and one for all."[40]

Reverend Father Michael Balogh, Windber's Greek Catholic priest, was an ethnic leader who supported the miners' strike. In April 1906 he wrote to the *Amerikansky Russky Viestnik* after Berwind-White's hired detectives had massacred four people and wounded many others on April 16. The bloodshed had led to occupation of the town by the newly formed Pennsylvania State Police, known as "Cossacks" to ethnics, martial law, and hysterical nativist reports in the national English-language press. Balogh was writing to counter these accounts and make known the miners' side of the story to his fellow countrymen. He himself had spoken at the miners' rally on the day of the massacre and been an eyewitness to it. Balogh laid responsibility for the deaths squarely on the company, which had tried to twist the truth and blame the miners. He claimed that the company had been trying to create a violent incident for a long time so as to blame the miners. In great detail he described the day's events and affirmed the peaceful nature of the assembled crowd upon which company gunmen had opened fire. In 1906, unlike 1922, ethnic priests in Windber supported the union drive.[41]

The pattern of organizing efforts in Windber suggests that, whenever organized labor was truly active in the region and the nation during the nonunion era, new immigrant miners noticed. Thus, both foreign- and English-speaking miners in Windber tried to get District 2 to come in and organize Berwind-White mines on several key occasions during World War I and afterward. In July 1917 organizer Pat Egan, who lamented that he was followed and unable to reach English-speaking miners, nevertheless noted that foreign-speaking organizers were meeting with such great success that he could optimistically conclude: "I think that Windber can be got." On May 13, 1918, a local unionist, Edward J. Robinson, asked John Brophy to "send a couple of good Italians in this town to help. . . . They are all waiting until someone gets it started." He asked Brophy to send union replies in care of an officer of the Slovak Hall. In February George Habeeb, a Syrian store owner, and other businessmen traveled to Altoona to meet with Brophy to ask him to organize the miners as part of their effort to break company autocracy and establish political democracy in town. Windber's miners and business people had suffered years of exploitation, and they now sought to apply the democratic ideology employed dur-

40. Martin Smolko, "[Letter]," *Slovák v Amerike* (April 17, 1906): 3.
41. Michael Balogh, "Oprava viesty podanej v zaležitosci kervprelievania v Windber, Pa.," *Amerikansky Russky Viestnik* (April 26, 1906), 4.

ing the war to their everyday lives. As Robinson wrote Brophy in one of his letters, "The people think that you ought to be able to get Windber Free for Democracy."[42]

From the standpoint of Windber's foreign-born miners, the decision to strike in 1922 was taken by them at the local level. District 2's John Brophy liked to think that he had aroused Windber's new immigrant miners from the outside and led them out on strike. But letters, oral histories, and other evidence indicate that Windber miners had been acting autonomously and trying to organize for some time. Heber Blankenhorn has described some of the many spontaneous actions local miners took on their own to join the union effort. Brophy himself acknowledged that no one had fully recorded the many heroic deeds of ordinary people in Windber and other places during the seventeen-month-long strike in 1922. Windber's immigrants mobilized in 1922, as they had in 1906, because they had hope. They were keenly aware of the gains organized labor had won in the war and of its postwar militancy. With the district and national UMWA organizations on the move, defending recent gains, they understood that they had a reasonable chance to succeed. They did not have to be isolated. Immigrant miners did not act because they were "isolated masses," but because they were in touch with the mainstream labor movement and wanted to become part of it.

From the strike's inception foreign-born miners had rallied to support the strike and soon took steps in their immigrant communities to discipline strike-breakers and ethnic leaders who supported Berwind-White. Slovak fraternals illustrate the case. On April 23 the St. Thomas chapter 304 of the National Slovak Society became the first of numerous Slovak societies to deny sick aid to members who worked during the strike. Fraternals also voted to expel those members who worked during the strike and were not up-to-date in the payment of their dues. The societies either contributed money directly to the UMWA or assisted their own members who were on strike. As the strike dragged on, ethnic miners and organizers sought aid from their national institutions and monitored foreign-language newspapers for misleading information or advertisements for strike-breakers. In his book, *The Strike for Union*, Heber Blankenhorn demonstrated that the bulk of strikebreakers in 1922 were American-born miners rather than new immigrants.[43]

42. Robinson to Brophy, May 13, 1918, UMWA Records; "Brophy-Committee from Windber," [Memo], February 9, 1919, UMWA, District 2, UMWA Records; Beik, "Miners of Windber," 467–95; and Edward J. Robinson, Windber, to John Brophy, Clearfield, November 12, 1918, UMWA, District 2, UMWA Records.

43. Sväti Tomas, Odbor 304, Národný Slovenský Spolok, Windber, Pa., "Zápisnica," Meetings, (April 23, 1922); 16 July 1922; Spolok Sväti Jána Kerstitela, čislo 48, Pennsylvánska Slovenská Katolícka Jednota, Windber, Pa., "Zápisnica," Meetings, May 7,1922; June 4, 1922; July 2, 1922; Spolok Sv. Jána Krstitela, čislo 292, Prvá Katolícka Slovenská Jednota, Windber, Pa., "Zápisnica," Meeting, May 21, 1922; Kunrad Valent, Mine 40, to Michael Lenko, First Catholic Slovak Union, June 20, 1922, Box 86, File 868, First Catholic Slovak Union Papers, The Czech and Slovak American Collection, University of Minnesota, St. Paul; [Michael Lenko], to Kunrad Valent, Mine 40, June 24, 1922, Box 86, File 868, First Catholic Slovak Union Papers; Slovenský Politický a Poučný Klub, "Zápisnica," Meeting, July 2, 1922; *Penn-Central News*, September 30, 1922; and Blankenhorn, 261.

The ethnic miners' fight for working-class solidarity quickly spread to the other bulwark of immigrant communities: the immigrant churches. Prominent priests who had been among the ethnic leaders who upheld the company's authoritarian rule were also disciplined. As a result, three priests soon lost their parishes. The Hungarian, Polish, and Italian clergymen had infuriated miners by preaching from the pulpit that the men should return to work. Miners responded by placing a bundle of miner's tools on the front steps of each parish. Attached to the bundle was a note to tell each priest to use the donated tools and "go to work."[44]

New foreign-speaking leaders, miners who had inhabited Windber's stratified ethnic communities, challenged company domination that had been sustained by American-born managers and the company's ethnic bosses. These new activists gave speeches, worked to coordinate the nationalities, and performed many other needed services. Joe Zahurak, subsequently president of the Windber local in the 1930s, and Alex Kada, a Hungarian, were two of the many men who took the initiative on their own to drive to different places to give speeches to urge the miners to stay out whenever they got word that some were considering returning to work. Between the two of them, they could speak Slovak, Hungarian, Polish, Russian, and English. Whenever possible, they got an Italian to join them.[45]

Such class-conscious activists understood the need to keep the nationalities together. Zahurak explained that he had learned the lesson when he was a young boy who overheard his parents and boarders discuss the failure of the strike of 1906, in which they had taken part. Their discussions had led him to conclude that Windber miners would really have to work hard to keep the various nationalities together. In his words, "They [the company] had the nationalities split up so they didn't stick together good enough. They came on strike [in 1906] but not 100%. The Italians dominated the 35 mine, the Hungarians mines 36 and 40, and the Polish and all them nationalities." What was more important than ethnic difference, however, was that "they couldn't get together and discuss things and it discouraged them" (ibid.).

If District 2 organizers had to discuss strategies for invading "Siberia," Windber miners had to find ways to break through those barriers and get outside help. Since organizers couldn't get into town in their own cars or on the streetcar, local miners had to take action to bring them in on their own. Zahurak and Kada were forced to go into hiding when company guards told them to get out of town. But Kada owned a car, and until that car was blown up in the middle of a night, the two men took it upon themselves to bring outside organizers to local union meetings. Zahurak explained: "We had to go to Beaverdale to get a Slovak organizer, Mr. Slivco. We had to go to Nanty Glo to [get] the Hungarian-speaking organizer, which was Joe Foster. In Homer City [there] was John Ghizzoni and Charles Ghizzoni, the Italian." The miners met in ball parks or farmers' fields, and they wanted outside speakers who spoke their own languages. Zahurak noted: "You had all them nationalities at that

44. Zahurak, interview, October 7, 1986.
45. Ibid.

time—that generation. You had to use the different nationality speakers to interest them [the miners] in staying out'' (ibid.).

Windber-area miners lost the strike of 1922, as that in 1906, through no fault of their own. Working men and women had democratically mobilized and asserted control over their old community institutions, even as they had adhered to a new one, the union. They had endured evictions, injunctions, harrassments, the hardships of living in tent colonies and chicken coops. Some had brought lawsuits, petitioned the government, and picketed Berwind-White's offices in New York City. District 2 was generous in its help, but that aid was not sufficient. The UMWA's national policy in regard to the unorganized and newly organized fields had proved bankrupt when Windber's miners were once again left out of the national settlement. Without greater outside help, there was no way that they, alone or with district help, could win the protracted struggle against the combined political and economic might of the corporate interests represented in Somerset County.[46]

Although Windber miners had won the battle but lost the war in 1922, a complete return to the status quo ante was impossible. The foreign-born miners' actions in support of unionization undermined the myth of new immigrant docility vis-à-vis the labor movement, betrayed the falseness of the company's claim to be a ''model'' town, and fueled intra-union radical dissent. Berwind-White's open-shop strategy, based on segregated ethnic enclaves and loyal ethnic leaders had failed. The company could never look at ethnic communities the same way. Foreign-born miners and their families were not docile creatures easily controlled by a few ethnic bosses. They could act independently in their own interest and would, under certain circumstances, even fight heroic battles.

After the strike, Berwind-White continued to rely on autocratic means to keep its diverse workers unorganized. In this sense, its policies remained intact. But it also opened a night school for its employees that was in part designed to curb dissent and co-opt potential ethnic union leaders whom it invited to attend. Ethnic miners and former strike activists did attend, but they were not co-opted. These same leaders successfully led the unionization drive in 1933 when permanent organization was effected.[47]

Windber's new immigrants were pragmatic people. Somerset County local unions had ended the lengthy strike of 1922 at a convention on August 14, 1923, when delegates adopted a resolution that recognized ''the circumstances making necessary the temporary abandonment of our fight against the coal operators for union recognition.'' The strike's failure, in their words, ''was not due to any defects in the principles of unionism, but rather to the brutal tactics and tremendous financial strength of the coal companies, as well as to the weakmindedness, selfishness and un-Americanism of strike breakers who took our jobs.'' Ethnic differences were

46. For a history of the Somerset County strike, see Blankenhorn, *Strike for Union.*
47. Zahurak, interview, October 7, 1986.

otherwise not mentioned. They concluded by reaffirming their belief in unionism and awaited "the first opportunity of winning a contract and union recognition."[48]

The masses of new immigrant and American miners judged that that opportunity had arrived in 1933 with the New Deal and passage of legislation that permitted collective bargaining and included the right to organize. Earlier, in April 1927, the masses of miners had not supported a massive strike because they had not considered the moment favorable. Their chances of winning were slim, and they were not prepared to live again so soon in tent colonies and undergo the necessary sacrifices to make the fight worthwhile. In 1933, their hopes were rekindled by Franklin Delano's Roosevelt's administration and, ironically, by the same UMWA leader, John L. Lewis, who had left them out in the cold in 1922. They appreciated the changed political atmosphere and legal changes brought about by the New Deal. The UMWA came to the Windber area without the drama of the strikes of 1906 and 1922 but with a rapidity that startled many.[49]

To attract and maintain an immigrant workforce and keep its miners divided and unorganized, Berwind-White had adopted a variety of ethnic policies that were designed to reinforce its overall authoritarian control throughout the nonunion era. The failure of these policies was revealed by the sporadic but ongoing organizing efforts of the miners and by those important occasions when District 2 had mobilized and offered Windber miners a viable chance for successful unionization. Then, immigrants defied ethnic stereotypes, joined the union en masse, and engaged in costly strikes for union recognition. The company's "ethnic" failure was also underscored by its regular reliance on repression and by its periodic need to resort to its massive economic, legal, and political clout in order to avert unionization. Ethnic differences had made organizing more difficult, and conservative national union policies did injure the union cause. Nevertheless, the company's restoration of the old nonunion order was achieved primarily through mass evictions and wholescale injunctions, company gunmen and the strike-breaking activities of the state police, violence and nativism, hunger and deprivation.

In the end, the company could only "curry favor" with new immigrants, not empower them. From the 1890s to the 1930s, the only viable route to self-determination for Windber's foreign-born miners and their families lay through an imperfect, broad-based, complex industrial union, the United Mine Workers. The same could be said for American-born miners and other nonminers who did not enjoy basic civil liberties or the right to exercise an independent franchise.

The integration of Windber's foreign-born and their children into American society was ultimately made possible by the American labor movement, not by the company, churches, government, public schools, or the passing of time itself. In the 1930s, a local UMWA leader, Joe Novak, founded a Miners' Roosevelt Club and

48. "Resolution Adopted by Delegates of Somerset County Local Unions," August 14, 1923, UMWA, District 2, UMWA Records.
49. Beik, "Miners of Windber," 571–77.

established a citizenship school so that Windber's new immigrant miners could become citizens, vote, support the New Deal, and win political control of the borough away from the coal company. He himself wrote away for booklets in various languages, taught many of the initial classes, and took many people to Somerset for the citizenship hearings. Hundreds of foreign-born men and women became citizens in the late 1930s and early 1940s in this manner. Novak's work represented the continuation of the union's best, ethnic-friendly, class-based policies.[50]

The citizenship schools are perhaps the most concrete and direct link between the UMWA and an "Americanization" that occurred "from below." Throughout its history the UMWA had served as an integrating force that, in theory if not always in practice, sought to unite members of all nationalities and races on a class basis in the American environment. It had not integrated disparate peoples into a class-based organization by imposing cultural uniformity or by destroying the immigrant communities in which many of its members lived. Instead, it had respected cultural and linguistic differences, even as it presented American- and foreign-born miners with a common objective: the ending of exploitation. Immigrants responded to the UMWA and to the New Deal because they seemed to offer a viable option for changing—not merely accepting—American industrial capitalism.

50. Novak, interview, May 19, 1985; UMWA Local 6186, Minutes, Meetings, August 13, 1935; August 20, 1935; September 3, 1935; September 9, 1935; October 15, 1935; November 4, 1935.

CHAPTER FOURTEEN

THE 1913–1914 COLORADO FUEL AND IRON STRIKE, WITH REFLECTIONS ON THE CAUSES OF COAL-STRIKE VIOLENCE

PRISCILLA LONG

This essay has two parts. In the first, I narrate a history of the Colorado Fuel and Iron (CF & I) strike of 1913–14, the bitter industrial conflict best remembered for the event known as the Ludlow Massacre.[1] In the second part I discuss the causes of violence during coal strikes. To do so, I present and evaluate an analysis offered by the economist Price V. Fishback.[2] Fishback's exploration of coal-strike violence covers more than sixty strikes that occurred between 1877 and 1928. I discuss his conceptual framework in light of the general history of American coal mining while

1. For a comprehensive account of the strike, see Priscilla Long, *Where the Sun Never Shines: A History of America's Bloody Coal Industry* (New York: Paragon House, 1989). All work on this strike remains indebted to George S. McGovern's Ph.D. dissertation "The Colorado Coal Strike, 1913–1914" (Northwestern University, 1953). McGovern's dissertation is not superseded (or quite represented) by the published version, George S. McGovern and Leonard F. Guttridge, *The Great Coalfield War* (Boston, 1972).

2. I thank Price V. Fishback for allowing me the use of his paper "An Alternative View of Violence in Labor Disputes in the Early 1900s: The Bituminous Coal Industry, 1890–1930" before its publication.

paying particular attention to how it does and does not fit the case of the Colorado Fuel and Iron strike.

THE COLORADO FUEL AND IRON STRIKE

"The only language common to all, and which all understand in Colorado, is the voice of the gun," declared Ethelbert Stewart in November 1913.[3] An official of the U.S. Bureau of Labor Statistics, he had just failed to mediate the southern Colorado coal strike then making headlines across the country. Organized by District 15 of the United Mine Workers of America (UMWA), the strike on the Rockefeller-controlled Colorado Fuel and Iron Co. and on two other firms began in September 1913. Even before April 20, 1914, it had attracted national attention.

On that day troops of the Colorado National Guard (CNG) attacked a strikers' tent village, the Ludlow Tent Colony, inhabited by more than one thousand men, women, and children. The troops fired on the tents throughout the day, and at dusk, burned them to the ground. Among those who died in what shocked the nation as the Ludlow Massacre were two women and eleven small children. The incident gave rise to a ten-day armed rebellion of strikers that ended when President Woodrow Wilson ordered the United States Army into the southern Colorado coalfield. "This rebellion," wrote a federal investigator, "constituted perhaps one of the nearest approaches to civil war and revolution ever known in this country in connection with an industrial conflict."[4]

Yet Colorado coal miners and their wives were neither revolutionaries nor radicals. They believed in democracy, and equated America with democratic values. Before Ludlow they had patriotically raised and lowered the American flag morning and night. They had begun all union meetings by singing the national anthem. Strikers claimed it was the coal operators who conducted their business in an un-American fashion.

Southern Colorado coal communities included Italians, Greeks, Eastern Europeans, and Mexicans, as well as English-speaking miners. Of the 14,000 Colorado mine workers in 1913, some 70% spoke a first language other than English.[5] The CF & I intentionally mixed nationalities in the mines to prevent solidarity among miners. Reporting on his interview with a manager, a federal official explained, "When too many of one nationality get into a given district they would so adjust their men that no very large per cent in any mine could communicate with the

---

3. Ethelbert Stewart to Louis F. Post in Post to President Wilson, November 22, 1913, Woodrow Wilson Papers, Library of Congress.

4. George P. West, "Report on Ludlow," File: "West Report," Box 10, Commission on Industrial Relations Papers, RG 174, National Archives (hereafter NA).

5. "Nationalities Employed in the Mines of Colorado," File: D15/1912," UMWA Papers, Washington, D.C.

others.''[6] The strategy was intended to keep people apart but in effect it brought them together.

The leading Colorado coal firms—the CF & I, the Rocky Mountain Fuel Co., and the Victor American Fuel Co.—had long opposed the UMWA without qualification. In 1904 they had defeated a great coal strike for the eight-hour day. A decade later they remained willing to fight the union at any cost.

These firms had produced one of the worst coal-mine safety records in the world. At 7.3 deaths per 1000 mine workers (in 1912), Colorado's fatality rate was double the average for America, which itself had the highest death rate of any coal-producing country.[7]

Gross neglect of safe practices was a leading cause of accidental death. A miner secretly reporting to the union wrote of one mine that there was ''no air to speak of in some places.'' Roof supports were absent or inadequate, the rooms, ''40 feet and not a timber in sight.'' Firms paid nothing for ''dead work,'' work not directly related to taking out coal such as setting timbers and attending to other safety matters. They disregarded the recommended practice of employing a single shotfirer to do all the blasting after most workers had gone home.[8]

Safety was one issue, poverty another. The companies controlled not only a family's income, but also its costs. To begin with income, they paid the miners by the ton, and they had found a simple method to reduce the tonnage rate: cheating in weighing the coal. In a typical report made in 1910, an inspector found that when he stood on a coal car being weighed at the CF & I's Starkville mine, his weight, which was 155 pounds, added only 35 pounds. At the Sopris camp his weight added 70 pounds to a car of coal.[9]

As for costs, the companies sold the mining people their necessities, from rent to coal to groceries, and by charging high prices, further reduced their standard of living. ''We are expected to trade at the company store,'' one unionist stated. ''We were compelled to buy shoes for 4.00 that my wife got elsewhere for 2.50. We were charged 45 cents for a bottle of 30 cent oil.'' Southern Colorado miners were among America's working poor. A miner scolded, ''some of the children are dressed in clothes made of gunny-sacks [feed bags] and their fathers are working every day.''[10]

In southern Colorado coal camps, democracy was unknown. The camps were built near the mines, high in isolated canyons where the company owned everything

6. The manager was L. M. Bowers. Frame 000265-000281, Reel 1, Ethelbert Stewart Papers, Microfilm Edition, Southern Historical Collections, University of North Carolina Library, Chapel Hill.

7. For a full discussion of fatality statistics see Long, *Where the Sun Never Shines*, 43–51.

8. Report from No. 94, Superior, Colo., September 18, 1913, U.S. Commission on Industrial Relations, *Final Report and Testimony* (Senate Doc. 415, 64th Cong., 2d Sess.), Washington, D.C., 1916 (hereafter, CIR *Report*), 7063.

9. Colorado Bureau of Labor Statistics (hereafter CBLS), *Twelfth Annual Report, 1909–1910*, 30.

10. Miners' conditions are taken from ''Read the Grievances of the Colorado Coal Miners, Trinidad, September 15–16, 1913,'' File D15/1913,'' UMWA Papers; and *Proceedings Special Convention of District 15 . . . 16 Sept. 1913*, 4, E. L. Doyle Papers, Env. 10, Western History Dept., Denver Public Library (hereafter WHD/DPL).

from houses to land to water. Superintendents ruled the camps and mineguards patrolled them. The coal companies hired, paid, and supervised the mineguards who were nevertheless deputized by county sheriffs and carried guns as county law enforcement officers. The companies called them camp marshals. The mining people called them gunmen, thugs, and scum of the earth.

Mineguards prevented outsiders from entering the camps unless they could give an unquestionable account of themselves.[11] They barred union organizers and suspected anyone unknown to the company of being one. Often they were right, particularly after the fall of 1912 when UMWA District 15 officers inaugurated an aggressive but clandestine organizing campaign a year before the great strike began. People posing as peddlers, house painters, religious personages, cousins, uncles, persons looking for work, and lost persons, not to mention working miners, were often union organizers, some of them paid and others volunteer.

To keep the union out, and for other reasons as well, the Colorado operators conducted surveillance in every town, saloon, and camp. State officials were not exempt. "One does not need to be a sleuth," a Colorado labor commissioner reported, "to become acquainted with the elaborate and complete system of surveillance that is maintained by the fuel corporations of this district. . . . Under this system of espionage it is an easy matter for one of the Trinidad agents to notify a mine when to expect a visit from the [State Coal Mine] Inspector."[12]

District UMWA officials were pursued, hounded, and harassed. "There was never a time that I wasn't followed constantly by one to three guards," fumed District 15 President John McLennan. "If I went to eat in a restaurant they stood at the door until I came out. . . . [M]any times five or six of them would stand for half a day in front of our office for the purpose of intimidating men from going up there. Every man who was seen going up there was . . . trailed until they found out what camp he went to, and immediately he was discharged."[13]

For the women, repression took the form of sexual harassment. In the daytime, with husbands underground, wives and children shared the camps with mineguards. "I have been told by women in Primero," reported a state official, "that there was no privacy in their home life, that whenever a representative of the company or deputy sheriff desired, they entered the house unannounced."[14] Incidents of rape were occasionally reported and probably underreported. One mineguard, Bob Lee, was a known rapist. A former undersheriff described him as "a brutal man, very brutal. . . . The miners' wives . . . who used to come up the hill to do washings for the American women, told hard stories on him of how he terrified certain miners' wives into submitting to him by authority of his star and threatening the loss of their

11. Moran, Fitzgibben, and Paulsen to John P. White, August 14, 1912, File: D15/1912, UMWA Papers.

12. CBLS, *Twelfth Biennial Report, 1909–1910*, Denver, 1911, 32.

13. McLennan Test., U.S. Congress, House Subcommittee on Mines and Mining, *Conditions in the Coal Mines of Colorado* (63d Cong., 2d Sess.), Washington, D.C., 1914 (hereafter House Subcommittee on Mines), 2074, 2077.

14. CBLS, *Twelfth Biennial Report, 1909–1910*, 27.

men's jobs. . . . Myself, I've heard him brag as some young Italian wife went by, 'She's a peach. I'm a goin' to get her.' "[15]

Any appearance of discontent on the part of miners resulted in immediate discharge. The UMWA estimated that in 1912 the coal companies fired twelve hundred Colorado mine workers on suspicion of their having union sympathies.[16] Nevertheless, managers maintained the illusion of a contented workforce. "So far as we can learn," a CF&I manager wrote his superior, "they [the miners] are satisfied . . . but the constant dogging of their heels by agitators, together with the muckraking magazines and trust-busting political shysters, has a mighty influence over the ignorant foreigners who make up the great mass of our ten thousand miners."[17] To keep the "ignorant foreigners" in line, mineguards broke up meetings of fraternal societies, disrupted socials, routed church meetings. Indeed, any of these activities may well have included clandestine union business.

The UMWA hired ethnic organizers, such as the Greek organizer Louis Tikas and the slavic organizer Mike Livoda. Livoda began walking out to the coal camps every night to recruit miners into the union. One night he was sleeping in the bachelors' quarters at the Ravenwood camp. He woke to a brilliant light shining in his face. Mineguards yanked him out of bed, pulled him out of the house, and severely beat him. To his cries for help they responded, "Shut up, you son of a bitch, or we'll kill you."[18]

Violence was one tactic; granting union demands before miners struck for them was another. In the midst of the organizing campaign, the CF & I granted a 10% raise to counter "unusual activity on the part of spies sent out by the union." L. M. Bowers elaborated to his superior: "You know our mines are non-union, and I know of no better way than to anticipate demands and do a little better by the men than they would receive if they belonged to the union."[19]

Nevertheless, organizing continued unabated. In March 1913 the firm inaugurated the eight-hour day, a change that cost the company nothing. By supplying more coal cars, the CF & I president told his executive committee, managers reduced the time miners had to spend waiting for cars to load. This enabled them to do work in eight hours that had previously required ten.[20] The irony was that a decade earlier the companies had spent more than a million dollars to defeat a strike (the 1903–4 Colorado strike) for this same eight-hour day.

15. John McQuarrie Test., CIR *Report*, 6782.

16. Doyle, McLennan, and Lawson to John P. White, July 10, 1913, Denver, File: D15/1913, UMWA Papers.

17. L. M. Bowers to John D. Rockefeller, September 30, 1912, Item 99, Box 28, L. M. Bowers Papers, Special Collections, Bartle Library, State University of New York, Binghamton.

18. This occurred in June 1912. Author interview with Mike Livoda, Denver, January, 1977; Livoda affidavit, CIR *Report*, 6950.

19. L. M. Bowers to Frederick Gates, April 15, 1912, Item 99, Box 28, Bowers Papers.

20. "President's Report, CF&I Executive Committee Meeting, April 12, 1913, File 58, Jesse Welborn Papers, Colorado State Historical Society (hereafter CSHS).

Most miners recognized the anti-union tactic for what it was—a gesture easily rescinded in the absence of the union—and continued to hope for a strike. By August 1913 excitement mixed with anxiety pervaded the coalfield. Mineguards from the notoriously violent Baldwin Feltz Detective Agency of Bluefield, West Virginia, began to appear in southern Colorado. The miners and their families waited. In the words of one organizer, "The miners here are ready at the word to drop their tools to the man."[21]

With both sides fully prepared for a strike, in August 1913 the first casualty occurred. A young organizer, Gerald Lippiatti, was shot dead on the streets of Trinidad by Baldwin Feltz detective, G. W. Belcher. After the strike began Belcher was himself killed, undoubtedly by someone on the union side.[22]

On September 2, UMWA organizer Mary "Mother" Jones arrived in Trinidad to work with local organizers to recruit the coal-mining people to the union cause. "They have my skull drawn on a picture," she wrote to a friend, "to tell me that if I do not quit they are going to get me. Well, they have been a long time at it."[23] Her easily recognized presence ended the clandestine phase of organizing. Soon union officials would invite the operators to negotiate. Everyone knew they would decline. The strike was about to begin.

At this time the UMWA appointed a policy committee to direct the coming strike in Colorado. The committee first wrote to the operators and requested a conference. The operators declined to reply. On September 5 the committee publicly urged the miners of the district to join the UMWA, "which has advanced the interests of its members in a hundred different ways and has brought sunshine and happiness into thousands of homes."[24]

The policy committee called a district convention to be held in Trinidad on September 15 and 16. The operators were invited but no one expected them to appear.

On the first day of the convention, three hundred miners cheered UMWA speakers in Walsenburg and then marched through the streets behind a brass band. In Trinidad hundreds of miners milled in the streets and talked on the street corners. That evening Mother Jones and other UMWA organizers were billed to speak at the West Opera House. As evening approached the large hall filled to capacity and many were turned away.[25]

Mother Jones held the audience spellbound for two hours, the *United Mine Work-*

21. Germer report to John P. White, September 2, 1913, File "1911–1913," Box 1, Adolph Germer Papers, University of Wisconsin, Madison.

22. For Lippiatti's death see "Town in Turmoil," *Rocky Mountain News* (hereafter *RMN*) (August 17, 1913); and "Mine Organizer Killed in Fight," Denver *Times* (August 17, 1913), 1, 3. For an account of Belcher's death see McGovern and Guttridge, *Great Coalfield War*, 149–50.

23. Mother Jones to T. V. Powderly, September 30, 1913, File: "Personal Correspondence, I–J," Box Al-118, T. V. Powderly Papers, Catholic University of America.

24. "An Appeal to All Mine Workers in District 15," Doyle Test., CIR *Report*, 7067.

25. "Hayes Predicts Strike Victory," *RMN* (September 15, 1913), 3; E. L. Doyle, "Minutes of the Policy Committee, September 14, 1913," Env. 11, E. L. Doyle Papers; *UMWJ* (September 25, 1913), 2.

ers Journal reported, "mercilessly scoring the operators and the Baldwin Feltz guards." She also pleaded for arbitration, urging the governor to use his influence to force the operators into a conference with the union. Then she built to the crescendo of her address. With fists clenched, she cried, "If it is strike or submit . . . why for God's sake, strike—strike until you win!" The cheers that greeted this utterance, reported the *Rocky Mountain News,* "ended in a veritable pandemonium. Springing to their seats the men shouted until they dropped back exhausted."[26]

On Monday morning organizers held open meetings directly outside the coal camps, which by now operators had enclosed in high barbed wire fences. In Trinidad 255 delegates to the convention paraded the streets behind a banner that read: "We Are Fighting For Our Homes."[27]

For two days the convention heard grievances. The delegates reduced these to seven demands. First, the miners demanded recognition of the UMWA as the legitimate bargaining agent for the mine workers. To outsiders this demand could seem arbitrary and unreasonable. Yet both miners and operators understood, if the public did not, that only with union recognition did the collective workforce have any real power. Otherwise companies could retract concessions arbitrarily, at times of weakness on the part of the workforce. Other demands included a 10% raise, the eight-hour workday, payment for "dead work," and a checkweighman elected by the miners, whose job was to check the work of the company weighboss. The miners also demanded the right to choose where to shop and where to live, and the right to choose their own doctor. Lastly, they demanded "the enforcement of the Colorado mining laws and the abolition of the notorious and criminal mine guard system which has prevailed in the mining camps of Colorado for many years."[28] Roughly half the demands echoed clauses in the unenforced Colorado mining law.

The strike was set for the following Monday. Organizers intensified their efforts, and coal operators began evicting coal-camp residents. On Monday, September 23, a freezing rain fell over the canyons, prairies, and rolling foothills of southern Colorado. On that day, the motley and bedraggled inhabitants of the coal camps struggled through the mud to begin one of the greatest industrial struggles the United States has ever known.

According to federal observers, 90 to 95% of the Colorado coal-mine workforce joined the strike.[29] Strikers draggled into tent villages set up by the UMWA on land rented just outside of company property. The Ludlow Tent Colony was the largest of eight. As strikers arrived cold and soaked to the skin, the women served hot coffee to the adults and milk to the children. A miner's wife, Mary Thomas, reported that the many nationalities pitched in to help each other get settled.[30] One Tony

26. *UMWJ* (September 25, 1913), 2; "Hayes Predicts Strike Vote," *RMN*, September 15, 1913, 3.
27. "Strike Crisis Near," *RMN*, September 16, 1913, 1.
28. E. L. Doyle Test., CIR *Report*, 7017.
29. W. B. Wilson, "Memorandum for the President," December 10, 1913, File x902, Series 4, Woodrow Wilson Papers.
30. Mary Thomas O'Neal, *Those Damn Foreigners* (Hollywood, Calif., 1971), 100–102.

Gorci was carried in on a mattress, the victim of a severe beating. Gorci had been pretending to spy for the company while actually organizing for the UMWA, a fact revealed to actual company spies during the convention.

The people emerged from the coal camps hungry. UMWA regulations stipulated that strike relief could not begin until the second week of the strike, but the union suspended the rule on September 24 when several hundred strikers presented themselves at the union office. "We are actually starving," they said. "We must have assistance."[31]

Difficult beginnings. Yet the union provided for basic needs, and before long a vibrant community came to life. The Ludlow Tent Colony evolved into an elaborately organized village of twelve hundred inhabitants, mostly young people under the age of thirty. Strikers and their families lived in white tents arranged in numbered streets. At the center a speaker's platform stood next to a large tent for meetings and church services.[32]

The union supplied coal, water distributed in barrels, and strike relief (three dollars per week for each miner, one dollar for his wife, and fifty cents per child). John Lawson, a District 15 official who at forty-two was one of the oldest people around, served as camp boss. Next in command was Louis Tikas, the Greek organizer, who served as resident camp boss. Both men actively helped organize the life of the community. After the tents were set up, they made lists of necessary tasks for the approval or disapproval of all. These included cleaning, guard duty for day and night, emergency squads, and the picket committee. Later a journalist marveled at how thoroughly organized the tent colony was. It even had its own police officers. The chief of police wore "a pie-plate badge with 'chief of police UMWA' emblazoned on it."[33]

The Ludlow Tent Colony evolved into a close-knit, multi-ethnic community. The strikers enjoyed themselves, a miner's wife recalled, preferring life in the Ludlow camp to that in the coal camps. Mary Thomas declared that she had never seen so many people get along so well. They played baseball, and one visitor watched a group of Croatians playing bolo. The women shared the work of caring for the children. Charles Costa, an Italian organizer, "kept everyone in stitches with his jokes. The children followed him around like Pied Piper." Organizer Mike Livoda spent his evenings walking around the Ludlow camp: "I used to get out and listen the songs," he recalled years later. "Sometimes they put on a dance, they used to polka. You just begin to feel like that even though they're out on strike, they're happy, because they're singing and enjoying themselves."[34]

The day after the strike began, on September 24, Bob Lee, the mineguard and

31. Hayes Test., CIR *Report*, 7196.

32. McGovern, 163; *UMWJ* (February 26, 1914); O'Neal, *Those Damn Foreigners*, 100, 109–10, 138.

33. O'Neal, *Those Damn Foreigners*, 108–9; author interview with Mike Livoda, January 1977; "U.S. Officers Came Back on It," *RMN* (October 21, 1913), 4.

34. "Mrs. Thomas Tells About Ludlow," *UMWJ* (July 1, 1964), 6; *RMN* (February 19, 1914), 2; O'Neal, *Those Damn Foreigners*, 115; author interview with Livoda.

reputed rapist, was shot dead, presumably by a group of Greek strikers who promptly disappeared in the direction of New Mexico. Immediately firm managers began praising Lee's upstanding character and the fine old family that had produced him.[35]

The strike settled into a daily routine. The union sought to prevent coal from being mined while the firms looked for ways to mine it. In the first weeks the union prevailed.

On October 7 the first gunbattle of the strike occurred. That morning John Lawson and Mother Jones had spoken at the Ludlow Tent Colony. In the early afternoon shooting broke out between strikers and mineguards and continued until dark. Each side accused the other of starting it. The union addressed a letter to the operators: "We deeply deplore the shooting that has occurred . . . and feeling you are likewise concerned, we wish to ask you to cooperate with us to prevent repetition of such occurrence. Both sides must work harder to keep their men under control."[36] The operators declined to respond.

Ten days later in a drenching rain, mineguards fired six hundred rounds of ammunition into the Forbes Tent Colony. A striker was killed. In the meantime buildings were blown up at one mine and shots fired into another. Mineguards spoke of "bloodthirsty Greeks" among the strikers and strikers accused mineguards of provocations to encourage the governor to call out the Colorado National Guard.[37]

Coal operators began to pressure Colorado Governor Elias Ammons into ordering the CNG into the strike zone. Governor Ammons, elected in part with labor's vote, was a Democrat, not the party of the coal companies. His reeducation now began. "There probably has never been such pressure brought to bear upon any governor of this state by the strongest men in it," L. M. Bowers reported to John D. Rockefeller Jr., "as has been brought to bear upon Governor Ammons." The CF & I secured the cooperation of every Denver banker, of businessmen, and of fourteen newspaper editors who visited "our hesitating governor" in a steady stream to urge him "to drive the vicious agitators from the state."[38]

The UMWA believed, from its experience with the Guard in the 1903–4 coal strike, that the troops would support the operators' side. The union began its own campaign to oppose the calling out of the Guard. Nevertheless, on October 28, Governor Ammons ordered the CNG into the southern Colorado strike field. He had assured unionists that the troops would not be used to escort strike-breakers into the mines, and for this reason, the strikers gave the troops a friendly welcome. But an ominous development damaged relations almost immediately. Within two weeks, CF & I mineguards began appearing in CNG uniforms. One observer reported that

35. "First Strike Death . . ." *RMN* (September 25, 1913); McGovern, "Colorado Coal Strike," 169.

36. Reported in *RMN* (October 12, 1913), quoted in McGovern, "Colorado Coal Strike," 189.

37. *UMWJ* (October 16, 1913); *RMN* (October 18, 1913); McGovern and Guttridge, *Great Coalfield War*, 114.

38. L. M. Bowers to Rockefeller Jr., November 18, 1913, Item 100, Box 28, L. M. Bowers Papers, McGovern, "Colorado Coal Strike," 195.

the entire force of mineguards at Sopris was enlisted in one day. The mineguard who had led the attack on the Forbes Tent Colony (whom strikers regarded as a murdering thug) now appeared in uniform. The bitterness of the strikers was intense.[39]

It became increasingly evident to strikers that CNG troops were acting on the companies' behalf. Troops were seen riding around in CF & I company automobiles and going in and out of the firm's Trinidad office. Before long strikers saw troops escorting strike-breakers into the mines. Within a month the governor rescinded his order against this practice. That which had been done covertly could now be done in plain view.[40]

The troops conducted daily weapons searches during which they dumped possessions on the floor, stole things, and vandalized property. (Testimony on the troops' abusive treatment of strikers fills seven hundred pages.)[41] In response, the women organized the children to taunt and curse the troops while they conducted searches. The women themselves had became aggressive picketers, not hesitating to express themselves in language considered unwomanly by the recipients of their verbal abuse.[42]

On October 24, strikers milling in the streets of Walsenburg devised the game of surrounding any isolated mineguard and disarming him. At midafternoon, mineguards were assisting a family of strike-breakers to load their things into a cart. Harassment by strikers had persuaded this family to move to a coal camp. As the mule pulled the cart out into the street, women and children threw nut coal and tin cans at it. A large crowd began to gather. Mineguards opened fire and four strikers were killed.[43]

The next day, strikers killed a mineguard. Out on the prairies, gunfire had become nearly continuous. On November 8 a group of strikers ambushed three mineguards and a strike-breaker and shot them to death.[44]

Discipline among the troops was lax and it gradually deteriorated. A former guardsman (who later regretted his own enlistment as a youthful mistake) recalled that "plain holdups on the street and armed robberies of the saloons became common. Once a crime had been committed, the uniformed thugs disappeared into a pool of 2000 militiamen, confident no one would betray them."[45]

By January 1914 the strike had settled into a standoff, with more and more strike-breakers entering the mines. This was bad news for the union side: the longer a

39. "Statement of Mr. Don MacGregor," File: "Colorado Strike, CIR *Report*," Commission on Industrial Relations Papers, RG 174, NA.

40. Ibid; McGovern, "Colorado Coal Strike," 239.

41. "Transcripts of . . . witnesses . . ." vol. 1, Box 1, Farrar Papers, WHD/DPL; Lt. Karl Linderfelt Test., CIR *Report*, 6883.

42. See for example Van Cise Exhibit No. 2, CIR *Report*, 7324–7326.

43. McGovern, "Colorado Coal Strike," 191, 193; CIR *Report*, 7334–7343.

44. Ibid.

45. George Minot, "Lifelines," February 11, 1969, Minot Papers, WHD/DPL.

strike lasted, the more difficult it became to hope for a victory: the strike drained enormous sums and required a high level of continuous organizing. By this time the companies had acquired a powerful ally: Colorado Governor Elias Ammons. As the strike lurched forward, it became impossible to distinguish the governor's voice from that of a coal operator. Before the strike was over, a Rockefeller-employed publicity man (Ivy Lee assisted by John D. Rockefeller Jr.) was writing the governor's pronouncements for him.[46]

In early January 1914 the CNG deported Mother Jones from the strike region. In response to protest telegrams pouring into his office, Governor Ammons defended the deportation on the grounds that, in his opinion, three-fourths of the strike violence could be blamed on Mother Jones's "incendiary utterances."[47]

However, the most "incendiary utterance" that either he or the operators could come up with was Mother Jones's statement to miners at Starkville: "We will lick the hell out of the operators. We are not going to take any guns; we will take picks along, and we will take the mines and own them." Referring to this speech, Jesse Northcut, attorney for the operators, grilled John Lawson during a Congressional investigation: "Didn't you hear her tell the men . . . that they would have to get their rifles out here?" Lawson denied this. Northcutt continued, "Didn't you hear her at Starkville tell them to use their picks and knives?" Lawson answered that she had mentioned only picks. The text, transcribed by the operators' side and available only to them at the time, corroborates Lawson's answer and reveals how unreliable these operators were on the subject of Mother Jones.[48]

Notwithstanding incidents of violence on the part of strikers, UMWA organizers, including Mother Jones, aggressively and consistently urged the strikers to act peaceably, even under provocation. "Boys, we must have no blows or bloodshed," Mother Jones urged at a Colorado labor convention in December 1913. "Live up to the law."[49]

Mother Jones returned to Trinidad, where the Guard detained her without charge at the local hospital. On January 22 the UMWA organized a women's demonstration to demand her release. CNG commander General John Chase comprehended the union's strategy perfectly: "The strikers had evinced a disposition to cause disturbance and disorder through their women folks . . . believing, as was indeed the case, that it would be more embarrassing for the military to deal with women than with men."[50]

Embarrassed or not, General Chase ordered the demonstrating women to halt, and

46. For this see Long, *Where the Sun Never Shines*, 300–301.

47. "Troops Deport Mother Jones," *RMN* (January 5, 1914), 2.

48. Operators entered the speech into the record of a subsequent investigation. Mother Jones speech at Starkville, September 24, 1913, CIR *Report*, 7252; Lawson Test., House Subcommittee on Mines, 290.

49. McGovern, "Colorado Coal Strike," 176, 189; Lawson Test., House Subcommittee on Mines, 295.

50. Report of the Commanding General, "The Military Occupation of the Coal Strike Zone," WHD/DPL.

when they refused, ordered the troops to charge. They obeyed, swinging their rifles and cutting several women with sabers. The women scattered into porches and yards. They began hitting the troops with sticks and throwing bottles. Mary Thomas was arrested while whacking a soldier repeatedly with an umbrella. General Chase reported that she used language that was "highly abusive, and to say the least, unwomanly."[51]

In early February 1914, one of the few hopeful signs to cheer unionists was the arrival of a Congressional delegation to investigate the strike. Strikers hoped the national publicity would influence public opinion in their favor. It did so, but public opinion had no effect on the coal firms. The investigation produced an illuminating record of the strike, its only accomplishment.[52]

The presence of five Congressmen had inhibited violence. Their departure seemed to set it loose. On March 11, twenty-three mounted troops of the Guard tore down the tents at Forbes. A woman who had just given birth to twins was thrown out into the sleet and snow along with everyone else. A District 15 official confessed his fear that this was the beginning of a reign of terror designed to drive the miners back to work.[53] Troops began surrounding the tent colonies every night after dark. The miners and their families lay awake in fear.[54]

The Guard was deteriorating as increasingly the more decent troops, their tours of duty completed, returned to their homes. The troops had begun receiving IOUs from the now bankrupt state of Colorado. Then Governor Ammons ordered a partial withdrawal of the Guard. Mineguards joined the remaining companies. A new company, Troop A, consisted of mineguards, pit bosses, mine superintendents, and mine clerks. Troop B consisted entirely of mineguards. "All that is left now," fumed one striker, "are the gunmen, scum of the earth, barrel house bums, professional killers from every part of the country who think nothing of human life."[55]

The troops went fearfully out of control. One officer of the Guard wrote to another: "The detachment at Sopris turned out just as I thought. They had a drunken brawl the first night and raised cain in general, shot holes in the walls and ran each other all over the place."[56]

On a visit to the strike zone, State Senator Helen Ring Robinson observed militiamen openly entering the office of the CF & I to receive paychecks. Both soldiers and strikers informed her that they expected the Ludlow Tent Colony to be wiped out. At Ludlow, the senator found an atmosphere of waiting, of dread. The women showed her cellars the men had dug beneath the tents for them to run into with the children in case of attack. But Senator Robinson also discovered, among the women

51. Ibid.; "Great Czar Fell," *UMWJ* (January 29, 1914), 4; *RMN* (January 23, 1914), 1.
52. House Subcommittee on Mines.
53. White, Hayes and Green to Woodrow Wilson, File 168733-A, RG 60, NA; Doyle to Green, March 11, 1914, Env. 4, E. L. Doyle Papers.
54. *UMWJ* (April 9, 1914), 1.
55. CBLS, *Fourteenth Annual Report*, 197; "Military Rule Ended," *UMWJ* (April 23, 1914), 1.
56. Lt. Conners to Capt. Frost, April 14, 1914, Frost Papers, WHD/DPL.

particularly, that the long winter had brought the nationalities together in a rather remarkable way. "I saw a friendliness among women of all nationalities—22 at least. I saw the true melting pot at Ludlow."[57]

Sunday, April 19 was the Greek Orthodox Easter. Everyone, not just the Greeks, took part in the service. A baseball game followed. It was attended, as usual, by CNG troops. One detail was out of place. The troops amused themselves by training their rifles on the players.[58]

Apparently the strike community was in the habit of sleeping late. At nine o'clock on Monday morning, April 20, not one-half of the tent colony residents were up and dressed. CNG Major Hamrock had asked Louis Tikas, the presiding camp boss whose duties included dealing with the Guard, to produce a particular man. Tikas informed Hamrock that the man was not in the tent colony. As the two men talked, troops seemed to be moving into positions relative to the tent colony. Then, three explosions went off. They may or may not have been signals.

The shooting began. "Suddenly the prairie was covered with human beings running in all directions like ants," Mary Thomas recalled. "We all ran as we were, some with babies on their backs . . . not even thinking through the clouds of panic."[59] Many women with small children ran into the cellars dug beneath the tents. Others ran out of the tent colony. The men went for the rifles they'd managed to keep through successive weapons searches. Some ran to a rifle pit they had dug purposely away from the tents, with the idea of drawing fire away from the tents. Others ran to another point away from the tents.

Yet the troops shot directly into the tents, hour after hour. By midafternoon the children in the cellars were becoming restless and hungry. Eleven-year-old Frank Snyder came up into the Snyder tent to get something to eat. He was shot in the head and killed. His father came up to lie down beside him for a while. Then he began running hysterically from tent to tent telling people to make their children lie down rather than have them be killed. After this, it seemed to one Mrs. Tonner that "the machine guns turned loose all the more. My tent was so full of holes that it was like lace, pretty near."

Meanwhile the strikers shooting back from the rifle pits were faring badly. At approximately 4:30 in the afternoon they ran out of ammunition. At dusk, the attackers entered the colony with war whoops. They looted the tents of quilts, musical instruments, and clothes. At 7:10, a CF & I manager in Trinidad received the following message: "Tent colony on fire."[60]

Louis Tikas and a 21-year-old wife, Pearl Jolly, ran from tent to tent trying to get people out. As they were leaving with a group of fifty they heard a rumor that one of Mary Petrucci's children had been shot. Tikas turned back with the idea of help-

57. Ibid.
58. "Pearl Jolly Speech," May 21, 1914, Ellis Meredith Papers, CSHS.
59. O'Neal, *Those Damn Foreigners*, 133–134.
60. Memo, File 145, Box 7, CF&I Papers, CSHS.

ing her. He was captured and killed in captivity. Troops killed two other prisoners just as the tents were starting to burn. In the meantime, strikers killed CNG Private Albert Martin and mutilated his body.

In the light of the burning tents, troops escorted a few families up to the Ludlow Depot. There, according to Juanita Hernandez, one of the soldiers took an accordion and "played on it before us." Some time after midnight soldiers came upon the Snyder family with their six children, five of them living and one dead. One soldier ordered them out of the tent with the comment, "You redneck son-of-a-bitch, I have a notion to kill you right now."[61]

The light of Tuesday morning revealed whiskey bottles strewn across the battle-field. Sometime after dawn, Mary Petrucci regained consciousness. Lying in the cellar beside her were thirteen corpses, including those of her own three children. She staggered out of the cellar toward the Ludlow Depot, not entirely in her right mind.

On Tuesday, other wives, cold, hungry, and half-dressed, straggled into Trinidad. They had spent the night on the prairie. One woman had given birth; mother and child came into town half-clad and freezing cold.[62]

"For God's sake," District 15 secretary-treasurer E. L. Doyle wired UMWA President John White, "urge the chief executive of this nation to use his power to protect the helpless men, women, and children from being slaughtered in southern Colorado."[63] CF & I Manager L. M. Bowers wired John D. Rockefeller Jr.: "An unprovoked attack upon small force of militia yesterday by two hundred strikers forced fight resulting in probable loss of ten or fifteen strikers, only one militiaman killed. Suggest your giving this information to friendly papers."[64]

As the news hit the front pages of the nation, an armed rebellion gripped the southern Colorado coalfield. Local UMWA officials along with other Colorado unionists issued a "Call to Rebellion," which asked volunteers to organize them-selves into companies "to protect the workers of Colorado against the murder and cremation of men, women and children by armed assassins in the employ of coal corporations." They openly distributed guns.[65]

Strikers set up camps in the hills and elected military officers. On Wednesday, Doyle wired the national office: "Battle raging now. Five large tipples said to be on fire. Five guards killed, two strikers wounded." The next day he wired: "Hell is loose in this state."[66]

61. Except where otherwise noted, all eyewitness accounts of the days events are taken from affidavits and testimony in CIR *Report*, 8186 (Dominiske); 7384 (Tonner); 8194 (Petrucci); 7371 (Snyder), 7365, 6853; and in manuscript affidavits found in Box: Colorado Strike, CIR Papers, RG 174, NA.

62. McDonald Test., CIR *Report*, 6777.

63. E. L. Doyle to John P. White, April 21, 1914, Env. 4, E. L. Doyle Papers.

64. L. M. Bowers to John D. Rockefeller, Jr., April 21, 1914, Item 101, Box 28, L. M. Bowers Papers.

65. "A Call to Rebellion," April 22, 1914, Env. 17, E. L. Doyle Papers.

66. Author interview with Livoda; Doyle telegrams to UMWA National Office, April 23–24, 1914, Env. 4, E. L. Doyle Papers.

"Campfires gleamed along the ridges at Aguilar, scene of the burning of the Empire Mine Property," reported the *New York Times* on Thursday, April 24. "At the Southwestern Mine, which broke into flames early this afternoon, a battle is raging between guards and a strong force of strikers."[67]

By Wednesday, the strikers controlled an area eighteen miles long and five miles wide, including the town of Trinidad. Trapped inside this territory were superintendents, mineguards, strikebreakers, and the troops who had attacked the Ludlow Tent Colony.[68] A minister ventured into the battle zone in an attempt to rescue strikebreakers; he commented of the armed strikers: "There were men there who had their children killed at Ludlow just two days previous. . . . [I]t is almost impossible for anyone to appreciate the intense excitement that prevailed among these men; in fact it would almost be right to say that some of them were insane in their grief."[69]

Demonstrations protesting the massacre were organized in cities from Chicago to New York to Washington, D.C. CNG troops were ordered back into the strike field. Company C refused to go. Its eighty-two troops stood at attention and hissed the troops departing Denver "to engage in the shooting of women and children."[70] By Friday UMWA officials were frantically trying to stop the fighting, with only marginal success. The rebellion had passed out of union control. After ten days, President Woodrow Wilson ordered the United States Army into the southern Colorado coalfield. Peace was restored, and eventually the strike was defeated.

The Rockefellers, chagrined by these events, took steps to improve the image of the company. John D. Rockefeller Jr. became the architect of the country's first important company union and first large-scale corporate public relations campaign.

The coal miners of Colorado had to wait for the New Deal to get union representation and union conditions. But the strikers—men, women, and children—had done their part to build the union movement. Mary Petrucci, grieving the death of her children, told a reporter that even now she and her husband supported the union: "You're not to think we could do any differently another time," she said. "We are working people—my husband and I—and we're stronger for the union than before the strike. . . . I can't have my babies back. But perhaps when everybody knows about them, something will be done to make the world a better place for all babies."[71]

The Guard conducted an investigation, questioning no one on the union side. They found the cause to be the character of tent colony inhabitants, "almost wholly foreign and without conception of our government. A large percentage were inassimilable aliens to whom liberty means licence." But the ultimate cause lay with

67. "1000 Strikers in Ambush for Troop Train," *New York Times* (April 24, 1914), 10.
68. George P. West Report.
69. Rev. James McDonald Test., CIR *Report*, 6776.
70. Col. Edw. Verdeckberg, "Report of the District Commander, Walsenburg, 28 Oct. 1913 to 5 May 1914," Verdeckberg Papers, DPL/WHD.
71. Clip., Huffaker interview with Mary Petrucci, File: Colorado 4, Box 2, Mother Jones Papers, Catholic University of America.

the coal operators, who had established in Colorado "a numerous class of ignorant, lawless and savage south European peasants."[72]

ON THE CAUSES OF COAL STRIKE VIOLENCE

With an account of the Colorado Fuel and Iron strike before us, I turn now to an examination of the causes of violence in coal-industry labor disputes. In doing so I present both a summary of and a challenge to the analysis offered by Price V. Fishback in his paper "An Alternative View of Violence in Labor Disputes in the Early 1900's: The Bituminous Coal Industry, 1890–1930." Fishback builds his explanation for violence in coal strikes by reviewing and evaluating previous explanations. He tests the previous explanations against his own ideas and against information on specific coal strikes drawn from a selection of books and articles. Fishback's rather cursory research on these numerous strikes by no means invalidates his complex and highly useful conceptual framework. But it does mean that the framework must be evaluated against actual events understood in the light of exhaustive archival research. I propose to do this for the CF & I strike.

Fishback argues that, in assessing the causes of violence in coal strikes, efforts to assign blame to one side or the other are misguided. Both operators and miners armed themselves in self-defense, perceiving a threat from the other side based on past bitter experience. Violent confrontations usually occurred in a series of steps, unintended by either side, that soon veered out of control. Neither operators nor union leaders exerted total control over all their members. On both sides there were bound to be a few hotheads. A small incident such as a shot fired by some trigger-happy individual could quickly escalate, with people on both sides joining the fray in the belief that they were defending their own people. Each side would blame the other for starting it. Fighting would continue to erupt until both sides tired of fighting and settled, or until ". . . an outside authority, like the state militia restored order. In some cases the state militia were perceived as choosing sides. Then federal troops were required" (3).

Fishback begins his review of previous explanations for what he terms "violent strikes" by stating that a "common explanation . . . is economic exploitation and oppression." He questions this, noting that coal miners' wages and working conditions were on a par with those of workers with similar skills in other sectors of the economy. He asks: "If coal miners were no more exploited than other workers, we have no explanation for why coal miners were more likely to commit violent acts than other workers" (5).

To call a strike marked by violent incidents a "violent strike" carries the implication that the UMWA would call a "violent strike" or that the mining community

---

72. Boughton Test., CIR *Report*, 6363; "Ludlow, Being the Report of the Special Board of Officers," File 168733-a, RG 60, NA.

would go out on a "violent strike." Of course this was not the case. Moreover, we have no evidence that "coal miners were more likely to commit violent acts than other workers." Such a statement makes coal miners responsible for all coal-strike fatalities, including violence done to them by others.

If miners were not exploited or impoverished then such conditions could not explain "violent strikes." Fishback notes that strikes often occurred during periods of economic growth. He suggests that strikes may have been undertaken, not in response to deplorable conditions but as attempts to raise wages above those of other workers. I would note, however, that strikes in the context of falling prices usually proved disastrous. To strike when prices were rising may have reflected nothing more than effective union strategy.

The question of how exploited or destitute the mining community *felt itself to be* pertains to its propensity to strike. In southern Colorado the men and women of the coal camps felt abused and described themselves as destitute. Their *felt* experience motivated them to take the considerable risk of joining the union and striking. But their conditions, exploitive or not, do not explain violence done by a few strikers (as Fishback notes), and they certainly do not explain violence directed against strikers.

Fishback then turns to frustration as a cause of coal-strike violence. It is worth noting that each of the frustration explanations carries the assumption that miners alone committed strike violence, since it is their frustration and not that of mine-guards or operators or detectives or troops that comes under discussion. Fishback begins with "the Davies J-curve explanation." According to this, workers "experience substantial growth in opportunities and expect the growth to continue. When their expectations are not met and wages don't rise or are cut, frustration leads to a greater likelihood of violence." Fishback rejects this explanation, arguing in particular that it does not apply to the CF & I strike since Colorado operators raised wages prior to the strike, but "the miners made union recognition the prime issue" (6). However, it is doubtful the wage increase raised expectations among most Colorado miners because they saw these improvements for what they were: a management tactic to defeat the union.

Another explanation involving frustration has to do with the deprivations attending the long duration of some strikes, and the problems of living in a tent colony. Fishback writes, "Strike benefits from the union, when available, were low and strikers whose savings had run out depended on fellow workers and sympathetic merchants for food." Fishback questions this explanation for violence, noting that some strikes erupted into violence early rather than late. He also points out that strikers could and often did leave the strike region, returning when the strike was over (7). I would add that this argument does not fit the CF & I strike because life in the tent colonies was better for these strikers than it had been in the coal camps.

Fishback next argues that coal miners who lived in company towns probably experienced more frustration with their employers than did urban workers who could blame their troubles on various parties and agents (storekeeper, landlord, police, etc.). In company coal towns, company agents filled every position of power. Fishback writes, "when the frustration was compounded by a sense that the operator controlled local law enforcement, a resort to violence was more likely" (7).

There is no question that life in the coal camps provided experiences perceived by southern Colorado miners and their families to be degrading, humiliating, undemocratic, and unfair. This contributed to the community's ability to form into a cohesive community of resistance. But did resentments stirred up in the undemocratic coal camps contribute to violence during strikes? There is little or no evidence that they did, although connections exist between life in the camps and certain violent incidents during strikes. When strikers shot Bob Lee they were repaying his habitual brutality toward miners and his violence against women. Again, the beating of Tony Gorci by mineguards at the inception of the strike related directly to his activities before the strike. But these cases (as well as the shooting of the Baldwin Feltz detective Belcher, probably by unionists) suggest, not outbursts resulting from frustration, but planned acts of revenge.

Fishback next turns to the classic explanation of coal miners' propensity to strike put forward in 1954 by sociologists Clark Kerr and Abraham Siegel.[73] This explanation holds that the isolation of certain types of workers in company towns explains their readiness to strike. (Kerr and Siegel explore mainly the propensity to strike, not violence, which they mention only twice and then rather casually. Fishback interprets their argument as one to explain violence, a reading I question.)

Kerr and Siegel describe miners as almost "a race apart." They characterize the community as an "isolated mass" and argue that miners lacked upward mobility and that their skills were not transferable to other industries. Their isolation from the moderating influence of the rest of society rendered them more strike-prone.

Fishback argues (correctly, I think) that the isolation of coal miners is exaggerated for the early years of the century. He notes the intense mobility of the workforce—miners frequently traveled from region to region, always carrying news from other places—and he also notes the melting-pot character of coal communities. I would add that by 1900, unskilled workers pouring into the industry from Europe and the South usually came to mining from other occupations such as carpentry or farming. Miners of Anglo-Saxon origin who had learned the trade from their fathers fit Kerr and Siegel's description of skilled workers with nontransferrable skills, but by 1900 these particular miners had many opportunities for upward mobility.[74]

It is true that in southern Colorado the remote, company-owned camps were economically and geographically isolated, even if mobility and diversity diluted the isolation. However, southern Colorado miners were not more strike-prone than miners who lived in less isolated communities. The isolation argument remains questionable.

73. Clark Kerr and Abraham Siegel, "The Interindustry Propensity to Strike—an International Comparison," in *Industrial Conflict*, ed. Arthur Kornhouser et al. (New York, 1954).
74. For a discussion of upward mobility among miners see Long, *Where the Sun Never Shines*, 128–29 and 157–58.

Isolation can also be psychological, cultural, or political. In its patriotism and in its belief in democracy the CF & I strike community was not isolated but rather identified with the larger community. This identification served to validate their criticisms of the firms and contributed, I think, to their propensity to strike. The April 20 attack by uniformed representatives of the state momentarily broke this identification. In the extreme instance of the ten-day rebellion, the isolation argument carries weight: strikers felt outraged, betrayed, and totally alone.

Finally, Fishback examines (and quickly disputes) the notion that coal workers were violent by nature. This notion mainly refers to Appalachian mountain culture famous for Hatfield and McCoy types of feuds. Whatever one might say about Appalachian mountain culture, after 1900 the majority of Appalachian coal workers had not grown up in the region. In West Virginia for instance, half were "new immigrants" from Europe and a quarter were blacks who had migrated from the south.[75]

This fallacious notion of the coal miner's violent nature could as easily be put forward to explain the violence in the shoot-'em-up Wild West, and can be refuted on the same grounds. The concept is overreaching, involves misconceptions about the composition of the mining population, and purveys stereotypes about coal miners. But the question remains, Was there a culture of violence in the coal camps?

It seems likely that southern Colorado mineguards were involved in a culture of violence, though one unrelated to regional culture. Before the strike it was entirely usual for mineguards to deal with a union organizer by beating him up. For many years anyone who dared defy the coal operators, according to one observer, "was in a constant danger of physical reprisal. More than one man was murdered, and scores were beaten and driven out of the county."[76] What adverse consequences could a mineguard expect for beating up a union organizer or for raping a miner's wife? In a word, none whatever. In southern Colorado the coal firms controlled the county legal systems from the sheriff's office to judges to courts. This was no coal miner's paranoia but a situation amply documented by state and federal investigators among others.[77] Violence on the part of mineguards did not result in criminal penalties, a situation that gave free rein to the more violent among them. Year after year mineguards enforced the company policy of excluding suspected union organizers by using force backed up by violence, a very effective strategy indeed. This is not strike violence but certainly it pertains to the discussion. There is simply no comparable record of systematic violence on the part of Colorado coal miners.

Fishback now turns to the question of whether violence was ever used by either side as a conscious decision, as a strategy for winning the strike. The use of aggres-

---

75. Kenneth R. Bailey, "A Judicious Mixture: Negroes and Immigrants in the West Virginia Mines, 1880–1917, *West Virginia History* 34 (January 1973), 144; Frank J. Sheridan, "Italian, Slavic and Hungarian Unskilled Immigrant Laborers in the United States." *Bulletin of the Bureau of Labor No. 72,* 1907, 1971, 435.

76. Congressman Edward Keating quoted in McGovern, "Colorado Coal Strike," 54.

77. See McGovern, "Colorado Coal Strike," 67–75.

sive violence had costs for both sides, he writes, "because it damaged relations between the two groups and often led to retaliation in kind" (12).

For miners, Fishback argues, there were many disadvantages of resorting to violence: retaliation of operators, the bringing in of state troops, the eventual loss of the strike. (I would add to the list the enormous legal defense costs the UMWA faced in the wake of violent incidents.) Fishback questions whether strikers used violence as a strategy without alluding to the UMWA, a mistake since the union determined the strategy. He questions whether violence was sometimes used by strikers as a last resort.

CF & I strike organizers such as Mother Jones, Mike Livoda, and John Lawson repeatedly urged strikers to hold together and to refrain from using violence.[78] On their part, operators repeatedly denounced Mother Jones for inciting violence. There is simply no evidence for this, and Colorado operators themselves could not find any.[79] She very effectively incited miners to strike, not to commit violence. One of the union's basic tasks during the long months of the strike was to prevent a violent response to provocation. The UMWA was well aware, as Fishback points out, that the disadvantages of using violence outweighed any possible advantages. This is not to suggest that strikers were never violent, but rather that violence was most emphatically not the policy of the union, district or national.

The exception to this well-documented UMWA policy was the use of physical aggression by women on the picket line and in other situations. Men on both sides of this conflict felt strongly that it was unmanly to strike a woman. Contemporary views about proper manly conduct went along with widely held views on womanly behavior. But, significantly, ideals for *womanly* behavior in the working-class communities of the coal camps diverged from those of say, middle-class or wealthy people in Denver. For such middle-class women, hitting a soldier with an umbrella or cursing him out would definitely not qualify as womanly behavior. In contrast, the women of the coal communities felt they were exercising their *womanly* and *wifely* prerogatives when they engaged in such activities.

Mineguards and CNG troops alike repeatedly castigated the miners' wives for their "unwomanly" language and for aggressive behavior on the picket line. They understood that the union used this class split in conceptions of ideal womanhood (to put it in 1990s terms) to pursue the aims of the strike. The women could enter volatile situations potentially deadly for their husbands and fathers, because their opponents could strike back only at the cost of violating their own strongly held values concerning manly behavior. (In my view, Mother Jones, who displayed physical bravado and "unwomanly" language, but who also held highly traditional views on women's roles, was so influential with miners in part because she repre-

78. See note 49.

79. For documentation of Mother Jones see Edward M. Steel, ed., *The Correspondence of Mother Jones* (Pittsburgh, 1985) and *The Speeches of Mother Jones* (Pittsburgh, 1986); Philip S. Foner, ed. *Mother Jones Speaks* (New York, 1983).

sented ideal womanhood exactly as it was conceived in coal communities. A militant "mother," she was a larger-than-life version of the typical miner's wife.)[80]

The detective Belcher's probable assassination arranged by out-of-region unionists notwithstanding, random violence by strikers worked to their disadvantage, and the UMWA opposed it, both officially and unofficially. The Ludlow incident changed this. Local union officers joined in the Call to Rebellion and helped collect arms for it. However, within three days District 15 officials were frantically trying to stop the rebellion. It is significant that the UMWA as well as the operators petitioned President Wilson to order federal troops into the strike field.

Were coal operators, then, inclined to use violence as a strategy? The possible benefit, Fishback notes, would be to intimidate miners to return to work, but the greater disadvantage was that "the miners were often willing to retaliate in kind" and that violence could prolong a strike. Furthermore, Fishback writes, aggressive violence damaged relations with strikers, most of whom would return to work. Firms that used violence gained a bad reputation among miners and this in turn compounded the firm's difficulties in attracting productive workers, an ongoing problem for firms. This would deter the operators from using violence as a deliberate tactic.

Fishback asks whether operators might have followed the more devious strategy of trying to provoke miners to violence so that the governor would send in militia to protect company property, thus shifting the cost to taxpayers. (Unionists persistently accused Colorado operators of this.) Fishback counters this by arguing that violence by militia had the same negative effect for operators with the added disadvantage that operators exerted less control over the militia than over their own mineguards. I would note here that whatever their real interests, Colorado operators lobbied intensely for the calling out of the Guard, perceiving it as functioning unequivocally in their interests.

What of detective agencies, including the Baldwin Feltz? Of them Fishback writes that agencies "who wished to continue in business for the long run had incentives not to provoke incidents because the vast majority of employers did not want to hire a firm that provoked violence" (21). This fits Fishback's argument but ignores the notorious violence of Baldwin Feltz detectives, who stayed in business for a very long time.

He concludes that "the self-defense option of hiring mineguards or paying supplements to local law enforcement may have been the least costly strategy." He adds "Throughout the strike the employer weighed the extra costs of acceding to the strikers' demands against the cost of maintaining the guard force and the lower productivity of replacement workers" (21).

These observations describe a hypothetical management functioning rationally, comparing the costs of various alternatives and pursuing them accordingly. They

80. For a description of the women's worldview see Priscilla Long, "The Women of the Colorado Fuel and Iron Strike, 1913–1914," in *Women, Work, and Protest: A Century of US Women's Labor History*, ed. Ruth Milkman (Boston, 1985).

are quite accurate for some coal firms, but do not fit CF & I management before 1915. CF & I managers opposed the UMWA with fanatical zeal. As Bowers expressed it, company managers were prepared to fight the union "until our bones are bleached white as chalk in these Rocky Mountains."[81]

Bowers did not give a hoot for anyone's opinion. He derided federal officials, despised strikers, one and all, and believed in his absolute right (given Rockefeller approval) to run the company as he pleased. Among miners, the reputation of the CF & I could not have been worse. It did not concern Bowers.

He represented a management style that the Rockefeller response to Ludlow would forever change. The public relations campaign instituted by John D. Rockefeller Jr. after the public relations fiasco of Ludlow gave the appearance of compromise with coal miners, and recognized the importance of public opinion. It deeply offended Bowers: his inability to adjust resulted in his removal from CF & I management. The new face of the company, put on after the absolute defeat of the union, inspired extreme distress among several lower managers. (The new policies did not recognize the union but did permit organizers into the camps). As these loyal managers expressed it, they had sacrificed a great deal for the *principle* of keeping out the union.[82]

What of the relationship between the CF & I and the CNG? Did the company exert less control over the CNG than over company-employed mineguards? Was the Guard neutral, or did it come into the fight on the side of the operators? Certainly, troops came into the strike field with a semblance of neutrality. Many of the original enlisted men were college students and others who genuinely had nothing against the strikers. But the neutrality of the Guard eroded as the strike wore on. By April 20 the Guard was abjectly in the control of the coal firms. Putting aside the issue of troops escorting strike-breakers, which to strikers put them on the operator's side but which to others may not, a neutral peacekeeping force cannot maintain credibility while accepting into its ranks combatants from one of the sides. Neither can it pretend to neutrality while one side is paying its bills and providing various services and favors.

How much control, if any, did coal firms exert over state governments? The Colorado government of course comprised a mix of forces. Labor interests had accumulated enough power to pass a mining law but not enough to get it enforced. Business interests—and the CF & I was Colorado's largest firm—wielded significant influence in the state government. But the CF & I's greatest power was in the southern Colorado county governments, which were thoroughly corrupted to coal-company ends.

What of the influence of coal firms on governors? Fishback states that in general governors were not pawns of the coal companies, although strikers might perceive

---

81. L. M. Bowers to Rockefeller, Jr., September 29, 1913, Item 100, Box 28, L. M. Bowers Papers.

82. For middle manager response to the company union see Long, *Where the Sun Never Shines*, 318–20.

them as such because the governor would call out militia troops who would in turn escort strike-breakers to their jobs. Governor Ammons certainly did not begin as a pawn, or even as a candidate, of Colorado coal firms. But tragically for everyone concerned, he lacked the strength of character required for the role history handed him. He soon crumbled under coal-operator pressure. Ultimately, he lost his independence entirely. He ended a pawn of the companies, unless there is a better term to describe a governor who would allow his policy statements to be composed by the public relations department of a coal firm.

Fishback concludes that violence worked equally to the disadvantage of both sides. In the case of the CF & I strike it seems to me that violence, though it came with heavy costs for both sides, worked greatly to the disadvantage of the union side and greatly to the advantage of the company side. Violence served operator interests in important ways. It resulted directly in the interventions of the CNG and eventually of federal troops. Both these interventions caused the defeat of the strike. With the entry of federal troops the violence ended, the (military) costs to the companies ended, and because federal troops began escorting strike-breakers to their jobs, the strike was defeated with no further ado. Because, as Fishback notes, the enforced laws of the time tended to protect property rights but not civil and human rights— the unenforced Colorado coal mining laws are an excellent case in point—any intervention by state or national government tended to accrue to the advantage of the company. Violence catalyzed these interventions, which in turn served the interests of the company.

It is also true that the Ludlow incident was damaging to the reputation of the company, embarrassing to the Rockefeller interests, and put the plight of the strikers on the national agenda, thereby serving the strikers' interests. Bowers himself paid the high price of losing his position in the company. Ultimately, the costs to the company, including financial costs, were extremely high. But the wild card in this result, the thing no one predicted, was that women and children died at Ludlow. What if only men had died at Ludlow? Would there have been a ten-day rebellion? Would the Rockefellers have responded as they did? Would the country have responded as it did?

After arguing that violence does not essentially serve the interests of either side (an argument that the case of the CF & I strike does not wholly support) Fishback concludes that the likelihood was that both sides armed in self-defense, seeking to deter the use of violence by the other side. He discusses in turn the considerations of operators and of unionists in deciding to so arm. Here he uses the "prisoner's dilemma" model: not to arm gives the advantage to the side that has armed, whereas to arm cancels that advantage. This dilemma develops in part because of limited communication between the two sides. Once both sides were armed, the probability of a confrontation escalating into violence increased. The act of one individual could quickly turn a peaceful confrontation into a violent one. Each side then believed the other was willing to use violence. Aggressive violence then became less costly because the employer-worker relationship was already damaged (13).

According to Fishback, anti-union operators armed in self-defense because they perceived the UMWA as a violent organization. In addition, they armed in self-defense because they feared local law enforcement would be inadequate to defend their property in which they had invested substantial capital and inadequate to defend replacement workers.

Fishback now lists the reasons miners armed in self-defense, or why, as he phrases it, "[t]he miners developed an ideological basis for resorting to violence." These reasons are that they considered the local government to be biased against them in strike situations, and that they distrusted the courts, as well as the local and state political process, claiming the coal operators dominated the state government. In some cases, Fishback writes, the constitutional rights of free speech, free assembly, and the right to bear arms had been infringed by deputies, mineguards, and/or state militia. In the company towns, Fishback writes, "[e]ven though the miners had signed away these rights voluntarily, they perceived the company's actions as stomping on their civil rights to peaceful assembly and free speech" (15, 16).

Leaving aside the question of whether requiring a worker to sign an agreement in exchange for a job is strictly voluntary, Fishback has here listed some miners' grievances against the company, along with, to take the case of Colorado, their accurate perception that neither the local or state government was rushing to their defense. It is unclear why such perceptions and grievances should constitute an "ideological basis for resorting to violence," as against an ideological basis for going on strike, or why Fishback has slipped into this language, forgoing, for the moment, "self-defense."

At the inception of the strike, the UMWA armed strikers just as the operators armed mineguards. No doubt the union thought the strikers would be shot at by mineguards. No doubt the mineguards felt unsafe around strikers. Once both sides were armed, the chances of violence increased. Fishback lays out the scenario as follows. A confrontation might develop and, through bad luck, someone trips and fires a shot into a crowd. In the confusion, others start shooting and the event explodes. Either side may have trouble controlling its more aggressive members. A hothead could catalyze the escalation of what had started as an accident or as a minor confrontation. Fishback points out that the advantage of such an explanation is that it does not seek to blame one side or the other. He emphasizes again that most strikes were entirely peaceful, and that most actors on either side wanted to avoid violence.

He now turns to a discussion of hotheaded individuals on both operator and union sides. Certainly there were hotheads on each side, trigger-happy mineguards, strikers difficult to control. Fishback projects a scenario in which strikers faced a "public bad" problem in which the actions of an individual impose costs on others because the person committing the bad act cannot be identified. Reactions to a shot fired, for instance, would be directed at all strikers rather than at the man who started the trouble.

Fishback's discussion centers on a particular hot-tempered union official in West

Virginia. To keep the focus here on Colorado, the evidence is overwhelming that organizers John Lawson, Mike Livoda, Louis Tikas and, most emphatically, Mother Jones were engaged in keeping strikers from violence or from violent retaliation. This persistent effort on the part of organizers provides evidence for Fishback's point that indeed there were hotheads among the strikers. In fact, the UMWA's letter to operators deploring the gunfire in early October virtually expresses Fishback's scenario.

However Fishback skates on thin ice when he begins to speculate on whether or not the UMWA was a violent organization. "The UMWA's attitudes toward violence are not easily documented," he writes. Yet he has utilized neither the extensive United Mine Workers papers (regional or national) nor recent scholarly books that provide elaborately documented histories of this important union.[83] Perhaps, he speculates, "national leaders might press for violence in West Virginia to enhance the chances of winning a strike later in time or in Pennsylvania" (19). A reading of the confidential, verbatim minutes of UMWA executive board proceedings would quickly convince any scholar of the absurdity of such a statement. E. L. Doyle, secretary-treasurer of District 15, flatly asserted to federal investigators that the UMWA was "absolutely opposed to violence either in labor troubles or otherwise."[84] He served as secretary to the strike policy committee: his minutes reveal no hint of planned violence.

Fishback then raises as a respectable scholarly view the possibility that Mother Jones instigated violence among strikers, the opinion of the anti-union operators of the time. To my knowledge (I have spent years researching Mother Jones) there is no evidence to support such a view. Fishback relies on a single, flagrantly unbalanced account to suggest that Mother Jones would "shout a call to arms" at miners' rallies, or that she would say one thing and wink to indicate another. His source, Howard Lee, former attorney general of West Virginia, claims that Mother Jones "was in the forefront inciting violence in every major labor disturbance in America."[85]

Mother Jones did not shout calls to arms at miners' rallies. No transcription of a Mother Jones speech, no letter, no reliable reminiscence indicates such an activity. Her task as a paid UMWA organizer was to get miners to fight the companies by sticking together, by striking. Fishback ignores the archival sources to put forward an opinion unsupported by them.[86]

What did happen at Ludlow? As in Fishback's hypothetical scenario, there were loud reports (never finally explained), and then the shooting started. We don't know who fired the first shot. Nevertheless, this was no real confrontation, there were no

83. See for instance, Long, *Where the Sun Never Shines*, Melvyn Dubofsky and Warren Van Tine, *John L. Lewis* (New York, 1977); Maier B. Fox, *United We Stand: The United Mine Workers of America, 1890–1990* (Washington, D.C., 1990), and others.

84. CIR *Report*, 6962.

85. Howard B. Lee, *Bloodletting in Appalachia* (Morgantown, W.Va., (1969), 189.

86. For documentation on Mother Jones see note 79.

two crowds facing each other. I term what happened an attack, not a battle (the term used by the operators and by many subsequent scholars) because troops were surrounding the colony; strikers were not surrounding a mine, or blocking a road. All day troops fired directly into the tents full of women and children, while strikers fired back from positions outside the colony. (Many families were saved by the pits.) I call it an attack because the colonists, not being up and dressed, were totally unprepared for the emergency; had it been a battle it would have ended at 4:30 when the strikers ran out of ammunition. What happened after 4:30 seems to me to involve a riot of CNG troops; that is, of mineguards in CNG uniform. The militia became, in the words of the strike's first historian, George S. McGovern, an "uncontrollable, murderous, pillaging mob."[87] Senator Helen Ring Robinson had reported that people from both sides had told her the tent colony would soon be wiped out. This was an accurate prediction of what happened, and I speculate that it was the intent of the troops gathering at Ludlow that day. In this case it is highly doubtful that "most actors on either side wanted to avoid violence."

Infusing these events was the virulent ethnic hatred (xenophobia) felt toward the strikers and expressed freely and publicly by the Guard, by operators, and by others. The strikers were seen as "foreigners," as ignorant, as childish, as "savage south European peasants," as "bloodthirsty." The commander of Troop B, a hated mineguard named Karl Linderfelt, habitually referred to the strikers as "wops." The managers, in their fanatical opposition to the UMWA, gave such troop-mineguards license for a rampage by their unequivocal defense of any behavior whatever on the company side.

Fishback's scenario does not seem to fit the Ludlow incident and his somewhat idealized view of operators disregards the benefits accruing to Colorado operators, at least from their point of view, from the use of systematic force and violence during nonstrike periods. These policies served to keep the union out. But his scenario does accurately describe many sorts of strike incidents, including many that occurred during the Colorado Fuel and Iron strike. The exchanges of gunfire in October, and incidents such as that in Walsenburg, provide illustrations of a tense confrontation veering out of control, with hotheads on either side.

Fishback's conceptual framework brings the scholarly discussion of strike violence to a new level of complexity. In general, its strength is that it seeks to explain violence on both sides of the struggle, in contrast to explanations that perhaps unconsciously blame coal miners for all coal-strike violence. New scholarly work done on the level of particular strikes ought to complicate this excellent if somewhat overreaching model to account for variations to it, as well as to confirm its generalizations where appropriate.

87. McGovern, "Colorado Coal Strike," 287.

CHAPTER FIFTEEN

LADIES IN WHITE
Female Activism in the Southern Illinois Coalfields, 1932–1938

STEPHANE E. BOOTH

In perfect order, each dressed in white, white band around her head, they assembled. They came marching from every corner of the state with their banners and their music. They came in rattletrap Fords, in trucks, on trolleys. They came from the Midlands, which has borne the brunt of the fight against the Peabody Company and John Lewis's strikebreakers the part of the country where militia and gunmen have been terrorizing the miners for a better part of a year.

These fighting women who had lived so long under terror saw with joy the banners of the women from all over the state. They came from fifty-one different communities. They marched eight abreast, and five coal-digger bands led them in their hour march from the state arsenal to the capitol. Watching the white-clad women streaming past with their banners and music was a congregation of miners. They were looking on a new sight, the miners' women taking up the men's fight and protesting against the four years of hunger, want, and the use of armed forces of the state to aid in breaking the rank-and-file union.[1]

1. Dee Garrison, ed., *Rebel Pen: The Writings of Mary Heaton Vorse* (New York: Monthly Review, 1985): 153–54.

This protest march on January 26, 1933, described by Mary Heaton Vorse in the *New Republic*, in which ten thousand women from the Illinois coalfields participated, is a testimony to the seriousness of the crisis that developed in Illinois District 12 of the United Mine Workers of America during the early 1930s, and of the strong concern felt by the women in these fields. Coal miners' wives and daughters were no strangers to deprivation. But the conditions that developed in the Illinois coalfields at the outset of the decade forced these women not simply to follow in the steps of Mary Harris "Mother" Jones, who urged "her boys" to take a courageous stand against the coal operators, but to go beyond her by forming a Women's Auxiliary to the Progressive Miners of America that would protect and advance their own position as women as well.

What prompted the Women's Auxiliary of the Progressive Miners of America to be established when it was, in November 1932? Throughout the 1930s, the need for a union that would be more representative of the true interests of the coal miners than was District 12 of the UMWA, and of an auxiliary to support it, was stressed generally through articles, letters to the editor, official union publications, resolutions, poetry and songs published in the *Progressive Miner*. But the issue that brought matters to a head, and that brought the Women's Auxiliary itself into being, was the crisis created by the betrayals of the UMWA leadership and in particular of John L. Lewis and of District 12 President John H. Walker after they forced the Illinois miners to accept an unwanted contract in August 1932. It was common to see John L. Lewis and John Walker referred to as despots, tyrants, and thugs. In a letter to the editor on February 17, 1933, for example, Marguerite Soustelle urged her sisters "to join the ranks of our brothers to help repulse the hordes of Huns and the modern Attilas—John L. Lewis. Help us to form one solid front line to stop the invasion of the gangsters, thugs and gunmen who under the leadership of the U.M.W. of A., usurp the right of our brothers, and help the coal corporations to bend down the miners to the deepest misery that human history has ever known."[2]

The years 1932–39 were some of the most violent in the history of the Illinois coalfields. It was a time marked by shootings, bombings, and the suspension of civil rights—an actual war between a new union, the Progressive Miners of America (PMA) and the old, the United Mine Workers of America (UMWA), which was backed by Peabody Coal Company, one of the largest coal companies in the country.

The foundations for this war, in which women were to play an important role, were laid in April 1932 when Illinois District 12 went on strike for higher wages leaving 43,000 miners idle.[3] The coal companies wanted to lower the pay scale 50–60% because Illinois miners were receiving higher wages than miners in other states. This caused Illinois coal to be sold at a higher price, thereby limiting demand for the coal.[4] In June 1932, the coal operators proposed a cut in wages from $6.10

2. *Progressive Miner*, February 1, 1933; hereafter cited as *PM*.
3. *Illinois State Journal*, April 1, 1932.
4. *Taylorville Daily Breeze*, June 9, 1932.

to $4.00 per eight-hour day. The union leadership in response proposed a cut in pay and working hours ($4.75 per six-hour day), thereby increasing the number of miners employed.[5] Each side rejected the other's terms. A commission was appointed and Illinois Governor Emmerson urged arbitration. The commission reached an agreement on a wage scale on July 8, 1932, setting the basic wage at $5.50 per eight-hour day.

A mass meeting of miners was immediately scheduled and held at the state arsenal in Springfield to ask John Walker, Illinois District 12 president of the UMWA, to allow a referendum on the proposed wage scale. The referendum was proposed because many of the rank-and-file miners were unhappy with the terms of the commission's agreement. These miners wanted a basic wage of $7.00 per eight-hour day.[6] Following this meeting, many of these miners decided to hold another meeting in Taylorville, in the evening, as they returned to southern Illinois. The purpose of this meeting was to protest the wage cut in the mining area dominated by Peabody Coal Company, a company strongly in favor of the wage cut. At the appointed time, approximately 1,500 miners (no women were reported to have participated) were met at the edge of Taylorville by the sheriff and 200 deputies, with drawn guns, and forbidden to hold their meeting.[7] The miners then gathered at the junction of Routes 48 and 24 east of Taylorville where several speeches were given. The battle lines were drawn and the mine war began.

Meanwhile, during the latter part of July 1932, District 12 held a referendum that resulted in the rank and file rejecting the proposed contract four to one. On August 10, 1932, the referendum was once again presented to the miners. After the election, the ballot boxes were shipped to the Ridgely Farmers State Bank in Springfield, where they were stored in a vault to prevent tampering prior to the actual count. While the ballot boxes were being transported from the Ridgely Farmers State Bank to District headquarters of the UMWA for the actual count, they were stolen by two armed men. The ownership of the automobile in which these two men were riding was traced to Fox Hughes, vice president of the Illinois district of the UMWA, and one of John L. Lewis's "henchmen."[8]

Lewis promptly declared a state of emergency, claiming that it would take too long to get hold of a duplicate copy of the ballots, to check out the actual vote. He signed the contract, which had the effect of putting it immediately into operation. With this usurption of power, all the negative feelings toward John L. Lewis surfaced once again. Illinois miners recalled how Lewis had imposed a contract on them in February 1924 forcing them to accept a wage scale that Illinois coal operators quickly repudiated after implementation, and how in 1928 Lewis replaced Franklin County local union officials with his own appointees. With Lewis's actions

5. Ibid., June 17, 1932.
6. Ibid., July 12, 1932.
7. Editorial, "The Illinois Miners' Revolt," *New Republic* 72 (September 7, 1932): 87.
8. Editorial, *Nation* 135 (August 24, 1932): 155.

in 1932, the prediction of Mother Jones in 1919 appeared to be true: "Mark my words, John Lewis will sell the miners out. I know John Lewis. He don't think a thing in the world but John Lewis. He's a strong man, and he's a bad man."[9]

In response to actions taken by Lewis, miners from various coalfields in Illinois met at Gillespie, Illinois, on September 2, 1932, and formed a new union that they felt was better suited to their needs, the Progressive Miners of America (PMA). The women quickly followed the lead of the men and formed auxiliaries for the Progressive Miners of America, with such groups active in Gillespie, Staunton, Mt. Olive, Carlinville, Kincaid, Taylorville, Panama, West Frankfort, Benld, and Springfield.

Even though women's participation in support of union activities was not new in the southern Illinois coalfields (as evidenced by their march through the Belleville area in 1919 to "encourage" women whose husbands were not supporting the strike to do so), a women's auxiliary that was more than a ladies' aid society, was a new concept for most of these women. Women's associations had formed for brief periods of time in Illinois in order to support local strikes (usually wildcat strikes) but the impetus for a more formalized approach was instigated after Pat Ansboury, a militant coal miner, returned from Indiana where he met Hazel Kimmell, who headed such an auxiliary in that area. The first auxiliary was formed in West Frankfort, Illinois, where a soup kitchen was started, in order to respond to the needs of striking miners and their families.[10]

The "Illinois Women's Auxiliary of the Progressive Miners of America was organized at the state convention in Gillespie, Ill, November 2–4, 1932."[11] In drafting the constitution for the Women's Auxiliary, the ideal of rank-and-file democracy prevailed. Auxiliary officers received no salary, nor could they continue in the same office for more than one year; and the president of the auxiliary, upon completion of her term, had to retire. The local auxiliaries also tried to maintain rule by the rank and file by encouraging all members to be actively involved through committee membership and active participation at meetings. Meetings often began with a song, followed by an update on the strike proceedings. Local business was then conducted with decisions made on strike relief efforts, political responses, and militant activities. The diverse political backgrounds of members made auxiliary meetings very exciting and unpredictable. Dues were collected at each meeting, but those unable to pay were still encouraged and expected to attend. Everyone's help was needed. The meeting closed with the energetic singing of "Solidarity Forever."

The woman elected as the first president of the Women's Auxiliary and faced with the challenge of bringing together into one organization women from diverse political, religious, ethnic, and geographic backgrounds was Agnes Burns Wieck. Wieck, often compared to Mother Jones, was an activist in the labor movement.

---

9. Mary Heaton Vorse, "Illinois Miners," *Scribner's Magazine* (March 1933): 169.

10. *Women's Auxiliary Progressive Miners of America First Annual Report*, 8–9. Agnes Burns Wieck Papers, Walter Reuther Archives, Wayne State University, Detroit, Michigan.

11. Ibid., 8.

Meeting Eugene Debs as a young woman, Agnes discovered an ideology—socialism—that matched her own vision of a world for workers, a world she would try to build.

While working as a reporter for the *Harrisburg Chronicle*, she was elected by the Illinois State Committee of the Women's Trade Union League, as a delegate to the league's national convention. While at the convention, she was awarded a scholarship to attend the league's school in Chicago. In 1916, after completing her training as a labor organizer, she was given an assignment to speak at the District 12 convention of the UMWA, where she drove home the point that women were essential to the success of trade unionism, a belief she would put into practice as a writer and as president of the Women's Auxiliary. Agnes began writing for the *Illinois Miner* under the name Mrs. Lotta Work, where she introduced the idea of a women's auxiliary, a idea that would reach fruition nine years later.[12]

It then became necessary to keep the miners and their families apprised of the situation. In order to help solve this problem, the new union established its own newspaper to disseminate the news of the organization under the editorship of Gerry Allard. Within the newspaper the Women's Auxiliary was given a page in which to report its views. The heading on that page read: "Devoted to the mothers, wives and daughters of the coal miners. Members are invited to use this column to inform the working women of the activities of the Ladies Auxiliary in mining struggles."[13] The page was edited by Joan Lee for two years and contained such things as editorials on the conditions in the coalfields, candidates to support for office, working conditions of women in industry, reports on auxiliary conventions, notification of activities planned by local auxiliaries, a copy of the auxiliary constitution, and the serialization of the *Autobiography of Mother Jones*. The tone of the page's editorials and articles depended upon who was in control of the organization at a particular time, the right wing or left wing.

However, the feelings of the PMA about Lewis and UMWA leadership was best expressed in the poetry and songs written by the female auxiliary's members. One such poem, "Fate of the U.M.W. of A." by Mrs. Jesse Wilson, portrayed the UMWA leadership in this way:

John L. Lewis and John H. Walker are our masters, we shall always want.

They maketh us to struggle in the darkness of coalfields. They leadth us in the paths of disaster for their name's sake.

Yea though we walk through the valley of starvation, we shall always fear the cold, for thou art against us; thy deputies and thy gang they torture us.

12. David Thoreau Wieck, *Woman from Spillertown: A Memoir of Agnes Burns Wieck* (Carbondale: Southern Illinois University Press, 1992): 100.

13. *PM*, September 16, 1932.

Thou preparest a vast check-off from our pay in the presence of thy cheaters, thou anointeth our heads with worry; our heads runneth over.

Surely disaster and terror shall follow all the days of our life; and we shall dwell in the house divided against itself forever.[14]

In the same vein, Lillian Burnette gave the auxiliaries a song to sing, "On to Victory," to be sung to the tune "Marching Through Georgia":

John Lewis and Peabody Coal
are working hand in hand
Stirring up dissension 'mongst
The miners of our land.
But we will not listen to
Their dictates and commands
For we are marching to victory.[15]

Another theme used in these writings to encourage miners and their women to join the PMA was the need to provide a unified front in order to obtain certain economic and social goals. As pointed out by Rose North, "In order to maintain what conditions we have won, to improve them, to insure more and better laws for the benefit of the working people, to strengthen the laws pertaining to child labor, the compensation laws, and other safety measures we must organize. All we have ever won or can hope to win was and is through organized effort."[16]

Mrs. I. J. Hoy's advice to miners and auxiliary members was to "hang together, stand up for each other, for if we don't we cannot expect others to stand up for us."[17] One way to "hang together" was for auxiliary members to participate in the march described in the introduction to this chapter. Agnes Burns Wieck, president of the auxiliary,[18] assessed the gains of this march by writing, "You demonstrated our solidarity. You proved beyond any doubt that the Progressive Miners of America is the dominant union in the Illinois coalfields, the union the miners want . . . You gave warning that the only government that can hope to endure is a government of the people, by the people and for the people."[19]

The need for a feeling of solidarity was also presented through song. Many auxiliary meetings either began or ended with the singing of "Solidarity Forever." During the mid-1930s one song a month was published in the *Progressive Miner* on the

14. *PM*, January 13, 1933.
15. *PM*, September 7, 1934.
16. *PM*, August 4, 1933.
17. *PM*, September 27, 1935.
18. Agnes Burns Wieck's militant activities for workers' rights are highlighted in her biography, *Woman from Spillertown: A Memoir of Agnes Burns Wieck* (Carbondale: Southern Illinois University Press, 1992).
19. *PM*, February 3, 1933.

auxiliary's page in hopes of stirring members' emotions. Many of these songs were written by members such as Mrs. Charles Peppard's "Add Another Name" (sung to the tune "Throw Another Log on the Fire") which provided the view:

> . . . United we will keep on fighting
> Till our glorious cause is won,
> So keep on adding names to our roll call
> Till John L. Lewis' force is outdone.[20]

Or Lillian Burnette's "The Union Forever" (sung to the tune "The Battle Cry of Freedom"):

> . . . Workers of the world unite
> In labor unions strong.
> That's the only way to gain our freedom
> Fight for equity and right,
> Opposing every wrong,
> That's the only way to gain our freedom.[21]

Still another theme used to inspire auxiliary members was to recall the work and vision of Mother Jones. Auxiliary members wrote poems, songs, and letters to the editor extolling the virtues of Mother Jones and the support she would be giving to the Progressives during this time if she were alive. As one member wrote: "Our boys are still your boys, still carrying on the fight against the forces trying to degrade the miners. You are gone from among us, mother, but your spirit still lives."[22]

The need for a new union that was more responsive to the social, economic, and political problems of the miners and their families was addressed by the Women's Auxiliary. These women were prolific writers on problems they felt their communities and workers in general were facing because of the present economic situation both locally (the mine war) and nationally (Great Depression). It is very difficult, however, to divide these problems into two distinct groups and discuss them individually as they are so closely related.

Auxiliary members in some areas of the state found themselves desperately trying to find ways of feeding families who had no income. This was a topic about which they wrote frequently. One auxiliary member attempted to answer the question "What are we fighting for?" in her poem "The Progressive Miners of America Our Only Salvation":

> . . . It's to keep the wolf
> From coming to our door.

20. *PM*, December 7, 1934.
21. *PM*, July 24, 1936.
22. *PM*, April 21, 1933.

> Peabody's trying to force us
> To work, By starvation;
> The Progressive Miners of America
> Is our only salvation.[23]

But with little provided in the way of federal or state relief funds, the specter of hunger was always present. In hopes of relieving the situation, the Women's Auxiliary leaders presented the following petition to Governor Horner during their march in January 1933

> for increased and more equitable distribution of state aid that will provide us more than a bare subsistence, that will guarantee us food that is nourishing, clothing that is adequate, and homes free from the constant dread of eviction.[24]

Other auxiliary members wrote to Horner themselves describing the situation:

> I am just one of the many thousands of mothers facing the cold winter months trying to figure out a way to keep her little ones in clothes, food and in a warm room, which in all probability will be a big problem indeed, without an income for the past nineteen months and none in sight.[25]

Others took the business community to task for its unfeeling behavior toward the miners:

> Yes, you call us deadbeats. Now just who is to blame? When we are forced to work for nothing or even for starvation wages, tell me, how can we pay our honest debts? You look down on the miners, but what about those who force the miners to work for nothing and the operators who fail to pay off? I suppose they must be loved and respected because they are "business men."[26]

And still others, such as Maud Land, in her poem "A Ton of Coal," tried to draw attention to the conditions under which the miner worked.

> Are you asking the price of a ton of coal?
> I'll tell it to you, as to me it was told;
> All day long in the damp dark earth,

23. *PM*, December 23, 1932.
24. *PM*, February 3, 1933.
25. *PM*, November 24, 1933.
26. *PM*, August 11, 1933.

Digging and toiling for all one's worth.

Maybe a price of a hand you'll pay,
"That all goes in the work"—they say;
Some times a life will be added too;
In this ton of coal delivered to you.

And yet you'll say coal's not high,
Maybe it has cost some one an eye
Or, lamed for life now who can tell,
The price of coal to you they'll sell?

The tears of a miner's widow maybe
Added to the price of coal you can see,
That a ton of coal can cost so dear,
In limbs and lives, and a bitter tear.

Did you ever stop and think, what price
When you sit by the warm fire so nice,
It has cost 'o bring you that ton of coal
From some dark, damp and dangerous hole?

Just breath a prayer for the miner man
And give him a kind thought when e're you can.
Ask yourself the price of a ton of coal
That costs life, and health, perhaps a soul.[27]

The task of providing aid for those on strike continued for years. Fund raising was a necessity and the various local auxiliaries were constantly searching for ways to collect funds in order to purchase food and clothing, or help pay emergency medical or funeral bills. Most auxiliaries held dances and charged a minimal admittance fee (25 cents per couple). Some auxiliaries sponsored dinners and still others raffled items such as box suppers and quilts. Other groups held local talent shows or put on plays. One such play, *Mill Shadows*, written by Tom Tippett, a prominent labor activist of the period, was performed in Gillespie, Illinois, on May 29, 1933. The troupe of players, who were local residents, performed in several towns throughout Illinois to raise money and the play was also broadcast over radio station KSD.[28] Card parties, where euchre and bunco were played, also generated funds. Even the monthly auxiliary meetings were used to raise funds. Part of the dues collected each month went to the relief fund and there was always a door prize to be won.[29]

Another activity in which some of the women engaged was sewing. Material was

27. *PM*, October 26, 1934.
28. *PM*, September 23, 1933.
29. *PM*, February 2, 1934.

solicited from members and townspeople to make clothing for miners' children. Other garments were remade to fit children and old shoes were collected and repaired. As the strike continued, clothes for adults were also made and distributed— usually one garment per person.

Soliciting food from local businesses and townspeople was a constant challenge. Many gave very generously. In the Benld area almost seven tons of food was collected in July 1933 containing such items as sugar, salt, cornmeal, rolled oats, rice, coffee, cereals, bacon, cheese, lard, macaroni, flour, and canned food.[30] Another way auxiliary members helped to alleviate the food problem was by canning food grown in local gardens. Auxiliary members in Staunton canned 285 quarts of food.[31]

A large amount of this food was used to operate local soup kitchens. Depending on the size and "wealth" of the auxiliary, these kitchens operated one to three times a week. In November 1932, the Mt. Olive auxiliary began operating a soup kitchen to feed children at noon. The soup kitchen in Kincaid fed more than three hundred children daily with the help of fourteen auxiliary members. In order to be fed, however, a child did not need to be a son or daughter of a Progressive. As was pointed out in the *Progressive Miner*: "No kiddies are discriminated against. Progressive, United Mine Workers, negro, white, non-miners, all elements are fed with the same impartiality."[32] At times the county governments that were unfriendly toward the Progressives made it almost impossible to operate the kitchens. In the DuQuoin area, local officials stopped the auxiliary from holding meetings and fund-raising activities that funded the kitchen. When the auxiliary in Dowell heard what was happening, they held a dance to provide funds to help keep the kitchen in DuQuoin operational. Enough money was raised in order to keep the kitchen operating until school was dismissed for the summer recess.[33]

Children were not forgotten at holiday time either. Donations of fruit and candy were solicited from local merchants. Many auxiliaries collected broken toys to be repaired and given to the children and usually some type of entertainment was held. Often times, auxiliary members also received treats—canned fruits and vegetables.

The auxiliaries also helped other groups that were in need. In December 1932, there was an explosion in a coal mine in Moweaqua, Illinois, where fifty-four miners lost their lives. Immediately upon hearing about the disaster various members of local auxiliaries from Gillespie, Tovey, Springfield, Benld, Stonington, Pana, and Staunton rushed to aid the families of the victims. These and other auxiliaries sent money to aid the relief work.[34] In 1937, when a flood hit the Benton area, money was sent from the auxiliaries. As the judicial problems in which PMA members found themselves entangled increased, the auxiliaries also established defense funds for these individuals.

30. *PM*, July 21, 1933.
31. *PM*, October 21, 1932.
32. *PM*, May 12, 1933.
33. *PM*, May 12, 1933.
34. *PM*, January 6 and 13, 1933.

Many of the other activities that the Women's Auxiliary members were involved with, however, took them beyond their conventional female roles. Women were involved in picketing, parades, and rallies, served as speakers at male union gatherings and were involved in organizational work. Still others became involved in the political sphere.

Women began attending meetings during the initial days of the UMWA-PMA dispute. Photographs of the crowds that included women were numerous. Around 1932 when violence was not a usual occurrence, women were left home if violence was expected. But by 1934 violence became a common occurrence, and women were found at most parades, meetings, and rallies to show their support for their men and the union. In fact, in the majority of instances, the women outnumbered the men at these parades.[35] At Carlinville on September 8, 1932,

> 545 women from several central Illinois cities, dressed in the immaculate white uniforms of auxiliaries to the Progressive miners' union, paraded through the streets . . . in protest against the new wage scale for miners in the Illinois district. The parade was led by Chief of Police Clarence Rasor, followed by the Gillespie band, several hundred men and a hundred automobiles filled with men, women and children. Each unit carried an American flag. . . .
>
> Starting at 1 o'clock at the courthouse, the parade proceeded to the county fairgrounds, where a crowd estimated at three thousand persons had gathered for the afternoon's program.
>
> Mrs. George Brown, president of the Carlinville auxiliary presided. . . . Mrs. Mary McKeever of Kincaid, one of the oldest women present praised the work of Mother Jones among the miners. Miss Agenline Gorella of Mt. Olive gave several readings and was later called on to make a short talk.
>
> Among other women on the program were Mrs. Maloney of West Frankfort who suffered a broken arm in a clash with Franklin county deputies, Miss Mary Casper of Taylorville, Mrs. Mary Robeck of West Frankfort who organized one of the first auxiliaries in the state, and Mrs. Joe Kobart, also of West Frankfort . . .[36]

Speakers were constantly reminding the women to "support their husbands and sweethearts" but Mrs. Mary McKeever took it one step further: "that if their menfolk did not have enough gumption to stand staunchly for their union, that they should take over the task themselves and refuse to pack their dinner buckets or to keep house for them."[37]

The most memorable march by the auxiliary was the Springfield march, which

35. *PM*, October 6, 1933.
36. *Illinois State Journal*, September 9, 1932.
37. *PM*, October 17, 1932.

occurred on January 26, 1933. One week prior to the march Auxiliary President Agnes Burns Wieck sent out the call for the women to rally in Springfield, Illinois, to present their demands to the governor. Five thousand were expected but 10,000 responded to the call. An organization that held its first convention in November 1932 was able to bring together representatives from fifty-one towns in Illinois to march en masse. They marched in their white uniforms from the state arsenal to the state capitol where the following demands were presented to the governor:

1. restoration of civil liberties in coalfields
2. increased and more equitable distribution of state aid
3. unemployment insurance paid by industry and state
4. defeat of the state's sales tax.[38]

Through press coverage, this march brought the Illinois miners' conflict to the nation's attention.

Women also participated as speakers at these meetings and rallies. Mary Casper of Taylorville spoke many times throughout the state urging miners to support each other and the PMA. Agnes Burns Wieck spent most of her time traveling from meeting hall to meeting hall urging women to join the auxiliary and vote for legislation that favored the worker, and also assuring the miners of the women's support. "If it's going to take courage, we've got it. If it's going to take guts, we've got that, and the women are ready at all times to do all in their power for a powerful organization of miners."[39]

Women were also involved in picketing mines that were still working under the UMWA contract that had been accepted by John L. Lewis and by District 12 President John H. Walker in August 1932. At times these women joined the men on the picket line and at other times they formed their own picket line. In one instance, women established picket lines at the Knoxville Mining Company near Galesburg, where they stoned truck drivers and miners that continued to work. It was reported that they tipped over a loaded truck and pulled the driver out and beat him. The mine operators then decided to shut down the mine.[40] In another instance, members of the auxiliary chased scabs through a cornfield. Throughout this seven-year ordeal, women were found on the picket lines, in all types of weather.

Participation in rallies and meetings as a speaker or supporter as well as on the picket line, put these women in constant peril. As stated earlier, this was one of the most violent periods in Illinois coal-mining history. More than thirty individuals, from both sides, were killed (including one woman) during the course of the Illinois mine wars, and hundreds were injured. The state militia and county governments in the areas still working under the UMWA contract were in many cases working

38. Mary Heaton Vorse, "Women's March," in *Rebel Pen: The Writings of Mary Heaton Vorse*, ed. Dee Garrison (New York: Monthly Review, 1985), 153–56. *PM*, February 3, 1933.

39. *PM*, June 9, 1933.

40. *Illinois State Journal*, June 9, 1933.

against the PMA, adding to the hostility in these war zones. Finding women participating in activities, whether picketing, or attending an auxiliary meeting, did not
promote less violence on the part of the soldiers or deputies. Many times those on
the picket lines were subjected to tear gas and those marching in parades stoned by
onlookers. Still others were clubbed and arrested at bayonet point as happened in
Taylorville. On October 12, 1932, several truckloads of PMA and auxiliary members went to Taylorville to try and convince those miners still working under the
UMWA contract to come out on strike. Many of the pickets were rounded up at
bayonet point, with the men taken to the county jail and the women held for varying
amounts of time at an auto repair garage. Some women were later released and told
to leave the county whereas others were actually transported out of the county in
troop trucks.[41] Some times women were also held in the county jail.

The Women's Auxiliary found it very difficult to hold their meetings in some
parts of the state because they were forbidden to do so by the county sheriff. That,
however, did not always stop them, and they found themselves in danger. For example, on February 5, 1933, a busload of women from Tovey returning from an auxiliary meeting in Staunton was stopped and searched by the militia. Others walked
twenty miles to attend an auxiliary meeting in Buckner only to have it broken up by
the sheriff who then arrested the evening's speaker, Agnes Burns Wieck, and severely beat many of the women who attempted to attend the meeting. The next day,
many of these women journeyed to Springfield to show the governor the results of
his promise to Wieck and other Women's Auxiliary officials on January 26, 1933,
to restore civil rights. That evening two women were hospitalized for their injuries:
a fractured skull and internal injuries.[42] This violence did not intimidate these
women and they continued to support the miners on the picket line and in their
organizational efforts.

By mid-1933 it was estimated that there were twenty thousand members in the
auxiliary. In addition, efforts continued to organize those areas still dominated by
UMWA and Peabody Coal Company. Mrs. Wieck and succeeding auxiliary presidents found themselves escorted by a committee of miners and women to ensure
their safety when trying to hold a meeting in an "unfriendly" area. Auxiliary members even went into the fields of West Virginia and established three auxiliary locals.

Besides participating in parades and rallies, on the picket line and in organizational activities, many women became involved politically. That is not to say that
any sought political office, though it might be argued that the auxiliary offices were
such, but rather that they lobbied state and federal officials through written resolu-

41. Interview with Mamie Sandretto, Gillespie, Illinois, February 6, 1981 and March 8, 1981; *Wom-
en's Auxiliary Progressive Miners of America First Annual Report*, 10–11. Agnes Burns Wieck Papers,
Walter Reuther, Archives, Wayne State University, Detroit, Michigan.

42. *PM*, February 24, 1933 and August 11, 1933. *Women's Auxiliary Progressive Miners of America
First Annual Report*, 19. Agnes Burns Wieck Papers, Walter Reuther Archives, Wayne State University,
Detroit, Michigan.

tions and in person. The topics of these resolutions were many but generally revolved around the situation in the Illinois coalfields.

As already suggested, one issue of primary importance to the auxiliary was the
restoration of civil rights in the areas of the state where troops were stationed, particularly in Christian and Franklin Counties in the southern part of the state. In these
counties the PMA and Women's Auxiliary were forbidden to meet; even meetings
of two or three people on a street corner were not allowed. Curfews were imposed,
and people from outside the area were expected to leave by nightfall. County deputies and National Guard troops forcibly searched homes for guns and "troublemakers." People were pulled from their cars and beaten while law enforcement officials
watched, and at times participated. Many of the auxiliaries passed resolutions concerning these action and had copies sent to local newspapers, county sheriffs, Governors Emmerson and Horner, State Attorney General Oscar Carlestorm, President
Franklin D. Roosevelt, and Secretary of Labor Frances Perkins. One such resolution
read in part: "Therefore be it resolved that we, the Women's Auxiliary of Zeigler,
Illinois, appeal to the law enforcement agencies of the State of Illinois that the
citizens of Taylorville are given their constitutional rights, and demand that you take
immediate steps to see that the same is carried into effect immediately."[43]

Other resolutions called upon the above-named individuals, as well as other state
and federal officeholders and Mrs. Roosevelt, to use their influence to convince the
National Labor Relations Board to allow a referendum to decide which union would
represent the miners in Illinois. This was the desire of many in the state since mid-
1933 when a solution to the problem did not seem imminent and most were convinced that the PMA would have no trouble winning such a referendum. However,
with the National Labor Relations Board ruling against the Progressives in 1934,
it became a moot point even though resolutions were still adopted urging such a
referendum.

Other areas of concern related to the mine war that were addressed by the auxiliaries included: protestation of PMA convictions; treatment of pickets and marchers;
inability to hold memorial services; and a call for an impartial investigation of the
Illinois situation. Not all resolutions adopted, however, had to do with the mine war.
A brief look at the topics of these resolutions gives an indication of the political
leanings of this particular group. The auxiliaries supported legislation regulating
child labor. Among other resolutions adopted were support for Unemployment and
Social Insurance Bill H.R. 7598, Old Age Pension bill, Veteran Soldier Bonus bill,
the Frazier-Lemke Farm Refinance bill, opposition to a large national debt, destruction of food and clothing material, purchase of foreign goods, Wagner Act, appropriations for war, Guffey coal law and strip mine legislation.[44] Many of these issues
were being pressed for passage by the Roosevelt administration. It is, therefore, easy

43. *PM*, December 16, 1932.
44. *PM*, November 9, 1936 and March 6, 1936.

to see why the PMA felt so frustrated, when the Roosevelt administration would not come to their aid.

Auxiliary members were also concerned with the plight of the working class as a whole. Some articles and editorials discussed the problems of the present economic system; others presented remedies. Resolutions were passed concerning these issues at the Auxiliary's annual conventions.

The Women's Auxiliary, through its recognition of the class struggle as stated in its constitution, continued the radical tradition of District 12, which had produced such Socialist leaders as Adolph Germer and Duncan McDonald and whose voting record showed a strong support for local and state Socialist candidates.[45] Because of this continued emphasis on class struggle, the capitalist system itself came under fire for its unequitable distribution of wealth. While some, like Rose North, called for "great changes in our economic system," others, such as Lillian Burnette encouraged all laborers to "work together and fight until this damnable capitalistic system is abolished from off the earth."[46] Others wrote about the need for all workers to "wake-up and see the necessity of demanding and getting the full social value of their labor";[47] even though the New Deal had promised a better standard of living for all and a redistribution of wealth, this had not taken place. This country still consisted of "the owner and the owned, the well-fed and the starved, the hunter and the hunted."[48] And the problems faced by the underclass—"despotism, exploitation, usurpations and oppression . . . all offsprings of the hell-born system of 'profits and usury' "—would be rectified if the government would "produce for use, not for profits."[49]

The politics and rhetoric of the PMA and the Women's Auxiliary is an example of a resurgence in radical activity after World War I with a particular emphasis on economics. As John Laslett has pointed out: "the contribution which the postwar radicals in District 12 helped make to the American tradition of dissent were their efforts to supplement these demands for political control with a partially new program of economic democracy."[50]

Not all auxiliary members were quite so vehement in their attack upon the existing system. The majority of the writings by auxiliary members were concerned with concrete ways to relieve the plight of the working class. The sentiments of Rose North expressed those of many auxiliary members: "We are our brothers' keepers.

45. Stephane E. Booth, "The Relationship Between Radicalism and Ethnicity in Southern Illinois Coal Fields, 1870–1940" (D.A. diss., Illinois State University, 1983), 175–77.

46. *PM*, August 17, 1934; August 31, 1934.

47. *PM*, December 7, 1934.

48. *PM*, December 14, 1934.

49. *PM*, June 21, 1935.

50. John H. M. Laslett, "Swan Song or New Social Movement? Socialism and Illinois District 12, United Mine Workers of America, 1919–1926" in *Socialism in the Heartland*, ed. Donald T. Critchlow (Notre Dame: University of Notre Dame Press, 1986), 187.

Man cannot live to himself alone. We owe a duty to our fellowmen, and this long depression has been showing us what this duty really is."[51]

Auxiliary members were also concerned about child labor legislation. Not only, according to auxiliary members, did there need to be laws regulating against "premature employment," there also needed to be changes in the system so that a family did not need to employ children at very young ages, a practice not uncommon in coalfields earlier in the century. These changes included "a wage earned by the father which will be sufficient to maintain a decent standard of living, and a system of state aid to widows and dependent children which will enable the children to remain in school up to the age of at least 16, or better, 18."[52] In conjunction with a concern over child-labor legislation must also come a concern with the educational system in this country. This system should include better facilities, better trained and paid teachers, curriculum suited to the capabilities of every child, vocational training, and evening classes for workers.

The Women's Auxiliary also endorsed an unemployment insurance plan but cautioned that it was not a "cure-all." Not only was unemployment insurance necessary but so were higher wages, a shorter workday and week (six-hour day, five-day week), a system of national economic planning and no sales tax, which was seen as a burden to the working class.[53] A minimum wage was also necessary to "make certain the physical welfare of the workers as well as contribute to a healthier mental attitude."[54]

The growth of unionism generally was also seen as vital for the survival of the working class, especially among young women and girls who produced garments under sweatshop conditions. Otherwise work would continue to be done in sweatshop conditions. One way to encourage manufacturers to deal with the unions was for workers to refuse to buy products that did not have a union label. Joan Lee instructed her readers:

> Some low prices are made possible by the employment of young children and girls, who work long hours in "sweatshops" where the light is poor, the air foul, and general conditions are unsanitary.
>
> If we as union people demand of merchants only products which bear a union label or which we know are produced under standard hours and wages, it will not be long before merchants will comply with our demands.[55]

Lee continues at a later date: "This is the consistent attitude of a true union man. What he desires for himself—good working conditions and pay equivalent to the

51. *PM*, September 15, 1933.
52. *PM*, December 2, 1932.
53. *PM*, December 16, 1932.
54. *PM*, February 17, 1933.
55. *PM*, May 5, 1933.

labor he gives—he must help secure for those workers whose finished product he must buy."[56]

During the latter part of the decade, as problems in Europe escalated, the Women's Auxiliary protested America's possible participation in a war abroad. As Lillian Burnette wrote: "The 'merchants of death' are again trying to agitate war. Evidently they didn't get rich enough as a result of the last wholesale slaughter of human beings. . . . Their greed and lust for gold have made them murderous beasts of prey."[57] In the January 7, 1938, issue Burnette tried another approach:

> Women of America, awake! Are you going to allow your son, brother, husband or father to be ruthlessly snatched out of your homes and maybe out of your lives forever by these heartless war-mongers? . . . All women of this nation should, in fact they MUST, organize against war. Let every women instill this well in her mind.
>
> THERE'D BE NO WAR TODAY, IF MOTHERS ALL WOULD SAY, "I DIDN'T RAISE MY BOY TO BE A SOLDIER."[58]

Thus the concerns voiced by the members through their articles, editorials, letters, and resolutions were not just those of a group faced with a life-and-death struggle (the mine war) but a group of individuals who saw their place in a much larger group (the working class) that was faced with the need to survive. These women were able to look beyond the immediate sufferings of their own families and see the problems of the workers of America and offer remedies to improve the situation.

In looking beyond their immediate families' sufferings, these women were assuming a role new to many of them. Very few of the local auxiliary officers had any experience as leaders, but the majority knew the deprivation of strikes and the importance of the role of the woman during a strike in trying to find food and clothing for the family. This belief in the importance of the home continued during the mine war. As Joan Lee pointed out, "marriage and homemaking are vital to social welfare and the family is proving the foremost line of defense in this present struggle for existence."[59] Because of the much more violent nature of this strike Lee warned auxiliary members that "a home should be a haven of peace and mental security for children. The constant nervous tension of the parents during the present crisis may leave indelible scars upon the minds of little children."[60] But because of the violent nature of the strike, it soon became apparent that women were not going to be bound to their homes. In order to close down the mines throughout the state, their presence was needed on the picket lines and in marches; as more and more miners and their families were affected, massive relief operations needed to be undertaken. This

56. *PM*, August 11, 1933.
57. *PM*, September 23, 1932.
58. *PM*, June 7, 1935.
59. *PM*, September 23, 1932.
60. *PM*, November 4, 1932.

could not be done from the home. PMA leaders urged husbands and fathers to
"allow" or encourage their wives and daughters to join the auxiliary. But few
needed prodding. Southern Illinois coal miners and their families participated in
numerous strikes prior to 1932; therefore miners were accustomed to their wives'
involvement in helping to provide for the needs of the community. Because of the
importance and nature of the UMWA-PMA dispute, a more organized effort by both
men and women was needed to ensure success and the Women's Auxiliary took a
leadership role in providing this solidarity. As the number of miners belonging to
the PMA increased, pressure on those remaining outside of the union and its auxiliary to participate, increased. For those who were reluctant, encouragement was
provided through a song by Nannie Parker, "Arise! Brave Women," to be sung to
the tune "John Brown's Body."

> Arise! Arise! Brave Woman!
> There is work for you to do.
> Show the world that love is wisdom
> and love's promises are true;
> Break the bonds that held you captive
> for the world has need of you,
> And we'll go marching on.
>
> (*Chorus*)
> All unite and fight for freedom!
> All unite and fight for freedom!
> All unite and fight for freedom!
>
> Do you need a sound to rouse you?
> Hear the little children cry.
> Do you need a sight to stir you?
> See the old who helpless die.
> Shall they call to you in misery
> While you stand heedless by?
> No, we'll go marching on.
>
> Man too long has fought unaided
> with the evil of the world;
> But together we shall conquer, all
> our strength against it hurled;
> And united march to victory, our
> banners bright unfurled
> As we go marching on.
>
> We will give the world fair daughters
> and those daughters shall be free;
> They shall stand beside their brothers

on the ground of liberty

And the cause of right shall prosper
on the land and on the sea
As we go marching on.

Then Arise! Arise! Brave Woman!
There is work for you to do;
Show the world that love is wisdom
And love's promises are true;
Break the bonds that hold you captive
for the world has need of you
And we'll go marching on.[61]

This song also exemplified the continued tradition of working-class women, from the millworkers at Lowell to the Women's Auxiliary of the PMA, as champions of the republican tradition of resistance to the rise of a corporate state.

The idea of female equality was also present throughout the writing that dealt with the role of women during this crisis. As Nannie Parker pointed out, victory will be obtained by marching together. And during a time of internal conflict, members were reminded that the auxiliary was founded "in behalf of these husbands of ours and their leaders to march side by side with them to victory"[62]—a reminder that also served to emphasize the equality of function given to women through the auxiliary. Even an officer of the PMA saw the auxiliary as an "opportunity for women to develop their ability in the struggle to make her equal to man."[63]

Within the auxiliary women saw themselves in a multifaceted role. One member felt "we can do wonderful work in securing for our men legislation that will be a great benefit to them." which they attempted to do.[64] Woman's role as voter was also stressed. Candidates who favored labor legislation were promoted by auxiliary leaders. Women were encouraged to vote for those candidates who would be of most benefit to workers, regardless of party, and not to vote for a candidate just because "our husbands voted that way" in the past. Middle-class and working women were urged to "band together now and work as never before for the party and the men who will revise the whole system of labor."[65]

Others saw their role as educator: to educate their sons and daughters to a class-consciousness and the importance of a union and to educate themselves and their children against war.[66] Other members testified to the importance of the auxiliary in their own education. Lillian Burnette testified that "through the auxiliary I have

61. *PM*, February 14, 1936.
62. *PM*, November 10, 1933.
63. *PM*, October 28, 1932.
64. *PM*, March 8, 1935.
65. *PM*, September 30, 1932.
66. *PM*, December 30, 1932.

learned how the Wall Street money masters have exploited the working class, and robbed them through low wages, high cost of living and usury. I have also learned that a clean, bona fide, rank and file labor union is a powerful weapon with which the workers are able to fight the 'bosses' or 'master class.' ''[67] Mary Lemmon admitted she changed her perception of woman's role, which she had originally believed should not be in public. Mildred Drudi found that she and other women ''learned to stand on our own feet and declare our rights as law-abiding citizens.''[68]

Another role of women in the auxiliary was that of mourner. The auxiliary took it upon themselves to memorialize the PMA men and women killed during the mine war through ceremonies at the cemetery at the time of burial and each year thereafter. They commemorated the dead in songs and poetry.

The support that the women gave the miners during this period, ''on the picket line, in the soup kitchen, on the parade grounds, at mass meetings'' was bound to make them victorious, or so they believed.

However, the fate of the auxiliary followed closely that of the PMA itself. Both were besieged by internal and external disputes. The auxiliary was faced with its first internal problem during the spring of 1933 when ''The Progressive Miner'' editor, Gerry Allard, was accused of being a Communist. Local auxiliaries, through resolutions, rushed to assure Allard of their support. However, by August of the same year, Allard was thrown out of the PMA and Agnes Burns Wieck's loyalties were also called into question. She was ousted as Women's Auxiliary president in November 1933. With her ouster the Women's Auxiliary became formally affiliated to the PMA itself. It was no longer a separate body.

As the courts continued to rule against the PMA, on the grounds that District 12 was the legitimate representative of the Illinois miners, the effects of this were felt in the Women's Auxiliary. As more and more miners returned to the UMWA, the number of women eligible for membership decreased. 4,000 members were reported in September 1937. Fewer auxiliary reports were found in the *Progressive Miner*, and conventions were no longer an annual event. The auxiliary was invited to affiliate with the Federation of Womens' Auxiliaries of Labor when the PMA was given an American Federation of Labor charter, but this did not serve to bolster membership.[69] The PMA and its auxiliary were on the decline.

Despite this, at its peak, the Women's Auxiliary of the Progressive Miners of America could claim a number of important achievements. For one thing, it was a democratic movement of the many. Even though a few names stand out—Agnes Burns Wieck, Catherine DeRorre, Celina Burrell, Mary Casper, and Mary Boetta—as providing leadership, this organization was one that operated through the hard work of its members: the women on the picket lines and in the soup kitch-

67. *PM*, November 22, 1935.
68. *PM*, December 6, 1935; December 13, 1935.
69. *PM*, September 17, 1937.

ens. And though these women cannot be labeled feminists, they provided a model for other auxiliaries in the strike-torn 1930s.[70]

In its first year, the auxiliary was completely independent from male authority. It provided an opportunity for many women to develop their organizational and leadership skills both within and outside the domestic sphere. And even within gender-related activities, women were allowed to operate independently (e.g., in matters of providing relief). An educational program was also instituted to develop the class awareness of these women and to instill in them the importance of their political role. Their participation in militant workplace activities (picketing, participating in marches and rallies), which put them in physical danger, served to heighten their awareness of the political situation, particularly in Illinois, and generate efforts on their part to change it. Auxiliary members also asserted their independence outside the domestic sphere in the initial weeks of the confrontation, when they began to participate strongly in these militant activities outside the home. At first this brought consternation to some of their more socially traditional spouses. But later it came to be accepted as necessary by most of them. Therefore, even though most of the activities in which the women participated were based on the traditional gender role (helping one's mate, providing for your children, and so forth), these women reached the outer boundaries set by that role and in some cases surpassed it.

In examining the writings and activities of the members of the PMA Women's Auxiliary, there is no recrimination or complaining about their plight because of the strike action. Recriminations instead were placed on UMW leaders, government officials, and the unequal economic system. The women were particularly critical of John L. Lewis and District President John Walker. Other issues on which the rank-and-file women expressed their opinions included: the need for unity to win the fight against the UMWA; the violence and suspension of civil rights in some counties in Illinois; and the need to provide for their children, not only food but the means to develop a higher standard of living. In examining the writings of the auxiliary leadership (district and local auxiliary officers), on the other hand it is apparent that they were more concerned about the problems of the laboring class in general. That wider concern, however, was consistent with two of the objectives found in the Auxiliary's constitution:

(1) To strengthen our class on the economic and political field, that we may secure equitable old-age pensions, workmen's unemployment insurance and health insurance; legislation that will surround our men with the utmost safety in their work in the mines, and such other labor legislation as will be beneficial to our members and other labor organizations.

(2) To educate our members and the workers of other industries to recognize the

70. Marjorie Penn Lasky, "Where I Was A Person: The Ladies Auxiliary in the 1934 Minneapolis Teamsters' Strikes," in *Women, Work and Protest*, ed. Ruth Milkman (Boston: Routledge and Kegan Paul, 1985), 181–205.

need of independent working class political action as an additional weapon in labor's struggle for emancipation.[71]

That is not to say that the rank and file were not concerned with these problems, as the type and number of resolutions passed by local auxiliaries attests. The language used by the leadership was also more representative of the radical working class rhetoric of the 1930s than that used by the rank and file.

Thus, the role that members of the PMA Women's Auxiliary developed for themselves during this time of crisis in the mid-1930s went well beyond the home. As PMA officer, Pat Ansboury, pointed out, "Another striking significance of the women's organization has been their emancipation from the old theory of 'the woman's place is in the home.' This theory has been forcefully dispelled by the efforts and organization of the mining woman in this struggle. They have proven that economic problems are their interest as well as the men engaged in the industry."[72]

Or as Agnes Burns Wieck stated: "As an educational force, the Auxiliary has accomplished wonders among the women of the Illinois coal fields. Forced to do things they thought they couldn't do, they have lost their shyness, their timidity, their feelings of inferiority. They preside over meetings, keep books, write records, letters, news reports, form committees to visit public officials, mount improvised rostrums and take their turns at spellbinding."[73]

Even though the economic crisis of the Depression took women out of their homes onto picket lines, marches, and meeting halls—giving them an education in economics, government and politics, and providing them with leadership training—the majority saw this as an extension of their role, not a new one. Miners' wives, daughters, and mothers were used to the demands put upon them during a strike, in particular that of caring for or protecting a family. Their participation in this mine war was an extension of that need to provide for the family, first by trying to provide for its immediate needs (food, clothing, housing, and safety) and second by providing for its long-term needs (education, a more equitable economic system, and so forth). During these particular years, however, the means needed to achieve these goals were unique. One had to leave the home to plan and participate in mass relief efforts, picket lines, marches, and meetings. Even though Pat Ansboury and other males within the PMA may have seen these activities and writings of auxiliary members as an emancipation from an old theory, these women saw it as doing what needed to be done to win protection for their and other workers' families, a goal which they had been working toward for many years. As the majority of these women defined their role, they had not developed a new one during this crisis, but had expanded upon a role they had defined for themselves as miners' wives—one that Mr. Ansboury and others had not recognized previously.

71. *PM*, September 29, 1933.
72. *PM*, October 28, 1932.
73. *Women's Auxiliary Progressive Miners of America First Annual Report*, 14. Agnes Burns Wieck Papers, Walter Reuther Archives, Wayne State University, Detroit, Michigan.

PART IV

INTERNATIONAL COMPARISONS

MONOPOLY, COMPETITION, AND COLLECTIVE BARGAINING
Pennsylvania and South Wales Compared

I S A A C   C O H E N

During the last quarter of the nineteenth century industrial relations in the South Wales coal industry were regulated by collective bargaining. Representatives of both coal-owners and coal miners met periodically to negotiate sliding scales; strikes were few and far between; and a relative state of industrial peace had become the hallmark of the industry. In Eastern Pennsylvania, on the other hand, industrial warfare became the rule in coal mining. From 1875 to 1902 industrial relations in the anthracite coalfields of Eastern Pennsylvania were marred by virulent anti-unionism, violence, and bloodshed. The critical difference in industrial relations in the two regions, I suggest, lies in the degree of unity among the employers. South Wales coal producers were deeply divided by competition whereas Pennsylvania coal operators were unified.

South Wales and Eastern Pennsylvania were quite comparable in many ways. Both were famous for their anthracite coal deposits, both industries expanded rapidly during the last three decades of the nineteenth century, and both were nearly equal in size. In the early 1870s the two coal regions had become highly unionized; both experienced three large-scale miners' strikes between 1870 and 1875.

The miners of South Wales had never been defeated. Rather, they reached an accommodation with their employers. The collectively bargained sliding scale had become the embodiment of the 1875 compromise, and as such, underlay the evolution of industrial relations throughout the remainder of the century. The Pennsylvania coal diggers, by contrast, were vanquished. By and large, their union was destroyed. The defeat of 1875 shaped the contours of industrial relations in Eastern Pennsylvania well into the twentieth century.

A comparative analysis of the two regions will shed more light on the Pennsylvanian experience. Such a comparison will enable us to identify important similarities between the two industries, isolate significant differences, and show how these differences contributed to union's defeat and victory.

The difference between the divided Welsh employers and the unified American operators had two profound effects on labor relations. First, Welsh coal producers were eager to cooperate with the miners' union in order to suppress competition between firms and thereby control output, regulate wages, and stabilize coal prices. The increasing cartelization of the American anthracite industry from 1870 to 1900, by contrast, made it unnecessary for the employers to cooperate with the union because the cartel itself regulated prices, wages, and output. Second, sharp divisions among the South Wales coal-owners weakened their resolve to oppose the union and undermined their power to do so. The oligopolistic structure of the Pennsylvania industry, on the other hand, enhanced the sheer power of the coal corporations and their willingness to fight the anthracite miners to the finish.

To claim that the fate of the Pennsylvania anthracite miners was shared by the bituminous coal miners as well would be wrong, however. After all, it was during the period under study that the bituminous coal companies signed the first interstate collective bargaining agreement with the United Mine Workers of America. Nevertheless the comparison is valid. The defeats of the Pennsylvania anthracite coal miners during the closing decades of the nineteenth century were not unlike those of other groups of American workers; for instance, the cotton mule spinners and the iron steel workers. Violent confrontations in American industry versus peaceful cooperation in British industry was the norm not only in anthracite coal mining, but in cotton manufacture, iron making, and steel production as well.[1] In all three industries, the degree of competition among firms played a key role in the evolution of labor relations, in all three cases, the more competitive the industry, the more likely were the employers to seek an accommodation with the unions.

THE COAL INDUSTRY

Eastern Pennsylvania, like South Wales, has been a coal-producing area since at least the eighteenth century. During the first half of the nineteenth century, the two

1. See for example, Isaac Cohen, *American Management and British Labor* (Westport, Conn., 1990); and James Holt, "Trade Unionism in the British and U.S. Steel Industries, 1880–1914," *Labor History* 18, no. 1 (Winter 1977).

regions had become major suppliers of coal for industry, and from 1870 onward their coal output expanded at a rapid pace. The South Wales coal output rose from 14 million tons in 1870 to 40 million in 1899; the corresponding figures for Eastern Pennsylvania were 13 million tons and 54 million tons. The number of miners employed in the coalfields of South Wales and Eastern Pennsylvania tripled during the period from 49,000 (S.W) and 36,000 (E.P.) in 1870 to 133,000 against 141,000 in 1899 (see Table 16.1). The two coal regions, it should be noted, were roughly comparable in size. The South Wales region covered nearly 1,000 square miles while the coal area of Eastern Pennsylvania stretched over 1,700 square miles, 483 of which were composed of the coalfields themselves.[2]

To be sure, there were important differences in the quality of coal extracted. First, the coalfields of South Wales produced a wider range of coals than did those of Eastern Pennsylvania. Anthracite and semianthracite were the sole products of Eastern Pennsylvania whereas South Wales coalfields yielded semi-bituminous and bituminous as well. All types and kinds of coals were classified by carbon content (which stands in inverse relations to the proportions of volatile gases found in coal such as oxygen and hydrogen) with anthracite containing from 91 to 98% carbon, semi-anthracite 80–84% and bituminous less than 80% carbon. Second, the dichotomy between anthracite and bituminous was far more pronounced in Pennsylvania than in Wales. In Pennsylvania one may observe a change in the coal quality from anthracite to bituminous as one travels from the eastern to the western part of the state. In Wales, on the other hand, such a change in the coal rank is evident within the southern region itself; the same coal seams become more anthracite and less bituminous as they move toward the western and northwestern boundary of the region. By contrast to Eastern Pennsylvania, finally, only a small proportion of the coal mined in South Wales was of the pure anthracite type. Rather, the bulk of South Wales coal output was made up of "steam coal," a variety ranging from hard or dry semi-anthracite to semi-bituminous "admiralty" coal.[3] Because South Wales was

Table 16.1   Output and Employees in the Coal-Mining Industry of South Wales and Eastern Pennsylvania, 1870–1899

	Output (million tons)		Employees	
	S. Wales	E. Penn	S. Wales	E. Penn
1870	14	13	49,000	36,000
1880	21	25	69,000	73,000
1890	29	40	110,000	109,000
1899	40	54	133,000	141,000

SOURCES: For South Wales, see E. W. Evans, *The Miners of South Wales* (Cardiff, 1961), 237, 241, and J. H. Morris and L. J. Williams, *The South Wales Coal Industry, 1814–1875* (Cardiff, 1958), 73. For Eastern Pennsylvania, Peter Roberts, *The Anthracite Coal Industry* (New York, 1901), 107.

2. Stanley Jevons, *The British Coal Trade* (1915; repr., New York, 1969), 93; Peter Roberts, *The Anthracite Coal Industry* (New York, 1901), 5.
3. Jevons, *British Coal Trade*, 31–40, 95–99, 660–74; Roberts, *Anthracite Coal Trade*, 4; Aurand, *From the Molly Maguires to United Mine Workers* (Philadelphia, 1971), chap. 1.

the only region in Britain to specialize in the extraction of anthracite, because its main product—smokeless steam coal—contained an important element of semi-anthracite, and because the region's output of bituminous coal was rather limited, South Wales may reasonably be viewed as comparable to Eastern Pennsylvania insofar as coal quality is concerned.

The quality of coal encouraged its use for industrial purposes. Unquestionably, the development of the two coal regions between the 1830s and the 1870s was stimulated by the growing demand for iron. In both regions, anthracite had been used for the manufacture of iron products from wrought iron bars, for refining wrought iron from cast pig iron, and since the 1830s, for converting iron ore into pig iron. Using "hard coal" to make pig iron had become feasible only with the application of hot blast to an anthracite coal-fired furnace—a technology transferred from Wales to Pennsylvania in 1839.[4]

Again, there were important differences between the two industries. The South Wales iron industry was older, more developed, and more diversified than its Eastern Pennsylvania counterpart; for example, it employed both anthracite and coke (bituminous coal from which most of the gases have been removed by heating) furnaces to smelt iron. In addition, the coal mined in South Wales supplied the local demand for iron whereas Pennsylvania anthracite dominated the vast Eastern markets. Still, the pattern of growth and decline of iron production in the two regions was similar.[5] Furthermore, in both regions, the declining importance of iron-making in the second half of the nineteenth century did not entail a decline in coal production. On the contrary, coal output tripled in South Wales and quadrupled in Eastern Pennsylvania during the last three decades of the nineteenth century. Just as the rising demand for export stimulated the British "steam coal" industry, so did the increasing demand for domestic heating fuel give the American anthracite industry a new lease of life.

The economics of coal mining was another issue affecting the industry. One market characteristic of coal was the inelasticity of demand. Another was the high elasticity of supply during booms and the inelasticity of supply during slumps. The demand for coal was price-inelastic (a large change in price resulted in a small change in output) because it was determined more by the level of industrial activity

4. J. H. Morris and L. J. Williams, *The South Wales Coal Industry, 1841–1875* (Cardiff, 1958), 2, 5–6, 9, 43–44; Jevons, *British Coal Trade*, 101–2; Ross Yates, "The Discovery and Process of Making Anthracite Iron," *Pennsylvania Magazine of History and Biography* 98, no. 2 (April 1974); James Swank, *History of the Manufacture of Iron in all Ages* (Philadelphia, 1892), chap. 41; Frederick Binder, *Coal Age Empire* (Harrisburg, 1974), chap. 4; Alfred Chandler, "Anthracite Coal and the Beginning of the Industrial Revolution in the United States," *Business History Review* 46, no. 2 (Summer 1972), esp. 159–63; Donald Miller and Richard Sharpless, *The Kingdom of Coal* (Philadelphia, 1985), chap. 3.

5. Morris and Williams, *South Wales Coal Industry*, 6, 48, 8; Jevons, *British Coal Trade*, 103; Parliamentary Papers (henceforth PP) 1973, vol. 10, *Select Commitee on the Dearness and Scarcity of Coal*, 58; Peter Temin, *Iron and Steel in Nineteenth Century America* (Cambridge, Mass., 1964), 266–69. For the rise and decline of the anthracite iron in the United States see Temin, 52–53, 58–61, 77–80, 120–21, 201–6, 246–48, 256; Chandler, "Anthracite Coal," 164–65, 179; and "A Reply," *Business History Review* 53, no. 2 (Summer 1979): 255–58.

and household consumption than by price (the cost of storage was prohibitive). At the same time, a short supply during booms could cause a sharp rise in prices, encouraging new entry into the industry and rapid expansion.[6] Under conditions of depressed trade, on the other hand, it was often more feasible to work a coal mine at an actual loss rather than stop production altogether.[7] The combination of volatile demand, ease of entry, and the high cost of exit resulted in chronic overcapacity, intense competition, and sharp variation in prices. Extreme competition, in turn, evoked repeated attempts on the part of the employers to control the market. The need to regulate the output and price of coal, as we shall see, became a major preoccupation of coal-mining firms in both South Wales and Eastern Pennsylvania, and as such, played a key role in their attitude toward unionism.

Finally, work relations. Notwithstanding the actual method of mining, the coal miner enjoyed an extraordinary degree of job control on both sides of the Atlantic. Unlike skilled workers in other trades and industries, the miners' autonomy at work was circumscribed by the actual design of the coal mine itself: underground gangways (tunnels) and chambers stretched over hundreds of yards, sometimes miles, isolating one work place from another.

Two methods of coal mining were practiced in the nineteenth century: pillar-and-stall (pillar-and-breast in the United States) and longwall. The pillar-and-stall method was commonly used in British and American mines up to the 1870s. Longwall mining had spread rapidly in South Wales after 1860 and by the end of the 1870s became the prevailing practice of coal cutting not only in South Wales but in most other British coalfields.[8] In the United States, by contrast, mine operators continued to rely heavily on the pillar-and-breast system. Neither in Eastern Pennsylvania nor in other American coal regions has longwall become the predominant method of mining.

Under the pillar-and-stall system one coal digger and his assistant (occasionally a pair of miners and their laborers) worked together in a stall: a room surrounded on three side by walls of coal. Under the longwall system, miners were not working in isolated chambers but shoulder to shoulder in a single unbroken line.[9]

Yet the change from pillar-and-stall to longwall in South Wales did not undermine the miner's control. Nor did it alter the organization of work. Under the longwall system the coal face was divided into distinctly separate sections, each constituting

6. Richard Hannah and Garth Magnum, *The Coal Industry and its Industrial Relations* (Salt Lake City, 1985), 18–31.

7. Morris and Williams, *South Wales Coal Industry*, 78–79.

8. Morris and Williams, *South Wales Coal Industry*, 57–62; J. W. F. Rowe, *Wages in the Coal Industry* (London, 1923), 8.

9. R. H. Walters, *The Economic and Business History of the South Wales Steam Coal Industry, 1840–1914* (Ph.D. diss., Oxford University, 1975; published, New York, 1977), 197–98; Jevons, *British Coal Trade*, 206–8; Dave Douglas, "The Durham Pitman," in *Miners, Quarrymen and Saltworkers*, ed. Raphael Samuel (London, 1977), 218; A. R. Griffin, *Coalmining* (London, 1971), 47–53; Anthony Wallace, *St. Clair* (Ithaca, N.Y., 1988), 11–12; Miller and Sharpless, *Kingdom of Coal*, 92–94; Roy Church, *The History of the British Coal Industry,* vol. 3, *1830–1913* (Oxford, 1986), 328–39.

an independent unit of work, each approximating the size of a stall, each having its own "gate" or roadway leading to the main gangway, and each placed under the total control of the miner.[10] Owning his own tools, buying his own powder, subcontracting his laborer, and getting paid on a tonnage-rate basis, the South Wales longwall collier, like the Eastern Pennsylvania anthracite miner, was an independent contractor, autonomous of management supervision and defiant of the foreman's authority.[11]

THE MINE WORKERS AND THEIR UNION

The miners' independence and management hostility to unionism helps to explain why in Eastern Pennsylvania, as in South Wales, labor-related violence was the antecedent to unionism. In both coal regions, miner-sponsored violence flourished as early attempts at unionization were repeatedly frustrated: in both, violence and early strikes went hand in hand; the failure to win the employers' recognition encouraged many union members to resort to violence, riots, and terrorism.

Acts of violence were committed by the Scotch Cattle movement in South Wales and the Molly Maguires organization in Eastern Pennsylvania. The first was a Celtic movement of Welsh (as opposed to "foreign," i.e., English) colliers, the second, a Celtic organization of Irish anthracite miners. The first had been active from 1822 (Monmouthshire strike) through 1850; the second from 1842 (Minersville strike) until 1876. E. W. Evans captured the essence of the Welsh movement when he wrote:

> The main object of the Scotch Cattle was to enforce solidarity among the workmen. Those who accepted a wage reduction during a strike, for example, would find warning notices posted at the level. If they remained at work after this warning they would be visited by the Herd. The Herd might comprise as many as 300 men, and was led by a Bull, chosen for his ferocity, and wearing horns on his head. Their arrival might be heralded by lowing, rattling chains or blowing horns, each man being either masked or having blackened his face. . . . Their first step was usually to break the doors and windows of the transgressor's house. Then every article of furniture within would be systematically destroyed, while the victim was mercilessly beaten if he offered any resistance.[12]

10. Rowe, *Wages in the Coal Industry*, 66; Walters, *South Wales Steam Coal Industry*, 204–5.

11. See Carter Goodrich, *The Frontier of Control* (New York, 1920), 137–38, and *The Miners' Freedom* (1925; repr., New York, 1977), 56; and John Goldthrope, "Technical Organization as a Factor in Supervisor-Worker Conflict: Some Preliminary Observation on a Study made in the Mining Industry," *British Journal of Sociology* 10, no. 3 (September 1959): 214–17.

12. E. W. Evans, *The Miners of South Wales* (Cardiff: University of South Wales, 1961), 49–50. See also Ness Edwards, *The History of the South Wales Miners* (London: Labour Publishing Company, 1926), 17–36; and E. J. Jones " 'Scotch Cattle' and Early Trade Unionism in Wales," *Economic Journal, Supplement (Economic History)* 1 (1926–29): 385–93.

While everything we know of the Scotch Cattle points to the ad hoc nature of the movement, the Molly Maguires was a secret society with sworn membership, formal organization, and lodges headed by bodymasters. By contrast to the Cattle, furthermore, the Mollies operated in small bands, often carrying out deadly attacks; consequently, the war waged against them by the authorities was bloodier than the war against the Cattle.

Yet the similarities between the Cattle and the Mollies overshadow the contrasts. In Eastern Pennsylvania, as in South Wales, roving bands of miners beat "black legs" during strikes and posted "coffin notices" signed "Molly" for strike-breakers. In addition, they frequently attacked mine bosses. In 1862 a mine foreman notorious for "short weighing" was stoned to death and a year later a mine-owner who had a reputation as a hard taskmaster was shot and killed by an armed band of men. Like the Cattle, the Mollies either blackened their face or wore masks; they often attacked their victims at home in front of their families; and in most cases, arranged for the attacks to be carried out by outsiders (that is, lodge members from a neighboring town).[13]

But unlike the Cattle, the Mollies survived well into the 1870s. While union recognition in South Wales acted rather powerfully against the revival of Cattle attacks, the 1875 defeat of unionism in Eastern Pennsylvania brought about an unprecedented revival of labor-related violence, and in turn, a sweeping repression of the Mollies.

The repression of the Mollies was preceded by a rapid union growth. Short-lived unions had appeared first in South Wales in 1831 and then in Eastern Pennsylvania in 1848, but only after the Civil War were relatively permanent organizations of miners established in each of the two regions, In 1868, the Workingmen's Benevolent Association (WBA) was formed in Schuylkill County, Pennsylvania, as a local union of anthracite miners. Two years later, the Amalgamated Association of Miners was formed in Lancashire, Britain, as a national union federation. A growing number of South Wales districts were enrolled in the federation. Within three years membership reached a peak of 40,000 in the WBA (1871) and 45,000 in the Amalgamated Association of South Wales (1873).[14]

The WBA and the Amalgamated had similar union goals. In both regions, the cornerstone of union policy was recourse to arbitration and the adoption of sliding scales: the first as a means of settling disputes, the second as a method of regulating wages.[15] Such a policy protected the miners from the employers' arbitrary control

13. Wayne Broehl, *The Molly Maguires* (Cambridge, Mass., 1965), 91–92, 94, 96, 187, 199; Miller and Sharpless, *Kingdom of Coal*, chap. 5, esp. 151–52, 162–63; and Marvin Schlegel, *Ruler of the Reading* (Harrisburg, Pa., 1947), 68–69, 89–91.

14. Evans, *Miners of South Wales*, chaps. 3 and 8; Edwards, *History of the South Wales Miners*, chaps. 1 and 3; Aurand, *Molly Maguires to United Mine Workers*, 66; Andrew Roy, *A History of the Coal Miners of the United States* (1905; repr. Westport, Conn., 1970), 75; Edward Pinkowski, *John Siney* (Philadelphia, 1963), 61.

15. Evans, *Miners of South Wales*, 104, 112; Morris and Williams, *South Wales Coal Industry*,

over wages and at the same time constituted a de facto union recognition. It was a policy adopted after midcentury by many British trade unions in the name of cooperation, accommodation, and industrial peace. It was carried over across the Atlantic by British immigrant union leaders.

Hence the similarity in the leaders' philosophy. The Welsh union was led by William Abraham, a native of Wales. The WBA was founded and led by John Siney, a Lancashire-Irish union organizer who immigrated to the United States at the age of thirty-two. Each of the two leaders was an ardent proponent of arbitration and a leading exponent of the sliding scale (the sliding scale was a list of tonnage piece rates based on a "standard" linked to the average price of coal). Siney spoke of arbitration as "the best means" of settling labor disputes while Abraham was confident that "the only salvation for capital and labor [was a] whole-hearted cooperation . . . in forming boards of conciliation and arbitration."[16] Siney and Abraham alike served as union representatives on their respective sliding-scale committees, Siney during a brief period in the early 1870s and Abraham from 1875 until virtually the end of the century.

Notwithstanding these similarities in union leadership and goals, the evolution of labor relations in the two coal regions took a sharply divergent route from the 1870s onward. The watershed year was 1875: a series of strikes that culminated in that year destroyed trade unionism and collective bargaining in Eastern Pennsylvania but not in South Wales. It is upon this difference that we now must concentrate.

The miners of South Wales struck three times in five years—1871, 1873, 1875— and eventually reached an accommodation with their employers. The strikes were all triggered by wage reductions. The 1871 strike was settled by arbitration that was clearly favorable to the miners; and in 1873, once again, the miners managed to oppose a wage reduction successfully (although the union accepted a token 5% wage cut for five days). The 1875 strike resulted in a landmark sliding-scale agreement. The union accepted a 12.5% wage cut for three months, but far more important, it reached an agreement with the coal owners that future wages should be governed by a sliding scale supervised by a joint conciliation board of representatives of employers and miners.[17] The sliding-scale agreement stabilized labor relations in the South Wales coal-mining industry for a period that lasted nearly three decades. Signed for the first time in December 1875, it was renewed eight times, in 1880, 1882, 1887, 1890, 1892, 1893, 1895, and 1898.

The Pennsylvania anthracite miners struck four times—1869, 1870, 1871, and 1875—and at the end were utterly defeated. An early union victory in 1869 had

---

283–84; Edwards, *History of the South Wales Miners*, 76; Alexander Dalziel, *The Colliers' Strike in South Wales* (Cardiff, 1872), 38, 154; Wallace, *St. Clair*, 419–21.

16. The quotations are, in order, from Pinkowski, *John Siney*, 75; and E. W. Evans, *Mabon (William Abraham, 1842-1922)* (Cardiff, 1959), 11.

17. Dalziel, *The Colliers' Strike*, especially chaps. 17 and 18; Edwards, *History of the South Wales Miners*, 65–72; Evans, *Miners of South Wales*, 107–14; Morris and Williams, *South Wales Coal Industry*, 280–84. In addition, the 1873 strike is discussed in details in PP 1873, 10:61, 200, 204–8.

granted the miners a sliding scale, and a year later, the first written contract in the industry's history. During the 1871 strike the employers had first agreed to refer the dispute to arbitration but were unwilling to cooperate further with the union. Rather, they were determined to wage an all-out war against the union. Acting unilaterally, they revised the sliding scale downward, cut miners' rates by 10%–20%, and deliberately provoked a strike that lasted five months.[18] The outcome of the "long strike" (1875) was an unmitigated union disaster: The Miners' and Laborers' Benevolent Association, as the WBA was now officially called, collapsed and twenty men—all thought to be connected with the Molly Maguires—were executed.[19] As a result collective bargaining had completely vanished from the anthracite fields of Eastern Pennsylvania for a quarter of a century. Not until 1903 were the anthracite operators forced to sign the first union contract with the United Mine Workers (UMW) as a result of federal intervention. Nonetheless, they adamantly refused to recognize the UMW or deal with its representatives for another seventeen years, until 1920.[20]

Why, then, were the Pennsylvania anthracite miners so badly beaten? How, on the other hand, did the South Wales miners manage to win recognition, collective bargaining, and a sliding-scale agreement despite the apparent weakness of their union? How, in brief, is one to explain the defeat of one union in the light of the triumph of another?

THE EMPLOYERS

Control over the anthracite coal industry of Eastern Pennsylvania was concentrated in the hands of six large corporations. All were railroad corporations with combined mining and transportation interests; together they formed "America's first cartel."[21] Five of the six corporations owned valuable coal lands and had operated large coal mines in the two upper fields (Wyoming, Lehigh) since at least the late 1860s. They had been authorized by the Pennsylvania legislature to do so either directly (by opening their own mines) or indirectly—(through the ownership of stock in coal-mining companies). They were prohibited, however, from taking control of any coal-mining firms operating in the County of Schuylkill—the southern coalfield.

This prohibition dated back to the early 1830s. The Philadelphia and Reading Railroad Company—the main road serving the Schuylkill coal basin and the largest in the region—was chartered in 1833 at the time the Pennsylvania legislature was

18. Pinkowski, *John Siney*, chaps. 4 and 6; Schlegel, *Ruler of the Reading*, 16–31, 62–76.

19. Harold Aurand and William Gudenlunas, "The Mythical Qualities of Molly Maguire," *Pennsylvania History* 49, no. 2 (April 1982): 93.

20. Marvin Schlegel, "The Workingmen's Benevolent Association: First Union of Anthracite Miners," *Pennsylvania History* 10, no. 4 (October 1943): 267; Arthur Suffern, *The Coal Miners' Struggle for Industrial Status* (New York, 1926), 85–93.

21. Marvin Schlegel, "America's First Cartel, " *Pennsylvania History* 13, no. 1 (January 1946).

investigating the abuses of conferring mine privileges on canal and railroad companies. The Reading Railroad, consequently, was not granted mining privileges, did not acquire coal lands and mines, and confined itself exclusively to the transport business. By 1870, the Schuylkill basin was the only coalfield in Eastern Pennsylvania where transportation and mining still remained completely separate, the only area still experiencing fierce competition among many small coal-mine operators.[22]

The fierce competition hurt the Reading, however, and it led its newly appointed president, Franklin Gowen, to embark on a new policy. The reasons for the new policy were spelled out by Gowen in an 1871 report to the stockholders: "The repeated and serious interruptions of the business of the company caused by strikes in the coal regions during the last few years, and the many fluctuations in the coal trade produced by alternative periods of expansion and depression . . . have directed the attention of the Managers of the Company to the necessity of exercising some control over the production of coal."[23] Control was exercised by forming a new shadow company, the Laurel Run Improvement Company, later known as the Reading Coal and Iron Company. The bill to incorporate the new company was prepared by Gowen, passed the legislature in March 1871, and allowed the new company to buy coal lands, operate mines, and sell coal. The bill, in addition, made it lawful for any of the railroads operating in Pennsylvania to purchase the stock of the new company. At once, the Reading purchased the total stock of the new company and thereby secured 70,000 acres of coal lands. By 1874 the Reading was in possession of one-third of the coal lands of the entire anthracite region: a year later—on the eve of the "long strike"—fewer than 36 of the county's 175 collieries were independently operated. Practically all were tenants leasing corporate land and the vast majority paid rent to the Reading.[24]

From the outset, the Reading Railroad led the employers' struggle against the union. In 1869, shortly after the WBM had won a sliding-scale agreement, the Reading took over Schuylkill Canal, hence achieving a monopoly over the transport of coal in the area. By virtue of this monopoly the Reading managed to suppress competition among individual mine operators, enforce solidarity against the striking miners, and punish backsliding employers. During the 1870 strike, for example, the Reading raised the transport toll by 25% in order to discourage operators from going back to work at the old union rates. During the 1871 strike, similarly, the Reading raised the charge for transporting coal to Philadelphia from $2 to $6 a ton, making

22. Eliot Jones, *The Anthracite Coal Combinations in the United States* (Cambridge, 1914), 23–28; Jules Bogen, *The Anthracite Railroads* (New York, 1927), esp. 19–27; Stuart Campbell, "Businessmen and Anthracite: Aspects of Change in the Late Nineteenth Century Anthracite Industry" (Ph.D. diss., University of Delaware, 1978), 137–46.

23. Cited in Jones, *Anthracite Coal Combination,* 29.

24. Schlegel, *Ruler of the Reading,* 32–43; Jones, *Anthracite Coal Combination,* 28–30; Bogen, *Anthracite Railroads,* 51–54; Clifton Yearley, *Enterprise and Anthracite* (Baltimore, 1961), chap. 6, esp. 212; U.S. Congress, House, *Labor Troubles in the Anthracite Regions of Pennsylvania, 1887–1888,* Report No. 4147, 50th Cong., 2d Sess., 1889, lxii–lxiv.

it absolutely prohibitive at twice the price of "lump coal" (coal as it comes out of the mine). Cooperating closely with the Reading and forming together a united front against the union, the five anthracite railroads did the same. Only a single railway line refused to participate in the 1871 agreement to raise the freight rates: the Northern Central, controlled by the Pennsylvania Railroad. Characteristically, the small group of Shamokin collieries that refused to adhere to the employers' strategy and instead resumed work at the higher union rates, were served by the Pennsylvania Railroad.[25]

But the amount of anthracite hauled by the Pennsylvania was too small to affect the outcome of the strike. On the contrary, following "Gowen's compromise" of 1871 and the subsequent takeover of the Schuylkill coal lands and mines by the Reading, the six major carriers consolidated their control over the anthracite industry under the leadership of the Reading. Together, they formed a cartel and divided the coal market among themselves according to fixed percentages. The largest share (26%) was in the hands of the Reading with the remainder divided among the Delaware and Hudson Company (18%), the Jersey Central Railroad (16%), the Lehigh Valley Railroad (16%), the Delaware, Lackawanna, and Western Railroad (14%), and the Pennsylvania Coal Company (10%).[26]

The cartel of 1873 (in existence until August 1876) was the combination that ruined the union. It was, in the words of Marvin Schlegel, "the first of the great monopolies which were to dominate the United States for many decades."[27] It represents the first successful attempt to regulate output, control coal prices, fix wages, and defeat unionism in the coalfields of Eastern Pennsylvania. The cartel was powerful enough to suppress competition among producers and maintain coal prices during the severe depression of 1873–75. By 1875, it was also strong enough to fight the union to the finish. Provoking a strike in the midst of an economic downturn and imposing a general lockout that lasted five months, the employers not only outlasted the miners but brought the Miners' and Laborers' Benevolent Association into a state of total submission, collapse, and disintegration. Gowen's threat to reject any compromise with the union even if the mines remained shut down for two years, was all too real.[28]

The South Wales story was markedly different. By and large, the ownership of coal, the operation of coal mines, and the business of coal carrying in South Wales remained separate during the period. Land-owners, to be sure, invested modestly in coal transport, yet they were reluctant to acquire collieries. Some of the large coal-owners, it is true, bought shares in canal and railroad companies, but again, their investments were far too small to facilitate close cooperation between mining and

---

25. Schlegel, "Workingmen's Benevolent Association," 249, 253–54; "America's First Cartel," 4, 8–9; *Ruler of the Reading*, 20, 24–25.

26. G. O. Virtue, "The Anthracite Combinations," *Quarterly Journal of Economics* 10 (April 1896): 301–2; Schlegel, "America's First Cartel," 7; Pinkowski, John Siney, 58.

27. Schlegel, "Workingmen's Benevolent Association," 259.

28. Jones, *Anthracite Coal Combination*, 44; Schlegel, *Ruler of the Reading*, 64.

transport interests, let alone combination.[29] In addition, the South Wales coal producers themselves were divided by conflict of interests, conflicts between iron-making and coal-mining firms, between large and small employers, between associated and nonassociated firms, firms of different structure, and firms selling coals of different reputation and quality.

To begin with, competition between iron masters and coal-owners revolved around the price of coal and the cost of labor. Ordinarily, the coal-owners favored high coal prices while the iron masters were interested in high iron prices, and—as substantial consumers of the product—low coal prices. Furthermore, because of the greater regularity of work at the iron mills, the iron-masters paid their coal miners lower wages than did the coal-owners. The growing tendency among iron-masters to produce coal for sale was another factor resented by the coal-owners: as coal sellers, the iron masters were able to utilize the "small coal" they could not sell and thereby gain an additional advantage. The iron-masters, it should be noted, played a very prominent role as coal producers in South Wales: of the region's total output of 16.2 million tons in 1873, iron firms were producing more than 5 million tons of coal (consuming 3 million internally and sending more than 2 million to market).[30] Such a large share in the hands of the iron-masters helps to explain why a united front between coal-owners and iron-masters was so indispensable. And why acting alone, the coal-owners were too weak to oppose the miners' union successfully.

But even among themselves the coal-owners were divided. They had not formed a homogeneous cohesive group at any time during the period. Rather, the coal-mining industry (in contrast to the iron industry) was made up of small individual firms and was easily accessible to new operators. As late as the 1870s, the average holding of a South Wales coal-mining firm was 1.6 collieries, roughly the same as it had been thirty years earlier. In 1873, ownership of the South Wales industry was divided among 256 coal-mining firms, the majority of which (183) owned but a single colliery. Of the remaining 73 firms, 40 owned 2 collieries each, 17 owned 3 pits, 5 owned 4 pits, 10 owned 5 to 8 pits each, and one large firm owned 12 collieries. An examination of the output returns of a sample of 103 colliers producing nearly 5 million tons of coal in 1874 shows that the thirteen largest firms accounted for just under 39% of the total coal output—a market share far too small to facilitate monopolistic control over the industry.[31]

And there were more divisions. Beginning in the early 1870s there developed a

29. Morris and Williams, *South Wales Coal Industry*, 125; L. J. Williams, "The Coalowners of South Wales, 1873–80: Problems of Unity," *Welsh History Review* 8, no. 1 (June 1976): 77; Jevons, *British Coal Trade*, 109–11; A. J. Tayler, "The Coal Industry," in *The Development of British Industry and Foreign Competition*, by Derek Aldcroft (Toronto, 1968), 65; Virtue, "Anthracite Combinations," 318.

30. Williams, "Coalowners of South Wales," 81, 91–92; Morris and Williams, *South Wales Coal Industry*, 91, 278.

31. John Benson, *British Coalminers in the Nineteenth Century* (New York, 1980), 19; Morris and Williams, *South Wales Coal Industry*, 134–35.

fierce competition between the newly established limited liability companies and the older, individually owned collieries. By 1875 the largest coal-mining firms and nearly all the iron-making concerns converted into limited liability companies. Altogether, about half the coal output of South Wales was controlled by limited companies and about a quarter of the coal-sale collieries were owned by the limiteds. In addition, there developed throughout the century a conflict of interests between producers selling coals of different qualities. Anthracite, steam, and bituminous coals were sold by different firms in broadly distinct markets and therefore the interests of these forms were not identical. Furthermore, even within the same broad type (for example, anthracite) the quality, standing, and market reputation of the product varied considerably, and so did the interests of the producers. The increasing dependency of Welsh coal on diverse export markets—in contrast to Pennsylvania anthracite's "captive market" of home heating—was another source of division among the producers. It is hardly surprising therefore, that the South Wales employers faced greater difficulties in building an effective organization than did their Pennsylvania counterparts. So competitive was the South Wales coal industry that no successful attempt at price control is recorded between 1850 and 1900. Indeed, when the Coal Owners Association of South Wales was formed as a permanent organization in 1873 it did not even include price control among its objectives. Nor was price control included at any time before 1914 in the association preamble.[32]

The association of 1873 was preceded by earlier organizations. Formed during the 1860s and early 1870s, the chief goal of these employers' organizations was neither the regulation of output nor the control of prices but rather the need to form a united front in dealing with mine workers. As such, these early employers' associations had two fundamental weaknesses: first, they were confined to the coal-owners and did not enroll any of the iron-masters (who had their own organization); second, their member firms controlled just a small proportion of the region's total coal output.[33] The strikes of 1871 and 1873 underscore these weaknesses.

In 1870 the coal-owners operating in the Aberdare and Rhondda valleys reorganized the South Wales Steam Collieries Association. The association was extremely vulnerable both because its members controlled just 15% of the South Wales coal output and because the iron-masters were excluded. The result was predictable. During the 1871 strike that spread throughout the Aberdare and Rhondda valleys and did not involve the iron-masters many of the strikers were able to obtain employment in nonassociated firms (ironworks and coal-sale collieries) despite repeated attempts of the steam collieries association to prevent them from doing so. Aided by contributions from working miners—strikers who found work elsewhere as well as nonstriking colliers—the miners of Aberdare and Rhondda outlasted their employers and won the strike. Two years later, during the 1873 strike, the positions of the iron-

32. Morris and Williams, *South Wales Coal Industry*, 148–54, 177; Williams, "Coalowners of South Wales," 81, 92, 79.

33. Williams, "Coalowners of South Wales," 75–83.

masters and coal-owners were reversed. The iron-masters were on strike while the coal-owners were working so that the miners on strike were supported by those at work. Once again, the union benefited from the split between the iron-masters and the coal-owners, achieved victory, and gained strength.[34]

But the defeats of 1871 and 1873 taught the employers a lesson. Intense negotiations between the coal-owners and the iron-masters led to the formation of the South Wales Collieries Association. The new association represented all sectors of the industry (anthracite, steam, bituminous), controlled about 70% of the region's coal output, and included among its members most of the large iron and coal companies.[35] Like the Eastern Pennsylvania cartel, the South Wales association had organized in 1873, remained active during the severe depression of 1874–75, provoked a strike in 1875 (at the time the union was weak and vulnerable), and imposed a general lockout that lasted five months. Unlike the anthracite cartel in the United States, however, the association of South Wales settled the 1875 strike by means of negotiations with the union. Why?

Negotiated sliding-scale agreements helped stabilize the coal-mining industry and acted rather powerfully against the competitive market forces. Because the South Wales employers were subject to fierce competition, they were unable to regulate production directly and were therefore looking for an indirect way to do so. The collectively bargained sliding scale provided them with such a machinery. The sliding scale linked wages to prices, produced a regionwide uniform wage system, and as such stabilized labor costs. Because labor costs in the coal-mining industry accounted for 60–70% of all operating costs, the leveling of wages was a critical element in the efforts to reduce competition.

Just as the union played a stabilizing role in the South Wales coal industry, so did the railroads in the Pennsylvania anthracite industry. The anthracite railroads, we have seen, divided the coal market among themselves according to fixed percentages and thereby regulated output, prices, and wages. Reducing competition drastically—at least between 1873 and 1876—the railroads managed to control mining labor costs and therefore had little to gain and a great deal to lose from reaching an accommodation with the union. This is one important reason why the anthracite corporations of Eastern Pennsylvania had stubbornly refused to recognize the mine workers' union until after World War I, as we shall see.

FROM 1875 TO 1903

During the next twenty-seven years Pennsylvania's anthracite corporations made repeated attempts to eliminate competition, not just to reduce it. By 1903 they were

34. Morris and Williams, *South Wales Coal Industry*, 277–81; "The Discharge Note in the South Wales Coal Industry 1841–1898," *Economic History Review* 10, no. 2 (December 1957): 288; Williams, "Coalowners of South Wales," 83.
35. Williams, "Coalowners of South Wales," 83; Morris and Williams, *South Wales Coal Industry*, 281–82, "The Discharge Note," 288.

fully successful. At the same time, they launched an all-out protracted war against the miners that culminated in one of the bloodiest workers' massacre in U.S. history (Lattimer, in 1897), and five years later, one of the greatest strikes of the Progressive Era (1902). The South Wales coal-owners too made concerted efforts to reduce competition. But they did so by means of contractual relations with the unions. The sliding-scale agreement of South Wales was renewed eight times between 1875 and 1898. In 1903 the scale was superseded by a conciliation agreement.

All through the period the South Wales employers continued to be deeply divided by competition. Consequently, the Coal Owners' Association experienced serious problems of unity. To begin with, the majority of associated owners were not prepared to cooperate with officers of the association during the 1875 negotiations on the sliding-scale agreement. As a result, the terms of the first agreement were not so favorable to the employers as they could have been had the employers been unified. The owners' negotiating committee had initially sought to tie wages to profits (rather than prices) through a sophisticated formula based on cost and profit information supplied by members. Most member firms, however, refused to disclose such confidential information; therefore the owners' negotiating committee abandoned the sophisticated formula in favor of the more straightforward procedure proposed by the miners: linking wages to coal prices.[36]

Second, during periods of continual fall in prices the unity of the South Wales Coal Owners' Association was seriously threatened. Member firms wishing to free themselves from the binding terms of the agreement left the association in an attempt to seek further concessions from their employees. During the steep decline in coal prices from 10s.8d. a ton in 1875 to 8s.3d. in 1880, for example, 37 of the original 84 associated firms defected. Subsequently, the share of the region's coal output controlled by the association dropped from 70% to 46%. In addition, some of the associated owners were tempted to breach the agreement outright and seek further wage cuts; others sought to impose longer hours or double shifts— arrangements that were clearly not in accord with the spirit of the agreement.[37]

Another problem creating disunity among the South Wales Collieries Association was the failure to regulate production. Twice during the period, in 1893 and 1896, at the time coal prices were falling to a "lamentable level," leaders of the South Wales industry put forward schemes of output control and price fixing. In both cases, however, the schemes of Sir George Eliot (1893) and D. A. Thomas (1896) were so divisive that they were not even seriously considered by the association.[38]

Divisions among the employers, finally, undermined the association efforts to blacklist strikers. Ever since its formation in 1873, the South Wales Collieries Asso-

36. Williams, "Coalowners of South Wales," 84–85, 93.

37. J. M. Morris and L. J. Williams, "The South Wales Sliding Scale, 1876–1879: An Experiment in Industrial Relations," *Manchester School of Economics and Social Studies* 28, no. 2 (May 1960): 171–73; Williams, "Coalowners of South Wales," 88–92.

38. J. H. Clapham, *Economic History of Modern Britain* (1938, repr., Cambridge, 1951), 3:220; Page Arnot, *South Wales Miners: A History of the South Wales Miners' Federation, 1898–1914* (London, 1967), 42–43.

ciation had instituted a policy of requiring striking miners to produce a "discharge note" before they could be hired. Using the discharge note as a "strike weapon" was nonetheless ineffectual because it could be easily evaded. First, many associated coal-owners were reluctant to look searchingly at new recruits during periods of trade revival, and second, nonassociated employers did not use the discharge note at all and therefore offered strikers an unrestricted choice of employment.[39]

But all these divisions did not put an end to the sliding-scale agreement. On the contrary, the agreement survived intact for twenty-seven years. It survived, paradoxically, because it was the one unifying force that brought the divided employers together, it was the raison d'être for their association, and significantly, it provided the employers with minimum unity necessary to compete successfully with rival coalfields both at home and abroad. Because it gave the employers reasonable guarantees that profits were forthcoming, promoted stability and growth, and secured industrial peace, the "automatic wage regulator" encouraged buyers to place long-term contracts with Welsh firms and thus ensure the competitive advantage of the industry.[40]

"It is worthy of record that during the 20 years whilst the [sliding-scale] system has been in vogue," the secretary of the Coal Owners' Association noted in 1895, "the workmen of the South Wales district have, with but very few exceptions, loyally abided by the arrangement and have resisted every attempt . . . [to secure] wages in excess of those justified by the actual state of trade." Praising Sir William Lewis, chairman of the Sliding Scale Joint Committee, for his "great work . . . in maintaining the cordial relationship existing between the employers and employed," the secretary surely exaggerated. Quite a few strikes, as a matter of fact, did occur during these years, some rather large and militant: for example, the 1893 haulers' strike and the 1898 colliers' strike. Moreover, the coal-owners showed a degree of unity confronting the miners in these strikes.[41]

Nevertheless this assessment is essentially correct. In contrast to the third quarter of the nineteenth century, the fourth quarter was indeed an era of industrial peace. Between 1875 and the 1900s many wage disputes were settled by the Sliding Scale Joint Committee without a recourse to a strike; furthermore, strikes, when they erupted, normally broke out at times of new contract negotiations. In addition, the sliding-scale agreement—which applied only to member firms—had considerable influence on the wage policy of nonassociation firms and consequently promoted harmony in the nonassociated sector as well. Collective bargaining over the construction of the scale thus, meant that the struggle over piece rates shifted from the coalfields to the bargaining table, hence reducing the level of industrial conflict. Collective bargaining, in short, facilitated the survival of South Wales trade union-

39. Morris and Williams, "The Discharge Note," 290, 293; *South Wales Coal Industry*, 266; Arnot, *South Wales Miners' Federation, 1898–1914*, 40–56.

40. Evans, *Miners of South Wales*, 226–27.

41. Arnot, *South Wales Miner's Federation, 1898–1914*, chaps. 1 and 2; the quotation is from page 27.

ism under the most adverse market conditions of the "great depression" of 1873–96.[42]

Trade unionism in Eastern Pennsylvania, we recall, was destroyed in 1875. The defeat of 1875 was followed by successive waves of strikes and riots and numerous attempts at unionization that lasted throughout the century. Four major strike waves may be identified during the period, 1877, 1887–88, 1897, and 1900–1902. The first two involved the Knights of Labor, the third was a spontaneous outburst led by local militants, and the fourth was made up of two general strikes directed by the United Mine Workers. Nowhere in the history of late nineteenth-century Wales is there a parallel to such a strike record.

42. Jevons, *British Coal Trade*, 512–13; Morris and Williams, "Discharge Note," 289; "South Wales Sliding Scale," 165; Williams, "Coalowners of South Wales," 92. Whether the miners too benefited from industrial peace and the sliding scale is a matter of dispute. To be sure, following the depression of the 1870s, the South Wales unions were broken up to independent feeble district societies that had scarcely any existence independent of the Sliding Scale Joint Committee. It is also true that several aspects of the sliding scale were unfavorable to the miners. The removal of the minimum wage clause from all agreements signed after the 1870s, the problem of the scale's sensitivity, the link between earnings and prices but not earnings and output, the narrow conception of the functions of the joint committee, and consequently, the policy of dealing solely with disputes over contract negotiations and not all disputes and grievances—all these elements were clearly adverse to the interests of the miners. Accordingly, a growing disatisfaction with the sliding scale among the miners was one of the elements leading to the formation of the South Wales Miners Federation (SWMF) in 1898. Jevons, *British Coal Trade*, 463; Sidney and Beatrice Webb, *Industrial Democracy* (1897, repr., London, 1902), 576. Other contemporary critiques of the sliding scale are L. L. Price's "Industrial Concilliation: A Retrospect," *Economic Journal* 8 (December 1898): 461–73; H. Read's "South Wales Sliding Scale: Its Advantages and Its Defects," *Economic Journal* 4 (June 1894): 332–35, and S. J. Chapman's "Some Theoretical Objections to Sliding Scale," *Economic Journal* 13 (June 1903): 186–96. Of all modern critics, the most influential has been J. H. Porter; see his articles, "Wages Bargaining Under Concilliation Agreements, 1860–1914," *Economic History Review* 23, no. 3 (December 1970): 460–75; "Wage Determination by Selling Price Sliding Scales 1870–1914," *Manchester School of Economic and Social Studies* 39, no. 1 (March 1971): 13–21, and "Coal and Conciliation," *Bulletin of the Society for the Study of Labor History* 26 (1973): 27–28. See also V. L. Allen, "The Origins of Industrial Conciliation and Arbitration," *International Review of Social History* 9 (1964): part 2, 237–54, and Keith Burgess, *The Origins of British Industrial Relations* (London, 1975), chap. 3.

On the other hand, the sliding scale did confer substantial benefits on the miners. Union recognition was an obvious one, especially during the long economic downturn of 1873–96. Moreover, the sliding scale limited the power of the employer to enforce reductions without consulting the miners; in other words, no matter what concession the miners were forced to accept, the principle that wage rates no longer be solely determined by the employers was now firmly established. Collective bargaining, furthermore, promoted a more steady employment in the mines. Collective bargaining, recognition, and local unionism, finally, laid the foundations of the SWMF. Reaching a total membership of 100,000 in 1899 (Evans, 177–78), the SWMF had become within a decade a formidable union organization famous for its militancy. To argue, therefore, that under the sliding-scale agreement "trade unionism was contained and disarmed at a significant stage of its growth," as one modern critic did (Allen, 254); or that "a more militant policy" on the part of the miners "would have secured greater gains" (Porter 1973, 27), is to miss the critical point: under the unfavorable labor market of 1873–96 South Wales unionism survived. It could have been destroyed. For a thorough and balanced assessment of the sliding-scale agreements see Evans, *Miners of South Wales*, 115–128.

The great railroad strikes of 1877 prompted a series of uncontrolled and violent coal strikes. The strikes affected all three anthracite fields with the most militant and violent protest taking place in the Wyoming field around Scranton, where the Knights of Labor had organized a local assembly in 1876. A Special Police force financed partly by the Delaware, Lackawanna and Western Railroad and partly by the Lackawanna Coal and Iron Company was mobilized against the strikers. Armed with "breech loading rifles," the police force fired into a crowd of strikers and sympathizers killing six and wounding twenty. Immediately following the shooting, 3,000 members of the Pennsylvania National Guard were sent to Scranton to occupy the area.[43]

The 1887–88 strike had broken out in the Lehigh Coal basin and four months later spread throughout the Schuylkill area. Altogether, the stoppage lasted over six months and at its peak involved some 50,000 mine workers—about half the anthracite workforce. Violence erupted as the strike began to collapse. Attempts to hire strike-breakers and reopen the collieries led to a riot in Shenandoah (Schuylkill) in February 1888, to the intervention of the operators' private security force—the Coal and Iron Police—and to the shooting and wounding of five protesters.[44]

Ten years later, during the 1897 strike wave, the anthracite miners experienced what two historians recently called "the worst disaster yet to befall American labor." The strikes of 1897 were rather small in scale, involving a maximum of 10,000–11,000 mine workers, mostly Slavic immigrants; were limited to the Hazelton area of the Lehigh coalfield; and erupted in succession during August–September 1897. On September 10, 1897, a group of 250 to 300 unarmed strikers marched peacefully toward the Lattimer mine patch to shut down the local collieries. The sheriff of Luzerne County (Lehigh field), accompanied by 150 deputies armed with Winchester rifles was waiting on the road blocking the way. When the strikers arrived and refused to turn back, the sheriff panicked, someone shouted "fire," and the deputies fired into the crowd killing eight men on the spot and wounding sixty, some with multiple wounds from which eleven more would die. All in all, the Lattimer Massacre claimed nineteen lives.[45]

The Lattimer shooting made the UMW's organizing efforts impossible to stop. Two giant strikes followed, both directed by the UMW. The first had taken place in the fall of 1900, involved 120,000–130,000 anthracite mine workers and lasted six weeks; the second broke out in May 1902 and put out of work 147,000 workers for 163 days. The UMW demanded a wage increase in 1900 and federal arbitration in

43. Samuel Logan, *A City's Danger and Defense or Issues and Results of the Strikes of 1877* (Scranton, Pa., 1887), 84–104.

44. U.S. House of Representatives, *Labor Troubles in the Anthracite Regions,* lxxv–cxiv; Victor Greene, *The Slavic Community on Strike* (Notre Dame, Ind., 1968), 87–91.

45. Michael Novak, *The Guns of Lattimer* (New York, 1978), especially part 3; Victor Greene, "A Study in Slavs, Strikes, and Unions: The Anthracite Strike of 1897," *Pennsylvania History* 31, no. 2 (April 1964): 203–12; Miller and Sharpless, *Kingdom of Coal,* chap. 7. The quotation is from *Kingdom of Coal,* 238.

1902, and both demands were granted. But despite a presidential intervention in support of the miners (in 1902 as in 1900) the UMW failed to gain recognition—the single most important strike goal.[46]

The UMW failure was rooted in the employers' unity, their willingness to use violence and their control of local government. Close cooperation among the anthracite railroads for the purpose of opposing unions dates back to the 1877 strike wave. The bloodiest unrest in 1877 occurred in the Wyoming coalfield where three railroads (Delaware and Hudson, Delaware, Lackawanna, and Western, and the Pennsylvania Coal Company) formed a united front in opposition to the miners. Refusing to grant the miners a wage increase, the three corporations held firm, kept the mines shut down for three months, fired the strike leaders, and starved the strikers into submission.[47]

Similarly, the Reading's monopoly over the Schuylkill coalfield played a critical role in the miners' defeat of 1888. Twice during the strike did the miners challenge the Reading's monopoly—first in the Pennsylvania legislature and then in the House of Representatives—and twice did they fail in their legal campaign to separate railroad from coal-mining firms. Evicted from company tenements, deprived of company coal, and replaced by strike-breakers under the protection of the Coal and Iron Police, the Schuylkill miners yielded to the enormous power of the Reading Railroad.[48]

The Lattimer Massacre did not involve the anthracite railroads but rather the independent coal operators. Independent operators remained in all three anthracite fields but only in the Hazelton area of the Lehigh coalfield (where Lattimer was located) did the independents rule. Control over the Hazelton mines concentrated in the hands of a few powerful families—Pardee, Markle, Cox, Van Wickle—who also owned the local banks, land trusts, ironworks, flour and powder mills, retail stores, and in addition, substantial shares in the railroads. Interconnected through a web of social marriages and interlocking directorships, members of the leading families formed a close-knit group. Together, they made a decision to crash the 1897 strike by force, delivered the message "loud and clear" to the sheriff of Luzerne, and paid for an armed force of deputies reinforced by both Pinkerton detectives and the Coal and Iron police to be placed under the sheriff's command.[49]

The unity among the employers reached its apex in the years following the Lat-

46. Roberts, *Anthracite Coal Industry*, 183–91; Roy, *History of the Coal Miners*, 396–440; P. Q. R. "The Anthracite Strike," *Outlook* 62 (November 8, 1902): 585–89; Robert Cornell, *The Anthracite Strike of 1902* (Washington, D.C., 1957); Robert Reynolds, "The Coal Kings Come to Judgement," *American Heritage* 11, no. 3 (April 1960): 55–62, 94–100; Joe Gowaskie, "John Mitchell and the Anthracite Mine Workers," *Labor History* 27, no. 1 (Winter 1985–86): 54–63.

47. Aurand, *Molly Maguires to United Mine Workers,* 112–13.

48. Herold Aurand, "The Anthracite Strike of 1887–88" *Pennsylvania History* 35, no. 2 (April 1968): 180, *Molly Maguires to United Mine Workers*, 127.

49. The quotation is from Novak, *Guns of Lattimer*, 90, but see also 35–43 and Greene, "Study in Slavs," 206.

timer Massacre. Between 1897 and 1902, the anthracite corporations had combined so effectively that by 1902, once and for all, competition had come to an end; thereafter coal prices remained remarkably stable from month to month and from year to year. The combination of 1902 was the result of four developments: railroad mergers, the removal of the independent operators, the growth in intercorporate linkages, and the increasing concentration of financial control over the industry. The largest merger of the period involved the Reading Railroad. In 1901 the Reading purchased the Central Railroad of New Jersey and thereby gained control over one-third of the region's anthracite output and 63% of Pennsylvania's anthracite coal reserves. Similarly, competition between the railroads and the independent operators was practically eliminated by means of coal-sale contracts (signed by the railroads and the independents) covering the entire future output of the independents at 65% of the tidewater price of coal. Between 1898 and 1902, moreover, the steep increase in the number of interlocking directorates among the boards governing the railroads further consolidated the anthracite combination. The growing concentration of financial control over anthracite production in the hands of J. P. Morgan and his associates was the final element in the drive to consolidate the industry, eliminate competition, and form a united front against the UMW. Morgan put together the cartel that imposed a lasting order on the industry.[50]

Morgan also made the decision to settle the strikes, first in 1900 and again in 1902. Initially he did not intervene personally in either dispute; rather, he left the matter in the hands of the railroad's presidents, with George Baer, president of the Reading and a Morgan appointee, leading the struggle. But in the end Morgan acted.

Only intense political pressure from the White House persuaded Morgan to seek a settlement. In 1900, Mark Hanna, chairman of the Republican Party, convinced Morgan that a prolonged anthracite strike was likely to hurt President McKinley's chances for re-election. In 1902, Secretary of War Elihu Root pressured Morgan to accept President Roosevelt's solution (federal arbitration by the Anthracite Commission) and hence avert a "coal famine" in the freezing eastern cities, which used anthracite for domestic heating. In both cases, union recognition was out of the question. In 1900 the UMW won a 10% wage hike but the operator refused direct negotiations with the union representatives. In 1902, the Anthracite Commission compromised on wages and hours, established labor-management boards, and again, refused to consider recognition. Characteristically, in his negotiations with Root, Morgan excluded any possibility of union recognition as a precondition for accepting the recommendations of the Anthracite Commission.[51]

50. Jones, *Anthracite Coal Combinations*, pp. 97, 109, 154, 156–57, 178–79. See also U.S. House of Representatives, *Labor Troubles in the Anthracite Regions*, lii–liii; and Subcommittee of the Committee on Interstate and Foreign Commerce, *The Alleged Combination of the Philadelphia and Reading Railroad Company*, Report No. 2278, 52d Cong., 2nd Sess., 1892–93, i–viii.
51. Robert Wiebe, "The Anthracite Strike of 1902: A Record of Confusion," *Mississippi Valley Historical Review* 48, no. 2 (September 1961): 236–37, 240, 243, 248–49. See also Elsie Gluck, *John Mitchell* (New York, 1929), 76, 156; Cornell, *Anthracite Strike*, chaps. 2 and 8; Lewis Gould, *The*

CONCLUSION

Historians have offered several explanations for the defeat of Pennsylvania's anthracite miners. One explanation identifies ethnic, regional, and occupational divisions among the miners as a key element in their failure to build effective unions. Ethnic animosities among Welsh, Irish, English, and Scotch miners, regional conflicts between the Wyoming, Schuylkill, and Lehigh miners, and occupational discord between miners and laborers—all these forces, it has been argued, tore apart every important union organization among the anthracite miners in the 1870s and 1880s: the Workingmen's Benevolent Association, the Knights of Labor, and the Miners' and Laborers' Amalgamated Association.[52]

The Welsh comparison casts doubt on this assessment. It shows that internal divisions among mine workers played at least as important a role in South Wales as they did in Eastern Pennsylvania. It shows, for example, that the geographical divisions of the South Wales region into deep isolated valleys checked the growth of a centralized union organization and encouraged the proliferation of a large number of small local districts, widely spread and loosely interconnected. It shows in addition, that rivalries among native Welsh miners, English immigrant miners, and Irish immigrant mine laborers created almost as much ethnic disunity in South Wales as they did in Pennsylvania. And it shows that there were further divisions between the anthracite, steam, and bituminous miners and between colliers employed by the iron-masters and those employed by the coal-owners.[53]

Another explanation identifies the anti-union ideology of the American employer as the principal factor contributing to the failure of the Pennsylvanian unions. "Ideology was the crucial ingredient" in management opposition to unionism, one labor historian concluded in his survey of the anthracite miners, and "the violence that attended strikes showed that industrial strife in the anthracite regions reflected an ideological clash."[54]

This explanation is hard to reconcile with the remarkable success of the UMW in the bituminous coalfields of Western Pennsylvania, Ohio, Indiana, and Illinois. Granted that ideology was indeed "the vital ingredient" of management hostility, why did the bituminous coal operators accept unionism and collective bargaining? Why did they grant the UMW recognition and accept peaceful cooperation with the union through the Interstate Joint Conference Agreement? What were the reasons,

---

Presidency of Theodore Roosevelt (Lawrence, Kans., 1991), 66–71; United States, Anthracite Coal Strike Commission, *Report to the President* (Washington, D.C., 1903), 60–63.

52. See Yearley, *Enterprise and Anthracite*, 192, Aurand, "Workingmen's Benevolent Association," 34; and his *Molly Maguires to United Mine Workers*, 81, 94, 164.

53. Morris and Williams, *South Wales Coal Industry*, 270, 236–37; Evans, *Miners of South Wales*, 125, Jevons, *British Coal Industry*, 130; T. M. Hodge, "The Peopling of the Hinterland of the Port of Cardiff," *Economic History Review* 17, no. 1 (1947): 65, 68–69.

54. Aurand, *Molly Maguires to United Mine Workers*, 168.

in other words for the contrasting attitudes of management toward unionism in the two sectors of the American coal-mining industry?

These reasons, it is easy to see, lie in the realm of competition and monopoly, not mere ideology, Ideology certainly played a role, but a role circumscribed by the competitive structure of the industry. The American bituminous industry, like the South Wales coal industry, was made up of hundreds of small operators, each typically running one or two collieries, each typically subject to cut-throat competition from local operators as well as rival coalfields. Unlike its impact on anthracite mining, the great merger movement that swept through American industry at the turn of the century left bituminous mining almost untouched. Divided by competition, the bituminous coal operators, like the South Wales coal-owners, sought to regulate production, stabilize coal prices, and reduce competition by means of collective bargaining; the interstate joint conference of the four participating states (Central Competitive Field), like the sliding scale of South Wales, was a labor as well as an industry agreement.[55] In both cases, collective bargaining reflected the mutual interests of operators and miners; in both, it acted powerfully against the competitive market forces; in both, it stabilized output, wages, and prices. In Eastern Pennsylvania, by contrast, stability was achieved by the railroads. There was no need to seek an accommodation with the union.

---

55. For an analysis of the bituminous industry along these lines see John Bowman, ''When Workers Organize Capitalists: The Case of the Bituminous Coal Industry'' *Politics and Society* 14, no. 3 (1985): 289–327, and David Brody, ''Labor Relations in American Coal Mining: An Industry Perspective,'' in *Workers, Owners, and Politics in Coal Mining*, ed. Gerald Feldman and Klaus Tenfelde (New York, 1990), 74–117. West Virginia of course, was an exceptional case. The diffusion of ownership of bituminous mines in West Virginia among ragged, ruthless, frontier-type individual capitalists did not encourage union recognition. For an explanation, see Brody 87–88, and sources cited there.

CHAPTER SEVENTEEN

"A PARTING OF THE WAYS"
Immigrant Miners and the Rise of Politically Conscious Trade Unionism in Scotland and the American Midwest, 1865–1924

JOHN H.M. LASLETT

In the spring of 1865, the opening of the northern Illinois coalfield lured several hundred Scots colliers, along with other Scottish and Irish emigrants, to board a sailing vessel for New York at the Broomielaw, on Clydeside in the heart of downtown Glasgow. Arriving in New York, they took the "emigrant train" for Chicago, and then traveled to unsettled prairie lands fifty miles southwest of the city where rich coal deposits had just been discovered. These southwestern Scottish miners were followed throughout the 1870s and 1880s, at irregular intervals, by other shiploads, many of whose occupants ended up in the Scottish enclaves of mining communities as far apart as Maryland, Alabama, and western Pennsylvania.[1]

Several of these emigrant Scottish colliers, most notably Daniel McLaughlin and John James, had earlier exerted a strong influence over the policies and outlook of

---

1. Gordon M. Wilson, *Alexander McDonald, Leader of the Miners* (Aberdeen: Aberdeen University Press, 1982), 113. See also Clifton K. Yearley, *Britons in American Labor: A History of the Influence of the United Kingdom Immigrants on American Labor, 1820–1914* (Baltimore: Johns Hopkins University Press, 1957), 128–29.

the small, scattered groups of unionized colliers in central Lanarkshire (located not far south of Glasgow), who later helped form the Lanarkshire County Miners Union. In turn, this became the backbone of the Scottish Miners Federation when it was formed in 1894. Scottish-bred, or Scottish-influenced miners' leaders like Duncan McDonald and John H. Walker also exerted a powerful influence over the founding and development of District 12 of the United Mine Workers of America. By 1919, this district had become the largest and most powerful, as well as the most radical, district union in the United Mine Workers as a whole.[2]

In their origins, work culture, and early political development, therefore, the men who founded the Lanarkshire County Miners Union (LCMU) in 1886, had much in common with those who established District 12 of the UMWA (1890). Hence a comparison of the social and political outlook of these men and the mining communities they came from, first in Lanarkshire and then in northern Illinois, provides a powerful insight into the factors that both united—but also separated—the subsequent historical development of the United Mine Workers of America (1890) and the Miners Federation of Great Britain (1889). In many ways these, the two largest and most powerful miners' unions in the English-speaking world, developed along similar lines. But in certain respects, most notably in the attitude they took up toward socialist, or third-party politics, they were different.

This essay analyzes the development of these two district miners' unions, one on each side of the Atlantic, in order to shed new light on this difference. In particular, it answers the question of why, despite the growth of almost equally strong class hostilities between miners and coal operators in Scotland and Illinois, the political solution to the economic problems from which both groups of miners suffered turned out to be different. After 1900, for a time at least, both coal unions were led by socialists of similar background and convictions. But whereas in May 1908, the LCMU committed itself to third-party politics under the leadership of the British Labour Party, District 12 of the UMW, while also politically very active, chose to commit itself—in that very same year—to the politically nonpartisan policies of the American Federation of Labor.[3]

This transatlantic parting of the ways, which was followed by a similar divergence between the UMWA and the Miners Federation of Great Britain as a whole, had momentous consequences for the differing political development of the labor movement in both Britain and America. The geographical concentration of colliers in specific regions of the two countries gave the two national miners' unions unique electoral clout. This was because, numbering more than half a million on each side

2. John H. Keiser, "John H. Walker, Labor Leader From Illinois," in *Essays in Illinois History*, ed. Donald F. Tingley (Carbondale: Southern Illinois University Press, 1968), 75–89; Duncan McDonald, "Early Experience" (Duncan McDonald Collection, Illinois State Library); McAlister Coleman, *Men and Coal* (New York: Arno, 1969), 90–93.

3. Roy Gregory, *The Miners and British Politics, 1906–1914* (London: Oxford University Press, 1968), 32; Eugene Staley, *History of the Illinois State Federation of Labor* (Chicago: University of Chicago Press, 1930), 180.

of the ocean, they controled sufficient votes in their local coalfields to elect to office whomever they liked, either to Parliament or to the legislatures of America's mining states. After the 1884 Election Reform Act gave British miners the ballot, the Scottish union followed the example of Illinois District 12 and elected quite a few of its members to political office, at first on behalf of the Liberal Party, which was the party of the left in Britain at the turn of the century. Then, between approximately 1906 and 1918, they slowly transferred their political loyalties from the Liberals to the British Labour Party, which was founded in 1900.

Indeed, the committment which the Lanarkshire miners finally made to the Labour Party in the years between 1918 and 1922 helped materially to transform that party from a minor irritant on the left flank of the Liberals, into the majority party of the British working class.[4] If the UMW had followed a similar course, the political history of the U.S. labor movement might also have been different.

Yet District 12 of the UMW, as well as the United Mine Workers generally, chose not to follow the example of their British cousins by lending their support to an independent party of labor. Why not? An important part of the answer can be found by comparing the fortunes of a similar group of miners, who historically had a great deal in common, yet who operated in two different countries and in two different political contexts. My essay begins by describing the common economic problems that miners on both sides of the Atlantic faced in the 1880s and 1890s, after growing industrial conflict in the pits exposed the inadequacy of the class-harmony doctrine of trade unionism that the colliers pursued in the mid-Victorian period, first in Britain and then in America. By 1900 both the LCMU and District 12 had adopted a similar type of militant, class-conscious industrial unionism. The essay then goes on to explore the gradual separation that occurred in the political strategy the miners of Scotland and the American Midwest followed in securing legislative solutions to their economic problems in the period leading up to and following the First World War. Among other things, I shall argue that it was differences in the way the two-party system operated in Britain and America, not any weaker measure of class-consciousness among U.S. workers, that accounted for the difference in political outcome.

I

Because the northern Illinois coalfield was unsettled prairie when the Scottish, Irish, and English miners first arrived there in the spring of 1865, they were able at first to imbue their new communities with very much the same philosophy of mining unionism they had learned from the great Scottish miners' leader Alexander Mac-

4. Henry Pelling, *A Short History of the Labour Party* (Harmondsworth: Pelican Books, 1964), 62–63.

Donald back home. MacDonald, who dominated Scottish mining unionism between 1855 and 1874, had been the mentor of both John James and Daniel McLaughlin. Let us look at his philosophy of unionism a little more carefully.

Drawing upon the autonomous workplace traditions of the skilled pick miner, in the 1850s MacDonald articulated what some historians have called the ideology of the independent collier. This was based on the idea that miner and mine-owner shared a common—and equal—responsibility for the running of the industry, and that each should share in the profits to be derived from it. By controlling his own level of output (usually between two-and-a-half and three tons a shift) the collier and his union could exert sufficient pressure on the coal-master both to keep wages high, and to limit the entry of unskilled workers into the trade. In return, MacDonald and his followers expected the mine-owners to bargain collectively with the union, and to submit any disputes that could not be settled by direct negotiation to the disposition of neutral arbitrators. He also expected the collier to be respected as a semi-autonomous, petty contractor, who could control his own output and way of life.[5]

In the rural mining villages of mid-Victorian Scotland, this class-collaborationist philosophy was for a time sufficiently acceptable to the paternalistic mine-owners and gentry to bring considerable rewards. But the social compact did not last for long. In the 1860s and 1870s improved technology, increased competition, and expanding Scottish export markets prompted large firms like Dixon's, Bairds, and Merry and Cunningham to introduce managerial supervision into the mines. Modern blasting powder was brought in to increase the output rate; men and ponies were replaced by steam engines for operating machinery; and improved winding gear, coupled with greater depth of pit, meant that colliers were less able to come and go from the mine when they pleased.[6]

It was disillusionment and anger at the loss of their traditional rights down the pit, coupled with a desire to limit the coal operators' access to unskilled labor by drawing off the surplus, that first prompted a minority of Lanarkshire miners to migrate to Maryland, Pennsylvania, and to the newly opened coalfields of the American Midwest. Besides the fact that wages were higher than they were at home, Scottish miners had special reasons for settling in northern Illinois. In the 1850s that region of the country had helped to establish the Republican party, whose radical wing was dedicated to the principles of "free labor, free soil, free men."[7] All three of these ideals evoked a sympathetic chord in the hearts of colliers who had a sentimental attachment to the land, and whose forbears had been bound in virtual perpetuity to their coal-masters before the Scottish Emancipation Act of 1799. Some Scottish miners were also keen to take advantage of the recently passed Homestead

5. Wilson, *Alexander McDonald*, chap. 6.

6. Alan Campbell, *The Lanarkshire Miners, A Social History of Their Trade Unions, 1775–1874* (Edinburgh: John Donald, 1979), chaps. 8, 10, and 12.

7. Eric Foner, *Free Soil, Free Labor, Free Men: The Ideology of the Republican Party Before the Civil War* (New York: Oxford University Press, 1970), 72–83.

Act of 1862, in order to establish farms of their own. Others were aware that their new place of settlement was the home state of the celebrated author of that act, President Abraham Lincoln. Lincoln was a self-made son of toil who had praised labor as superior to capital in his public speeches, seeming thereby to endorse the dignity of the workingman in much the same way that Alexander MacDonald had done back home.[8]

Besides this, the Civil War had drawn many American miners into the Union Army, creating a scarcity of labor and driving wages up still higher in the northern Illinois coalfield. By contrast, wages had suffered a major decline in the Lanarkshire field in the late 1850s. By the time of the Civil War, quite a few Scottish colliers (particularly young, single men) had already developed the technique of going out to the northern states for a ''run'' in the winter mining season (when wages tended to be higher), and returning home in the summer. They were aided in this by the increasing number of Clyde-built iron passenger ships, which had been steadily displacing wooden vessels throughout the 1850s, and had brought a safer, quicker, and cheaper method of emigration closer to hand.[9]

As a result of these advantages, for several years after they settled in the northern Illinois coalfield, the emigrant English, Scottish, and Irish miners were able to reproduce the informal work relations they had enjoyed in Scotland in the 1840s and 1850s. Indeed, in some respects they were able to implement their independent collier philosophy more successfully in the United States than they had back home. The first pits sunk in northern Illinois were small family concerns that enabled the immigrant miners to preserve their petty-contractor role in ways that were no longer possible in Scotland. Coal seams were narrower than they were in Lanarkshire, but they were also nearer to the surface. This meant that the immigrant miners were once more able to determine the length of their working day, and to come and go from the pit as and when they pleased.[10]

Because of their ability to reproduce, or even to extend, the sense of independence and pride in craft they had enjoyed in Britain, the northern Illinois miners at first chose to adopt the same moderate, class-collaborationist brand of trade unionism that Alexander MacDonald had taught them back home. They were helped by the fact that the first large miners' union in the Midwest, the American Miners Association (1861), had already blazed the way. At its founding convention held in St. Louis in 1861, this union outlawed strikes, and advocated output restriction and arbitration and conciliation as the best means of resolving disputes.[11] But the growing scale of

---

8. David Montgomery, *Beyond Equality, Labor and the Radical Republicans, 1862–1872* (New York: Vintage Books, 1967), 302.

9. Wilson, *Alexander McDonald*, 112.

10. Modesto Donna, *The Braidwood Story* (n.p., n.d.), 57–59; Richard P. Joyce, ''Miners of the Prairie: Life and Labor in the Wilmington, Illinois, Coalfield, 1866–1897'' (M.A. thesis, Illinois State University at Normal, 1980), 12–28.

11. Edward A. Wieck, *The American Miners Association, A Record of the Origins of Coal Miners Unions in the United States* (New York: Russell Sage Foundation, 1940), 112–14.

production in the American mines soon caused the situation to change. By the end of the 1870s the development of modern mining methods had brought in its train the same kind of class separation, degradation of work, and recriminations over the unfair distribution of profits that had occurred in Scotland twenty years before.

The key to the these new developments, as in the Lanarkshire coal and iron industry in the earlier period, lay in a rapid expansion in the market for coal; in technological innovations that rendered obsolete many of the small slope or drift mines that had been present in northern Illinois in the 1860s; and in the replacement of small, locally owned coal companies by large absentee-owned mining corporations. In the early days the Scottish colliers of Braidwood and Streator—the two Illinois towns where they were most influential—had enjoyed more or less unchallenged access to the Chicago coal market via the Chicago and Alton railroad line. By the mid-1870s, however, numerous other railroads had been built, bringing higher-grade coal to Chicago from newly opened pits in the southern Illinois coal mines, as well as linking them to a broader midwestern market via St. Louis.

By the end of 1873, for example, the Wilmington Coal Mining and Manufacturing Company had sunk a deep mine shaft in the newly laid-out village of Diamond, southwest of Braidwood. In 1874 the Coalfield Coal Company, organized by a group of New York financiers, purchased one thousand acres of land along the railroad in Grundy County, leased 640 acres to the Wilmington Star Company, and laid out the town of Coal City. In the early 1880s, the slumbering village of Braceville was awakened when the Chicago, Milwaukee and St. Paul Railroad purchased 14,000 acres, and undertook large-scale mining operations nearby. In 1878 the coal companies of Will and Grundy Counties produced 478,000 tons of coal with a labor force of 5,422 men. For a brief period this made them the two largest coal-producing counties in Illinois.[12]

Technological innovations came about as a result of the ingenuity of Alexander Crombie, the superintendent of the Wilmington Star Company, who in 1876 obtained a patent on "a machine for digging coal." The machine proved to be impractical, but it set a precedent for the development of more efficient coal-cutting equipment soon afterward. Two years later Crombie invented a device to prevent the sudden and deadly descent of miners' cages when the cable broke. Later on, Richard Raney of Braceville put together a new machine for trimming coal cars, reducing from seven to two the number of men needed for this task. These changes made it possible to increase both the efficiency and the scale of mining operations, as well as the number of employees engaged at any one pit. In 1882, for example, the four largest coal companies in Grundy County employed, respectively, 330, 287, 234, and 150 miners. These were larger figures than the numbers for the Scottish pits in which the men had worked earlier. All of these new mines were shaft pits, using

12. Herbert Gutman, *Power and Culture, Essays on the American Working Class*, ed. Ira Berlin (New York: New Press, 1987), 122–23; Jasper Johnson, "The Wilmington, Illinois, Coalfield," *Transactions of the American Institute of Mining Engineers* (Easton, Pa.), no. 3 (1874–75), 186–202.

steam-driven machinery rather than horses to move the coal, and all of the shafts went down more than a hundred feet. All of them also made use of professionally trained supervisors.[13]

No company reflected this transition to modern corporate methods more clearly than the Chicago, Wilmington and Vermilion Company (CW & V), which had been formed as a result of a merger of two earlier firms. Capitalized at two million dollars, by 1876 its five Braidwood shafts provided employment for more than half the 1,665 miners living in the town. Not only were the company's stockholders absentee owners in Boston and other eastern cities. Both its president, James Monroe Walker, and its general manager, A. L. Sweet, lived in Chicago, more than fifty miles from Braidwood.[14] The emergence of the CW & V as the corporate giant of the northern Illinois coalfield signaled the demise not only of the small, single-family firm as typical of the U.S. coal industry; it also marked the end of the coal town as a harmonious, face-to-face community displaying a sense of mutual respect between mine-owner and employee. A further, if indirect, blow to the emigrant miners' belief in the class-harmony ideal was administered by the violent, nationwide railroad strike of 1877, which coincided with a bitter strike in the northern Illinois coalfield.[15]

The miners themselves were fully aware of the negative implications of these changes for their position in the industry, both in Scotland and the United States. John James of Braidwood, who had been one of Alexander MacDonald's main disciples in the Old World—and had sought diligently to carry out his trade union philosophy in the New—showed this in a poignant letter he wrote back home to MacDonald on January 27, 1876. Noting that the Miners National Association on the U.S. side of the ocean (of which he was himself a national officer), was on the verge of collapse, he went on: "Capitalists are the same the world over. The same desire to trample roughshod over the man who toils is evidenced here to a large extent." James concluded, "I am thoroughly satisfied," "that whether it be under a republic or an empire, labour, if it will have fair, honest dealings at the hands of its employer must put itself in a position to command it."[16]

II

But how, in the new economic circumstances of the 1880s and 1890s, were these "fair, honest dealings" to be secured? What kind of new collier outlook could be

---

13. *History of Grundy County* (Morris: Grundy County Board of Supervisors, 1968), 162–74.

14. Gutman, *Power and Culture*, 142.

15. Quite a few miners in railroad towns like Spring Valley, who shared with the colliers a common hatred of the corporate arrogance of railroad companies like the Illinois Central, were also radicalized later on by Eugene Debs's American Railway Union, which conducted the 1894 Pullman strike. See Almont Lindsey, *The Pullman Strike* (Chicago: W. Kerr, 1942), 181–83; *Spring Valley, Illinois: An Ethnic Heritage Made From Coal* (Spring Valley: Spring Valley Centennial Committee, 1986), 41–42.

16. *Workingmen's Advocate* (February 3, 1976), 3.

fashioned that could both preserve and defend the traditional skills and dignity of the pick miner in the community and at the coal face, and at the same time provide a sufficient antidote to the power of the modern mining corporation?

The answers to these questions emerged slowly on both sides of the Atlantic. They did not all come at once. Instead, they developed out of a period of turmoil and conflict in the coal industry that lasted from approximately 1873 until the turn of the century. During the first half of this period the older generation of miners, represented by Alexander MacDonald in Lanarkshire and by John James in northern Illinois, sought unsuccessfully to maintain the basic elements of the class-harmony ideal, despite growing evidence that the coal operators were no longer willing to uphold it. During the second period, which ran from about 1890 to 1908, a more militant philosophy was espoused that culminated in the adoption of openly social democratic policies in Scotland, but in something short of this in the United States.

Several factors exposed the growing class divide that now separated the economic interests of miner and mine-owner in both Scotland and Illinois. They included the growing insistence of the operators on controlling the pace and character of underground work; the downward pressure on wages generated by the international economic recession of 1873–97; and the unwillingness of the coal operators to continue using the informal methods of conciliation and arbitration that had hitherto settled most disputes between masters and men.

In Illinois, for example, the newly enlarged mining corporations in Braidwood and Streator, like their Lanarkshire equivalents in Larkhall and Wishaw, pressed their employees for greater industrial discipline, so as to be able to compete successfully with other regional coal companies. In the spring of 1873, the managers of the CW & V in Braidwood asserted that the company had the unilateral right to shut down its pits at any time. It required its men to "perform a full day's work of ten hours," unless they had special permission to do otherwise. And it insisted that the terms of employment would be determined by the company's officials alone. "No person will be allowed to interfere with the employers' just right of employing, and discharging from employment any person or persons whom the Superintendent may consider proper," the company's contract read.[17]

These demands were rendered even more unpalatable by the severe mining depression that began with the financial panic in New York in the summer of 1873, and that led to the most drastic round of wage cuts to be inflicted on miners on either side of the Atlantic for more than twenty years. By the end of the year coal and iron prices had collapsed all over Britain and America. They continued to fall until 1887. The consequence was wage cuts that drove the earnings of Lanarkshire miners down from about eight shillings a day in 1873 to about four in 1874 and three in 1878. Comparable cuts occurred in northern Illinois.[18]

17. *Workingmen's Advocate* (April 4, 1873), 2.

18. Campbell, *Lanarkshire Miners*, chap. 12; Joyce, "Miners," 123–29; Fred Reid, *Keir Hardie* (London: Croom Helm, 1978), 88.

The resulting human suffering was extensive on both sides of the ocean. In the autumn of 1879, for example, large numbers of miners from Wishaw, Larkhall, and several other Lanarkshire mining towns were evicted from company housing owned by Dunlop's and other big iron companies after they had protested a wage cut. Slack times among the Braidwood miners began as early as June 1873. By December of that year John James reported sadly that only two out of every five miners was working in the local pits. Throughout northern Illinois, noted the *Wilmington Advocate* in April 1874, "there are many families at the mines . . . in want of the necessities of life." In Streator, miners were being discharged at the rate of twenty a week, leading many either to migrate further west in hope of work, or even to return to Great Britain. Several dozen Braidwood miners moved to Colorado in 1876, causing a local paper to ask: "Will Braidwood and Gardner be depopulated?"[19] Tales such as these were to become even more commonplace among miners on both sides of the Atlantic during the recession of 1893–96.

As a result of the prolonged recession, a series of bitter strikes took place in both Scotland and Illinois, most of which ended in humiliating defeat. The first strike in the series took place in Lanarkshire at the end of 1872. Over a thousand miners from Wishaw, Larkhall, Motherwell and elsewhere struck unsuccessfully against a wage cut of two shillings in some areas, and one shilling in others. They were forced back to work without the cuts being rescinded. The second Lanarkshire walkout occurred two years later, in the spring of 1874, when another wage cut was imposed by the coal and iron companies, producing an almost identical result. Miners who worked for large-scale iron companies like Bairds, Merry and Cunnihnghanm, and Dixon's endured another two shilling cut, while those who worked for the sale-coal companies lost another shilling a day.[20]

The third strike in the series took place in northern Illinois between June and September 1874. It was the only one that could be called a victory. On June 1, 1874, the Chicago, Wilmington and Vermilion Co. cut its pick-mining rate from $1.25 to $1.10 per ton, and the price for "pushing" coal cars (hauling them from workplace to pit bottom) was cut in half. On this occasion the immigrant Illinois miners were able to drive a wedge between the smaller and the larger coal companies, enabling them to gain the upper hand. In late August 1874, the Wilmington and Diamond Coal Companies, and a few days later the Eureka Coal Company, agreed to a compromise settlement. This isolated the CW & V, thereby forcing it into a compromise agreement on September 4. The digging rate was cut by a small amount, but all employees were rehired without discrimination.

In the summer of 1877, however, a second major, districtwide strike took place in the northern Illinois coalfield, which resulted in a resounding defeat. It began on May 1, 1877, when CW & V managers in both Streator and Braidwood announced that the pick-mining rate for the following season would be 25% lower than it had

19. *Wilmington Advocate* (April 11, 1874), 2.
20. Campbell, *Lanarkshire Miners*, 290–92; Reid, *Keir Hardie*, 25–26.

been in 1876. They also refused in advance to negotiate with the miners' union, insisting instead that the colliers sign a yellow-dog contract repudiating any attempt at union organizing. Angered by this demand, as well as by those of other coal operators in the area, more than fifteen hundred miners walked out. In response Alanson Sweet, the CW & V's general manager, imported first some white strike-breakers from Chicago, and then a larger number of blacks. The Illinois state militia was brought in to protect the black strike-breakers, a move that doomed the stoppage to defeat. Although it limped on until November 1877, the miners were forced back on the employers' terms, amid much suffering.[21]

The final strike in this series took place in Lanarkshire in 1879–81. In November 1879 the Lanarkshire Coal Masters Association cut its employees' wages by another sixpence a day, with further cuts threatened in the weeks that followed. Several hundred miners promptly walked out of the pits. Alexander MacDonald advised the miners to accept the sixpence-a-day cut, meanwhile sending agents into Fife, Clackmannon, and other mining districts to urge the miners there to press for a wage increase. The idea was to bring their pay up to the same level as in Lanarkshire, thereby reducing competitive pressure on the operators there. But the miners were not satisfied with this timid response. Instead, increasing numbers of the rank and file went out on unofficial strike. The coal-masters were not intimidated, however: at the beginning of December they imposed a third reduction of sixpence, the effect of which was to bring wages in many pits down to three shillings a day. This level was as low, if not lower, that the extremely low rate the colliers had been forced to accept in the late 1860s. Once more, the miners expanded the strike, but to no avail. Early in 1881, several of the big iron-masters put their furnaces out of blast. This tactic, coupled with the introduction of extra police to keep pickets away from the mine gates, forced all of the Lanarkshire miners back to work.[22]

In these changed circumstances, the advocates of class harmony among the miners on both sides of the ocean found their ideas increasingly difficult to defend. In Scotland, open quarreling broke out between the aging Alexander MacDonald and his opponents over two main issues: the use of the strike weapon, and role of the sliding scale. The most important of his opponents was the young James Keir Hardie, who was soon to become a Lanarkshire County Miners Union official. In 1892 he was elected the first truly independent Labor MP in the British House of Commons.[23]

In both the 1872 and the 1874 disputes MacDonald had attempted to limit the use of the strike by advocating selective stoppages: striking those pits where a two shilling cut had been demanded, but keeping the men at work where there was a one shilling cut. Given the ability of those pits still working to take up the slack in the coal supply, this seemed in any event a futile policy. But the important development

21. Gutman, *Power and Culture*, 148–56, 168–91.
22. Reid, *Keir Hardie*, 47–48.
23. Ibid., 130.

was the increased willingness of the rank and file to make use of the extended (i.e., coalfield-wide) strike, first on an unofficial, then on an official basis. This initiated a broader basis for union growth and miner solidarity, and it effectively buried the idea of resolving disputes between miners and operators without open confrontations between them.

More important than the strike issue, however, was the question of the sliding scale. This mechanism for setting wages, by which wage rates rose and fell automatically with changes in the market price for coal, was widely used at the time, and it was endorsed by MacDonald. The sliding scale was quite popular during periods of mining prosperity when coal prices moved up and down within a fairly high range, guaranteeing a decent average level of wages. But when the bottom dropped out of the coal market, as it did during the 1870s depression, wages fell to near starvation levels in Scotland. In a bitter August 1880 speech dismissing MacDonald's sliding scale and output restriction policies as viable solutions to the miners' problems, Keir Hardie for the first time invoked the desirability of state intervention to provide a minimum wage as an alternative to market mechanisms for setting the rate.

"There were two different kinds of sliding scale," Hardie said. "There was the sliding scale that was always sliding down, and there was a fair one, and they [the Lanarkshire miners] did not object to the latter." The sine qua non of a fair sliding scale, he went on, was that it should enforce a minimum level of wages below which the miner's pay should not fall. "In Australia," he added significantly (referring to the socially progressive policies of the Labour Party that had already come into existence there) "the sliding scale had been brought into force by the Government, who had appointed a Minister to look after the mining community."[24]

Taken together these two lines of attack, coupled with the ongoing recession, effectively discredited MacDonald's class-harmony policies. He retired from the scene, and the search began for more collectivist solutions to the problems of the miners. In Lanarkshire the search was given political momentum when Keir Hardie put his name forward as an independent Labour candidate for the mining constituency of mid-Lanark in April 1888.[25] No such dramatic outcome followed the strike defeats of the late 1870s in northern Illinois. The quarrel over how far, and in what manner, the strike weapon should be used, which was to be an issue between Knights of Labor National Assembly 134 and the National Progressive Miners Union, had not yet been fully joined. Nevertheless, there were echoes of the MacDonald versus Hardie conflict in the disagreement that emerged between John James and Daniel McLaughlin in northern Illinois over what direction the miners' new militancy should take.

John James maintained his opposition to the indiscriminate use of strikes, and repeatedly showed his distress at the growing signs of class division between the

24. Ibid., 51–52.
25. James Kellas, "The Mid-Lanark By-Election (1888) and The Scottish Labour Party (1888–1894)," *Parliamentary Affairs* 17 (1965): 318–29.

mine owners and miners in Braidwood. He did tolerate the 1874 strike. But he openly opposed the 1877 one, and he was highly critical of the support the Braidwood miners gave to the Greenback Labor Party in the 1877–78 local elections. This party succeeded in electing a municipal ticket to office in Braidwood and several other coal towns in the Illinois river valley in the latter year. James was ostracised by McLaughlin, as well as by the younger miners for his stand, much as MacDonald had been in Scotland. As a result, he left Braidwood permanently in 1880 to become a mine manager in Carthage, New Mexico.[26]

Daniel McLaughlin, on the other hand, was radicalized by the strike defeats of the 1870s. He did not abandon the class-harmony ideal altogether. He remained critical of strikes, upheld the sliding scale, and never became a socialist in the way that Keir Hardie did in Scotland. He did, however, fully support the Greenback Labor third-party ticket in local elections, even though that party proved to be only a flash in the pan. In fact, he was elected mayor of Braidwood for a time on that party's ticket. And in the winter of 1878 we find McLaughlin talking of more than the need to increase the circulation of paper currency, to deny free land to speculators, and to expand free public education for "rich and poor alike"—all standard parts of the Greenback Labor program. He went further: "It does not require much logic or reason to prove that the wage workers and wealth producers are defrauded and robbed out of the wealth they create; the basis of our social system requires to be remodelled and founded upon industrial equality."[27]

In June 1878, northern Illinois miners held a mass picnic and demonstration to show their defiance of the employers, with banners proclaiming: "A Republic Forever," "Never a Monarchy," "We Use No Coercion to Get Votes." Two years later, after the infant Socialist Labor Party had established itself in Chicago, fifty miles to the northwest, they invited the radical anarchist Albert Parsons to address them. None of this added up to the dramatic action James Keir Hardie had taken in running for Parliament on an independent ticket. But it was a significant step forward.[28]

III

If the 1870s and 1880s saw the emergence of a somewhat more ambiguous response to growing class conflict in the Illinois compared to the Lanarkshire coal pits, the following two decades saw the beginnings of a political shift that was to end up crystallizing mining politics in the two areas along quite separate lines. The Scottish miners continued their shift toward independent political action, while their midwestern counterparts remained committed, for the most part, to working within the existing two-party system.

26. Gutman, *Power and Culture*, 194–97.
27. *National Labor Tribune* (February 14, 1878), 3.
28. Gutman, *Power and Culture*, 198.

For a period of time, it did not appear that such a policy split would occur. In the late 1880s and early 1890s it seemed as if the common experience of high unemployment, low wages, and growing employer intransigence—coupled with the special solidarity that had always characterized the miners' way of life—would continue to lead the Lanarkshire and Illinois miners down the same leftward path. During the depression of the mid-1890s, for example, colliers on both sides of the Atlantic once more suffered from savage wage cuts. After a bitter 1889 strike in the northern Illinois mining town of Spring Valley, miners in both Scotland and Illinois suffered other, equally humiliating defeats. With a market glutted with coal even before the depression began, hundreds of mines in Ohio, Indiana, and Illinois were closed down, and so many colliers were thrown out of work that the governors of several midwestern states had to issue public appeals for aid.[29]

Desperate to avoid further wage cuts the UMWA, with only 13,000 paid-up members and $2,600 in its treasury, called a national strike for April 21, 1894. More than a hundred thousand colliers came out in response. "The miners are on strike because they must," Daniel DeLeon's SLP newspaper *The People*, declared. "Their condition is unbearable."[30] He went on to describe the starvation conditions of a family of miners in central Ohio. The American strike was a complete failure, however. President McBride failed to get a nationwide conference with the operators, and wages in most areas continued to fall. Two months later the Scottish miners also went on strike, the employers pressing for a one shilling a day cut. At first the MFGB voted financial support from England, but when that dried up the Scottish strike also collapsed. Deep anger, and a growing sense of disillusionment in the fairness of the capitalist industrial system accumulated on both sides of the Atlantic as a result of these defeats.[31]

For a brief time, it also seemed as though Illinois District 12, like the Lanarkshire County Miners Union, might build upon local agrarian discontent to move toward radical politics. In Lanarkshire the idea of land reform had an attraction for immigrant Irish miners whose families had lost their potato farms to the Protestant gentry back home. Anti-aristocratic sentiment was also present among the native Scots colliers, who were angered by the large sums the Duke of Hamilton—the largest land-owner in the area—made from the mineral royalties he charged coal-owners for the use of his coal lands. Sometimes, the need to pay their royalty fees out of the profits they made from selling their coal was used by the Lanarkshire mine-owners as a reason for not raising wages.[32]

29. Coleman, *Men and Coal*, 91–93; *Spring Valley, Illinois, 1886–1986: An Ethnic Heritage*, 36–37.

30. *The People* (June 10, 1894), 1.

31. David J. McDonald and Edward A. Lynch, *Coal and Unionism: A History of the American Coal Miners Unions* (Indianapolis: Bobbs-Merrill, 1971), 118–19; R. Page Arnot, *A History of the Scottish Miners, From the Earliest Times* (London: George Allen and Unwin, 1955), 76–88.

32. T. W. Moody, "Michael Davitt and the British Labour Movement, 1882–1906," *Transactions of the Royal Historical Society*, 5th ser., 3 (1953): 204–15; David Lowe, *Souvenirs of Scottish Labour* (Glasgow: W. & R. Holmes, 1919), 1–38.

In the summer of 1894, a Labor-Miner-Populist political alliance, under the leadership of Progressive reformer Henry Demarest Lloyd, seemed also to be in the making in the state of Illinois. Populist declarations for the nationalization of both mines and railroads were enthusiastically endorsed, and President J. A. Crawford of District 12 was nominated on the Populist ticket in Springfield.[33]

Most significant of all, by the turn of the century a new generation of miners' leaders was coming to power on both sides of the Atlantic who not only rejected the class-harmony doctrine espoused by their predecessors, but who in one way or another also advocated an explicitly socialist philosophy. In Scotland, after Keir Hardie the most important of these young men was Robert Smillie of Larkhall, who in 1894 became president of the Scottish Miners Federation. A second radical leader was William Small, a former Cambuslang draper who became secretary of the LCMU in 1886. His cottage in Blantyre became the venue for animated discussions of the mining problem by such national socialist luminaries as William Morris, Henry Hyndman, and Edward Aveling.[34]

Now a high-profile Labour MP for a London constituency, Keir Hardie still influenced Scottish mining opinion. In 1894, for example, he ended an editorial in his *Labour Leader* on the great Scottish strike of that year by urging Scottish miners to follow his example and abandon the Liberal Party for the Independent Labour Party (one of the constituent elements of the Labour Party). "Don't forget your trade union," he wrote, "But after you have done all this, carry your principles to their logical conclusion by acting politically as you do industrially. It is foolish to form a union to fight the coalmasters and then send one of those masters or his friend to make the laws for you."[35] As if in response, at the 1897 MFGB conference held in Leicester, the Scottish miners' delegation proposed a resolution declaring it "absolutely necessary that the Land, Minerals, Railways, and instruments of wealth production should be owned and controlled by the State for the people."[36] Although defeated, it got a significant amount of support.

District 12's equivalent of Keir Hardie, with much the same ethical view of socialism, was John H. Walker, who had also been born in the heart of the Lanarkshire coalfield. He was elected president of District 12 between 1906 and 1913. Another Scots-born socialist was Duncan McDonald, who became secretary-treasurer of the district between 1910 and 1917.[37]

After its founding in 1900, the Socialist Party of America vote among Illinois miners also rose markedly, just as the Labour Party vote was doing in southwest Scotland. Analysis of SP of A voting returns in Illinois's mining counties shows that Eugene Debs secured more than 15% of the vote in a steadily rising number of

33. Chester M. Destler, *American Radicalism, 1865–1901* (Chicago: Quadrangle Books, 1966), chap. 9.

34. "William Small Papers," National Library of Scotland, File 5.

35. Page Arnot, *History of the Scottish Miners*, 88.

36. Ibid., 91.

37. See note 2.

coal counties in the four presidential elections between 1900 and 1912. A similar pattern developed at the municipal level. In the thirteen Illinois mining towns known to have elected Socialists to local office (which included Riverton, Thayer, Glen Carbon, O'Fallon, Buckner, and Herrin), the victories were all won between 1906 and 1914. In February 1914, the Canton *Daily Ledger* estimated that 650 of that town's trade unionists were members of the UMW. George L. Mercer, a Socialist and frequent candidate for Third Ward alderman, served as secretary-treasurer of Sub-District 12. John Spargo, a Socialist alderman in Canton, was also a subdistrict board member.[38]

Despite all of the similarities we have noted in the rise of trade union solidarity and militant class-consciousness among Scottish and Illinois miners, however, in the end the Lanarkshire County Miners Union and District 12 took different political paths. As noted at the outset, in June 1908, one month after the Scottish miners had voted to affiliate with the British Labour Party, Illinois District 12 affiliated itself with the Illinois State Federation of Labor.

The significance of this decision lay in the fact that it officially committed the district to the AFL's long-standing political policy of shunning the Socialist Party of America, and of advocating the nonpartisan policy of "reward-your-friends-punish-your-enemies" instead. From 1908 on, the miners of District 12 were officially encouraged to vote for those candidates in either the Republican or Democratic Party who favored mining legislation, and to vote against those who did not.[39] This was precisely the opposite advice from that which the LCMU gave to its members after its May 1908 decision to affiliate with the Labour Party. It does not follow, of course, that the miners on either side of the Atlantic always followed the political direction of their union leaders. Large numbers of miners in Lanarkshire, in particular, continued to vote Liberal up until the First World War. But in the long run it made a major difference. In 1922, for example, the Lanarkshire miners elected no fewer than five Labour MPs to the House of Commons.[40]

Part of the reason for this difference in political behavior lay in the greater degree of class collaborationism that characterized relations between District 12 and the midwestern coal operators than was present in Scotland. This was due to the particular character of the U.S. Central Competitive Field Agreement, which had been negotiated between the coal operators and the entire midwestern coalfield in the spring of 1898, and which lasted up until the First World War and beyond.

By 1898 northern Illinois coal, which was inferior in quality to that in other parts

38. Robert F. Hoxie, "The Rising Tide of Socialism," *Journal of Political Economy* (October 1912): 613, 618; Lee M. Wolfle, "Radical Third-Party Voting Among Coal Miners, 1896–1940" (Ph.D diss., University of Michigan, 1976), 74; Errol W. Stevens, "The Socialist Party in Municipal Politics: Canton, Illinois, 1911–1920," *Journal of the Illinois State Historical Society* 72, no. 4 (November 1979): 257–58.

39. *Proceedings of the Twenty-Third Annual Convention of District 12, U.M.W.A.* (Springfield, Ill., 1912), 78–82.

40. I. G. C. Hutchinson, *A Political History of Scotland, 1832–1924: Parties, Elections and Issues* (Edinburgh: John Donald, 1986), 277–83.

of the Midwest, was in danger of being priced out of the market. Hence in order to eliminate competition from cheap, nonunion coal, the Central Competitive Field Agreement contained a carefully balanced, compensatory pay scale that equalized wage costs between the coalfields of Illinois, Indiana, Ohio, and western Pennsylvania. This succeeded in stabilizing prices, and hence wages, at a fairly high level throughout the entire area. But it also put pressure on the leaders of District 12 not to jeopardize the interstate agreement by antagonizing coal operators in the annual negotiations for a new contract. Although radical rank and filers frequently railed against this agreement, they were unable to prevail on the leaders of District 12 to make any real break with the employers. Since wages were generally higher in Illinois than they were elsewhere in the Midwest, this had the effect of reducing the level of class tensions considerably below what they had been in the 1880s and 1890s.[41]

A second reason for the difference in political outcome derived from differences in the political outlook and tactics of the SP of A, compared to those of the British Labour Party. Whereas the former was, ideologically speaking, a fairly rigid political party committed to an explicitly socialist program, the latter was a pragmatic alliance of trade unionists, Lib/Lab MPs (socially progressive working-class MPs who, on most issues, voted with the Liberal government of the day), and radical intellectuals that was more broadly based than the SP of A, more tolerant of ideological differences, and more gradualist in its approach. This contrast showed up in various ways. One was the division of opinion that appeared between the moderate radicals in District 12, led by President John H. Walker, and the more doctrinaire socialists led by German-born Adolph Germer, who regarded the British Labour party as insufficiently revolutionary. For example, in a debate that took place at the union's 1909 national convention over what political course the UMWA should follow, the influential Walker—who was in touch with his former friends in Lanarkshire, and who openly admired the British left—urged his fellow delegates to follow the Lanarkshire miners' example, not by endorsing the SP of A, but by helping to establish a trade union–based political movement similar to Britain's Labour Party.[42]

Adolph Germer, on the other hand, (who in 1916 became national secretary of the Socialist Party, and admired the German Social Democratic Party) opposed the labor party idea. The right course was for the UMWA to endorse the SP of A, which was the only true party of the left in America. "The abuses of which we complain," he stated, "spring from the capitalist class, and as long as this class struggle exists, . . . you can organize as many labor parties as your mind is able to invent, and so long as you fail to strike at the vital issue, so long will your independent labor party be of very little value."[43]

41. Louis Bloch, *Labor Agreements in Coal Mines: A Case Study of the Administration of Agreements Between Miners and Operators Organizations in the Bituminous Coal Mines of Illinois* (New York: Russell Sage Foundation, 1931), chaps. 1 and 9.

42. *Proceedings of the Nineteenth Annual and Eighth Biennial Convention of the United Mine Workers of America* (Indianapolis, Ind., 1909), 243–44.

43. Ibid., 245.

The British Labour Party, by contrast, including its affiliates in Scotland, had been deliberately designed as a broad coalition whose immediate purpose was not to implement a doctrinaire socialist program, but to elect trade unionists to the House of Commons. In addition, given the preponderant financial power of the trade union movement within the Labour Party, it almost never disciplined its trade union leaders for failing to toe the party line, as the SP of A—which lacked comparable support from the AFL—sometimes did. In 1912, for example, and again in 1916, President Walker of District 12 endorsed Illinois Democratic Governor Edward F. Dunne because of his pro-labor legislative record. This included a washhouse law for miners, better safety legislation, and a law granting women the vote in state elections. In 1916, he went on to support President Woodrow Wilson for national re-election, also because of his pro-labor record. For these actions Walker was expelled from the Socialist Party of America, thereby angering many miners and weakening the party statewide.[44]

A third differentiating factor was the conservative popular culture that dominated many of the small rural coal towns in the southern part of Illinois, where much of District 12's strength lay. By World War I the industrial area surrounding Glasgow—which lay just to the north of the Lanarkshire coalfield—was teeming with disaffected engineering and munitions workers, as well as miners, whose postwar militancy earned them the name of "Red Clydesiders."[45] Southern Illinois, by contrast, particularly the Little Egypt area, was a sparsely populated agricultural region that had been settled by poor tenant farmers who came from the mountainous regions of Kentucky and Tennessee. These miners were no more averse to joining the UMWA than their upstate counterparts. Nor were they unwilling to challenge the coal operators: some of the bloodiest mine-labor conflicts in the state took place in southern Illinois during and after the First World War.

However, many of the miners in Williamson and Franklin counties were Southern Baptists, or religious fundamentalists who disapproved of the liberal politics, Catholic faith, and whisky-drinking habits of the Irish and Scottish colliers who worked in the northern part of the state. Antiwar sentiment, which in Lanarkshire helped galvanize support for the Labour Party (because of plans for a negotiated peace advocated by an influential minority within the party) was also far more muted in southern Illinois than it was in the industrial towns of southwest Scotland. Unlike the official leaders of the Labour Party, who supported the war, the SP of A actively opposed it. In April 1918, this led to the public lynching of German-born miner Robert Paul Prager by a group of hysterical native-born colliers in Collinsville, dividing the Illinois left still more.[46]

Thus local politics in these southern Illinois coal towns tended to revolve more

44. Pelling, *Short History of the Labour Party*, 23–26; Keiser, "John H. Walker," 91–93.

45. Keith Middlemas, *The Clydesiders* (London: Macmillan, 1965), passim.

46. Carl Weinberg, "The Tug of War: Labor, Loyalty and Rebellion in the Southwestern Illinois Coalfields, 1914–1920" (Ph.D diss., Yale University, 1995), 451–524.

around ethno-cultural issues associated with patriotism, local drink laws, and religious affiliation than they did with the politics of class. The Red-baiting tactics of the Ku Klux Klan also became popular in the region after the First World War. In these isolated mining camps, where the local farmers were mostly out of sympathy with the mining population, getting a regionwide socialist culture to take root was particularly difficult.[47] The Lanarkshire mining community, where Scottish Protestant loyalists often quarrelled with Catholic Irish miners in their nationalist struggles over the Orange and the Green, also suffered from religious and cultural conflicts, although admittedly of a somewhat different kind.[48] But since both groups were industrial workers, these sectarian differences did not ultimately prevent both sides in the nationalist dispute from giving their political support to the Labour Party.

However, the critical issue that kept District 12 from committing itself to third-party politics was not religious or political sectarianism. It was probably not even ideological aversion to socialist ideas. It was the issue of how best to go about securing protective legislation for the miners underground. Questions associated with mine ventilation and inspection, safety and accident prevention, and the qualifications and training of those who work underground, have traditionally been the touchstone of politics for miners all over the world, often taking precedence over party affiliation.

Given this fact, the issue becomes, not whether the American colliers were just as deeply involved in seeking favorable mining legislation as their British counterparts; the evidence suggests strongly that they were. The question becomes, rather, how best to secure the same legislative goals? To answer this question, we must take a brief look at the differences between lobbying and third-party politics, as well as at differences in the way that British and American miners viewed their relations with the state.

Ironically, colliers on both sides of the Atlantic began their quest for mine-safety legislation almost identically. Beginning in the mid-1860s, Alexander MacDonald was paid by the Lanarkshire miners to travel to London when Parliament was in session to lobby before it for favorable mining laws. Following suit, Illinois miners retained Yorkshire-born lawyer John Hinchcliffe to represent them at the 1871 Illinois constitutional convention. Partly as a result of Hinchcliffe's lobbying efforts, a package bill was passed by the Illinois General Assembly that provided for ventilation and escapement shafts, and for the reporting and investigation of mine accidents. Then, in 1874, Alexander MacDonald was elected to Parliament, sitting as a de facto Liberal in the House of Commons. Again following suit, at the turn of the century Illinois miners elected almost a dozen of their fellows as state assemblymen to Springfield.[49]

47. Daniel J. Prosser, "Coal Towns in Egypt: Portrait of An Illinois Mining Region, 1890–1930" (Ph.D diss., Northwestern University, 1973), 32–59; Paul M. Angle, *Bloody Williamson: A Chapter of American Lawlessness* (New York: Knopf, 1980), passim.

48. For sectarian conflicts between Protestant and Catholic miners in the Lanarkshire coalfield, see Campbell, *Lanarkshire Miners*, chap. 7.

49. Wieck, *American Miners Association*, 14–23, 191–94; Wilson, *Alexander McDonald*, 54–73.

So far, so similar. The difference was that whereas the eleven miners elected to Springfield between 1872 and 1911 were more or less evenly divided between Republicans and Democrats, the miners' MPs in Britain—whose numbers increased by 1908 to fourteen—were all either Liberals, or the so-called Lib/Labs. In 1918 these Lib/Labs, including most of the MPs sponsored by the Miners Federation of Great Britain, broke decisively with the Liberals, and threw in their lot with Labour.[50] Given the absence of any comparable number of miners' representatives in the Illinois General Assembly at this time, no such electoral swing to the left was likely in the politics of post–World War I Illinois.

In fact, whatever their personal political predilections, the leaders of District 12, following the nonpartisan political tactics that had been developed by the leaders of the Illinois State Federation of Labor (ISFL) moved in exactly the opposite political direction from their fellows in Scotland. After 1900, the miners' earlier habit of electing their own representatives to the General Assembly at Springfield faded into the background. Between 1908 and 1924, only two coal miners out of sixty representatives from the eight most populous Illinois mining counties were elected to Springfield. One was a sympathetic Democrat, the other a Republican.[51] Why did this happen? The most important reason was that District 12's leaders had by now become persuaded of the superior efficacy of the AFL's "reward-your-friends, punish-your-enemies" strategy. In turn, this flowed from their June 1908 decision to join the ISFL. For a time, District 12's lobbying representatives collaborated with the ISFL's Legislative Committee members, who spent several weeks a year in Springfield, lobbying state legislators of both major parties to pass laws favorable to labor, and defeat those that were not.[52]

In 1909, District 12 took another step that removed the issue of mining legislation still further from the arena of partisan, class-driven politics. In the preceding legislative session of the General Assembly, District 12's lobbyists had found themselves locked in protracted and apparently irreconcilable differences with the coal operators' own lobbying representatives over efforts to improve the state's mining code. Early in the year, in an attempt to break the deadlock, District 12's leaders agreed to a three-way negotiation between its own representatives, Republican Governor Deneen, and delegates from the Illinois Coal Operators Association. The result was the establishment of a body called the Mining Investigation Commission. The purpose of this organization was to get the main provisions of new mining laws agreed to in advance between the union and the coal operators, before they were submitted to the General Assembly. The result was not simply to render the discussion of new mining legislation a nonpartisan issue. It was to remove it from the area of electoral

50. Pelling, *Short History of the Labour Party*, 49.

51. In 1914 William T. Morris, a British-born miner, was elected as a Democrat from Duquoin, Perry County; and in 1914–24 William J. Sneed was elected as a Republican from Herrin, in Williamson County. See *Illinois Blue Book* (1916), 155; (1922), 270.

52. *Proceedings of the Twentieth Annual Convention of District 12, U.M.W.A.* (Springfield, Ill., 1909), 201–9.

conflict—where the opposing class interests of both sides were pretty clear—and to place it, instead, in the private arena of committee bargaining and bureaucratic compromise. In Britain, by contrast, new mining laws resulted from a largely open, class-driven, political contest in Parliament between the Lib/Lab miners' MPs, on the one hand, and Liberal and Tory mine-owners and their allies, on the other.[53]

The acid test, however, was whether or not District 12's nonpartisan political policy was as successful in securing favorable legislative results as the MFGB's commitment to the Labour Party was. The answer is that it was, both in the arena of general labor legislation, and as regards the Illinois mining code. Regarding general labor legislation, in three years between 1909 and 1911 the lobbying efforts of the ISFL helped to secure the Health, Safety and Comfort Act for Chicago's factory workers, a new child labor law, as well as the Women's Ten Hour Law and the Occupational Disease Act. As a result of the work of the Mining Investigation Commission, District 12 also secured some new and highly valuable legislation. One was the improved Shot-Firer Law, making it the responsibility of the coal operators, not the UMWA, to hire and pay these men. Another was the greatly strengthened Miners Qualification Act, which barred the use of untrained and uncertified labor in any Illinois coalfield. In 1911, the Illinois Mining Code was described by one expert as "probably superior to . . . the mining code of any other state or country."[54]

Under these circumstances, save for the ideologues among them the majority of voting colliers in the mining counties of Illinois—which in 1912, the Socialists' peak year, probably amounted to more than 20,000 men—had little, if any incentive to vote for the Socialist Party of America. They could get most of what they wanted by supporting Progressive-oriented Democrats and Republicans. Nor was this all. The refusal of the miners to vote for the Socialists, even though many of them supported progressive social legislation, meant that they took few steps to join up with others who sought to create an active counterculture to prevailing capitalist values.

After World War I even John H. Walker, although still personally a socialist, showed the effect of these successes on his own political strategy. At the March 1920, District 12 convention, a debate took place over a proposal that the Illinois miners emulate their British comrades by adopting the check-off political contribution system. Under this system, Labour Party dues were automatically deducted from the paychecks of MFGB members throughout Great Britain, thereby providing it with thousands of pounds annually. In the case of Illinois, the proposal was put forward by the more militant socialists in District 12 in order to provide financial

53. Staley, *History of the Illinois State Federation of Labor*, 273–78; Henry Pelling, *Labour and Politics 1900–1906, A History of the Labour Representation Committee* (London, Macmillan, 1958), chap. 9.

54. Earl R. Beckner, *A History of Labor Legislation in Illinois* (Chicago, University of Chicago Press, 1929), 281; *Proceedings of the Twenty-First Annual Convention of District 12. U.M.W.A.* (Springfield, Ill., 1910), 47–51; Frank Bealey and Henry Pelling, *Labour and Politics, 1900–1906* (London: Macmillan, 1958), chap. 9.

support for the nascent Illinois Farmer-Labor Party, which seemed then to have a chance of capturing several offices in the state. Indeed, had the check-off system been adopted, it would have significantly improved the Farmer-Labor Party's financial and political prospects.

But the influential Walker, who was now president of the Illinois State Federation of Labor himself, rejected the idea. If District 12 endorsed the check-off system, he argued, not only would it be Red-baited by the Farmer-Labor Party's ideological opponents; it would also sacrifice all of the political clout it had painstakingly built up over the years by endorsing pro-labor candidates in both the Republican and Democratic Parties. By adopting the check-off proposal, Walker stated, District 12 would lose far more political influence than it would gain. The District 12 convention upheld Walker's objections by a large majority.[55]

Four years later, in January 1924, the first Labour Government took office in Great Britain, with the full support of the Scottish miners' MPs who had been elected to Parliament by the colliers of the Lanarkshire County Miners Union. The Illinois Farmer-Labor Party, on the other hand, was stillborn.[56] No new left-wing party that had a serious chance of capturing the miners' votes en masse appeared again in Illinois, not even during the period of the New Deal. The British Labour Party, by contrast—with the undivided support of more than fifty miners' MPs— went on from strength to strength. The parting of the political ways between the miners of Scotland and Illinois was now complete.

55. *Proceedings of the Twenty-Eighth Consecutive and Third Biennial Convention of District 12, U.M.W.A.* (Springfield, Ill., 1920), 303.

56. R. W. Lyman, *The Labour Government of 1924* (London: Macmillan, 1952), 81–84; Charles R. Green, "The Labor Party Movement in Illinois, 1919–1924" (M.A. thesis, University of Illinois, 1959), 83–110.

CHAPTER EIGHTEEN

INDUSTRIAL DEMOCRACY AND INDUSTRIAL LEGALITY
The UMWA in Nova Scotia, 1908–1927

DAVID FRANK

I

In 1922 Selig Perlman underlined the significance of the United Mine Workers of America for understanding twentieth-century labor relations: "In no other industry has a union's struggle for 'recognition' offered a richer and more instructive picture of the birth of the new order with its difficulties as well as its promises than in coal mining."[1] In the early twentieth century the UMW was one of the new facts of life in industrial North America. From barely 10,000 members in 1897, the UMWA had come to represent a majority of the coal miners on the continent. By 1920 the UMW, boasting 393,600 members, was the largest single union in North America—and this figure included 19,800 members in Canada.[2] The early history of District 26 in

1. Selig Perlman, *A History of Trade Unionism in the United States* (New York, 1929 [1922]), 167.
2. Leo Wolman, *Growth of American Trade Unions, 1880–1923* (New York, 1924), 85, 137, 146. For the traditional hagiography on the UMW, see Rex Lauck, *John L. Lewis and the International Union United Mine Workers of America* (1952), which was still being distributed twenty-five years later. A good sympathetic history of the union, however, was published by the labor journalist McAlister Cole-

Nova Scotia provides a regional perspective on developments in the international union; in this case study the view from the hinterlands sheds light on the challenges facing the UMW as a whole in the early decades of the twentieth century. Nova Scotia was not a typical district or a significant one in the UMW. It was situated in an outlying coalfield that did not participate in the national energy market in the United States, and the history of the Nova Scotia coal miners was often governed by the shape of labor and politics in a separate country. But the controversies over industrial democracy and industrial legality that were fought out in District 26 belonged very much to the larger history of the international organization in this period.[3]

The interaction between industrial democracy and industrial legality offers a framework for considering the larger history of the union and also for examining some of the characteristic dilemmas of unionism in the twentieth century. The term "industrial democracy" was probably originated by Sidney and Beatrice Webb in Britain and popularized by sympathetic intellectuals and adopted by contemporary labor leaders. They saw unions as logical expressions of the evolving liberal-democratic tradition. While the Webbs focused on the internal democracy of unions, others made a broader argument. In this view the formal institutions of political democracy, rooted in the constitutional struggles and compromises of the seventeenth and eighteenth centuries, did not adequately meet the needs of an industrial society in which large corporations exerted extensive power over the lives of individuals. The full application of established principles of citizenship required appropriate reforms of the capitalist system to ensure, in Jett Lauck's words, "self-government and equality of opportunity in industrial as in political life." As a program, industrial democracy could be interpreted to include everything from minimum wage and workers' compensation legislation to full employment policies and workers' control, but at the center of the concept was the recognition of trade unions and the achievement of collective bargaining. The achievement of high levels of unionization and of state support for the recognition of unions thus represented a "logical supplement to political democracy." It was in short, as Eugene Forsey put it in the Canadian context, an extension of responsible government and constitutional democracy to the world of work.[4]

---

man, *Men and Coal* (New York, 1943). For more recent work, see the discussion of sources, 593–600, in Melvyn Dubofsky and Warren Van Tine, *John L. Lewis: A Biography* (New York, 1977), a book that is itself a major contribution to the history of the union. The standard history of the union, which draws usefully on recent literature, is Maier B. Fox, *United We Stand: The United Mine Workers of America, 1890–1990* (Washington, D.C., 1990).

3. The present study focuses on the coal miners of eastern Canada. For an introduction to the coal miners of western Canada, see Allen Seager, "Miners' Struggles in Western Canada, 1890–1930," in *Class, Community and the Labour Movement: Wales and Canada, 1850–1930*, ed. Deian R. Hopkin and Gregory S. Kealey (St. John's, 1989), 160–98.

4. See Elsie Gluck, "Industrial Democracy," in *Encyclopedia of the Social Sciences*, ed. E. R. A. Seligman (New York, 1932), 7:691–92; Sidney and Beatrice Webb, *Industrial Democracy* (London, 1902); W. Jett Lauck, *Political and Industrial Democracy, 1776–1926* (New York, 1926), 56, 343–46;

This optimistic perspective was shared by the early labor historians such as John R. Commons, and the idealism of the approach is also applauded in more recent work. Bruno Ramirez, for instance, has described the arrival of collective bargaining and the trade union agreement as a democratic solution to some of the inherent instabilities of the labor-capital relationship. Ramirez also points out, however, that the great difficulty faced by early twentieth-century advocates of industrial democracy was that some of the essential conditions for such a historic compromise were not present in early twentieth-century America: first, union membership was limited in scope and often restricted by craft forms of organization; second, employers were not prepared to make permanent concessions of authority unless they were forced to do so (and by the 1920s many preferred to explore the possibilities of a modernized paternalism); and third, the state was not prepared to apply the force of law to the achievement of union recognition or collective bargaining. From this perspective the rights of workers and of unions under the capitalist system were limited and contingent.[5]

The concept of industrial legality proceeds from these more pessimistic conclusions. The phrase can be traced back to the observations of the Italian Marxist Antonio Gramsci who saw trade unions not so much as the outgrowths of liberal-democratic idealism but as "the form which labour as a commodity is bound to assume in a capitalist system, when it organizes itself in order to control the market." By organizing themselves into unions, workers placed themselves in a position to establish "a favourable balance between the working class and the power of capital," but in negotiating agreements and accepting responsibilities, unions were engaging in a form of historical compromise: "The emergence of an industrial legality is a great victory for the working class, but it is not the ultimate and definitive victory. Industrial legality has improved the working class's standard of living but it is no more than a compromise—a compromise which had to be made and must be supported until the balance of forces favours the working class."[6]

Gramsci was writing in 1920, yet the term anticipated the critical perspective that later writers would apply to the achievements of unions in the 1930s and 1940s. The extension of union membership and the achievement of union contracts in this later period has been most widely interpreted in both the United States and Canada as a democratic reform. In Canada, Justice Ivan C. Rand, in a key statement of industrial relations ideals in 1946, indicated that unions now occupied an accepted place in industrial civilization "within a framework of labour-employer constitutional law based on a rational economic and social doctrine"; but it would also be the case that "capital must in the long run be looked upon as occupying a dominant position." In

Eugene Forsey, "The History of the Canadian Labour Movement," in *Lectures in Canadian Labour and Working-Class History*, ed. W. J. C. Cherwinski and G. S. Kealey (St. John's, 1985), 10.

5. See Bruno Ramirez, *When Workers Fight: The Politics of Industrial Relations in the Progressive Era, 1898–1916* (Westport, Conn., 1978).

6. Antonio Gramsci, *Selections from Political Writings (1910–1920)* (London, 1977), 265–68.

short, labor unions were there as partners to "redress the balance of social justice."[7] For much of the union leadership at this time, this was an acceptable compromise; unions had fulfilled their aims and indeed even reached "the end of history." Already in the 1950s, however, C. Wright Mills was raising questions about the extent to which the new unions and their leaders, as agents, were implicated in the administration of the capitalist system and the discipline of their members. This critical perspective informs much recent work on labor law and industrial relations.[8]

The attempt to reconcile the promise of industrial democracy with the requirements of industrial legality is a central theme in the history of organized labor in the twentieth century. For the purposes of this discussion it is notable that much of this debate had already been articulated in practical terms in the coalfields of North America, where a strong union had succeeded in organizing a diverse and substantial workforce and obtaining recognition from both employers and governments. By the 1920s these achievements were in question, threatened in part by the changing attitudes of employers and governments but also frustrated by the sometimes inconsistent ideological expectations that union leaders brought to the ongoing conflict.

As early as 1903 UMW President John Mitchell had proclaimed the ideal of industrial democracy in these words: "Trade unionism stands for liberty, equality, and fraternity; it stands for the liberty of workingmen to arrange their own lives and to contract jointly for the manner in which they shall be spent in mine or factory." In the early twentieth century the union's general goals were roughly captured by this ideal of industrial democracy. The underlying assumption was that the achievements of political democracy must be strengthened and extended.[9] Of course, the usage of the term was not consistent. At one extreme the Canadian industrial relations expert William Lyon Mackenzie King appropriated the term to describe anti-union employee-representation plans, such as the one he engineered for John D. Rockefeller in Colorado in the wake of the Ludlow Massacre. But within the UMW, industrial democracy referred to some of the more general aims of the union to improve the lot of the coal miner and the quality of industrial life, such as the enforcement of the eight-hour day and the minimum wage. Second, ideals of industrial democracy were also reflected in the inclusive organizational practices of the

7. Justice Ivan C. Rand, as quoted by Leo Panitch and Donald Swartz, "Towards Permanent Exceptionalism: Coercion and Consent in Canadian Industrial Relations," *Labour/Le Travail* 13 (Spring 1984): 137.

8. C. Wright Mills, *The New Men of Power: America's Labor Leaders* (New York, 1948). For a general discussion of the problem, see Melvyn Dubofsky, "Legal Theory and Workers' Rights: A Historian's Critique" and the accompanying statements by Karl Klare and Staughton Lynd, *Industrial Relations Law Journal* (1981): 449–502. See also Christopher Tomlins, *The State and the Unions: Labour Relations, Law, and the Organized Labor Movement in America, 1880–1960* (Cambridge, 1985) and, in the Canadian context, Panitch and Swartz, *The Assault on Trade Union Freedoms* (Toronto, 1988) and Ian McKay and Michael Earle, "Industrial Legality in Nova Scotia," in *Workers and the State in Twentieth Century Nova Scotia*, ed. Michael Earle (Fredericton, 1989), 9–23.

9. Mitchell, *Organized Labor*, as cited by Milton Derber, *The American Idea of Industrial Democracy, 1865–1965* (Urbana, 1970), 123–24.

union. The UMW endorsed the organization of all workers in the industry, skilled and unskilled, craftsmen and laborers, underground and surface, in and around the mines, and without regard to creed, color, or nationality. Finally, for many coal miners industrial democracy also implied the more radical goal of democratic reform within the management of the industry. Workers' control was a kind of philosophy of common sense, embedded in the coal miners' daily work and in instruments of local democracy such as the pit committee. Under the influence of progressive and socialist thinking, as early as 1909 public ownership and democratic management of the industry had also become a formal policy of the union and a standard reference point in internal union debates.[10]

The ideal of industrial democracy constantly interacted with the goal of industrial legality. More than any other objective labor leaders wanted statutory protection for the right to organize. The UMW in particular was the victim of numerous legal challenges in this period, and the balance of the law did not begin to turn in favor of unions until the reforms of the New Deal in the 1930s. In general the union accepted the rule of law in industrial relations and simply aimed to reform its biases and extend its scope. The legislative demands of the union were specific: laws to prohibit child labor and company police, to protect the health and lives of the coal miners. Short of statutory reforms, the acceptance of the union could also be signified in informal ways: the elevation of John Mitchell by the National Civic Federation symbolized the arrival of union leaders on the national stage, and the appointment of UMW President John P. White to the Federal Fuel Board under wartime conditions in 1917 was a form of de facto recognition of the union in managing the coal industry.

Most important, industrial legality aimed to establish the collective agreement as the code of law in the coalfields. The strongest practical argument unions could offer in return for the right to organize was that industrial legality was a guarantee of class peace. In negotiating agreements unions were not only extracting concessions from their employers but were also undertaking to regulate and discipline their own members. Under the union constitution any major strike, even in a single district, required the sanction of the executive board or an international convention. The union contract thus bound members to respect a negotiated peace and as a result in some measure to suspend the class struggle.

In the case of the coal miners in Nova Scotia in the early decades of the twentieth century two historical moments illustrate the tensions surrounding the interaction between industrial democracy and industrial legality. In the first of these periods the appeal of the UMW rested on its reputation as a defender of industrial democracy. In a long struggle for recognition the union challenged the employers and govern-

10. Fox, *United We Stand*, passim.; "Constitution of the United Mine Workers of America," in Louis Bloch, *Labor Agreements in Coal Mines* (New York, 1931), appendix 3. For full texts of the documents from 1892 onward, see Bernard G. Naas, comp., *American Labor Unions' Constitutions and Proceedings* [microform edition, 1980], part II, reel 65. See also Carter Goodrich, *The Miner's Freedom* (Boston, 1925) and David Montgomery, *The Fall of the House of Labor* (Cambridge, 1987).

ments who supported a discredited regime of industrial legality in the Nova Scotia coalfields associated with an established local organization. In the second period, however, the international union itself appeared primarily as the defender of a reconstituted industrial legality and as the opponent of an increasingly radical version of industrial democracy favored by the membership and officers of the district.

II

The UMW entered Nova Scotia by invitation and with some early reluctance. When the international office began to charter locals in 1908, it was responding to Nova Scotia coal miners who saw the union as the carrier of industrial democracy. They saw the UMW as the vehicle for bringing about reforms such as the eight-hour day and weekly pays, as well as tougher bargaining with the companies. Internally they also wanted reforms such as the election of officers by general membership ballot and more efforts to organize the unorganized in the rapidly growing workforce.[11]

Originally the UMW responded cautiously to suggestions that the union be extended into Nova Scotia, partly because an indigenous union, the Provincial Workmen's Association (PWA) was already present there. As early as 1901, President Samuel Gompers of the American Federation of Labor was urging John Mitchell to bring the Nova Scotia coal miners into the UMWA. In Gompers's view, "the United Mine Workers of America make no distinction as to Canada and the United States. It seems to me that the miners' union referred to, as well as all unions of miners, ought to be a part of the United Mine Workers of America." Mitchell did not disagree but his response was a cautious one: "If there were any possibility of our organization obtaining jurisdiction over the miners of Canada without entering into a contest with the national union now established there, we would do so; but unless they would withdraw from the field or amalgamate, we would not care to spend any money in a fight with them for control, as we have a wide field yet remaining uncovered in the United States."[12]

One of the strongest supporters of the UMW in Nova Scotia was J. B. McLachlan, an active local officer of the PWA who admired the achievements of the UMW in advancing the coal miners' cause. A Scottish immigrant and socialist, McLachlan's

11. For the early history of unions in the Nova Scotia coal industry, see Eugene Forsey, *Trade Unions in Canada, 1812–1902* (Toronto, 1982) and Ian McKay, " 'By Wisdom, Wile or War': The Provincial Workmen's Association and the Struggle for Working-Class Independence in Nova Scotia, 1879–1897," *Labour/Le Travail*, 18 (Fall 1986): 13–62. For an earlier account of the entry of the UMW into Nova Scotia, see Robert H. Babcock, *Gompers in Canada: A Study in American Continentalism before the First World War* (Toronto, 1974).

12. Samuel Gompers to John Flett, January 18, 1901; Gompers to John Mitchell, January 18, 1901; Rosa Lee Guard to Flett, January 23, 1901; Samuel Gompers Letterbooks (1901), 41:488, 365, Library of Congress, Washington, D.C.

views of international cooperation had been shaped by the collaboration between Scottish and English miners in the 1890s as well as by the principles of working-class internationalism. "I am strongly in favour of international unions," McLachlan argued in 1907, "There should be no dividing line between workingmen, and the more international we become, the greater power will we be able to exert."[13]

From the perspective of industrial legality, however, this placed the UMW in the position of challenging the PWA, whose roots in Nova Scotia dated back to 1879; employers and governments saw the UMW as an alien and disturbing force aiming to overthrow the existing industrial-relations regime in the coalfield. The summer of 1908 produced a showdown between PWA loyalists and UMW reformers. The outcome was a victory for the reformers in a membership vote in favor of joining the UMWA. The PWA refused to recognize the result and proceeded to make a new agreement with the coal operators. In McLachlan's view, the PWA's claims to recognition were now spurious: the PWA had lost its moral authority to represent the coal miners and had been voted out of existence.[14] At this stage the UMW might have withdrawn from the field, and this was probably John Mitchell's intention. But in the summer of 1908 Mitchell was replaced by his rival T. L. Lewis, who lacked Mitchell's enthusiasm for class harmony and regarded expansion into Nova Scotia as an opportunity to strengthen his own support within the UMW. The new district was formally established in March 1909; by the end of the year union ledgers showed that 4,500 miners had joined the UMW.[15]

The conflict settled down into a long battle of endurance, with UMW miners on strike for recognition and PWA men at work under their own agreement. There was never any doubt that the coal companies would oppose the UMW. They at once proclaimed that the UMW was engaged in a conspiracy to weaken the position of Nova Scotia coal in its export markets in central Canada and New England: "the agitation carried on by . . . the United Mineworkers of America to gain control of the labour at the mines, is fraught with much danger to the Nova Scotia coal mining industry, and is likely to result in the loss of a large part of our trade to the Americans . . . the attempt of a foreign organization to control our mines should be resisted in every way possible."[16] As far as the law was concerned, there were no procedures for determining which union was to represent the coal miners. Employers were fully entitled to blacklist union members and hire strike-breakers. And there was ample provision under the law for the requisition of military aid to the civil power, the most common peacetime use of the Canadian armed forces. With the arrival of the troops, strike-breakers would be escorted into barracks behind barbed wire and electrified fences. Strikers would be evicted from company houses and their posses-

13. Grand Council Minutes, Provincial Workmen's Association (September 1907), 3:577–642, Labour Canada Library, Ottawa.

14. *Labour Gazette* 9 (July 1908): 12; PWA Grand Council Minutes (September 1908), 3:668–74.

15. *Eastern Labor News*, July 3, 1909; District 26 Ledgers, December 1909, UMWA Archives, Alexandria, Virginia.

16. *UMWJ* (December 2, 1909).

sions confiscated for back rent. Union parades would march in the face of fixed bayonets and mounted machine guns. At Inverness a union organizer would be jailed for supplying food and clothing to striking coal miners.[17]

The benefits of the international union were obvious when the coal companies advertised far and wide for strike-breakers. The union countered with its own advertising campaign. A front-page notice in the *United Mine Workers Journal* warned: "A strike has been on in Nova Scotia and at these mines since July 6 with every prospect of winning. Don't go there and try to defeat your brothers who are fighting for the right to organize and better conditions of employment." The district office distributed tens of thousands of circulars, notices, and pamphlets in Britain, Europe, and North America. When McLachlan learned of company plans to import one thousand miners from Belgium, he telegraphed Samuel Gompers of the AFL, to enlist his support. Gompers in turn cabled the secretary of Belgium's Federation of Labor about the Nova Scotia situation, "urging him to take such steps as would prevent the miners of Belgium coming to take the places of the striking miners there."[18]

Furthermore, the UMW provided substantial financial support. From the sidelines John Mitchell remained skeptical of "our president's pet achievement." But union money continued to flow into Nova Scotia throughout the winter, and by May 1910 the bills amounted to more than $800,000, most of which was spent on food, clothing, and shelter for the members on strike.[19]

The more radical themes of industrial democracy also won some attention. The Socialist Party of Canada gained a strong following among the coal miners in Nova Scotia, its message ably promoted by *Cotton's Weekly*, Canada's version of the *Appeal to Reason*. The coal miners also crowded into local theaters to hear speakers such as Big Bill Haywood, who pressed home the idea of "making the union an industrial school in which the workers study and develop themselves in such a manner that when the Socialist Party has achieved political emancipation, the industrial union would be prepared to efficiently and economically man and administer the means of production."[20]

The Nova Scotia strikes ended in defeat for the UMW in 1910 and 1911. District 26 did not stand alone in its defeat; battles were also lost in West Virginia and Colorado and Vancouver Island in these years. The achievements of the UMW were

---

17. *Report of the Deputy Minister of Labour on the Industrial Conditions in the Coal Fields of Nova Scotia*, House of Commons Sessional Papers, 1910, vol. 19, No. 36A; Dan Moore, "The 1909 Strike in the Nova Scotia Coal Fields" (unpublished honours paper, Carleton University, 1977), 80.

18. *UMWJ* (September 9, 1909); Gompers to J. Bergmans, March 30, April 1, 1910, Gompers to McLachlan, April 1, 1910, Nat. Union/No. 7, National Union Files, AFL-CIO Papers, Washington, D.C.

19. John Mitchell to Harriet Reid, August 9, 1909, John Mitchell Papers, Reel 16, Catholic University of America, Washington, D.C.; UMW Executive Board Minutes, March 30, June 26, September 27–30, 1909, May 23, 1910 [stenographic report], UMWA Archives, Washington, D.C.; *International Socialist Review*, April 1910, 952.

20. *Cotton's Weekly* (December 23, 1909).

not universal: in 1910 only one-third of the coal miners in the United States were organized and by 1920 this would increase only to slightly more than 50%.[21] The UMW closed the books on District 26 in February 1915. Yet the UMW had won enormous and lasting prestige among the Nova Scotia coal miners. The union's praises were sung in locally composed industrial folk songs such as "Arise Ye Nova Scotia Slaves," which was still being performed a generation later at the fiftieth-anniversary convention of the union in 1940: "And when the strike is over we'll march in grand array, / And we'll ring ten thousand cheers for the U.M.W.A. / And the scab will go under like the man before the gun / And the miners they will flourish when the dreary strike is won."[22]

III

Five years later everything had changed. In 1919 District 26 received a new charter from the UMW, and the international union was accepted by employers as the bargaining agent for the coal miners of Nova Scotia. The achievement owed much to the persistence of the UMW supporters in Nova Scotia and to the effects of the First World War. Under wartime conditions the local coal industry enjoyed unprecedented importance in the Canadian economy. The UMW veterans reorganized independently as the United Mine Workers of Nova Scotia. On this occasion they received timely assistance from the federal government. In Ottawa the miners were aided by J. C. Watters, another Scottish immigrant who had worked in the West Virginia and Vancouver Island coal mines and later became president of the Trades and Labor Congress of Canada; he was now working as a troubleshooter for the Dominion Fuel Controller. With the local UMW threatening a strike, Watters brought the government into the situation in the spring of 1917 and helped arrange for an amalgamation of the PWA and its rival UMW supporters. This was a remarkable achievement, as the Canadian government had generally failed to support the principle of collective bargaining in other wartime industries.[23]

The new union, the Amalgamated Mine Workers of Nova Scotia, proved to be a transitional body and soon voted to join the UMW as a unit. All the officers elected in 1917 were men associated with the old District 26. The senior member of the new leadership was the secretary-treasurer of the old district, J. B. McLachlan, commonly regarded as the guiding force behind the UMW in Nova Scotia for the previous ten years. The new president was Silby Barrett, a Newfoundland fisherman's son who had worked in UMW mines in Ohio before returning to Nova Scotia; with

21. Wolman, *Growth of American Trade Unions*, 137.

22. David Frank, "The Industrial Folk Song in Cape Breton," *Canadian Folklore canadien* 8, nos. 1–2 (1986): 31–34.

23. Developments in District 26 in this period are discussed in David Frank, "The Cape Breton Coal Miners, 1917–1926" (Ph.D. diss., Dalhousie University, 1979), chap. 5.

his salty wit, Barrett belonged to the most recent generation of recruits to the coal industry, men for whom the PWA had never possessed any appeal and for whom the UMW alone represented the principles of trade unionism.

When company officials proved reluctant to accept the UMW, the astute union leaders again turned to the state for assistance. With the encouragement of the Dominion government, in February 1919 the coal operators agreed to recognize the union they had fought so hard to exclude from the province; they would continue the union check-off and introduce the union's standard eight-hour day. At the same time operators also insisted on a statement which specified that "the local districts will receive complete autonomy" within the UMW.[24] The establishment of a new regime of industrial legality in the coalfield was confirmed in the Montreal Agreement between the coal operators and the union in 1920. The new contract included modest rate increases as well as a series of clauses guaranteeing managerial authority in the mines and limiting some of the existing forms of workers' control in the pits. Company and union officials were both reluctant to embrace the contract and did so under pressure from the federal government, still concerned about the stability of the fuel supply in Canada. Indeed the union officers found themselves forced to defend the contract against a storm of protest in the coalfields. Despite his reputation as a radical, McLachlan was accused of selling the miners short and betraying some of the miners' freedoms. He defended the contract by pointing out that the new agreement for the first time offered a guarantee of union security: the coal operators were required to meet the union before the end of the contract to negotiate a new agreement. Under the influence of the union officers, the new agreement was approved in a district vote.[25]

But it was an uneasy peace. The British Empire Steel Corporation, which by 1921 controlled virtually the entire coal industry of the province, was soon proposing large reductions and was ultimately determined to drive the union out of the industry entirely. The coal miners' struggle to defend their wages and their union precipitated a period of labor war that underlined the tensions between industrial legality and industrial democracy in the UMW.

The year 1922 began with a unilateral wage reduction of about one-third on the prevailing scale. The union charged the company with violating the existing terms of industrial legality, since the company was guilty of altering wages and conditions before submitting the dispute to conciliation procedures under the Industrial Disputes Investigation Act. An extended struggle followed, including both a dramatic slowdown strike in the pits and the return of the Canadian army; a new agreement finally restored most rates to the 1920 scale. The agreement violated the interna-

24. *Labour Gazette* 22 (February 1922): 164.

25. David Frank, "Contested Terrain: Workers' Control in the Cape Breton Coal Mines in the 1920s," in *On the Job: Confronting the Labour Process in Canada*, ed. Craig Heron and Robert Storey (Kingston and Montreal, 1986), 103–4.

tional union's "no backward step" policy of 1922, but the provision for local autonomy was recognized in this case and the outcome was considered to be a victory.[26]

During this struggle the district also took a strong turn to the left and endorsed
radical views of the potential for industrial democracy in the coal industry. Consistent supporters of public ownership in the industry, in June 1922 the union's leaders
denounced the chaotic condition of the coal industry and concluded with a sweeping
repudiation of the entire capitalist system: "we are out for the complete overthrow
of the capitalist system and capitalist state, peaceably if we may, forceably if we
must." Also, the district endorsed the sensational idea of applying for affiliation
to the Red International of Labour Unions, although this flamboyant gesture was
abandoned under pressure from UMW headquarters. This turn to the left did not
discredit the radicals among union members; in August McLachlan and his comrades were returned to office by large majorities.[27]

These events placed the district on a collision course with the international office.
McLachlan and several other district leaders (with the important exception of Silby
Barrett) had become members of the Workers' Party of Canada, the Canadian affili-
ate to the Communist International. The new UMW president, John L. Lewis, was
watching District 26 with misgivings. It is notable that during these months his
chief lieutenants were secretary-treasurer William Green and vice-president Phillip
Murray, who would of course later head respectively the American Federation of
Labor and the Congress of Industrial Organizations. As his local ally Lewis adopted
Barrett; defeated as international board member for District 26, he would become
Lewis's personal representative first in Nova Scotia and later on the national scene
in the CIO unions.

Meanwhile, the international union also raised the uncomfortable fact that District
26 was the only district that had worked without a contract and then accepted a
wage cut in 1922. The international's efforts to reopen the contract failed, but in
June 1923 the district convention voted to fight for the 1921 rates, even at the cost
of repudiating the existing agreement. McLachlan had justified this position in terms
that challenged the accepted version of industrial legality: "The 'sanctity' of contracts has become of late years a vanishing quality. Where is the mine worker who
in his every day toil does not find his employer continually interpreting the contract
to his own financial advantage, if not openly violating it?"[28] In response to the

26. David Frank, "Class Conflict in the Coal Industry: Cape Breton 1922," in *Essays in Canadian Working Class History*, ed. G. S. Kealey and P. Warrian (Toronto, 1976), 161–84.

27. "Minutes, Third Annual Convention of District 26, United Mine Workers of America, 20–24 June 1922," 23–25, Beaton Institute, University College of Cape Breton, Sydney, N.S.; *Maritime Labor Herald*, July 1, 1922. On the events of 1923 see also David Frank, "The Trial of J.B. McLachlan," *Communications historiques/Historical Papers* (1983): 208–25. For one recent study that overlooks de-velopments in Nova Scotia, see Alan Singer, "Communists and Coal Miners: Rank-and-File Organizing in the United Mine Workers of America During the 1920s," *Science and Society* 55, no. 2 (Summer 1991): 132–57.

28. McLachlan to Lewis, February 2, 1923, February 3, 1923, President's Correspondence: District 26, 1923, UMWA Archives, Alexandria.

district announcement, corporation president Roy Wolvin at once contacted Lewis to point out that the contract remained in force until January 1924. Lewis replied: "the United Mine Workers of America had never repudiated a contract." He also warned district officers by telegram against "ill-considered action which will violate every rule of honourable joint relationship and bring our union into public disrepute."[29] As a sign of reassurance, Lewis also sent a copy of the telegram to Wolvin's office at the Canada Cement Building in Montreal. The Besco president replied with enthusiasm: "Permit me to say that your action is the one which I fully expected the United Mine Workers to take, but taking it in the vigorous manner which you have, it is very much appreciated."[30]

The stage was set for a fullblown test of the principle of industrial legality in District 26. But when it came in July 1923, the explosion was set off by an entirely different set of circumstances. On July 4, 1923, the district leaders appealed to all mine workers in the province to come out in a sympathetic strike in support of embattled steel workers. When mounted police beat back union pickets at the local steel plant gates and rode down unarmed citizens in the streets of Sydney, the miners' union rallied to their support in a sympathetic strike.[31]

When he received the news Lewis was at the Ambassador Hotel in Atlantic City negotiating an important agreement with the anthracite coal operators. He sent urgent inquiries to District 26, but there were no replies. The two principal union officers had been arrested by provincial authorities. McLachlan would later be convicted of seditious libel. Lewis took steps to contain the rebellion. He warned District 18 in western Canada, where a sympathetic strike was being planned, that the Nova Scotia strike was "a pure violation of the existing contract between the miners and operators in that field." He also made plans for the appointment of Barrett as head of a provisional district. Before doing so, Lewis also reached an agreement with Besco to ensure that the company would maintain the union contract and pay union dues directly to the provisional officers.[32]

For Lewis events in District 26 were a distraction that threatened to undermine his credibility in the ongoing anthracite meetings and he said as much in one of his telegrams: "Situation district twenty six is doing serious injury to United Mine Workers in anthracite conference here and elsewhere." As Lewis later explained, "the matter became bigger than District 26": he had been placed in a difficult

29. Proceedings [stenographic report], June 1923 international board meeting, 268–69, 296, UMWA Archives.

30. Lewis to Wolvin, June 22, 1923, Wolvin to Lewis, June 23, 1923, President's Correspondence: District 26, 1923, UMWA Archives.

31. Frank, "The Trial of J.B. McLachlan." For oral accounts see "The 1923 Strike in Steel and the Miners' Sympathy Strike," *Cape Breton's Magazine*, no. 22 (June 1979): 1–9. For the general history of work and struggle in the Canadian steel industry see Craig Heron, *Working in Steel: The Early Years in Canada, 1883–1935* (Toronto, 1988).

32. Barrett to Lewis, July 5, 6, July 16, 1923; Lewis to Barrett, July 5, 15, 20, 1923, President's Correspondence: District 26, 1923.

position in the anthracite negotiations, where the fate of 158,000 workers was at stake: "The press was belabouring the organization for asking this recognition on the one hand, while in Nova Scotia there was widespread defiance of contract obligations."[33]

Finally, on the night of July 17, Lewis delivered a sweeping attack on what he considered to be the mad revolutionaries of District 26: "Your deliberate breach of the existing contract between the operators and miners of Nova Scotia is indefensible and morally reprehensible. Your assault upon the laws and institutions of your Provincial and Dominion Governments cannot be countenanced by the United Mine Workers of America. . . . You may as well know now as at any time in the future that the United Mine Workers is not a political institution and cannot be used to promote the fallacious whims of any political fanatic who seeks to strike down the established institutions of his Government." The charter of District 26 stood revoked and all the elected officers were removed. District 26 had temporarily ceased to exist.[34]

For the Nova Scotians the timing could not have been worse. Lewis had acted on the very day that the union leaders were meeting in a railway car with the governor-general—the titular head of state in Canada who was at the time on a ceremonial tour of Nova Scotia—and attempting to reach a basis for a peaceful settlement of the strike. McLachlan believed he had succeeded in arranging a symbolic victory for the coal miners and that Lewis was drawn into the picture that day through the agency of Besco. Certainly in Atlantic City, Wolvin's appeals for intervention were well received and Wolvin was in communication with Lewis up to and including the final day. The evidence of collaboration is circumstantial. Lewis himself had been considering drastic action for months and did not need to be pushed hard.

The strikes fell apart. It would be tempting to conclude that Lewis received a guarantee of continued recognition of the UMW in return for disciplining the radicals, but this was not the case. It would be another four years before the future of industrial legality in the coalfield was settled, and the international union played little part in this outcome. When the contract expired, the company posted a 20 percent reduction and set off a strike; when the provisional officers made a new agreement the coal miners voted it down two-to-one, and the international board was forced to impose the agreement. There were more headaches when the local courts ruled that Lewis had the right to discipline elected officers but no power to appoint provisional officers.[35]

Meanwhile, the radicals in District 26 failed to abandon the UMW. At the Indianapolis convention in January 1924, the Nova Scotians received support from other dissident districts in the union and forced the convention to debate the Nova Scotia

33. Proceedings of International Executive Board [stenographic report], November 1923, 241–42, UMWA Archives.
34. For the full text see *UMWJ* (August 1, 1923).
35. Frank, "The Cape Breton Coal Miners," 357–59.

situation at length. By the summer of 1924 a breakaway movement led by the One Big Union, a new Canadian-based radical industrial union movement, was also making headway. Preferring to contain the rebellious local elements within the UMW rather than face another long interunion struggle, the UMW restored the district's independence in September 1924. The coal miners then returned an executive composed entirely of McLachlan's supporters. A month later one of the district officers, Joseph Nearing, would run against William Green for international secretary-treasurer on a reform slate representing several dissident districts within the UMW.[36]

The following year, 1925, was marked by the longest and grimmest strike in the history of District 26. With the closing of the company stores, the miners were sustained for more than five months by public subscriptions and support from the international union. The strike finally erupted in a violent battle between union pickets and company police at Waterford Lake on June 11, 1925; coal miner William Davis was shot dead and several others were injured. Then the company stores went up in flames and the Canadian army returned. Later that summer the provincial government was overthrown at the polls in a sweeping victory for the Conservative Party, who pledged to bring peace to the coal industry.[37]

In the royal commission hearings that followed, the corporation president made it clear that he had no confidence in the UMW and no wish to continue union recognition. These views were rejected by the inquiry, which took a more optimistic view of the prospects for acceptance of industrial legality by the coal operators and urged the company to provide an "open and frank acceptance of the men's union." In the new agreement the company was forced to back down and include the union check-off in the contract. Behind the scenes the provincial government also took action by amending the Mines Act to authorize continuation of the union check-off. This amendment only confirmed existing practice but prevented the company from again attempting to abolish this symbol of union security.[38]

By 1927 the labor wars had come to an end in Nova Scotia. The union was battered but it was not broken. In Canada the coal miners' struggle was a large step toward the establishment of the modern system of industrial legality in Nova Scotia. Ten years later the provincial government would introduce the Trade Union Act, which protected the right to union membership and collective bargaining. The act was partly inspired by the Wagner Act in the United States, but it was also rooted in the local industrial conflict. Premier Angus L. Macdonald was anxious to redeem the Liberal Party in the eyes of Nova Scotia workers and also to avert another catastrophic industrial conflict involving an alliance between the coal miners and steel workers. Ironically the steel workers, whom Lewis had abandoned in the sum-

36. Ibid., 360–61.

37. Ibid., 362–75.

38. *Report of the Royal Commission on the Nova Scotia Coal Industry* (Halifax, 1926); E. N. Rhodes to W. S. Thompson, February 25, 1926, E. N. Rhodes Papers, Public Archives of Nova Scotia, Halifax, N.S.; *Statutes of Nova Scotia, 1927*, chap. 1, sect. 97.

mer of 1923, would now become, as Local 1064, one of the strongest units in the new Lewis-sponsored Steel Workers' Organizing Committee.[39]

The age of public ownership in the Nova Scotia coal industry was still more than a generation away and it would be achieved in 1967 under circumstances very different from those hoped for by the earlier advocates of industrial democracy. But the coal miners could also take some comfort in the collapse of the British Empire Steel Corporation. Their long resistance had helped to bring the hated corporation to the edge of collapse. As the local poet Dawn Fraser wrote in a grim spirit of vindication: "The bosses couldn't stand the gaff / Oh let me write their epitaph."[40]

IV

Like all coal miners in North America in the 1920s, those in Nova Scotia faced the ravages of an economic crisis and searched hard for a means of resistance. In a highly competitive market, marked by excess capacity and overproduction, the coal miners were held hostage by economic forces they could not control. In the 1920s every UMW district struggled to defeat reductions and maintain contracts. In the process the UMW itself became divided over tactics and strategies. For some the crisis demonstrated the irresponsible anarchy of the capitalistic system; they advanced the claims of industrial democracy for the complete reconstruction of the coal industry. For others it was necessary to defend the achievements of industrial legality as vigorously as possible by preserving strong agreements in the best-organized coalfields; this would enable the union to weather the storm and emerge with strong claims for recognition in a restructured industry.[41]

Foremost among the proponents of new forms of industrial democracy were supporters of John Brophy, president of District 2 in Pennsylvania. Brophy represented a body of pragmatic socialist opinion in the union, which was prepared to welcome large-scale state intervention. By 1922 the union's Nationalization Research Committee had prepared a detailed plan, at the heart of which was the proposal to buy out the coal operators and reorganize the coal mines under a federal commission. Much along the lines of the precedents of economic management in the First World War, the aim was to establish economic planning and national standards. This was a highly centralized, even bureaucratic, form of industrial democracy, far from revo-

39. For an oral account of these developments, see *George MacEachern: An Autobiography* (Sydney, 1987), chap. 4.

40. *Maritime Labor Herald*, July 1, 1926. See also Dawn Fraser, *Echoes from Labor's Wars: The Expanded Edition* (Wreck Cove, 1992), 55.

41. See Coleman, *Men and Coal*; and Dubofsky and Van Tine, *Lewis*. A useful account of the internal politics of the union in this period is A. C. Everling, "Tactics Over Strategy in the United Mine Workers of America: Internal Politics and the Question of the Nationalization of the Mines, 1908–1923" (Ph.D. diss., Pennsylvania State University, 1976).

lutionary in its underlying assumptions. In Brophy's view this was the most constructive alternative to the anarchy which threatened to overwhelm the industry and extinguish the rights of labor in the coalfields.[42]

For his part Lewis was eloquent in proclaiming the cause of the coal miners as part of the American struggle for human emancipation. The cause was fully defended in Lewis's 1925 book, *The Miners' Fight for American Standards*, written in cooperation with Jett Lauck. He agreed that the problem of the industry was an economic one, "a superfluous horde of incompetent and irresponsible coal operators." But he also believed that the industry must work out its own salvation with minimal interference from the state. In his view any effort to expropriate the coal operators, even at market prices, was a violation of the relationship that should prevail between employers and employees. Unlike the radicals, he defined industrial democracy narrowly and believed that the union's responsibility was limited by the collective agreement. This was the key to stability and Lewis was determined to demonstrate that the union was devoted to the maintenance of this form of industrial legality.[43]

By the time of the 1927 convention at Indianapolis, the internal battle within the UMW was all but over. The Brophy Plan was buried, undebated at conventions and unexamined in the union newspaper, and those, such as Brophy in 1926, who had run against Lewis had gone down to defeat. At the 1927 convention there were extensive constitutional changes, most of them designed to strengthen the authority of the executive board and the president. The most symbolic of the amendments, though, was a change in the preamble in the constitution. The phrase "full social value of their product," which had been installed by the socialists in 1912 to indicate the far-reaching goals of the union's wage policy, was replaced with the original, and more temperate, "equitable share of the fruits of their labor." The restoration of the original phrase from the 1890s represented a symbolic repudiation of the socialist influence in the union. As in the past, a short resolution on public ownership was also endorsed. Although "the principles of democratic management" were reaffirmed, no revolutionary change was anticipated. The endorsement of "equal representation in the management of the industry" implied a form of co-management between labor and capital and the state rather than a more radical form of industrial self-government or workers' control. The resolution concluded cautiously that "the development of this idea, like in Great Britain, is not rapid."[44]

But the union's policy of protectionism was ending in failure. In district after district, agreements were being repudiated by the coal operators and the coalfields were being plunged into industrial anarchy. Lewis continued to deliver lectures on

42. See J. B. S. Hardman, ed., *American Labor Dynamics* (New York, 1928), 173–91; and John Brophy, *A Miner's Life: An Autobiography* (Madison, Wisc., 1964).

43. *Proceedings of the 30th Consecutive Constitutional Convention of the UMWA, 1927*, 75. See also John L. Lewis, *The Miners' Fight for American Standards* (Indianapolis, 1925) and the discussion in Dubofsky and Van Tine, *Lewis*, 136–39.

44. *Proceedings, 1927*, 269, 215–16.

the benefits of industrial legality, but now his stern words were aimed not at his dwindling membership but at the undisciplined operators: "Trade unionists from time immemorial have been lectured by statesmen, employers, economists and moralists upon the virtue of carrying out the obligations of industrial agreements when negotiated. The United Mine Workers of America in the thirty-seven years of its existence has never repudiated an agreement once entered into, and yet our organization sought in vain for a friendly public opinion to inflict moral chastisement upon great corporations who thus violated the basic and cardinal principle of industrial relations."[45] This was the voice of frustration. The battles of the 1920s were ending in evictions and beatings, injunctions and defeat. No membership data were published by the union, but historians have estimated that membership fell to less than 100,000 members.[46] Industrial democracy had lost most of its meaning in the UMW, yet the promise of industrial legality had delivered no guarantees of stability to the coalfields.

In the view of many labor historians, trade unions are by nature conservative, protectionist organizations whose objectives must be limited to the defense of their members and the maintenance of the union contract. But there was also much in the history of the UMW to contradict this view. In these years at the beginning of the twentieth century the union presented a sometimes ambivalent image to its members. The Nova Scotians like many others had seen the fraternal face of industrial democracy give way to the disciplinary visage of industrial legality. Like Mitchell before him, Lewis defined industrial democracy narrowly, in terms of the acceptance of industrial legality; but others had given the cause a broader meaning, not only at the international level but also in smaller districts such as District 26.

There the radicals had some limited success in reconciling the claims of industrial democracy and industrial legality. The main achievements of industrial legality in Nova Scotia, including the recognition and preservation of the union, were brought about by leaders who supported a radical interpretation of industrial democracy. They did so by pressing hard for favorable state intervention at moments of strategic opportunity. Despite their enormous defeat before the war, they succeeded in gaining union recognition in the course of the First World War. Then in a protracted series of labor wars in the 1920s they kept the spirit of class solidarity alive in the coal country and aroused public support in the political domain; in the end they helped bring down an unpopular corporation and a government and were able to win guarantees for the maintenance of collective bargaining and the legal status of the union. By the end of the 1920s many districts in the UMW had given up more and accomplished less.

Industrial democracy? Or industrial legality? History did not offer such a clear choice of alternative strategies. Industrial democracy represented a broad vision that

45. *Proceedings, 1927*, 70–71.

46. Dubofsky and Van Tine, *Lewis*, 133, 147, have estimated that union membership declined to less than 100,000 members, most of them in Illinois.

could be shared, in their own eyes and interpreted in their own ways, by labor leaders as different as Samuel Gompers and Bill Haywood. Where leaders differed was in the importance they attached to the second concept, industrial legality. For John L. Lewis, industrial legality was a sufficient goal in the quest for working-class citizenship; with the achievement of industrial legality, industrial democracy would, in a sense, take care of itself. For McLachlan, however, the rule of law was too severely compromised under capitalism ever to bring a lasting solution to the labor question; the achievement of industrial democracy must finally await more revolutionary changes. These differences were not resolved by 1927, nor have they been answered since that time. As in so much else, however, the history of the coal miners casts a broad light on the history of labor and industrial relations in the twentieth century. As Selig Perlman had observed already in the 1920s, the rise of large and powerful unions such as the United Mine Workers in many ways marked "a new order" in North American labor history: "with its difficulties as well as its promises."[47]

47. Perlman, *History of Trade Unionism*, 167.

PART FIVE

DEVELOPMENTS SINCE 1960, AND THE STRUGGLE FOR RENEWAL

CHAPTER NINETEEN

LEGACY OF DEMOCRATIC REFORM
The Trumka Administration and the Challenge of the Eighties

PAUL F. CLARK

Much like its members who work in the unstable environment of underground coal mines, the UMWA experience has long been one of adapting to constantly changing conditions and challenges. And like the miners it represents, the continued survival of the union has always depended on its ability to respond to these changes. This is as true today as at any point in the union's long history.

Among the challenges the UMWA has faced in recent years are adverse markets for coal stemming from falling energy costs, the decline of the American steel industry, and imported coal; technological improvements in the mining of coal that have increased productivity at the expense of jobs; and changes in the composition of the industry itself, resulting from a wave of mergers and acquisitions, that have important ramifications for bargaining structure and tactics. The union has responded to these challenges by developing a comprehensive program of innovative strategies that have strengthened the union's hand at the bargaining table. This program was conceived and implemented by a new generation of leaders and staffers who took control of the union in late 1982.

The leadership of the union during the period, led by Richard Trumka, and the new tactics they spawned, were legacies of the democratic reform movement that substantially overhauled the UMWA in the 1970s. I shall examine both in light of the structural and policy changes instituted during the reform period.* In an effort to put the current state of the union in perspective, I shall also briefly examine the history of the union and the manner in which its past administrations, most notably the one led by the legendary John L. Lewis, have given leadership to the union during times of adversity.

THE LEWIS YEARS

During the forty years of John L. Lewis's presidency (1920–60), the UMWA won significant gains for its members and Lewis became a revered figure among American coal miners. Lewis's achievements at the bargaining table were considerable. In the 1930s, Lewis resisted the concession wave sweeping the country and won small, but symbolically important, wage increases from coal operators anxious to cut miners' pay. Lewis also won a significant measure of strength and security for the UMWA by establishing the union shop for a large segment of his membership.[1] During the coal boom brought on by World War II, Lewis pressed his advantage in an effort to increase the wage levels of UMWA members substantially through wage hikes and the institution of portal-to-portal pay. Lewis's finest performance as a negotiator probably occurred in the postwar era with the establishment of the UMWA Welfare and Retirement Funds in 1946.[2]

While Lewis's victories on behalf of coal miners were substantial, they were not without cost to the union and its membership. UMWA members surrendered a great deal of control over their union by gradually permitting Lewis to centralize power in his office.

In theory, Lewis won these gains while employing a formal bargaining structure that provided an opportunity for input from the membership.[3] The reality of contract negotiation in the UMWA during most of the Lewis years, however, was much different. When an agreement was due to be renegotiated, or when John L. Lewis felt an agreement should be renegotiated, he would assess the situation, formulate contract demands, present them to the coal operators, and proceed to bargain. If an impasse was reached, Lewis would command his troops to lay down their tools and man the picket line, which they did without question. When Lewis was satisfied with the terms he would accept the operators' offer, sign the final and binding agreement, and present it to the men who had to live with it.[4]

*I thank Mark Wardell and Bradley Nash Jr., for their editorial assistance.

1. Melvin Dubofsky and Warren Van Tine, *John L. Lewis: A Biography* (New York: Quadrangle, 1977), 374–75, 378–81.

2. Ibid., 389–490.

3. Paul F. Clark, *The Miners' Fight for Democracy: Arnold Miller and the Reform of the United Mine Workers* (Ithaca: Cornell University Press, 1981), 15–16.

4. Dubofsky and Van Tine, *John L. Lewis,* 389–490.

The membership had virtually no role in the formulation of demands and no right to ratify or even review the terms of an agreement before it was signed by Lewis. Lewis justified his omnipotent role in bargaining this way, ''I work harder than anyone else in this union, and I know more about the problems of miners than anyone else. Therefore, I should think that my decisions would mean more than those of anyone else.''[5] Without question, they did.

Perhaps the greatest challenge of Lewis's career, in this sense, occurred during the last ten years of his presidency. The American fuel market had shifted during the postwar era, with oil and gas challenging the dominance of coal in both the industrial and the domestic energy market.[6] To improve the industry's competitive position the coal operators looked to increase productivity. Mechanization of the work process, and the reduced labor costs that would accompany such a move, was one obvious answer to the productivity problem. While the economic benefits of mechanization were potentially great, these benefits could only be achieved at the cost of thousands of jobs, as miners would be replaced by machines. Lewis made the decision to grant the operators a free hand to mechanize the industry, reasoning that ''it is better to have half a million men working in the industry at good wages and high standards than it is to have a million working in the industry in poverty and degradation.''[7]

While it can be argued that Lewis had a practical responsibility to the welfare of the industry that employed his members and that both mechanization and the resultant layoffs were inevitable, Lewis did little to shield his members from the savage effects of this process. By 1964, close to three hundred thousand miners had lost their livelihood as a result of Lewis's acquiescence. The coal companies introduced machinery rapidly and with little regard for the men the machines displaced. Neither they nor the union provided retraining or rehabilitation programs for those thrown out of work. In many cases the union cut benefits from the Welfare and Retirement Funds that the unemployed or prematurely retired miners needed desperately.[8] The industry essentially discarded thousands of union miners, and the UMWA looked the other way. It is only possible to speculate whether the union's response to the challenge of mechanization might have taken a different form had the thousands of miners affected had some influence or input in deciding their fate.

APRÈS LEWIS, LE DÉLUGE

When John L. Lewis stepped aside in 1960, after forty years as UMWA president, he was succeeded by Thomas Kennedy, the union's elderly vice president. The new

5. Saul Alinsky, *John L. Lewis: An Unauthorized Biography* (New York: Putnam, 1970), 350.

6. Joseph E. Finley, *The Corrupt Kingdom: The Rise and Fall of the United Mine Workers* (New York: Simon and Schuster, 1972), 170–71.

7. ''John L. Lewis Goes to Bat Again,'' *Business Week* (October 4, 1958): 97.

8. Finley, *The Corrupt Kingdom*, 188–197.

vice president, and heir apparent, was W. A. "Tony" Boyle. When Kennedy died in early 1963, Boyle became the eleventh president of the United Mine Workers union. Although ambitious, Boyle lacked the brilliant mind and genius for leadership that Lewis had brought to the union's presidency. Ironically, however, it was simple for Boyle to assume the same control as his larger-than-life predecessor, since the mechanisms of power had been so thoroughly institutionalized during Lewis's reign.

Without the checks that characterize democratic union structures, neglect and unresponsiveness came to characterize the Boyle administration as corruption spread throughout the organization. In terms of collective bargaining, Boyle conducted negotiations in the same manner as Lewis. The same rituals of internal process were observed, allowing for the same amount of rank-and-file involvement—virtually none.[9]

Unfortunately, Boyle was unable to deliver as Lewis had. Open discontent began to emerge as wage agreements negotiated by Boyle caused miners' wages to slip behind their counterparts in the steel and auto industries.[10] In 1964 and 1966, UMWA members walked off the job to protest agreements signed by Boyle.[11] The opposition that continued to build in response to substandard contracts, the leadership's neglect of such basic issues as miner health and safety, and ongoing revelations of corruption and fiscal abuse, eventually coalesced into a movement for the democratic reform of the union. This movement took wing in May 1969 when Jock Yablonski, a longtime UMWA official from western Pennsylvania and former administration loyalist, announced that he would challenge Boyle for the presidency of the union.[12]

Jock Yablonski's election loss to Boyle in December 1969, and the brutal killing of Yablonski, his wife, and daughter twenty-two days later by Boyle-hired gunmen, have been well documented.[13] At Yablonski's funeral, miners who had worked with him during the election challenge decided to form a new organization, Miners For Democracy (MFD), to carry on the struggle in which he had fallen. In 1972, the Department of Labor ordered the 1969 election rerun due to massive irregularities committed by Boyle and his followers. Later that year Arnold Miller and the MFD slate of candidates defeated the incumbent Boyle administration. The reform administration took office in December 1972, only months before Tony Boyle was indicted

9. "Miners Seek a Pact in Cool, Quiet Talks," *Business Week* (September 28, 1968): 109; John Paul Nyden, "Miners For Democracy: Struggle in the Coal Fields" (Ph.D. diss., Columbia University, 1974), 475, 483.

10. UMWA, *It's Your Union, Pass It On: Officers' Report to the Forty-seventh Constitutional Convention, Cincinnati, Ohio, September 1976* (UMWA: Washington, D.C., 1976), 27.

11. Nyden, "Miners For Democracy," 475, 483.

12. Brit Hume, *Death and the Mines: Rebellion and Murder in the United Mine Workers* (New York: Grossman, 1971), 173.

13. Hume, *Death and the Mines;* Trevor Armbrister, *Act of Vengeance* (New York: Dutton, 1975).

for the murder of Jock Yablonski.[14] While the election of the MFD slate was indeed a significant achievement, the task it faced in rebuilding the UMWA into a democratic labor organization was an even more formidable challenge.

THE REFORM PERIOD

The MFD ticket was elected on a reform platform that called for the reestablishment of democratic procedures that would return control of the union to the membership and force the leadership to be more responsive. In its early days in office, the reform administration moved to restore the right of UMWA members to elect their district officials, a practice that had been largely discontinued when previous administrations placed the districts in trusteeships and appointed their officers. Supervision of elections by elected union tellers, equal use of the union's official publication by all candidates for International office, a bona fide appeals process, and voting at the mine site—all helped to make subsequent UMWA elections legitimate exercises in union democracy.

The new leadership, recognizing that top-down reform was inconsistent with the principles of democratic unionism, moved quickly to involve the rank and file in the reshaping of their union. The UMWA's constitutional convention was seen as the mechanism that could best serve this function. The convention, which had been a largely orchestrated, pro forma affair under Lewis and Boyle, was badly in need of reform. Toward this end, the delegate selection process, the convention committee system, and the rules by which the convention was governed were revamped to ensure that it would truly be a representative forum.

Given the opportunity, the delegates to the 1973 and 1976 conventions made significant changes in union structure and policy, laying the foundation for democratic unionism. Among the measures taken were provisions to place tight control over the International's power to bring a district or local under trusteeship; steps to ensure honest elections at all levels of the union; and guidelines delineating the powers and responsibilities of elected union officials. Important to note, these changes were made by UMWA members in what one veteran of UMWA conventions testified was "the most open and democratic convention that I have ever attended."[15]

The "imperial bargaining" arrangement of Lewis failed during the Boyle years, and many UMWA members realized that if the union's bargaining strategies were going to reflect the sentiments of the rank and file, the rank and file had to be involved in the process. The bargaining procedure created by the 1973 UMWA Convention embodied this thinking.

14. Finley, *The Corrupt Kingdom;* Nyden, "Miners For Democracy."
15. UMWA, *Proceedings of the Forty-Sixth Consecutive Constitutional Convention of the United Mine Workers of America, Pittsburgh, Pennsylvania, December 3–14, 1973* (UMWA: Washington, D.C., 1974), 439.

The procedure began with rank-and-file miners electing representatives to a district bargaining conference that met to transmit the sentiments of the membership to the next step in the procedure, the Bargaining Council. The Bargaining Council, composed of all district presidents and International Executive Board (IEB) members, served to advise the International officers and other members of the negotiating team on bargaining strategy. When an agreement was reached with the coal operators, the proposed contract started back through the internal bargaining procedure— requiring the approval of the Bargaining Council before being sent again to the district conferences for explanation and clarification. The final step was ratification by all members covered by the agreement. This step fulfilled one of the basic promises of the MFD campaign by ensuring that no miner would have to work under a contract on which he had not voted. The UMWA's bargaining procedure remains one of the most democratic in the American labor movement.[16]

The transition to democratic unionism was not without problems. Not all of the membership, or leadership, supported the reform movement, and the new democratic framework provided a forum for dissenters to make their case openly. In addition to the factionalism that resulted, the UMWA experienced a dramatic increase in wildcat or unauthorized strikes during the reform administration's first term. These problems were compounded by the sometimes ineffective response of a still inexperienced leadership.

Nowhere were the problems so visible, or fundamental, as on the collective bargaining front. The first contract negotiations conducted under the revised bargaining format took place in 1974. The union went in well prepared and, with the help of a highly capable staff, Miller eventually negotiated a solid contract that included impressive gains in a number of areas. While the new bargaining procedure sputtered a bit (in fact, the newly formed bargaining council twice rejected proposed agreements), this was not unexpected as both members and officers were learning their roles in the new bargaining process. And, for the first time, rank-and-file members and local and district officers were more than just spectators in the negotiation of the contract.[17]

Unfortunately, things did not go so smoothly in 1977–78. Following a bitter campaign in which Miller defeated two challengers to retain the UMWA presidency, the union faced another round of contract negotiations. The union that entered these talks was already a union in crisis. The wave of wildcat strikes that had plagued the union from 1974 to 1976, the recent cutbacks in health benefits caused by an income shortfall in the Welfare and Retirement Fund, and the highly politicized atmosphere resulting from the recent election campaign had set the UMWA back on its heels. To make matters worse Miller, beset by a wave of staff resignations, came to the bargaining table unprepared, without adequate staff support, and tied by campaign

16. *The Miners' Fight for Democracy,* 45–56.
17. Ibid., 52–56.

pledges to demands the operators rejected out of hand.[18] The result was a disastrous 111-day strike, that included a very erratic performance by the UMWA president and three rejections of Miller-endorsed settlements, two by the Bargaining Council and one by the membership. The end product of the painful and costly strike was an agreement that fell far short of the expectations of most of the union's members.[19]

Some observers were quick to blame this failure on the democratic reform movement generally, and the new bargaining procedure in particular. In retrospect, the problems the union experienced both prior to, and during, the 1977–78 negotiations appear to have been the growing pains that any dramatic change would be likely to encounter. It would be naive to expect the transition from autocracy to democracy to proceed quickly and painlessly. Also, democratic organizations are dependent on strong and capable leadership. This is something the union appeared to lack, at least in the latter years of Arnold Miller's administration.

Miller resigned as UMWA president in November 1979, plagued by health problems and buffeted by political infighting following the 1977–78 contract debacle. Sam Church, a former Boyle loyalist who had been brought to the union's headquarter's staff by Miller and elevated to the vice presidency in the 1977 election, assumed leadership of the union. At the time Church took office, the coal industry was experiencing a number of structural and market changes that would play a role when the union and the BCOA met in 1980 to renegotiate the industrywide agreement. Despite this unstable environment, optimism prevailed on the part of both the parties and outside observers that a settlement could be reached without a strike. This view was based on leadership changes at both the UMWA and the BCOA, on the previous resolution of the wildcat problem, and on the vivid memory of the 1977–78 strike, an occurrence both sides desperately wished to avoid.

When talks began in 1980, the issues were fairly clear. The union wanted to achieve a ''substantial'' increase in wages and a cost-of-living clause, greater benefits for widows of pensioners, a dental plan, the adoption of a new absenteeism policy, and the elimination of the Arbitration Review Board. The BCOA went into negotiations willing to give a reasonable wage settlement, but adamantly opposed a cost-of-living escalator clause. In addition, the operators wanted to substitute individual company pension plans for the existing multiemployer pension funds and to eliminate the nonsignatory royalty clause, which would effectively allow unionized coal companies to market nonunion coal without penalty.[20]

Just days before the contract expired in March 1981, the UMWA Bargaining Council approved a tentative agreement negotiated by Church and sent it to the membership for ratification. To the great surprise and dismay of both the union leadership and the BCOA, the miners voted the proposal down by more than a 2 to

18. Ibid., 114–37.

19. Ibid., 117–31.

20. Charles Perry, *Collective Bargaining and the Decline of the United Mine Workers* (Philadelphia: Industrial Relations Unit, 1984), 244.

1 margin. In retrospect, the only thing that is really surprising about this turn of events was that the contract was sent to the membership in the first place. The proposed contract contained a great many of the BCOA's demands, demands that had significant ramifications for the security of both the union and unionized miners' job. Among these provisions was language that would have given the operators a free hand to subcontract work heretofore performed by UMWA members and a clause that would terminate the requirement that BCOA firms pay a royalty on all non-BCOA coal they bought and resold. The members clearly saw these provisions as an effort to circumvent the contract at the cost of UMWA jobs.[21]

After more than two months of acrimonious negotiations, the union and the BCOA arrived at a second proposed contract. This contract was unanimously approved by the Bargaining Council and won membership ratification by a two-thirds vote on June 6, 1981. The revised contract retained the nonsignatory royalty payment and offered greater protection against the subcontracting of jobs, as well as added benefits like a modest dental plan and widows' pensions. While the union was forced to give some ground in important areas, the second proposed contract was a significant improvement from the initial agreement that had been rejected by the membership.[22] Clearly, most of the credit for these gains was due to the miners themselves. They had used the democratic process to force the operators to come up with a contract that would not threaten the security of their union or their jobs. And they had accomplished this, once again, despite a weak performance by their leadership at the bargaining table. It was a profound statement for democratic unionism.

Unfortunately for Sam Church the fallout from the 1981 negotiations was deep. Resentment of that contract smoldered as the Church administration geared up for its fall 1982 reelection bid. The November 1981 announcement by IEB member Richard Trumka that he would challenge Church for the union's presidency fanned this resentment into an open flame. Focusing on Church's handling of the 1981 contract talks, especially his failure to win job security guarantees, Trumka castigated the incumbent for providing "weak leadership."[23] For his part, Church attacked his challenger on a number of fronts, charging Trumka with being a militant with leftist associations and a fomenter of wildcat strikes.[24] Despite the charges and countercharges, at least some observers credited the candidates with demonstrating relative restraint, compared to past UMWA elections.[25]

21. Curtis Seltzer, *Fire in the Hole: Miners and Managers in the American Coal Industry* (Lexington: University Press of Kentucky, 1985), 194–95.

22. Seltzer, *Fire in the Hole*, 198–99.

23. Carol Hymowitz, "UMW Chief Is Facing Strong Challenger Who Criticizes Handling of Contract Talks," *Wall Street Journal* (August 3, 1982): 12.

24. Kathy Sawyer, "Mine Workers, After Bitter Campaign, To Vote Today on Chief, Challenger," *Washington Post* (November 9, 1982), A2; Seltzer, *Fire in the Hole*, 202.

25. Kathy Sawyer, "Trumka: Suited For Mining In a New Era," *Washington Post* (December 22, 1982), D1.

When the ballots were counted following the November 9 election, Trumka had outpolled Church 68% to 32%. Running on promises of no concessions and tougher, more militant leadership, the challenger had defeated the incumbent in twenty-three of the twenty-six UMWA districts. In terms of the coal industry, the union and the labor movement this was a milepost.

Trumka's election was a significant story for at least two reasons. The media, however, focused a great deal of attention on only one of these: the contrasting styles and personae of the two candidates. Typical was a *Wall Street Journal* article that saw the election as a contest between the incumbent Church, a "tobacco chewing," "brawling coal miner who made it big," and the challenger Trumka, "an articulate and sophisticated . . . miner-lawyer who favors pin-striped suits and French restaurants."[26] Such contrasts did have significance, inasmuch as they symbolized the rise of a new breed of UMWA leader. Richard Trumka was different from his predecessors. College-educated and a law school graduate, Trumka represented both the gradual evolution of the union's membership and the UMWA's need for a leader who could drag the union into a new era.

Still, the media, among others, missed the second part of the story. The seeds of Richard Trumka's election to the UMWA presidency had been sown in the unsuccessful challenge of Jock Yablonski and in the eventual triumph of the MFD movement. Without the democratic mechanisms put into place by the reform movement, and without the democratic consciousness raised in the process, the 1982 elections would have been business as usual. Viable challenges to sitting union presidents are unusual in the American labor movement. Successful challenges are considered extreme anomalies. Yet here, rank-and-file miners had the opportunity to evaluate, in the course of a relatively civilized election campaign, the merits and qualifications of two candidates for the presidency of their union. They had the opportunity to vote, without coercion, for the one they felt could best lead the union in the very difficult years ahead. They had made their choice and a relatively orderly transition of power had taken place. This was one of the most important legacies of the democratic reform movement in the miners' union.

THE TRUMKA ADMINISTRATION

When Richard Trumka and his slate of officers were sworn into office on December 22, 1982, exactly ten years to the day after the Miller-led MFD team had taken their oath, they faced a coal industry in the midst of fundamental change. Between 1970 and 1980, the BCOA-UMWA share of industry production fell from 424 to 365 million tons, while national output increased from 603 to 824 million tons. Over the

---

26. Susan Carey, "Mineworkers' Election on Tuesday Pits A Brawler Against Young, New Breed," *Wall Street Journal* (November 5, 1982): 18.

previous twelve years, the percentage of UMWA-mined coal had fallen from 65% to 40% of total output. Membership in the union, which had peaked in the Lewis era at over 400,000 members, was down to 230,000, of whom 70,000 were pensioners. Many of these shifts had their roots in the ascendancy of surface coal produced in the western states. In addition, falling demand for underground coal mined by UMWA members, due to the declining steel industry and environmental concerns, and the advent of new ''labor-saving'' mining technologies, combined to exacerbate an already difficult situation. Finally, the union's misfortunes had not escaped the attention of the coal operators, who were fully prepared to exploit these circumstances in an effort to shift the balance of power within the industry even more in their favor.[27] The future faced by the union at this juncture was so grim as to cause one observer to comment: ''Unless the UMWA and its members do something different, their union cards are likely to be souvenir items in twenty years.''[28]

To their credit, Trumka and his supporters had recognized the need for new directions prior to their taking command of the union. Once in office, the Trumka administration moved quickly to put its plans into action. During his first year, Trumka addressed the union's financial crisis by cutting the headquarters' payroll by nearly 50%. This step, combined with other organizational efficiencies, had the union once more operating in the black by year's end. In addition, Trumka completely revamped the union's important organizing and safety departments, cutting their budgets but increasing their effectiveness. Being aware of how his predecessor's lack of support among the union's executive board had hampered their efforts, Trumka also took steps to mend fences and improve communications with the IEB. Common to all of these moves was a leadership style that, according to one staffer, had made UMWA headquarters ''an electrifying place to be.''[29]

Trumka's First Term

The first significant opportunity for the Trumka administration to present its plans for the future came at the union's December 1983 convention. Held in Pittsburgh, the meeting presented an opportunity for Trumka to consolidate his leadership and to put in place, constitutionally, the tools he would need to confront effectively the coal operators at the bargaining table. While the delegates to the convention did not give their president everything he asked for, Trumka came away from the meeting with much of what he wanted.

Delegates voted to give Trumka authority to implement a selective-strike strategy in the upcoming contract talks with the BCOA. A related resolution required a two-thirds vote of the IEB to reverse any decisions made by the president regarding the

27. Seltzer, *Fire in the Hole*, 205–8.
28. Seltzer, *Fire in the Hole*, 207.
29. ''The UMW's New Boss Starts to Dig Out From Under,'' *Business Week* (December 12, 1983), 90.

selective strike-strategy. Also, after much discussion, the delegates reluctantly gave authority to President Trumka to assess working miners up to 2.5% of their wages to build a 70 million dollar strike fund. And in a move of great significance to the new administration, the delegation abolished the union's Bargaining Council, an intermediate step in the contract ratification process that had proved a stumbling block in the past. Finally, the convention agreed to break with tradition by supporting the leadership's call not to discuss bargaining priorities publicly. Instead, the delegates voted to go on record as rejecting any contract concessions.[30]

The Trumka administration had one additional goal for the 1983 convention, but here it overreached. Early in the convention the delegates rejected, by a two-to-one margin, an administration-inspired proposal that would have required a two-thirds vote of the IEB to overturn a presidential decision, instead of the simple majority then needed. Wary of past abuses, the delegates voted, by a two-to-one margin, to retain what they saw as a check on the power of the president. As a miner from District 2 observed, "there is a little in Rich that is like ol'John L. (Lewis). We couldn't give him absolute control. He got a mandate in his landslide election last year, but it wasn't a blank check."[31]

The 1983 UMWA Convention put Richard Trumka firmly in control of the union as it geared up for negotiations in 1984. Specifically, it gave him a virtual free hand to shape and implement a bargaining strategy that was vastly different from any employed by the union in modern times. At the heart of this strategy was the concept of the selective strike.

A New Bargaining Strategy

Traditionally, the UMWA's approach to bargaining with the bituminous coal industry had been very straightforward. The union would negotiate until its contract expired, at which point all miners working under that agreement would lay down their tools until a new contract was agreed upon. This strategy was built upon the credo of "no contract, no work," a sort of Eleventh Commandment among UMWA members. This catechism had become such an article of faith that when Trumka's predecessor Sam Church merely suggested that the union examine the effectiveness of this approach, he was quickly and firmly rebuffed.[32] In this context, Trumka's proposal of a new bargaining strategy employing selective strikes, in the course of his first round of contract talks, was a bold step.

The selective-strike strategy called for choosing particular companies, and sometimes particular operations within those companies, to shut down. In practice, the

30. Susan Carey, "UMW's Trumka Is Voted More Powers, But Test Lies in Control of Labor Talks," *Wall Street Journal* (December 19, 1983): 12.

31. Nicholas Knezevich, "Fired Up: UMW President's New Power Revives Shades of John L.," *Pittsburgh Press* (December 1983), B1.

32. Merrill Hartson, "Church Facing His Greatest Challenge," *Valley News Dispatch* (Tarentum, Pa.) (March 27, 1981), A3.

"no contract, no strike" philosophy would be abandoned. If those companies and operations selected as strike targets were in fact struck, miners at the remaining companies would continue to work. UMWA members at the companies closed would receive strike benefits from the selective-strike fund. These benefits would be pegged at levels high enough so as to not inflict economic hardship on the strikers and their families.

The rationale for the selective-strike strategy lay in the fact that changing conditions in the industry had reduced the potential impact of a nationwide coal strike. In a February 1984 article in the *United Mine Workers Journal*, the UMWA president explained to the membership the need for such an innovation:

JOURNAL: Why does the union need a selective strike option right now?

TRUMKA: The biggest reason is that the nature of the coal industry has undergone a dramatic change in recent years.

The UMWA used to negotiate primarily with coal companies, companies whose only business was mining coal. In that situation, it was comparatively easy for the union to put a lot of economic pressure on these operators just by shutting down their coal production.

For the past several years, we've been negotiating with a different coal industry, one made up of giant corporations. Island Creek is owned by Occidental Oil; Consol is owned by DuPont; and so on down the line.

Anyone who remembers 1978 and 1981 knows that our old strategy of a nationwide strike doesn't work in the same way when the corporations who own the mines have other sources of income besides their coal production.

JOURNAL: What's different about a selective strike?

TRUMKA: With a nationwide strike, one company doesn't have any advantage over another. They're all shut down. In that case, as we've seen, they all bite the bullet together and come after us.

But in a selective strike, we only strike one, or a few, companies. Those companies whose mines are on strike face a loss of revenues, and possibly a loss of their share of the coal market, because all the other companies are working.

I don't know of any coal company that will sacrifice its own profits to protect the rest of the industry when all the other companies are working and making money. These companies will have a lot of incentive to negotiate a fair contract and get back to work.[33]

By striking only selected coal companies the union would be able to use the competitive forces of the coal market to pit one company against another. Most of its members would be able to continue to work at full wages since labor law prohibits an employer from making cuts, even after a contract expires, as long as negotia-

33. *UMWJ* (February 1984): 5–6.

tions are ongoing. Those on the job would then be in a position to indefinitely support those chosen to strike. One possible problem with the strategy was that the coal operators might not choose to cooperate with the union in this economic jujitsu. If, however, the industry decided to shut down in unison (in essence to lock out a workforce willing to work), miners would in most instances be eligible for unemployment compensation. And, finally, if this strategy did not prove effective, the union would still have the option of the time-honored national shutdown.

Armed with the selective-strike strategy and a well-prepared bargaining team, the UMWA entered talks with the BCOA in April 1984, five months prior to the September 30 contract expiration date. Among the challenges facing the union was an industry bargaining structure that had changed significantly from past years. The BCOA, which traditionally represented most of the companies operating in bituminous coal, had suffered defections since the last agreement. By the time negotiations began, this bargaining group had been reduced to 32 coal companies, employing approximately 70,000 union miners.[34] These companies came to the bargaining table with the goal of winning a contract that would boast productivity in the mines. On the BCOA wish list were changes in absenteeism policies, manning levels, job classification and bidding procedures, vacation days, and rules prohibiting Sunday work.[35]

While the union had made an early decision not to publicize its bargaining priorities, two issues appeared paramount: job security and resistance to concessions. With between 25 and 50% of its members out of work, and with membership levels falling to crisis levels, it seemed certain that the union would strenuously resist any changes that would mean fewer jobs for UMWA miners. Also, the union had made clear, both by convention resolution and presidential decree, that it would accept "no backward steps."

Initially, with the parties bringing seemingly conflicting goals to the talks, prospects for settling a UMWA-BCOA contract without a strike for the first time in nearly twenty years did not seem good. Chances for a peaceful settlement appeared even more remote when both parties came to the table well prepared for a strike. This was evidenced by the UMWA's creation of a selective-strike fund and by the industry's extensive stockpiling of coal. When talks broke off in mid-August (a result, the BCOA contended, of UMWA President Trumka introducing "an expanded list" of demands), even the most optimistic observers predicted a strike.[36]

However, when talks reconvened on September 10, quick progress was made and eleven days later, the parties reached a tentative agreement. Speculation as to whether the union's membership would reject the contract, as they had so often in

34. Susan Carey, "Coal Industry Negotiators Push to Reach Pact a Month Before Sept. 30 Expiration," *Wall Street Journal* (August 18, 1984): 5.

35. Susan Carey, "Coal Industry Is Preparing for a Strike When UMW Agreement Expires Sept. 30," *Wall Street Journal* (July 16, 1984): 7.

36. Susan Carey, "Trumka's Polished Style of Negotiating Is Tested as UMW Pact Deadline Nears," *Wall Street Journal* (September 10, 1984): 20.

recent years, was great. The proposed agreement's chief selling point, however, was a strong one: no givebacks. At a point in time when many, if not most, major unions were granting contract concessions, the Trumka administration had negotiated a contract with a distressed industry that included modest wage increases totaling 10% over the life of the 40-month agreement. There were concerns on the part of some that the union had traded provisions that would hurt laid-off miners, but, for the most part the UMWA had resisted the labor-saving proposals put forward by the industry. In addition, the union won language that would require operators subleasing mines from a unionized coal company to give first hiring rights to UMWA miners laid off by the company leasing the mine.[37]

The union's membership apparently liked what it saw. When the results of the contract ratification process were tallied, more than 83% of miners voting approved the agreement. On September 28, 1984, President Trumka, and his fellow officers, signed their first contract with the BCOA.

Most observers saw the settlement as a great boost for the union and the Trumka administration. The UMWA had bucked the trend and negotiated wage increases without giving ground on job security or work practices. It is difficult to tell what impact the union's well-organized and innovative approach to the talks ultimately had. There was, however, little question that Richard Trumka had impressed many people, both in the industry and without. Clearly, the union's performance in the 1984 negotiations with the BCOA was a cut above its recent performances.

A New Organizational Strategy

In the period following the 1984 talks, the strength of Trumka's leadership continued to be evident as the union moved in new directions. One example of this dynamism was the union's frontline role in the American labor movement's opposition to the system of apartheid in South Africa. While the union's involvement in this issue was undoubtedly tied to the fear that South African coal imports, mined by cheap, black labor, were a threat to the jobs of American miners, the scope and intensity of the union's involvement seemed to transcend pure self-interest. The UMWA instituted a nationwide boycott of Royal Dutch/Shell, a company with massive investments in the South African energy industry; organized a South African Miners Aid Fund to help striking black miners in that country; helped build a coalition on the issue with other unions and social and religious organizations (like the World Council of Churches); and hired full-time staffers to coordinate the union's efforts.

President Trumka and the union's two other International officers, Cecil Roberts and John Banovic, also took part in demonstrations at the South African Embassy in Washington, D.C., undergoing arrest in a show of support. The UMWA's active

---

37. Bill Keller, "Mine Workers and Coal Operators Reach Agreement on Pact," *New York Times* (September 22, 1984), 10.

involvement in an international social justice issue, and the working relationship it developed on the question with progressive elements of the labor movement, was something that had not been a part of the union's experience since the early seventies.[38]

In addition to its involvement with other unions on the South Africa issue, Trumka's reputation and activism helped draw the UMWA closer to the mainstream of the American labor movement. Rumors began circulating that the UMWA's return to the AFL-CIO was imminent. AFL-CIO President Lane Kirkland's invitation to speak at the 1983 UMWA Convention, and his direct appeal to the delegates to rejoin the "House of Labor," fueled the rumors.[39]

While Trumka did not lead the union back into the AFL-CIO until October 1989, possibly because of a reluctant membership still clinging to the tradition of independence glorified by Lewis, he clearly was not afraid to make significant breaks with the past when necessary. This was evident in his decision to sell the UMWA's controlling interest in the National Bank of Washington. Always of symbolic importance to the union, and a source of pride since John L. Lewis purchased it in 1949, selling the bank could not have been an easy decision for the UMWA leadership. Yet the union's ownership of the bank was, in many ways, an anachronism, particularly at a time when the UMWA's finances were in a precarious state and the bank itself was struggling. With the support of the IEB, Trumka put the bank up for sale, and at the end of 1985 the deal was complete. Most observers agreed that the bank's sale was a prudent move and one that could only help to consolidate the union's financial position.[40]

A Special Convention

During its first three years in office the Trumka administration had accomplished much. In the process, it had demonstrated an astute political sense, a talent for organization, and a willingness to break new ground. All of these qualities were evident as the administration geared up for its second round of negotiations with the BCOA. Although the contract was scheduled to expire in January 1988, the union was already preparing for talks when it made the surprise announcement in the summer of 1986 that it would call a "Special International Convention" for October of that year. The announcement was a surprise because the UMWA had never held a special convention in its more than ninety years of existence. Traditionally, UMWA conventions were held every three or four years. That would mean that the next

38. *UMWJ* (February 1986); Karlyn Barker, "UMW to Escalate Protests Against South Africa," *Washington Post* (July 26, 1985), C5; Karlyn Barker, "UMWA Sets South Africa Miners' Fund," *Washington Post* (September 5, 1985), A28.

39. Drew Von Bergen, "UMW Urged to Rejoin House of Labor," *Washington Post* (December 13, 1983), D7.

40. Michael Abramowitz, "End of an Era: Sale of NBW Becomes Final." *Washington Post* (December 23, 1985), B1.

regular convention would, most probably, have been scheduled for sometime in 1987. According to the *UMWJ*, the union decided to hold a special convention because:

> It takes nearly a year to plan, organize, select delegates and conduct a regular International convention.
>
> The IEB felt that, because of the rapidly changing nature of the industry with which the union will be bargaining in 1987 and 1988, it was necessary to have our bargaining goals and strategies determined as early as possible.
>
> A special convention, limited to these issues, can be organized within a short period of time, and the Board determined it would be the best way for the union to get ready for the next round of negotiations.[41]

Constitutionally, a special convention is limited to considering only matters specifically stated in the convention call. The UMWA Special Convention Call listed four issues that would be discussed: the establishment of job opportunity and economic security as the union's bargaining priorities for upcoming negotiations, the removal of the cap placed on the Selective Strike Fund by the previous convention, the granting of authority to the IEB to approve the merger or affiliation of the UMWA with any other labor organization, and the scheduling of the next UMWA Constitutional Convention for sometime in 1990.

When the Special Convention convened in Atlanta, each of the four resolutions were overwhelmingly approved after only a half-hour of debate. No one spoke from the floor to oppose any of the four resolutions. While some delegates complained that the administration had stacked the microphones with loyalists, Trumka's support and popularity among the delegate-members was obvious. Things went so smoothly that the convention, originally scheduled for two days, was adjourned before the first day was over.[42] The second day of the meeting was devoted to caucuses and a two-hour labor "songfest." The UMWA leadership had obviously done their homework in planning and conducting the Special Convention.

The two most significant actions taken at the Convention involved the strike fund cap and potential merger agreements. The $70 million cap was put in place by delegates to the 1983 Convention who only reluctantly agreed to the creation of the fund in the first place. The Trumka administration proposed that the lifting of the cap was "necessary to fight the huge multi-national energy conglomerates and utilities that are now the dominant coal field owners."[43] Clearly, in the three years since the fund was created, the union's leadership had convinced the membership of its importance.

41. *UMWJ* (October 1986): 18.
42. Jim Woodward, "Mine Workers Boost Strike Fund For 87–88 Contract Talks," *Labor Notes* (December 1986): 1.
43. Jim McKay, "UMW to Increase Strike Fund, Permit Mergers," *Pittsburgh Post-Gazette* (October 28, 1986), 1.

Perhaps the most surprising aspect of the meeting was the ease with which President Trumka was able to win a virtual free hand to negotiate merger or affiliation agreements. The UMWA has always been a fiercely independent union; its members have taken great pride in their organization's autonomy. Ten years earlier, at the 1976 Convention, a resolution authorizing the officers to explore re-affiliation with the AFL-CIO was soundly defeated. In 1986, the Trumka administration skillfully made its case that having the flexibility to pursue mergers, particularly with other unions in the energy industry, would strengthen its hand at the bargaining table. Given the presence of the Oil, Chemical, and Atomic Workers (OCAW) president at the convention, speculation centered on a possible UMWA-OCAW merger. The Special Convention of 1986 provided further evidence of the Trumka administration's willingness to explore new approaches to the problems facing the union.

As the Trumka administration neared the end of its first term in office, it had successfully negotiated its first contract, taken bold and innovative steps to deal with the many challenges facing the union, and solidified its position politically. Not surprisingly, when nominations were held for the upcoming International elections, no opposition stepped forward to challenge the incumbent officers. In December 1987, Richard Trumka was installed for a second term, becoming the first UMWA president to win reelection by acclamation since John L. Lewis.

Trumka's Second Term

As their second term commenced, the challenges did not lessen for the Trumka administration. At the time of their re-installation, negotiations with the BCOA were well under way in an effort to beat a January 31 contract expiration date. By this time, extensive preparations for bargaining had become a hallmark of the Trumka-led UMWA. The groundwork for these, and other, talks had been laid much earlier. As in the recent past, the focus of these preparations were the continuing changes in the industry.

Many of the trends the union had faced at the time of the 1981 and 1984 negotiations continued to present problems for the union. UMWA members continued to lose their jobs at an alarming rate at the same time that coal production soared to record levels. The ongoing introduction of technological improvements and the continued growth of western coal played a role in this trend. The dismal job situation for UMWA miners was further exacerbated by overexpansion in the industry that resulted in fierce competition, falling prices, and massive layoffs. For the union, this meant a drop in active members of approximately 50% from 1980 levels. In 1987, it was estimated that the share of coal mined by the roughly 73,000 miners still on the UMWA rolls, had fallen to 35%.[44]

At the same time, the coal employers, were experiencing significant changes in

44. Alison Cowan, "Weaker U.M.W.'s Hard Task," *New York Times* (August 10, 1987), sec. 4, p. 1; Kim Moody, "Mine Workers Push for Job Security," *Labor Notes* (February 1988): 1.

their ranks. First, the players themselves were changing. As small or inefficient employers were forced out of the business, large employers, often owned by multi-national corporations not dependent solely on coal, became even more dominant in the industry. In addition, the BCOA, in the past the bargaining representative for most of the industry, was being decimated by defections. Where, as recently as 1981, the organization represented 130 companies, the BCOA had fallen to 30 members in 1984, and to only 14 by 1987. Although much smaller, the fourteen companies that remained in the bargaining group were some of the largest in the industry and the contract they negotiated still was the benchmark for the wage-and-benefit package in the industry.[45]

While the union publicly hoped for a peaceful settlement and the initiation of a "non-adversarial relationship" with the industry as talks got under way, it had prepared extensively for a difficult round of negotiations. The 1986 Special Convention had given the Trumka administration some of the tools it felt it needed to bargain from a position of strength. It had set the bargaining priorities that the union could unite behind and had given the leadership a weapon in the form of an uncapped strike fund. In addition, while the union did not move to merge or affiliate immediately, at least partly in the spirit of the convention resolution, it did announce a cooperative agreement with OCAW to share information on common employers.

In an effort to expand its "arsenal of weapons," President Trumka announced the formation of a new International Department of Corporate Strategies. The new department was composed of three offices, each responsible for a different strike strategy. One of the offices would organize the selective-strike strategy at all levels of the union. A second office would focus on inside campaigns, coordinating on-the-job pressure campaigns by locals at mines targeted by the union. Among the activities that might fall under this heading were working to rule, the daily reporting of any and all mine violations to state and federal authorities, and other actions designed to capture the attention of the company. The third office was created to coordinate "corporate campaigns." These campaigns involved "concerted efforts to pressure an operator by publicizing its corporate tactics before its shareholders, its creditors, or the public."[46]

These programs were conveyed to rank-and-file members through regular articles in the *UMWJ* and through a series of regional and district conferences. The formation of this new department suggested that the innovative approaches to bargaining, initially developed by the union on an ad hoc basis, had now become an integral and systematic part of the union's multifaceted bargaining strategy.

A New Contract

Prior to the beginning of negotiations with the BCOA in the fall of 1987, the UMWA had further strengthened its hand by signing the "Employment and Economic Se-

45. Jim McKay, " 'Pivotal' Negotiations," *Pittsburgh Post-Gazette* (November 10, 1987), 23.
46. *UMWJ* (December 1987): 6–7.

curity Pact (EESP)'' with Island Creek Corporation, the nation's thirteenth-largest coal producer. Island Creek was one of the companies that had broken with the BCOA in 1984. At the heart of the agreement was a provision giving first hiring preference at new Island Creek operations to UMWA miners laid off by the company at other locations. In addition, lessees or licensees mining on Island Creek coal lands would be required to offer jobs to laid off Island Creek miners first and operate under the economic terms of the UMWA contract. Finally, Island Creek agreed to be bound by any agreement reached between the UMWA and BCOA in 1988. In return, the UMWA agreed to allow Island Creek to reduce its royalty payment to the union's 1950 Pension Fund from $1.11 a ton to $.25 a ton. This move was made possible when, in May 1987, the Pension Fund reached a level at which all of its obligations could be met without additional funding.[47]

Between the April signing of the Island Creek agreement and the January 31 expiration of the BCOA contract, some fifty to sixty coal operators agreed to similar ''me-too'' contracts. These operators either agreed to accept the contract to be negotiated with the BCOA or sign agreements containing elements of the EESP. In either case, the UMWA agreed not to strike these early signees. This divide-and-conquer strategy was designed to isolate and pressure the BCOA and was a significant departure from past strategies of taking on the industry en masse.[48]

Talks with the BCOA began on November 12, 1987. That left the union and the employer association less than three months in which to negotiate a new agreement before the old contract expired on January 31, 1988. Clearly the union's goals were to pursue job security for its members by extending the provisions spelled out in the previously negotiated EESP's and to do so without having to agree to wage and benefit concessions. For its part, the industry was reported to want ''continued productivity improvements, as well as some relief from its pension obligations.''[49] The talks continued throughout December and January in relative secrecy, as a news blackout was imposed by the parties. On January 30, the UMWA and the BCOA announced tentative agreement on a new contract, beating the contract expiration date by one day. Although the union's ratification process would take several days, the union pledged not to strike until the ratification vote was complete. On February 8, UMWA miners employed by the fourteen BCOA companies accepted the proposed agreement by a 63 to 37% vote. For the second time in succession, the UMWA and the BCOA had settled a contract without a strike. Combined with the 1984 contract, this new five-year agreement signified the longest period of labor peace in the coalfields in decades.[50]

The terms of the 1988 contract suggest that the union had been successful in extending many of the provisions in the EESP's to the new agreement. Included in

47. Kim Moody, ''Mine Workers Push for Job Security,'' *Labor Notes* (February 1988): 1.

48. Ibid.

49. McKay, '' 'Pivotal' Negotiations.''

50. *UMWJ* (March 1988): 17.

the contract was a clause allowing laid-off miners to claim new jobs at nonunion mines operated by their employers. UMWA miners would also have the right of first refusal at all operations subcontracted by their employer to another employer. Consistent with the union's priority of creating job opportunities, the new agreement created an employer-funded training and education program for furloughed UMWA miners. In addition, the contract provided for a $1.05 per hour wage increase over the first three years of the contract, as well as improved pension benefits. The union traded off reduced employer payments into the 1950 Pension Fund in exchange for its gains.[51]

As in its first round of negotiations with the industry, the Trumka administration's performance in bargaining was viewed by most observers as impressive.[52] Not only had the union's leadership helped bring stability and labor peace back to much of the industry, it had done so without granting concessions, while simultaneously winning gains in job security for its members. This occurred during a period of time when employers in the coal industry and beyond held most of the cards and unions, for the most part, were on the defensive. In addition to the tangible gains won by the Trumka administration, the union's leaders also appeared to have won the confidence and trust of their members, as well as the respect of their counterparts on the opposite side of the bargaining table. One coal-industry official described Trumka as a welcome change from the "disorganized mess" other UMWA presidents brought to the bargaining table.[53]

A Proposed Merger

On the heels of the contract settlement with the BCOA, the UMWA's leadership quickly embarked on yet another ground-breaking venture. On February 21, 1988, President Trumka assembled the union's IEB in Denver to consider a proposed merger with OCAW. Informal merger discussions had begun shortly after the administration won approval to pursue such agreements at the 1986 Special Convention. Formal talks commenced in the early summer of 1987 when Trumka appointed a Special Exploratory Merger Committee. By mid-February 1988, this committee, and a similar group representing OCAW, had reached tentative agreement on a merger proposal that would have created the United Mine, Energy, and Chemical Workers of America with Trumka as president. At their Denver meeting the IEB overwhelmingly approved the proposal. However, two days later, OCAW's Executive Board surprised the UMWA by rejecting the merger.[54] News accounts suggested that critical among the reasons for the rejection was the question of future dues increases. Officially, the union reacted to OCAW's decision by expressing its disap-

51. *UMWJ* (March 1988): 16.

52. Frank Swoboda, "Tentative UMW Contract Averts Coal Mine Strike," *Washington Post* (January 31, 1988), A3; "Peace in the Coal Fields," *Pittsburgh Post-Gazette* (February 15, 1988), 6.

53. McKay, " 'Pivotal' Negotiations."

54. *UMWJ* (March 1988): 20.

pointment in the most diplomatic of terms. Unofficially, there were expressions of anger and frustration. As one UMWA official noted, ''We came out of the mines with a vision, and this is our first failure. We're used to winning.''[55]

Pittston

In character with its history, the UMWA ended the 1980s engaged in a pitched battle with a hard-nosed employer in the midst of the southern Appalachian coalfields. The Pittston Coal Group, a subsidiary of the Pittston Company, is one of the largest producers of coal in the United States. Although its corporate offices are in Greenwich, Connecticut, most of its production facilities are in southern Virginia and West Virginia. In May 1987, the Pittston Group announced that it would pull out of the BCOA by January 31, the date Pittston's contract with the UMWA was to expire. The UMWA initiated separate talks with Pittston in November 1987. When the parties were unable to reach a settlement by the January 31 expiration date, the union asked its members to stay on the job while talks continued. Among the points in dispute were Pittston's demands to contract out work to nonunion labor and to drop the successor clause in the contract so that if the company sold part of its operation the new owner would not be bound by the union contract. On April 5, 1989, 1,700 Pittston workers walked off the job.[56]

Over the next nine months the UMWA would conduct one of the most remarkable job actions in its long history. Taking on a large diversified corporation at a point in time when the UMWA and the rest of the labor movement were just beginning to regroup from a decade of devastating defeats, the union conducted an ingenious campaign against Pittston that captured the imagination of much of the American labor movement. The union's strategy centered on a tactic—mass civil disobedience—that was far different from the UMWA's traditional strike strategy. The union combined this approach with a number of other creative and innovative strategies and actions: the organization of a women's brigade that actively participated in all aspects of struggle, the involvement of the community at large on behalf of the strikers, the setting up of a ''camp'' to house supporters from all over the country who were invited to come and back the union, and the occupation of a key Pittston production facility by employing the rarely used sitdown strike.[57]

On February 19, 1990, more than nine months after the strike had begun, Pittston miners voted by a nearly two-to-one margin to accept the contract negotiated by their union. The agreement contained a very favorable clause on contracting-out that

55. Frank Swoboda, ''Oil Workers Union Rejects Plan to Merge With Miners,'' *Washington Post* (February 25, 1988), A3.

56. Maier Fox, *United We Stand: The United Mine Workers of America, 1890–1990* (Washington, D.C.: UMWA, 1990); Phil Wilayto and Dave Cormier, *We Won't Go Back: The Story of the Struggle of the United Mine Workers of America Against the Pittston Coal Company* (New York: United Labor Action, 1990).

57. Fox, *United We Stand,* 528–30; Wilayto and Cormier, *We Won't Go Back.*

would give union miners considerable job security. In addition, companies purchasing unionized facilities from Pittston would be required to honor contracts in effect at those job sites.[58]

In evaluating the Pittston struggle, it is clear that Richard Trumka and the International union provided considerable leadership and support for the strike, including the fending off of efforts by courts at both the federal and state levels to intervene. It is, however, difficult to assess credit for the imaginative tactics used in the course of the conflict. Overall, it seems fair to conclude that this was an effort that deeply involved all levels of the union, from the International leadership to the rank-and-file.

ANALYSIS AND CONCLUSION

In examining the UMWA's experience from the early seventies to the 1990s, two themes seem apparent. The 1970s were a period during which much of the union's energy was consumed in the movement to return control of the organization to its members. Instituting democratic reforms, and learning to operate under this new system, was a process that touched all aspects of the union through much of the decade. The 1980s were a period during which the UMWA responded to a difficult set of challenges within the industry. These responses were, in many cases, innovative and dramatic departures from the past.

During this period, the Trumka administration made major strides in several areas. The union adapted to changing circumstances in the structure and economics of the coal industry by developing a multifaceted program. The key to this response was its approach to collective bargaining. This approach included the formulation and implementation of a selective-strike strategy and the creation of a massive strike fund to support this plan, the institution of a program to coordinate "inside campaigns" or on-the-job pressure, and the organization of corporate campaigns, designed to bring public pressure to bear on operators. The UMWA's innovative approach to bargaining was readily apparent during the Pittston campaign.

The union also pressured BCOA companies by negotiating early settlements with independent companies. In terms of issues, the union made strides toward greater job security for its members through the creation of Employment and Economic Security Pacts (EESP) and related contract provisions. And the union, under Richard Trumka's leadership, came to the table much better prepared and organized. It streamlined its own bargaining procedure by eliminating the Bargaining Council and, if two consecutive successfully ratified contracts are any indication, it won the trust of its members in this area.

---

58. Ibid.

Internally, the Trumka administration pulled the union back from the brink of financial crisis by instituting budget cuts and organizational efficiencies, as well as by selling the union's controlling interest in the National Bank of Washington. Politically, Trumka brought stability to the UMWA by solidifying his administration's position in the union by reducing the factionalism and turmoil that had been a fact of life in the recent past, and by winning the support and respect of the union's IEB. The leadership's efforts to bring about a merger with OCAW was further proof of ongoing efforts to strengthen the union by moving in new directions.

The experience of the UMWA over the past several years is instructive on several levels. While no two unions face exactly the same set of circumstances, the willingness of the UMWA to explore bold and innovative responses to its problems is a lesson that should not be lost on other labor organizations. Of equal significance, however, was the relationship between the union's involvement with democratic reform in the 1970s, and its success in meeting the challenges of the 1980s.

Some observers of the democratic reform process see the movement, retrospectively, in the context of a good idea that went too far. The internal factionalism, the leadership problems, and the strikes of that era can all be attributed to an excess of democracy, according to this point of view. Another view, however, suggests that the problems the UMWA experienced in the 1970s were necessary, if painful, learning experiences for an organization that had chosen to rapidly evolve from one of the most autocratic institutions in the American labor movement to one of the most democratic. In this context, the innovations of the 1980s can be viewed as a direct result of the union and its membership eventually becoming more comfortable with the democratic process and using it to face the difficult challenges facing the organization.

There is other evidence to suggest that the democratic structure and spirit that are the legacy of the reform movement of the 1970s played a significant role in the UMWA's response to the problems it faced in the 1980s. Perhaps most obvious is that the union's membership used the revamped election process to elect Richard Trumka as UMWA president. Trumka is viewed by many as one of the brightest and most capable of the cadre of national union leaders that have emerged in the last twenty years, a perception underscored by his 1995 election as secretary-treasurer of the AFL-CIO.[59] Yet, it is quite probable that in most American unions, Trumka would not have been able to rise through the ranks, at least so quickly as he did, to assume a top leadership position. The reasons for this are many. In all but a handful of unions, the top officers are not chosen directly through a referendum vote of the members, but rather through a vote of delegates to the union's convention. This method puts the selection process in the hands of a group of local union officers, field staff, and headquarters officials that are sometimes beholden to incumbent officers. Also, in many labor organizations, the rigid pecking order of the union's

59. On December 22, 1995, Cecil Roberts succeeded Richard Trumka as UMWA president.

bureaucracy makes progression through the union's ranks a long, sometimes a life-long, process.

Although the UMWA's referendum election process was established well before the emergence of the democratic reform movement in the union, free and fair elections were the very rare exception, not the rule. This was clearly the case when Jock Yablonski took on the incumbent Tony Boyle in 1969. The Miller administration revamped the election process to ensure that the union's membership would have the opportunity to elect their leadership unfettered by corruption. In addition, the Miller administration restored the election of all district leaders. Without these reforms in the election process, and without the emphasis placed on democratic practices in the union, Richard Trumka would most probably not have been elected to office, first at the district level, and then at the International level.

Beyond presenting an opportunity for the union's membership to choose a capable leader, the UMWA's recent tradition of rank-and-file democracy played a critical role in the programs proposed and implemented by the Trumka administration once it was in office. In the 1970s, the union's bargaining procedure was completely reshaped in an effort to provide UMWA miners with an opportunity to influence and participate in this important process. Most significant, rank-and-file members were able to ratify any contract they were to work under. In addition, critical decisions involving the direction of the union's new bargaining strategy, like the creation of a selective-strike fund, first had to win support from the union's convention. And consistent with the union's emphasis on membership participation, the UMWA's new bargaining strategies—selective strikes, on-the-job pressure, corporate campaigns, and so forth—are now heavily dependent on the active support and involvement of its members. In organizing and implementing these programs, the union's leadership made a great effort to inform, involve, and mobilize the union's membership.

Any discussion of the UMWA in the 1980s, particularly one noting the contributions of the union's democratic traditions, should also note that the role of democracy within the union has changed. Throughout much of the 1970s democracy and democratic reform were considerations that influenced all aspects of the union's experience at all levels. The democratic gains made by the membership were carefully guarded. Some argued that on occasion, to the detriment of the union and its membership, the focus on democratic process became an end in itself. Certainly, this period of adjustment was not without problems.

Beginning in the late 1970s and early 1980s, the focus on democracy that had pervaded the union became less intense. The UMWA's leaders were granted more latitude. Members did not automatically see efforts by the leadership to run the union more efficiently as efforts to chip away at membership prerogatives. As external threats to the union's existence mounted, other issues became of paramount concern to the rank-and-file miners.

Under Richard Trumka, the role of democracy in the UMWA clearly changed from the period when the union was undergoing reform. While the democratic procedures enacted in the 1970s largely remain in place, there has been a subtle change in the union's collective democratic consciousness. Within the UMWA the emphasis on union democracy, which at times in the past had bordered on the obsessive, has dwindled. This would seem to be at least partly a function of the union's democratic process becoming a routine part of the member's experience and of the level of trust the membership places in the hands of its elected leaders. This phenomenon could be interpreted as evidence that democracy in the UMWA has entered a new phase of maturation in which both the members and the leaders have become more adept in their respective roles.

In sum, it seems readily apparent that the UMWA's concern for democracy and the structural provisions instituted in the 1970s has been one of the strengths underlying the union's relatively successful performance in the 1980s. The UMWA's experience seems to support the premise that democracy is the most appropriate and, in the long run, the most effective form of governance for a labor organization. In fact, the case of the UMWA raises the question as to whether the lack of creativity and innovation demonstrated by many unions facing similarly fundamental problems is related to the absence of the kind of democratic tradition found in the UMWA.

CHAPTER TWENTY

WOMEN GO UNDERGROUND[1]

MARAT MOORE

In late 1973, a West Virginia woman crossed a coal-mine portal to become the first beneficiary of federal affirmative action mandates that opened high-wage jobs in the coal industry to American women.[2] The entrance of more than 4,000 female workers into coal-mining jobs over the next two decades challenged deep-seated prejudice in the industry and introduced a new dynamic into the United Mine Workers of America (UMWA).

The 1970s generation is the largest and longest-lasting group of women to work in U.S. mines, but it is not the first. In the 1920s and 1930s, women toiled in various

This is a revised and expanded version of author's introduction to *Women in the Mines: Stories of Life and Work* by Marat Moore. Copyright © 1996 by Twayne Publishers. Used by permission of Twayne Publishers, an imprint of Simon & Schuster Macmillan.

1. The oral interviews in this chapter were conducted as part of an independent oral history and photography project initiated by the author in 1980, which evolved a decade later into a collective effort with the nonprofit Coal Employment Project.

2. Statistics on women's hiring in the coal industry are based on records of chest X-rays given to new miners conducted by the National Institute for Occupational Safety and Health (NIOSH), Chest X-Ray Division in Morgantown, W.Va.

capacities: as unpaid laborers in family mines, as operators of small mines, and as temporary workers during wartime.

But women's entry into U.S. mines during the 1970s and 1980s as permanent production workers marked a significant change in policy and practice in the coal industry and in the UMWA. It was not a smooth transition for the virtually all-male industry or for a union that historically had opposed opening its membership to women. The first wave of women hired by unionized companies earned the same paycheck as male new hires, but they routinely faced obstacles the men did not: entrenched cultural taboos, community opposition, discrimination in training opportunities, sexual harassment, and lack of support from union officials. Added to these stresses for most women were the family responsibilities of raising children and maintaining a household.

Women miners developed individual and collective ways to respond to those pressures. Individually, they chose responses ranging from withdrawal to humor and rapid-fire repartee. Collectively, many women miners participated in the Coal Employment Project (CEP), a grassroots organization through which they built leadership, educated themselves on political and union issues, and provided a network of emotional support.

Libby Lindsay, a member of Local Union 633 who has mined coal in West Virginia since 1976, reflected on two decades of struggle and achievement in a CEP newsletter published in December 1993:

> Has it really been 20 years? Sometimes I think, already? And sometimes I think: Is that all? Sisters, we fought some big battles to get jobs and keep them, to make the mines safer for all miners, for parental and family leave, for workplace justice and human dignity. . . .
>
> We fought sexual harassment from innuendo to peepholes, fought for bathhouses and for training on equipment. We fought for the union, and sometimes we fought the union itself. Some women were jailed for strike activity. Some women moved up and on. Some women were forced out through injury, and many through layoff. Some were killed. Some have died. . . .
>
> Those who came later . . . owe a tremendous debt to those first women. I'll bet they didn't think what they were doing was remarkable. I wonder if they realize it now.[3]

FEMALE LABOR AND TABOO: THE EARLY YEARS

Written records indicate that women worked in European mines as early as the thirteenth century, and artwork depicting women miners dates to the fifteenth cen-

---

3. Libby Lindsay, "20 Years In The Mines: A Tribute To Women Miners," *CEP News* (January 1994): 3.

tury.[4] Women workers hauled baskets of coal, operated windlasses, and performed other heavy labor at coal mines for centuries in Germany, Belgium, France, and Great Britain.

By the nineteenth century, a backlash to women's mining employment developed in parts of Europe. In 1842, an investigatory commission issued in Great Britain a report on children and women working underground that shocked the public. The outcry prompted Parliament to pass a law immediately banning children and women in British mines. Women were still allowed to work on the surface, but the "pit brow lasses" were stigmatized by their link to earlier conditions. The pit brow lasses became the center of a national debate in the 1880s on the right of women to become paid manual workers. The upper classes condemned them as an example of degraded womanhood, the opposite of the refined Victorian "lady."[5] The exclusion campaign intensified in the 1880s and forced most of the approximately 5,000 pit brow lasses from their jobs, except for a small number who continued working past the turn of the century.

In Belgium, female miners staged strikes and demonstrations to protest laws banning their employment. One newspaper blasted the workers with a venom laced with fear: "Look at them with their sagging breasts, huge thighs, shrill voices, impudent looks and shameless movements. They are the cause for the revolts and social upheaval!"[6]

Historian Christina Vanja suggests that public opposition grew to women miners when industrialization and higher wages made mining jobs more desirable for men. Cultural ideas of femininity accordingly changed, and women were no longer identified with their capacity to work. Instead, the ideal woman was submissive and idle, and working-class women suffered lower status for not conforming to the emerging feminine ideal.[7]

Vanja argues that the economic pressures that forced women out of mining jobs developed its own mythology, a system of misogynist taboos and superstitions later enforced through prohibitory laws. According to the superstition—one of the most common in mining folklore—the presence of a woman around a mine is bad luck and can bring disaster. Once viewed as able coworkers, women were transformed into agents of disaster. The origins of the taboo are unclear; the belief has been documented in the coalfields of Europe, Japan, South America, the former Soviet Union, and South America.[8]

    4. *Frauen und Bergbau: Zeugnisse aus 5 Jahrhunderten,* Ausstellung des Deutschen Bergbau-Museums Bochum vom 29. August–Dezember 1989 [Women in mining: Evidence of 500 years; an anthology of articles published in conjunction with an exhibit at the Mining Museum in Bochum, Germany].
    5. See Angela V. John, *By The Sweat Of Their Brow: Women Workers At Victorian Coal Mines* (London: Routledge and Kegan Paul, 1983).
    6. *Frauen und Bergbau.*
    7. Ibid.
    8. Sources included George Korson, *Coal Dust On The Fiddle: Songs and Stories of the Bituminous Industry* (Hatboro, Pa.: Folklore Associates, 1985); Barbara Kingsolver, *Holding The Line: Women In The Great Arizona Mine Strike of 1993;* and *Frauen und Bergbau.*

In the United States, questions persist concerning the role of African-American slave women in coal production. One Virginia slave owner who died in 1821 included three women and four children in a list of slaves who labored at his coal mines in his will; historian Ronald L. Lewis suggests that "the women and children probably cooked and cleaned for the pitmen."[9]

Industrialization fueled a U.S. coal boom in the last half of the nineteenth century, drawing European immigrants who carried with them from their native cultures a tradition of women's labor. In 1895 a German miner in Pennsylvania told a local reporter that he "introduced the customs of the fatherland" in utilizing the labor of his four daughters to operate the family mine. The use of female labor proved profitable, enabling him to buy the mine "and a large amount of timber land besides."[10]

Immigrants also brought entrenched taboos against women in mining that proved to be stronger than the tradition of their labor. The belief spread through folk tales like the following, recorded by folklorist George Korson among Cornish miners in Pennsylvania: Long ago a race of beautiful women existed whose siren calls made men betray their families. The gods burned the sirens' forest homes into carbonized rocks and imprisoned their spirits in coal seams. A mine explosion was "a sign that more of these mythological sirens were escaping from the wall of coal, accompanied by the poisonous gases which carried death to every miner in their path."[11]

Folk tales and sexist taboos did not stand up, however, before the economic pressures of World War I, when European mines reopened mine portals to women. In the United States, the industry magazine *Coal Age* lobbied for women's employment after thousands of miners enlisted in the armed services. Faced with a drastic drop in anthracite production, Lehigh Coal and Navigation Company in 1918 took the bold step of hiring forty-two girls and women in Nesquehoning, Pennsylvania, to work as timekeepers, weighscale tenders, switchtenders, and on other outside jobs.[12]

The hiring of the "bloomer girls"—so named because the company provided bloomer uniforms—stirred up immediate protest from the male workforce and brought an indignant response from the UMWA. As the news spread, miners throughout the Panther Valley region threatened to strike. The *UMWJ* charged that the company planned to pay the women lower wages and attacked the operators' "sham patriotism," which risked "sowing the seeds of industrial discord."[13]

UMWA District 7 president Thomas Kennedy cited a Pennsylvania law that banned women's employment and asked the attorney general's office for a legal ruling. The matter was referred to the state's chief mine inspector, Seward E. Button.

9. Ronald L. Lewis, *Black Coal Miners in America: Race, Class and Community Conflict 1780–1980* (Lexington: University Press of Kentucky, 1987), 5.

10. *Black Diamond* 15, no. 335 (September 14, 1895).

11. George Korson, *Coal Dust On The Fiddle*.

12. *Coal Age* 13, no. 18: 841.

13. *UMWJ* 29, no. 1:11.

On April 27, 1918—four days after they were hired—Button suspended the young women and instructed the state's twenty-five anthracite inspectors to order an immediate halt to the employment of women.[14] According to a local newspaper, the bloomer girls faced harassment even after it became clear that their presence would be short-lived. A reporter wrote that "the girls quit work on Thursday following a hard afternoon when the boys jeered and poked fun at [them]," and noted that several of the boys were arrested.[15]

Both the union and the industry laid the issues of patriotism and women's morality like a thin veneer over the deeper economic struggle. The *UMWJ* declared that the employment of girls on the breakers would subject them "to an atmosphere of immorality," but later revealed its deeper worry: that the industry was trying "to disrupt the union at the conclusion of the war."[16] The *Journal* charged that women's employment was "an insult . . . while thousands of men are idle in this country and seeking a job. The union argued on class lines that "it was the daughters of workingmen who were sought as an entering wedge to beat down the wages of labor."[17] After the dismissal of the female workers, *Coal Age* decried the "exultation of a certain element of labor over this outcome" in a front-page editorial and predicted the war would result in "a victory—for the Huns." But the industry journal also admitted its underlying concern: that the union's opposition represented "unnecessary interference with the attempts of companies to maintain their working forces."[18]

COAL MINING AND FAMILY LABOR

Despite continuing UMWA opposition, taboos and a host of state laws barring female employment in the late nineteenth and early twentieth century, American women did work underground. But they toiled for the most part invisibly as undocumented laborers in small family contract mines on the periphery of the burgeoning coal industry. Women helped their fathers, brothers, and husbands mine coal to ease their family's economic hardship. Oral history evidence suggests the practice increased during the Depression years, especially in Appalachia, where hillside coal seams were more easily discovered and mined.

In Ohio during the Great Depression, John Zofchak took his children into a leased hillside mine, including his thirteen-year-old daughter Elizabeth. She recalls standing in the family's kitchen while her mother snipped off her long brown hair and dressed her like a boy to evade state mine inspectors. For three years, the children helped their father dig coal to trade for flour, coffee, and other staples. With his children, John Zofchak would kneel at the mine entrance to offer a prayer in Slovak for the family's safety.

14. *UMWJ* 29, no. 2:11. See also *Coal Age* 13, no. 18.
15. Pottsville, Pa., *Republican* (3 May 1918).
16. *UMWJ* 29, no. 1:11.
17. *UMWJ* 29, no. 2:11.
18. *Coal Age* 13, no. 19:1.

Six decades later, Elizabeth Zofchak Stevens recalled the experience: "Coal mining was different then. This was hand-diggin' times. We all had a pick and shovel.
Dad would put us in a room and we would undermine the coal. We worked a lot
kneeling down or lying on our sides, with a potato sack as a cushion. We'd dig
underneath the coal so it would come loose. We'd make a trench at the bottom, and
take our picks and knock it out. We didn't even have an auger to bore with, and we
very seldom shot the coal."[19]

The mine served another purpose for her mother: as a child care center. "My
father was like a babysitter," she said. "On Saturdays . . . we took George [the
youngest] mainly so Mother could get her work done at the house." Young Elizabeth
played hide-and-seek with her brother in the mine, and played the same game with
local mine inspectors. When the inspector arrived, she said, "I would run and hide
in places we had already dug out. At that time, my father could have gotten arrested
for having a girl in the mine, but I never got caught." Her father went to work at a
larger mine in 1939 with one of her brothers, but Elizabeth stayed behind. Girls
could work out of sight in a contract mine, but risked flaunting state law at larger
operations.

One Ohio woman who leased her own mine openly challenged a state ban and
won in the state with the nation's stiffest restrictions on women's employment. In
1934 Ida Mae Stull defied state mine inspectors who evicted her from the mine and
cited her as "a danger of immediate and extraordinary character."[20] She challenged
the eviction in court, and the ruling was overturned. Newspapers hailed her as
"America's First Woman Coal Miner" and her story appeared in the *New York
Times* and the *Chicago Tribune*. Stull's jubilant reentry to the mine in 1935 spawned
more publicity, and she declared to reporters, "I prefer coal dust to a powder puff.
. . . It may sound unladylike, but every woman to her own desires, and mine is
digging coal." The victory was short-lived, however; inspectors later shut down
Stull's mine for safety violations, and she struggled against poverty until her death
in 1980.[21]

Ida Mae was not the only Stull daughter to mine coal. Her younger sister Elizabeth worked underground over a period of thirty years. The poverty-stricken family,
which was raising more than a dozen children from two marriages, sent Elizabeth
to live with and work for a cruel woman. At age thirteen, Elizabeth rebelled and
followed a male cousin to Pennsylvania to obtain a mining job. In 1920, she went
to work as the only child among forty miners. Wearing her cousin's baggy clothes
and a lard-oil cap lamp, she hauled water and loaded coal for a few dollars a day.
She married soon after, but later returned to the mines as a young widow with three
children. During the 1930s she helped her sister Ida at her mine near Cadiz, Ohio,
making pit cuts and using a breast auger. In her forties a decade later, she toiled on
her knees in a three-foot seam with her son to handload coal.[22]

19. Interview with Elizabeth Zofchak Stevens, Woodside, Ohio, October 1, 1982.
20. *UMWJ* 88, no. 17:12.
21. Interview with Elizabeth Stuff Crawford, Dillonvale, Ohio, July 31, 1982.
22. Ibid.

Migrating to find work was common among miners during the Depression years. Irene Adkins Dolin recalled her West Virginia childhood, when she hitchiked and walked with her family on job-hunting treks between eastern Kentucky and southern West Virginia. When the family settled in West Virginia, Irene's father developed tuberculosis. Irene, age ten, and her seven-year-old sister ventured into a hillside mine to dig coal for family fuel. From 1937 to 1942, Irene remembers, the girls dug coal with no adult supervision in near-total darkness:

> Daddy had carbide, but he wouldn't let us use it because it was too danger-ous. We just went to the face and felt our way until we hit coal. We knew the mine like a book. We dug [coal] in the dark, sacked it in the dark, and we dragged it out in the dark in coffee sacks. We could see the opening of the hole, and it would guide us back out. . . . The coal hole was about three foot high. We'd take picks, and we'd start digging back in there, and we'd peck on the rooftop like Daddy told us. We would be lying down digging out the coal, and we'd hear it falling.

If the girls stayed underground too long, their mother would call to them from the coal bank:

> She'd holler, "Hurry up, girls!" And we'd holler back, "Just wait, Mommy. We'll get a little more." She was scared. She thought we'd been in there too long and it might fall in. But we didn't know no time when we were in there. And it was better for us to be in there than for her. Mommy couldn't have done it in that low-down coal. We got all the wood, too. And we felt like we had accomplished something when we got done. . . . We dug coal in blue-cold weather, with snow knee-deep. Sometimes we had to dig out the snow to get into the hole. Lots of times it was so cold, we'd crawl in that coal bank just to get warm.[23]

While Adkins and other women labored underground, social taboos persisted against their employment. When First Lady Eleanor Roosevelt traveled to the Illinois coal-fields in 1936, she planned to tour a working mine, but changed her plans and inspected an idle mine when she realized the strength of the local superstitions against women in the mines.[24]

"THE FEMALE ON THE TIPPLE": WORLD WAR II

The entry of the United States into World War II in 1941 opened the door for mil-lions of women to obtain jobs in defense industries until the war ended four years

23. Interview with Irene Adkins Dolin, Julian, West Virginia, May 23, 1992.
24. "Mrs. Roosevelt Visits Mine Pit in Illinois," *New York Times* (17 June 1936):28.

later. The *UMWJ* reported wartime employment of coalfield women in traditionally male jobs, and even published occasional job openings. But the union's tone changed abruptly when coal operators offered mining jobs to women. In an article titled "Necessity for Women in Coal Mines Does Not Exist" published in December 1942, the *UMWJ* blasted "two recent grandstand publicity plays" in western Canada and West Virginia where women were hired as outside workers.[25]

One group was hired on the tipple at Algoma Coal and Coke Company in southern West Virginia. Alice Fulford was forty years old when she was hired to pick refuse from coal on outside conveyor belts at the Algoma tipple, where she worked with four other women. Her husband's disability had prompted Fulford to seek work as a "bone picker." The workers were represented by the UMWA, and Fulford joined the union.

> It was during the time of the war, the Second World War. The boss said we would help the soldier boys if we went to work, because most of them was gone. . . . I was married at the time, but my husband was crippled up with a bone disease. He'd had his leg taken off. Since he didn't have no job, I thought, Well, I can make more money working at the mines. We were paid as much as the boys was paid. If they hadn't paid us as much, we wouldn't have worked. . . . [The coal] would come down through the tipple, onto these shaker tables. The table would shake back and forth and we would pick the bone out of the coal. . . . We learned fast, and we worked fast.[26]

As it had in World War I, the UMWA condemned women's wartime employment in union mines. George Titler, president of UMWA District 29 in southern West Virginia, demanded that Algoma general manager William Beury immediately stop the practice of hiring women, invoking a moral standard and citing the grievous example set by Great Britain. After a strike was threatened, Beury dismissed the women.[27]

Fulford recalled receiving a visit from a district union official: "A head union man came over from Beckley to talk to me. I told him that I needed work to support my children. The union asked me if I would quit if they got my husband a job at the tipple, with his artificial leg. I told them I would. . . . They went to talk to my niece at the same time, and she quit too. I don't know what they offered her. The union didn't want the women working in the mines. I never did know why."[28]

In the western coalfields of Wyoming and Utah, companies hired women in larger numbers for surface work. In November 1942, Union Pacific hired twenty-five women to work in mine shops and tipples in Wyoming, and Utah Fuel Company hired female "bony pickers" in Carbon County, Utah. The women, most of whom

25. *UMWJ* 53, no. 23:9.
26. Interview with Alice Fulford, Columbus, Ohio, July 30, 1982.
27. *UMWJ* 53, no. 23:9.
28. Ibid.

were married, received equal pay with the men and the company built them their own restrooms. Forty years later, Madge Kelly described her work at a tipple near Superior, Wyoming as "one of the happiest times of my life" and the job as carrying both responsibility and a decent wage.[29]

Esther Snow worked on a Utah Fuel Company tipple in 1944 and 1945. She wrote a poem that appeared in the company newsletter with the byline, "Written by Esther Snow, Boney Picker."[30] An excerpt appears below, and ends on a note of nostalgia for women's brief employment at the mine:

> *The Female On The Tipple*
> It was in September in forty-three
> When Dan and Duwayne decided to see,
> If women couldn't replace the men,
> That "Uncle Sam" had taken from them.
> So for a week with hammer and saw
> A rest room was built in one sidewall.
> To care for the women who'd be there soon,
> To sweep the stairs and the boney room . . .
>
> The men all smiled and even laughed
> To think that Females might stand the gaff.
> The boom, the clamor, the roar and clang
> Of machinery moving and going bang!
>
> "Wait til the snow piles white and deep,
> They'll stay at home," says little Pete.
> But we proved to them we could stick it out
> Even the boney we soon learned about . . .
>
> When the boys come back from the war and strife
> We'll quit and go back to being a wife.
> To sweep our floors and dust and groom
> And think as we sweep of the boney room.[31]

At a 1944 meeting of the UMWA's governing International Executive Board (IEB), President John L. Lewis noted with satisfaction that the situation was "promptly adjusted" in West Virginia after an IEB policy committee had voted to oppose women's employment. But he raised the specter of women's employment in Wyoming, where the number working on Union Pacific Coal Company tipples had grown from a mere handful to nearly one hundred.

29. Interview with Madge Kelly, Rock Springs, Wyoming, June 1985.

30. The occupational dialect differs by region. West Virginians called coal refuse "bone" while western women referred to it as "boney."

31. From author's correspondence with Esther Snow.

Lewis expressed concern that a precedent on women's employment in mines could be established by the federal War Manpower Commission, who was examining its policy on the issue. A commission was appointed to investigate the problem and to stop the spread of women's hiring.[32] Decades later, Madge Kelly recalled a story she heard at the mine during the war years that John L. Lewis opposed women in the mines "because his mother had worked in a mine when he was young."[33]

Despite Snow's poetic suggestion, not all the female tipple workers returned to keeping house. Many stayed in the workforce and were forced into lower-wage jobs after the war ended when returning veterans flooded the job market. Madge Kelly's later jobs included making "spudnuts" (potato-based doughnuts), tending bar, cooking and working in a gift shop. She said none of the jobs offered comparable wages to her wartime work on a mine tipple.[34]

Women also worked with family members during World War II, and some were openly acknowledged by mine bosses. In Harlan County, Kentucky, Ethel McCuiston began working full-time in 1941 as her husband's helper in a unionized mine. In 1980 she reflected on her dual roles in the home and underground:

> During wartime they all had to work overtime. I persuaded him to let me go in one Sunday evening, just to look it over. I started taking meals in to these miners. I'd go over there and find out no one was helping my husband, and I'd get dressed and go to the lamphouse and put that big old battery on my hip. I'd climb on the deck of the motor and go hunt my husband. I just couldn't stand the thought of Arthur working over there by himself. During the war, about all the miners were drafted into service, and he lost his helper.
>
> With both of us in there, if one got hurt, the other could go get help. I thought, "Well, fiddle, there's my husband in there making our living, working for our children." Arthur knew how desperate they were for coal. He would go in there and undertake to do the whole job himself.
>
> I'd go in there and help Arthur shoot coal. I'd make the dynamite dummies, and I'd get down on my knees and shovel coal just like any man. I was really scared sometimes, with that [mine roof] popping and cracking. Sometimes there wouldn't be anyone in the mine but me and my husband. I would be in the back shoveling dust and watching those big steel poles holding the top up, and if I seen them a-giving, I'd always holler.[35]

Other miners complained about her presence, but the mine boss defended her right to work.

32. Minutes of UMWA International Executive Board, April 17, 1944.
33. *UMWJ* 53, no. 23:9.
34. Ibid.
35. Interview with Ethel McCuiston, Cumberland, Kentucky, May 6, 1980.

Some of the men would . . . be a-cursin' and going on. But the boss said, "If Ethel didn't help Arthur cut coal last night, there wouldn't be no work today. What would you think if your payday came up small?" Some threatened to quit. The boss told them to go ahead, that I could work any time I wanted to. He told them it was a great honor that a woman would come into the mines to work.

I was even secretary of the union for awhile. My husband would take notes, and I would do the bookwork. I wrote all the signs for the men to come to special union meetings. The men didn't care as long as the work got done.

Besides mining coal, she raised her children, kept six boarders, and ran the family farm. "I didn't need much sleep," she wryly observed. McCuiston worked at the mine for more than a decade after the end of the war. She became pregnant with twins in the 1950s and finally left the mine after fourteen years' employment.

The postwar decades of the 1950s and 1960s were marked by layoffs created largely by mechanization in the coal industry. Unemployment triggered a massive outmigration of mining families from Appalachia and other coalfield regions to the nation's industrial centers. The collected oral histories show little evidence of women working during this period.

CROSSING THE PORTAL: THE NEW MINERS

The 1973 oil crisis fueled a coal boom of historic proportions. Hiring of new miners ballooned and the migration reversed, as thousands of people returned to the coalfields to seek jobs. Coal operators hired 150,031 new underground coal miners from 1973 through the end of the decade, with 45,500 new workers added in 1974 alone.[36]

The first wave of women hired by unionized companies in the mid-1970s joined a workforce—and a union—that had undergone significant changes. The new hires included more young workers, and college degrees were more common. Despite their youth, the new generation brought into the mines a breadth of life experience, with large numbers of Vietnam veterans, black miners affected by the civil rights movement, Navajos employed at newly opened western pits, and women.

Change was also brewing at the UMWA after a revolt by members fed up with the union's international leadership. The Miners For Democracy (MFD) fielded a successful slate of reform candidates headed by Arnold Miller to take the reins of power from Tony Boyle. In 1974, the rank and file regained their right to vote on contracts and to operate union districts autonomously.

36. Statistics on coal-mine hiring have been compiled by the National Institute for Occupational Health and Safety (NIOSH), Chest X-Ray Division in Morgantown, West Virginia. Annual hiring statistics were published each year in *CWST News!*

The legal push to hire women miners followed a battle by black workers to end discrimination in the steel industry. Consent decrees signed in 1970 forced nine major steel companies to implement affirmative action hiring programs in the steel industry.[37] The successful fight pressured steel-owned "captive" coal mines to begin hiring women in their mines to forestall further lawsuits. The consent decrees provided the legal means for women to enter the mines in significant numbers.[38]

The first women who sought jobs grappled with deeply entrenched gender prejudice about their right to work. In May 1973, the *UMWJ* chronicled the efforts of four textile workers in southwestern Virginia—including a mother and daughter—to obtain coal-mining jobs.[39] The article was followed by reactions by three male miners, who opposed the idea on the grounds that the women wanted the jobs for "cosmetics money" and that women would have to shower with men.

After companies began hiring women a few months later, the *UMWJ* published a series of letters to the editor from miners' wives on both sides of the issue. Wanda Harless of Bluefield, West Virginia, wrote to remind readers that women were still under men and that "God never wanted them to be equal," and added that women miners "are very ugly or don't care" about their looks and "have no respect for themselves as a woman."[40] The letter prompted three responses from coalfield women in the following issue; two supported women's employment, including the mother of one of the first women hired. A month later, a woman miner wrote an eloquent defense of her right to work and her commitment to the UMWA.[41]

The first women showed grit and determination to get hired, and faced tremendous obstacles from the time they arrived at the portal. Shirley Boone went to work in 1976 as the first woman at a mine near her home in Boone County, West Virginia. On her first day, she was abruptly reminded of the strength of local taboos: "I'd heard all those old superstitions, about how it was bad luck for a woman to go in. . . . The first day I rode into the mine on the mantrip to the mantrip station, a man stepped out of the mantrip car and had a heart attack. He just keeled over, and he never did come back to the mines to work. . . . The boss said, 'That's what you get when you start having women in the mines—trouble.'"[42]

Having grown up in the local community, she found it easier to adapt in some ways, and harder in others. "Nobody around there had ever done anything like that before. I grew up there, too. That made it easier to get on at work, but harder to deal with people in the community. . . . I was threatened with being shot when I first went in."[43]

---

37. Kipp Dawson, "Women Miners and the UMWA, 1973–1983," Center for Labor-Management Policy Studies Occasional Papers 11, City University of New York, July 1992.

38. Ibid.

39. *UMWJ* (May 25, 1973): 12.

40. *UMWJ* (June 1–15, 1974): 21.

41. *UMWJ* (July 16–31, 1974): 12.

42. Interview with Shirley Boone, Crichton, West Virginia, September 22, 1983.

43. Dawson, "Women Miners."

Superstitions often had a local flavor. Cosby Totten of Local 6025 recalled a legend still alive in the 1970s when she started mining coal in a large Consolidation Coal mine in southern West Virginia: "There was a story about a red-headed woman and a couple of kids who went into the mine and got lost and supposedly starved to death. If you saw this red-headed 'haint,' you didn't have to work that day. It went way back, and was part of the company's policy of past practice. The company would let the men go home." When her coworkers tried to scare her with the tale, she used the taboo to support the idea of women in the mines: "The men tried to get me scared on the hoot owl shift, telling me somebody had seen her coming out from under the rocks. I said, 'If y'all ever see that red-headed woman in here, it's a vision of things to come. She's here to tell you that women are in the mines, and we're here to stay.' "[44]

Many women miners expressed gratitude and pride about belonging to what they perceived as a strong union and felt they had more job protection than nonunion women, who could easily be fired as soon as companies met their affirmative action quotas. Sandra Bailey, an Ohio native who moved to eastern Kentucky and took a mining job, felt proud to join the UMWA: "I had always heard about the United Mine Workers being a strong union. So when I knew that I was going to get to join this famous United Mine Workers of America, I was really happy about it, because I knew the benefits they had in the coal industry, and I felt an obligation to at least attend the meetings."[45]

She was not prepared, however, for the community's opposition, which was preached openly at a local church:

> Not being from here, I didn't realize the social stigma attached to women miners. I didn't know what a disgrace it was going to be. My kids didn't realize it either. They learned afterwards when people made fun of them at school. I'd hear comments from them about people saying I was just in the mines to get a man.
>
> Then there was the sermon preached against me in the church. They didn't use my name, but I was the only woman coal miner in the community. People came up and told me that the preacher said it was sinful, women stepping out of their place, wearing pants and trying to take men's jobs. It was meant for me. I was the issue, pointing at me to tell these other women not to go astray.[46]

Women from UMWA families grew up in a rich mining tradition that specifically excluded them from mining labor. What would have been a natural occupational choice for a male child was unacceptable for a daughter. Linda Raisovich was eigh-

---

44. Telephone interview with Cosby Totten, August 16, 1994.
45. Interview with Sandra Bailey, Mayking, Kentucky, March 2, 1981.
46. Telephone interview with Cosby Totten, August 16, 1994.

teen years old when she was hired by U.S. Steel. Her family had deep roots in the UMWA: "My grandfather came from Yugoslavia to this country to work in the mines. . . . [He] was one of the first from this area to join the union. When anyone joined, they were thrown out of their company house. I think it makes you a more dedicated union member when your whole family has struggled and suffered to organize and make the union what it is today. You feel like you have to support it and do the most that you can to preserve it. . . . My dad and I were real close when I was growing up. That had something to do with the fact I went underground. He used to sit and tell me all these stories about the mines."[47]

When she took a mining job, her mother was more supportive of her choice: "My mom encouraged me. She felt that if I wanted to do it, she was all for it. But my dad didn't really want me in the mine. I was sent to work right beside him. He made it kind of rough on me, to make me quit. We were on a back up crew, and he was the crew leader. . . . The shift foreman told him, 'Well, we have to have a woman here, and I'm not gonna let you run her off.' . . . My dad finally realized that I was there to stay. He never gave me a hard time after that."

But her relationship with her father was strengthened by the shared time and common interest in mining. "After I started working, we became closer, because we worked the same shift. We rode together. When he worked and I was in school, he was on the evening shift and by the time I got home, he was gone to work. I never saw him, except on weekends. But when you work right beside him, and ride with him, you get the chance to really know each other." Although she was unaware of it at the time, her father's presence at the mine helped shield her from sexual harassment: "My dad working at the mine made a difference in how I was treated. He was respected. And he was a big man. I heard later that my dad overheard somebody at the mine talking about me and he like to got into a fight over it. But my dad never told me about it."

The pioneer women of the 1970s represented, in some cases, an entirely new type of miner that combined previously gendered traditions. From their fathers, coalfield women learned mining lore, union history, and manual skills. From their mothers they absorbed the domestic arts, and the skills of building family and community life. Together, these customs forged workers strongly grounded in union history and mining skills, and yet whose lives were shaped by family and community values.

Like most working women, UMWA members struggled to meet family and job responsibilities, shouldering the extra burdens of life-threatening job hazards and long commutes that could add hours to a workday. Lack of seniority meant many women worked second and third shift, which cost family time and robbed them of much-needed sleep.

Despite the job's physical demands, many women reported mining was preferable to working two or three low-wage jobs just to make ends meet. Elizabeth Laird of Cordova, Alabama, went into the mines at age fifty-four after working nearly

47. Interview with Linda Raisovich, Welch, West Virginia, August 12, 1982.

twenty-five years in textile plants. After her divorce, she worked five years on day shift in a textile mill, and then worked until 2:00 A.M. in a diner. She said if the coal industry had let women in earlier, "I wouldn't have had to work two full-time jobs and gone five years without a decent night's sleep."[48]

Minority women miners shouldered the additional burden of racial prejudice in their work lives. Patricia Brown, an African-American, took a mining job in Alabama in 1980 after she was widowed while pregnant with her third child. She was one of two black women in a workforce of more than three hundred. In 1983, she noted that race seemed to be a factor in her early job assignments:

> Certain things I was given to do, the white women weren't. There were two white women hired when I was, and they would put them together shoveling, and put me by myself to do the same work. They would get a pallet of rock dust to unload together, and I would get one to unload myself. I would have to haul concrete blocks, whereas they would be shoveling a little around the feeder. There was a difference. . . . Another thing to contend with in the mines is the Ku Klux Klan. Some of them boast about it, but it doesn't have the power that it used to have. We say, "To hell with the Ku Klux." This one Ku Klux on our section is friendly toward me. We get along fine on the section. He don't seem to show any prejudice. I mostly drive by myself to work. There are no women from here working, and I never tried to ride with the white men. The wives wouldn't have approved of us riding with their husbands.[49]

In Arizona and New Mexico, Navajo women were first hired at large strip mines that operated on reservations in the 1970s, when Peabody Coal Company opened the Kayenta and Black Mesa mines. The company began mining the coal-rich Black Mesa, which was sacred land to the Navajo. For Evelyn Luna, taking a mining job challenged the tribe's gender roles and her own religious beliefs:

> The traditional Navajo belief is that women stay home and do the inside work, and the men work outside in the garden, or herd sheep. I was raised with the traditional beliefs, but my father was a uranium miner. I'm sure that was part of why I became a miner—and the fact that I was left with two kids in a divorce.
>
> The Kayenta mine is on the Black Mesa, and in Navajo tradition the Black Mesa is a sacred mountain. We call it the Mother Mountain. Digging out coal is seen as tearing up the mother mountain, tearing out an organ like a liver.

48. Interview with Elizabeth Laird, Cordova, Alabama, August 23, 1983.
49. Interview with Patricia Brown, Bessemer, Alabama, August 25, 1983.

Being a woman, it's an even worse thing to torture the Mother Mountain. It's worse for women because it's like torturing our own body and the body that gave us life. It is common among the Navajo at Kayenta to call the medicine man to come for a blessing. You have it somewhere away from people. You need it because you're destroying the things of nature.[50]

Luna sought the advice of tribal elders, and found a way to keep the job and live with her job choice: "I have talked with the older Navajo, and they say that driving a water truck is all right because I'm not tearing up the mountain, I'm just wetting it down. It's the women's role in some of the blessings to carry the water, and I tell myself that is what I'm doing."[51]

THE COAL EMPLOYMENT PROJECT

From 1973 until 1977, women entered the mines in small numbers, and received little public attention. That dynamic changed with the birth of the Coal Employment Project (CEP) in 1977, a nonprofit group formed when Appalachian activists accidentally stumbled upon evidence of widespread gender discrimination in the coal industry. Citizens' groups had requested an underground mine tour from a Tennessee coal operator, who was helpful until he discovered that one visitor was female. He reportedly said, "Can't have no woman going underground. The men would walk out. . . . If you insist on bringing her, forget the whole thing."[52]

An all-male tour proceeded, but the activists later dug through federal affirmative action policies until they found Executive Order 11246, a Johnson administration directive that barred sex discrimination by companies holding federal contracts. Since many Tennessee and Kentucky coal operators held contracts with the federal Tennessee Valley Authority (TVA), the group hired lawyer Betty Jean Hall to work full-time on the project.

From this effort emerged the Coal Employment Project (CEP), a nonprofit women's organization that has supported women miners in their efforts to gain jobs, combat discrimination, build a support network, and educate themselves and the public. Through the 1980s and early 1990s, CEP addressed a broader range of issues facing the labor movement, and grew to be a closely knit network with international links. In 1978, Hall and her small staff filed a landmark sex discrimination complaint with the U.S. Labor Department's Office of Contract Compliance Programs (OFCCP).[53] The complaint charged that the coal industry as "one of the most bla-

---

50. Interview with Evelyn Luna, Kayenta, Arizona, November 11, 1986.
51. Interview with Patricia Brown, Bessemer, Alabama, August 25, 1983.
52. *Southern Exposure* 9, no. 4:48.
53. *CWST News!* 1, no. 1:2.

tantly discriminatory employers'' in the United States and targeted 153 coal companies and mines representing about half of the nation's coal production.

Among the companies named in the OFCCP complaint were Peabody Coal Company and most of the steel-owned coal firms. The complaint pressed for a hiring
plan that would mandate hiring one woman for every three inexperienced men until
women made up 20% of the workforce.[54] At the same time, the Kentucky Human
Rights Commission aggressively pursued coal operators who discriminated against
women.[55]

CEP's broad-based legal strategy worked. By December 1978, Consolidation
Coal Company had agreed to pay $360,000 in back wages and benefits to seventy-
eight women who had been refused jobs between 1972 and 1976, and was forced
to implement an affirmative action plan. Other lawsuits followed. The widespread
publicity informed coalfield women about employment opportunities. By the end of
1979, 2,940 women had been hired as underground coal miners in the United States,
with the highest number of women hired in West Virginia, Pennsylvania, Illinois,
and Alabama.[56]

Shortly after the complaint was filed, a delegation of UMWA women traveled to
the UMWA's national headquarters in Washington, D.C., to ask President Miller for
an official statement of support. Miller promised his support but later rebuffed
CEP's request to approach the International Executive Board for an official support
resolution. Union officials claimed the request arrived too late to be placed on the
agenda.[57] CEP members protested, and published a follow-up story in the group's
newsletter entitled, "Which Side Is The UMWA On?" Women lobbied their IEB
representatives, who unanimously passed a support resolution at the next quarterly
meeting.[58]

After the Washington, D.C., meeting, CEP worked on projects including the formation of local support teams of women miners, publication of the monthly *Coal-
mining Women's Support Team News!* and the first-ever national conference for
women miners scheduled for June 1979. This inaugural CEP conference at Institute,
West Virginia, drew two hundred UMWA rank-and-file activists of both sexes, national media, and a scattering of leftist political groups—all new to most of the
participants. Guests included singer Florence Reece, who wrote the labor anthem,
"Which Side Are You On?" and Bill Worthington, an African-American UMWA
activist in the black lung movement. Participants made clear that their goals were
not restricted to women's issues. Mary Zins, a West Virginia miner, told the group
the debate on maternity benefits needed to be broadened: "What it comes down to

54. *Southern Exposure* 9, no. 4:48.
55. "Women Miners," 15.
56. *CWST News!* 2, no. 6:2. CEP newsletters carried extensive coverage of legal settlements in the
Consol case and others.
57. *CWST News!* 1, no. 2:2.
58. *CWST News!* 1, no. 5:1.

is we need benefits for sickness, as do our brothers. . . . We need assurance for our safety. We need a better grievance procedure. That's not a matter of sex. That's a matter of being a miner."[59]

In November 1979, the UMWA International held its own women's conference, a daylong event that mirrored CEP conferences in format. It was never repeated. Shortly afterward, the reins of power at the UMWA headquarters shifted to Vice President Sam Church when Arnold Miller suffered a stroke. Church's attitude about women miners was inadvertently revealed a month later at the UMWA's constitutional convention in Denver, Colorado, where nine women were among the 1,267 delegates. At a hospitality room hosted by CEP, women delegates pressed Church for an affirmative action hiring clause in the contract and improved sickness and accident benefits, and he responded with an off-color joke.[60]

In 1982, Church was unseated by Richard Trumka, a young lawyer and miner who promised reform. Women miners vigorously campaigned for Trumka, especially in his home state of Pennsylvania. In 1983, the UMWA officially endorsed the annual CEP conference.

SEXUAL HARASSMENT IN THE MINES

Soon after women entered the mines in sizable numbers, reports of sexual harassment emerged. At every CEP conference, workshops on the topic drew large crowds and elicited gut-wrenching testimonies about harassment from bosses and coworkers. Problems with management often were viewed as more serious, because they could affect a woman's employment and daily working conditions.

In oral history reviews, women miners described a wide range of hostile behaviors: sexual comments and jokes, unwanted advances, an initiatory rite of "greasing," groping, bathroom peepholes, verbal abuse, physical assault, and other problems, such as finding human feces in a dinner bucket. Women reported that some male coworkers opposed the harassing behavior, but did not openly object because they were outnumbered. Women miners who worked on a regular crew for longer periods had more opportunity to find a solution; the loss of mining jobs in the 1980s, however, left fewer women working, and many were placed with different crews, which brought new reports of sexual harassment.

By sharing their struggles, women miners forged strong bonds that helped them find emotional support from their peers and develop strategies to combat the problem. Most vulnerable were women outside the CEP network who also lacked union representation; however, even UMWA women complained that local and district

59. *CWST News!* 1, no. 10:1.
60. *CWST News!* 2, no. 5:3.

officials did not take sexual harassment seriously, especially when it involved co-workers.[61]

The collected oral histories of women miners suggest harassment is affected by a variety of workplace conditions: the number of women employed at the mine; the length of time a woman has worked at the mine; a connection to a support network such as CEP; the strength of the local and district union; local management attitudes; the presence of a male relative at the mine; and a woman's awareness of legal and contractual remedies.

Like pornography, certain types of sexual harassment are expressed through voyeurism and secrecy. In the women's bathhouse at Consolidation Coal Company's Shoemaker mine near Benwood, West Virginia, a group of bosses had drilled a pencil-sized hole through a wall into the women's shower area. On one side, women miners dressed and showered under the illusion of privacy. On the other side, men secretly watched them in their most private moments.

In 1981, eight UMWA women filed a $5.5 million lawsuit against Consol, accusing the company of invasion of privacy. The group also filed a grievance through their local union, but the contract included no privacy language. The case was widely publicized, and CBS' ''60 Minutes'' featured the story in October 1982.

The courtroom drama ''took on many aspects of a rape trial,'' with the defense attacking the characters of the plaintiffs, according to the CEP newsletter.[62] Company witnesses included foremen, other women miners, and union brothers —even the chairman of the local union mine committee. The two parties reached a settlement during the trial, and a gag order was placed on the plaintiffs.

Sexual harassment more commonly was directed at individual women, often creating feelings of shame and increasing a woman's isolation. Sheila (not her real name), an Alabama miner, recalled her early years of employment:

I have a big bust. Of course, I never thought I was that big-breasted until I got down there. They made me feel . . . ashamed. They would tease and comment. They drew pictures. Some guy on the shift before would go down and draw pictures of my body, and somebody else would come and tell me, so everybody would get a big laugh.

The first time I saw it, I went home and cried all night. When I would get upset, it would come out in such a way that I was hostile at home. It put a great strain on my four children. I would wake them up and make them do things that were unnecessary because I was angry. At one point, I thought about getting an operation. But then I decided to ignore it.

I did have this one guy who was very supportive. If he went down before me, he would spray paint the pictures off so I couldn't see them.

61. This issue was raised at almost every CEP conference from 1979 to 1993, and addressed in a meeting between fifteen CEP members and UMWA Vice President Cecil E. Roberts in Washington, D.C. on April 15, 1994.

62. *CWST News!* 5, no. 5:3.

... And they try to feel on you. I've had some walk up and pinch me on the butt, or try to grab my breasts, but I stopped that. I told them that if I ever caught one of them putting their hands on me, it would be over for them. And I meant it.

Along with her workclothes, Sheila donned psychological armor:

One thing about coal mining for women, you can't go in there and just be yourself. You have to always put on an act. . . . When I hit that bottom and get on the portabus, if somebody punches me, I punch them back. You have to stay on the defensive all the time.[63]

She received threats, and felt she had no effective remedies and no one in whom she could confide:

They would take my bucket, or my jacket, and they would put them in a hangman's noose, to give me a message. My life was threatened. More than once, a man tried to run me down with a track car. I was crossing the track with a heavy piece of water pipe, and this guy ran the track car right at me. I was told later he was planning to run me down and make it look like an accident.

She never approached the union about the problem "because then the company brands you a troublemaker. If I had gone to them with a discrimination grievance, it would have meant a hard time . . . it would have meant more discrimination."

The threats abated once she left the track and joined a face crew. Although it was known as a "tough" crew, Sheila adapted and gradually became an accepted part of the group. In the process, she allowed her real feelings to emerge, and deeper friendships developed. The process took nearly a decade.

At first, I let them know we could tease, we could talk, but they could not touch me. I threatened them. They laid in wait for me and would tear up things. It was a hard fight all the way, to show them I would not be broken down. . . . I became part of that group. I learned to fit it. And finally I was accepted as myself, not by doing things they did or thinking the way they thought. I eventually earned their respect. . . . I wasn't going to change my personality or beliefs or anything to fit in the group. I decided to do that after seeing how things worked for so many years in the mines. I decided I was not going to be changed.

I worked on that section [crew] for nine years, and we were close-knit.

63. Interview with "Sheila" in Birmingham, Alabama, August 1983.

They got to the point where they would defend me from anybody. They were my protectors. I learned to love them and they learned to love me.

Sheila, who is African-American, had never worked with white men before, and had never been friends with a white man. At the worksite, she found common ground with men who had wives and children, and she also became close to several of her coworkers' wives.

In some cases, male attitudes to women miners appear to differ with the coworker's age, as a New Mexico woman explained: "I was surprised because the old-timers took care of me, and I had trouble with the young ones. Everybody told me it would be the old-timers who would give me a rough time because they didn't want women in the mine. But they took me under their wing. I think they were raised to take care of women."[64]

Young local union leaders staged a protest strike to try to take away her job: "My own union walked out on me. I started on the longwall because the company thought if they put the women there, they'd run us off. We had a union official that hated the idea of women being in the mine. He convinced the guys to walk out on me because I couldn't lift a bale of wire that weighed 150 pounds, even though very few men could do it. The union was trying to hang me, but I kept my job."

She combated sexual harassment by quick comebacks, threats, support from coworkers, and in one case, help from the harasser's wife:

I had problems with one of the guys. When I went to the bathroom in the mine, he would be watching. Once he came right at me. I let out a scream, and the guy I worked with took care of him.

I've had union guys walk out of [the men's bathhouse] door naked, shaking their clothes, so that I would see them. One man said, "Do you like what you see?" I looked at him and said, "With what you have to offer, you probably have to squat to pee like I do." The guys cracked up laughing.

One man continually pestered me underground, trying to manhandle me. Outside, he made comments. One day I ran into his wife, and she said, "If he gives you any trouble, call me." And so I got fed up one day and called her. She said, "There's no reason for that," and afterward I had no trouble with him.

It was easier for me because some of the men's wives are my cousins, and a lot of people at the mine were related.

The National Bituminous Coal Wage Agreement (NBCWA), negotiated approximately every three to five years between the international union and the Bituminous Coal Operators' Association, provides limited protections for victims of sexual harassment. Article 25 flatly prohibits discrimination against an employee by the em-

64. Interview with Martha Horner, St. Louis, Missouri, June 24, 1994.

ployer or the union, and then lists sex, age, race, and other factors as protected categories.[65]

Article 25 contains the NBCWA's strongest language on discrimination, but other supporting provisions are contained in Article 19 (d), which bans the employer from making a temporary assignment for the purpose of disciplining or discriminating against a worker, and Article 1, an enabling clause that states that management will not abridge the rights of employees as set forth in the contract as a whole. If the harassment created a safety hazard for a worker, she could file a grievance citing violation of individual safety rights in Article 3 (i), which gives an employee to remove herself from an "immediately hazardous" situation.

In their first years of employment, few women miners used the grievance procedure to address sexual harassment or other problems. As time passed, some grew more knowledgeable and confident about using the contract to protect their job rights.

As UMWA member Bonnie Boyer explained, "I didn't start filing grievances until about the seventh year. I think it takes that long to learn the company's whole system of discrimination. I've talked to other women miners. It's a turning point. It's like you've taken all you can tolerate, and you start filing grievances, and you starting pushing things to the limit. You turn your whole attitude around, and you don't care anymore. You're going to fight the company."[66]

The UMWA grievance procedure is a four-step process. In the first step, the grievant attempts to resolve differences through the immediate supervisor/foreman. If that is unsuccessful, she files a grievance and a meeting takes place between the union mine committee and management. Failure at the second step means the grievance is referred to a union district representative, who sets a meeting with a different management official for third-step action. The fourth step is a hearing by a district arbitrator, who rules on the grievance after reviewing relevant evidence and testimony.[67]

The degree of discrimination faced by women seeking union representation is difficult to document because of lack of consistent documentation of grievance procedures by UMWA advocates. One CEP member elected as a member of the local union grievance committee said her local union tried to ignore sexual harassment when it involved another union member:

> In any industry that has nontraditional jobs for women, you should be able to sit down and talk to your own sex about what's going on. Sexual harassment was really big at that time [the early 1980s] and women needed to know they had a recourse. The UMW didn't know how to face a woman

65. See the National Bituminous Coal Wage Agreement of 1988, for example. The antidiscrimination language has remained intact in the subsequent two agreements.

66. Interview with Bonnie Boyer, Shelocta, Pennsylvania, November 19, 1991.

67. This procedure is described in Articles 23 and 24 of the 1993 National Bituminous Coal Wage Agreement.

being harassed. They turned their back. They said, ''That's a union brother you're talking about.'' So women had to take measures into their own hands. Most time you had to go through an agency outside of the union. We shouldn't have to do that after all these years.

When I got into the union, I took an oath to uphold my union brothers and sisters. That means something to me, and it will mean something to me until I die. The men take the oath to help a sister in need, but when the sister is in need, they won't help you.[68]

HEALTH AND SAFETY ISSUES

Since the 1970s, women miners have been outspoken on mine-safety issues, including ventilation regulations, dust sampling, and black lung reform. Individually, many were elected to serve on local union health and safety committees. CEP filed amicus briefs in several mine-safety cases, and helped the UMWA fight the Bush administration nomination of an unqualified female candidate as assistant secretary of labor to oversee federal mine safety and health enforcement.[69] Mine safety has drawn women to work as state and federal inspectors, company and union safety specialists. Mine safety has also been a central focus of the Coal Employment Project.

Since 1973, at least seven women have been killed in mining accidents.[70] The first underground woman miner killed on the job, Marilyn McCusker, drew national media attention in 1979 and, for women miners, raised the issue of spousal benefits for men. In the early 1980s, CEP launched a study of lost-time accident rates among women miners. It concluded that 4% of all female coal miners were involved in lost-time accidents from 1978 to 1980, as compared to 7% of all male miners. Female workers lost approximately 1.1 days apiece as compared to 2.4 days for males.[71] Several women interviewed said they felt their concerns about safety reflected their early training in caring for other family members.

Working mothers who were interviewed frequently voiced anxiety about how a mining accident would affect their children. A West Virginia miner whose arm was nearly ripped off in a shuttlecar accident described the effect of her accident on her year-old son: ''It was a month before I saw my baby, and it was a bad scene. He wouldn't recognize me. He wouldn't let himself hug me. Near the end of the time I

68. Interview with Carol Davis, Waynesburg, Pennsylvania, October 14, 1992.

69. *Journal of Commerce*, July 31, 1987.

70. Data compiled by Linda Raisovich-Parsons of the UMWA Department of Occupational Safety and Health. From 1973 through 1993, the victims include: Marilyn McCusker (1979); Eleanor Bowen (1980); Jackie Herran (1980); Mary ''Cat'' Counts (1983); Linda Thompson (1984); Nannette Wheeler (1984); and Gloria L. Smith (1990).

71. *CWST News!* 7, no. 4:2.

was in the hospital, though, he was really hanging onto me. For a couple of years after that, he didn't want me out of his sight. I think he didn't want to go through losing me again. It was hard for people to understand, but for him Mommy had gotten up and gone to work and disappeared for a month."[72]

Among health issues, pregnancy was a major concern since many women entered the mines at childbearing age. As early as 1980, CEP conference delegates passed a resolution instructing CEP to conduct a study on coal mining and pregnancy.[73] Little was known about the effects on a pregnant worker of airborne coal dust, vibration, electromagnetic fields, chemical agents, noise, and other hazards common in the mining environment. With the support of the UMWA, in 1985 CEP and the National Institute for Occupational Safety and Health (NIOSH) released a report based on a preliminary health survey of twenty-six women coal miners who had been pregnant on the job.[74] The results were not conclusive, pointing to the need for further research.

At mine sites, women were often surprised at the strong reactions pregnancy provoked from male coworkers. Brenda Brock was single and in her late twenties when she worked nearly eight months into her pregnancy at a non-UMWA mine in Harlan County, Kentucky.

> When I told my boss I was pregnant, he jumped up and said, "You can't work! You'll be up here with morning sickness!" And I said, "I've puked for two months and you haven't even noticed."
>
> At that time, I had just been put on a belthead that would spill fifteen to twenty tons of coal a day, and I was cleaning it up with a shovel. Before I knew I was pregnant, I'd feel my side hurt whenever I lifted that shovel over my head. And every time I'd sit down, I'd fall asleep. I'd go to bed an hour early and I still keep falling asleep. So I went in about a week later and told everybody. The men were shocked. They said I should quit, that I shouldn't be working.
>
> And they talked bad about me. So I said, "If any one of you wants to talk about me, fine, but I can make your life perfectly miserable because I'll go straight to your wife and tell her it's yours. And for nine months, you'll be miserable because they won't be able to see the kid, and for the next two years your wife will be staring at it." When I told the men that, it shut them up good.[75]

72. Interview with "Angie," Morgantown, West Virginia, February 1981.

73. *CWST News!* 3, no. 1:6.

74. Jan L. Handke and June Rostan, "Survey of Pregnant Women Miners: Report of a Preliminary Study." Researchers interviewed twenty-six self-selected women who had been pregnant while in a mining job. A reproductive history interview was administered to interviewees for information on reproductive outcome and occupational exposures.

75. Interview with Brenda Brock, Highsplint, Kentucky, May 9, 1980.

She found that her pregnancy was an effective organizing tool among the women at the mine: "I decided to use the pregnancy as a way to get the women together. I wanted the women to know that the men had changed the policy of Southern Labor Union about donations for sickness. When a person is off five weeks, they get an automatic $1,100 donation from the [SLU]. But the men told me they weren't giving no five dollars for a baby they didn't have the pleasure to make."[76]

A West Virginia miner noticed that some men felt protective toward her after her pregnancy became known, but felt it necessary to disguise their feelings:

> The ones who wouldn't harass me were embarrassed to work with me. Some of them felt sympathetic, but they couldn't really express it because so many of the men were resentful. They did what they could in a very unobtrusive way. Others would help if I had to hang brattice curtain above my head. They didn't say anything, and I didn't say anything, but we both understood. . . . After I came back from having the baby, the men were very supportive. They knew I wasn't getting anything from the father. He was a foreman, and in the mornings the guys would be lined up ready to go in, and they'd yell, "Child support, child support!" at him, and he would run into the shop.[77]

SISTERHOOD AND SOLIDARITY

The 1980s proved to be a decade marked by decline and retrenchment for labor unions in the United States, but women miners organized aggressively within CEP and in the UMWA on a wide range of social issues. CEP conference participants debated the environmental impact of acid rain, international solidarity with striking British miners, and race and gender discrimination. CEP members also discussed women's issues outside the union's sphere of interest, such as abortion rights.[78]

The CEP earned the union's support and involvement on the issue of family leave, and the successful campaign is a landmark achievement in the labor movement. Women miners first raised the issue of extended maternity benefits at their first national conference in 1979, and at subsequent conferences broadened the concept to "maternity/paternity leave." In April 1983, CEP sponsored a three-day workshop in Washington, D.C., for seventeen UMWA women representing fourteen of the union's districts.[79] The group studied the UMWA constitution and drafted contract language on maternity/paternity leave that also protected the jobs of parents of seri-

---

76. *CWST News!* 3, no. 1:6.
77. The interviewee asked for anonymity. The interview took place in February 1981.
78. A list of resolutions passed by conference delegates was published annually in *CWST News!*
79. *CWST News!* 5, no. 11:1.

ously ill children. They developed a strategy to educate their union brothers and to lobby for the issue through local and district unions.

In choosing to launch a campaign for family leave, women miners deliberately chose an issue that would benefit all union members. "Family leave is about equality—for men," said CEP member Cosby Totten of UMWA Local 6025. CEP members lobbied union members and officials. By publicizing the stories of men whose jobs were threatened because of a family illness, women miners earned the union's support. The family leave provision was passed unanimously in 1983 by delegates to the UMWA constitutional convention for contract language on family leave. Early the next year, a UMWA contract was ratified that included a letter of intent for a union/industry committee to study the issue. CEP members lobbied for representation on the committee and were appointed to two of five union seats.[80]

Women miners also influenced the drafting of federal legislation. After initiating a meeting in 1984 with ten women's groups, leaders of those groups decided to expand proposed language on "parental leave" to include time needed to care for seriously ill children.[81] After more than a decade of work, women miners finally celebrated President Clinton's signing of the federal Family and Medical Leave Act in February 1993.

In the 1970s and 1980s, CEP's activist agenda was frequently promoted by UMWA women who also belonged to the Socialist Workers Party (SWP), which generated an internal debate within CEP.[82] UMWA women's activism, however, grew to extend beyond ideology, becoming a natural expression for women who had fought to get hired, trained, represented, and to be heard as a collective voice.

The wildcat strikes of 1977 and the 111-day national strike in 1977–78 were the first strikes many women miners had personally engaged in. As relatively new hires, many women reported being discouraged by local union leaders from picketing, and being instructed to prepare food or engage in other "safe" strike duties. But some women interviewed were highly visible on picket lines and in mass confrontations, particularly in volatile strike zones in Illinois, Alabama, and West Virginia.

The 1980s brought mass layoffs to women miners, who suffered from the "last hired, first fired" rule of union seniority. But despite unemployment and a declining U.S. labor movement, UMWA women built solidarity in strikes against A. T. Massey, Canterbury Coal, and Decker Coal Company. Women miners also forged links with striking meatpackers from Local P-9, who had challenged their international union, the United Food and Commercial Workers.[83]

Beyond the U.S. borders, women miners also made contact with embattled British

80. *CWST News!* 8, no. 4:3.

81. Cosby Totten, "For Our Children: The Coal Miners Fight For Parental Leave," *CWST News!* 5, no. 11:3.

82. The role of the Socialist Workers Party in the Coal Employment Project is an important chapter of history that has not yet been published in written form. This information comes from the author's conversations from 1979 until 1994 with CEP members and SWP members.

83. See coverage in the July–August 1986 issue of *CWST News!*

miners striking to prevent the closing of union pits. In 1985, a delegation of British miners' wives representing the activist Women Against Pit Closures made the first in a series of trips to CEP conferences. The CEP also sponsored fact-finding trips to the coalfields of China, the former Soviet Union, India, Europe, Canada, and the *maquiladora* region of Mexico.

By the early 1980s, women miners had gained enough union experience to begin running for elected local union offices. The exact number of women who have served as officers and as elected committee members is unknown, but at the 1988 CEP national conference, the chairperson asked for all women who had ever held local office to stand up; nearly the entire roomful of women rose to their feet.[84]

The CEP in particular worked to promote and educate women for positions of leadership in the UMWA. In 1986, CEP member Joy Huitt added her name as an independent candidate for secretary-treasurer of the UMWA's District 22, which spanned four western states and a diversity of cultures: Navajos, Mormons, Mexicans and migrants from the eastern coalfields. She ran against a slate of candidates organized by the incumbents, but won by a narrow margin.[85]

In a 1986 interview, Huitt credited CEP with building skills and confidence that later helped her run a successful political campaign: "I don't think I would have been prepared to tackle this campaign without the training I had from the Coal Employment Project. Through CEP, I've learned administrative and accounting skills, helped put on a national conference, and traveled overseas to observe mining conditions in England, India and the Soviet Union. CEP has worked to provide opportunities like that to women miners. Without our organization, women would have had a lot further to go in becoming a recognized force in the union."[86] After serving one term, she lost her bid for reelection in an even closer race with a slate-endorsed candidate, who was also female. Afterward, Huitt filed a workers' compensation claim for stress for alleged harassment from District 22 officials.[87]

Another CEP organizing effort focused on UMWA auxiliaries, groups of miners' wives associated with union locals. Despite their innocuous-sounding name, UMWA women's auxiliaries have a militant history. From West Virginia to Colorado, wives of strikers have confronted strike-breakers and mineguards, and faced arrest and physical assault to defend the union and their families.

During the historic Pittston strike, the UMWA supported a large-scale organizing of UMWA auxiliaries by assigning the author and two CEP members to coordinate the effort. An estimated 1,000 strikers' wives volunteered for strike duties. In 1989 auxiliary members staged a peaceful occupation of the Pittston regional office in Virginia, went to jail in civil disobedience protests, conducted vigils, and staffed

84. From author's notes of the 1988 conference.
85. *CWST News!* 8, no. 7:1.
86. Interview with Joy Huitt, Crystal City, Virginia, September 1986.
87. From conversations with Joy Huitt during and after her reelection bid.

Camp Solidarity, which hosted more than 50,000 visitors before the strike ended in early 1990.[88]

As the strike progressed, however, some auxiliary leaders privately complained that the UMWA did not support women's organizing efforts.[89] After the successful early takeover of the Pittston building, auxiliary members found themselves assigned to less activist roles. During the later men's occupation of the Moss 3 preparation plant, women reportedly were deliberately excluded from the strategy discussions.[90]

Cosby Totten worked for the union to organize the Pittston auxiliaries, and found herself disillusioned with the UMWA: "It was frustrating, because the women found a voice in the strike and then were kept from using it. After [the women's occupation] was over, [the strike leader] said he wanted the occupation carried out so that the women could show up the men. I didn't like that, because a wife does not want to be used to humiliate her husband. It seemed like most of the men in the decision-making part of the union would use the women when they needed them and when they didn't, they wanted all of us to get back out of the way."[91]

Four years later, women miners were visible during the 1993 selective strike against companies of the Bituminous Coal Operators Association (BCOA), which affected miners in seven states. UMWA women served as strike captains, outreach coordinators, and as key organizers in strike relief efforts. While the union's efforts to organize auxiliaries in 1993 appeared perfunctory, women miners stepped in to help organize the groups, with at least one woman miner serving as auxiliary president in her dual capacity as UMWA wife and striking miner.[92]

CONCLUSION

Perhaps fewer than one thousand women remain employed in union and nonunion mines in the United States, although accurate statistics are difficult to obtain.[93] Of

88. This is from the author's personal experience. In 1988, at the beginning of the corporate campaign against Pittston, the author raised the issue of broad auxiliary organizing with Joe Jurczak, coordinator of the corporate campaign. He agreed to hire on lost-time wages two UMWA women from southwest Virginia, Cosby Totten and Catherine Tompa. Totten, Tompa, and the author helped organize a regional network of approximately twelve local union auxiliaries, and participated in the occupation and other acts of nonviolent protest.

89. Marat Moore, "Ten Months That Shook The Coalfields: Women's Stories From The Pittston Strike," *Now & Then Magazine* 7, no. 3:6.

90. From discussions in September 1989 with male UMWA organizers, who informed the author that the UMWA strike chief ordered in all-male meetings that no women would be informed or involved in the occupation planning.

91. Interview with Cosby Totten, Tazewell, Virginia, May 25, 1992.

92. From the author's conversations with auxiliary members during the 1993 strike. For example, at one local in Illinois, UMWA member Martha Vaughan was elected president of the local union auxiliary. She was both a miner and a miner's wife.

93. National Institute for Occupational Safety and Health.

those hired in the peak years of the late 1970s, the women still working are nearing retirement as the unionized industry continues to shrink, endangering mining wages and the future of the UMWA.

By crossing mine portals into a high-wage, virtually all-male occupation, women expanded the horizons of nontraditional work in the wake of affirmative action mandates. The oral histories evidence suggests that women as a group exercised a high level of safety awareness and activism, and that they strengthened solidarity in labor struggles during the antilabor decade of the 1980s. In addition, women broadened the UMWA's social agenda through the campaign for family leave, and found vital support and educational opportunities through their nonprofit organization, CEP.

Perhaps it is too soon to know whether women miners have had a lasting impact on the UMWA and on the U.S. coal industry. More research and discussion is needed in key areas of women miners' history: the degree of union representation of UMWA women in grievance and arbitration procedures; community and spousal attitudes about women in mining over a twenty-year period; and the relationship between women coal miners and their male coworkers, to name a few.

Although most of the approximately four thousand women who were hired as miners since 1973 have lost their jobs, the occupational identity remains strong years after they have departed from mine portals. "Once a woman miner, always a woman miner," noted laid-off miner Carol Davis in a comment often repeated by CEP members.[94]

Women like Cosby Totten continue to pay UMWA dues long after their layoffs because of loyalty and a commitment to working for social justice: "I was laid off in 1982, and I have stayed a dues-paying member of the United Mine Workers. I intend to stay a member, because I love my union. I stay active for my mental health, although sometimes being active makes me think I'm crazy. I stay involved because I want to make life better for my children. . . . An injury to one is an injury to all. Our children need to understand those words."[95]

Writing in late 1993, Libby Lindsay—who was still working in the mines in early 1996—concluded an editorial in the CEP newsletter by noting that the twentieth anniversary of women miners had almost slipped by without her realizing it: "No wonder I nearly forgot. We've been busy! We're getting older. We have more health problems than we used to. We're burned out. But we're still here. We're still saying, 'Si, se puede'—Yes, we can."[96]

94. Interview with Carol Davis, Waynesburg, Pennsylvania, October 14, 1992.
95. Telephone interview with Cosby Totten, August 16, 1994.
96. Lindsay, "20 Years In The Mines."

CHAPTER TWENTY-ONE

"TYING THE KNOT OF SOLIDARITY"
The Pittston Strike of 1989–1990*

J A M E S   R .   G R E E N

When Richard Lewis Trumka became the president of the United Mine Workers of America in 1982 at the age of thirty-three, he inherited a union with a reputation for "bitter political infighting" and a declining membership. A third-generation coal miner with a law degree and a great deal of charisma, Trumka wanted to "turn the members' attention to external threats," including the rapid growth of nonunion, western coal. Although the union had implemented democratic reforms, it lacked leadership at the top and had lost the active participation of the rank and file. Trumka spent his first year trying to restore the members' belief in the union and in themselves and in negotiating a new contract with the Bituminous Coal Operators Asso-

*The author thanks the following officers and staff members of the United Mine Workers of America for their help in providing information and making suggestions: President Richard Trumka, Vice President Cecil Roberts, Marat Moore, Ron Baker, Gene Carroll, Ken Zinn, Lanny Shortridge, John Duray, Greg Hawthorne, and Eddie Burke. He also thanks Alex Lubin for research assistance and John Laslett for helpful editorial suggestions.

ciation (BCOA). In 1984 the membership ratified the agreement without a strike—for the first time in twenty years.[1]

But soon after signing this contract, the UMWA faced an attack by the A. T. Massey Company, a renegade BCOA member. Unprepared, the union plunged into a bitter struggle that would test Trumka's leadership. Massey had been taken over by Royal Dutch Shell and the Fluor Corporation whose directors wanted a higher return on coal investments. Massey refused to sign the 1984 national agreement, ending payments to the 1950 pension fund and denying employment rights to union miners in its new nonunion mines.[2] When the coal company fortified its operations and hired replacements for its 2500 striking workers, a war broke out that raged along the Tug Fork River on the West Virginia–Kentucky line just as it had in 1920–21 when Sid Hatfield shot it out with the Baldwin-Felts gunmen at Matewan and when the UMW's armed forces marched up Blair Mountain on the way to liberating Mingo County. Massey spent $200,000 a month on security, including a helicopter and an armored personnel carrier, but it would only run scab coal trucks during daylight and then with state troopers riding shotgun.[3]

Alarmed by the spiral of violence, the union leaders experimented with massive civil disobedience and for a while in early 1985 the strike gained momentum. But court injunctions and fines persuaded the UMW to return to less confrontational tactics. An impressive international boycott against Shell Oil helped bring Massey back to the table, as did pressure from the National Labor Relations Board. After a tough fifteen-month strike the union settled but it "lost jobs, suffered massive fines and had to accept a labor contract less favorable than the national agreement."[4] The UMWA's leaders feared that the war with Massey would encourage other coal operators to break out of the old multiemployer agreement and even attempt to break the union.

PREPARING FOR WAR AT PITTSTON

In less than two years a similar conflict emerged when the Pittston Coal Group withdrew from the BCOA and stopped paying into the industrywide health insurance fund for retirees. Pittston's new coal division President Mike Odum said he

1. "Today the Mine Workers—Tomorrow, The AFL-CIO," *Business Week* (February 15, 1988): 65–66. Author's interview with Richard Trumka, Washington, D.C., January 19, 1994, transcript in author's possession.

2. "Today the Mine Workers," 66; and Richard A. Couto, "The Memory of Miners and the Conscience of Capital: Coal Miners' Strikes as Free Space," in *Fighting Back in Appalachia: Traditions of Resistance and Change,* ed. Stephen L. Fischer (Temple University Press: Philadelphia, 1993), 172, 176.

3. Couto, "The Memory of Miners," 178–79; and Nicolaus Mills, "War in Tug River Valley: A Long and Bitter Miners' Strike," *Dissent* (Winter 1986): 52.

4. Couto, "The Memory of Miners," 178–79, 173.

wanted a contract like Massey's because his firm, unlike most BCOA members, needed to compete in international markets where it sold a great deal of low sulphur coal, used to make coke for steel producers. The company intended to shave five to six dollars a ton from the costs it incurred under the BCOA agreement.[5]

The new UMWA-BCOA national agreement, signed on January 30, 1988, gained some job security, won a modest 6.8% wage increase and established an unprecedented Education and Training Trust Fund to pay for educating unemployed miners and their dependents. The rank and file ratified the contract and Trumka secured another agreement without a strike. But Pittston rejected the new pact and the UMW had to continue frustrating negotiations while trying to penetrate the corporation's "baffling web of subsidiaries."[6] With the old contract due to expire on January 31, 1988, a strike seemed inevitable.

The mines Pittston owned were concentrated in the southwestern corner of Virginia in some of the most beautiful country in the Appalachians, mainly in Buchanan and Dickenson counties wedged up against the West Virginia and Kentucky borders. These mines had been working under a UMW contract since 1939 and labor relations had been stable. The company earned a bad name, however, after the Buffalo Creek tragedy in 1972 when waste from one of its mines caused a dam to burst, flooding a hollow and drowning 125 people in West Virginia. In 1984 a new management team took over headed by CEO Paul W. Douglas and Coal Operations Vice President Joseph Farrell. Douglas had spent thirty-one years with Freeport-McMoran in New York where he had risen through the ranks to become chairman and chief executive. In Douglas's first year Pittston lost $26 million and accumulated $104 in debts. In 1987, when Pittston left the BCOA, it took a $133 million loss.[7]

Pittston had acquired other companies, including Brinks Security where it eliminated the Teamsters Union, but coal accounted for more than half the corporation's profits. The demand for Pittston's metallurgical coal rose, especially among Japanese steelmakers who bought 57% of the company's fuel. Productivity had increased 72% in the union mines. Still, Douglas wanted a much higher return on investment from coal operations. He developed a corporate restructuring plan that created a "complex web of over 50 coal mining subsidiaries, holding companies and land companies" designed to cut down dependence on coal reserves mined by

5. On Pittston see *Betraying the Trust: The Pittston Company's Drive to Break Appalachia's Coalfield Communities* (Washington, D.C.: United Mine Workers of America, 1989); and Martha Hodel, "The Pittston Company," *Charleston Gazette* (August 29, 1989).

6. United Mine Workers of America, "The United Mine Workers' Strike Against the Pittston Coal Company," 1989, Background Briefing Paper, unpublished manuscript in author's possession.

7. "In Midst of Strike, Pittston Chairman Plans for Future," *Journal of Commerce* (August 7, 1989); and Alecia Swasy, "Pittston Chief Digs In Against UMW," *Wall Street Journal* (August 22, 1989). On the Buffalo Creek tragedy see Kai T. Erikson, *Everything in its Path: Destruction of Community in the Buffalo Creek Flood* (New York: Simon and Schuster, 1976).

UMW members and to move work to Pittston's nonunion subsidiaries. Through restructuring and cost cutting Douglas reduced the union mining force by four thousand. But he wanted more. Specifically, he wanted out of the BCOA agreement and he wanted concessions in a new contract that would cut labor and health care costs. The company also wanted to run coal seven days a week and to escape from the costly health care fund.[8]

If Paul Douglas represented a new breed of managers who wanted to push up returns on investment and break unions to do it, Richard Trumka represented a new brand of union leader. Well-educated and well-spoken, sophisticated in public relations and legal affairs, he broke new ground in 1988 when he negotiated an innovative contract with Island Creek Coal Company that emphasized labor-management cooperation and enhanced productivity incentives in return for access for UMW members to new mines that had employed only nonunion workers. By then even A. T. Massey's CEO praised Trumka as a progressive labor leader who had reduced strikes and increased productivity in the industry. *Business Week* touted him as a future head of the AFL-CIO. But those who thought Trumka had left behind the UMW's militant traditions were mistaken. Still a vigorous young man with the build of a fullback and a striking dark complexion, Trumka talked often of the stories his Polish father, a miner, and his Italian mother told him of growing up in a poor Pennsylvania coal patch called Nemacolin. He retold stories of striking families being put out of their houses, described the Catholic Church as the only place in town where miners felt equal to the foremen and remembered eating nothing but government cheese in hard times.[9]

Trumka had been tracking Pittston's corporate strategy for three years and he feared another Massey strike in which the employer would try to break the UMWA as it had the Teamsters. On January 27, 1988, Pittston confirmed his suspicions when it announced that it would hire permanent replacements in the event of a strike. The union offered to work under an extension of the old contract, but Pittston refused. When the existing agreement expired on January 31, 1988, the company ended pension contributions for working miners; eliminated arbitration of disputes; stopped the check-off union dues; and cut off health benefits to fifteen hundred widows, retirees, and disabled miners.[10]

This last action would later become a central moral issue in the strike, arousing deep anger in the coalfields and moral condemnation from churches; at the time, however, it attracted little attention. Pittston was confident that a strike could be isolated, that many of its union employees would cross the picket lines and come back to work and that the courts and police would limit pickets and protect replacement workers.

8. Ibid.; James Green, "Corporate Culture's Failure in Dealing with Coal Miners," *Boston Globe* (June 21, 1989), and Moe Seager, "One Day Longer Than Pittston," *Z Magazine* (October 1989): 14.

9. "Today, the Mine Workers, Tomorrow the AFL-CIO," and author's interview with Richard Trumka, Nemacolin, Pennsylvania, July 12, 1990.

10. "The United Mine Workers Strike Against Pittston," 3; and *Betraying the Trust*.

But the company had misread the lessons of the Massey strike and underestimated the union's leaders. Though steeped in labor history and UMWA tradition, Trumka was not a prisoner of the past. He was enormously popular with the members, having won re-election to a second term in 1987 without opposition, and he believed they would follow him even if he broke with tradition. Contrary to UMW custom, which required members to strike immediately after a contract expired, Trumka decided to keep the Pittston miners on the job working without a contract. He surprised the company's managers who had hoped to goad the UMW into a strike for which it was unprepared.[11]

The UMW needed a new strategy to avoid a repeat of the Massey strike. Together with Vice President Cecil Roberts and a remarkably gifted staff, Trumka planned an ambitious, multifaceted strategy. Since it would be difficult to win the strike on the picket line (though quite possible to lose it there), the union planned what Trumka called a "sophisticated" corporate campaign against Pittston on a national level and, because of the company's export business, on an international scale as well. Unions had waged corporate campaigns and boycotts before, but the ambitious Shell Boycott against Massey's owners had not produced a victory in that bitter strike. Nor had the corporate campaigns against Hormel and International Paper earlier in the 1980s prevented striking employees from losing their unions and their jobs.[12]

The brutal concessionary strikes of the eighties also convinced Trumka that nothing less than a total mobilization of UMW members and their allies could win. He believed the union had been too isolated from its allies in the Massey strike. That conflict also demonstrated that even aggressive UMWA picket lines could be decimated by court orders and violated by heavily guarded strike-breakers, who could become permanent replacements. Trumka knew that unless he was willing to take big risks, defeat would be certain. He drew two lessons from recent movement history. From the 1980s he learned that playing by the rules meant defeat for striking unions and from the 1960s he learned that nonviolent movements could mobilize and energize ordinary people and win support from the public and the media. All this pointed toward civil disobedience, toward building something like a 1960s protest movement around the strike.[13]

11. Dwayne Yancey, "Thunder in the Coal Fields: The UMW's Strike Against Pittston," a special report of the *Roanoke Times & World News* (April 29, 1990), 2.

12. Ibid. Other information on strike strategy is from an interview with strike coordinator Ron Baker, July 15, 1993. For an overview of concessionary bargaining in this period, see Kim Moody, *An Injury to All: The Decline of American Unionism* (London: Verso 1988). On the International Paper and Hormel strikes, see Jane Slaughter, "Corporate Campaigns: Labor Enlists Community Support"; and Peter Rachleff, "Supporting the Hormel Strikers," in *Building Bridges: The Emerging Grassroots Coalition of Community and Labor*, ed. Jeremy Brecher and Tim Costello (New York: Monthly Review, 1990), 47–69.

13. Trumka later said that he was attracted to what Harris Wofford wrote on Gandhi in the 1950s, writings that had influenced Martin Luther King; Trumka interview, January 19, 1994. Also see David Moberg, "Envisioning a New Day for the Labor Movement," *In These Times* (August 30–September 5, 1989).

But Trumka, a creative labor lawyer and student of military as well as union history, also wanted to use laws when they could help the union. If the UMW struck Pittston over the contract, the courts would regard it as an economic strike (that is, a conflict over contract issues, not over violations of labor law) and therefore would allow Pittston to hire permanent replacements for the strikers. With disastrously high unemployment in Appalachia, the company could easily find those replacements and if it held out long enough, it could break the union. So UMWA lawyers immediately filed unfair labor practice charges against Pittston with the NLRB. If the board ruled against the company, then, in a strike over unfair labor practices, Pittston would not be allowed to hire replacements permanently. On March 23, 1989, the National Labor Relations Board agreed to hear the union's unfair labor practices charge.[14]

During the fourteen months Pittston miners worked without a contract (from January 1988, to April 1989) they suffered various kinds of harassment from company managers trying to provoke a strike. The union attempted an inside strategy trying to slow production while its members were still on the job, but these efforts failed to bring Pittston to the bargaining table. While the inside strategy bogged down, the union's outside strategy patiently prepared miners and their families for a new kind of strike, the likes of which the UMWA had never seen. In late 1988 and early 1989 the union "braintrust" grappled with how to avoid another Massey strike, which had remained an isolated conflict publicized mainly for its violence. Marty Hudson, the executive assistant to Vice President Cecil Roberts, was appointed strike coordinator, with strict orders from the president to keep the strike nonviolent.[15]

But the strike strategists had more in mind than avoiding violence. They wondered if they could use a campaign of civil disobedience to defy the courts but still gain public support and mobilize the masses of people it would take to win the strike on the picket line. Vice President Cecil Roberts thought so. Though he was a devoted student of labor's past whose family had helped make working-class history in West Virginia, he drew on a different history now. The civil rights movement, he argued, taught lessons that could help win the impending strike. He had devoured *Parting the Waters*, Taylor Branch's book on Martin Luther King, and he carried a dog-eared copy with him to staff meetings where he insisted that everyone read it until they could quote easily from the words of both King and Gandhi. Trumka agreed fully. He later recalled the lessons of the violent Massey strike: that unless the top leaders gave strong direction to a strike the "infinite number of clashes" that would take place on the picket lines could lead to violence. But if members were to follow their leaders' nonviolent strategy, the union would have to develop in "a continuous process of education and re-education."[16]

UMWA attorney Judy Scott and corporate campaign director Ken Zinn proposed

14. Yancey, "Thunder in the Coal Fields," 2–3.
15. Ibid., 3.
16. Ibid., 3, and Trumka interview, January 19, 1994.

a training program in nonviolent protest tactics. Another staffer, Gene Carroll, who had worked for the nuclear freeze campaign, brought in two peace activists who met with UMW leaders in Washington and told them how civil disobedience could involve entire families and communities, even children and the elderly, and how it could win allies. They talked about ways of occupying offices and blocking roads. On February 18 they conducted training in Charleston, West Virginia, for seventy union field reps from the eastern coalfields. The leaders had to be convinced that civil disobedience would work and that the strikers would not reject it as being "unmanly." Some union leaders thought civil disobedience would seem too timid to Appalachian miners accustomed to violent picket-line struggles. Nonetheless, UMW staffers and officers, impressed by the training in Charleston, fanned out to preach the new gospel of nonviolence in the union halls and homes of Pittston's miners in southwest Virginia, West Virginia, and Kentucky.[17]

While union leaders expounded the ideas and tactics of the civil rights and peace movements, others adopted the approaches of the women's movement and community-organizing struggles. The union hired Cosby Totten and Catherine Tompa, who had been underground miners, to organize miners' wives, daughters, and other women in the community to raise consciousness about what was at stake. Together with UMW organizer Marat Moore, they drove hundreds of miles through the coalfields to talk with union members about setting up local women's auxiliaries and then linking them up in district organizations. "They held fund raisers, staged convoys, and established a regular presence at local company headquarters" in Lebanon, Virginia, that started in July 1988 and lasted for the whole strike. Even before the strike began "the knot of solidarity had been tied."[18] The stage was now set.

Pittston's managers wanted a strike all along and on April 5, 1989, they got one. But as Cecil Roberts said later, "it wasn't the one they were looking for."[19] Officially, the union began an "unfair labor practices" strike against the company's alleged violations of federal labor law. But the enthusiastic response of the strikers showed that much more was at stake: the health and welfare of their elders on retirement; the survival of their communities, which depended on union wages; and even the future of their union. In the fourteen months the Pittston miners worked without a contract the union had made an extraordinary effort to educate the coal communities about these grave stakes. It paid off almost immediately.

On the first day of the strike the battle lines were drawn at McClure mine No. 1, the company's biggest operation. Vance Security guards in blue jump suits and sun glasses guarded the mine and heard curses rain down on them from the massive crowd of pickets; they were denounced as "gun thugs," like the Baldwin-Felts who

17. Yancey, "Thunder in the Coal Fields," 3.

18. Marat Moore, "Ten Months That Shook the Coal Fields: Women's Stories from the Pittston Strike," unpublished manuscript, n.p. An edited version appeared as "Women's Stories from the Pittston Strike," *Now and Then* (Fall 1990): 6–12, 32–35.

19. Roberts quoted in "Out of Darkness: The Mine Workers' Story," Video produced by Barbara Kopple, directed by Bill Davis (New York: Cabin Creek Films, 1990).

had terrorized the Appalachian coal camps in Sid Hatfield's day. Across the road a detail of Virginia state troopers looked on warily at a large group of miners all dressed alike—in camouflage. This uniform had become popular during the Massey strike and it served a useful purpose. During that strike scab truck drivers whose rigs had been stoned identified alleged assailants by describing their dress. So from day one, the Pittston strikers wore camouflage as their uniform for tactical reasons; but the fatigues came to have rich symbolic meaning as well. The uniform signified a state of mind, a feeling of solidarity among people ready to wage an all-out war—a war without firearms—to defend their way of life.[20]

FROM CIVIL DISOBEDIENCE TO CIVIL RESISTANCE

The strike's first day passed peacefully, but organizers were tense. Pittston's lawyers went to court to stop the mass picketing. On April 12, Donald McGlothin Jr., the circuit court judge for Dickenson and Russell counties, issued his first order limiting pickets to ten. In the meantime, other supporters took action. Someone shot out a transformer at Lambert Fork, cutting off power to the mine. A scab truck convoy headed for Pittston's Moss 3 coal preparation plant came around a bend in the road and "ran into a barrage of rocks that hit us like a hailstorm," according to one truck driver. "Jackrocks" turned up on mountain roads, puncturing the tires of coal trucks, Vance security vans, and state police cars. For those unfamiliar with jack-rocks in the state capitol, the Richmond paper described these objects, often called "mountain spiders" by miners, as "nails welded together so they puncture truck tires." "Miniature versions" were "fashioned into ear rings," and were worn proudly by female strike supporters.[21]

It was time to begin civil disobedience in order to discourage violence, maintain discipline, and boost morale. The women of the strike moved first on this front perhaps because the strike organizers thought wives and sisters of the miners would be more willing to experiment with nonviolent protest than the men. On April 18, thirty-seven women occupied the Pittston offices in Lebanon where they had maintained a tent site picket for months. These wives, widows, and daughters of miners confronted a startled receptionist; after a moment of silence they started singing "We Shall Not Be Moved," the old CIO-civil rights song. They expected to be arrested by the police and, if that occurred, they had decided not to cooperate by giving their names: they would all say they were "Daughters of Mother Jones."[22]

20. Moore, "Ten Months That Shook the Coal Fields," 13; Yancey, "Thunder in the Coal Fields," 4; and Nicolaus Mills, "Solidarity in Virginia: The Mine Workers Remake History," *Dissent* (Spring 1960): 238.

21. Yancey, "Thunder in the Coal Fields," 4.

22. Ibid., and Moore, "Ten Months That Shook the Coal Fields."

The sit-in lasted all night, and the next morning it made headlines across the state. When the women left at 4:00 P.M., Marty Hudson was delighted. "It let me know what you can do with civil disobedience," he recalled. After this, the women "became the backbone of the strike."[23]

When the women's occupation ended, civil disobedience began on a mass scale. On April 24, three hundred strikers in full camouflage sat down in front of the McClure mine. They locked arms, so that when the state police waded in to make arrests they had to pull people apart. There were injuries. James Gibbs, the only black miner, suffered a broken arm. The actions of the police at McClure angered and, according to one report, "radicalized" many citizens in the area. Next day the community mobilization expanded. To protest the arrests and the brutalities at McClure a crowd of students from three area high schools walked out and over a hundred gathered at Dickenson County courthouse wearing camouflage uniforms. The school superintendent ordered a three-day suspension for those absent without leave.[24]

The next morning nearly five hundred pickets gathered at the Moss 3 coal preparation plant. Violating Judge McGlothin's order, they sat down in front of a convoy of replacement workers. Again, police waded in and hauled off sit downers as the crowd's anger swelled. John Cox, an international organizer, took the bullhorn and persuaded people to submit to arrest. He kept a scary moment from exploding in violence. When the crowd started rocking the buses, UMWA District 28 President Jackie Stump ordered them to stop. State police arrested 457 people at Moss 3 that day, including Stump, "whose strong lungs and stern countenance probably prevented a riot that day."[25]

One of the miners told the reporters who had gathered: "They talk about violence and all, but look who's getting hurt." The strikers had begun their campaign to win hearts and minds to their cause. A few days later the strike made the *New York Times*. It was a short story on the inside pages, but it reported on the seriousness of the strike, and it attracted other media to the remote coalfields of southwestern Virginia.[26]

At this moment the union organized its biggest demonstration to celebrate and legitimatize the new resistance movement. On April 30, some ten thousand people braved a driving rainstorm and crowded into Wise County Fairgrounds on an old strip mine near Norton, Virginia, to hear the Reverend Jesse Jackson and the strike leaders. Two separate car caravans, each one with four hundred vehicles, arrived from West Virginia and Kentucky. Traffic backed up for miles on the roads leading to fairgrounds. Echoing the themes of his 1988 presidential campaign, Jackson urged the wet sea of people, in forest green and earthy brown, to "keep hope alive"

---

23. Yancey, "Thunder in the Coal Fields," 4.
24. Ibid., 4–5; John Clarks, "Students protest for UMWA," *Cumberland Times* (April 26, 1989), and Moore, "Ten Months."
25. Yancey, "Thunder in the Coal Fields," 5.
26. Ibid., 5.

even in the hardest times, and to unify across all boundaries, including race. When miners went down in the mine every day, everyone looked alike. These workers learned to "live together eight or nine miles underground." If they could do this deep below the ground, he said, "we must learn to live together above ground." Celebrating the fusion of the labor movement and the civil rights movement, Jackson proclaimed: "When we look around today we see the tradition of John L. Lewis and Martin Luther King have met together, and we will not go back." Aware that civil disobedience had led to many arrests, Jackson glorified the defiance of unjust laws. He did so not only as a black civil rights leader but as a preacher who could speak in familiar Baptist idiom to a throng of faithful Christians. Ever since his first presidential campaign in 1984 Jackson had aroused an almost religious fervor among hard-pressed union workers, who thrilled to his jeremiads against corporate greed and his exciting appeals for radical change.[27]

Jackson also stressed the wider significance of strike. "This is not just your strike; it's the people's strike. Workers everywhere identify with this strike." Then Trumka spoke, calling Pittston a "turning point for labor" in the United States. In his best stem-winding style, he took aim at Democratic Governor Gerald Baliles who had earlier won labor's political support but then had sent in state police to occupy the coalfields. Trumka joined Jackson in emphasizing the power of nonviolent protest. It was working. He also took pains to distinguish civil disobedience from "civil resistance." The strike involved more than disobeying unjust laws; the strikers were resisting wrongs caused by corporate greed.[28]

The strikers dramatized their cause by attending the Pittston stockholders meeting in Greenwich, Connecticut, on May 10, where union members who had been given small shares of stock introduced resolutions to embarrass management. One proposal, to allow for secret ballot voting, actually won significant support, and suggested that some of Pittston investors might be vulnerable to the union's corporate campaign aimed at the company's executives in Connecticut, and its board members around the country.[29]

The union explained the strike as a moral defense of decency and tradition, a struggle for community survival, not for wages. Cutting off the benefits became a key issue in the UMWA's public campaign against Pittston. In 1988 Pittston had reported $59 million in profits yet, the union charged, it was breaking "a delicately

27. McKelway, "Jackson Makes Pledge to Miners," *Richmond Times-Dispatch* (May 1, 1989); "The Message Comes to the Mountains," *Herald-Courier* (Bristol, Va.) (May 1, 1989); and Greg Edwards, "Jackson to Miners: Don't Go Back," *Roanoke, VA Times and World News* (May 1, 1989); and Tracy Wimmer, "Miners Lifted by Jackson Magic," *Roanoke, VA Times and World News* (May 1, 1989). On Jackson's appeal to white union workers in the 1980s see James Green, "Campaign '88: For Jackson Populism is a Class Act," *Boston Sunday Globe* (April 3, 1988), 63–64.

28. Dana Priest, "Jesse Jackson Joins Forces With Striking Miners in Va.," *Washington Post* (May 1, 1989); and Wayne Barber, "Westmoreland Workers Will Remain Off Jobs," *Bristol Herald Courier* (May 1, 1989).

29. Yancey, "Thunder in the Coal Fields," 7.

forged social pact'' with coalfield communities just to make more money. Demanding Sunday work and scorning the traditions of a churchgoing people, it had become "just one more mega-corporation with micro-vision.''[30]

But Trumka knew the crusade to win the moral high ground would fail if the strikers acted violently. He also knew however that the courts would make peaceful civil resistance a costly strategy to pursue. On May 16 Judge McGlothin fined the UMW more than $600,000 for violating his order banning mass picketing. He also threatened to add $200,000 for each day union members violated his order and $100,000 for every rock-throwing incident or other act of violence. Trumka knew what to do. The UMW might lose its treasury but it would not lose this strike by caving in to court orders.[31]

In the Massey strike the union responded to court orders by limiting mass picketing and ending civil disobedience, but it would not make that mistake now. It would mobilize all strikers, their families, and their supporters to circumvent or to directly challenge court orders. The picket lines at Moss 3 and other Pittston operations remained jammed with strikers and their families. The union's tactics allowed thousands of people to "discover the democratic potential in their own power to say 'No' to corporate power,'' Richard Couto observed. The actions of April and May involved people who had never been activists but were now "mesmerized by their newly discovered power to stand up for what they thought was right.''[32]

The strikers created a new sense of community in their region. An exciting "culture of solidarity'' emerged in defense of traditional rights and standards. The strikers spoke of these things in plain language with the moral clarity of evangelical Protestantism. Initially, they drew upon their "deep bonds'' as coal-mining families with common stories and tragedies, and with shared religious traditions and moral values. In these ways, Marat Moore recalled, "people were harmonically tied with one another.'' You could feel it, she said, when people would spontaneously sing "Amazing Grace'' when someone was being arrested. But there was also something new in how people expressed this "spiritual commonality.'' The union borrowed an idea from the civil rights movement and organized weekly evening rallies on a ball field in St. Paul. Like civil rights activists inspired by black preachers, these strike activists expressed their religious values on the new terrain dictated by social struggle and civil resistance. In defending a way of life the UMW had earlier created, the strikers crossed the boundaries between work and community, established novel associations and allies, experimented with alternative roles and relationships, and clarified the meaning of values like solidarity.[33]

30. *Betraying the Trust.*
31. Yancey, ''Thunder in the Coal Fields,'' 7.
32. Couto, ''The Memory of the Miners,'' 179, 180.
33. Yancey, ''Thunder in the Coal Fields,'' 8–9. Author's interview with Marat Moore, Washington, D.C., December 15, 1993. For a discussion of this process in other strikes, see Rick Fantasia, *Cultures of Solidarity: Consciousness, Action and Contemporary American Workers* (Berkeley and Los Angeles: University of California Press, 1988), 218–19, 230–31, 236–37.

The strikers also created their own heroes and found their own leaders in Marty Hudson and Jackie Stump, two men who spoke in the idiom of mountain evangelicals using the words of Martin Luther King. Their leadership would soon face its toughest test. On May 24 Federal Judge Glen Williams issued an order to the strikers at the request of the Republican-dominated National Labor Relations Board: stop blocking Pittston gates, and end the new tactic of impeding coalfield roads with slow-moving vehicles. When the union ignored the order, Williams was incensed. A Republican schooled in the hard-edged politics of southwestern Virginia, the judge called Hudson, Stump, and strike coordinator C. A. Phillips into court to face contempt charges on June 5. When they refused to order their members to end civil disobedience and invoked their Fifth Amendment rights to avoid self-incrimination, Williams sent them off to jail in handcuffs and leg-irons. The *Roanoke Times* report suggested later that the fines and jailings had hurt Pittston's cause because the court had created martyrs and turned the strike into a conflict "like no other in the Virginia coal fields."[34]

EXPANDING THE STRIKE

It would soon become one of the most unusual strikes in recent U.S. history. Ever since the air traffic controllers' strike of 1981, labor people had bemoaned a lack of union solidarity that helped employers isolate and defeat unions. Trumka shared this bitter memory, and reflected on it often during the strike. "If we play by their rules," he would say, "we lose." On June 11 he spoke to a militant rally of fifteen thousand UMW members in Charleston, West Virginia, and called on them to "rise up and fight back."[35]

The next day ten thousand union miners in West Virginia started a wildcat strike to protest the jailing of the Pittston strike leaders and to show sympathy with the strikers. Mingo and Logan counties, the battlefield in the 1921 civil war, reported 98% of the miners on strike. David Evans of Logan County said the workers walked out to protest "the excessive fines and the jailings of three union officers down in Virginia. They're going to shut down all the union and non-union mines by the end of next week . . . , whatever it takes to get this settled." Before the week ended the wildcat had spread to six more states involving another twenty thousand miners.[36]

The union now risked even more astronomical court fines; it also jeopardized relations with BCOA members, who had just negotiated a new contract. When questioned, Trumka said he had met his legal duty by asking the thousands of miners to return to work. He said the rank and filers simply refused. "They believe their

34. Yancey, "Thunder in the Coal Fields," 8.
35. "Wildcat Strikes Break Out in West Virginia," *Bristol Herald Courier* (June 13, 1989).
36. "Miners Defiant," *USA Today* (June 14, 1989); and "Wildcat Coal Strike Continues Despite Order," *New York Times* (June 15, 1989).

union is threatened and they walked off their jobs because of that," he said. "They genuinely believe the rules are written for them to lose every time."[37]

It was not clear at this point that the UMWA would win its battle with Pittston, but "It had taken a local strike in Southwest Virginia and stirred up a national ruckus." Important media began to cover the story. The prime-time television program *48 Hours* aired a segment on the dispute, and one of the strike's most eloquent philosophers, a preacher and retired miner named Harry Whitaker, appeared on the *Donahue* show.[38] At first, civil disobedience seemed necessary to ensure a nonviolent strike, but it soon became apparent that such tactics also attracted the media. At an early training for strike organizers, peace activists "suggested the union cultivate local heroes, who could personalize the strike for the public so it wouldn't be just another anonymous dispute between the company and the union." The media, struck by the romance of mountain life, readily focused on the spectacle of lawabiding rural folk sitting down in front of gigantic coal trucks and kneeling down on a roadside with troopers holding shotguns to their heads.[39]

Some reporters exaggerated strike violence and blamed it on the union, but many media people reported favorably on the strikers' commitment to nonviolence.[40] However, the positive media coverage and public support the UMW won through civil disobedience could have ended with just a few rounds of gunfire. The union prohibited alcohol, firearms, and strangers in picket shacks, and it put a picket captain on duty twenty-four hours a day. Top leadership was crucial. One reporter wrote that miners on "the picket line say their new style of conducting a strike has percolated down from the union president Richard Trumka who has brought them a sense of dignity and pride not felt since the glory days of union founder John L. Lewis."[41]

The union's strike strategy seemed to be winning favorable media attention and public support, but tension and anxiety still gripped the strikers and their leaders. Eddie Burke, coordinator of the Massey strike who had come over from West Virginia to help, worried that history would repeat itself. The month began with Pittston breaking off negotiations, strike leaders jailed, the coalfields occupied by state police and another Massey strike on people's minds. But "it ended with the entire labor movement rallying behind the UMW" and Pittston hurting.[42] The wildcat strikes had even begun to affect those operators who supplied Pittston's overseas

37. Martha Hodel, "Wildcat Walkout: Trumka Not Doing Enough to Get Miners Back, Companies Say," *Sunday Gazette Mail* (July 9, 1989).

38. Yancey, "Thunder in the Coal Fields," 8.

39. Ibid., 2–3.

40. For reports unfavorable to the strikers see James Buchan, "A Marriage of Coal and Violence," *Financial Times of London* (July 10, 1989), Wayne Barber, "Explosion Rocks Pittston Building," *Bristol Herald Courier/Virginia-Tennessean* (July 6, 1989); and the discussion in William J. Puette, *Through Jaundiced Eyes: How the Media View Organized Labor* (Ithaca: ILR Press, 1992), 117–39.

41. Jules Loh, "UMW Now Negotiates from a Position of Civility," *Allegheny Journal* (July 23, 1989).

42. Yancey, "Thunder in the Coal Fields," 9.

customers with metallurgical coal.[43] A Wall Street investment firm's report expressed surprise that the UMW, thought to be weakened over the 1980s, had fought Pittston to a standstill for two months. "After more than 2,200 arrests and $3 million in fines for civil disobedience, the UMW's perseverance is starting to pay off where it counts most—in the financial community which could pressure Pittston to compromise."[44]

As the sympathy strikes postponed shipments to foreign customers and threatened the industry's export market, Federal Judge Williams got the two sides back to the table. For the first time since the UMW and Pittston began negotiations in 1987 the top people from both sides attended the talks. They refused to sit at the same table, however, and a federal mediator took messages between labor and management teams sitting in separate rooms.[45]

BUILDING A MOVEMENT

As wildcat strikes rolled across the midwestern coalfields, the imprisoned strike leaders Hudson, Stump, and Phillips were released. However, they had to promise the judge not to advocate illegal strike tactics, and so they could no longer take the lead in directing the civil resistance movement. A crisis of leadership loomed, because no one in Virginia enjoyed their moral authority with the miners. But there was someone in Washington who did. In modern labor history few top national officers had ever taken leadership of a strike on the ground. But on this occasion Vice President Cecil Roberts boldly assumed command. No one could have been better suited to do so. Born in Cabin Creek, West Virginia, Roberts had been one of the young militants in the turbulent 1970s when conflict raged through those mine fields. His father had been a coal miner who remembered seeing airplanes drop bombs on the miners' army as it marched to free Mingo Country from the gun thugs in 1921. His great uncle was Bill Blizzard, the UMW commander who led that historic march. Cecil grew up hearing stories about Mother Jones sitting on his family's front porch and about Baldwin-Felts guards shooting up strikers' tent colonies. He was a crack negotiator who knew the industry inside and out and he was an old-fashioned radical orator—one of the few national labor leaders who still used

43. Richard Trumka, speech at Harvard Trade Union Program, March 4, 1990, and Ken Zinn, "International Labor Solidarity and the Pittston Strike," presentation at International Confederation of Free Trade Unions Conference, Elsinore, Denmark, March 26, 1990. Manuscript in author's possession.

44. *Roanoke Times* (June 7, 1989); and Richard Phalon, "Mis-Calculated Risk?" *Forbes* 142 (June 12, 1989).

45. Yancey, "Thunder in the Coal Fields," 9; and "Producers Fear Lengthy Strike, Loss of Sales," *Journal of Commerce* (June 7, 1989).

the words "working class" and "class war." It was a class war that he came down to fight that June.[46]

Roberts arrived in the nick of time. "The strikers weren't losing their resolve but some were starting to lose their patience," said a local attorney. The UMW vice president took on the difficult task of escalating militancy while keeping the strike activity nonviolent. He constantly told the strikers they were part of something much bigger than a strike against Pittston and a fight with scabs. Like Trumka, he made the whole legal system an issue. In one speech, on June 17 in Norton, Virginia, Roberts declared: "It's the system that's really at issue here as much as the contract. The country desperately needs labor law reform that will at least level the playing field."[47]

Roberts boldly defended direct action tactics as wildcat strikers poured into the area from the other coalfields; they escalated the "rolling road blocks," which cut the haul to Pittston Moss 3 coal treatment plant by one-third. Speaking to a crowd of three thousand including many wildcatting midwestern miners, Roberts stood in the bed of a flatbed truck and looked out over a muddy field at the men and women in fatigues. "It's not just a strike any more, it's a movement," he said. "Everybody has been wanting to rally around something for years and this is it."[48]

At a big Fourth of July rally in St. Paul, the UMW introduced the last union leader to arouse the labor movement and the national conscience. Joining the hundreds who now came to be arrested on the region's back roads, United Farm Workers President Cesar Chavez declared that with nonviolence social struggles took on a transcendent, spiritual dimension. "Your commitment to nonviolence and the use of passive resistance has captured the attention of organized labor," he declared. "People are attracted to nonviolence. They want to come and help you. If the judge likes to put people in jail, let him. He can't put the whole world in jail."[49]

Judge Williams had already fined Roberts $200,000 for refusing to take responsibility for the road-blocking effort. On July 5, he added another $800,000 to the union's fines which, it now seemed, would bankrupt the UMWA. The judge blamed Roberts and UMW leaders for threatening the legal system and creating a situation "bordering on anarchy." On his orders federal marshals were dispatched to aid state police in enforcing court injunctions. Roberts said the courts were threatening to fine the union out of existence because members refused to give up their jobs to other men. But still the resistance grew. The *Richmond Times-Dispatch* reported

46. Author's interviews with Cecil Roberts, April 22, 1990, on the road from Norton, Virginia, to Welch, West Virginia, and December 15, 1993, Washington, D.C.

47. Yancey, "Thunder in the Coal Fields," 9; and Wayne Barber, "UMW Official Calls for Law that at Least Levels Playing Field," *Bristol Herald Courier* (June 18, 1989).

48. David Reed, "UMW: Pittston Strike is More than Labor Dispute," (AP) *Williamson Daily* (June 29, 1989), and Yancey, "Thunder in the Coal Fields," 4.

49. Martha J. Hall, "NLRB Ruling May Protect Union Jobs," *Kingsport Times-News* (July 5, 1989); and Deborah Rouse, "Striking UMWA Miners Hear Encouraging Words from Cesar Chavez of United Mine Workers," *Coalfield Progress* (July 6, 1989).

that UMW strike supporters who said they were "tourists" were clogging the region's coal-hauling roads with their cars, "defying federal court orders against the practice and subjecting the union to $500,000 in daily penalties."[50]

By now the union's stakes in the Pittston strike were enormous. Federal court fines against the UMW had reached $960,000 which, when combined with state court fines, equaled a total of $4 million. Still, the union's leaders did not waver. As Trumka later said, "we did what we thought we had to do to win the strike." On July 9 he spoke in Charleston and said he was willing to go to jail. "They've done everything they can to me except take away my personal freedom." "It's win this fight or be stampeded to death in the very near future." If the fight bankrupted the union, then so be it, Trumka declared. "If we aren't successful," he added, "if justice and legal redress are totally denied here, I submit to you that from the crumbled blocks will arise a movement" as it had in the past when the UMW faced hard times with no money.[51]

At this point, 2,265 felony charges had been filed against strikers and their supporters, many of them out-of-state sympathy strikers. The arrest of law-abiding citizens for blocking traffic aroused special concern. Some had to post $10,000 bonds for minor violations and others were forced to sit in hot buses for long periods of time. The most sensational case came on July 12 when police arrested Sister Bernadette Kenney for impeding traffic. She was a nurse driving a mobile unit for dispensing medication. Sister Kenney's arrest received national publicity and aroused even greater support for the strike among religious people.[52]

Kenney's story also added weight to the union's charge that Governor Baliles had sent one-fourth of the state police to "occupy southwestern Virginia." One of the most photographed picket signs, nailed to a shack outside Moss 3, read: "Governor Baliles! This is Southwest Virginia not South Africa!" The governor had won the region's traditionally Democratic vote with the support of the UMWA, but, according to one report, "Sentiments have run so high against Baliles in the coal fields that the governor has cancelled at least one visit" and had made no plans to tour the strike zone. A frustrated Baliles wrote to Pittston's Douglas expressing disappointment about his failure to bargain and asking him to return to the table because the strike was hurting the growing foreign market for Virginia coal.[53]

50. Jonathan Gill, "Union Leaders Stress Merits of Non-Violence," *Williamson Daily* (June 30, 1989); "U.M.W. Fines Again in Virginia Coal Fight," *New York Times* (July 6, 1989); Bill McKelway, "Defiant Miners Clog Roads," *Richmond Times-Dispatch* (July 7, 1989), and "Extra Police Sent to Coalfields as Acts Spread to West Virginia," *Richmond Times-Dispatch* (July 14, 1989).

51. Mike Wright, "49 Strike Related Cases Dismissed by Greenwalt," *Dickenson Star* (July 13, 1989); and "Union Set for Memorial Period, President 'Willing' to Go to Jail," *Bristol Herald Courier/ Virginia-Tennessean* (July 10, 1989); and Harry E. Stapleton, "It Was Old Men That Made This Union," *New York Times* (July 9, 1989).

52. "U.S. Marshals Halt Strikers' Convoys," *Bluefield Daily Telegraph* (July 7, 1989); and Jeff Moore, "Nun Arrested; Community Angered," *Coalfield Progress* (July 13, 1989).

53. "Baliles' Appearance Postponed," *Bristol Herald Courier* (July 7, 1989); and Jeff Moore, "Export Clients told Shipments Can't be Filled," *Coalfield Progress* (July 11, 1989). Also see "Baliles Calls for New Bargaining," *Bristol Herald Courier/Virginia-Tennessean* (July 11, 1989).

"The nation's worst coal strike since the mid-1970s arrives at a crossroads," a July 10 article in *Journal of Commerce* observed. "The great majority of the coal hauling" had reportedly ceased in West Virginia where one company laid off ten drivers who refused to cross picket lines. At this point, the Pittston strike had become even more than a survival struggle for the UMWA. Sympathy strikes and massive civil resistance helped accomplish what Roberts and Trumka had hoped: turning a local strike into a national cause for the labor movement. After extending the national walkout several days, Trumka called the wildcat strikers back to work. He then joined Senator Jay Rockefeller in a New York meeting with Japanese steel officials to assure them that the West Virginia coal supply was not in jeopardy. Trumka appealed to their respect for the elderly. "We're fighting for the health care of our parents and grandparents," he told them. "Would you have me turn my back on them?" He thought that this particular appeal touched the Japanese and that they in turn put some pressure on Pittston to settle the strike.[54]

Later that month Trumka issued a "national call of conscience" inviting the entire labor movement to come to support the strikers in Southwest Virginia. The response was surprising. All through July, reported the *Washington Post,* "Miners and their supporters from around the country continue[d] to pour into Camp Solidarity, the strike's makeshift headquarters in a lush meadow outside Castlewood, Virginia." Many activists traveled to the war zone to witness what one local journalist called the "Appalachian Intifada." They went to be arrested for the cause, to bear witness for justice and against corporate greed. Besides the attractiveness of the strikers' civil resistance campaign, other unionists plunged in because, Trumka suggested, the UMWA was still a symbol of militancy and solidarity—still seen as the group most willing to take on the toughest fights, the first group to be targeted by anyone "who wanted to kill the labor movement." Thousands of supporters came to believe that if the miners lost at Pittston, the labor movement might lose its vanguard.[55]

To accommodate the wildcat strikers motoring into the region, the union opened Camp Solidarity on a ten-acre parcel of land near the Clinch River. While the wildcat strikers rolled into the camp with convoys hundreds of cars long, other unions began sending delegations from all over the country. The strikers, emotionally drained from their confrontations with scabs and police, at first seemed overwhelmed by the flood of visitors who needed a place to eat and sleep. But then

---

54. "Coal Miners Strike Reaches Critical Point," *Journal of Commerce* (July 10, 1989); and Trumka interview, January 19, 1994.

55. "Miners' Union Cooling-Off Period Starts With Gunfire and Explosion," *New York Times* (July 11, 1989); David Reed, "UMW: Pittston Strike Is More than Labor Dispute," *Williamson Daily* (June 29, 1989); Dana Priest, "Striking Coal Miners Fear End Of Union, Way of Life in Va.," *Washington Post* (July 6, 1989); and Moberg, "Envisioning a New Day for the Labor Movement"; Trumka interview, January 19, 1994. Also see Denise Giardina, "Coal Field Violence: Myths and Realities," *Christianity & Crisis* (August 14, 1989), and "Strike Zone: The 'Appalachian Intifada' Rages On," *Village Voice* (August 29, 1989), 31–36.

seeing "people from all over the country with different accents and different licence plates, gave the miners and their families renewed determination."[56]

The women of the strike rose to the challenge and spent every day at the camp cooking for the pilgrims. "They spent their own money to come here and help us," organizer Cosby Totten recalled. "Could we let them down?" The women had already been mobilized by the auxiliaries and the Daughters of Mother Jones to feed and care for the local strikers at the Binns-Counts Community Center. The Daughters started "as a traditional UMW women's auxiliary and 'just caught on fire.' " For months they had prepared for the strike as a struggle for community survival. Linda Adair, a hairdresser in St. Paul who gave up her business and devoted all her time to the strike, explained that the Daughters wanted to avoid slipping back into the "powerlessness" that "ruined the lives" of their grandparents—into what she called "the days of slavery." The group included a core of fifty women willing to be arrested and at least two hundred more who acted as supporters. Like the Ladies' Auxiliary in the Flint sit-down strike of 1937, which transformed itself into an emergency brigade, the Daughters wanted to take direct action in the strike.[57]

They did take direct action and in the process they "helped transform the strike into a movement of wider dimensions." Despite all they seemed to have in common, most did not know each other because they lived in isolated rural areas. The Daughters of Mother Jones brought them together literally and symbolically. Being arrested gave some a common experience and "had become pretty much a badge of honor among people." Wearing camouflage gave them all a uniform, "a fashion of discontent" in Marat Moore's words. As more women became more involved in the strike "camouflage underwent a sex change" as the colors worn by hunters and soldiers appeared on cakes, quilts, afghans, umbrellas, bathing suits, and baby clothes. The women made one thing clear, Moore wrote: "In the coal fields camouflage would never again be simply military, or simply male."[58]

56. Yancey, "Thunder in the Coal Fields," 9; Jenny Burman, "The Daughters of Mother Jones," *Z Magazine* (November 1989); Fred Brown, "Striking Miners Gather to Relax at Camp Solidarity," *Knoxville News-Sentinel* (July 22, 1989); and Gene Caroll, "Camp Solidarity: The Heart of the Pittston Strike," *UMWJ* 100, no. 10 (November 1989): 15.

57. Quotes from Moore, "Ten Days"; Burman, "Daughters of Mother Jones"; and Yancey, "Thunder in the Coal Fields," 9.

58. Quotes from Moore, "Ten Months that Shook the Coal Fields." Women's role in the Pittston strike remains to be studied in more detail. It seemed as though the Daughters might emerge as a kind of autonomous organization that would not only break down female isolation but create a real public role for women in the strike beyond the supportive role women's auxiliaries had played in the past. This happened earlier in the 1980s for women in the British coal miners' strike and in the Arizona copper strike. See Jill Evans, Clare Hudson, and Penny Smith, "Women and the Strike: It's a Whole Way of Life," in *Policing the Miners' Strike,* ed. Bob Fine and Robert Miller (London: Lawrence and Wishart, 1985), 18:203 and Barbara Kingsolver, *Holding the Line: Women in the Great Arizona Mine Strike of 1983* (Ithaca: ILR Press, 1989). The Daughters certainly overcame their isolation during the strike, emerged as highly public activists, and experienced empowerment, but they did not act on their own advice or command their "own ship" like the highly effective Morenci Miners Women's Auxiliary did during the 1983 Phelps-Dodge strike; see 140.

"The Daughters have made this [strike] a people's movement," said Linda Adair. They did this in part by making Camp Solidarity "the heart of the strike," and before it was over, a point of contact for the strikers and thousands of supporters who visited during the summer. "This strike could really be depressing, but our people have been brought together like never before because of the spirit that comes from what goes on in the camp," said Peggy Dutton, the spouse of a striking miner. "It's a place where we demonstrate how much we care about one another—not just the families on strike at Pittston but all working people." In this free space the union staked out in Carterton Hollow strikers created a culture of solidarity that touched supporters who came from far and wide to bear witness and offer help. Camp Solidarity gave them all something to remember, a taste of movement experience to carry back home. "On summer evenings, as the heat soaked into the hills, the smell of burning charcoal and the twang of banjos drifted across the wild field," wrote reporter Dwayne Yancey. "Kids chased a stray dog named Jackrock. A garbage-bag effigy of Judge Williams swung from a branch. An Alabama coal miner brought his bride on their honeymoon." "It was like a hillbilly Woodstock," Eddie Burke remembered. By midsummer forty thousand people had already visited the camp. Not even the mass strikes of the early 1930s had attracted this many allies to participate directly in strike support.[59]

POLITICIZING THE STRIKE

Although the Pittston strike took place in an isolated part of Appalachia, its leaders not only insisted on its national significance; they placed it in an international context as well. They compared the striking miners to those striking for democracy in South Africa, Poland, and the USSR. They even compared their struggle with the pro-democracy movement in China, which generated intense interest and concern after the Army massacred protesters on Beijing's Tiananmen Square early in June. By bringing international attention to the violations of labor law and the anti-union use of court injunctions arising from the strike, the union hoped to embarrass the Bush administration, which claimed to support the Chinese students, the striking Soviet coal miners, and the Polish Solidarity movement, but opposed trade unions back at home. The passionate protest Pittston strikers made against their oppression by the U.S. legal system helped make the Bush administration vulnerable to the charges of hypocrisy in its defense of democracy abroad. It was deeply ironic, Trumka often said, that our officials protested the treatment of workers in the USSR but ignored workers' rights violations in the United States. Only two industrialized

---

59. Quotes from Burman, "Daughters of Mother Jones"; Brown, "Striking Miners Gather"; and Yancey, "Thunder in the Coal Fields," 9. See also James Green, "Camp Solidarity: The United Mine Workers, The Pittston Strike, and the New People's Movement," in *Building Bridges,* ed. Brecher and Costello, 15–24.

countries allowed employers to replace workers when they struck, South Africa and the United States. "To tell a worker you have the right to strike and then replace him in the next breath is a cruel hoax," he charged.[60]

Trumka believed that U.S. unions had failed to use international labor organizations effectively. He asked staff lawyers to file charges with the International Labor Organization against the U.S. government for failing to stop labor law violations during the strike. The UMWA had already been more involved in international solidarity work than most unions, especially in South Africa, where black workers supported its Shell boycott in the mid-eighties. Trumka wanted to build on this work. In July he addressed an international conference to "tell the miners' story" and promote "global labor solidarity." Heads of unions all over the world pledged their help. The Australian miners' union persuaded employers not to supply excess metallurgical coal to Japanese steelmakers hurt by the strike. The International Confederation of Free Trade Unions pledged its support. The International Metal Workers Federation urged its affiliates to demand support for a settlement from those of their employers who were Pittston customers. The steel company Italsider telexed Paul Douglas on June 20 from Italy threatening legal action if Pittston's intransigence continued to reduce its coal supply.[61]

For three months pressuring the state and national political systems had seemed totally ineffective. Then, on July 11, the NLRB found Pittston guilty of unfair labor practices. The company had violated federal labor law twenty-eight times and was "failing and refusing to bargain in good faith." The board's ruling made the walkout an "unfair labor practices strike" and thus prohibited Pittston from offering permanent jobs to replacement workers.[62] This decision eliminated a key element of Pittston's strike-breaking strategy and gave the union an important legal victory.

A day later Congressman William Clay (D-Mo.), chair of the House subcommittee overseeing labor law, announced an investigation of the dispute, stating that "the Pittston strike and the sympathy strikes by thousands of other UMW workers have raised concerns about the administration of labor laws, the involvement of Virginia

60. Greg Edwards, "UMW Chief Faults Labor Law," *Roanoke Times & World News* (July 9, 1989). Author's interview with Ken Zinn, December 15, 1993. Local miners wrote many letters to local papers and gave many interviews to local media putting their struggle in an international context. See, for example, letter to editor likening the strike to protests of Beijing students for democracy, *Coalfield Progress* (July 6, 1989). These points also appeared in media outside the state. The Charleston, West Virginia, paper quoted an editorial by radical journalist Alexander Cockburn comparing the favorable press coverage of the Soviet miners' strike with the union slurs in the Pittston media coverage. Alexander Cockburn, "Their Miners and Ours," *The Nation* (August 21, 1989), quoted in "Wrong Strike Site," *Charleston Gazette* (August 12, 1989).

61. Zinn, "International Labor Solidarity and the Pittston Strike"; and John F. Harris, "Trade Unions Pledge Support to Striking Miners," *Washington Post* (July 9, 1989); and "World Wide Support for Miners," *Free Labour World*, no. 13 (August 31, 1989); and "Foreign Miners Chief Supports UMW," *Washington Times* (August 23, 1989).

62. "Labor Ruling Finds Coal Company Guilty in Strike," *New York Times* (July 12, 1989). Also see, Phil Primack, "UMW Chief to Drum up Hub Support," *Boston Herald* (July 12, 1989).

state and federal courts in the conflict and the increasing threat to the national economy.''[63]

In early August, a report for Clay's subcommittee criticized the federal government's inaction in prosecuting Pittston for violating labor law. While it could be years before a court ordered the company to correct unfair labor practices, the report said, ''the striking miner has seen union leaders jailed and is confronted each day with a massive display of state police and company security forces who are present for the express purpose of assuring that the company can continue to operate.'' So the strikers and their families ''are understandably perplexed and frustrated by this apparent discrepancy in how the legal system is working.''[64]

While the union gained in making labor law reform and court bias a national issue, its leaders also worked to increase national concern over the matter of miners' health care. Pittston had followed other major employers in demanding reduced health care costs. When it cut off health benefits to retirees the company unwittingly provoked the most publicized of many health-care related strikes. It also gave the union an opportunity to take the moral high ground, and its leaders pressed the advantage in Washington. Senator Jay Rockefeller introduced a bill that would force Pittston to contribute to industrywide health funds. Later in the summer a *New York Times* article on the strike featured health care as an emerging national crisis, especially in labor relations.[65]

Whatever the long-term hopes the strike inspired, the short-term costs reached intimidating levels. Pittston's lawyers presented Judge McGlothin with new evidence that strikers were violating his orders and on July 27 he fined the union another $4.5 million—one hundred times what Pittston had been fined after the 1983 explosion that killed seven miners at McClure. In early August the UMW announced it was spending $4 million each month on strike support (while taking in about $500,000 per month from miners not on strike).[66]

In response to a request by Federal Judge Glen Williams, strike talks resumed on August 6, but again the two sides met in separate rooms. The union offered a new proposal to discuss more flexible hours but the company stood on its last offer. Chief union negotiator Roberts emerged ''disappointed and disillusioned.'' *Coal Outlook* worried about the possibility of a national strike.[67]

63. Bill McKelway, ''Pittston Mum on Plea for New Talks,'' *Richmond Times-Dispatch* (July 12, 1989); ''Report on the Strike at the Pittston Coal Company,'' prepared by the Majority Staff Subcommittee on Labor-Management Relations, August 31, 1989, 22.

64. Martha J. Hall, ''Report Questions Aspects of Strike,'' *Kingsport Times-News* (August 5, 1989).

65. Michael Freitag, ''The Battle Over Medical Costs,'' *New York Times* (August 17, 1989). Also see ''Health Care, Pensions Key Issues in Strike Against Pittston Group,'' *Washington Post* (July 6, 1989).

66. Wayne Barber, ''More than $4 Million in UMW Fines Imposed,'' *Bristol Herald Courier-Bristol Virginia/Tennessean* (July 28, 1989).

67. ''UMW official pleads innocent in Virginia,'' *Charleston Gazette* (August 4, 1989); ''Efficiency Panel Proposed by UMW,'' *Richmond Times-Dispatch* (August 9, 1989); ''UMW Makes New Proposal to Pittston in Coal Strike,'' *Washington Post* (August 9, 1989); and ''UMW Officials 'Is a National Strike in the Offing?' '' *Coal Outlook* (August 7, 1989).

The union's resistance took on a more defiant tone. In August Cecil Roberts made news all over the coalfields when he directly challenged court authority and dared Judge Williams to jail him for contempt. As he came to appear before the federal judge on August 21, Roberts gave a rousing speech before six hundred people at the courthouse. "I don't fear going to jail because when you're right, going to jail is okay. Regardless of what happens today, you keep your heads up, keep your hearts beating like they've been beating and stay on fire for this cause because this is a class struggle between the working class and the very rich."[68]

Roberts's confident words and bold actions heightened a mood of militant engagement but discouraged violent acts of revenge. During the weeks he had been in command Roberts showed an unabashed affection for the people on strike. He seemed as moved by their courage as they were by his eloquence. "I've never felt this way about any group of people in my entire life," he declared before facing the court. "I think you are the finest group of people in the entire world. The solidarity movement in Poland has nothing on you people here today." The affection and admiration was returned. Strikers told the media that if the courts put Cecil Roberts in jail, there would be hell to pay. Judge Williams shrank before Roberts's challenge and dismissed the contempt charges against him.[69]

The continuing defiance of state and federal courts politicized the strike in one way; the all-out attack on Governor Baliles did in another way. Citizen anger grew because the state police had arrested so many people, including many nonstrikers. One merchant erected a sign: "We respectfully refuse to serve troopers during the course of the strike." According to a federal report, hundreds of state police, along with the federal marshals, had created "a sense that the coal fields" were "occupied by a massive security force from outside the . . . region."[70]

Trumka blasted Baliles on many occasions, and he questioned the Democratic Party's commitment to working people. In an article headlined "Miners' Discontent gets Political," the *Washington Post* reported: "Sentiments against Baliles have run so high in the coalfields that the governor has cancelled at least one appearance in the region and has not visited the region at all since the strike began." The Dickenson County Sheriff even criticized the governor's use of state troopers and complained about "unofficial martial law."[71]

68. "UMW Vice President Arrested," *Kingsport Times-News* (July 26, 1989); "Mine Workers Officers, Others Are Arrested," *Wall Street Journal* (July 26, 1989); Yancey, "Thunder in the Coal Fields," 9; Tim Sansbury, "Pittston Coal, Miners' Union To Resume Talks Today," *Journal of Commerce* (August 1, 1989); and "UMW Vice President Dares Federal Judge to Jail Him," *Charleston Gazette* (August 9, 1989).

69. "Labor in America, 'We Won't Go Back': The UMWA/Pittston Strike, 1989–90," *Dickenson Star* (Clinchco, Va.), 1990, 69, 98.

70. Ibid., 69; House Subcommittee Report on the Strike at Pittston, 17; and Mike Wright, "Trumka's 'Call To Conscience' Answered."

71. "The Strike at Pittston," *Trade Union Advisor* 2, no. 15 (July 25, 1989); Ken Jenkins Jr., "Coal Miners' Discontent Gets Political," *Washington Post* (August 6, 1989); and "Sheriff Blasts Coalfield Troopers," *Roanoke Times and World News* (September 24, 1989).

Governor Baliles's role in the strike fueled labor's discontent with conservative Democrats. Although the union endorsed the Democratic ticket in 1988, many had supported Jesse Jackson and others favored a labor party. When the fall political campaigns began in Virginia, strikers wanted to take political action. Don McGlothin Sr., the incumbent Democratic representative from Buchanan County to the Virginia House of Delegates, stood unopposed for re-election. A conservative who had held that seat for over two decades, McGlothin was a power in the House, but he was the father of the judge who had fined the union $31 million during the strike. Trumka wanted a union candidate to run against the elder McGlothin. Strike leader Jackie Stump reluctantly agreed, announcing his candidacy on September 18 at the John L. Lewis Building in Oakwood. No one thought Stump had a chance of upsetting a powerful incumbent like McGlothin with a last minute write-in campaign, but the strike and the civil resistance movement had shaken up the status quo in southwest Virginia, and within a few weeks people were talking about a UMW leader going from the jailhouse to the state house.[72]

"STIRRING UP THE LABOR MOVEMENT"

The union exerted surprising power against Pittston in the coalfields, but it could not win the strike on the picket line, at the ballot box, or in the courts. The company seemed willing to lose millions of dollars to break the union. To crack Pittston, the union had to hit its directors and investors with a corporate campaign more effective than those conducted by other striking unions in the eighties.[73]

When the strike began the union launched an intense campaign against the company where its executives lived—in Greenwich, Connecticut, and in other cities where its board of directors resided.[74] The union hired Pat Speer to run its campaign in Greenwich. A devout Catholic and community organizer involved with the Campaign for Human Development in Appalachia, Speer roused the religious community in Connecticut against Pittston. In late June twelve local clergy sent a letter to CEO Douglas protesting the company's efforts to blame strike violence on the union; the twelve boldly suggesting that he was "like the Pharaoh" who had enslaved people, and wondered why a pestilence stalked his land. The company dismissed the letter as "absolutely ridiculous." It was harder to dismiss another letter, signed by eighty-six area clergy, calling for a fair contract and condemning Pitts-

72. Yancey, "Thunder in the Coal Fields," 4, 17–20.

73. Zinn, "International Labor Solidarity and the Pittston Strike."

74. Two months before the strike started in April the union targeted the Crestar, a major Pittston lender. The campaign cost Crestar money, according to the union staffer who directed the campaign, and put the bank in frequent communication with Pittston about the strike's negative effects. "Mine workers vs. Manny Hanny," *ABA Banking Journal* (August 1989); author's interview with Ken Zinn, December 15, 1993.

ton's decision to cut off health benefits because it was "not the will of God . . . that . . . persons should be used this way."[75]

The strikers and their supporters haunted the Pittston executives in Greenwich. "When they went to church, some heard sermons from their priests and ministers against their company," wrote one reporter. "When they commuted to and from work, they ran into strikers passing out leaflets." The minister of the Methodist Church in Greenwich thought the moral campaign "jarred the Pittston Company people who just kind of assumed this would be a safe haven from the strike. There was just no escape. They just couldn't get away from it."[76]

The union also pressured the board of directors in cities across the nation dispatching striking miners and their families to work with local supporters. Along with investors and lenders these directors were principal targets of the corporate campaign headed by UMW staffer Ken Zinn. He came to Boston in April to begin an effort against board member William Craig, a vice president of Shawmut Bank. Craig was a good target because his bank had extensive dealings with the public, including unions and city governments. A strike support committee formed to carry on the campaign. The feuding labor factions in Massachusetts buried their hatchets, not deeply but long enough to unify behind the strikers.[77]

On July 12 Trumka came to Boston for a spirited rally at the Shawmut's downtown bank and testified before the Boston City Council urging that municipal funds be withdrawn from the bank unless Craig agreed to work for a settlement. On July 26 the City Council passed a resolution to remove $20 million from Shawmut Bank because of Craig's links to Pittston and his refusal to work for a fair strike settlement. The resolution passed unanimously and made headlines. Boston Mayor Ray Flynn did not act on the resolution immediately, but he was sympathetic to the strikers, so much so that he visited the coalfields and made a controversial statement comparing the use of state police in Virginia to their use against Solidarity in Poland. Encouraged by these developments, the Boston support committee put added pressure on Craig by picketing his home and encouraging the cities of Somerville and Cambridge, along with several unions, to withdraw their funds from the Shawmut Bank. Within a few weeks $280 million had been withdrawn and the political phase of the corporate campaign began to take its toll on one of Pittston's directors. Meanwhile, protest mounted against Shawmut's subsidiary in Connecticut when several unions announced major withdrawals to protest Craig's connection with that bank. The union also targeted the firms of other board members and some parent

75. Charles Isenhart, "A Coal Strike Comes to Affluent Greenwich, Conn.," *National Catholic Register* (August 1989); and Yancey, "Thunder in the Coal Fields," 10; and "A Letter to Paul Douglas, Chairman the Pittston Company," by Religious Leaders of Fairfield County, leaflet in author's possession.

76. Yancey, "Thunder in the Coal Fields," 10.

77. Paul Cannon, "Miners Reach Out for Our Help," *New England Labor News & Commentary* (July–August 1989); and Green, "Camp Solidarity."

companies reportedly complained that Pittston's hard-nosed tactics were hurting them and "stirring up the labor movement."[78]

The Pittston strike had stirred up a labor movement deeply frustrated and angered by the series of defeats that began when President Reagan broke the PATCO strike in 1981. The UMW's willingness to risk everything in a final confrontation aroused deep sympathy in union ranks. Trumka received boisterous responses wherever he spoke, often in tandem with Jesse Jackson. He called upon "people across the country to visit southwest Virginia and see 'a system that doesn't have room for workers in it.' " National AFL-CIO leaders took note of the groundswell of support for Pittston strikers and for the use of civil disobedience. They also recognized that their affiliates and major media organs like the *Washington Post* had come to see the Pittston strike as a last stand for the UMWA and even for the labor movement itself. On August 30, just before Labor Day, AFL-CIO President Lane Kirkland and Secretary-Treasurer Thomas Donahue, joined Trumka and eighteen other top labor leaders in blocking Dickenson County courthouse as a crowd of more than one thousand miners and supporters cheered. Their arrests received national media coverage. Kirkland, who had never been arrested in a strike, hoped the UMW would reaffiliate with the AFL-CIO and he wanted to show that federation could offer real support to the miners' strike. Trumka and Roberts were convinced, partly by the example of Martin Luther King, that a civil resistance strategy could work only if the rank-and-file activists knew that their leaders would also disobey the law and take the penalty.[79]

After five months, the striking miners remained united, according to the *Baltimore Sun,* and Pittston continued to take a beating in the press and from politicians like Senator Rockefeller, who demanded government prosecution of Pittston for unfair labor practices. But as the summer waned, a settlement still seemed to be remote. With court fines still mounting, some experts began to doubt the UMWA's chances for victory or even for survival. This was a fight the union had to win, but it might not, said the *Los Angeles Times.* The strike had become a "cause célèbre of organized labor" but it now attracted a lot less attention than it had when tens of thousands of miners had wildcatted earlier in the summer. "[T]he strike is bogged down," the report said, "attracting few headlines outside the coal country." The Pittston miners now stood in isolation, clustering in wooden shacks they built at

78. Joe Sciacca, "Council Votes to Close Its Shawmut Accounts," *Boston Herald* (July 27, 1989); "Flynn Remarks Anger Mass. Cops," *Boston Herald* (July 22, 1989); "Flynn Visits Miners," *Boston Herald* (July 21, 1989); "Boston Council Cites Pittston-Bank Link," *Journal of Commerce* (July 28, 1993); and "AFL-CIO Threatens to Sever Tie with CNB," *Greenwich Time* (August 23, 1989). Zinn quoted in Yancey, "Thunder in the Coal Field," 10.

79. Mike Wright, "Trumka's 'Call To Conscience' Answered," *Dickenson Star* (August 31, 1989); Frank Swoboda, "Organized Labor Toughens Its Stance," *Washington Post* (September 3, 1989); "Labor Leaders Arrested at Rally Held to Support Striking Union," *New York Times* (August 25, 1989); Dana Priest, "Labor Leaders Arrested in Va.," *Washington Post* (August 24, 1989); and author's interview with Cecil Roberts, Washington, D.C., December 15, 1993.

each Pittston mine entrance. The arrest of Lane Kirkland and other labor leaders appeared to the *Times* to be just a "desperate" attempt to keep the issue alive.[80]

Indeed, after mobilizing an entire region, creating a powerful resistance movement and hurting Pittston's production, the UMW seemed no closer to reaching an agreement. The union needed to do something to keep the pressure on Pittston, to keep morale strong and maintain nonviolence. Faced with this situation, union leaders made a bold plan to seize and occupy the Moss 3 coal treatment plant near Carbo, the site of the biggest resistance actions.

Eddie Burke, who organized the operation, was a keen student of labor history who knew what the sit-down strikers of the 1930s had accomplished. Burke and three team leaders spent nearly a month in secret meetings on the plan, code-named Operation Flintstone after the UAW occupation of a Fisher Body plant in Flint, Michigan, in 1937. The action was organized in military fashion and on September 16, 1989, ninety-nine carefully chosen miners and one clergyman, Jim Sessions, gathered at Camp Sol to receive their secret orders. They arrived at Moss 3 on schedule and Burke, his heart pumping wildly, led his teams through the gate toward the huge six-story structure as supporters cheered from the road. Anxious about the possibility of gunfire, Burke shouted over his bullhorn that the group was peaceful and unarmed and, rather audaciously, that it was a group of Pittston stockholders coming "to inspect their property."[81]

Surprisingly, only three troopers patrolled the area and only two private guards stood watch. The security men quickly fled as occupiers marched through the gates and clambered up the stairs of the huge facility. In twenty minutes they had locked themselves in the control room. Cecil Roberts assumed command of the crowd outside. He asked 2,000 supporters to stay all night to protect the occupation. By nightfall the crowd had grown much larger as state troopers arrived belatedly on the scene. Tension swelled as supporters worried about a police assault.[82]

On the second day, the miners, surprised that they had not been evicted, rigged makeshift showers and set up dorms in the processing plant. While the NLRB sought an injunction to end the illegal sitdown, Roberts dealt with the police and the large crowd that had gathered. On the third day U.S. marshals served subpoenas

80. For critical news coverage of Pittston see Martha Hodel, "The Pittston Co.," Alexander Cockburn, "Their Miners and Ours," *The Nation* (August 21–28, 1989), and "Corrupt Firm," *Charleston Gazette* (August 18, 1989); Wayne Barber, "Religious Leaders Rally Behind UMW," *Bristol Herald Courier* (September 10, 1989); and Stephen Coats, "Churches Respond to the Pittston Strike," *Christianity and Crisis* (September 25, 1989). Quotes from Carol Schoettler, "After Five Months, Striking Miners remain United," *Baltimore Sun* (September 5, 1989); and Bob Baker, "Coal Strike a Fight Union Has to, but May Not, Win," *Los Angeles Times* (August 23, 1989).

81. Author's interview with Eddie Burke, Norton, Virginia, April 20, 1990, video taped by Cabin Creek Films; Jim Sessions and Fran Ansley, "Singing Across Dark Spaces: The Union/Community Takeover of Pittston Moss 3 Plant," in Fischer, *Fighting Back in Appalachia,* 199–222; Yancey, "Thunder in the Coal Fields," 10–11; and "Striking Coal Miners Hold Pittston Processing Plant," *Washington Post* (September 19, 1989).

82. Yancey, "Thunder in the Coal Fields," 10–11.

on Roberts and Burke, while Mike Odum, Pittston's chief in Virginia, denounced "this latest act of violence by the union," calling the occupiers "common terrorists." Federal Judge Williams, sitting in Abingdon, gave the sit-downers twenty-four hours to "walk out honorably." If they did not accept this offer of amnesty, the union would be fined $600,000 a day and the union leaders would face jail sentences. Meanwhile, state police made plans to storm the plant. Roberts met with the men inside and said there was an immediate possibility of a police attack on the plant and that they should probably leave. Judge Williams's 7:00 P.M. deadline passed and then the men came out at 9:00 P.M., cheered wildly by the big throng that had gathered to protect them.[83]

The union helped restore the strikers' militancy and tighten the knot of solidarity; and it had once again caught Pittston and the police offguard. Moss 3 was Mike Odum's crown jewel and he seemed stunned that the union could capture and hold it. The occupation did not get the national media coverage the union wanted, even though the UMW deluged papers and television news with information. The occupation had not delivered a knockout blow to Pittston, but it let the company know the union was still willing and ready to hit anywhere at any time without regard to legal constraints.[84]

SIGNS OF HOPE

As the Appalachian hills turned brilliant colors of crimson, brown, and yellow that October new signs of hope appeared. On October 2 a bi-partisan group of senators introduced a bill to take health benefits to retirees off the bargaining table, proposing that the federal government assume responsibility for two debt-ridden health funds covering 161,000 retired miners. Two days later the Senate Finance Committee endorsed the plan, which Senator Rockefeller succeeded in attaching to the budget bill, thus ensuring its quick passage.[85]

On October 12 a delegation of international labor leaders arrived in the coalfields. The group, which included a Solidarity member newly elected to Poland's Senate, denounced the Pittston's violations of labor law, promised to file a complaint with the International Labor Organization, and to work through the International Confed-

83. Ibid., 11–13, Dana Priest, "Miners Heed Court Order, End Va. Plant Takeover," *Washington Post* (September 21, 1989); and Priest, "Striking Miners Settle In At Va. Processing Plant," *Washington Post* (September 20, 1989); and Paul Kwik, "Pittston Power," *The Nation* (October 16, 1989).

84. Author's interview with Ron Baker, Washington, D.C., July 15, 1993; and with Trumka, January 19, 1994.

85. Dana Priest, "Senate Bill May Settle Big Issues in Coal Strike," *Washington Post* (October 3, 1989); "Coal Accord?" *Charleston Gazette* (October 5, 1989); Pamela Porter, "Panel OKs Plan to Salvage Miners' Fund," *Bluefield Daily* (October 10, 1989); and Joel Chernoff, "Miners Fighting for Health Plans," *Pensions & Investment Age* (October 30, 1989).

eration of Free Trade Unions to discourage Pittston's customers and allied suppliers.[86]

The next day the international delegation visited Secretary Elizabeth Dole and made a forceful presentation about the violations they had witnessed. Dole then announced that she would go to the coalfields herself. International scrutiny was beginning to make a difference. On October 14 Dole convened the first meeting attended by both Trumka and Douglas and announced she would soon appoint a supermediator to put federal pressure on the parties to settle. After returning from an "emotionally wrenching" tour of the coalfields, she said, "I saw families against families, brothers against brothers. This is tearing entire communities apart." Dole's comments seemed newsworthy if only because they represented the most sympathetic words unions had heard from a federal official in nearly nine years. In a few days Dole appointed William Usery as her supermediator. He had worked for both Republicans and Democrats, and had "earned a reputation as one of the nation's top labor dispute troubleshooters." If anyone could wrench an agreement out of the warring adversaries, Bill Usery could. But he soon found this strike to be one of his toughest assignments because, he said, the parties found themselves stuck in a "deep hole full of animosity."[87]

On October 20 the corporate campaign claimed a victory when William Craig announced in Boston that he would resign as a vice president of the Shawmut Bank. Ken Zinn recalled later that Craig's resignation marked a turning point. "It sent a very strong message to the board of directors that there was a personal cost" to the strike. "What we did in this campaign was to take the coal mines to him in Boston and it cost him."[88] Investors wondered about the costs of the strike too. Pittston's income had fallen by 79% in the third quarter of 1989 from $14.7 million to $3.1 million.[89]

By late October Jackie Stump's write-in election campaign against incumbent House Delegate Don McGlothin began generating some excitement in the strike

86. "Secretary Dole to Visit Site of Pittston Strike," *Daily Labor Report* (October 13, 1989); "ICFTU tour Appalled at Pittston, U.S. Law," *AFL-CIO News* (October 14, 1989); and William Keesler, "Foreign Unions Pressure Firms to Cut Purchases from Pittston," *Louisville Courier Journal* (October 13, 1989).

87. Yancey, "Thunder in the Coal Fields," 14; "Dole Leads Cole Strike Summit," *Washington Post* (October 15, 1989); and "Ex-Labor Secretary Usery to Mediate Va. Coal Strike," *Washington Post* (October 25, 1989).

88. Joe Battenfeld, "Mine workers Applaud as Shawmut Exec Resigns," *Boston Herald* (October 20, 1989), 10; Doug Bailey and Bruce Butterfield, "Shawmut Boycott Off as Craig Quits," *Boston Globe* (October 20, 1993).

89. "Pittston New Plunged 79% in 3rd Quarter, Coal Strike is Cited," *Wall Street Journal* (October 23, 1989); and "Pittston Income Falls 79%," *Greenwich Time* (October 21, 1989). Six weeks later the UMW won a suit against Pittston when a federal district judge ruled that the company had violated securities regulations when it conducted votes on three proposals submitted by striking miners at the annual stockholders' meeting in May. "Judge Says Pittston Co. Violated Securities Rules," *New York Times* (November 30, 1989).

zone. The energy mobilized for civil resistance had been redirected into the campaign, just at a time—"crunch time" Trumka later called it—when the strike strategists had exercised nearly all their tactical options. "People told me they'd gotten four phone calls prior to the election," a McGlothin supporter said with amazement. It was one of the best orchestrated campaigns he had ever seen.[90] All of the movement-building energy that Cecil Roberts and his zealous followers had generated in the spring and summer powered Stump's insurgent campaign against the senior McGlothin. It was the clearest expression of how political the strike had become.

Campaign manager Eddie Burke was surprised and delighted when his phone banks reported that 75% of the people called said they would vote for strike leader Stump. On November 7 the miners' write-in candidate won every precinct except the incumbent's home town. "It was a landslide beyond anyone's imagination: Stump 7,981; McGlothin 3,812," wrote an observer. As Stump said to a rally of supporters: "The work has just started because now people throughout the United States have realized that if the politicians that are supposed to help working people don't help working people then we can take them out of office."[91]

Two days later, after news of Stump's election "hit like a storm," Supermediator William Usery reopened contract talks in the Washington area with Cecil Roberts and Joseph Farrell heading the union and company teams. Usery began by declaring a news blackout for both sides and insisting on a cease-fire in the war zone. The mass picketing and road blocking ended. No trucks were stoned. Most of the state troopers left and nearly all of the hated Vance security guards departed.[92]

Now, time seemed to be on the union's side. In November a UPI story predicted that Pittston could lose up to $60 million by the end of the year. One expert said: "Douglas believed the law would take care of everything" in what should have been a "small strike." But "Pittston apparently misread how fast the courts could move" and it "underestimated the union's resolve." UMW officials and other union leaders had "targeted the Pittston strike as a place to take a stand" and now that they had forced government intervention, the corporation could not expect "a clear-cut victory."[93]

After a week of intensive negotiations that lasted late into the evening, Usery declared a week's suspension to talk independently with both sides. When the parties returned, a more cooperative atmosphere developed. After eight months on strike and great financial losses on both sides, the two parties realized that this might

90. Trumka, speech at Harvard Trade Union Program; and Yancey, "Thunder in the Coal Fields," 14.

91. Yancey, "Thunder in the Coal Fields," 15; and "Labor in America: 'We Won't Go Back,' " 90, 91.

92. Dana Priest, "Va. Coal Miner Strikes Gold in Politics," *Washington Post* (November 20, 1989); and Yancey, "Thunder in the Coal Fields," 15.

93. "Pittston Company Misread Strike," UPI, *Charleston Gazette* (November 21, 1989); Dana Priest, "Big Machines, Ready Replacements and the Strike's Bottom Line," *Washington Post* (November 26, 1989).

be their last chance to settle and avoid a struggle to the death. The sticking point remained Pittston's withdrawal from the health care fund. Usery talked to Elizabeth Dole and she said that the government might be able to look into the problem; this possibility opened up new progress in the talks. Usery set a Christmas deadline to create a sense of urgency and Trumka joined the talks, a sign of progress.[94]

As Christmas in the coalfields approached, union caravans arrived bringing toys and clothes to the strikers and their families. But the holiday was a somber one. The hatreds stirred up by the strike hung over the region like the coal dust stirred up by giant trucks still hauling "scab coal" to Moss 3. Judge McGlothin, no doubt angered by his father's stunning defeat by Jackie Stump, handed out $33.4 million more in fines in the eighth, ninth, and tenth rounds of criminal contempt hearings and called UMWA members "thugs" and "terrorists." A spokesman for Usery criticized these fines and said they might hurt negotiations.[95]

After a Christmas break the parties reconvened in Washington at the Capitol Hilton and on New Year's Eve, just before midnight, Trumka and Roberts reached across the table and shook hands with their enemies, Douglas and Farrell. On New Year's Day 1990, the union and company announced a tentative agreement. Trumka, "who had staked his reputation and the future of the union on the strike's outcome, called the settlement 'a victory for the entire labor movement.' " The miners appeared to "score a major victory," *U.S. News* said, "leaving the company with relatively meager gains won only at great expense."[96]

Other reporters saw losses for both sides in the settlement that gave the company some of the flexibility it wanted in work rules including two alternatives to the conventional eight-hour, five-day week and the freedom to run coal twenty-four hours a day except Sunday during daytime. On the other hand, the company agreed to maintain the 100% health care coverage the union insisted on. On the difficult issue of the trust funds, the employer agreed to pay $10 million into the funds that covered those who retired before 1976 if it could then drop out. To address the long-term problems of the troubled funds, Secretary Dole agreed to appoint a commission, chaired by Usery, to explore other solutions. On the critical union issue of job security Pittston and its subcontractors agreed to hire laid-off union miners for four of the first of every five job openings at Pittston's new operations; subcontractors would provide the first nineteen of every twenty jobs to UMW miners. It also agreed to limit but not end transfers of coal reserves from union to nonunion subsidiaries.[97]

Union leaders discussed the contract proposal with strikers intensively and on

94. Yancey, "Thunder in the Coal Fields," 15.

95. Yancey, "Thunder in the Coal Fields," 15; *Camo Call* (December 8 and 29, 1989), and "Union 'Santas' Aid Striking Miners," *Bridgeport Post-Telegram* (December 10, 1989).

96. Yancey, "Thunder in the Coal Fields," 15, and "A Healthy Settlement for Mine Workers," *U.S. News & World Report* (January 15, 1990).

97. "A Healthy Settlement," Yancey, "Thunder in the Coal Fields," 16; Peter Kilborn, "Pittston and Miners in Accord to Resolve Bitter Coal Strike," *New York Times* (January 2, 1990); and Dana Priest, "Light at the End of the Tunnel," *Washington Post* (February 26, 1990).

February 20, 1990, the Pittston miners ratified it by a 60% majority. Trumka announced the results at the AFL-CIO meetings in Florida and a celebration erupted. "One line of labor leaders after another at meetings in Bal Harbor said they saw the accord as a break in the long decline of trade union membership." Critics of the labor establishment also saw the strike as a great victory and a turning point for labor.[98]

Trumka, who knew the strike's costs, said the results were "bittersweet." There had been great suffering, hard feelings, millions of dollars lost, thousands of people arrested, but Pittston's union busting drive had been stopped and the UMWA had been saved. The strike "caught fire" and became a movement that inspired union workers all over the United States, he recalled. The strikers even "twanged the nation's conscience." Moreover, Trumka concluded, "the union had convinced the public that it spoke for the working people of America and that the UMW's defeat would have weakened the position of all working people." Few labor leaders in the modern era could have made such a claim with so much credibility.[99]

From the seeds planted by the Pittston strikers, Trumka hoped, would spring "nothing less than a movement for the overhaul of U.S. labor law." He thought the strike demonstrated the futility of abiding by existing laws and that it highlighted an "outrageous" contradiction: corporations made products that killed people but suffered no fines while UMW people went on strike, sat down in the roads, or drove slowly on the highway "and they ended up getting fined 64 million bucks." Trumka believed it was so outrageous that many unions began pushing harder for labor law reform and making it a number-one priority for the AFL-CIO.[100] In addition, the attention the strike drew to the health care crisis led to a very surprising outcome: the passage of legislation recommended by Elizabeth Dole's commission on miners' health care and sponsored by Senator Jay Rockefeller to guarantee health benefits for 120,000 UMW people covered by the bankrupt funds. It was, Trumka said, the "greatest victory the Mine Workers have had in fifty years." It also gave impetus to the move for "national health care" reform with full coverage.[101]

However, the massive court fines levied against the union lingered like a dark cloud into 1994. In the strike settlement Pittston agreed to drop most of the charges that led to fines. Others would be appealed. But the courts insisted on holding the

---

98. Dana Priest, "Striking Miners Vote on New Contract," *Washington Post* (February 19, 1990); "Labor in America: 'We Won't Go Back,' " 98, 99; David Reed, "Pittston Miners OK Contract," *Greenwich Time* (February 21, 1990); Dana Priest, "Contract Approved By Miners," *Washington Post* (February 21, 1990); Lionel Barber, "Miners' Settlement May Herald New Era," *Financial Times* (January 3, 1990); Greg Tarpanian, "Pittston: Rebirth of the Unions?" *Wall Street Journal* (November 20, 1989); and Jane Slaughter, "Is the Labor Movement Reaching a Turning Point?" *Labor Notes* (January 1990).

99. Trumka interview, January 19, 1994. Also see Richard L. Trumka, "On Becoming a Movement," *Dissent* (Winter 1992): 57–60.

100. Marianne Lavelle, "The New Coal Wars," *National Law Journal* (November 20, 1989), 28 and Trumka interview, January 19, 1994.

101. "Keeping the Commitment," *UMWJ* (February 1992): 4–9.

UMW accountable for over $60 million in fines. In 1993 the union's legal appeal went all the way to the Supreme Court. The case is still undecided. But if the Court rules against the union, Trumka said in early 1994, it would discourage the use of civil disobedience as a peaceful form of protest. The Court will be saying to unions, "Don't you ever sit in the street to protect health care of elderly people because we will fine you into oblivion."[102]

Even a short time after the settlement in early 1990 it is difficult to re-create the mood of anger and passion the Pittston strike aroused in union labor across the land. It came in the context of antiworker Republican rule and an anti-union onslaught organized labor had not seen since the 1920s; it also came after a series of defeats in which top labor leadership had failed to support local strikers or to mobilize fully against the employer. Strikers from Arizona to Minnesota felt abandoned and betrayed by their national leaders and this feeling produced a bitterness far deeper and more destructive to the labor movement than the tough opposition of the employers, the courts, and the Republican administrations in Washington. Although local cultures of solidarity blossomed in many of these desperate strikes, at the national level "legal strategies predominated over strategies for mass mobilization."[103] The United Mine Workers, led and inspired by their national leaders, shattered this discouraging trend in 1989 and thus renewed hope in the union movement. They retied the knot of solidarity between local strikers and national unions.

In the struggle with Pittston the UMWA demonstrated how old forms of struggle could be blended with new ones. The union had organized ladies' auxiliaries, community allies, and local officials before, but it had never mobilized churches and the rest of the labor movement so effectively. It perfected strategies used in the 1970s and 1980s, like corporate campaigns, and it expanded them to the international scene with unusual effectiveness. It returned to the sympathy strike rank-and-file miners used in the wildcats of the 1970s and it reached back to the 1930s to resurrect another illegal maneuver: the plant occupation. But it also added new tactics like civil disobedience, borrowed from the civil rights movement, and renamed them civil resistance to harmonize nonviolent tactics with the militant traditions of coalminer protest in Appalachia. It relied on familiar forms of political influence with remarkable success at a national level (notably in the form of Secretary Dole's intervention) and returned to an old practice of running a union miner for state office. But it also politicized the conflict in unprecedented ways so that it became much more than a strike. What began as a contract fight became a people's movement against corporate greed and an oppressive legal system, a movement many hoped would provide a model for the revival of organized labor in the United States.

102. Ibid.

103. On the problems of local strikers with their international unions, see Fantasia, *Cultures of Solidarity,* 218–25; quote, 242. On the failure of national unions to support Phelps Dodge miners on strike in Arizona and Hormel packinghouse workers in Minnesota, see 278–79, and Peter Rachleff, *Hard Pressed in the Heartland: The Hormel Strike and the Future of the Labor Movement* (Boston: South End Press, 1993).

CHAPTER TWENTY-TWO

AFTERWORD
Prospects for the UMWA

MAIER B. FOX

For 105 years, the United Mine Workers of America has been at the center of the country's industrial system. For that reason alone, it has received more attention than is normally accorded a labor union. But the UMWA has been of even greater importance than that simple fact suggests.

The UMWA, after the turn of the twentieth century and again in the 1930s and 1940s was one of the largest labor unions in the world. Nearly a half-million men (and all were men in those days) were covered by UMWA agreements with coal-mine operators at the union's peak. Because the existence of coal deposits is geographically restricted, the relative size of the union varied tremendously. Where mining was a mainstay of the local economy—as in much of Pennsylvania, West Virginia, and Kentucky—coal miners and their families often *were* the people.

And conditions in those geographical areas were among the worst in the country. As has often been the case in areas where the economy is based on extractive industry, wealth was also extracted from coal-mining communities. For generations, the American image of the coalfields was dominated by ramshackle housing, malnourished children, a devastated environment, crippled and short-breathed workers. The image reflected reality far too closely. Because the UMWA accepted this reality as its challenge, the union had extraordinary influence among people in the communities where miners worked, and then in the country as a whole.

The union used its strength in negotiations to modify and then eliminate the company town. When miners' families were allowed to live where they wished, and when miners' incomes rose to allow them to take advantages of options, mining communities started to improve.[1]

When government studies[2] confirmed the lack of quality health care available in many coalfield communities, the UMWA took it upon itself to solve the problem. With the government in control of the mines—an outgrowth of the inability of miners and operators to reach agreement during World War II—the union insisted on the creation of an employer-financed fund to aid injured and ill or retired coal miners. The funds that were created, as noted by George Goldstein (Chapter 10) were extraordinarily influential. Under the control of union trustees, the program expanded to provide rehabilitation programs, build hospitals, and develop a fee-for-service medical care coverage system that was opposed by much of the traditional medical care community but succeeded in attracting idealistic young practitioners who made a long-term difference in the coalfields.

This UMWA creation set the standard for negotiated benefit programs in other industries, at least for a limited period (see Chapter 6). And its multiemployer, "portable" approach continues to be at the center of our debate over the appropriate system of health care coverage a half-century later.

But it was not unusual for the UMWA to set the pace for the American labor movement, either by devising new approaches to workers' problems or by setting a standard that other unions sought to meet. For example, even before the creation of the UMWA, organized miners fought to organize the operators and develop regional collective bargaining systems. These were well established in the 1890s and became identified with the first great UMWA president, John Mitchell.[3] Fully national multiemployer negotiations were not quickly gained even in coal mining, but the concept was fully accepted by about 1950 and the importance of large-scale bargaining became something of an article of faith in much of the labor movement.

A repudiation of racial discrimination was among the actions of the founding UMWA convention of 1890.[4] The union was also quick to admit Asian workers,[5]

1. As is true of the majority of historians, I do not accept Price Fishback's benign view of the company town; see Chapter 8.

2. See Coal Mines Administration, *A Medical Survey of the Bituminous-Coal Industry* (Washington, D.C.: GPO, 1947).

3. Arthur E. Suffern, *Conciliation and Arbitration in the Coal Industry of America* (Boston: Houghton Mifflin, 1915). Also see Phelan, Chapter 4.

4. *Proceedings of Joint Convention of N.P.U. and N.T.A. 135, K. of L., January 23–27, 1890* (Pennsylvania State University, Pattee Library, The Pennsylvania Historical Collections and Labor Archives, United Mine Workers of America Papers; hereafter, UMWA Papers). For later manifestations of this attitude, see Lewis, Chapter 12, and Trotter, Chapter 11.

5. Uji Ichioka, "Asian Immigrant Coal Miners and the United Mine Workers of America: Race and Class in Rock Springs, Wyoming, 1907," *Amerasia* 6 (Fall 1979): 1–23.

but its progressive attitude was not adopted by most American institutions for many years. The UMWA's repudiation of racial discrimination was for practical as well as ideological reasons. So was its decision to adopt a structure of "industrial" organization rather than the more common "craft" approach dominant in early American unionism. This also made it easy for the union to adopt a leading position in the creation of the Congress of Industrial Organizations in the 1930s.[6]

The UMWA also played a central role in some of the most important federal labor legislation ever passed in the United States. The New Deal's repeated guarantee to workers of the right to bargain collectively (as in the National Labor Relations Act) was drawn from wording originally prepared by Henry Warrum and W. Jett Lauck of the UMWA.[7] And the Taft-Hartley Act, restricting union rights, was probably passed in reaction to the UMWA's post–World War II strikes.

Finally, the UMWA's acceptance of mechanization, which began even before the turn of the century (and the "downsizing" that accompanied it) seems to have set a pattern for other industrial unions, though none seems to have fully accepted it and changes are still sought.[8]

One factor in the UMWA's willingness to set precedents was its militant self-image. Members believed they were willing to put themselves on the line whenever necessary—and often gave substance to this belief. Multiemployer strikes in the anti-union 1890s and the 1919 nationwide coal strike in the face of a government ban were proof of this militancy. Another factor in the UMWA's tendency to go in unexpected directions was recognized by longtime labor activist Len DeCaux when he described John L. Lewis as "an irreverent pragmatist."[9] Lewis may have been particularly irreverent, but the pragmatism was already traditional in the UMWA.

The miners and their union have often been militant and confrontational, though the periodic differences between the approach of the members and the institution they have built have often been documented and sometimes stressed.[10] The tendency toward pragmatism has been noted less often—and continues to be less appreciated. Among the essays in this book, David Frank has provided a great service in reminding us of the constant potential for tension between militancy and practicality (see Chapter 18), and I look forward to historians in the United States adopting (or reacting to) his insights as a starting point for a broader interpretation of the pressures on labor unions as institutions.

Perry Blatz (see Chapter 3) suggests that the basic ambivalence of the American people toward unions helps explain the lack of greater militancy of the UMWA and

6. UMWA Papers, CIO collection. Also see Singer, Chapter 5, above.

7. W. Jett Lauck Papers, University of Virginia Library, Special Collections Department. For a review of the legislative development of this idea, see Maier B. Fox, *United We Stand: The United Mine Workers of America, 1890–1990* (United Mine Workers of America, 1990), 307–12.

8. See the *UMW Journal* and the *Proceedings* of UMWA national conventions for the period 1900–1912, especially. Dix, Chapter 7, and his earlier publications, discuss many of the key factors in the mechanization process, particularly in later days.

9. *Labor Radical: From the Wobblies to CIO: A Personal History* (Boston: Beacon, 1971), 217.

10. See, among others, Singer, Chapter 5, and Phelan, Chapter 4.

that possibility, too, should be explored further. I would hope that such a study would take into account what seem to be—at least in terms of union membership and labor laws—fairly wide differences in the views of Canadian and U.S. citizens about labor organizations.

However, the ambivalence of *historians* about this pragmatism, which has often characterized their treatment of the UMWA, continues to be evident in other contributions to this volume. Alan Derickson, for example (see Chapter 9), underlines the importance of compensation, rather than prevention, in the UMWA approach to the diseases suffered by coal miners. This protected the jobs of people in the early stage of disease who had no employment options. Unstated is the regret (shared by others) that the union could not take a longer-term approach. The UMWA's long struggle with occupational disease included more than a century of compromise, of trade-offs to maintain economic opportunity.

Others who are ambivalent, but less understanding, include Alan Singer, Craig Phelan, and Keith Dix. Singer (Chapter 5) recognizes the willingness of John L. Lewis to use miners' militancy to rebuild the union in the 1930s and to counter the effect of government controls in 1942. He overstates the evidence that the miners were willing to make new departures. There is in Singer (and many others) an assumption that the militancy of American miners is synonymous with miner radicalism, an assumption whose truth they have not sufficiently demonstrated. Though certainly to the "left" of Lewis, John Brophy, Frank Keeney, John H. Walker, and Adolph Germer—even Mother Jones—were something less than radical. Patricia Long recognized the absence of radicalism even in the midst of the bloody Colorado strike of 1913–14 (Chapter 14).

Phelan (Chapter 4) reports that the "economic reality of the soft-coal industry" necessitated the interstate trade agreement and he clearly regrets John Mitchell's approval of the system and desire to maintain it. Miners even before Mitchell understood that the signing of an agreement for the Central Competitive Field, which stretched from western Pennsylvania to Illinois, was basic to their ability to share in whatever work was available.

Dix (Chapter 7) knows that mechanization was inevitable and that the refusal of the union to accept it would simply have led to the replacement of unionized coal production by nonunion companies. Yet his dislike for this compromise—manifested in his suggestion that miners either should or could have pressed for greater control of their workplace—is palpable. Richard Trumka, current UMWA president, believes greater worker control is destined to return: if companies are serious about putting productivity first, they will need to provide more freedom to workers to adjust to conditions.[11]

Ronald Lewis's investigation (Chapter 12) of the bi-racial nature of the early UMWA in Alabama, on the other hand, is refreshingly realistic. Instead of approaching his subject with a preconceived philosophical absolute, he uses the prevailing

11. Interview, January 5, 1995.

attitudes of Alabama society to explain the options open to the union and the almost inevitable results of the union's actions. Working with materials from 1920s West Virginia, Joe Trotter, while noting that individuals did not always follow the union's lead, describes the "interracial character" of the miners' fight (Chapter 11). And Mildred Beik shows that the insistence on interethnic organizing reflected the reality in the coalfields (Chapter 13). Paul Clark's look at the last decade of the union's first century also aptly summarizes the record as a history of "adapting to constantly changing conditions and challenges" (Chapter 19).

The UMWA has completed the first five years of its second century. It is not now the huge organization of 1905 or 1935, but it is as large or larger than it was in 1895 and 1930. What does the future hold for an organization that has affected America more than any other labor union—and is increasingly unknown outside of the coalfields today?

Two predictions seem particularly likely to be valuable. First, the UMWA's approach will be practical. Second, the members' militancy will be the key to success. Just as in the union's early years, practicality has been a hallmark of recent UMWA efforts. A willingness to take new approaches, to break from tradition, has been central to the union's attitude for more than a decade. It clearly surfaced in a series of decisions made in the early to mid-1980s. These included the selective-strike concept and the strike fund created to make it effective, the sale of the National Bank of Washington (NBW) and the decision to affiliate with the American Federation of Labor–Congress of Industrial Organizations.

Each of these was a practical decision that struck at tradition. The insistence on nationwide strikes had earlier been one of the keys to the miners' sense of solidarity. The NBW had been an innovation of the revered John L. Lewis, a guarantee that the union would be able to borrow money even when in a contest with employers who were allied with bankers. And Lewis's disdain for the unwillingness of the "House of Labor" to challenge government edicts was widely shared in the coalfields, making the decision to become part of labor's mainstream somewhat problematic.

Nevertheless, many of the union's present and probable future priorities represent a continuation of traditional policies. First and foremost will be the need to negotiate agreements that provide miners the opportunity to make a living. Improved health and safety is a second continuing commitment, currently focusing on the dangers presented by the introduction of diesel equipment into the underground environment.

Clean air legislation that does not destroy the coal industry and maintenance of a health and retirement program that protects both current and past miners and their families are also basic. Along with the rest of the labor movement, the UMWA will—to the extent the political situation permits—fight for labor law reform that would place it on "a level playing field" with the coal operators when it comes to organizing new members and to protecting the jobs of strikers from replacement. The Coal Miners Political Action Committee, a modern version of UMWA and CIO pioneering efforts, has proven quite successful in making the case for miners on Capitol Hill.

In the long run, however, new programs, perhaps most important the future role of the Office of Allied Workers (OAW), will determine the future of the UMWA. In the late 1980s, OAW was designed to represent a group that had shrinking work opportunity in the coalfields. Coal-mine construction workers had little work opportunity because new coal mines were seldom being opened. But these union members had abilities that could be used outside of the mining industry, and OAW sought to find those opportunities for the construction workers.

By the early 1990s, people in the coalfields knew that the UMWA was representing these nonminers. Some called upon the UMWA to provide representation to a wider spectrum of workers. The union, new to the AFL-CIO and hesitant to become embroiled in jurisdictional disputes, was slow to respond. But the administration of Richard Trumka quickly found an approach that proved satisfactory. The UMWA would organize outside of its original coal-mining jurisdiction, but restrict itself to coal-mining areas where its reputation was a built-in advantage and other unions had little or no presence.

In the strictest sense, OAW was not a new departure but hearkened back to "District 50," a John L. Lewis creation in 1936. As with District 50, OAW was designed to provide representation within the UMWA to workers who were not coal miners. District 50 had been a challenge to other labor organizations and a potential challenge to both the AF of L and the CIO. The impetus behind OAW was different. In many coal-mining communities, there were few other employment options. Perhaps for that reason, other unions seldom appeared to try to organize the small number of workers with other occupations. But those workers often needed and wanted union protection—and the union with which they were most familiar was the UMWA.

The UMWA was slow to expand outside of coal mining. The decision to welcome nonminers into the union may prove to be one of the most important ones made by the union under Trumka. While usage of coal has been expanding consistently, the number of miners has been shrinking. At present, total nonsupervisory employment in coal mining is less than 100,000. That number is likely to decline further, as mechanization continues to lead to productivity increases in surface as well as underground mining.

Moreover, clean air concerns threaten to destroy the industry. Coal's primary market is the utility industry. Utilities, in recent decades, extended the life of coal-burning plants rather than build new ones. Increasingly, these will need to be replaced. Primarily because of concern over air pollution, current law discourages the use of coal, largely because of the expense involved in burning coal cleanly, and the popular perception that it can't be done. Meanwhile, evidence of abundant supplies of clean-burning natural gas suggest that utilities will turn more to that fuel.

The shrinking of the coal-mining population will be gradual, but it seems inevitable. If the UMWA is to remain an independent force in the American labor movement, the workers who have joined the union through the OAW—still a small proportion of the membership—will play an increasingly important role. In its second century, a successful UMWA will include, among others, the members who worked on Hoover Dam, the hospital workers in Dickenson County (Virginia), the public employees of Walker County (Alabama) and Sheridan (Wyoming), and the people in the Housing Authority of Evansville (Indiana), along with the country's coal miners.

The OAW may also prove to be important because of the difficulty the UMWA has had in finding other unions with which to merge. In the late 1980s, the UMWA and the Oil, Chemical, and Atomic Workers Union nearly consummated a merger agreement. It made sense for these unions to join forces because both were relatively small, both were in the energy field, and they negotiated with some of the same employers. On the other hand, their geographic strengths differed, and a merger would have created a union with greater national influence. The failure of those discussions leaves no such "natural" partner and the UMWA's growth is likely to be circumscribed.

Pragmatism has also proved to be the key to the bargaining goals in recent negotiations. The UMWA continues to make health care the centerpiece of negotiations, and is likely to do so until such time as the nation's health care system ensures proper care to all. This is a particularly important issue for miners because of the multigenerational tendency among coal miners. Miners will brook no system other than lifetime health care because the retirees in the industry are the parents and grandparents of the current workforce. But other leading goals have grown from the decline of the industry.

The Employment and Economic Security pacts that date from the late 1980s recognize that employment opportunity is declining and are designed to ensure that future opportunities will be given to UMWA members. The promise of first opportunity to unemployed union coal miners has been central to UMWA bargaining strategy and will likely continue to be in the near future. Still, the declining number of available jobs will continue to cost some UMWA members their livelihoods. The union's current answer to this problem is a second innovation in contracts, the Training and Education Fund, which provides college (or technical school) tuition and some expenses for laid-off members and, since 1993, for the dependents of active miners.[12]

For a job protection/job training strategy to bear fruit, it is important that employees and employers recognize a reciprocal commitment. Miners need to work toward greater productivity while employers provide increased security and opportunity. History makes the trust implied in this cooperative approach difficult for miners. Often, greater productivity has meant fewer miners or longer hours, and the union continues to react strongly to the mandatory overtime that has come to the indus-

12. See *UMWJ* (March–April 1995).

try.[13] Other efforts at cooperation collapsed because the operator approach was seen as divisive—as a new attempt in the old effort to "bust" the union.[14] Modern efforts have been successful when both sides have accepted the goodwill of the other.

Some years ago, for example, a Canadian UMWA local and mine management had established a cooperative relationship called "Relationship by Objective." It differed from traditional worker-involvement programs in that it was not mandated by the company and that changes had to be accepted by both parties. The program did not spread quickly, probably because of management dislike for modifying its prerogatives and miner distrust of management's objectives.[15]

However, the concept received a new lease on life at a western Pennsylvania mine in 1992. The miners got a new safety program, tuition payments, increased job security, and an end to mandatory overtime. The operators got better productivity, fewer conflicts needing resolution through the arbitration procedure and ten more years added to the life of the mine.

UMWA President Trumka indicates the union's desire to blend pragmatism with militancy in his approval of such programs and by his insistence that there are prerequisites. These are that the operators must be serious about their willingness to cooperate, and show it by putting an end to mandatory overtime. He feels that the industry is sometimes held back by an outmoded tradition of paternalism and by an insistence on centralized control that may not be useful in a given situation.[16]

Trumka's comments bring into question the commitment to better labor-management relations that has been displayed to date; in broad outline, however, the UMWA and the Bituminous Coal Operators Association (BCOA) accepted the need to cooperate in the National Bituminous Coal Wage Agreement of 1993.[17] Included in that pact was an updated cooperation program, the Labor Management Positive Change Process.

This program was based on the agreement that both the operators and the union "must discard old ways of dealing with each other in mistrust, and foster a new environment of mutual trust and good faith acceptance. In order to achieve these objectives, the parties recognize the need for new and creative approaches to labor-management cooperation." Labor-management committees, aided by expert consultants, work to improve productivity, protect job security, and otherwise encourage cooperation without encroaching on grievance procedures or other contractual dispute-settlement procedures. Similar provisions were included in agreements signed with non-BCOA members. Such a provision was successfully invoked at the

13. Interview with Richard Trumka, January 5, 1995.
14. See, for example, the discussion of the Rushton experiment in the *UMWJ* (December 16–31, 1976).
15. This (and following material) is based on coverage in the *UMWJ* (May 1993).
16. Interview with Trumka, January 5, 1995.
17. Available through the UMWA or the BCOA.

Kellerman mine in Alabama but there has not been a strong indication that labor-management relations in the coalfields have changed fundamentally.[18]

Although the NBCWA of 1993 encompasses the union's willingness to be pragmatic and innovative, the events that led to that agreement underscore the continued militancy of America's coal miners. After a series of long and bitter contract strikes, the union and the BCOA reached agreement without a work stoppage in both 1984 and 1988. This did not herald a new cooperative era in the relations of coal miners and operators. In fact, there was a new threat to cooperation: the decline of the BCOA. The decline of the BCOA was central to the two large strikes that took place in the last half of the decade. With the splintering of the employers' association, individual operators with deep pockets thought they would be better off negotiating independent agreements with the union (or working nonunion) than by following the association's lead.

The union engaged in long and bitter strikes, first with A. T. Massey (a company particularly active in Virginia that had both union and nonunion mines), then with Pittston (see Chapter 21). In both instances, attempts to eliminate the union were beaten back. Complete victory was delayed nearly a decade in the Massey strike, but sale of the mines brought even nonunion former Massey miners into the UMWA fold in the 1990s. Extraordinary fines imposed in the Pittston strike hung over the union long after it was ended, until finally cancelled by action of the U.S. Supreme Court in 1994.[19]

Victory in these two strikes was not so important as the union's demonstration that it would stand by member militancy in the face of judicial threats to incarcerate the UMWA's officers and destroy the union economically. A threat that extreme had not faced the union since the days of John L. Lewis, and it was accepted as the price of doing business.

The union proved in both the Massey and Pittston strikes that it still had the will to avoid ''give-backs.'' But Trumka's willingness to pit the union against the united employers may not have been recognized until 1993. In that year, the UMWA engaged in its first strike with the BCOA companies in more than a decade. It was a long and difficult confrontation. Still, membership—and leadership—militancy in the Massey and Pittston contests may well have moderated the 1993 contract strike, lengthy and difficult as it was. And that strike may have been less destructive to long-term harmony between the union and the operators, for the operators did not make the error of assuming they could eliminate the union as a force in the industry.

Militancy has always been ingrained in American and Canadian miners.[20] There are probably many different reasons that miners see themselves—and others see miners—as militant. Trumka refers to the danger that has always been inherent in

18. See *UMWJ* (April 1994).

19. See *UMWJ* (August–September 1994), on the decision handed down June 30, 1994.

20. Unless otherwise indicated, all material in the rest of this essay is drawn from the Trumka interview of January 5, 1995.

mining and the resultant closeness among those who share the danger. Miners have faced the real possibility of accidental death on a daily basis. The dangers of confrontation with management pale in comparison. The forms that the miners' militancy will take in coming years are likely to be based on their history. Trumka recognizes this in statements that reflect his own familiarity with UMWA history. He speaks of the union rejecting the traditional paternalism of the operators and of the union's role as champion of the "working class," a term largely out of favor today.

Even the "innovations" in recent UMWA activity seem grounded in the union's history. The "Office of Allied Workers," for example, is not a carbon copy of the District 50 created more than a half-century ago. But it does recall the origins of that departure, organizing among gas and coke by-product workers who were considered part of an allied (or competing) industry, natural constituents of the UMWA. And the approach to the conflict with the Pittston Company, while it was a change from "normal" union procedure, also would have been recognized by earlier generations of UMWA miners.

As far back as the 1920s, the UMWA pioneered aspects of the "comprehensive campaign," picketing the New York City offices of Berwind-White and Consolidation Coal (along with the office of John D. Rockefeller Jr., principal stockholder of "Consol") during an organizing strike. Again in the 1970s' "Brookside" strike, the UMWA broadened the target from the Harlan County mine to the owners, Duke Power. There has been increasing sophistication in the tactics used by the union, but the basis for this kind of union action has clear precedents.[21]

Even the UMWA's role in the recent dispute over the future leadership of the AFL-CIO has historical precedent. The union has provided both leadership to the labor movement as a whole and challengers to that leadership. Samuel Gompers's leadership of the AFL was challenged successfully by the UMWA's John McBride and unsuccessfully by John L. Lewis. William Green of the AFL came out of the UMWA—and Lewis's antipathy for Green was repeatedly evident in the formation of the CIO. Both Lewis and Phil Murray headed the CIO. Trumka's recent election as secretary-treasurer of the AFL-CIO suggests that a larger role for the UMWA in the labor movement is again likely.

The UMWA is a proud institution, proud of its past and proud of the image of militant leadership it has maintained within the labor movement. It will likely maintain the same role.

21. Early examples of the "comprehensive campaign" are reported in many sources, including the *UMWJ*; John Brophy, *A Miner's Life* (Madison: University of Wisconsin Press, 1964); and Lynda Ann Ewen, *Which Side Are You On?* (Chicago: Vanguard Books, 1979).

FURTHER READING

The most comprehensive institutional history of the UMWA is Maier Fox, *United We Stand: The United Mine Workers of America, 1890–1990,* which was published by the union in its centennial year. A broader and more colorful account of the union's early years can be found in Priscilla Long, *Where the Sun Never Shines: A History of America's Bloody Coal Industry* (New York: Paragon House, 1989). Briefer and more anecdotal is McAlister Coleman, *Men and Coal* (New York: Farrar and Rinehart, 1943). On anthracite miners, see Perry K. Blatz, *Democratic Miners: Work and Labor Relations in the Anthracite Coal Industry, 1875–1925* (Albany: State University of New York Press, 1994). The UMWA's decline and its internal struggles in the modern period are delineated in Joseph E. Finley, *The Corrupt Kingdom, The Rise and Fall of the United Mine Workers* (New York: Simon and Schuster, 1972), and in Paul F. Clark's *The Miners Fight for Democracy: Arnold Miller and the Reform of the United Mine Workers* (Ithaca: New York State School of Industrial and Labor Relations, 1981).

For the UMWA's major leaders, see Melvyn Dubofsky and Warren Van Tine, *John L. Lewis* (New York: Quadrangle/The New York Times, 1977), Craig Phelan, *Divided Loyalties: The Public and Private Life of a Labor Leader* (Albany: State University of New York Press, 1994), and John Brophy, *A Miner's Life* (Madison: University of Wisconsin Press, 1964). Brophy was the main opposition leader to Lewis in the 1920s, then collaborated with him in creating the CIO. Regarding UMWA treatment of racial and ethnic minorities, see Ronald Lewis, *Black Coal Miners in America: Race, Class, and Community Conflict, 1780–1980* (Lexington: University Press of Kentucky, 1987), Mildred Beik, *The Miners of Windber: The Struggle of New Immigrants for Unionization* (University Park: Penn State Press, 1996), and Uji Ichioka, "Asian Immigrant Coal Miners and the United Mine Workers of America: Race and Class in Rock Springs, Wyoming, 1907," *Amerasia* 6, no. 2 (June 1979).

Readers interested in mine mechanization and its consequences should consult Keith Dix, *What's a Coal Miner to Do? The Mechanization of Coal Mining* (Pittsburgh: University of Pittsburgh Press, 1988). On accidents, safety, and health issues, as well as on miners' wages and the role of the company town, see William Graebner, *Coal-Mining Safety in the Progressive Period: The Political Economy of Reform* (Lexington: University Press of Kentucky, 1976), and Price V. Fishback, *Soft Coal, Hard Choices: The Economic Welfare of Bituminous Miners* (New York: Oxford University Press, 1992). The role of women in mining is touched on in Dale Featherling, *Mother Jones, The Miner's Angel* (Carbondale: Southern Illinois University Press, 1974). It is dealt with at greater length in Marat Moore, *Women in the Mines: Stories of Life and Work, 1920–1994* (New York: Macmillan/Twayne,

1996). An excellent study of community life in a Pennsylvania anthracite town is Anthony F. Wallace, *St. Clair* (New York: Knopf, 1987). See also Carl D. Oblinger, *Work, Community, and the Mining Wars in the Central Illinois Coal Fields During the Depression* (Springfield: Illinois State Historical Society, 1991).

NOTES ON CONTRIBUTORS

MILDRED A. BEIK, a miner's daughter, is an independent scholar living in Atlanta, where she occasionally teaches at Emory University and Georgia Tech. She is the author of *The Miners of Windber: The Struggles of New Immigrants for Unionization, 1890s–1930s,* forthcoming from Penn State Press.

PERRY K. BLATZ is Associate Professor of History at Duquesne University and director of its program in Archival, Museum, and Editing Studies. He is the author of *Democratic Miners: Work and Labor Relations in the Anthracite Coal Industry, 1875–1925* (1994).

STEPHANE E. BOOTH is Assistant Professor of History at Kent State University and Director of Women's Studies at the Salem campus. Among her articles is "The American Coal Mining Novel: A Century of Development," in *Illinois Historical Journal* (1990).

PAUL F. CLARK is Associate Professor of Labor Studies and Industrial Relations at Penn State University. He is the author of *The Miners' Fight for Democracy: Arnold Miller and the Reform of the United Mine Workers* (1981).

ISAAC COHEN, an Associate Professor in the School of Business at San Jose State University and author of *American Management and British Labor* (1990), is completing a new book on the airline industry and the New Deal.

ALAN DERICKSON, Associate Professor of Labor Studies and History at Penn State University, has written *Workers' Health, Workers' Democracy: The Western Miners' Struggle, 1891–1925* (1988) and "Health Security for All? Social Unionism and Universal Health Insurance, 1835–1958," in *Journal of American History* (1994).

KEITH DIX, author of *What's a Coal Miner to Do? The Mechanization of Coal Mining* (1988), is now farming in northeastern Ohio.

PRICE V. FISHBACK is Professor of Economics at the University of Arizona and Research Associate at the National Bureau of Economic Research. He is the author of *Soft Coal, Hard Choices: The Economic Welfare of Bituminous Coal Miners, 1890–1930* and is writing a book on the origins of workers' compensation legislation.

MAIER B. FOX is Associate Director for Analysis at The Wilson Center for Public Research in Washington, D.C. As a consultant to the UMWA, he authored the official history of the union, *United We Stand: The United Mine Workers of America, 1890–1900* (1990). Fox also co-authored "Employer Tactics and Labor Law Reform," which appeared in *Restoring the Promise of American Labor Law* (1994).

DAVID FRANK teaches at the University of New Brunswick in Canada. He has published several articles on Canadian working-class history and has served on the editorial boards of *Acadiensis* and *Labour/Le Travail.*

GEORGE S. GOLDSTEIN was for thirty years director of group practice clinics in the UMWA Health and Retirement Funds program. Now Adjunct Assistant Professor at the

Graduate School of Public Health at the University of Pittsburgh, he has also written "Defining Managed Health Care," published in the H.M.O. *Magazine* (1992).

JAMES R. GREEN teaches labor history and directs the Labor Studies Program at the University of Massachusetts at Boston. Active in 1989 in the Pittston strike support network, Green is the author, among other works, of *The World of the Worker: Labor in Twentieth-Century America* (1980) and *Grass-Roots Socialism: Radical Movements in the Southwest, 1895–1943* (1978).

RONALD L. LEWIS is Eberly Professor of History at West Virginia University. He has published a number of books and articles, including *Black Coal Miners in America: Race, Class, and Community Conflict* (1987), *Coal, Iron, and Slaves: Industrial Slavery in Maryland and Virginia, 1715–1865* (1979), and *The Black Worker: A Documentary History from Colonial Times to the Present,* 8 vols. (1978–84).

PRISCILLA LONG is an independent writer living in Seattle. Her publications include *Where the Sun Never Shines: A History of America's Bloody Coal Industry* (1989) and *Mother Jones: Woman Organizer and Her Relations with Miners' Wives, Working Women, and the Suffrage Movement* (1976).

MARAT MOORE is the author of *Women in the Mines: Stories of Life and Work, 1920–1994,* forthcoming from Macmillan/Twayne. She is a former associate editor of the *United Mine Workers Journal* and winner of the prestigious Max Steinbock Award for labor journalism.

CRAIG PHELAN is Lecturer in American Studies at the University of Wales, Swansea. He is author of *William Green: Biography of a Labor Leader* (1989) and *Divided Loyalties* (1994), a study of John Mitchell, He is currently working on a new biography of Terence Powderly.

ALAN J. SINGER is Assistant Professor of Education at Hofstra University. His articles include "Class-Conscious Coal Miners: Nanty-Glo Versus the Open Shop in the Post–World War I Era," *Labor History* (1988) and "Communists and Coal Miners," *Science and Society* (1991).

JOE W. TROTTER JR., a member of the editorial board of *Labor History,* teaches history at Carnegie-Mellon University. He is the author of *Black Milwaukee: The Making of an Industrial Proletariat, 1915–1945* (1985) and *Coal, Class, and Color: Blacks in Southern West Virginia, 1905–1932* (1990), and editor of *Migration in Historical Perspective: New Dimensions of Race, Class, and Gender* (1991).

ROBERT ZIEGER is Professor of History at the University of Florida. His major works are *Republicans and Labor, 1919–1929* (1969), *John L. Lewis: Labor Leader* (1988) and *The C.I.O., 1935–1955* (1995).

INDEX

A. T. Massey Company, 514, 516–20, 523, 525, 553

Abraham, William, 402

absentee coal owners, impact on mining, 422–23

accidents and injuries in mining: among African-American miners, 272–74, 285–86; Colorado Fuel and Iron strike and, 347; rates of, 178–79, 202, 205; Southern and Eastern European miners, rates of, 336; types of accidents, 202–3

Adair, Linda, 530–31

Adamic, Louis, 145–47

Adams, K. C., 106, 113, 146

Adkins Dolin, Irene, 490

AFL-CIO, UMWA links to, 2

African-American miners: biracial unions in Alabama and, 297–301, 548–49; earnings disparity for, 284–85, 309–10; employment statistics on, 270–71; exclusion from supervisory positions, 280–81; geographical mobility of, 286–87; Hawk's Nest Tragedy and, 278–80; health and safety issues for, 285–86; immigrant miners' attitudes toward, 48–49; Mitchell's attitude regarding, 85–86; productivity of, 285–86; racial discrimination against, 7, 16–17; settlement patterns for, 34; strike actions by, 288–92, 301–3, 310–19; UMWA relations with, 303–19; unionization efforts of, 287–88, 549; in West Virginia, 269–96, 549; women miners among, 487, 498–99; working conditions of, 281–84

age levels of miners, union militancy and, 67–71

Alabama: biracial unionization in, 297–301, 548–49; mine working conditions in, 296; social equality issues for miners in, 297–319

Alabama Ancient Free and Accepted Colored Masons, 314

Alford, John, 206–7

Algoma Coal and Coke Company, 491

Allard, Gerry, 375, 390

Allen, J. V., 316

Altmeyer, Arthur, 244n.13

Altoona Diocese, 326

Amalgamated Association of Miners and Mine Laborers, 53, 401–2

Amalgamated Mine Workers of Nova Scotia, 446

American Association for Labor Legislation (AALL), 228

American Federation of Labor (AFL) (later AFL-CIO), 23–24, 448; Committee for Industrial Organization, 119–20, 122; ILGWU joins, 130; labor militancy in mass-production industries and, 119–20; Lewis's relationship with, 106, 109–10, 116–17, 120–22, 136–37, 152–56, 554; "Little Steel Formula" and, 143; Pittston strike and, 537; PMA charter granted by, 390; UMWA charter granted by, 86, 101–2; UMWA District 12 affiliation with, 431–33, 435; UMWA links to, 23–24, 140, 152, 418, 473, 475, 549, 554; wartime no-strike pledge and, 139

American Federationist, 120

American Friends Service Committee, 219

American Miners' Association, 9, 29, 421

American plan for open shops, 187n.49

Americanization, ethnic miners' resistance to, 326–27

Amerikansky Russky Viestnik, 339

Ameringer, Oscar, 115

Ammons, Elias (Governor), 353, 355–56, 366–70

Amsden, Jon, 53

Anderson, S. R., 277, 293

Andrews, John, 228–29

Ansboury, Pat, 374, 392

Anthracite Coal Strike Commission, 68–69, 90–92, 414

Anthracite Health and Welfare Fund, 234

anthracite (hard coal) mines: cartelization of industry by owners, 403–8, 413–14; health issues for miners in, 230–31; Mitchell's involvement with miners, 82–85, 97–98; strike actions by miners in, 52–54, 62–71, 82–85, 89–90, 141–42; task segregation in, 55–56; UMWA and, 51–71; underemployment in, 57–58; Welsh and Pennsylvania miners compared, 395–400, 403, 408–16

anthraco-silicosis, 232

antitrust laws, U.S. coal industry and, 194